Mexico and the United States
in the Oil Controversy, 1917–1942

Mexico and the United States in the Oil Controversy, 1917–1942

by Lorenzo Meyer

Translated by Muriel Vasconcellos

University of Texas Press Austin & London

Translated from *México y los Estados Unidos en el conflicto petrolero (1917–1942)*, 2d ed.

© 1972 by El Colegio de México

Library of Congress Cataloging in Publication Data

Meyer, Lorenzo.
  Mexico and the United States in the oil controversy, 1917–1942.

  Translation of México y los Estados Unidos en el conflicto petrolero, 1917–1942.
  Bibliography: p.
  Includes index.
  1. Petroleum industry and trade—Mexico. 2. Mexico—Foreign relations—United States. 3. United States—Foreign relations—Mexico. I. Title.
HD9574.M6M64513   338.2′7′2820972   76-18690
ISBN 0-292-75032-3

A Don Daniel Cosío Villegas (1898–1976)

mexicano e intelectual ejemplar

Contents

Introduction to the First Edition

Objectives

The investment of capital by one or several countries in others that are economically less developed is a mode of international relations that arouses special interest among scholars. This phenomenon, especially when it takes the form of direct investment, amounts in effect to an extension of the investing country's national interests beyond its borders. It may take place between similar systems or between societies of differing potential and degree of development. When it is a question of extending capital from economically powerful states to "peripheral" areas for the purpose of extracting raw materials, two things in particular are likely to happen: first, certain economic sectors in the less developed countries that were hitherto inactive or inadequately exploited because of lack of capital and markets begin to grow; and, second, a situation of economic dependence is created, which gives rise in turn to the formation of "economic enclaves."[1] Such enclaves, for their part, set the stage for the development of a politically dependent relationship between the investing and the receiving country. Sometimes, when both foreign and domestic circumstances are propitious, the dependent societies may attempt to turn the situation around in their favor—that is, they may try to minimize the political dependence by controlling the activities that originally created their economic dependence. A situation of this kind is ripe for setting off a conflict at the international level.[2]

The study of the development of the oil industry in Mexico from its beginnings in the first years of the current century up to the time of nationalization offers an opportunity to examine one of these processes at close range. The phenomenon unfolds as follows: a dependent country, motivated by changes in its internal structure, attempts to diminish its economic dependence by gaining control of an enclave, but this action leads sooner or later to repercussions at the international level, where forces are mobilized to stave off the change in the status quo. The result is a conflict between the dominating country and the peripheral one. In the Mexican case, the fact that the development and expansion of the economic enclave that is the subject of this study coincided with the advent of a tremendous internal political and social upheaval—namely, the Mexican Revolution, which had as one of its main objectives the elimination of certain colonial characteristics of the national economy—gives added interest to the inquiry. Moreover, the fact that the process was to culminate, after a prolonged struggle between opposing international forces, in the desired transformation at the hands of the new leadership lends even greater interest to the review of the emergence, growth, and denouement of what may be considered a typical case of economic and political dependence in the first half of the twentieth century. It is not intended here to generalize from the results of the present study. Nevertheless, while recognizing that every situation is unique and qualitatively different, it is hoped that this essay, along with other similar ones, may help to provide a better understanding of the special relationship between industrialized and developing nations that characterized international capital investment during the first half of the present century.

Compared with other modern revolutions, the Mexican one was haphazard and inconsistent in its ideological orientation. It was an unplanned rebellion against exploitation by landowners, public officials, foreign capitalists, and the Church. Little by little the movement's leadership came to be concentrated in the hands of the middle classes that had been emerging during the era of Porfirio Díaz. These groups wanted to replace the Porfirian system of domination—from which they had been excluded—with another in which they would be the leaders and the popular classes would participate to a certain extent. Their overall goal, they said, was to speed up Mexico's transition from an outdated rural economy to a modern capitalist one—although hopefully without having to go through all the steps traditionally followed by the industrialized countries of the West. Despite the vagueness of the Revolution's aims, there is no doubt that one of its main objectives, in addition to establishment of a political democracy and attainment of a more equitable distribution of wealth, was the subordination of foreign interests to national ones.[3] These three basic planks in the Revolutionary platform met with widely differing success. The outcome of the last one has been the subject of rankling debate up to the present day: Did Mexico's economic dependence decline, increase, or remain the same as a result of the Revolution? Whatever the answer—and there are proponents of all three points of view—there is no question that the new leadership took issue squarely with the tremendous economic dependence that had come to exist under the former regime. Its power would never have become firmly established if it had not succeeded in bringing under its control the most modern and dynamic sector of the Mexican economy. For, unlike the old regime, it was sworn first and foremost to get the country's development out from under the sway of Anglo-American capital. This was at least one of the objectives on which the popular masses mobilized by the civil struggle were in agreement: national capital had to be the basis of development. The strategy of this policy—not always followed with equally firm resolve by all the administrations, their hands too often tied by adverse conditions on the international scene—consisted in trying directly or indirectly to gain control of the main economic sectors hitherto dominated by foreign interests and to keep that domination from reappearing in the future.

The reform of the oil industry's juridical status was the most important weapon used by the post-1917 administrations to challenge the hegemony of direct foreign investment. The nationalist faction and the new interests emerging after the fall of the old order were calling for foreign capital to turn over its lucrative fields to national elements, to limit its activities to the supplementing of domestic investment, to keep out of strategic economic sectors, and, finally, to subordinate itself to the public interest as defined by the new leadership. Under the new concept of national interest, foreign capital and technology could no longer be allowed to be the driving force of Mexican economic development. The oil industry, whose great prosperity clearly was not shared either with the state or the new groups in power, did not meet the criteria for the role now to be played by foreign capital. Nor was this the only industry to find itself in such a position: the mining companies were in the same situation. But the marked concentration of power in the case of oil, the industry's newness and bright prospects for the future, the boom it had experienced in the second decade of the century, and the fact that a natural resource was at stake which was expected to run out sooner than the metals—all these elements helped to focus public attention on this activity more than any other. Almost from the beginning the oil companies were made the villains in an international plot to despoil Mexico of what was considered its greatest natural resource. Thus the Revolutionary governments, from Venustiano Carranza down to Lázaro Cárdenas, saw themselves committed to this issue, which we shall call the "oil reform," in such a way that the concept of property as defined in the Constitution of 1917, and to a great extent the whole program of economic and political reform, hinged on its solution. Indeed, the entire hope for recreating an economic system whose guiding reins would be essentially in the hands of the new hegemonous groups depended on the outcome.

Limits of the Present Investigation

This study deals solely with the controversy in regard to oil between the governments of Mexico and the United States of America. The role of the European groups is therefore touched on only superficially. Given the political nature of the study, the economic aspects are dealt with only to the extent that they contribute to an understanding of the main subject. Although the presence of American interests in the Mexican oil industry did not entirely end with the signing of the compensation agreements in 1942, for present purposes the "oil question" between Mexico and the United States is considered to have come to a close with that act. Later a few minor American companies were to be asked to return, but on the condition that they accept the expropriation as a fait accompli.

Sources

The literature on the Mexican oil question is extensive. In the case of a large part of it—perhaps because its original purpose had been more to propagandize than to present an objective analysis of events—the quality leaves much to be desired. Because of this fact, and also because none of the many studies that have dealt with the oil problem have drawn to any significant extent on the rich material deposited in the Mexican and U.S. public archives, I decided that it was worth the trouble to explore once again a path that would seem to have been trodden over many times before. I am confident that the results have borne out the merit of this decision. The secondary sources examined were mostly works by Mexican and American authors; only exceptionally will the reader find references to European works. Apparently, Europe's loss of political influence in Mexican affairs was paralleled by a declining interest on the part of Old World scholars in this area, even though materially speaking there was still very much involved.

The published primary sources used in this work consist mainly of articles from Mexican and American newspapers and pamphlets published in the two countries. The European press devoted a certain amount of space to the analysis of Mexican oil matters during the various crises, but as far as I have been able to determine their reports do not add enough new elements to warrant an exhaustive study of this source. The Mexican newspapers most extensively consulted were *El Universal*, *Excélsior*, and *El Nacional*. In addition, some reference was had to other dailies, such as *El Demócrata*, which were published during the period of the study. Only on occasion were provincial newspapers examined. Of the American papers consulted, the *New York Times* and the *Wall Street Journal* were felt to have the greatest importance. The *Nation* was reviewed with attention to certain periods; though a rather secondary publication, it was of interest because it systematically sympathized with the Mexican point of view as against that of the U.S. government, the oil companies, and the press at large. Outstanding among the Mexican serial publications and pamphlets was the *Boletín del petróleo*, published by the Ministry of Industry, Commerce, and Labor from 1916 onward, which until 1933 printed very important articles on political, juridical, and economic, as well as technical, aspects of the subject. The oil companies, especially Standard Oil of New Jersey, put out numerous pamphlets, particularly during the different crises, which were useful for gaining an understanding of their position on the many problems that came up between the firms and the Mexican government.

The unpublished primary sources included documents on file in the Mexican Ministry of Foreign Affairs, the U.S. National Archives in Washington, D.C., and the Manuscript Division in the U.S. Library of Congress, also in Washington, D.C. In addition, occasional reference was had to some of the documents in the General Archives of the Nation in Mexico City and diplomatic exchanges between Mexico and Spain. While I believe that this work is based on the most important collections of primary sources, I am aware that it does not cover all of them. The British archives, as well as the papers of some of the main principals in the drama, are yet to be investigated. Although I feel that the omission of this material has not made for any significant lacuna in the study, when it is ultimately explored it will no doubt add to a fuller understanding of the subject. The documentation from the American archives is unquestionably the richest and the most complete. It consists mainly of State Department papers on the oil question, which are kept in the U.S. National Archives in Washington under the classification 812/6363. Although this file is the most directly related, there is also a good quantity of documents on the subject under other headings (Revolutionary Movements, Labor and Economic Matters, etc.). The papers of Josephus Daniels, U.S. ambassador to Mexico from 1933 to 1941, are found in the Manuscript Division in the U.S. Library of Congress and constitute an interesting supplement to the State Department records, particularly for the period when the controversy was at its height.[4] The first part of the study also draws on the papers of President Woodrow Wilson, which are likewise kept in the Manuscript Division. The archives of the Mexican Ministry of Foreign Affairs, as has already been pointed out, are not as rich or as well organized as their U.S. counterparts, but they contain some very interesting material that supplements the more complete and voluminous documentation on file in Washington. The Mexican papers referred to in the study are almost exclusively those found under headings related to oil. Undoubtedly there is material elsewhere which is relevant to the subject, but deficiencies in classification and the lack of an index made consultation impractical.

Mexico City, 1967

Introduction to the Second Edition

In this present edition the original work published in 1968 has been revised and substantially enlarged—and, I hope, improved in the process. It reflects, in addition to certain necessary modifications in style, some secondary changes in the general framework within which the various phases of the oil controversy are presented. It also incorporates a few significant changes in the last chapters based on findings from primary sources that were not available when the original study was carried out. Although some of them are rather important, I do not feel that they fundamentally alter the substance of the original work. On the contrary, the new material strengthens the central theses and at the same time gives a more complete view of the circumstances leading up to the oil conflict.

The secondary modifications, as I have said, have to do mostly with the framework within which the various chapters have been set. They stem from reflections developed in a smaller work in which I attempted to tie in some of Mexico's problems of contemporary political and social development with the attitude of the political elite toward direct foreign investment.[1] This attitude was, and is, largely a product of the social forces that are at work in the national and international systems and that at any given moment constitute the climate in which the oil controversy or any of Mexico's other international problems evolves. Through an awareness of this context it is possible to understand to a certain extent the pressures and restrictions that faced the various Mexican administrations as they dealt with the foreign problem.

Most of the important changes are found in Chapters 8, 9, and 10, which cover the final phase of the oil conflict between the United States and Mexico—namely, the administration of Lázaro Cárdenas and the beginning of that of Manuel Avila Camacho. They are based on new material from the U.S. National Archives in Washington, D.C., and from the Mexican Ministry of Foreign Affairs. In 1966 when I was perusing the State Department documents on file in Washington I had not obtained permission to consult those related to the last phase of the investigation—that is to say, the period from 1937 onward. The only way to make up for this lacuna was to refer to the papers of the U.S. ambassador in Mexico at the time, Josephus Daniels, which I did. Four years later, when I was able to gain access to the rest of the State Department material, I found it sufficiently important to warrant a reorganization of Chapters 8 and 9.

My consultation of the official archives in Mexico had also been hampered at the time I did the original research, since the documents were in the process of being transferred to a new location. It was necessary to wait several years before access could be had to them. My review was therefore limited to those papers which had been generously placed at my disposal by the Modern History Seminar at the Colegio de México. Unfortunately, this material, abundant as it was, also failed to cover the period beginning with the Cárdenas administration, and, even though the Mexican government had published some of this documentation, direct consultation was absolutely necessary. In 1970 the Ministry of Foreign Affairs archives were once again open and I was able to peruse them fully with respect to the subject of oil. As in the case of the American documents, the material was voluminous and of great value. As a result of this additional investigation into the two sets of archives, Chapter 8 is now much more complete and has sixty-three new footnotes. The original Chapter 9, to which it was necessary to add more than two hundred new footnotes, had to be divided in two, giving the present edition one chapter more than that published in 1968.

As I said earlier, the study's central theses have not been fundamentally altered by the inclusion of the new material, but those readers who have the patience to compare the two versions will not fail to observe some important changes. Perhaps the most notable of these has to do with the nature of the economic pressure that Washington exerted on the Cárdenas government starting in March 1938, pressure which was in fact more severe than we had originally been able to determine. The new material enabled me to see how the State Department interfered continuously and decisively in the Mexican government's efforts to place part of its fuel on the Latin American market. I was also able to see that the Mexican failures in this area were due not only to American interference but also to the national oil company's inefficient system of distribution during the early years of its existence. It was interesting to learn, as well, that the State Department's action had not been limited to obstructing the sale of Mexican oil on the foreign market and to keeping the U.S. Treasury from continuing to buy Mexican silver; it also tried to thwart the efforts of independent oil companies to market Mexican fuel in Europe and to put a stop to any official or private American loans intended for Mexican development in general.

These findings, and others that need not be mentioned here, made it necessary to reevaluate the influence of the various elements contributing to the formation of the U.S. policy toward Mexico during the period in question. For example, the new documentation shows that, once the initial impact of the 1938 expropriation had passed, Ambassador Josephus Daniels' moderating influence was less important than had been imagined earlier. The State Department bureaucracy gave little heed to the recommendations of the ambassador, who, unlike his superiors in Washington, sought to identify U.S. national interest in Mexico not with the intransigent defense of the oil companies' cause but rather with the need for hemispheric solidarity against the impending threat of war in Europe and Asia. While Daniels favored applying the least pressure possible on Mexico, the secretary of state and his advisers were inclined to use as much as they could within the limits of the Good Neighbor policy. Only the urgent demands of World

War II led them to switch to Daniels' position, and by then the effects of their earlier stand had left permanent results.

With the new documentation in hand, Cárdenas' resistance to U.S. demands seems even more extraordinary than before. However, the additional information does shed light on the circumstances that led him to back down on his internal reform programs starting in 1938. The American attitude appears to have been a fundamental factor, but not the decisive one. At least as important or more so was the pressure of conservative elements both within the army and outside it, which did not let up even after General Saturnino Cedillo's defeat following nationalization of the oil. This conclusion had been pointed to in the original version of the study, but not with sufficient clarity. The price Mexico paid for expropriation included far more than just the monetary compensation awarded to the companies; it comprised all that went into winning out over the forces opposed to Cárdenas' changes in the development model which had been decided on twenty years earlier by the victors of the Mexican Revolution.

Austin, 1971

Note on the English Edition

A sharp reader, on comparing the second Spanish edition with the present one, would find here and there differences that are the result not of translation but of interpretation. The reason is that since I wrote the book I have been dealing with problems of Mexico's recent history, and I could not resist the temptation to modify some of my previous ideas about the political processes that constitute the background of the oil controversy between Mexico and the United States. However, there has been no alteration in regard to the facts and interpretations of the controversy itself. A second but important group of changes has been the result of the zealous and sensitive translation of Muriel Vasconcellos, who found some errors and inconsistencies in the Spanish edition. She also decided very wisely to present a chart listing the main diplomatic actors of the drama in order to save the reader from unnecessary mistakes and confusions (see Appendix).

I am quite aware that there is no possibility of objectivity in the social sciences and that this is especially true in a study like this one, involving the relationship of a strong nation and its weak neighbor. The study of the U.S.-Mexican relationship has been a very emotional one on the Mexican side. I have tried to be as objective as I could, but I am quite aware that the oil controversy—which for me is important because it shows the distinctive characteristics of the unequal relations between the two countries—is presented here from the Mexican side. Nevertheless, I hope that the sense of balance is still sufficiently strong to allow foreign readers to form their own opinions about this event of contemporary history.

This book does not pretend to be the "definitive work" on the nationalization of the Mexican oil industry. There are still possibilities of exploring new fields through the analysis of the oil companies' archives; the memoirs of or interviews with former managers or employees of the companies, as well as any of the other actors; and diplomatic archives of other nations that had some interest in the exploitation of Mexico's oil. However, I am confident that the reader of this book is being presented with the central themes and basic facts of the problem.

Mexico City, 1976

Mexico and the United States
in the Oil Controversy, 1917–1942

Chapter 1

Evolution of the Mexican Oil Industry

It is generally agreed that the history of the modern oil industry began in the United States that famous day in August 1859 when black gold gushed forth from a well in Pennsylvania. Some time was to pass, however, before the activity was to take on the characteristics and proportions that are associated with it today. It was the invention of the internal combustion engine that made this modest operation the pivot of great fortunes and conglomerates and turned oil, which had been used since ancient times as a remedy and simple illuminant, into one of the principal sources of energy for the modern world. And it just so happened that the beginning of the industry's boom, which came with the mass use and assembly-line production of the automobile in industrialized societies, was to coincide with the gathering storm of the Mexican Revolution.

The first attempts at industrial exploitation of Mexico's tar sands date back to 1863. Two decades went by, however, before these efforts took on a more serious nature. By then a number of Americans and Britishers had arrived on the scene and were heading up the activity.

The first American entrepreneurs came to Mexico for a variety of reasons: to begin with, the worldwide demand for oil was already great and becoming greater, especially in the industrialized countries; in the second place, the Mexican deposits were the natural geographic extension of the Texas oil fields; and, finally, by the end of the nineteenth century the United States had clearly become a capital-exporting country,[1] and its next-door neighbor, Mexico, was not averse to being on the receiving end. At the same time, it is a fact that during the period when the Mexican oil industry was dominated by foreign capital—namely, from the end of the nineteenth century until 1938—the United States produced two-thirds of all the petroleum extracted in the world and took care of its domestic needs mostly from its own national output. In this sense, then, Mexican oil was not essential to the Americans. However, given the worldwide nature of the markets supplied by the U.S. industry, it was necessary to have whatever could be gotten from Mexico and other regions if the ever-increasing demand was to be met.[2]

The first firm to be established in Mexico was Waters-Pierce Oil Company, a subsidiary of Standard Oil founded in 1887. The original purpose was not to work the Mexican deposits but rather to import oil from the United States and refine it in Tampico for local use, mainly by the railroads. Until 1906 Waters-Pierce was the only company that had a refinery.

The enterprise formed in 1901 by Edward L. Doheny, an American, was the first to produce oil in Mexico.[3] Mexico's president at the time, Porfirio Díaz, looked favorably on this new undertaking, since it promised to put an end to the country's dependence on coal as a principal source of energy for the railroads and the mining and electric power industries. Indeed, between 1900 and 1910 coal accounted for from 2.2 to 3.7 per cent of all Mexican imports.[4] His government offered various fiscal incentives to encourage the nascent industry.[5] The oil companies were granted the right to import all the equipment they needed tax free, and they were exempted from all internal levies except the stamp tax for a period of ten years.

From the very beginning the oil activity in Mexico was dominated by American and British interests.[6] The companies established by Doheny (Pan American Petroleum and Transport and its famous subsidiary, Huasteca, among others) and Weetman D. Pearson, the Englishman who some years later was to bear the title of Lord Cowdray (El Aguila, S.A., or Mexican Eagle Oil Company, and its group) opened the way for the arrival of Standard Oil of New Jersey and Royal Dutch–Shell (Royal Dutch Petroleum and Shell Transport and Trading) in the late 1920's.

Progress was rapid. In 1901 the first commercially profitable well was in operation, and by 1908 there were already signs of an imminent boom. By 1910 success was assured. Doheny had discovered the El Ebano field and Pearson had found the Campoacán and San Cristóbal deposits. Photographs of wells gushing uncontrollably, launching 100,000 barrels of oil a day into the air, circulated throughout the world and spread the news of the enormous riches in the Mexican subsoil. The producers, with Pearson in the lead,[7] stepped up extraction at a vertiginous pace. The companies amassed their fleets of tankers—some of them among the best in the world—and began to set up distribution agencies abroad. A glorious future was predicted. Doheny alone estimated the reserves in his fields at no less than 5 billion barrels.[8]

The world's great oil consortia began to look toward Mexico.[9] In both 1913 and 1916 Standard Oil made attempts to acquire El Aguila and its affiliates. Pearson rejected these offers and tried instead to talk the British government into going into partnership with him. London, however, was not interested in the plan. Washington vetoed a similar arrangement. But, even though the British government turned down Pearson's proposal, it had no intention of letting the Americans gain a monopoly on Mexican oil. These sentiments were strongly echoed by Henry Detering, who had a controlling interest in Shell, and in 1919, with the blessing of the king of England, he bought out Pearson's interest.[10] The absorption of Doheny's interests by the large companies took a little longer, but in 1925 his Pan American Petroleum and Transport group was acquired by Standard Oil of Indiana, which in turn signed the purchase over to Standard Oil of New Jersey.[11]

The Development of Foreign Domination

Since the very beginning the world's great oil deposits have been dominated by a handful of giant firms. (The situation in the United States, mitigated in part by the antitrust laws, was somewhat of an exception.) The power struggle that emerged in Mexico between Standard Oil of New Jersey and Royal Dutch–Shell, with other less important companies competing as well, led in time to a series of agreements aimed at stabilizing prices and delimiting their respective areas of influence.[12] Although Latin America was the natural sphere of operation for the American companies, just as the Near East was for the British firms,[13] the latter continued to have significant interests in Mexico until the very end. Indeed, after the discovery of the Poza Rica beds in the 1930's their interests equaled and even surpassed those of the Americans.[14] Up to 1920 Mexico was almost the only foreign scene of operations that interested the American oilmen,[15] and by that date nearly all the important U.S. oil firms had made investments in Mexico. From the Mexican standpoint oil was the only activity through which the effects of American capital exportation were felt during the period from the end of World War I up to the Depression. In the other economic fields potential investors were discouraged by the civil disturbances and the generally nationalistic climate.

The sale of Doheny's and Pearson's rights brought the main oil firms in Mexico under worldwide consortia.[16] The most important groups were Royal Dutch–Shell, Standard Oil of New Jersey, Gulf Oil Corporation, Sinclair, Cities Service, and Warner-Quinla. Others that also figured prominently were Continental Oil, Union Oil, South Penn, Mexican Seaboard, and Pierce Oil. These firms together produced more than 90 per cent of the oil extracted in Mexico from 1901 to 1938.[17] The output of the rest—small independent enterprises belonging to both foreigners and Mexicans and numbering in the several hundreds—was insignificant.[18] Many of them never reached the production stage, and those that were successful in their drilling had to depend entirely on the big companies for transportation, refining, and distribution of the fuel. Sometimes their disappearance was also the work of the large consortia.[19] The participation of Mexican capital, which was limited to these independent enterprises, never accounted for more than 3 per cent of the total from the beginning of the industry up to its nationalization.[20]

The association that existed in the beginning between the oil industry and domestic economic activity in Mexico very quickly began to break down. Within a short time the industry was almost wholly devoted to meeting the needs of foreign markets. It was not until the 1930's that the domestic market was to have any real importance—and then only because production had declined. Meanwhile the oil industry's relationship to the national economy (which was predominantly agricultural) was limited exclusively to the payment of taxes, salaries, and lease rents. These wage and tax flows were important for Mexico, however. Even though they corresponded to a relatively small part of the total value of oil production, for a time they were a significant item in the overall fiscal income picture.

Three factors came together to work against the establishment of a strong partnership between the oil industry and the national economy: first, the discovery of large deposits on the Gulf coast, where nearness to the seaports provided uniquely favorable circumstances for exporting the fuel; second, the high world demand for oil at the time; and, finally, the inconsequential domestic requirement, typical of an economy in its early stages of development. Thus the oil industry was able to forge ahead during the Revolution while other foreign companies, engaged in mining, railroads, and agriculture, were obliged to cut back or suspend their activities—some of them permanently.

Traditionally minerals had always been Mexico's principal export. The new ascendancy of oil only accentuated this fact.[21] When the boom was at its peak, Mexican fuel was being shipped to twenty-six countries. It went mainly to North America and Europe, especially England, with only a small part to the rest of the world. The North American ports, however, were largely a way station, the oil being subsequently reshipped to Europe.[22] Until 1922 the bulk of U.S. petroleum imports came from Mexican fields, but from that date onward cargoes from Venezuela, Peru, and Colombia began to increase. Meanwhile declining production was causing Mexican oil to lose the importance it had previously enjoyed in foreign markets.[23] This then, was the situation that prevailed at the time of the takeover in 1938. Table 1 traces production levels over the period under study and shows the distribution between exports and domestic consumption in selected years.

As it has been pointed out, when production declined, domestic consumption began to pick up, especially in the early 1930's. By that time oil accounted for about 65 per cent of the energy being used in the country.[24] The shift toward domestic consumption was the result of an absolute decline in production and, in the years following the Depression, an increase in local demand for the nation's incipient industrialization (prompted in large part by the scarcity of foreign exchange, which had encouraged import substitution).[25]

The new situation gave rise to frustrated attempts by the Abelardo Rodríguez administration to foster the establishment of national oil companies.[26] It was believed that such enterprises would be better able to meet the needs of the internal market, since the rate of exploration was slow and the foreign firms were oriented toward markets abroad. (Indeed, some of the regions in Mexico that were far from the production centers, particularly those on the west coast, had to bring in fuel from other countries to meet their needs.)[27] After the 1938 takeover oil production was radically rechanneled: the industry began to devote itself mainly to meeting the domestic demand, not only because of the loss of the foreign markets but also, and more importantly, because of the increase in internal consumption from stepped-up industrialization in conjunction with World War II. By the time the conflict was over the domestic market was claiming more than 90 per cent of the total output.[28]

The Broad Periods in the Industry's Evolution

Four stages can be identified in the development of the oil industry in Mexico over the span 1901–1938. The first, from 1901 to 1910, corresponding to the last years of the Porfirio Díaz regime, was characterized by relatively low production and a modest rate of growth. The second, which may be set at 1911–1921, was the industry's golden era. The levels of 1921 were never again to be equaled. During these years the output of the Mexican fields was exceeded only by that of the United States. In the third period, which ran from 1922 to 1932, production underwent a sharp and uninterrupted decline, while in the fourth and final stage, from 1933 to 1938, it saw a slight but steady comeback (Table 1).

During the initial phase Doheny and Pearson discovered fields in the Gulf area and drilled the first commercially profitable wells. At first the market for their modest output was limited (at the time it was only intended to meet local needs), but this situation changed when the international market was opened to the companies that were operating in Mexico. The last two years of the period saw a temporary decline in production owing to saltwater invasion of some of the early wells. Production was to rally again sharply, however, with the discovery of new deposits toward the end of 1910 and in 1911.[29] At the time this first period came to a close, British participation accounted for 61.5 per cent of total investment in the industry, while the U.S. oilmen's share was only 38.5 per cent.

The finding of the new beds coincided with the start of assembly-line production in the automobile industry and the advent of World War I. And so it was that the increased reserves coupled with the rise in demand opened the way for the Mexican oil boom of 1911–1921. By the time the war was over in Europe, Mexican fields were contributing 15.4 per cent of the world's supply, a percentage that rose to 25.2 in 1921 when the initial Texas boom had begun to taper off and the Middle East reserves were not yet being fully explored.[30] If production was already impressive, the estimates for the future—at a time when a worldwide shortage of hydrocarbons was feared[31] —added even greater importance to the Mexican industry. In 1917, when exploration in Venezuela was just getting started, it was calculated that Mexico would be able to produce a million barrels a day for the next forty years. The only possible problem that could be seen on the horizon was transportation.[32] The Spanish embassy reported to Madrid, on the basis of expert opinion, that Mexico was on its way to becoming the number-one producer of oil in the world.[33] Doheny predicted that production would continue to climb for another twenty years. Word got around that without the Mexican fields there would be a worldwide shortage of petroleum.[34] Suddenly, however, in 1921, when production was at its peak, doubts began to appear. Some of the experts started to take an opposite view, forecasting that the beds then under exploration could well run dry in another two years and warning that new fields would have to be found in their place.[35]

When the oil deposits in Venezuela's Lake Maracaibo were discovered in 1922 the euphory in Mexican circles began to fade, and not long afterward, in the face of an unprecedented decline in production, it gave way to outright pessimism. By 1924 the Mexican output had dropped to 13.7 per cent of the world's total, and by 1930 it had plunged to 3 per cent. The turn of events was due both to a local cutback and to the increased activity in other

TABLE I. *Oil production, Mexico, 1901–1937, and breakdown between exports and domestic consumption in selected years*

Year	Production (Barrels)	Exports (%)	Domestic Consumption (%)
1901	10,345	—	—
1902	40,200	—	—
1903	75,375	—	—
1904	125,625	—	—
1905	251,250	—	—
1906	502,500	—	—
1907	1,005,000	—	—
1908	3,932,900	—	—
1909	2,713,500	—	—
1910	3,634,080	—	—
1911	12,552,798	—	—
1912	16,558,215	—	—
1913	25,692,291	—	—
1914	26,235,403	—	—
1915	32,910,508	—	—
1916	40,545,712	90.0	10.0
1917	55,292,770	—	—
1918	63,828,326	81.0	19.0

Sources: For the figures on production: Miguel Manterola, *La industria del petróleo en México*, p. 97. For the figures on exports and domestic consumption: *Boletín del petróleo* 1; 24; 31; 35; Gustavo Ortega, *Los recursos petrolíferos mexicanos y su actual explotación*, p. 43; Merrill Rippy, "El petróleo y la Revolución Mexicana," *Problemas agrícolas e industriales de México* 6, no.

parts of the world. During this period American interests dominated the scene (Table 2). Not only did they gain control of more than half the investment, but by 1927 they had taken over 77 per cent of all production and 80 per cent of the total reserves as well.[36]

The causes for the sharp fall were both political and economic. Not only the oil companies but also certain officials in Mexico chose to attribute the phenomenon to political causes, though each for different reasons. The companies and their spokesmen alleged that the hostility shown them by the revolutionary governments from 1912 onward had been the cause of the flourishing industry's sudden decline—although they failed to explain why it had had most of its greatest boom during the administration of Venustiano Carranza, who had been personally very antagonistic toward the oil interests.[37] The Mexican government and certain authors who sympathized with its position also attributed the crisis to political origins. The decline,

Year	Production (Barrels)	Exports (%)	Domestic Consumption (%)
1919	87,072,954	—	—
1920	157,068,678	—	—
1921	193,397,587	—	—
1922	182,278,457	99.0	1.0
1923	149,584,856	—	—
1924	139,678,294	89.3	10.7
1925	115,514,700	—	—
1926	90,420,973	89.3	10.5
1927	64,121,142	—	—
1928	50,150,610	79.0	21.0
1929	44,687,887	—	—
1930	39,529,901	—	—
1931	33,038,853	70.0	30.0
1932	32,805,496	62.5	37.5
1933	34,000,830	—	—
1934	38,171,946	—	—
1935	40,240,563	—	—
1936	41,027,915	—	—
1937	46,906,605	61.0	39.0

3 (July–September 1954): 93; Mexico, Secretaría del Patrimonio Nacional, *El petróleo de México: Recopilación de documentos oficiales de orden económico de la industria petrolera, con una introducción que resume sus motivos y consecuencias,* p. 94.

according to their interpretation, reflected an attempt on the companies' part to pressure the government by reducing the total amount of taxes paid and generating unemployment in the sector. In this way, it was claimed, the firms hoped to force the administration to change the constitutional legislation in their favor. The overproduction elsewhere in the world, they said, facilitated this deliberate cutback in the Mexican industry.[38]

Without entirely rejecting the arguments on either side, one can say that the factors mainly responsible for the situation were technical and economic rather than political. In the first place, the extraordinary prosperity of 1911–1921 was the result of intensive exploitation of relatively modest reserves.[39] Second, the vast area known as the "Golden Lane," which in 1921 and 1922 was the first oil-producing region in the world, could not be saved once salt water had started to invade it, despite the companies' efforts to step up extraction. Thus the output was coming almost exclusively from

TABLE 2. Direct American investment, total and in the oil industry, and percentage of overall investment in national oil, Mexico, 1896–1940

(Estimated figures, in millions of U.S. dollars)

| | Direct American Investment | | | Investment in Oil Industry | | |
| | Total in | In Oil Industry | | Total in | American | From Other |
Years	Mexico	Value	% of Total	Mexico	(%)	Countries (%)
1897	200	1.5	0.75	—	—	—
1908	416	50	20.0	—	—	—
1909	394	—	—	—	—	—
1910	745	15	2.0	—	—	—
1911	794	20	2.5	51.9	38.5	61.5
1912	792	49	6.2	—	—	—
1913	784	—	—	—	58	42.0
1914	587	85	14.4	—	—	—
1915	—	—	—	—	—	—
1916	584	—	—	—	—	—
1917	—	59	—	90.7	65	35.0
1918	—	200	—	266.7	75	25.0
1919	643	200	31.1	—	—	—
1920	535	—	—	—	—	—
1921	652	500	76.0	819.6	61	39.0
1922	—	303	—	522.4	58	42.0
1923	—	500	—	862.0	58	42.0
1924	735	250	34.0	438.6	57	43.0
1925	735	224	30.0	393.0	57	43.0
1926	1,123	231	20.5	405.0	57	43.0
1927	—	—	—	—	—	—
1928	—	303	—	—	—	—
1929	709	206	29.0	—	—	—
1930	672	200	29.7	—	—	—
1931	1,000	—	—	—	—	—
1932	887	—	—	—	—	—
1933	—	142	—	273.1	52	48.0
1934	—	175	—	330.2	53	47.0
1935	652	—	—	—	—	—
1936	479	69	14.0	346.0	—	—
1937	—	40	—	133.3	30	70.0
1938	—	42	—	107.7	39	61.0
1940	300	5	1.7	—	—	—

Sources: Cleona Lewis, America's Stake in International Investments, pp. 588, 606; Gastón García Cantú, El pensamiento de la reacción mexicana: Historia documental, 1810–1962, p. 931; Edgar Turlington, "Foreign Investments," in Mexico Today, ed. Arthur P. Whitaker, pp. 104–106; Frank Brandenburg, The Making of Modern Mexico, p. 206; Frank Tannenbaum, Mexico: The Struggle for Peace and Bread, p. 231; Tomme C. Call, The Mexican Venture: From

old wells.[40] Meanwhile the firms' investments in exploration and drilling reached unprecedented levels. After 1926, however, activity began to fall off noticeably. To the failure of the new explorations was now added the depression in the world oil market resulting from the discovery of large new deposits in Texas, California, and Oklahoma and the rise in Soviet and Venezuelan production. According to the U.S. Bureau of Mines' *Minerals Yearbook*, the wholesale price index of petroleum and petroleum derivatives fell by 28 per cent between 1926 and 1927 and by more than 60 per cent between 1926 and 1930. This drop in price led the oil companies to shift their attention to Venezuela, where production costs were lower than they were in Mexico.

After 1921 the companies stopped making new fixed capital investments in Mexico and began to concentrate their financial resources in Venezuela. Some of the medium-sized enterprises left Mexico entirely.[41] Refineries and terminals were closed, pipelines were dismantled, and more than half the workers were let go. A few of the firms—Huasteca, for example—went so far as to import crude oil from Venezuela for a time. Only the asphalt-rich heavy oil from the Pánuco region continued to be in significant demand in

---

Political to Industrial Revolution in Mexico, p. 239; Hubert Herring, *México: La formación de una nación*, pp. 79–91; James Neville Tattersall, "The Impact of Foreign Investment on Mexico" (Master's thesis, University of Washington, 1956), pp. 62, 115–117; Luis Nicolau d'Olwer, "Las inversiones extranjeras," in *Historia moderna de México: El porfiriato; La vida económica*, ed. Daniel Cosío Villegas, pp. 1137–1141; Samuel Eliot Morison and Henry Steele Commager, *Historia de los Estados Unidos de Norteamérica*, III, 20; Josephus Daniels, *Shirt-Sleeve Diplomat*, p. 213; Merrill Rippy, "El petróleo y la Revolución Mexicana," *Problemas agrícolas e industriales de México*, no. 3 (July–September 1954): 93–94, 96; William English Walling, *The Mexican Question: Mexico and American-Mexican Relations under Calles and Obregón*, p. 159; Miguel Manterola, *La industria del petróleo en México*, pp. 38–47; *Boletín del Petróleo* 10; 14; 33; Max Winkler, *Investments of United States Capital in Latin America*, p. 225; AREM L-E-533, vol. 1, Leg. 2, f. 195; Leopoldo González Aguayo, *La nacionalización en América Latina*, p. 297; Antonio J. Bermúdez, "The Mexican National Petroleum Industry: A Case Study in Nationalization," *Hispanic-American Report* (1963); William S. McCrea, "A Comparative Study of the Mexican Oil Expropriation (1938) and the Iranian Oil Nationalization (1951)" (Doctoral dissertation, Georgetown University, 1955), p. 43; Upton Close, "La expropiación petrolera y los Estados Unidos," *Excélsior*, November 7, 1938; *New York Times*, March 23, 1923; December 10, 1937; March 22, 1938; United States, Department of Commerce, report of October 7, 1918; United States, Tariff Commission, *Foreign Trade of Latin America*, p. 174; George Ward Stocking and Jesús Silva Herzog, *Mexican Expropriation: The Mexican Oil Problem*, p. 512; Manuel González Ramírez, *La revolución social de México*, I, 680; report of the U.S. consul in Tampico, NAW 812.6363/R221/E0041-0042; Ernesto Lobato López, "El petróleo en la economía," in *México: 50 años de revolución*, I, 323.

Note: For some of the years there were serious contradictions in the sources consulted. The calculations made in 1923 by the U.S. consul in Tampico and the Mexican consul in Galveston indicate that American investment in the oil industry at that time ranged between 500 million dollars and a billion—the more conservative of which figures was opted for here, since it was more consistent with the rest of the series. For the following year, 1924, McCrea estimates an investment of a little more than double the figure shown in the table, which coincides with the data provided by the U.S. Department of Commerce for 1919, but once again the sum is inconsistent with the rest of the series. The figure for the industry's total in 1918 was taken from Winkler and could be a bit high. In 1938 the companies estimated the value of their expropriated holdings at 450 million dollars, which would make the American investment about 200 million, but this amount included the value of the hydrocarbons still in the subsoil.

the United States.[42] While in American oil circles a small minority still thought in terms of the Mexican fields' "unlimited potential," others were taking the prospect of bankruptcy as an accepted fact.[43]

The decline in oil exports, coupled with the slacking off of overall exports to the United States as a result of the Depression, led the companies to ask the Mexican government for a basic change in its tax policy. Only a big cut in assessments, they felt, could check the losses they were suffering and revive the industry. Otherwise they could not compete against the lower cost of the Venezuelan product. However, although a degree of prosperity could be recovered, they warned that the old times were gone forever.[44] They also conditioned their continued stay in Mexico on a series of concessions, legal and other.[45] In the end their arguments worked, and the Mexican government reduced its taxes, although not to the extent they had wanted.

The fourth phase, which was marked by a relative comeback, began with the discovery and exploitation of the Poza Rica beds by El Aguila (Mexican Eagle Oil Company, by that time controlled by Shell) in 1933, which finally put a halt to the downward slide.[46] Never again, however, were the 1922 levels to be matched. Except for the Poza Rica and El Plan fields, all the known deposits were running dry, and the firms were disinclined to undertake any new large-scale exploration in Mexico despite the rally. In 1933 the companies themselves pointed out that there were important beds yet to be explored in the north of the country, in Tampico, in the Tehuantepec Isthmus, and in other regions, but that low market prices, U.S. tariffs, Mexican taxes, and uncertainty about their property rights made such exploration not worth their while.[47] (It is interesting to recall this lack of enthusiasm on the companies' part in regard to the development of new fields when we examine the causes that led to the national takeover in 1938.) In this fourth and last phase the British interests, which controlled the new fields, took on importance once again. In 1935 they were responsible for 54 per cent of all output, and in the next year their share rose to a high of 71 per cent. In 1936, 64 per cent of the known reserves were in their hands.[48] After 1934 the Americans were never again to occupy first place in the Mexican oil industry.

The Investment Pattern

There is no way to know exactly how much the American firms invested in the Mexican oil industry between 1901 and 1938. Even the Mexican government itself admitted on occasion that it did not have at its disposal this information which is so essential to setting national policy.[49] It has therefore been necessary to use data from a number of different sources—some of them contradictory at times—in order to put together an overall picture. Although statistics developed in this way are subject to a wide margin of error, in the present case they do reveal general trends that may be useful in determining the investment pattern over the period in question.

In 1911, at the time the oil industry was first getting under way, 80 per cent of the American and British investments in Mexico were concentrated in mining and railroads.[50] Oil accounted for only 2.5 per cent, and this sliver was largely dominated by the Doheny and Pearson groups.[51] However, these were the years when the industrialized nations were abandoning coal in favor of oil and electric power. Before long, between the growing world demand and the new wells' impressive output, the oil industry had become the most dynamic sector in the Mexican economy. There was no longer any problem of markets for the product, especially after hostilities broke out in Europe. During that period Mexico claimed 60 per cent of all American investments in foreign oil. Later, however, when production began to fall off, the American firms started to reinvest their profits outside the country. Hence, by the time of the Depression their real investments in Mexico had dwindled considerably. By 1924 the country's share of total U.S. capital in foreign oil had dropped to 24 per cent, and it remained at this level until 1934.[52]

As it happened, the decline in oil investment coincided with a much wider phenomenon: foreign capital was beginning to lose the importance it had once had in all branches of economic activity in the country.

During the period when the foreign companies were operating in Mexico the oil industry's earnings reached a peak that was never again to be equaled in that country or possibly even elsewhere in the world.[53] It is estimated that over the period 1900–1937 the firms' total real investment came to 100 million dollars. On the basis of this original sum and successive reinvestments, they were able to export net gains (exclusive of what was reinvested in Mexico) that have been estimated variously at from 1,000 to 5,000 million dollars during those same years.[54] According to data furnished to Ambassador Josephus Daniels by Deputy Foreign Affairs Minister Ramón Beteta, for example, production from the first decade of operations alone was enough to pay off everything the companies had put into the enterprise. The rest was clear profit.[55]

Earnings, like production, followed a cyclic pattern. From 1910 to 1915 they averaged around 8 per cent on the capital invested. As the industry prospered the proportion went up. In 1916 they doubled to 16 per cent, the next year they reached 20 per cent, in 1918 they jumped again to 25 per cent, and in 1919 they soared to 45 per cent. During the peak years 1920–1921, distributions after expenses had been met and large funds set aside for reserves and amortization actually attained levels of from 45 to 60 per cent.[56] El Aguila, the biggest of the companies, had the highest gains of all. This firm began to operate successfully in 1911 and started to distribute its profits in 1914. In 1918, after having set aside a reserve of 100 per cent, it paid dividends at 25 per cent. In 1920, with earnings reported at 28 million dollars, it paid 60 per cent to holders of preferred stock and 18 and 206 per cent to common shareholders.[57] After 1922 the returns began to decline— although investment in the industry certainly did not cease to be lucrative. In 1926 Shell and Standard Oil of New Jersey reported that they had suffered losses in their Mexican operations, and from that year until 1936 their average declared earnings were a modest 4.25 per cent.[58] Still, studies on the subject conducted by Mexican experts indicate that between 1930 and 1938 profits were actually of the order of 16 per cent or higher.[59]

The Oil Industry and the National Economy

As Raymond Mikesell and Douglas C. North have pointed out,[60] a review of direct private foreign capital investment during the first decades of the present century leads to the conclusion that those enterprises engaged in the production of raw materials for export contributed very little to the economies of the underdeveloped countries in which they were operating. Their activities were not conducive to, or accompanied by, significant development in other sectors of the economy or the creation of infrastructure. There is no reason to think that the oil industry in Mexico was an exception to the rule. However, although statistics on the subject are lacking,[61] it may be assumed that the industry did contribute indirectly to the growth of other sectors of the economy to the extent that the income derived from its exports was used in development projects. The measurement of this contribution is a very complicated task and goes beyond the framework of the present study. On the other hand, since the large government projects did not begin in Mexico until the end of the 1930's, it may be argued that the resources generated by the exportation of oil from the beginning of the century to the middle of the third decade were not used for development spending. Naturally, this situation was not due to any policy on the part of the oil firms; rather, it stemmed from decisions taken by the national government during the period. In any case, the oil industry's contribution to economic progress in Mexico does not appear to have paralleled the magnitude of its earnings. The data in Table 3 show that in the early 1920's this handful of foreign firms accounted for more than 6 per cent of the gross national product. The sector's contribution to the federal treasury should not be underestimated. According to the figures available, it amounted to 10.8 per cent of total revenue in 1918 and rose to as high as 33.6 per cent in 1922 (Table 4). Although the proportion declined notably in the years that followed, the Calles and Cárdenas administrations—which carried out the first large infrastructure programs—were to get between a fifth and an eighth of their income from taxes on the production, consumption, and exportation of oil. (The tax on consumption is not included here, since it is considered to be a contribution of the consumer rather than of the industry.)

The history of the oil companies' tax payments to the Mexican government is one of continuous accommodation of conflicting interests. Before the Revolution the government's sources of revenue consisted mainly of duties on imports and exports and a stamp tax. Under the new regime public expenditures grew. To meet them, it was necessary to increase the traditional taxes and put new ones—property taxes, assessments on the exploitation of natural resources, etc.—into law. Outstanding among the new sources of income were the imposts on oil.

TABLE 3. *Participation of the oil sector in the gross national product, Mexico, 1901–1937 (in millions of 1950 pesos)*

Year	Gross National Product	Oil	Percentage of Total	Year	Gross National Product	Oil	Percentage of Total
1901	10,741	*	—	1924	15,159	851	5.61
1902	9,975	*	—	1925	16,102	737	4.58
1903	11,092	*	—	1926	17,335	647	3.73
1904	11,287	1	0.01	1927	16,932	436	2.57
1905	12,460	1	0.01	1928	17,240	359	2.08
1906	12,319	2	0.02	1929	16,666	326	1.96
1907	13,042	5	0.04	1930	15,538	321	2.06
1908	13,022	21	0.16	1931	16,106	261	1.62
1909	13,405	14	0.10	1932	13,494	269	1.99
1910	13,524	19	0.14	1933	14,943	297	1.99
1921	14,560	1,007	6.92	1934	15,927	354	2.22
1922	14,988	949	6.37	1935	17,039	362	2.12
1923	15,411	937	6.08	1936	18,491	338	1.83

*: Less than 500,000 pesos.

Source: Enrique Pérez López, "El producto nacional," in *México: 50 años de Revolución*, vol. 1, *La economía*, pp. 587–588.

Note: Data for 1911–1920 were not available in the source consulted.

Under the Porfirio Díaz regime the oil firms had enjoyed almost total exemption from taxes, having had only to make a small payment for revenue stamps. It was Díaz's successor, Francisco I. Madero, who in 1912 first levied a tax on oil production—20 cents a ton. This amount was increased shortly thereafter under the Victoriano Huerta administration. In 1914 Venustiano Carranza, taking still another step in the same direction, established a duty on petroleum exports. After the constitution was promulgated in 1917, the system for taxing the oil industry was totally revamped, and assessments thenceforth were based on the value of each of the products. The new system continued in effect until the national takeover, although it underwent nine different reforms during the period from 1917 to 1931, the percentage varying in accordance with world market conditions and the economic and political requirements of the moment. The government, which from time to time would assert the state's right as owner of all hydrocarbons, attempted to collect royalties from the industry on various occasions. However, contravening political pressures kept these efforts from being successful. A tax decreed in 1921 had to be repealed the next year for the same reasons. In 1925 a levy was placed on gasoline consumption, and in 1934 another tax was imposed on oil earnings.[62]

By world standards, the oil firms paid relatively little in taxes to the Mex-

TABLE 4. *Effective income of the federal government and total taxes paid by the oil industry, Mexico, 1912–1937 (in thousands of pesos a year)*

Year	Effective Income of Federal Government	Total Taxes Paid by Oil Industry	Taxes as Percentage of Income
1912	—	494	—
1913	—	767	—
1914	—	1,234	—
1915	—	1,943	—
1916	—	3,088	—
1917	—	7,553	—
1918	111,182	12,008	10.8
1919	130,980	17,332	13.2
1920	238,243	51,314	21.5
1921	279,833	62,725	22.4
1922	261,252	87,779	33.6
1923	266,955	62,394	23.4
1924	266,907	54,467	21.1
1925	317,315	46,798	14.7
1926	312,018	41,438	13.3
1927	306,873	25,538	8.3
1928	310,739	18,349	5.9
1929	322,335	19,390	6.0
1930	299,499	22,372	7.5
1931	256,089	22,236	8.7
1932	212,347	24,211	11.4
1933	228,010	27,935	12.1
1934	309,127	45,610	14.7
1935	330,602	41,618	12.6
1936	385,175	50,012	13.0
1937	451,110	57,998	12.8

Sources: For figures on effective income of the federal government: Mexico, Secretaría de Hacienda y Crédito Público, Dirección General de Ingresos, "Egresos e ingresos del gobierno federal, 1900–1958" (mimeographed, Mexico City, 1959). For taxes paid by the oil industry: Mexico, Secretaría del Patrimonio Nacional, *El petróleo de México: Recopilación de documentos oficiales de orden económico de la industria petrolera, con una introducción que resume sus motivos y consecuencias*, pp. 18–19; Guy Stevens, *Current Controversies with Mexico: Addresses and Writings*, p. 280; *Boletín del petróleo* 15 (January–July 1923): 339; Miguel Manterola, *La industria del petróleo en México*, pp. 55, 385; Mexico, Cámara de Senadores, Sección de Estadística y Anales de Jurisprudencia, *El petróleo: La más grande riqueza nacional*, p. 288; report of the Association of Producers of Petroleum in Mexico, October 20, 1922, NAW 812.6363/R218/E0003.

ican government during the period under study. On the average, the total amount represented less than one-fourth of the assessments paid by producers in the United States.[63] At times during the history of their operations south of the Rio Grande the American firms paid more to the U.S.

authorities than to the Mexican ones on the fuel they were extracting.[64] The Mexican oil industry's total remittances, added up over the years, amount to 275 million dollars. If its earnings before taxes were 1,275, 2,275, or 5,275 million dollars—depending on which estimate one chooses to go by—then what they paid to the Mexican treasury was 21.5, 12, or 5 per cent. Even so, from 1912 right on up until the expropriation the companies never ceased to complain about the high rate of taxes.

Mexico tried, with some success, to use the tax structure as a means of forestalling losses and obliging the companies to refine as much oil as possible inside the country before they exported it. Through the latter effect the system did, in fact, help to increase the industry's contribution to the national economy. At the same time, however, there was no loss to the producers, since they were thus able to cut their transportation costs considerably.

Up until 1926 the industry's refining capacity climbed steadily—partly because of the tax policy and partly because the companies themselves considered it desirable to diversify their activities in Mexico. After 1926, however, the drop in production triggered a decline in this area that continued until 1933. The activity had developed at a frenetic pace. Whereas in 1916 there had only been four refineries, by 1921 there were already fourteen; three years later, nineteen (two of which were among the largest in the world); and in 1926, twenty. Almost all of them were located near the port of Tampico. With the downturn, the number dropped back to sixteen, and in 1933 there were fifteen all told. The discovery of the Poza Rica beds sent the activity upward again. The first refineries in Mexico were primary distillation plants for making gasoline, kerosene, and fuel oil—this latter mainly for railroad use. The cracking plants, which utilized natural gas and could produce asphalt, came later.[65]

From the very beginning it had been Mexico's wish that its oil be used to meet domestic needs rather than serve as a source of energy for foreign economies.[66] However, it was not until the 1930's, when the fall in production was accompanied by a spurt in internal growth, that the national market was to claim a significant share of the total. Between 1925 and 1937 gas and oil accounted for 46 per cent of the energy consumed in Mexico.[67]

The oil activity generated income not only through taxes but also through the payment of salaries, lease-rents, and royalties. Unfortunately, data on wages and salaries paid by the oil companies were not found, so that it has been impossible to reconstruct this important item over the period covered by the present study. However, estimates of the total spent on national manpower in selected years may give at least some idea of its importance. For example, for 1936 it was estimated that 14,000 oil workers received salaries and benefits amounting to 49 million pesos. The following year the figure rose to 55 million—no small sum in those days. It represented an average salary three times greater than the national median. Looked at from another angle, the sector's work force in 1940 represented only an insignificant fraction of the available manpower reserve of 6 million. Although the income generated by the industry in the earlier years may have had greater relative importance, the picture still does not change very much. During the time when production was at its absolute peak, the sector gave jobs to from 30 to 50 thousand workers—that is, between 0.7 and 0.8 per cent of the overall labor force. After that the figure dropped to less than half, and by 1927 the workers numbered a scant 12,500.[68]

Data on the total amount of rents and royalties paid are also lacking. Large tracts of land were leased rather than acquired outright by the companies. In some cases a fixed rent ranging anywhere from 2.50 to 200 dollars a year per hectare was set, while in others there was an agreement to pay royalties, which usually ran from 5 to 15 per cent of the value of output.[69] If El Aguila, the largest of the companies, is considered a fair example, these contributions do not appear to have amounted to a great deal. In the mid-1930's this firm was paying between 1.10 and 1.25 million dollars a year in rents and royalties.[70] In some of the other cases the compensation was really ridiculous. For example, the total rent paid for the Cerro Azul fields from which Huasteca extracted 182 million barrels of oil came to only 200,000 pesos. Worse still, the owner of a tract in Chinapa, Veracruz, that yielded 75 million barrels got only 150 pesos a year.[71]

At the time the Constitution of 1917 gave the subsoil rights back to the nation, the companies were in possession of practically all the areas that were to be exploited up to 1938. Officially it was recognized that in 1917 they leased or owned a total of 6,222,063 hectares.[72] After the oil reform they were to obtain concessions on an additional 2 million hectares, but their activities were always concentrated on the lands that had been acquired prior to 1917. The oil-producing areas were located mostly along the Gulf coastal strip, exploration in other parts of the country such as Lower California, Sonora, Chiapas, and Yucatán having proved unfruitful.[73]

An aspect of the oil industry's contribution to the Mexican economy that is still more difficult to measure is the technology introduced in the country. While it is true that most of the jobs calling for a high degree of technical skill and training were filled by foreigners, a certain amount of know-how did filter down to the national employees and the workers—which ultimately enabled them to keep the industry going after the takeover in 1938. The Revolutionary governments had made it a point to deny visas to foreign workers whenever possible in order to force the foreign bosses—in all sectors of the economy—to start training nationals. This Mexicanization of the companies' staffs was one of the first nationalist measures of the new administrations, and in the case of the oil industry it paid off following the expropriation.

Over the entire period—from the time the first rig struck oil up until nationalization of the industry—the foreign firms drilled 5,743 wells, of which 2,716 were productive,[74] and extracted nearly 2 billion barrels of petroleum. During the years from World War I to 1922 the Mexican oil fields, owing to their vital role for the economies of certain industrial countries of the West, took on international importance. The industry's returns on its investments in Mexico were among the highest it was getting anywhere in the world. However, the situation changed dramatically after 1922, when production started to plummet. It is difficult to agree 100 per cent with either the companies' point of view—namely, that Mexico shared in their prosperity to the fullest—or the opposite contention—that is, that they contributed little to the economic activity of the country. But, between the two, it is easier to find elements to support the latter assertion than the former. Finally, it should be pointed out that the greater part of the income generated by Mexican oil left the country in the form of profits, without adequate compensation to justify the intensive exploitation of such an important nonrenewable natural resource.[75] As it turned out, however, Mexico's general situation as a developing country was to stand in the way of optimum utilization of the hydrocarbon wealth that did remain in the country.

Chapter 2

Establishment of the First Oil Companies:

1900–1914

From the beginning of the war for independence in 1810 up until the triumph of General Porfirio Díaz' rebellion, the political and economic scene in Mexico could only be described as one of endemic anarchy. Foreign invasions by the United States and France and an uninterrupted civil struggle—centralists against federalists, conservatives against liberals—nearly led to the total breakup of the old Viceroyalty of New Spain. In 1876, however, the picture began to change. The liberal faction, after repelling the French invasion, defeating the conservative wing, and overcoming the internal divisions within its own ranks, managed to put together the first relatively strong and effective national administration. At the center of this new government was the figure of General Porfirio Díaz, hero of the struggle against the conservative forces and the armies of Napoleon III. After his takeover in 1876, Díaz rapidly consolidated his position and was to remain in power as the absolute and undisputed leader of the country until 1910.

Díaz' success may be attributed in large part to the facts that the old antagonists had finally been reconciled; the newly established government was a strong, central, authoritarian one; and the political and social climate was right for attracting foreign capital in substantial amounts and opening the doors to modern economic activity so that the course of development interrupted sixty years earlier by the war for independence could be taken up once again. This climate, so propitious for foreign capital, was to be both the cause and result of the famous "Porfirian Peace." Díaz believed that only the United States and the industrial nations of Europe could contribute the capital necessary to pull Mexico out of its economic stagnation, and that only through economic development could the country cease to be the easy prey for the imperialist powers that it had been up to then.[1] The potential enemy itself was to provide the tools with which to consolidate the nation's independence.

By the end of the century the effects of this policy were already becoming apparent. To begin with, national and foreign capital had started to carve out their respective areas of activity. A review of the 170 most important corporations in existence at the time is very illuminating. Only 23 per cent of their combined capital was Mexican. Moreover, the bulk of this share was taken up by government railroad operations, and only 9 per cent of the total corresponded to private investment. There was virtually no national industrial bourgeoisie. The economy was in foreign hands.[2]

The foreign companies' activities were concentrated mainly in mining, railroads, and banking. American capital predominated.[3] The Mexican affluent class had left the modern sectors of the economy—those sectors that linked the country to international markets—to the foreigners, preferring instead to focus their efforts on agricultural pursuits. In a country where 70 per cent of the economically active population was engaged in agriculture, the agrarian policy was fundamental. But it was in this area that Porfirio Díaz made his greatest mistakes.

Díaz picked up and elaborated on the policy initiated by his liberal predecessor, Benito Juárez, which favored the concentration of tillable land in the hands of a few as a means of speeding up rural development. As a result, the large haciendas soon acquired unprecedented power and the landholding elite became a major political force. It was this group that made the rules in the system of internal domination which was to prevail during the Porfirian regime. The agrarian policy advocated expropriation of all lands whose users did not hold proper title thereto. At first the sector that was affected most severely was the Church, especially under the Juárez administration, but later on the Indian communities were the ones to suffer the most from the policy. By the end of the Porfirian era more than 90 per cent of the heads of family in rural areas had no land, while 97 per cent of Mexico's tillable soil was in the hands of 1 per cent of the population.[4]

Outside the agricultural sector Díaz' program had spectacular results. All the internal impediments created by the localized interests that had flourished during the years of anarchy were finally removed, and there was at last a true national market. Whereas up until 1876 the modern sector of the Mexican economy had consisted of 400 miles of railroad track and a few mining companies and plantations,[5] the situation changed dramatically with pacification and the opening of doors to foreign capital. This was a time when large sums of money were available in the United States and the industrial countries of Europe. "Peripheral areas" such as Mexico offered attractive opportunities to investors from those countries that were looking for ways to provide their metropolitan industries with raw materials or else to actually gain control of the raw-material sources in order to protect their domestic markets. Thus in Mexico by the end of the nineteenth century foreign capital had begun to develop its mineral resources (precious and industrial metals), grow exportable agricultural products on large plantations, and explore the oil deposits in the area of the Gulf. At the same time, foreign entrepreneurs set about developing the transportation systems (railroads) and other services (electric power, telephones, banking, etc.) that these activities required. The economy had begun to move ahead.[6] By the end of the Díaz regime the country had more than 150 mining or metallurgic centers, 12,000 miles of railroad track, electric power plants, a sizable banking system, and a telephone and telegraph network. Mexico was now a participating member of the world market.

As it has been said, in this process of incorporation into the international economy national capital was almost totally absent. In 1910 Mexico's share in the local mining industry was about 2 per cent, and similar situations prevailed with respect to oil and electric power.[7] The railroads were the only exception, part of the system having been acquired by the government for strategic reasons. Although in 1911 only 27.4 per cent of the capital invested in this sector was foreign, nationalization of the railroads had been accomplished mainly thanks to a loan from the United States, so that indirectly the real participation of foreign capital in this activity was on the order of 61 per cent.[8] The only important industrial sector oriented toward the foreign market was the textile industry, but this was largely in the hands of the French.

In Mexico, as in Cuba and Canada as well, American capital was dominant. It is estimated that total U.S. investments in this country as of 1911 came to no less than 1 billion dollars. British capital was in second place, with 300 million dollars. The French, German, and Spanish had smaller stakes. Nearly half the national wealth was in foreign hands.[9] And these investments were highly concentrated. Three companies—two of them American and one British—were in control of oil production, while five other American firms were at the head of the mining industry. With the railroads the situation was a little different because of the government's large interest.[10]

The striking contrast between the modern sector, which offered bright new perspectives for workers, and agriculture, with its immobile peasant masses earning a bare subsistence on the haciendas, created a relative conflict between the administration and the foreign sector on the one hand and the landholding leaders on the other. This internal division was aggravated by the cool state of relations between Díaz and President Taft in the United States. After the turn of the century Díaz had started to show special favoritism toward European investors with a view to offsetting what was considered to be the dangerous predominance of U.S. interests.[11] These difficulties with the very sectors thanks to which he had originally come to power were taking place in the context of a serious new situation: despite all the economic development, the standard of living of the vast majority of the people was probably lower than it had been before, and there was widespread discontent in the small but ambitious middle sectors, which resented being outside the framework of the Porfirian system.[12] In 1911 all these elements came together to put an end to the more than thirty years of "peace" and open the floodgates to one of the great revolutions of the twentieth century.

The Early Days of the Oil Industry

There are at least two reasons why the Mexican oil industry was developed by foreign rather than national capital. In the first place, those "in the know" in Mexico, with only a few exceptions, had been convinced for some time that the country's oil resources were not worth exploring. Second, there was virtually no national entrepreneurial group, and Mexican capital was in short supply—while drilling rigs, refineries, pipelines, equipment, and so on called for large amounts of capital. The few local investors who might have had sufficient resources to go into this activity gave no sign of being disposed to commit themselves to an undertaking whose outcome at the time appeared dubious. Hence it should not be surprising that the person who ended up taking the lead in this enterprise was Edward L. Doheny, who had capital he was prepared to risk and had had experience with oil in the United States. Doheny was the perfect stereotype of the foreign capitalist in Latin America at the end of the nineteenth century: devoid of scruples, it was said, and ready to use any means within his reach to "get rich quick," with no concern whatsoever for legitimate owners of this natural resource. It must be admitted that this "black legend" has some basis in truth. He was certainly one of the most adventurous and rugged pioneers in the long history of U.S. investment in Latin America. According to his own testimony before a U.S. jury in the 1920's, he had been a surveyor in Kansas, a horse trader in Oklahoma, a soldier in the Indian campaigns, a schoolteacher, a law student, and, finally, an oil prospector. He made and lost great fortunes. In the end he was the biggest tycoon in Mexico.[13] He made his first trip there, prospecting for minerals, in 1887. Five years later he went back with his partners, C. A. Canfield and A. P. McGinnis, this time looking for oil in the Tampico and San Luis Potosí regions. The three men, together with Herbert G. Wylie, bought 450,000 acres of oil land at El Ebano, near Tampico, in 1900.[14] By Doheny's own admission, part of this tract was purchased at a dollar an acre from the former owners, who had no idea that it harbored oil.[15] Eventually his companies came to have 1,500,000 acres under their control. On December 20, 1900, Doheny founded the Mexican Petroleum Company of California to explore the deposits under all this land. It was registered in the United States as a foreign firm, and thus it had the right to appeal to the U.S. government for help in all matters in which diplomatic intervention might be helpful.[16] Doheny was to spend 3 million dollars before his efforts yielded any rewards. In the meantime one of the original partners became discouraged and sold out his share, so that Doheny then had control of 40 per cent. Shortly after the company began its operations Doheny made a deal with the Mexican Central Railroad to supply all the fuel for the 500-mile Tampico-Aguascalientes run.[17]

After the U.S. ambassador introduced him in official circles, Doheny soon stood in high favor with the Díaz administration. The Mexican president encouraged him in his undertaking—but not without asking him, if he should decide to put his shares on the market, to offer them first to the government rather than letting them get into the hands of a large monopoly like Standard Oil.[18] This official support was to be translated into the form of a complete exemption from all taxes except the stamp levy for a period of ten years. It was at about this time that Doheny began to set up subsidiaries: Mexican Petroleum, the famous Huasteca Petroleum, and, operating on leased properties, Tamiahua Petroleum and Tuxpan Petroleum. The first was capitalized at 15 million dollars and the others at 1 million each. In 1907 Mexican Petroleum of California and the three subsidiaries were absorbed by Mexican Petroleum of Delaware, which controlled all the interests of the Doheny group and had an authorized capital of 60 million dollars.[19] Eventually Doheny, who had interests outside Mexico as well, was to become the biggest oil magnate in the United States after John D. Rockefeller.[20] In the wake of Doheny's firms there soon appeared Oil Fields Company, a British enterprise, and Standard Oil of Mexico. However, the only entrepreneur who was to rival the American oilman was the wealthy railroad king Weetman D. Pearson. This clever Englishman, also known as Lord Cowdray, began his oil activities while he was building the Tehuantepec line. A law passed in 1901 authorized foreign businessmen to explore vacant national lands and extended to all the oil companies the same tax exemptions that had been granted to Doheny.[21] Thus in 1902 Pearson began some oil exploration in the isthmus as a sideline. Originally he planned to invest only about 1.5 million pounds in the venture (by that time his fortune was already large enough to let him run such a risk without any worry), but before he met with any success he had spent 5 million.[22] In 1908 he organized the Compañía Mexicana de Petróleo El Aguila (registered also as Mexican Eagle Oil Company), which before long was to absorb a number of other smaller firms. It was this company, with its famous strike at Dos Bocas, that was to launch the historic Mexican oil boom. Pearson, too, enjoyed the goodwill of President Díaz—especially because the dictator's son was on his company's board of directors and because the Mexican administration was anxious to maintain a certain balance of power among the foreign companies, playing the European and American interests against each other whenever it could.[23]

Hydrocarbon Legislation

The Porfirian laws on oil broke with a tradition which had prevailed in Mexico since colonial times—a tradition that Díaz regarded as an impediment to capitalist development. Up until 1884 the rights to subsoil resources had belonged first to the crown and afterward to the nation.[24] In that year, however, President Manuel González (Díaz' stand-in) decreed the first mining legislation under the independent republic. Following the French example, Article 10, paragraph iv, of the new law stipulated that coal and oil were the exclusive property of the surface landowner. Thus, with no opposition from the Congress, which wanted to encourage the production of fuel for the railroads, the nation was deprived of its time-honored right to the resources of the subsoil.[25] Contrary to what some authors have said, this first law cannot be seen to be the result of a maneuver on the part of the oil interests, since production was not yet really in full swing. It was simply a fruit of the Porfirian economic policy.[26]

The second mining statute, enacted in 1892, was contradictory to a certain extent in that it did not specifically recognize the surface landholder as owner of the subsoil hydrocarbons. It simply said, in its Article 4, that the oil could be exploited without the need to obtain any concession. On the basis of this provision, the first law dealing exclusively with oil went into effect on December 24, 1901. By this time a few American companies were already in operation. The law gave the surface landowner the right to extract the oil, and it gave the executive the power to grant concessions for the exploitation of national lands. Still, it was not very precise with respect to ownership of the subsoil hydrocarbons. Finally a measure passed in 1909, when the oil boom was nearly in full swing, put an end to the ambiguity and declared that the "fields or deposits of mineral fuels," including "bituminous materials," were the "exclusive property" of the surface landowner. The 1909 law, although it was the subject of bitter controversy after Díaz' fall, was to remain in effect until 1926, when it was replaced by another, a product of the Revolution, which was far less generous in its concessions to the oil firms. Nevertheless, from the time that this new legislation—namely, the law implementing Article 27, paragraph iv, of the Constitution of 1917—was enacted up until 1938 the Mexicans were to have to stand by and wait while the rich but exhaustible oil was rapidly draining out of the country[27]—not to mention all the benefits that its revenue would have provided for the people. Although the theorists of the Revolution had clearly declared the 1909 law null and void, the power of vested interests was time and again to stand in the way of any substantial modification in the Porfirian system.[28]

The First Attempt at Modifying the Hydrocarbon Code

While the change in the juridical and economic status of the oil industry that was to bring it more in line with the interests of the national economy was the work of the Revolution, the first attempts in this direction, though motivated by other than nationalist considerations, actually took place a number of years earlier. In 1905 Lorenzo Elízaga, Luis Ibarra, and Manuel Fernández Guerra presented the government with a proposed text for a law designed to place the subsoil hydrocarbons once again under the legal code that had existed prior to 1884. Contrary to what the companies said later, this measure was not an attempt by Mexican "radicals" and socialists to nationalize the industry.[29] Its authors' intention was just the opposite: namely, to make sure that private owners of the oil lands would not hold up exploitation of one of the country's principal sources of energy.[30] President Díaz showed little enthusiasm for the proposed legislation and appointed a committee to study it. The committee in turn appealed to the Mexican Academy of Jurisprudence for an opinion. All this ado gave rise to an interesting debate which, although it did not reach the general public, was considered sufficiently important by Doheny for him to follow it personally. The consensus was in favor of maintaining the status quo, and the Ministry of Development ended up discarding the proposal. What is interesting, however, is that in the process there emerged some legal arguments that justified returning to the earlier code without having to take "vested" rights into account. These arguments were later to be used by the Revolutionary writers in their struggle against the companies.[31]

Toward the end of the Díaz regime an open anti-American sentiment began to develop and was expressed in writings published in intellectual circles, in the platforms of the opposition parties (especially the Mexican Liberal Party [PLM—Partido Liberal Mexicano], and even in popular demonstrations.[32] However, there does not appear to have been any specific brief against the oil industry, perhaps because of the little importance it still had at the time.[33]

Díaz and the Americans

Although the Porfirian administration had always had some difficulties with the United States, they increased notably in 1910 with the stepping up of internal conflict. The Mexican government accused Washington of sympathizing with the rebel groups operating inside the United States near the border, while the U.S. government for its part resented Díaz' inability to control his domestic situation and, above all, his failure to take a firm stand on behalf of American interests.[34] In one aspect of his policy Díaz was consistent: he was determined to use Europe as a moderating force against the growing American influence in Mexico. To this stand were added a number of specific things that were not particularly to U.S. liking: the Mexican government's purchase, partly with American capital, of the major portion of the railway network; the unsympathetic attitude toward the Guggenheim interests on the part of Treasury Minister José Ivés Limantour; the support of the British oil firms in their disagreement with Waters-Pierce; and the rumors of secret negotiations between Mexico and Japan. All these factors taken together helped to foster the idea in certain American circles that the time had come for a political change in Mexico.[35]

In oil, as in other areas, the Díaz administration felt it was best not to let the capital of any one foreign country dominate the industry exclusively.[36] With this policy in mind, it canceled a drilling permit that had been granted to Standard Oil, thus forcing the company to carry on its operations through Waters-Pierce.[37] Pearson's arrival on the scene was clearly welcome. This situation, together with the growing importance of El Aguila and a tax on oil imports that was handicapping Waters-Pierce (the only firm affected, since it was the only one bringing the finished product back in from the United States), opened the way for a price war between Pearson and Henry Clay Pierce. The competition ended in 1913 when the American was abandoned by his ally, Standard Oil, and lost for good the monopoly he had enjoyed up to then selling petroleum and its derivatives in Mexico. By that time Pearson controlled more than 50 per cent of the Mexican oil industry.[38] Some authors have hinted at a bitter struggle between Pearson and Doheny, but the truth seems to be quite the opposite. Pearson's biographer states that, on the contrary, there was a certain degree of cooperation between the two oilmen. It is not difficult to imagine that the end of the Pierce monopoly was welcomed by Doheny, who was also a new arrival on the fuel market.[39]

The Pierce monopoly seems to have had the support of the U.S. State Department right from the beginning. As far back as 1887 Washington had already protested the granting of refining concessions to a Mexican company. The competition, claimed the State Department, was prejudicial to the American company's interest.[40] Thus, it is more than likely that Washington was displeased to see Water-Pierce now in a contest with El Aguila. However, the British firms had taken great care to build up good relations in official American circles so as to forestall any open hostility on Washington's part,[41] and it is a fact that the U.S. diplomatic machinery was not brought into play to protest the blow that had been dealt to Pierce. He and Standard Oil ended up taking the matter in their own hands, timing their action so as to make best use of the anti-Díaz sentiment that was rapidly building up in Mexico. In 1911 they entered into contact with the opposition forces led by Francisco I. Madero, which had already declared themselves openly against the regime, and offered them a loan for half a million to a million dollars to help along Díaz' overthrow and assure for themselves "certain concessions" under a new government. There is no documentary proof that the transaction actually took place, although the State Department did hear about some negotiations and was sufficiently concerned to call Standard Oil on the carpet.[42] In any case, it is clear that at least one of the American oil firms in Mexico was seriously enough affected by the Díaz administration to want to put it out of business. The companies' role, however, should not be overestimated, since there is a misleading tendency to regard Díaz' fall as simply one more episode in the worldwide struggle between British and American oil interests. Still, it is interesting that the dictator's own son, in a letter addressed to Pearson after Madero's victory, accused Pierce of having been the architect of his father's overthrow.[43] The friction between Díaz and the American oilmen was only part of a much broader situation which had given rise to a certain "resentment"—as Treasury Minister Limantour put it—against the dictator in official Washington circles and which led ultimately to the decision to no longer support his government. This decision was an important factor in the rise of the same Revolution which eventually, after a long struggle, was to put an end to foreign domination of Mexican oil.[44]

Madero

The uprising led by Madero in 1910 began as a rift between Díaz and a faction of the leadership, supported by the emerging urban middle class, that wanted to introduce reforms in the prevailing system so as to make it more open and institutionalized. Before long, however, this purely political reformist movement had created a breach far wider and deeper than had ever been intended.[45] The idea of Madero, a young member of the Porfirian establishment, and his recently organized Antireelection Party had been to assure the continuity of the system, not to make any radical change. It was only the intransigence of the old dictator and the unexpectedly successful operations of the guerrilla bands led by Pascual Orozco and Francisco Villa in the north that turned Madero into what he had never set out to be: the leader of a revolution.

The conduct of Madero and some of his nearest collaborators after the surprising fall of the Porfirian regime—surprising because its army was left intact—shows that they had failed to understand the tremendous importance of the movement they had started. Díaz' decision to resign virtually without resistance—prompted by the fear that a protracted civil struggle would lead to U.S. intervention—placed Madero in a position where he could heed the growing forces opposed to the status quo, whose existence until then had scarcely been noted. Indeed, very soon the Revolutionary leader was obliged to deal with these factions, which wanted to go from formal change to structural change. His break with Emiliano Zapata, who was for an agrarian reform on behalf of the landless peasants, was symbolic of the new turn of events. However, his rejection of this group, which had in fact been the driving force behind his victory, was not followed by a rapprochement with the other end of the political spectrum. He was never able to reach an understanding with this latter sector—the landholders, the Church, the bureaucracy, the army, the American investors—whose backing was vital to the survival of any government in Mexico at the time. This failure was due not only to his own lack of skill but also to the inflexibility of the Porfirian group, which refused to accept any reform whatsoever.

The United States and the New Regime

Washington's policy toward Madero was under influences from more than one source. There was a lack of coordination, at times clear, between President Taft, on the one hand, and the State Department and the U.S. ambassador in Mexico, Henry Lane Wilson, on the other.[46] While Taft, former governor of the Philippines, was an advocate of "moderate imperialism,"[47] Wilson was an aggressive and uncompromising spokesman for "big business," a clear partisan of "dollar diplomacy," and an enemy a priori of any change in the system that had prevailed under Porfirio Díaz. And in the formulation of Washington's policy, the decisions of the U.S. embassy in Mexico City were fundamental.[48]

In some circles Díaz' fall was seen not as a triumph for Madero and his men but rather as a victory for the United States.[49] Generally speaking, the American political and financial groups that were interested in Mexico did not regret his going. Hence Madero was able to look forward to a certain amount of good will from these quarters when he took over from the old Oaxacan leader—a situation that did not go unnoticed by a certain sector of the press, which accused him of having sought aid from Washington.[50] However, the repudiation of Díaz did not mean repudiation of his system— that is to say, internal peace and support of foreign capital. Before long a series of factors had militated to put an end to the cordial relations between Madero and the American group. To begin with, the Orozcan rebellion and the damage it caused to American interests in the north led Washington to doubt Madero's ability to ensure internal peace.[51] Taft had all he could do to hold back former president Theodore Roosevelt, who was determined that

Mexico should have "the punishment she deserves"—that is, invasion— and indeed he persuaded Taft to threaten Madero, as he had done before with Díaz, by deploying troops along the border.[52] The shadow of an American intervention was to hover in the background of U.S.-Mexican relations for many years to come.

A number of factors led up to Ambassador Wilson's decision to encourage his government to support an overthrow of the new Mexican regime. In the first place, he considered it inadmissible for Madero to be so indifferent to suggestions from the U.S. embassy. He took the Mexican president's independent attitude as a sign that the new government was thinking of changing the status of American investments in the country. Wilson accused Vice President José M. Pino Suárez and the ministers of war and development of heading up an anti-American faction in the cabinet.[53] It is true that the U.S. envoy was closely identified with the Guggenheim family in the States, and it may be that this personal conflict of interests with the Madero family interests[54] helped to fan his zeal. In any case, he was quick to interpret any new official move as an attempt to undermine overall American influence in Mexico.[55] This situation, added to the election campaign going on in the United States (in which Taft was accused of being lax in his protection of U.S. interests in Mexico), brought relations between the two countries nearly to the boiling point. The ambassador delivered a strong note to the Mexican government demanding increased measures to safeguard American interests and lives; Taft warned the Mexican ambassador in the United States that his patience was not eternal; and American warships appeared along the coast of Mexico.[56] However, the pressure actually did not go much further than this. By early 1913 the situation had begun to cool off considerably, in large part as a result of talks held between Foreign Affairs Minister Pedro Lascuráin and President Taft and Secretary of State Philander C. Knox on January 2 and 4 of that year. At the same time it appeared as if the Madero government had succeeded in overcoming its major difficulties and was on the way to being firmly established.[57] The threat to stability had gotten gradually diffused within the overall political picture. At this point, however, the U.S. ambassador, without any instructions from Washington on the matter, decided it was time to put an end to a situation that, according to him, continued to be potentially dangerous. Little did he imagine that the elimination of Madero at the hands of officers from the old federal army under the leadership of General Victoriano Huerta would unleash the forces of a real revolution—forces that the Madero regime had been on the verge of putting down for good.

Victoriano Huerta's takeover as chief of state represented the culmination of the American ambassador's efforts. Wilson believed that with this one stroke he had achieved at least three all-important objectives: the dissipation of the potential danger that he saw in the timid Madero reforms, the formation of a new regime responsive to the wishes of the U.S. embassy, and the restoration of the stable conditions of the pre-1911 days. He also had a hand in dictating the terms of an agreement that was signed between the two big anti-Madero, anti-Revolutionary leaders, Huerta and Félix Díaz;

in selecting the cabinet; and in setting down the broad lines of what was to be the Mexican government's policy.[58] The magnitude of his success led him to declare in an address to the diplomatic corps following Madero's fall: "Mexico has been saved! From now on we will have peace, progress, and prosperity!"

Madero and the Oil Companies

In a country where foreign interests controlled more than half the national wealth, it was difficult for any change in the status quo, however slight, not to affect them. Thus, when Madero came to power a few members of the foreign community had seen certain hopes for a favorable reaccommodation, but the great majority of them had their doubts, especially in the light of his reformist intentions and the continued civil strife. During the campaign against Díaz, Madero and his confederates had discreetly manifested their opposition to excessive foreign domination, but they were not extreme at all in their position, when it is considered that their interests were directly threatened by the competition and privileged status of foreign capital.[59] The policy followed by Madero once he was in power could hardly be characterized as "antagonistic" or "discriminatory" toward U.S. capital, as Ambassador Wilson had reported to his superiors.[60] While it is true that Madero did try to "Mexicanize" the railroad personnel and raise the federal revenue collected from the oil industry, during the short time he was in office it does not appear that he was bent on putting an end to foreign influence—which indeed had been precisely one of the main issues, as cited by Carranza's aide Luis Cabrera in 1911, that had led to the rebellion which put him into power in the first place. Rebel leader Pascual Orozco went so far as to accuse the Madero administration of being no more than an "arm of the government in Washington."[61]

At the time Madero made his triumphant entrance into Mexico City the oil deposits already being worked were of considerable importance. The industry was expanding geometrically, and the interests of the companies that controlled it were zealously guarded by the U.S. ambassador. However, there was no reason for a conflict over these interests to have developed with the new government. In the first place, Díaz' overthrow had been rather welcomed by those American companies that had looked unkindly on the old dictator's favoritism toward the British. The Orozco faction went so far as to accuse Madero of having made commitments to the foreign firms.[62] Madero never once attacked the oil companies' basic interests as his successors were to do.

In his strongest display of concern over the matter, Madero did take exception to the tax breaks that the firms were enjoying. The slight changes introduced in this area were followed soon after by a serious confrontation. Toward the end of 1911 the companies had begun to hear unsettling rumors. Moreover, in the Chamber of Deputies José María Lozano spoke up strongly against Pearson and Standard Oil of New Jersey, pointing out that if the latter were to absorb the interests of the former—which he claimed was a real possibility—the result would be an empire that could come to dominate the country entirely. And even if they did not merge, he went on to say, in any case the British interests, through Pearson, could grow to a point of becoming incompatible with Mexican sovereignty. To avoid these eventualities, the legislator proposed that oil be reincorporated into the legal code governing the rest of the minerals, that the taxes on oil production be increased, and that any exemptions still in effect be eliminated. His slogan, "Mexican oil for the Mexicans!" was widely cheered.[63] Days earlier, the State Department had been informed by its consul in Tampico that the Madero family was buying up oil lands in that area with the intention of organizing a company which could become a serious threat to the established interests.[64] Although this was only an unfounded rumor, it certainly did not help to calm things down.

But it was a small and unexpected tax in 1912 that was to trigger the oil firms' open hostility. Before deciding to decree it, Madero had arranged for a series of talks with the parties concerned to sound out their views and soften up their resistance to the measure. However, the firms refused to agree to any fiscal levies whatsoever. (It should be remembered that up to that time the industry had paid nothing but a stamp tax.) Discouraged at not having been able to reach a prior agreement, Madero decided to carry his proposal forward anyway and call for payment of 20 cents on each ton of oil extracted, or approximately 10 cents on a dollar's worth of earnings, to the national treasury.[65] Among his reasons for risking such a step was the fact that the new regime, faced with heavy military expenditures and all the other costs of government, was in severe economic straits. However, in view of the unstable internal situation and the enmity in Washington, it was hardly wise to court the displeasure of the oil sector.[66] No sooner was the tax announced than the companies launched a vigorous campaign against it. According to their figures, 20 cents on the ton was equivalent to 17 per cent of their annual dividends—a virtual "confiscation."[67] In view of the actual amount of the tax, the statement seems exaggerated. Indeed, it is not difficult to imagine that their real objection was not to paying the tax itself but rather to setting a precedent whereby the Mexican government could change fiscal policy unilaterally in the future. The companies took the matter to court. El Aguila was the only firm to pay the tax outright. When the case came before the Supreme Court in 1914—after Madero was already out of the picture—the legality of the measure was upheld. The companies had to pay, but they did so under protest.[68]

The discontent prevailing in the oil circles in 1912 was augmented by an air of restlessness that had begun to be felt among the foreign investors in general.[69] Madero did not limit his oil reforms to the fiscal field. Shortly after the new tax went into effect he took still another step and decreed a law calling for all the companies and landowners to register with the government and declare certain information about the value and makeup of their holdings. Its purpose, according to the text of the law itself, was to establish a basis for calculating how much the company or individual should be indemnified in the event the property were taken over by the government. If the terms of the decree were not met within the time stipulated, the party concerned would be subject to a fine equivalent to 5 per cent of the value of the property, which would be held without arraignment.[70] This time the oil companies' refusal was equally definitive, and the order was not complied with. Surely they were not going to facilitate a future government intervention in the oil industry by providing such vital information as what was being called for in the decree! The firms claimed that it was impossible for them to make the appraisal asked for. Again Madero had to give in; relations with Washington were very strained at the time. Similarly, resistance on the part of the companies kept the state of Veracruz from carrying forward certain fiscal plans that it had drawn up in regard to its hydrocarbon resources.[71] The firms' anxiety was total. They were so sure that their position was seriously threatened that they decided to forget their old feuds and join together in a "united front" against the Mexican government. This coalition was not a passing thing: it was to be crystallized in the form of a regular organization, and the spirit of alliance among the companies was to survive up to and beyond the expropriation in 1938, even though the struggle between U.S. and British interests and the rivalry among the American groups themselves continued to smolder under the surface.

Washington and the Oil Companies

The State Department, diligently and consistently protecting the interests of its nationals in Mexico, soon saw in the Madero administration a cause for concern. The first sign of trouble came in early 1912 when Washington heard that Shell might be going to win a concession to lay a pipeline, which would be a severe setback for the American companies. Secretary of State Knox asked Ambassador Wilson to investigate the matter. Thanks to the latter's intervention, the project was held up and U.S. interests were safeguarded.[72] Shortly afterwards the State Department learned that a propaganda campaign was being waged by the Tamaulipas authorities against Waters-Pierce. It began when a fire broke out in one of the company's storage tanks and the local town officials, claiming that the Waters-Pierce and Huasteca installations were a danger to the nearby populace, launched a vigorous drive against the two firms. Waters-Pierce promptly took the case to the federal authorities, and the Ministry of Government reported in short order that the state governor had already received instructions and that the attacks against the companies were going to stop.[73] Although on this occasion the firms' pressure had an immediate and positive result, the incident itself served to add just that much more fuel to their discontent. Soon thereafter still another problem came up in the form of an oil tax imposed by the state government of Veracruz. The U.S. consul in Veracruz took exception to it, and days later he was informed that the matter had been settled in the companies' favor.[74] These events were followed in turn by the tax on output that has already been discussed.

By August 1912, when Ambassador Wilson informed Washington that he was leaving for Tampico to investigate the companies' numerous complaints, his communiqués had already built up a degree of antagonism in the State Department toward the Mexican government's oil policy. The 1912 federal tax on oil production put an end to any doubt that the officials in Washington might have harbored with respect to Madero's intentions. In their opinion, his objective was clear and inadmissible: to ruin the American oil companies in Mexico.[75] On returning from Tampico, Wilson confirmed this conclusion by reporting to his superiors that an "almost confiscatory" tax was being levied. Secretary Knox's answer was immediate, and Ambassador Wilson delivered a violent note—virtually an ultimatum—to Foreign Affairs Minister Lascuráin demanding that a stop be put to the hostile measures against the American firms and that the "confiscatory" tax of 20 cents on the ton be withdrawn.[76] The Mexican minister rejected his American colleague's arguments[77]—and, though it is any government's sovereign right to impose taxes, he went on to explain carefully that the levy was necessary in view of pressing economic considerations. The tax remained on the books, but the Taft administration had made it clear that it would not let Madero make any other change in the industry's status.

Madero's Fall

In view of what they considered to be dangers to American lives and property, a group of oilmen and other people with business interests in Mexico got together with Ambassador Wilson and appealed to President Taft to resort to what they felt had become the only possible solution—namely, pacification by U.S. forces.[78] However, the president preferred not to rush into such a serious decision. Since the Democrats had won the election in November, he felt it would be best to leave the solution of the Mexican problem to the new Woodrow Wilson administration. The ambassador disagreed strongly with his chief and decided that, come what might, it was time to bring the Madero government to an end.

Madero's fall at the hands of the old Porfirian army, plotted in the U.S. embassy itself, was to be the last attempt by the dominant groups from the old regime to stop the trend that was under way. It had been their unwillingness to adapt to the new state of things that had led them to this solution, which proved to be the wrong one. Their inflexibility gave rise to a reaction of such magnitude that it was to definitively unleash the forces of the Revolution. Manuel Márquez Sterling, Cuban ambassador at the time and perspicuous observer of the events, said: "The coup was an absurd conspiracy by richlings, omnipotent industrialists, wealthy bankers, and favored businessmen who went after their goal as if it were a fetish and unwittingly wrought their own ruin."[79] Victoriano Huerta, the new leader, sought to prolong the Porfirian period and to keep the 1876 social structure intact. It was natural, therefore, that at the beginning he and the foreign interests considered themselves mutually allied; the latter's satisfaction with the political change was undisguised. The *Mexican Herald*, a paper published by the American colony, trumpeted its joy over the new government from the front page of the February 19 edition: "Viva Díaz! Viva Huerta! After a year of anarchy, a military dictator looks good to Mexico!"[80]

Huerta and President Wilson

The fate of the Huerta regime was to hinge in large measure on the course charted by the U.S. government: it came into being partly as a result of an American decision and was to disappear because of another. It is not difficult to imagine Huerta's surprise and irritation when, after having come to power with the unconditional backing of the U.S. ambassador and the approval of the American investors, he found the new administration in the White House refusing to endorse Taft's Mexican policy and actually questioning his permanence at the head of the government. The radical shift in U.S. position was a reflection of the dramatic contrast between Taft's conception of U.S. interests in Mexico and Woodrow Wilson's. Wilson, though an old-line aristocrat,[81] was alert to the changes taking place in his time. Rejecting totally the outdated conservatism of the Republicans, he had set himself to the task of making his "New Freedom" a reality. The industrial revolution had made for spectacular growth and progress in the United States after the Civil War, but it had taken a social toll of equal magnitude. Wilson represented that school of thought which believed that the time had come to put a rein on things if the future of the democratic system was to be preserved. The new president declared that the government had frequently been used for private and selfish ends, and that those who had so used it had neglected the people. In order to restore the balance that had been upset, he proposed to put a stop to the most serious abuses of the system, imposing certain restrictions on the big economic interests so as to favor the "common man," who so far had gotten little or no benefit at all from the country's great industrial development. These decisions were reflected in his foreign policy as he pursued it at first, especially since he took upon himself a large share of the duties of the secretary of state. In regard to Latin America—which was becoming increasingly an area of American rather than European influence—he believed that one of the responsibilities of the United States was to aid in the establishment of "democratic" governments, which were most compatible with the national interest. In theory at least, the new administration was committed to burying the "dollar diplomacy" of its predecessors once and for all. In this climate the programs of the Mexican revolutionary groups met with a fair amount of tolerance and even sympathy in the White House, since to some extent they coincided with the New Freedom. Wilson wasted no time in changing the U.S. policy toward Mexico: the first thing he did was to ask Huerta to step down.[82]

Washington versus Huerta

Counter to the opinion of his professional advisors in the State Department, the press, and the American investors in Mexico, all of whom advocated recognition of Huerta, Wilson decided to take a less simple course but one that he believed in the long run would be much more advantageous.[83] The former professor of political theory thought to create conditions favorable to U.S. interests by using an approach entirely different from that of his predecessors. He was convinced that stability would never be achieved by supporting the "strong man" of the moment, since all the dictatorships in Mexico had ended up being overthrown. He reasoned that the best way to put an end to the string of civil wars was to back the establishment of a democratic (in the Wilsonian sense) government, since only by attending to the interests of the large popular groups would true and lasting stability be achieved. Within this context, Huerta had to go. In the event that pressure did not work, one more revolution would have to be tolerated, or even supported, in order to put an end to all future ones. Wilson recognized that in the short run some American interest groups would be adversely affected, and it would be necessary to see that damages were kept to a minimum.[84] This new policy was not understood at the time, and Wilson was accused more than once of having fomented the "civil war, robberies, and murders" that were to play havoc with foreign interests in Mexico.[85] The "moral imperialism," as Howard F. Cline has called it,[86] that sought to protect American interests by creating a political and social structure in Mexico patterned after the U.S. system was likewise espoused by Wilson's two special emissaries whom he sent to get on-the-spot reports of what was going on.[87] Both William Bayard Hale, the first one, and John Lind, who went later, agreed basically that Wilson's approach was the only way to achieve the stability in Mexico that everyone wanted.[88] For all this, however, the American president's actions were not always in perfect harmony with the political line that he proclaimed, and on more than one occasion the steps he actually took gave the lie to his words. The pressures of the American interests affected by the struggle and the splitting up of the anti-Huerta front into dissident factions were two important factors behind the contradictions that were to appear in his Mexican policy.

Taft, in the last days of his administration, had the chance to consolidate the work of his ambassador, Henry Lane Wilson, by granting immediate recognition to the new Mexican government—especially since Huerta had personally assured him that the sole purpose of Madero's ouster had been "to restore peace in the republic and protect the interests of its sons and of the foreigners who have produced so many benefits for us." However, Washington chose to try to get the most it could out of the new situation and hold out for favorable solutions to all the problems that were pending between the two countries before extending diplomatic recognition. At first Huerta refused to agree to the U.S. requests. The matter was under negotiation when Taft's term came to an end.[89] Woodrow Wilson, on taking office, decided to meet the problem with a very simple solution: the discreet removal of Huerta—though not necessarily his entire faction. To that end he asked Huerta to hold immediate elections, leaving his own name off the slate. From an absolute master he was to be turned, by an order from Washington, into a mere provisional president.[90] Meanwhile, Wilson made his position known to the rest of Latin America: the United States would systematically oppose all governments established by force and against the will of the people; at the same time, no private American interests would ever again be placed before the legitimate interests of the peoples in this or the other hemisphere.[91] When Huerta refused to hold elections as Washington had asked, Wilson then set about finding allies for his anti-Huerta policy among the Mexican revolutionary groups, the European governments with interests in Mexico, and the other Latin American countries. In each case, however, and for different reasons, he failed to find the response he was counting on.[92]

In the face of a barrage of notes—"ultimatums," as they were called by Edith O'Shaughnessy, wife of the U.S. chargé d'affaires—sent by Wilson to Huerta at the end of 1913 and the beginning of 1914, the latter appeared to be concerned and tried on several occasions and in various different ways to explain to the U.S. embassy that what was needed in Mexico was order, not democracy.[93] Since Huerta refused to step down, Wilson seized upon the first opportunity—the USS *Dolphin* incident in Tampico, in which a shore party of U.S. Marines was briefly detained, followed shortly thereafter by the unloading of an arms shipment for Huerta from a German vessel at Veracruz—to back up his demands with a display of force just short of an open declaration of hostilities: in April 1914, U.S. troops occupied the port of Veracruz.[94] While all this was going on, the revolutionary forces under the command of Venustiano Carranza were advancing toward the capital of the republic.

The occupation of Veracruz was the culmination of Washington's campaign against Huerta. At least this is the way it was understood by his confederates, who wasted no time in asking the dictator to give in so that negotiations could be started with Wilson and at least something could be saved in the face of Carranza's advance. It was already too late, however, and before long the country was in the hands of the revolutionary forces.[95] The failure of the Huerta movement to ward off the breakup of the Porfirian structure was the product of a complex set of circumstances, both foreign and domestic, but there is no doubt that U.S. policy was one of the deciding factors.[96] Without American arms, the peasant masses from the north who occupied the capital in 1914 would have had a hard time standing up to the Porfirian army—especially if instead it had been the latter which had had the support of Washington.

The Oil Interests in Mexico and the Washington-London Conflict

The Mexican problem was reviewed in Wilson's meeting with his cabinet on April 18, 1913, and it was decided not to recognize Huerta. The suspicion was voiced that the Mexican civil struggle was being stimulated by the rivalry between the British and the American oil companies, but the point was not explored much further.[97] Though it was in the oil industry that American businessmen in Mexico were most acutely resentful of British competition, there is nothing to indicate that Wilson's initial decision to get Huerta out of power was connected with this problem. Still, the subsequent course of events was to indissolubly link the Anglo-American dispute over control of the oil with the destiny of the Huerta regime.[98] According to Josephus Daniels, who was later to be ambassador in Mexico, the American firms had definitely tried to get Wilson to recognize the Huerta government.[99] Wilson came to suspect that Doheny and other oilmen were furnishing aid to the dictator contrary to White House policy. Huerta, for his part, did not show any antagonism toward the American companies, nor did he resort to the old Porfirian technique of playing European interests against the pressures from Washington until the very end, when he realized that Wilson was trying to get rid of him in order to make way for the revolutionaries.[100]

While Huerta basically maintained the legal status quo with regard to oil, in the Congress the voices of protest that had been raised during Madero's regime continued to make themselves heard: Deputy Querido Moheno from Chiapas proposed the creation of a government oil corporation that would absorb the private companies. Luis Zubiría y Campa, and Félix Palavicini demanded a review of the exemptions and concessions that were being granted to the industry.[101] These moves, together with the general climate of hostility toward the American firms, aroused sufficient concern for Washington to give orders to Chargé d'Affaires Nelson O'Shaughnessy to be on the alert.[102] As a matter of fact, the only measure that the foreign companies really resented—and one that bothered the Americans and British alike—was a tax increase that Huerta had declared, which was even greater than Madero's levy of 1912. The State Department had known about his intention to put it into effect since October 1913 and had made its disapproval clear. Nevertheless, Huerta's budgetary difficulties were such that he felt obliged to go through with his plan.[103] The Association of Producers of Petroleum in Mexico (APPM) sent a delegation to speak to Huerta about the problem, and the State Department ordered its representative in Mexico to make a formal protest.[104] On this occasion, however, the pressure was to no avail, and Huerta held his ground on the tax. Up to the time his government fell, the American companies refused to pay it, invoking as an excuse his strained relations with Washington.[105]

In view of the continued hostility of the U.S. government, Huerta saw no other alternative but to seek British support. It was then that Great Britain made its last serious attempt to counteract the growing American influence in Mexico. Since oil was England's main interest there, it was only natural that Pearson became the intermediary between Huerta and His Majesty's government. The first thing to come out of this alliance was that Sir Lionel Carden—Pearson's friend, and, according to Jean-Baptiste Duroselle,[106] also a friend of the big English oil interests—presented his credentials to Huerta as ambassador of Great Britain—against the express wishes of President Wilson. Other European countries promptly followed suit. This new turn of events reinforced the American decision to get rid of Huerta. Invasion would be resorted to if necessary before Mexico would be allowed to become a satellite of Europe.[107]

Washington's displeasure focused on Carden and Pearson, especially when it was learned that the latter was negotiating a sizable loan for Huerta in London.[108] President Wilson, Secretary of State William Jennings Bryan, Colonel Edward M. House, and Ambassador John Lind at the Court of St. James's were all convinced that Pearson was out to get a monopoly over Mexican oil with the help of Huerta and his government.[109] However, Pearson's biographer, Desmond Young, claims that this was not the case. He insists that the British magnate had nothing to do with the fact that his government had decided to support Huerta. Young admits that Pearson and Carden were friends, that he had access to the British prime minister and the Foreign Office secretary, and that he believed Huerta was the man most capable of maintaining order in Mexico, but he claims that at no point and in no way did these circumstances lead the English lord to arrange for financial or any other kind of support for the Mexican leader—though these denials are not entirely convincing. Pearson, on learning that Washington had him at the top of its list of enemies in Mexico, hastily assured the U.S. government that he had no wish to jeopardize American interests by furnishing support to Huerta. Meanwhile, a Foreign Office envoy made similar disavowals to Wilson directly. The American president did not change his mind, however, feeling also that it was dangerous to let Pearson's interests be extended to other countries in Latin America.[110]

Not long later the British government was to abandon its position on Mexico. Considerations of far greater import—namely, the threat of war in Europe—obliged it to make up with Washington. At the end of 1913 Sir Lionel Carden—who according to Mrs. O'Shaughnessy had been in a veritable "love feast" with Huerta—went to the Mexican chief of state, together with a group of his European diplomatic colleagues, and asked him to consider complying with Wilson's request, explaining that Great Britain could no longer remain on his side.[111] Still, England, even though it had taken the "formidable decision" (as First Lord of the Admiralty Winston Churchill had phrased it) to run its fleet on coal instead of oil, could not give up on these valuable oil fields[112] without asking Wilson to offer a quid pro quo—namely, removal of certain discriminatory toll charges on foriegn ships passing through the Panama Canal.[113]

With the spheres of influence now divided up between the United States and Europe, it was not difficult to come to secondary agreements. For example, the governments of the United States, Great Britain, the Netherlands, and Sweden concurred not to recognize the advantages that some of the oil companies might obtain over the rest as a result of the abnormal conditions created by the civil war in Mexico.[114] In subordinating itself to U.S. policy in Mexico, England was essentially acknowledging the supremacy of American interests there, and this acknowledgment was accompanied by a request for assurance that British oil properties in Mexico would be protected by the United States. Wilson complied with a statement issued on December 2, 1913.[115]

With England "subdued," as some would have it, another European power, Germany, now came forward with an offer to Huerta of military support and any other kind of assistance he might need, in open defiance of Wilson. Clearly this German overture fitted in with the country's world strategic needs. Admiral Paul von Hintze went further and offered war matériel to Mexico in return for a promise that it would cut off the oil supply to the British fleet in the event of a war between the two powers. However, like so many other dubious German projects that were to come up, this one did not lead to any concrete results.[116] The United States' position remained unassailed.

U.S. Protection of the Oil Zone

The threat of U.S. intervention in Mexico—above and apart from the Veracruz incident—hung ominously over relations between the two countries throughout the Huerta administration.[117] Foremost among the reasons that could have led the United States to take this step was the need to protect the oil fields in the midst of the struggle between federal troops and the forces led by Carranza. In reality, during the ten years over which the armed conflict was to last, the companies' lands were in one of the most untroubled areas of the country.[118] One of the few interruptions in this tranquillity took place in April and May 1914 when Carranza besieged the Tampico area. In view of the danger to the oil rigs and other installations, Wilson's military advisers suggested that this section at least be occupied by American troops. The firms, hoping for such an eventuality, had sent maps of the oil region to the State Department with locations of their properties carefully marked, and these charts had been passed on to War Secretary Lindley Garrison.[119] When a tanker belonging to Waters-Pierce was sunk, Secretary of State Bryan warned both sides that the oil zone was neutral territory and that if this neutrality were not respected his country would be obliged to take steps to prevent the destruction of a resource that was of great interest not only to the companies and to Mexico but to the rest of the world as well. On April 2, 1914, the foreign technicians abandoned the oil fields and left the industry in charge of its Mexican employees. The companies demanded protection vociferously and at all levels.

On May 7, 1914, the representatives of 58 oil firms met in New York to review the "difficult situation" in Mexico. A committee of five spokesmen was appointed to call on President Wilson and urge him to obtain assurances from the Mexican government that their employees could safely return to the oil fields, making his stand fully known to the appropriate authorities in both Mexico and the United States.[120] At the same time they asked the State Department to try to get the British government to join it in insisting on the neutral status of the oil zone. Finally, they accompanied all these representations with urgent appeals to the Senate, claiming that they could not get to their wells to cap them, and that the oil was overflowing and flooding out over the countryside to as far away as Pánuco. A fire would be fatal, and the irresponsibility of the forces fighting in Mexico made such a catastrophe almost inevitable.[121] In response to Washington's demands, Carranza and Huerta both assured Secretary of State Bryan on repeated occasions that all the necessary guarantees would be extended to the foreign technicians, but no formal recognition of the neutral status of the oil zone was ever given.[122] The State Department backed up its warnings by sending down several warships, which were joined along the way by some European vessels, to sit at anchor off the coast of Tampico. For two weeks the American technicians stayed on board out of harm's way while the consul in Tampico took care of paying the Mexican employees and similar tasks. He had orders to do whatever he could to help the oil companies.[123] This was in fact the only time when the revolutionary struggle actually disrupted the industry's operations, and the protective machinery mobilized on the firms' behalf by the interested world powers was such that they hardly suffered any losses at all.[124] No one doubted that if the trouble had continued much longer the forces aboard the warships would have landed.

The Oil Interests and Huerta's Fall

While Huerta's overthrow was not the exclusive work of the American oil firms, still there is no doubt that they had a hand in it, especially after the encounter between Wilson and Huerta had led to the threat of British competition. Two facts should be kept in mind in this connection. First, even before the conflict developed between the two presidents, Ambassador Henry Lane Wilson himself had suggested to the State Department, as a possible solution to the Mexican problem, that the oil-producing region and surrounding area in the north of Mexico be constituted as a buffer state.[125] And second, quite apart from any resentment the firms may have had toward Huerta for his preferential treatment of Pearson, they were also bitter about the fact that he had upheld the tax decreed by Madero and, to make matters worse, actually taken steps to increase it.[126]

As the oilmen were later to testify before the Senate subcommittee chaired by Albert B. Fall of Arizona, President Wilson had never consulted them about his policy toward Mexico.[127] Doheny maintained that the companies had been totally powerless in the matter and had had no alternative but to submit to the decisions of their government. Given Washington's declared intentions, the only thing they did was to stop payment of their taxes to Huerta. They had not supported him, as they had been accused of doing. On the contrary, they had specifically helped Carranza, Doheny having advanced him 100,000 dollars in cash and 685,000 dollars' worth of fuel to be applied against future levies.[128] Nevertheless, there are indications that the oil firms had not limited themselves to suspending the payment of taxes and that they had probably had a part in the move for U.S. military occupation of the oil region. In 1913 their champion in the U.S. Congress, Senator Fall, came out in favor of a hard line with respect to the neighbor to the south. He appealed for a policy of zealous protection of American interests in Mexico and urged that the possibility of armed intervention not be ruled out.[129] (In 1921 Senator Fall, who for a number of years had been one of the main spokesmen for the oil interests in Congress, went on to occupy the post of secretary of the interior, where he had charge of the federal oil reserves. When it was discovered that he had taken advantage of his position to secretly lease the naval reserves at Elk Hills, California, and Teapot Dome, Wyoming, to Doheny and Sinclair, respectively, he was sentenced to prison and disappeared from the political scene.)[130] A similar opinion was expressed to Wilson personally by oilman William J. Payne.[131] In March, 1914, Fall called for occupation of the neighboring country in order to deliver the reigns of government into "capable and patriotic" hands.[132] For a while it was rumored that the USS *Dolphin* incident had been trumped up by Admiral Henry T. Mayo and the oil firms to justify an invasion of the oil region from the Gulf. While it is true that the possibility of armed intervention was raised several times in 1914 and afterward,[133] still the documents examined do not substantiate the thesis that the American oil firms had a significant role in the dispute between Wilson and Huerta.

In summary, it can be said that the establishment of the American and British oil companies in Mexico in the first decade of the century took place under favorable conditions that were to arouse the resentment of the successive nationalist regimes that came to power following the Revolution of 1910. These conditions were, essentially, the legislation prevailing with respect to subsoil property rights and the minimal contribution to the national treasury that was required of the companies. This situation was to give rise to a long and bitter struggle between the oil companies and the different governments in power from the fall of Porfirio Díaz onward. The tax imposed by Madero in 1912 was not the main cause of the antagonism between him and the Americans, but it did not fail to be a contributing factor. The change in U.S. policy toward Mexico following the election of Woodrow Wilson in 1912 does not appear to have been very much to the oil firms' liking at first, but in the long run Wilson's stand with respect to Huerta turned out to be beneficial, since because of it the British yielded the upper hand to Washington once and for all, and thus the American companies indirectly gained the advantage over their competitors. In addition to contributing to Carranza's victory over Huerta, Wilson's policy had helped Doheny's Mexican Petroleum to win out over El Aguila. Certainly British investments in Mexican oil did not disappear, but the danger of the firms entering into a special relationship with the Huerta government as before under the Porfirian regime—a possibility that had arisen as a result of the initial clash between Wilson and Huerta—was avoided.

Chapter 3

The Formulation of a New Oil Policy

The elimination of Madero, far from putting an end to the movement he represented, was to irreversibly unleash the forces of the Revolution—forces that he had almost succeeded in bringing under control. When the federal army surrendered to Carranza at Teoloyucan on August 13, 1914, it was forced to demobilize totally. The victory of Carranza, Villa, and Zapata brought down the buttress of what was left of the system held over from the Porfirian era. Subsequent blows were to seriously weaken other central elements of the old order—the hacienda, the Church, foriegn capital. The second phase of the struggle began in 1913 when Carranza, an old Porfirian politician converted to the Madero movement, challenged Huerta from his position as governor of the northern state of Coahuila, and it was to last until his own government eventually toppled at the hands of his lieutenant Alvaro Obregón in 1920. Historians have referred to it as the period of "social revolution," as distinguished from the "political" phase that began with Madero. The economic situation within which it unfolded was quite critical up until 1920. The demand for raw materials brought about by World War I did not benefit the Mexican economy as it did those of the other more stable countries in Latin America. The whole national production system was in chaos, important sectors were destroyed or paralyzed, inflation wrought havoc, and in some places people were close to starvation. The flow of foreign capital nearly came to a halt, and to make matters worse national as well as foreign money was leaving the country.[1] Only a handful of the large mining and oil companies were able to do business without serious disruptions during the second decade of the century.

The coalition of Constitutionalist forces under the leadership of Carranza was never a very solid one, and after their triumph over the common enemy the differences that had surfaced during the Madero regime came to the fore once again. On the one hand there were the peasant movements, headed in the north by Villa and in the southeast by Zapata, whose demands were not always the same, while on the other there was Carranza, Madero's official heir, who in the beginning represented the interests of the emerging middle class which was being victimized by the landowners and the big industrialists, most of them foreign. This latter sector came around to accepting some of the peasant demands and those of the incipient labor movement only when its supremacy was threatened. Only at that point did Carranza concede to deal with his opponents. At the Aguascalientes Convention in 1914 he attempted to reach a compromise on the selection of the new president, but when Villa and Zapata's candidate, Eulalio Gutiérrez, was chosen, he withdrew his support from the meeting. A violent struggle broke out between the Carranza faction and the forces led by Villa and Zapata in 1915, as a result of which the peasant leaders were to be defeated once and for all.[2]

Carranza and his group were forced to put aside their nineteenth-century positivist philosophy and yield to opportunism, accepting more radical solutions to the problems that faced them. Thus it was that Carranza, despite his scant sympathy for the labor movement, entered into a pact with the most important organization in this sector at the time: the House of the Workers of the World (Casa del Obrero Mundial). According to this accord, signed in 1915, the workers agreed to take up arms for the Constitutionalists, while the latter, for their part, promised to back the workers in their economic demands. A decree proclaiming the need for rural land reform which appeared later that same year had no other purpose than to take the agrarian banner away from Zapata. Only Carranza's need to secure a stronger base among the urban lower classes and to hold Zapata and Villa in check led him to make such concessions. He paid a high price indeed for his victory over the peasant leaders.

Carranza and the Foreign Interests

The general discontent over the privileged position enjoyed by foreigners in the Mexican social and economic structure was heightened with the Revolution. Carranza and the interests he represented had an essentially nationalistic philosophy. Their objectives centered on the creation of a new system in which they, not the foreigners, would have full control of both political and economic activity. Carranza was to go down in history as one of the great guardians of the Revolution. Unlike Zapata and Villa, moreover, he knew how to use nationalist sentiment to gain support for his regime.[3] When he first appeared on the scene as commander-in-chief of the Constitutionalist army, the foreign colony in Mexico already knew that he was not particularly sympathetic toward their interests.[4] And indeed, relations between the Americans and the Constitutionalist leader went far from smoothly. Immediately after assuming command of the anti-Huerta forces, he let the Americans know that he considered them largely responsible for Madero's fall.[5] In view of the international situation, he kept in touch with Washington through special agents. His dealings with the U.S. government were characterized by constant clashes and outright distrust.[6] He sought to create a new order in Mexico in which foreign influence would be neutralized to the greatest extent possible. Washington, on the other hand, wanted to see this new order established with a minimum of disturbance to the vested interests of its citizens.

The Americans in Mexico found it difficult to understand or accept the long-range considerations that guided President Wilson's policy. On more than one occasion they expressed their disagreement with him over how to solve the problems posed by the chaotic situation in Mexico. When the struggle broke out against Huerta, Wilson's position basically was that it should be left to run its own natural course, following which a constitutional regime that would once and for all put an end to the threat of new revolutions in Mexico could finally be established. This apparent tolerance of the revolutionary movement was not shared by the American investors in Mexico.[7] With Huerta defeated, Wilson's main interest was in seeing peace among the factions that had originally made up the anti-Huerta alliance so that he could then give his support to the building of a stable and democratic government. However, when it became evident that conciliation was impossible, no recourse was left but to back one faction or another in order to bring the civil war to an end. For a while Wilson debated about the choice, which in the end boiled down to Villa or Carranza.[8] Carranza was quite moderate, and the Americans appreciated this fact, although they did not much like his nationalism. It was not an easy decision. In one way or another, all the contending forces in Mexico tried to court Wilson's favor, since it was clear that with his open opposition it would be impossible to remain in power. Zapata and Villa were the ones who appeared most disposed to accept the demands on which Washington was conditioning its support,[9] and accordingly both Secretary of State Bryan and his successor, Robert Lansing, were in favor of backing Villa. But the rapid series of victories by Obregón, Carranza's most brilliant general, over the leader in the north in mid-1915 prevented any decision in this direction.[10] In October 1915 Wilson decided to give de facto recognition to Carranza, but only after he had first obtained certain assurances from him.[11]

It was at this point that the war in Europe intervened. Mexican problems had to be relegated to second place, and Wilson, who until then had personally directed the policy toward Mexico, was obliged to leave the situation almost entirely in the hands of his secretary of state.[12]

The European Conflict and Its Repercussions in Mexico

The "Great War" had a decided effect on the situation in Mexico and on the oil industry there: although from the beginning Mexican fuel had never been considered essential to the British fleet, the English maintained constant surveillance over the oil routes in the Gulf. The German embassy and its agents in Mexico were closely watched by the U.S. and British intelligence services and by Carranza himself so as to prevent any damage to the oil installations. In the end only a few minor acts of sabotage were committed.[13] The oil strike that broke out in Tampico at the beginning of 1917, however, was blamed in part on the Central Powers.[14] Meanwhile, the rumor went around that Mexico and Germany were planning to destroy the oil fields. The famous Zimmermann telegram—in which Germany held out the offer of territorial advantages to Mexico in the event the latter were to declare war against the United States—was the most spectacular piece of evidence, although not the only one, showing that the Germans did in fact have plans to mobilize Mexico against the United States and/or to cut off the

Allied oil lines.[15] Carranza, for his part, was not particularly satisfied with the situation in the oil sector. Already on December 12, 1914, in his "Additions to the Plan of Guadalupe"—the document which had marked the beginning of his struggle with Huerta—the oil reform was cited as one of the goals of the Carranza movement.[16] Moreover, at the time the United States entered the war a number of officials within the Constitutionalist government and a broad sector of the Mexican public were sympathetic to the Central Powers.[17] The incipient new Mexican nationalism was favorable to this attitude. For a while the word was spread that Carranza, taking advantage of Mexico's neutral status, intended to stop the exportation of oil to all the belligerents. The U.S. embassy warned him against such a measure, and nothing ever came of the threat.[18] Indeed, there is no record to indicate that the Mexican government ever actually considered entering into an alliance with Germany. Still, these facts did not keep the companies and a fair representation of the American press from accusing it of complicity with the Germans in their efforts to deprive the Allies of fuel.[19] Secretary of State Lansing believed these rumors and informed Wilson that the pro-German attitude of Carranza's military staff left the United States no alternative but to occupy the oil region, take over the Tehuantepec railroad, and deploy troops along the border. Wilson disagreed, however, both with respect to the characterization of the Carranza movement and on the need to use force against it at that particular time. It was unthinkable that the champion of self-determination would invade its next-door neighbor! He explained to Lansing that in the circumstances "the United States cannot afford to be too 'practical'" in the case of Mexico. Only "the mot extraordinary circumstances of arbitrary injustice" could lead him to order the occupation of Tampico or Tehuantepec.[20] Still, Carranza's denials that his government was contemplating an embargo or any other such move did not entirely allay suspicions against him within the United States.

In Mexico Carranza's enemies took advantage of Washington's fear of German activities and did their best to fan the flame. Manuel Peláez, a rebel chieftain of no particular convictions who was operating in the oil region, saw a chance to curry favor with the Americans. He was soon joined by Félix Díaz (the dictator's nephew), who had forces under his command near Veracruz. In a joint "proclamation to the president and people of the United States of America" they declared that it was in fact Carranza's intention to wrest the oil from Allied control in order to turn it over to the Germans and offered to protect the Americans against this sinister scheme.[21] The oil companies, for their part, consistently protested Carranza's efforts to get Peláez out of the area and complained in Washington that this campaign was a German plot. Accordingly, the State Department made it known that it was indispensable for Peláez to remain in the oil region and protect the fields against the threats both of Carranza and of the German saboteurs.[22] The supposed activity of German agents in the oil fields and an imagined plan for a Mexican-German alliance continued to be hinted at in the United States right up until the end of the war, conveniently providing a basis for the companies' reiterated demands that Carranza be kept out of power.[23]

As a result of the war, two contradictory trends in U.S.-Mexican relations were to emerge. On the one hand, the entry of the United States into the European conflict helped to speed up withdrawal of the forces under General John J. Pershing, who in 1916 had conducted a punitive expedition into Mexico following a series of raids by Villa against towns on the American side of the border. On the other hand, it increased the possibility of an Allied occupation of the oil region to protect it against the threat, real or supposed, of Germany. The fact that there was no real sabotage to the oil installations, either because it was never actually attempted or else because it was averted by joint Allied-Mexican surveillance, considerably reduced the danger of occupation. Nevertheless, the companies did not stop worrying entirely about the "German threat," even after the war was over, and for some time they continued to use it as an argument to justify their demands to the State Department for protection.[24]

The Revolution's First Attempts to Change the Status of the Oil Firms

The policy designed to secure greater national participation in the benefits from the oil reserves, at the time considered to be unlimited, was a constant feature of Carranza'a administration. It had been enunciated even before his victory over Huerta, despite his dependence on the goodwill of Washington, and the steps that he took in this direction from 1914 on were to determine the definitive cast of the "oil clause" under Article 27 of the new constitution.

At the time of Huerta's overthrow, it was believed in the United States that Mexico had the largest oil region in the world and could supply it with fuel for many years.[25] Carranza and his confederates imagined likewise and thought to save the faltering economy by increasing their control over this wealth. To put their oil policy into effect they utilized such devices as taxes, drilling permits, application of the Calvo clause (whereby the firms had no right to diplomatic protection in the event of a dispute with the government) to titles and leases, etc. They also sought to get even further to the bottom of the problem by substituting government concessions for all the companies' former property titles through a draft law that nationalized the oil. These measures were to be the subject of heated dispute between the Carranza administration on the one hand and the oil interests and their governments on the other from 1913 until 1917.

Recognizing Wilson's need for support in his opposition to Huerta, Carranza sent one of his prominent supporters, Luis Cabrera, to Washington to confirm that it was his intention to respect all the foreigners' "just" claims in Mexico—a vague commitment in which he did not define what he meant by "just."[26] The first contacts between the Constitutionalists and the American oil companies were relatively cordial, particularly when the firms refused to go on paying their taxes to Huerta.[27] Nevertheless, there were tensions owing to the revolutionary struggle itself,[28] which increased when fighting broke out near the oil region in 1914 and obliged the foreign technicians, as we have noted before, to evacuate the area and leave the fields in the hands of their Mexican employees, taking refuge aboard American and British warships that were stationed in the harbor in order to protect the oil installations. Washington, confronted with mounting pressure from the companies, appealed to the combatants to respect the neutrality of the oil zone: the burning of the wells in the course of the struggle would be a catastrophe of worldwide proportions. Still, Carranza, despite his need for Washington's goodwill, refused to make such a commitment. Instead, he simply reiterated that the forces under his command would do whatever was necessary so that the oilmen could resume their activities.[29] This did not satisfy them, and for some time afterward Carranza was to receive American protests over the damage suffered by the companies as a result of the conflict that ensued following the fall of Huerta.[30]

Soon, however, the fear of possible damage to the oil installations as a result of the armed struggle ceased to be the main source of friction between Carranza and the Americans. The threat of a change in the industry's legal status took first place. In 1914 the Mexican Ministry of Development, Colonization, and Industry, at the express order of the president, began to prepare and even to put into practice a series of measures designed to restore ownership to all combustible minerals to the nation.[31] Luis Cabrera, who was an important force in the new administration, publicly supported these measures and advocated increased state participation in the industry's profits, as well as solicitation of investment capital from sources in other countries, as means of combating American domination.[32] It was a new version of the old Porfirian strategy designed to minimize Mexico's position of dependence, but it was not to meet with any greater success than its predecessor had. By the end of another two years the idea of substantially changing the industry's legal status had begun to take shape. In April 1916 the Technical Commission on the Nationalization of Oil, an agency established by order of Carranza to help set government policy on the subject, presented a report that ended with the following declaration: "For all the reasons stated, we believe it is only right that that which belongs to the nation—the subsoil resources of coal and oil—be restored to it . . . ."[33] And so the issue was joined in a controversy that was to last until the 1940's.

Of more immediate impact were the decrees relating to the oil industry issued by Carranza and his ministers during these early years. While in 1913 Cándido Aguilar, the governor of Veracruz, had had to give up in his effort to raise taxes, by 1914 the situation had changed. Following their victory at Tampico that year, the Constitutionalists, ignoring the foreign fleet anchored in the harbor, levied a *derecho de barra*, patterned after a tax on minerals assessed in colonial times, and demanded that the firms pay it in gold.[34] When the latter refused, the revolutionary forces threatened to seal off the pipelines carrying fuel to the tankers in the port.[35] At the same time Governor Aguilar came out and declared all the oil concessions from the Huerta regime null and void, and shortly thereafter he forbade the sale or leasing of oil lands without prior authorization from the government of the state. His aim in both cases was to keep private parties unaware of the land's value from turning their property over to the companies on terms prejudicial to themselves and to the nation.[36]

The real beginning of the oil controversy, however, according to J. Reuben Clark, Jr., U.S. ambassador in Mexico from 1930 to 1933, dates from the decree of September 19, 1914.[37] According to this instrument, ostensibly designed to gain a more precise determination of the national wealth and set up an equitable tax structure, all owners of land and industries were asked to file an assessment of their holdings. It was similar to the Madero decree, and, like the earlier one, it too was disregarded by the oil companies. As in the former case, the information asked for would have provided the government with the necessary criteria not only for levying taxes on the flourishing oil industry but also for applying all other manner of legal and administrative measures. The companies simply refused to give the data requested.

Again, as in 1912, the oil firms' stand was backed by the State Department. Though the 1914 *derecho de barra* was finally paid under protest, Carranza gave in under U.S. pressure and agreed not to insist on the gold or dollars that he had originally wanted as well as to recognize the validity of the tax payments made to Huerta in the past.[38] Cándido Aguilar's refusal to honor the concessions from the Huerta regime was likewise the subject of strong protests from Washington, and in the end the decision was never put into effect.[39] Moreover, Washington ordered Admiral Frank F. Fletcher, whose ships were at the mouth of Tampico harbor, to warn Carranza not to carry out any reprisals against the British interests that had supported Huerta.[40] Finally, the White House stood behind the companies' refusal to furnish information about the extent of their holdings as called for in the September decree, claiming that such an assessment would be "very difficult" to make.[41] Madero's troubles with the oil industry were being repeated step by step all over again with Carranza. The new leader's problems were aggravated that same year by the uprising of General Manuel Peláez, who took control of the entire oil region, except for the ports, and was to keep it out from under the central government's jurisdiction for six years.

By 1915 Carranza, despite his political vulnerability because of his continuing difficulties with Villa and Zapata, was already seriously committed to the oil reform. On October 8, 1914, he created a corps of oil inspectors. This move was followed on March 15, 1915, by establishment of the Technical Commission on the Nationalization of Oil. In the midst of the political chaos a control system characterized by increasing official surveillance over and interference in the oil industry began to take shape. In expectation of forthcoming legislation, a Carranza decree of January 7, 1915, ordered a halt to any new drilling and demanded that permits be obtained in order to continue the operations already under way.[42] Carranza had taken these steps in the midst of the civil struggle since ". . . they gave the government unquestioned control over the exploration and industrial exploitation of oil."[43] Both the companies and the State Department in Washington understood the dangerous implications these requirements could have if they were applied to established interests. The firms, of course, were willing to take the chance of resisting the decree, in as much as by obeying it they would be committing themselves to complying with future legislation on the subject. The State Department protest did not take long in coming.[44]

When some of the companies were obliged to suspend their activities because they could not dig any new wells, the protests increased.[45] The Carranza government had no alternative but to give in, and gradually it began to grant "provisional permits."[46] The companies thanked the State Department for its intervention.[47] Washington was also successful in its effort to prevent confiscation of their rigs, which were being operated without proper permits in "federal zones."[48] At the end of 1915 Mexico made one more try to get the firms to give in and provide the information that had been being asked of them since January.[49] It was in the form of a circular, issued on November 15, urging them to comply and register their holdings—this time the alleged reason being to prevent the establishment of bogus companies that would issue worthless shares of stock. Again, no one was fooled: the real objective was for the government to gain increased control, and the firms were of no inclination to cooperate.[50] By 1915 Carranza's oil strategy was clear. He intended to put on as much pressure as he possibly could to get the vested interests to accept a reform in favor of the state. By this means he hoped not only to bring in some new income but also to consolidate his position in power. Given the existing balance of forces, however, it would be necessary to retreat to a point at which open conflict would be avoided—though not, of course, to go all the way back to the beginning. The results would not be the spectacular ones envisaged in the decrees but rather more modest ones. However, this was the most that could be done given the situation within which he had to work.

The year 1916 began with renewed protests from the State Department: Governor Aguilar had issued an order requiring that all purchases of oil lands in Veracruz be authorized by his administration. The companies claimed that the real reason behind this move was that the lands in question were known to be valuable and some of the generals in the army wanted to take them over. This accusation is not entirely beyond the realm of the possible. Carranza's generals were not necessarily noted for their probity. On February 2 the U.S. government informed Carranza that his efforts to modify the foreign firms' legal status left it with no alternative but to reserve all the vested rights of its citizens involved in the Mexican oil industry.[51] The subsequent cancellation of several leases granted to American companies by Huerta, coupled with efforts to oblige them to accept terms similar to the later Calvo clause added fuel to the fire in Washington.[52] What worried the companies and the State Department most was the possibility of an imminent change in the oil legislation that would entail nationalization of all the deposits. In January 1916 Secretary Lansing asked the U.S. consul in Querétaro, where Carranza's government was temporarily headquartered, to see if there was any truth to the rumor about a takeover, telling him to point out to the Constitutionalist leader that any move of this kind would have exceedingly dangerous consequences. The consul's reply, based on a personal meeting with Carranza, set the secretary of state's mind at ease: definitely no such action was contemplated.[53] However, rumors to the effect that such a plan—supposedly conceived by a prominent lawyer in the Carranza movement, Pastor Rouaix—did in fact exist continued to be alluded to in the Mexican and foreign press.[54] Throughout the rest of the year alarming bulletins reached the State Department at regular intervals.[55] Washington remained on the alert.

Although Carranza's faction was the most nationalistic among the revolutionary forces, it was not alone in its desire to modify the status of the oil industry. To a greater or lesser degree, the different movements were unanimous on the subject, since the foreign sector stood to lose the most, while any group that might come to power was bound to gain. As far as the Zapata and Villa factions were concerned, however, land reform was the main issue, and the oil question for them was only marginal. The one time they actually referred to the problem was at the Aguascalientes Convention in 1914. As a matter of fact, after Carranza, those who were most adamant on the subject were the conservative journalists and writers of the time.[56]

Anti-Carranza Movements in the Oil Region

In addition to the pressures exerted directly by the companies and the State Department, Carranza had a third element to face that was against his oil policy: the independent armed movements in the Tamaulipas and Veracruz areas. In 1914, precisely when the Constitutionalist leader's decrees aimed at modifying the status of the oil firms began to appear, Manuel Peláez rose up against him and proceeded to take control of the region in which the companies were operating. Was this a coincidence? There is no doubt that the Peláez rebellion was linked to the conflict between Carranza and the oil firms, but the precise nature of the connection is not very clear. Did the companies themselves organize the insurrection? Or was it Peláez who seized on a situation that he saw was to his advantage and offered them protection against Carranza in exchange for some form of compensation? From the beginning the Carranza officials seemed to have no doubt and openly accused the companies of having fomented and abetted the uprising.[57] The firms, for their part, always insisted that they had nothing to do with the Peláez movement. According to them, they were forced to accept the situation and pay the tribute he was demanding or else see their property destroyed.[58] There is no definitive documentary proof one way or the other, but, quite apart from the question of which side was responsible for starting the rebellion, there is no doubt that once it was underway the companies knew how to take advantage of it. The protection of the oil zone in the midst of a full-scale civil war cost the firms about 15,000 dollars a month. However, the protection and freedom they gained was well worth the price.[59] Unfortunately for them, the Carranza forces were always strong in the cities and never lost control of the ports. The relationship between the companies and Peláez seems to have been very close. In addition to the exchange of money, a number of employees from the industry actually joined in the fighting.[60] Moreover, on several occasions the firms pointed out to the State Department that it was in the U.S. interest to keep Carranza from undertaking a formal campaign against Peláez.[61] Up until 1918 the companies were entirely on his side, singing praises of the good treatment and protection he gave them.[62] Indeed, on May 5, 1917, the rebel leader issued a manifesto rejecting the new Carranza constitution and declaring his intention to keep the oil from being wrested from its legitimate owners. Carranza, for his part, maintained that the companies not only supplied the "forced loans" to Peláez willingly but also furnished him with arms, munitions, and other forms of assistance.[63] Believing this to be the case, Carranza's men threatened the firms more than once,[64] but the constant intercession by the U.S. government prevented any real move against them. Carranza was told that he had no right to take steps against the companies, since they were obliged to cooperate with Peláez precisely because of the Constitutionalist forces' inability to maintain control of the entire country.[65] Moreover, the State Department demanded assurances that its requests would be heeded. U.S. warships stood ready to back up Washington's words and protect the companies. The alliance between Peláez and the oil firms was looked on with favor by both the State Department and President Wilson himself,[66] although Washington did not go so far as to accept the rebel leader's proposals for a mutual aid pact.[67]

In 1918, however, when Peláez started to cap the wells and destroy some of the oil installations,[68] relations between the companies and their protector took a turn for the worse. It would seem that the insurgent, worried about the growing threat of Carranza, who had already gained control over Villa and Zapata, decided that U.S. intervention in the area was the only way to save his cause. Accordingly, with a view to provoking such an occurrence, he undertook to block the production of oil.[69] At the same time, his increased demands for payments from the companies also contributed to a breakdown in relations.[70] From that point up to 1920, when Carranza was assassinated, the situation remained more or less the same. When differences developed between Carranza and his most brilliant general, Alvaro Obregón, over the succession to the presidency, Peláez cast his lot with the latter. With Obregón's victory at Agua Prieta, he laid down his arms before the Adolfo de la Huerta provisional government, and neither he nor anyone else was ever again to take the oil zone out from under the central government's control. Two other generals—Félix Díaz and Higinio Aguilar—also tried at this time to capitalize on the conflict between Carranza and the oil firms through a similar maneuver, but they were much less successful— mainly because they did not have the strength to permanently control a territorial base as Peláez had.[71] Díaz not only accused Carranza publicly of taking sides with the Germans and attempting to confiscate the oil companies' properties, but he went so far as to supply Albert B. Fall in August 1919, through his agent in the United States, Pedro del Villar, with information that was used in the U.S. senator's campaign against Carranza.

There were also some vague agreements between Francisco Villa and the oil firms, but they never led to anything concrete. In 1914 word went around to the effect that Standard Oil and Waters-Pierce were negotiating a series of concessions with this important revolutionary leader.[72] A news item appearing in the press at about that time indicated that the oil interests, along with American Smelting and Refining, planned to lend support to Villa in his struggle against Carranza.[73] In 1916 an American publication alleged (with no conclusive proof) that Villa's raid on Columbus, New Mexico—which was answered by the Pershing punitive expedition—had been plotted with the oil firms in order to provoke an incident that would lead Wilson to intervene and send troops.[74] In the years that followed there were other rumors of talks between the oilmen and Villa.[75] In the absence of any further evidence, the only thing that can be said is that if any sort of arrangement did in fact exist between Villa and the oil firms, it was not at all important and certainly nothing ever came of it.

The Threat of U.S. Intervention in Behalf of the Oil Companies

From the outset Carranza had had to deal with the threat of an American intervention in defense of the oil interests. Even after the fall of Huerta, the Constitutionalists' clash with federal troops at Tamaulipas had been overshadowed by the specter of a U.S. landing to prevent damage to the oil installations. Warships not only from the United States but also from England, France, Germany, Spain, and even Cuba were lying at anchor in Tampico Harbor. More than once the officers in the chain of command appealed to Navy Secretary Josephus Daniels (who was later to be the U.S. ambassador in Mexico) for permission to warn the Constitutionalists to respect American lives and property.[76]

After Huerta's fall, President Wilson made it clear on various occasions that he intended to do everything in his power to avoid a war with Mexico.[77] Although he was supported in this position by some sectors of American public opinion,[78] the endorsement was by no means unanimous. His military advisers, for example, dissented vehemently, maintaining exactly the opposite: in the national interest it was imperative to invade Mexico or at least to take over the region where the main oil fields were located.[79] To these military voices were added others, such as those of former president Theodore Roosevelt, the Catholic Church fathers (displeased by Carranza's anticlericalism), and, of course, the oilmen themselves, especially through their friend in congress, Senator Fall.[80] Although the oil fields provided an excuse for demanding invasion, they were also an Achilles' heel, and Carranza took advantage of this fact. At the beginning of 1915, for reasons unrelated to the oil conflict, Wilson went so far as to seriously reconsider the desirability of a landing at Veracruz.[81] Carranza met the situation by threatening the potential adversary at its most vulnerable point: the oil fields. If U.S. troops were to actually land, he warned, the rigs would be set afire.[82] In 1916 Villa's raid on Columbus, New Mexico, in which seventeen Americans were killed, coupled with the gunning down of several U.S. engineers at Santa Isabel on orders from the guerrilla leader, caused the pressure for intervention to mount sharply. In Wilson's cabinet, Interior Secretary Franklin K. Lane tried his utmost to persuade the president that he must show "strong leadership" and use force with Mexico. Britain, for its part, anxious to protect its own investment, did everything possible to induce the United States to cast the die and take over the oil region once and for all. Back in congress, Senator Fall reacted to the Villa incursion in the strongest possible terms and demanded that Mexico be taught a lesson.[83] Following the Santa Isabel slayings, he and his colleague from Texas Senator James L. Slayden had already sponsored a resolution calling for an army of half a million to be sent immediately to occupy Mexico.[84] When Wilson, in order to avoid an invasion, dispatched General Pershing and his expeditionary force with the limited objective of capturing Villa in 1916, Fall personally went to the border in search of his own "information" and demanded complete success of the mission. He declared that if the U.S. troops returned without having captured Villa he would "open up a bombardment in the Senate which would make the past revolutions in Mexico look like a sane Fourth of July celebration."[85] These activities led him to be identified as the driving force behind the interventionist movement.[86]

Wilson never ceased to be aware of the main origin of the problem: the oil and mining interests. In conversations with Ray Stannard Baker in May 1916 he said that "the greatest trouble is not with Mexico but with people here in America who want the oil and metals in Mexico and are seeking intervention in order to get them." He went on to say that he intended to do what he could to see that they did not attain their objective.[87] There is no indication that after the Veracruz landing the U.S. Army or Navy ever made any serious plans to take over the Mexican oil region.[88] It is a fact, however, that in 1916 the State Department did call for warships to be deployed along the Gulf coast of Mexico, having heard that the plan to set the oil wells on fire in the event of an American attack was still in effect.[89]

In conclusion, it may be said that the events of the Carranza period prior to the promulgation of the new constitution in 1917 were decisive with respect to the oil industry, for it was during this time that the seeds of paragraph iv of Article 27—the basis for the oil reform to be attempted by future governments—were sown. The respective positions that the oil interests and the U.S. government were to take and the strategy they were to follow in the years to come were also outlined during this period. The lines of the conflict were already drawn by the end of 1916 when Carranza's group, the most nationalistic of the revolutionary factions, won out over their peasant rivals. In 1916 both parties, Carranza on the one hand and the Americans on the other, seemed to be equally determined to stand up for their convictions. In the end, Wilson's attitude and the war in Europe were largely responsible for keeping the situation from reaching the point of open war, but the possibility of an armed intervention in the oil zone was a real one that Carranza never ceased to take into account in setting his policy.

Chapter 4

Carranza and the Oil Reform

The Constitution of 1917, which is still in effect today, was the work of Carranza's victorious faction. It was to provide the legal basis for putting into effect the political and economic reforms that had been included in one way or another in the potpourri that was the Constitutionalist platform. It synthesized all the different views, frequently in conflict, predominating within the various groups that had supported Carranza in his struggle first against Huerta and later against Villa and Zapata. Practically all the most important political philosophies were found represented among the Constitutionalists, and this eclecticism was to come through in the final text of the new supreme law. The attack on the old order went beyond what Carranza and his close followers had wanted, but it still did not completely satisfy the radical group[1] (which to a certain extent represented the incipient labor movement emerging as a result of the industrialization fostered by foreign capital and of the influx of people from rural areas to work in factories).

In their concern to rehabilitate a bankrupt economy, the planners of the new government prepared the way for putting an end to the former system based on a large-landholding economy and excessive domination of foreign capital. The Constitution of 1917 maintained the basic structure of the previous one, which had been drafted by the liberal party in 1857, but it departed considerably from its predecessor's individualism in the economic and social changes that it propounded. The principle of private property was upheld, but on the condition that it serve a "social purpose." Individual rights were subordinated to the common good. The most important concrete changes besides this new concept of individual rights were those related to education and the place of church in society, workers' rights, land ownership, and the possession and exploitation of subsoil resources. In effect the constitution legitimized the changes that were going to take place. The new government's role was not only to *preserve* but also to *promote*.

For the most part the reforms were concentrated in Articles 3, 27, 123, and 130 of the new document. Revolutionary policy centered on establishment of the ejido system designed to give land to the peasants who until then had been merely a source of cheap labor for the large landowners, protection and support of workers, mitigation of the power of the Roman Catholic clergy, and drastic curtailment of the role to be played by foreign capital in the new society. Basic to the change proposed was the return of the rights to the subsoil—in other words, the oil—to the nation, and this was precisely the purpose behind paragraph iv of Article 27, which will be examined later in detail.

For a variety of reasons, the new constitution's program of reforms was never wholly implemented. To begin with, in certain areas the opposition was strong enough to totally block or at least partially hinder application of the new provisions. This was especially true in the case of the measures designed to work against the foreign interests, and particularly those with respect to oil. The Constitution of 1917 was a very ductile instrument, far from precise in many of its points. Its application depended on the interpretations that the different succeeding administrations would see fit to give it—interpretations that, insofar as the reform of subsoil rights was concerned, would be basically determined by external factors. The constitutional provisions with regard to oil were to be applied to the extent that the different governments felt they could withstand the combined pressure brought to bear by Washington and the oil companies—a pressure that was constant and varied only in its intensity.

For the Constitutional Assembly meeting at Querétaro in 1916–1917, Article 27 was the cement which held together the whole set of reforms that it sought to put into effect. This article—whose language was unfortunately not very clear—contained a series of principles which, though not immediately related one to another, were all designed in some way to effect a thoroughgoing transformation in the concept of private property that had prevailed up to that time. The right of private property—as it had already been said by others—existed mainly by virtue of its social function and was subject to the will of the body social, expressed through its political organs. And so it was that an order was created in which the state had a role vastly different from that which it had in the political systems of the great Western powers, in which nineteenth-century Anglo-American jurisprudence made the right of property entirely dependent on "natural law" and placed the interests of the individual above those of the community. Although the most radical faction within the Constitutional Assembly failed in its attempt to have the concept of private property thrown out entirely, the reform that did pass was already sufficiently far-reaching to produce violent reactions on the part of the foreign interests affected.

Article 27, in its paragraph iv, made a distinction between surface and subsoil property and gave the latter to the nation. Thus oil was brought under the legal system that governed the exploration of the rest of the minerals, and all existing legislation on the subject drawn up by previous governments was automatically invalidated.

At first glance it would appear that this particular reform had been imposed on Carranza by General Francisco J. Múgica and the rest of the radical group associated with Obregón, since the list of draft amendments to the earlier constitution which Carranza had presented to the assembly did not include the oil clause that was finally adopted.[2] However, a more careful review of the situation rules out this possibility. Carranza had been forced to go along with the agrarian and labor reforms, but as far as the foreign interests were concerned he was the first one to press for a change. Indeed, the measures that he and his party had taken in regard to oil prior to 1917 already showed a clear intent to turn around the favorable situation that the oil companies were enjoying. There is no question that the origin of the provisions which were eventually to make up paragraph iv can be traced to these earlier Carranza decrees. Moreover, the 1915 "Additions to the Plan of Guadalupe" promised that the movement's victory would bring reforms in the exploitation of minerals, petroleum, water, forests, and other natural resources. This precedent alone, however, was not enough to oblige the Constitutional Assembly to act as it did. It should be remembered that Múgica, the head of the constitutional-reform committee, was aided in the drafting of Article 27 by men from Carranza's own inner circle: Pastor Rouaix, José N. Macías, and Andrés Molina Enríquez (this last in the capacity of adviser). According to Rouaix, it was Carranza himself who had suggested nationalization of the oil.[3]

Because of its economic importance and its special legal status, the oil industry was singled out by Carranza as the focus of his attack against the favored position of foreign capital.[4] The chief executive was undoubtedly motivated by political considerations when he took the decision to attempt to regain control of the economic system and secure for the nation a greater participation in the benefits from the oil. This foreign-dominated sector, in which there were practically no national interests that could be affected, was the logical place for a leader reluctant to apply radical measures to assume a firm nationalistic stand in order to keep favor with the extremists who were demanding changes in more controversial areas. This strategy did not lack hazards, but it did offer the prospect of new fields of activity for the middle sectors that had begun to emerge during the Porfirian regime, while at the same time providing a means for winning the popular support that had been slow in coming because of the half-hearted nature of the reforms applied in other fields, such as land redistribution. Both Carranza and the drafters of the constitution were aware from the beginning that the oil reform involved serious international implications.[5] It is perhaps for this very reason that the new leader did not propose paragraph iv directly. External pressure could be exerted less easily on the Constitutional Assembly than on the executive. He preferred to appear as the simple executor of a higher-level mandate which must be fulfilled, rather than as the actual promoter.

When the committee charged with drafting the oil provisions presented its text to the plenary on January 1, 1917, there was virtually no debate. Nor did subsequent modifications provoke any considerable discussion. On January 25 the Constitutional Assembly announced that the right of property provided for in Article 27 permitted the nation to keep for itself the mines, the oil, and everything else in its domain that might be necessary for "social development."[6] Shortly thereafter the article's sponsors stated their position more specifically: "The nation has ceded the right of ownership to private individuals, but in so doing it has not given up the right to the products of the subsoil."[7] Thus, without discussion, the assembly in a single stroke of the pen completely wiped out the ownership rights to the hydrocarbon subsoil reserves which up until then had been held by private parties and, furthermore, empowered the executive to review and cancel all the concessions and other contracts entered into since 1876 between private individuals and the state if the public interest should so require.[8]

In view of the clear-cut position taken by the assembly—according to which all individual property rights to the oil deposits were to be abolished —the subsequent protracted controversy over whether or not paragraph iv applied to rights acquired prior to 1917 under the old legislation[9] is difficult to understand. Those in the Revolutionary camp who later, spurred by U.S. opposition, were to maintain that vested rights could not be infringed upon, took advantage of the drafters' imprecise language to block the attempts of future governments to put the Constitution of 1917 into effect.[10] This "conservative" thesis of nonretroactivity continued to be upheld despite the fact that in 1918 Pastor Rouaix, in response to a question regarding interpretation of the phrase "direct dominion" used in relation to oil in Article 27, declared that "from the moment the Constitution of 1917 was promulgated, legal ownership of the oil and other hydrocarbons was returned to the nation," later adding that "there is no basis for this much-talked-about retroactivity . . . The only thing that matters is to recover and rebuild the essential property of the nation which one of its leaders [Porfirio Díaz] unrightfully attempted to turn over to private parties."[11]

To fully understand the importance of the decision taken in 1917 with regard to the hydrocarbons, one should keep in mind that more than 90 per cent of all the oil properties affected either belonged to or were controlled by foreign corporations.[12] Moreover, practically all the lands that the oil companies were to explore up until 1938 had already been acquired under the Porfirian legislation. According to a draft law proposed by the executive in June 1917, at the time the new constitution was promulgated the companies held rights over 2,151,025 hectares of oil lands.[13] This is why the new code was never attacked for its effect on future acquisitions: all the lands known to have oil were already in the companies' possession by 1917.

In order to enforce Article 27 it was necessary for the Congress to approve both the organic and the regulatory laws implementing paragraph iv. However, the pressure exerted by the vested interests against the various texts proposed was so great that the government was to wait eight years before the first of these acts finally went into effect. Even then, the text was substantially modified by the opposition that had been aroused. Nevertheless, the attempts to get the law and its regulations on the books were to begin early on with Carranza himself. Though accepted today in developing countries throughout the world, the policy in regard to natural resources set forth in the Constitution of 1917—namely, that they should be taken out from under foreign control and put to use in behalf of national development —had a long and difficult road to traverse before it was to become a reality.[14]

Reaction of the Companies and the State Department

Article 27 immediately encountered opposition from the various groups that were affected: the landowners, the Church, and the foreign interests.

The last-mentioned sector, however, was the only one that was to have the forces necessary to stand up to the Revolutionary governments. In examining the U.S. reaction to the new constitutional provision, it is well to consider the companies and the State Department separately—even though in actual practice there was no such clear-cut distinction. From the outset the firms had done their best to keep the law from seeing the light of day. According to Francisco Múgica, the oil lobby had tried hard but unsuccessfully to suborn the different members of the Constitutional Assembly at Querétaro.[15] Once the new law was adopted, the companies, now on the defensive, contacted the State Department and demanded protection.[16] The latter, which had already been studying the situation, quickly mobilized its entire political armamentarium in their behalf, and for more than two decades the oil firms were to satisfactorily resist the Mexican government's drive, turning the application of Article 27 into the subject that was to be Mexico's major international concern over this whole long period. To channel their efforts more effectively, the foreign interests had formed an Association of Producers of Petroleum in Mexico (APPM), which brought together the principal American and British firms involved[17]—indeed, all the important producers in Mexico.[18] This organization had offices in both New York and Mexico City. In Tampico, the main oil port, an Oil Managers Association made up of ranking executives from the APPM member firms was also established. During its last years in Mexico, this organization changed its name and became the Sindicato Patronal. Now united, the firms took the position that the new Mexican constitution had been adopted irregularly and illegally[19] and that therefore they were under no obligation to abide by Article 27. In 1918 a spokesman for the oil industry in Mexico told the State Department that the new constitution, and Article 27 in particular, was in fact the work of the German minister in Mexico, Heinrich von Eckhardt, and was designed to deprive the United States and its allies of Mexican oil.[20] This was the beginning of a long and vigorous propaganda campaign designed to discredit the new Mexican constitution and persuade the American public to support the firms' petitions in Washington. Basically, it denounced the Carranza government's "confiscation" of the oil reserves in bald disregard for the sanctity of private property.[21]

When it was first rumored in January 1916 that the Carranza government might attempt to modify the legal status of the oil deposits being worked by the American companies, the State Department had warned the Mexican executive of the dangers that such a measure could entail and asked for his reassurance that nationalization was not being contemplated.[22] The presence of Pershing's troops along the border at the time gave the U.S. government special leverage with which to extract a guarantee regarding the property rights of its citizens in Mexico. In talks held in New London and Atlantic City at the end of 1916 and the beginning of 1917, the United States insisted that Mexico promise, in exchange for Pershing's withdrawal, to protect the property of Americans not only against armed attack but also against any possible "confiscatory measure." Carranza refused. In October 1916 the Americans proposed a draft agreement with a clause expressly recognizing the rights acquired in the past by Americans and foreigners in general. Alberto J. Pani, one of the Mexican delegates, claimed that the oil companies had pressured the U.S. envoys into trying to get these assurances from Mexico.[23] Carranza stood firm and refused to enter into any commitment until the U.S. troops were recalled. In the end President Wilson was forced to order Pershing's unconditional withdrawal because of looming conflict in Europe. Thus World War I was instrumental in opening up the future course for the implementation of Article 27.

Following closely the deliberations of the Constitutional Assembly, Washington was to learn shortly thereafter that despite all its efforts the threat of nationalization had materialized in the form of Article 27. The State Department immediately lodged a protest and demanded assurances that the new code would not be applied retroactively. In any case, the United States warned, it did not feel it was under any obligation to abide by the provisions approved at Querétaro.[24] The State Department's efforts were focused on getting the interests of its citizens (and to a lesser extent those of the Europeans) excluded from the application of Articles 3, 27, 33, and 130.[25] Carranza felt obliged to yield to some extent, and on February 20, just before the constitution was to enter into effect, he sent word through his minister of foreign affairs to Ambassador-designate Henry P. Fletcher (who was in Mexico awaiting Washington's decision so that he could go ahead and present his credentials) that it was unlikely the new legislation would affect any long-established interests in Mexico. The United States took this to be a definite assurance, and a few months later it extended de jure recognition to the Carranza government.[26]

Theoretical Bases of the Carranza Oil Policy

Meanwhile, the fact is that the Carranza government set about doing everything possible to develop the legal bases that would justify retroactive application of Article 27 in the eyes of the world. The authors of the various different theories that were advanced—and there were several, not necessarily consistent one with another—were typical members of the Carranza group: middle-level lawyers and engineers, most of them serving in the Ministry of Industry. The arguments they conceived to back up the nation's claim to the subsoil did not disappear with Carranza. Subsequent regimes were to fill in his roughly outlined policies in all fields, and, in one way or another, as circumstances permitted, they were to invoke these legal arguments time and again over the ensuing decades.[27]

Foremost among the theoretical bases evolved for Article 27 were those related to retroactivity. To begin with, there was the line of reasoning based on the supremacy of national interest, which claimed that retroactivity was entirely legitimate. It held that when the national interest comes into conflict with private interests—as it had done in the case of the oil companies—the latter, no matter how much weight they may carry, are secondary, and that a new system of ownership can rightfully be instituted regardless of whether or not private interests are affected by its retroactive application. Those who supported this point of view maintained that the Constitutional Assembly was sovereign and had every authority to make its provisions retroactive. Article 14 (which the oilmen were to consistently invoke in their favor) was directed against the retroactive application of any secondary law, but not against the provisions of the constitution itself. It was intended as a check against those who might try to change the new system in the future.[28] This thesis had been advanced on occasion in classical treatises on international law and also, even more to the point, in precedents in which the United States itself had enacted measures retroactively.[29] Another school of thought argued, on the contrary, that Article 27 was far from retroactive: true, its proponents said, the subsoil hydrocarbons belong to the nation, but this has nothing to do with retroactivity. This conclusion is reached entirely on the basis of different considerations. In the first place, it is a physical impossibility to own the subsoil petroleum, the argument went, since it is constantly shifting from one place to another under the surface; the only thing that can be owned is the oil once it is extracted. Thus Article 27 did not affect the companies, referring as it did to rights they had never had.[30] Still another line of logic leading to the same conclusion was based on the questionable legality of the Porfirian laws of 1884 and 1909, which allegedly had not been adopted in accordance with the procedures in effect at the time. Hence, the reasoning went, the oil still came under the old colonial code.[31] In either event, it was argued that in order to contemplate retroactivity at this point Mexico would have to have demanded compensation for the oil extracted prior to 1917—which was beside the point. What was at issue was the future output under the new legislation.

Slightly different in approach from these largely legalistic lines of reasoning—intended to clothe a Revolutionary measure in the garments of traditional international law so as to be able to deal with the great powers on their own terms—was the radical interpretation, which claimed simply that there was no valid moral argument to prevent the new constitution from affecting certain private interests if necessary, since "in all of society the first duty of its members is to sacrifice individual interest in behalf of the collective welfare."[32] Mexico had to be free to govern itself in the best interests of the majority of the people.[33] Only arguments of force, not of law, could prevent the new precepts from being put into effect.

Political and Economic Background of the Carranza Oil Legislation

The economic factors leading up to the attempt to modify the status of the oil industry were both mediate and immediate. The most pressing one was the need to raise funds for the public purse. Carranza had to have a budget big enough to comfortably take care of his military and bureaucratic needs, pay off the foreign debt, and undertake certain projects and reforms. Otherwise the stability of his administration would be in constant jeopardy. There were times when his fiscal problems were grave indeed. For example, in mid-1918 the treasury did not have money to meet the government pay-roll. Only the army—the generals in particular—received their salaries regularly. Even the pay for senators and representatives in Congress fell behind.[34] A loan from abroad was out of the question, since Mexico's credit had fallen to nothing. Meanwhile, the oil companies were an ideal source of income, since they were the only industry that had not been affected by the civil struggle. Moreover, they were prospering at a dizzying pace. In 1917 oil was Mexico's number-one export. The world war had created a tremendous demand for fuel, and there was a big market for the light Mexican oil. An average of 3,700 barrels a day were being taken from the 174 wells in operation, which placed them among the most productive in the world.[35] However, all this wealth had fled the country, leaving behind a mere 7.5 million pesos (less than 4 million dollars in the exchange of the time) in taxes collected that year.[36] As it had already been pointed out much earlier in the decree of January 7, 1915, in justifying the need for an oil reform, "the fruits of its exploration were being carried away without the nation or the government receiving their just harvest." The Constitutional Assembly's action of 1917 opened the way for the state to demand a greater share, through taxes and royalties, in the proceeds from this thriving industry. A second economic consideration, not so pressing but perhaps more important than the first in the eyes of the nationalists, was the fear that the foreign companies might take all there was of Mexico's oil, exhausting the deposits which in the future would be of vital importance to the nation.[37]

There were also purely political motives that led Carranza to take a nationalistic stand in regard to oil. He needed greater support than he was getting from the army, and he also needed to provide his government with a broader popular base. His halfhearted agrarian and labor reforms had not been enough to win the people over. Thus he was to concentrate his best efforts as guardian of the Revolution on the campaign to put an end to the privileged position of foreign capital—especially the oil industry. And it was in this area that he was to have his greatest popular response, at least in the cities, where anti-imperialist sentiment had been aroused at all social levels, especially once the Revolution had brought hitherto latent anti-American feelings out in the open. Carranza echoed and encouraged this spirit.[38] However, the obverse of the popular-based nationalistic policy was the quite real possibility of getting into an armed conflict with the most powerful nation in the world—a struggle that would have been the undoing of the Carranza regime.

Article 27 in Practice

Carranza used two approaches in trying to put the provisions of paragraph iv into effect. To begin with, he issued a series of decrees which through purely fiscal measures attempted to promote immediate and genuine implementation of the new constitutional precept—meaning a prolongation of the policy followed since 1915. In addition, he set about drafting proposed texts of its organic law.

The decrees constituted a direct approach to the problem posed by Article 27 and at the same time afforded a means of raising some of the money that the treasury needed. As Alberto J. Pani, who was industry minister at the time, later told President Obregón, it had not been Carranza's intention to follow a radical policy at first: he already knew it would be impossible to get the companies to fully accept the provisions of paragraph iv, but he thought that he should at least try to get them to agree to an important part of them. However, in the end, said Pani, "this radical point of view ceased to be just a tactic and became a true objective within the Carranza policy."[39]

The first steps, as we have said, broached the question from the purely fiscal standpoint. However, the tax decreed at the beginning of 1917—paid under protest—was a milestone in that once and for all it put an end to the exemption status that had been granted by Porfirio Díaz in an effort to stimulate the industry's development and perpetuated in spirit during the Madero and Huerta administrations through the companies' refusal to pay the successive new taxes that were decreed.[40] Still, the most important measure of all was to come a year later with the decree of February 19, 1918. In issuing this order, which did not have the support of the entire cabinet,[41] Carranza had availed himself of the extraordinary powers granted to him by the Congress in matters affecting the treasury.[42] If the firms had had misgivings about the earlier fiscal measures, the February decree was to give them real cause for alarm. In addition to setting a new tax in the form of a royalty on lands acquired prior to 1917, its Article 14, considering that the state had again come into possession of the oil deposits, explicitly declared that the subsoil petroleum belonged to the nation and that private parties wishing to exploit it must recognize this right by applying for a government concession before undertaking any new operations, regardless of whether their leases or property titles had been formalized prior to May 1, 1917 (the date on which the new constitution went into effect). If this measure was not complied with, it went on to say, the landholder in question would lose his rights, and third parties could lay claim to his land after a certain date. Thus the decree of February 1918 attempted nothing less than to change the land titles granted during the Porfirian administration to mere concessions.[43]

The big companies responded by maintaining that they did not need to apply for the concessions. Carranza—powerless to insist in the matter, since the firms had Washington's full support, but at the same time disinclined to revoke his decree—decided to extend the period before allowing third-party claims, hoping for more favorable political circumstances when it expired later.[44] No such circumstances presented themselves, however, and as the pressure continued to mount the Mexican government had no alternative but to recant—though it did not do so entirely. On August 12 it was announced that those oil lands in relation to which investments had been made prior to May 1, 1917, for purposes of exploitation were exempt from the new provision.[45] Thus, for a while at least, the most valuable lands —those for which concessions had already been approved and those that the companies were working or in the process of working—had been made subject to a loose interpretation of the decree. The status of important reserves, however, could still be challenged under it.

Carranza had given in at the critical moment, but only to the minimum, indispensable degree. He continued to insist that the companies apply for concessions in order to start new drilling. The question was taken to the courts.[46] If he had wanted to retreat with dignity and save appearances, he could have easily asked for a decision calling for amendment of the decree (the principle of separation of powers was never to be put into practice in the new regime). But he did not, and when his government fell in 1920 the Supreme Court had not yet handed down its verdict.[47] Meanwhile, the deadline set in the decree (November 14) was extended to the end of the year, and in January 1920 an agreement was reached with the companies on a modus vivendi. It was decided to extend the date before which third-party claims could be filed until such time as the laws implementing paragraph iv were passed—hopefully soon. The Mexican press was optimistic about a government victory. Both sides had saved face: the companies were mollified,[48] and Carranza had not had to give up his commitment, even though in fact the government had no way of forcing the companies to comply with its dictates.[49]

Although the firms' legal rights remained unaltered, still they could not go about their business of drilling as usual.[50] They had clearly been asked to apply for permission first. However, they felt that the support they had from the State Department enabled them to disregard this request, and some of them went ahead and drilled new wells. On learning of this, the Ministry of Industry warned that force would be used if necessary to stop them, since the deposits they proposed to exploit without permission were now the property of the nation.[51] Although back at the beginning of 1919 the Congress had authorized Carranza to call out the army if necessary in order to make the oil firms comply with the new laws, so far Anglo-American pressure had kept him from doing so.[52] On this occasion, however, he decided to run the risk. And a real risk it was indeed. He ordered his troops to occupy the companies' oil fields and cap the recently drilled wells. The U.S. consul in Tampico informed Washington that Mexico seemed to have finally decided to impose Article 27 by force. The embassy protested immediately.[53] The Mexican authorities in Tampico prepared themselves for an American invasion, which they were powerless to stop.[54] This tense and uncertain situation was to last until the end of the year, when provisional drilling permits were finally granted.[55]

Thus the Carranza decrees had no immediate practical result except for a small tax increase, since the companies, with the support of the U.S. government, were able to get out of complying with them—though not without having to suspend new drilling operations for a time. After Carranza, no attempt was ever made to directly impose a law implementing Article 27. However, the specter of the basic principles contained in the decrees was to hang imminently in the background, coming out into the open from time to time over the decades that followed.

While the oil problem was being tackled through Carranza's executive orders, at the same time efforts were being made to develop a more suitable instrument with which to set in motion the overall reform contained in paragraph iv—namely, its organic law and its regulatory legislation. Although the first of these was not to see the light of day until 1925,[56] bills began to be proposed one after another. Naturally, the central point in these texts was their position with respect to the rights acquired by the companies prior to May 1, 1917, and the widely ranging variations that appeared were a faithful reflection of the confused state of the controversy itself.

The first of the texts was presented by Alberto J. Pani in his capacity as minister of industry at a congress of important businessmen.[57] It had been prepared by the Petroleum Department in his ministry without any regard for the companies' opinions in the matter[58] and it embodied the full radical spirit of Article 27. Not even Carranza himself dared to hope that it would pass.[59] In the preamble retroactivity was justified simply because it was for the common good. Those who held titles from before May 1917 were granted only the preferential right to request a government concession, and in all cases the state would collect an annual rent.[60] The companies' protest was quick to follow,[61] and the government did not insist any further on this first draft, which was actually part of a broader strategy. The oil firms and the U.S. embassy kept the situation under constant surveillance and promptly informed the State Department of any development in regard to this and subsequent proposals, which they frequently knew about before the public did, thanks to their spies in the government agencies.[62]

More than once during 1917 the companies' lawyers asked that a formal diplomatic protest be lodged against the bills under study, but it would appear that Washington turned a deaf ear to these appeals and chose instead to simply keep a close watch on the events as they developed.[63]

On November 19 Veracruz Governor Cándido Aguilar, the chief advocate for a moderate approach to the oil question within the Carranza circle, sent a bill to the local congress in his state which, had it been approved, would have fundamentally altered the oil policy of the Revolution. It was his belief that the nation could not claim direct ownership of the oil deposits unless it were to pay a substantial indemnization. It simply had a higher claim, the right of "direct dominion," which meant it could collect reasonable royalties (about 6 per cent) on the gross output.[64] In Aguilar's opinion the problem centered on increasing state participation in the industry's profits, and the measures designed to modify its actual legal status were not only gratuitous but dangerous as well. The proposal was never fully discussed in the national Congress, and the Ministry of Industry was openly against it from the start.[65]

From the records of Spanish embassy communiqués it may be inferred that from the moment the new constitution was promulgated the oil firms were in a state of constant anxiety over the prospect of a law implementing paragraph iv.[66] In 1917, after the draft presented to the industrialists had been put aside, several texts were prepared in the Ministry of Industry for presentation to the Congress, which was pressuring Carranza to get on with the matter.[67] Apparently three different versions, affecting the established interests in varying degrees, were developed. None of them was presented that year, however.[68] It was not until November 1918 that Carranza sent the Ministry of Industry's definitive text to the legislature. (It should be kept in mind that during that time the decrees he had issued on the strength of his extraordinary powers were systematically resisted by the companies and the State Department.) The preamble of this document specifically upheld the laws affecting those vested interests which were prejudicial to the rest of the body social and insisted that concessions be applied for and that royalties be paid to the state. It went on, however, reflecting the realities of the power struggle that was then going on, to give assurances that properties in relation to which capital had been invested prior to May 1917 for purposes of exploring for oil were not subject to third-party claims or to the other provisions of the present law, though their titles would have to be confirmed and they would not be exempt from the payment of rents or royalties. In this text, as in the executive decrees, the most valuable lands were largely excluded from the applicability of Article 27. But even so, it still contained elements that the companies did not like, and they wasted no time in showing their displeasure.[69] However, the State Department, which had closely followed the preparation of the draft, felt that, despite everything, it was an improvement over the previous proposals and decrees, and it chose not to file any protest.[70] The bill was studied for over a year by a committee of the Senate, which finally decided against modifying the foreign firms' vested rights in any way.[71] It presented an alternative version that was heatedly debated in the Congress and in the press and ended up not being approved either.[72] These events took place in an atmosphere of great tension, since a new clash with the United States was feared. The U.S. embassy interpreted the vote against the Senate committee's version as a Carranza victory over the moderates.[73] And correctly so: the text that was finally approved by the Senate and sent to the Chamber of Deputies in December 1919 was almost the same as the one presented by Carranza a year before.[74] However, the bill was fated to remain in the Chamber of Deputies until after Carranza's fall. It was returned to the Senate slightly amended in 1923 and wound up being shelved in favor of a new draft presented by the executive that was to become law in 1925.[75]

In reality, the various bills remained in the Congress only as long as the president wanted them to. Once he decided to promulgate the law, it was promptly passed. It could not be any other way in the highly centralized presidential system that had emerged from the Revolution.[76] Therefore it must be concluded that if the congressional debates and studies were drawn out at length it was because the president had chosen to hold off on his reforms—no longer so very radical—until the international situation was more propitious.

The Companies' Defense

The oil industry's defense was waged using the established tactics. The firms protested and sought protection against the fiscal measures and the change in the status quo called for in the Carranza decrees.[77] At no point did they agree that their acquired rights could be exchanged for mere "mining licenses."[78] As for the taxes, some of them were totally disregarded, while others, with the State Department's concurrence, were paid under protest in the form of an advance, as had been done with the 1917 stamp tax. The companies called them "legalized theft" and maintained that they were confiscatory.[79] In private, however, they admitted that the amount itself was not their main concern; they were afraid that their compliance might constitute recognition that the state had a right which in reality it did not possess—namely, ownership of the subsoil.[80] In a word, they felt that Carranza, whose extraordinary powers did not go so far as to allow him to promulgate the law implementing Article 27, was attempting illegally, through his decrees, to establish the bases for expropriation at some future date, enforcing his measures through the power to grant drilling permits. To make their position more effective, they mounted a vigorous propaganda campaign against Carranza and the new constitution.[81] Their main forum was the U.S. Senate investigating committee presided over by Albert B. Fall,[82] but they also took advantage of the media in Mexico in their attempt to discredit the government's position.[83] The Mexican national press, always conservative, went to work against Article 27, claiming it was an invitation to armed conflict with the United States.[84]

In addition, the companies used direct negotiations with the Mexican government in the defense of their interests. In 1917 they held talks in Tampico with representatives from the Ministry of Industry to explore the possibility of paying their lease rents to the state rather than to the landowners directly. In the course of these sessions the oilmen hinted to the government that if it were to maintain the current state of affairs they would be prepared, in exchange, to lend a hand in the pacification of the Huasteca region—that is to say, in putting down Manuel Peláez.[85] The suggestion was not very well received. Talks were resumed following the decree of February 1918—this time at a higher level. From then on, for more than two decades, this approach was to be frequently used in the search for solutions to the various conflicts that arose. To reach this point, the companies for the first time had come to an agreement among themselves and presented a united front to the Mexican government.[86] This front was to be maintained, though not without difficulty, until 1939. The 1918 talks—in which two oil company spokesmen, James R. Garfield and Nelson O. Rhoades, met with Pani—ran from March to August. The Carranza government had asked that they be kept secret, and the Americans agreed.[87] The secrecy was necessitated by the same nationalistic fervor that had originally been Carranza's source of support, for by now the nationalists were convinced that negotiations spelled double-dealing, and these were not the only talks that the Revolutionary governments were to keep from the public. In the end a tax cut was agreed to after an exchange of memorandums between the companies and the Mexican government in which the former threatened to close down operations and move to Venezuela and Colombia. On this occasion, strange as it may seem, the firms agreed to the principle that the subsoil belonged to the Mexican nation. It was a short-lived victory for Carranza's side, however, for soon afterwards the companies were to recant, and relations ended up even more strained than before.[88]

Since the companies considered that Carranza's oil policy and the decrees he had issued left them "no choice but to commit suicide or be murdered," they appealed to the U.S. government for support. While it was in the State Department—both in Washington and at its embassy in Mexico City—that they were to find their stoutest champions, this did not keep them from cultivating other contacts elsewhere in the federal system: in the Fuel Administration, the Congress, and the presidency itself.[89] They maintained that they were entitled to protection from Washington because Mexico was violating their rights through its confiscatory policy. "In the name of thousands of shareholders" they vociferously protested Carranza's decrees and the measures he was taking to keep them from drilling new wells.[90] They did not limit themselves to legal arguments: as was to become their custom in the future, they underscored the parallel between U.S. national interests and their own, pointing out that any letup in Mexican oil production would set back the Allied war effort, and that such an event was imminent if they did not receive the support they were asking for.[91] When the war ended they continued to use the same line of reasoning, claiming that the U.S. economy would be severely disrupted by any halt in the supply of oil from Mexico. Washington, successfully convinced, was also made to see the dangerous precedent that could be set if Mexico were allowed to carry out its proposals: other countries might try to follow suit, and this could threaten the entire international investment system.[92] The firms were not content simply to make their viewpoints known in Washington through the normal channels; they also sent spokesmen to the Peace Conference at Versailles to present their case against Mexico before the great world powers.[93]

To better understand the State Department's unconditional support of the companies, it should be kept in mind that at the time all the world powers considered that one of the chief functions of their embassies was to defend the economic interests of their nationals abroad. But, more important still, the U.S. government was genuinely convinced that an uninterrupted flow of Mexican oil was necessary to maintenance of the Allied front in Europe: 75 per cent of the British fleet's energy needs were being met from this source.[94]

Mexican oil was no less important after the war ended. In the years immediately following the conflict, the United States produced and consumed three-fourths of the world's hydrocarbons, and some geologists thought that the earth's supply would be exhausted within the generation. It was necessary, therefore, to control substantial reserves abroad,[95] and Mexico's deposits, these experts believed, were among the largest and best located anywhere. In 1919 the U.S. Shipping Board informed President Wilson that Mexican oil was indispensable to the U.S. naval and merchant fleets.[96] Hence, Carranza's attack against the American firms' position had to be seen in part as a threat to vital U.S. economic interests and national security.

Once the new constitution had been promulgated, the State Department, with the tacit support of certain European chanceries, went to work to try to stop Carranza from applying the provisions that would be prejudicial to American interests, especially in the case of oil and mining.[97] Washington's diplomatic intercession in behalf of the oil interests in Mexico was justified on the basis of the same arguments that the companies had used. According to an official State Department declaration, President Wilson made a clear distinction between armed intervention and diplomatic pressure: the latter was regarded as a friendly means of protecting legitimate U.S. interests in Mexico.[98] And the State Department did not fail to exercise it—both through formal notes and, most importantly, through constant verbal protests lodged by Ambassador Fletcher or the chargé d'affaires. Economic pressure was also applied, but it was not decisive. In 1917 Fletcher told Carranza that his government would approve a U.S. loan to Mexico, but only if respect of the property rights of foreigners were guaranteed.[99]

As a first step, the State Department instructed its embassy to let Carranza know it was confident that Mexico had no intention of applying the new constitution retroactively. At the same time it went on record against the tax of April 13, 1917, asking that the promulgation of any future decrees be held up until Washington had had an opportunity to study them.[100] Some of the European countries gave thought to more drastic steps, such as recalling their diplomatic representatives, in order to pressure Carranza into guaranteeing the property rights of their citizens, particularly miners, bankers, and railroad men, but in the end no such measures were taken.[101] It was the decree of February 1918, however, that brought formal protests. Notes from the United States, England, the Netherlands, and France followed in the wake of Fletcher's failure to keep it from going into effect.[102] Secretary of State Robert Lansing, in his initial note and subsequent ones dated August 12 and December 28, 1918, attacked both the tax increase and the implied distinction between surface and subsoil property rights. Making it clear that there was no objection to normal fiscal measures, he claimed that the new decree was nothing short of confiscatory. The State Department underscored its protest by warning that if Mexico persisted along these lines the United States would be obliged to protect the property of its citizens.[103] It did not say specifically what form this "protection" would take, but no one had much trouble imagining what was meant. The Spanish embassy believed that an armed U.S. intervention was a very real probability.[104] In fact, Lansing was not completely convinced that the Mexican measures were confiscatory. (The companies had no such doubts: they assured him that the new Mexican taxes were the highest in the world.) This detail, however, did not stop him from formulating a clear-cut policy. The important thing, he decided, was to keep the Mexican position, legal or not, from becoming firmly established: confiscation had to be prevented before it could happen.[105] In the end the notes and threats were effective, since they led to postponement of the effective date of the new law. Although Carranza let it be known to Fletcher in August 1918 that neither the protests of the affected parties nor the threat of an armed conflict with the United States—which he most certainly did not want—could make Mexico go back on its decrees, the fact is that the extensions continued.[106]

Washington was concerned about other aspects of the problem as well—

namely, Pastor Rouaix's interpretation of Article 27, as reflected in the language of the bills he was drawing up for the executive, and the possibility that in the course of the controversy concessions might be given to third parties for lands belonging to the rebellious firms.[107] Ambassador Fletcher zealously defended the companies' rights, encouraging them to remain united and disregard all of Carranza's decrees.[108] More than once his superiors had to restrain this zeal and dissuade him from going beyond his instructions.[109] If only the action of the ambassador is taken into account, it is very difficult to see any difference between the policy of Taft and that of Wilson.

During 1919 the conflict got worse. The ambassador protested the suspension of drilling permits for the companies that had defied the February 1918 decree and demanded that force not be used to halt their continued activities. Washington maintained that the firms did not have to apply for permits, since the conditions therefor amounted to renunciation of their legitimate rights; it was the government, not the firms, that was in the wrong. Mexico for its part insisted that the provisional permits would be readily granted if only the firms would agree to comply with the provisions of a future law on oil; it did not matter if their request for the permits were made under protest.[110] These assurances were in vain, however, and Fletcher's position finally had to be accepted: the provisional permits would be granted unconditionally.[111] Also the subject of protest were the third-party claims to the rebellious companies' lands and attempts to collect royalties on properties acquired prior to May 1917.[112] Finally it was agreed to recognize the validity of these protests. In the end, no lands were taken from the firms, nor were any royalties paid.

There is some evidence that the State Department was not completely intransigent in its defense of the oil firms' interests. In any case, some of the companies thought the support was insufficient and were to say so in Senator Fall's Senate committee and on other later occasions.[113] This position was extreme, however, and not unanimous. Indeed, in the same Fall Committee hearings Doheny himself and other oilmen expressed their appreciation for the protection and guidance given by the authorities in Washington.[114] It was the representatives of the smaller firms who were the most demanding: in their opinion the use of force would have been the best solution to the problem created by Carranza's nationalism.

Possibility of U.S. Intervention in the Oil Firms' Behalf

If even before 1917 the desirability of occupying the Mexican oil region had been hinted at in certain circles within the industry, Article 27 and the policy developed by Carranza after that date by all means fanned the interventionist fire. Moreover, the entrance of the United States in the European conflict and the consequent need for Mexican oil to support the war effort presented the companies with a good excuse to urge Wilson to take over Tampico.[115] In public the firms systematically denied any interventionist intentions.[116] Even though allegations to the contrary abounded, there was never sufficient concrete proof to really show their hand.[117] Such proof was to appear only years later, fragmentarily, in archives and documents.

During the 1924 investigation of the scandal resulting from Fall's sale of the Teapot Dome naval fuel reserves to Doheny and others, Charles Hunt, one of Fall's associates, testified that in 1917 the senator and a group of oilmen had worked on a plan to partition off the northern states of Mexico (Lower California, Sonora, Chihuahua, Coahuila, Nuevo León, Tamaulipas, and the northern part of Veracruz) and, with the help of anti-Carranza elements, form a separate oil republic. Only in this way, they were said to have claimed, would their interests be safe.[118] Evidently, even if such a plan did exist, it did not get very far. Manuel Peláez had forces enough to hold Carranza at bay, but he most certainly did not have it in his power to make the whole northern part of the country independent.

At the beginning of 1917, against the background of a strike by the Mexican oil workers, then under the influence of the Industrial Workers of the World[119] and of an electoral struggle in the state of Tamaulipas, four U.S. warships showed up in Tampico. In addition, four others, plus two British vessels, stood in wait on the high seas not too far away. In response to this warning, the Constitutionalist authorities did everything they could to keep the workers under control.[120]

The appearance of Carranza's decrees in 1918 had prompted the oil firms to insist once again on the need for a show of force. Wilson refused to consider the possibility, however. It was not desirable, he argued, for the champion of self-determination to adopt a course of action that at bottom was not very different from what the Germans had done when they invaded Belgium.[121] Still, the note delivered to Mexico on August 12, 1918, clearly contained the threat of intervention.[122]

In 1919 it began to appear more likely that those who were pressing for the use of force would get their way. Pursuant to a U.S. Senate resolution, a committee was set up on July 6 to investigate the Mexican situation vis-à-vis American interests. It was headed, as we have already seen, by the famous Senator Albert B. Fall. For no real reason, many people regarded the creation of this committee as the prelude to an invasion.[123] Fall cleverly used witnesses from both sides—sympathizers and enemies of the Carranza regime (though a rather larger proportion of the latter)—as the basis for a large-scale propaganda campaign in support of all the points in the companies' line, including the need for intervention.[124] Nothing that could be used against the Carranza regime was left unsaid. The oilmen figured prominently among the witnesses, and they took great pains to elaborate on the injustices suffered at the hands of Carranza. In tones of injured righteousness they pointed out that his government failed to take into account the important service they were rendering to the Mexican economy.[125] Fall culminated his work with the publication of a monumental preliminary report —characterized by some as "the last word in imperialist propaganda"— which ended up concluding that the Carranza regime was a threat to U.S. national security.

The oil firms utilized the Fall Committee proceedings and the stories on Mexico appearing in the *New York Review*, the *Washington Star*, the *Chicago Tribune*, the *New York Times*, and the like to good advantage in their efforts to influence the White House. To outward appearances it would seem that Fall and the oil firms were only asking for Wilson to withdraw recognition of the Carranza government;[126] however, their real intentions were promoted indirectly. The governor of Texas was to suggest that nothing short of armed occupation of Mexico would bring about the order that different parties in question were so anxious to secure.[127] In an interview with Secretary of State Lansing the oilmen requested that warships be sent to the Mexican coasts so as to give greater impact to U.S. diplomatic representations.[128] The pressure went even further. Exactly how far can be seen in two communications from then Secretary of the Navy Franklin D. Roosevelt to the State Department in which it was asked that advance notice be given in the event it was decided to go ahead with the invasion of Mexico.[129]

In November Wilson and his close advisers came to the conclusion that the intervention the companies were asking for was not justified.[130] Shortly thereafter the president, following an exhausting trip around the country, fell ill, and it was while he was confined to his bed that the famous "Jenkins affair" (the kidnaping of the U.S. consul in Puebla) took place.[131] This incident gave rise to a brief but intensive campaign in the American press against the Carranza administration and the disorder in Mexico in general. Secretary of State Lansing informed Wilson that in his opinion diplomatic pressure against Carranza had reached the limit and war should be declared. This solution, he pointed out, would not only put an end to the problems with Mexico but also solve some of the Democratic administration's domestic difficulties by rallying the whole nation around the government. Wilson and most of his cabinet were against the idea.[132] Before any decision could be reached, Jenkins turned up and Lansing left the State Department in protest over Wilson's failure to approve his Mexico policy and in particular his handling of the Jenkins affair, which could have served as an excuse to provoke an open conflict.[133]

Years later Wilson's secretary of the navy, Josephus Daniels, was to tell President Franklin Roosevelt and Secretary of State Cordell Hull that the oil interests were behind Fall's active role in the campaign to have Wilson removed from office on the grounds of his illness.[134] In any case, it would seem that the president was able to keep Washington's Mexico policy under his control, successfully rejecting Lansing's and the oil industry's suggestions.[135] Still, if Carranza had stayed in office after 1920, or if the new Mexican president had carried on his policy, it is quite possible that the armed conflict would in fact have occurred,[136] especially with the Republican Party in power in Washington after 1921. Indeed, at the beginning of 1920, after the interventionist pressure had abated somewhat, the struggle between Carranza and his chief of armed forces Alvaro Obregón once more led the companies to ask for warships to be sent to Tampico, and again American vessels were dispatched to the scene.[137]

Main Factors in the Evolution of the Carranza Oil Policy

As it has been said before, Mexico's oil policy was rooted in the urban mid-dle-class militant nationalism that the Carranza movement stood for. This nationalism was an indispensable complement to his faction's offensive against the Porfirian political system, which had entrusted the develop-ment and management of the modern sectors of the economy to foreign capital. One of the motives behind the revolutionary movement had been to gain maximum possible control over the economic system, and to this end foreign capital had to be dominated and subordinated. This general ex-planation is understood better if the group that worked with Carranza on the formulation of the new oil policy is examined in detail.

Only a handful of men took part directly, but they were important be-cause of their closeness to Carranza. The most influential members of the group were extremely nationalistic, and their goal was none other than total nationalization of the oil. Others, who took a more moderate stand though they were equally nationalistic, were afraid of a conflict with the United States lest it undo all the achievements of the Revolution. This more moderate faction was in favor of increasing taxes somewhat but not of changing the industry's legal status. On the other side there were those leaders from the old regime who had been associated with the oil firms and who went on record in defense of their interests, but they were utterly pow-erless because they were outside the Revolutionary coalition.

Pastor Rouaix, Francisco Múgica, and Luis Cabrera may be considered some of the main spokesmen for the radical group. They exercised their in-fluence through the Constitutional Assembly and later the Ministry of In-dustry, particularly its Petroleum Department.[138] This group also had rep-resentatives in the Congress, especially on the Chamber of Deputies' Petro-leum Committee, and their ideas were reflected in the various tax propos-als, in the draft law on oil, and in their surveillance of the industry's day-to-day activities. Their principal propaganda organ was the *Boletín del petró-leo*, published by the Ministry of Industry.

Among the chief proponents of the more moderate view were General Cándido Aguilar and Alberto J. Pani. The latter, as industry minister in Carranza's cabinet but with no power base of his own, refrained from insist-ing too much on his point of view in order not to antagonize the president, whose sympathies were always with the radicals.[139] General Aguilar, how-ever, was able to be more open, and he drew up and presented his own draft proposal for the law on oil, which, as it has already been seen, was rejected by Carranza. He summed up his views on the subject in a letter to Carranza written on July 2, 1919, from New York, where he was serving as a special ambassador—and from where he could well appreciate the interventionist atmosphere created by the companies—in which he concluded that the pro-gram for reforming the economic system should never have begun with the oil sector, which was the one that presented the most difficulties from the international standpoint. However, he said, since it was too late for the government to retrace its steps without seriously endangering the entire Revolutionary movement, the constitutional principle should be insisted on. He went on to suggest that for the time being pressure should be brought to bear on the firms only through fiscal measures, without touching as yet on the question of property rights. The United States had come out of World War I as an unrivaled power, and at any moment it could impose its will on Mexico and put an end to the Revolution itself. Aguilar was fully conscious of this fact, and he pointed out in his report that "only on this side of the border can the enormous importance of a change in attitude be appreciated."[140] This point of view was not without its echo in the press. While none of the Mexican papers was strongly enthusiastic about the reform, *El Heraldo de México* was the one that perhaps most supported it during the course of the Carranza regime.

As it has already been said, those in Mexico who were opposed to any change in the status of the subsoil deposits were, generally speaking, those who had been affected by the Revolution and who hence were natural allies of the firms. But for the very reason that they were associated with the old order they had no influence in the new administration. Carlos Díaz Dufoo was perhaps their best-known spokesman. Seizing on an idea used by the companies in another context, he saw fit to equate Mexican national interest with maintenance of the oil status quo. He claimed that the oil industry, a source of great wealth to Mexico, was being irresponsibly endangered by the government's attempts to persecute and extort from the foreign companies.[141] This group was not without support in the Congress, and it is even possible that some of the more conservative Carranza legislators had been directly influenced by its members.[142] Moreover, it had the best press: the firms' interests were defended by *El Universal, Excélsior, El Demó-crata,* and *El Monitor Republicano*—except when government pressure obliged them to do otherwise.

While there was a group in Mexico that stood up for the foreign oil interests, in the United States it had an inverse counterpart in that sector of the American public which disagreed with the criticism being waged against Carranza and used what influence it could in Washington to try to prevent an armed conflict. In this movement the Protestant church leaders, represented especially by the Federal Council of Churches of Christ in America, had a prominent place. There were also some labor groups, but their participation was not so important.[143] A liberal—though not very influential—segment of the American press echoed the denunciations of the oil companies' activities in Mexico.[144] This current of American opinion, which had its origin in different local situations within the United States, was encouraged by the Mexican government whenever possible.[145]

Carranza's intention in regard to the hydrocarbon reserves had been clear all along: his goal was to bring this highly important natural resource, which was being exploited without any benefit to the nation, under state control—that is, under the control of the victors in the struggle against the old regime and against the peasant armies of the north and south. The culmination of this policy was found not so much in the Constitution of 1917 as it was in the decrees of 1918. Although the nearly unbearable American pressure totally thwarted any plan to put the new provisions into effect, the government was able to retreat without abandoning its principles. For a number of years the conflict over the attempt to apply the precepts of Article 27, and its paragraph iv in particular, was to dominate relations between the Carranza government and the United States, and the policy developed by Mexico over this period came to be known as the "international doctrine of the Revolution." The principles of nonintervention, equality of all nations under law, and equal rights for nationals and foreigners which Carranza constantly cited made up the basis of the defensive theory which from that time on was to govern Mexico's relations with the greatest power in the world—a theory that to a certain extent continues to be applied up to the present day.

The State Department, despite a few broad declarations in line with Wilson's foreign policy, supported the oil companies unconditionally and set about to systematically and vigorously oppose any measures that might constitute a potential threat to these firms, even before they were promulgated or the interests of its citizens had actually been affected. Mexico, while it regarded this policy as interventionist and claimed that it was against international law, was powerless to put up an effective resistance. Only the international situation, which led the United States to commit its resources to the struggle in Europe, was to finally give some maneuverability to the new nationalist government which was trying to free Mexico from its dependent position in relation to the United States. These circumstances enabled it to survive and keep from having to revoke its new legislation, but nothing more. The new theory would have to wait a number of years before it could be put into actual practice.

Chapter 5

From Obregón's Victory
to the Bucareli Agreement and the 1924 Accord

The triumph of the Agua Prieta movement (Obregón, Calles, and their followers) over Carranza in 1920 was the last successful military uprising in Mexican history. The years in power of the victor, General Alvaro Obregón—including the brief interim administration of Adolfo de la Huerta—were the beginning of what historians have called the "reconstruction period," during which the bases of the present-day Mexican political system were firmly established. The victory over Carranza in no way implied a change in the leadership's basic structure or program; it simply represented the outcome of an internal struggle over the succession. Carranza had wanted to pass the reins on to one of his more obscure deputies, while Obregón, head of the army, had had other ideas. Obregón's victory marked the beginning of the "Sonora dynasty" (Obregón and Calles), which was to hold sway until 1935, when Calles was run out of the country by Lázaro Cárdenas. During this period Mexico's leadership was in the hands of the victorious military faction—that is to say, those who after defeating Huerta had fought successfully against Villa and Zapata under the Carranza banner and eventually took the power into their own hands. In addition to this military clique, the new ruling group also included some intellectuals, a few representatives of the small but important urban middle class, spokesmen for the most important labor movements, and several agrarian leaders who acted in the name of the peasant sector. These varied elements provided the regime with a base of support much broader than that which it enjoyed from the army alone.[1]

Obregón was the first to start to put the provisions of the new constitution approved at Querétaro into effect, and he did so gradually, always favoring a minimum of reform. For example, the token support he gave to organized labor made very little real difference, since the sector was already completely tied to the government and the peasant movement, but it was nevertheless a small step beyond what Carranza had done. The halfheartedness of these revolutionary efforts was obscured by a smokescreen of official rhetoric that was considerably more exuberant than Carranza's had been and abounded with catch phrases such as "socialism," "government of the proletariat," "class struggle," "anti-imperialism," and the like.[2] But as the years went by the members of the Agua Prieta group began to accumulate large personal fortunes and more and more to see a parallel between their interests and the status quo. In the end they concentrated their efforts not on destroying what was left of the Porfirian structure—which was still a great deal—but rather on coming to terms with the forces from the old order.

For more than a decade this fragile and not very happy alliance was maintained, and the Revolutionary flame was not to be rekindled again until Cárdenas came to power in the 1930's.[3]

The first order of business in the Obregón administration was to build up a strong central authority once again, the ten years of struggle having led to a proliferation of local caudillos, some of them highly independent.[4] This effort was to take more than a decade. The Revolutionary governments were little different from the Porfirian regime in their eagerness to centralize the base of power. Obregón's success in this regard was particularly notable: he was able to bring the interior of the country largely under his control.

The reconstruction program was to run into a number of problems, one of them being that the beginning of this period coincided with a decline in certain of Mexico's exports.[5] Nevertheless, the oil boom during these years kept the foreign trade volume at a good level, and the federal treasury fared somewhat better than it had under Carranza. Obregón made a concerted effort to regain the confidence of foreign investors, with a view to speeding up the reconstruction,[6] but to little avail: quite some time was to pass before Mexico would again be attractive to foreign investors.

At the beginning of the 1920's the country's political situation was precarious and the international climate was hardly propitious for a program of big reforms. The United States was no longer preoccupied with World War I. The Sonora group, despite their cries of "Mexico for the Mexicans!" were obliged to make significant concessions to the American interests in order to avoid a direct confrontation with their government—or at least to keep them from mobilizing support in Washington.[7] Moreover, the new leaders soon found themselves more interested in reaping the benefits of their recently acquired power than in risking it to the winds of international fate—although this does not mean that their interests were ever to completely coincide with those of the foreign group. The oil problem continued. And while it was not the only problem that Obregón had with the United States, it was certainly the most important one, and was to set the tone for relations between the two governments for many years to come.[8] In a sense, despite the fact that the reform of the economy's foreign sector was being carried forward less vigorously than in the past, the overall course of the Revolution during this decade was to hinge in large part on developments in the oil controversy.[9] Obregón, like Carranza, was to be prevented from applying the new oil legislation in its full Revolutionary sense—although he did not have to go so far as to revoke it.

The New Administration in Washington and Its Effect on Mexico

The Mexican problem figured as an issue in the 1920 U.S. election campaign and was included in the platforms of both the major parties. While the Republican candidate was the more aggressive, both of them called for the traditional "firm hand" in relations with the restless neighbor to the south.[10] It could be said that what was to become the Republican policy began to be implemented even before the new president, Warren G. Harding, took office—that is, with Wilson's decision to pursue a hard line not unlike that advocated by the Republican politician least sympathetic toward Mexico, Senator Fall, after Carranza's overthrow.

In the United States the decade following World War I has been likened to the post-Civil War period. A time of conservatism both in politics and in social philosophy, it was characterized to a considerable extent by conspicuous political and economic corruption, a certain decadence of the liberal spirit, resurgence of an intolerant nationalism, and stagnation in the social reform program.[11] At the same time, the Republican administrations in Washington, without any extrahemispheric conflict to distract their attention, were only too ready to focus their energies on the Mexican Revolution. Despite the fact that the government by now was under the firm leadership of moderates, the Republican administration viewed it with scant sympathy and maintained that it was a threat to the interests of their citizens on the other side of the Rio Grande. And so it was that between 1920 and 1930 Mexico's government labored under the shadow of a possible U.S. intervention, either direct or through support of a counter-revolutionary movement.[12] The Republicans' aggressive stand—the classic "dollar diplomacy"—stemmed both from the decision to abandon Wilson's reformist policy toward Latin America and from the Harding and Coolidge administrations' close ties with the oil interests, especially in the case of the former.[13] Still, it is well to keep in mind that there was more than one important influence at work within the Republican administrations and that the oil sector's demands had to compete with those of the powerful banking group, whose main objective was to see that Mexico resumed payment of its foreign debt. Within the United States the two groups' interests were not in conflict, but when it came to matters outside the country, specifically those having to do with Mexico, such was not always the case, and they sometimes ended up lobbying on opposite sides in Washington.

The U.S. foreign policy that took shape after Wilson left the presidency reflected a certain obtuseness in regard to the postwar situation in Europe. World peace was to be sought through a series of treaties with the principal European powers and Japan for arms reduction and the peaceful settlement of disputes. Typical of this thinking was the unique Kellogg-Briand Pact, which actually went so far as to propose the "outlawry" of war.[14] However, this trusting, pacifist attitude, bordering on naïveté, did not prevent the continuation of an aggressive policy toward Mexico, Central America, and the Caribbean countries. Samuel Flagg Bemis claims that the U.S. foreign policy of the time was favorable to Latin America in the long run, since it brought an end to protective American imperialism, which was curtailed wherever strategic considerations would allow.[15] This conclusion would appear to be open to question. However, even if it is accepted, the policy toward Mexico must have been an exception, since in the relations between the two countries there was no sign of toning down the more notorious aspects of American imperialism that had prevailed at the end of the nineteenth century and the beginning of the twentieth. It is possible to try to defend Professor Bemis' thesis by arguing that in the Mexican case there were strategic factors at work that precluded any change. This may be a valid argument, but the truth is that these factors lost their importance very early in the story, and the tension still did not abate. What, if any, were these "strategic" American considerations? It would appear that in the early 1920's some of the American political experts thought it was necessary to accumulate oil reserves beyond the U.S. borders.[16] During the first two years of the Obregón administration, with oil production nearly at its peak, Mexico's reserves were believed to rank among the most important in the world and were looked upon as the solution to an anticipated energy shortage in the United States—it being expected that the oil fields in that country were soon to run dry.[17] At the instance of the U.S. Shipping Board, the State Department ordered an investigation of the oil situation in Mexico.[18] The Shipping Board sent a technician to Salina Cruz to study the possibility of running a pipeline across the isthmus of Tehuantepec, which would open up a supply of fuel for U.S. naval and merchant fleets in the Pacific.[19] Before long, however, these plans were abandoned. As it turned out, the American deposits did not run dry, and the Mexican reserves, on the contrary, proved to be less important than had originally been thought. Hence by 1922, or at the latest 1923, Mexican oil had ceased to be of strategic interest to the United States.

To these observations on the Republican administrations' policy toward Mexico it should be added that the European countries, confronted with the problem of whether or not to recognize the new Mexican government, chose to take their cue from the United States rather than act independently. The Obregón government was not to establish diplomatic ties with them until after it had done so with the United States, even though in several cases the situation was decidedly inconvenient for the Europeans.[20] At the same time, the government in Washington kept constantly on the watch to see that the American oil interests in Mexico did not fall into European hands.[21]

The Interim Administration of Adolfo de la Huerta

On June 1, 1920, Adolfo de la Huerta, titular head of the movement that deposed Carranza, was sworn in as interim president of Mexico. His six months in office gave Obregón a chance to develop a base of support and take over the leadership in the assemblies that were being held at the time. This short period also saw pacification of all the internal rebel forces in Mexico. Members of Zapata's army, which had ceased to be a serious threat, began to be incorporated into the government both at the local and the national level, as did some of the remaining Villa followers, who by then had also laid down their arms. General Pablo González, the only Carranza man capable of standing up to the Agua Prieta group, was forced to retire from the political scene, leaving the way open for Obregón. And finally the "oil state" in the north disappeared with the surrender of Manuel Peláez and Félix Díaz to the central government.

At the international level the new government's most pressing problem was to reinstitute regular diplomatic relations with the United States, which had been interrupted as a result of Carranza's fall. This was no easy task, since Wilson was demanding as a condition for recognition of the new Mexican government a series of commitments whose acceptance to the letter would have dealt an irreparable blow to the Revolutionary program and discredited Obregón in the eyes of the nationalist forces. In essence, Washington was asking De la Huerta for a formal promise not to enforce those provisions of the Constitution of 1917 that would affect the vested rights of the American companies. Indeed it was Wilson himself—who on more than one occasion had declared that the aim of his Mexico policy was not to defend private interests but rather to improve conditions for the "common man" in that country and who had agreed publicly that Mexican natural resources should be developed in behalf of its people—who in the end was largely responsible for keeping the objectives he espoused from being achieved. For even though he insisted that he had scant sympathy for American capitalists in Mexico, he consistently defended them.[22] In fairness, he really had no other choice. No great power, either then or now, has ever been able to stand by and fail to react to a threatened expropriation of such magnitude, regardless of how disinterested and altruistic its rhetoric might be.

In 1920 Fernando Iglesias Calderón and Roberto Pesqueira, the new government's envoys in Washington, held a series of talks with officials from the State Department in which they assured the American representatives that Mexico intended to honor all commitments to foreign businessmen made by previous administrations, including the Porfirio Díaz regime. In the particular matter of oil, Pesqueira promised that the case against the companies' tax shelters would be withdrawn from the courts, that the Supreme Court would hand down a ruling in the firms' favor, and that future laws on oil would be framed in accordance with this decision.[23] But even these assurances, which virtually did away with the oil reform provided for in Article 27, were not enough for the White House. It maintained that the De la Huerta government could not be recognized until they were incorporated into a formal treaty (such as the one that Fall was insisting on).[24]

While the Mexican leadership—Obregón and his collaborators De la Huerta and Plutarco Elías Calles—was not opposed in principle to a treaty with the United States that would guarantee and protect the interests of American citizens, nationalist fervor was running so high in the country that the leaders did not dare sign such a document until after their government had been recognized by Washington. The United States, for its part, refused to agree to any change in the order of precedence, believing apparently that its bargaining power would be diminished if the treaty were negotiated after diplomatic relations had already been resumed. In the end, De la Huerta turned the office over to Obregón without having made much progress toward the solution of this vital problem.[25]

At the time of the Agua Prieta movement's victory Mexico was producing 22.7 per cent of the world's oil, and it was the uncertainty regarding the ownership rights to this valuable resource that was mainly behind Washington's reluctance to recognize the De la Huerta government. The White House's position on the matter was fully set forth in a State Department memorandum delivered to a De la Huerta envoy in 1920. It called for: (1) repeal of the Carranza decrees; (2) cessation of the requirement to file claims for the oil properties; (3) cancellation of the concessions granted to third parties on the companies' properties for which claims had not been filed; (4) assurance that drilling permits would not be held up or refused; (5) reversal of the executive's position in regard to the injunctions filed by the companies; (6) elimination of concessions in "federal zones"; (7) establishment of a fair tax policy; (8) abrogation of Article 27 of the constitution; (9) restoration of the rights of foreign citizens affected thereby; and (10) assurance that future legislation would not run contrary to the foregoing nine points.[26] It was made clear that unless these points were agreed to there would be no recognition, and, what was more important, there would be no aid forthcoming in support of Obregón and his group against the opposing internal forces in Mexico.

Although it would appear that Obregón did not in fact receive any assistance from the firms in his struggle against Carranza,[27] their satisfaction over his victory was clear,[28] and they wasted no time in suggesting to the State Department that advantage be taken of the new power structure to once and for all settle the situation with Mexico that had been festering since 1917.[29] Not waiting for an answer, they entered directly into talks with the provisional government, but no conclusive agreement was reached.[30] In 1920 Industry Minister Jacinto B. Treviño, who had attended these sessions, accompanied President-elect Obregón on an unofficial visit to the United States and continued the negotiations with the oil group there.[31] Still no agreement was reached. However, on October 26 the De la Huerta government sent a note to Washington in which it clearly stated its intention to respect the vested rights of U.S. citizens. Although the text made no specific reference to oil, there was no doubt that this was the issue in mind.[32]

While in fact, as historian Jesús Silva Herzog has said, relations with the oil companies did take a turn for the better under the De la Huerta administration,[33] they were actually less cordial than is commonly thought. The points of contention were several. In the first place, De la Huerta did not agree to revoke the 1918 decrees outright. Instead, he insisted that the companies wait to obtain the corresponding concessions from the government before going ahead with their operations—failure to follow this procedure still making the properties subject to third-party claims.[34] The State Department, for its part, addressed a series of notes to the De la Huerta government protesting both the granting of concessions to third parties on the companies' properties and the executive's refusal to issue drilling permits unconditionally to those firms whose rights had been acquired prior to May 1917.[35] A second problem which came up constantly during the six months of the De la Huerta administration was that of the "federal zones." These were lands alongside rivers or stream beds running through the properties owned by the American companies which presumably belonged to the nation and on which the government saw fit to grant oil concessions to persons friendly to the new regime. The companies alleged that these grants violated their property rights, while the government maintained that the lands in question were national patrimony. At first it appeared that De la Huerta was going to give in to the oil firms' demands, but as it turned out he was to continue with the same practice, granting third-party concessions up to the last hours of his administration.[36] The State Department kept up a constant protest against this policy.[37] At the same time, some of the British companies (El Aguila and La Corona) took advantage of "federal zone" concessions at the Americans' expense, and this irritated Washington even more.[38] These small conflicts only served to strengthen the American firms' desire to keep Obregón's government from being recognized unless he first acceded to a formal agreement that would settle the oil question once and for all.[39] They wanted an accord that would put an end to all the causes of friction: the delays in the issuance of drilling permits, the charging of royalties, and the continuation in office of the Ministry of Industry staff who were originally responsible for formulating and executing the Carranza oil policy.[40]

The provisional De la Huerta government followed the example of its predecessor and launched on an effort to break up the companies' united front. As part of this campaign, it made overtures to Joseph F. Guffey, head of the Atlantic Gulf and West Indies Company (AGWI), which ever since its arrival in Mexico in 1917 had consistently broken ranks with the rest of the oil firms in exchange for official support.[41] Through Guffey an attempt was made to attract the Anglo-Persian Oil Company to Mexico, it being thought that this firm might be prepared to accept the new oil legislation in return for generous concessions. The scheme broke down, however, when Sinclair dissuaded it from aligning with AGWI.[42] Despite the latter's friendly relations with the Mexican government, it ended up joining the united front against the De la Huerta administration by the end of 1920. The same thing happened with El Aguila, which for a while had also made an attempt to turn the situation to its own advantage.[43] The provisional government hesitated between the need for recognition and support from Washington and the desire to cut itself in for a greater share of the oil industry's fabulous earnings, and in the end it failed to take a firm course in either direction. When De la Huerta left the presidency the American oilmen were just as much on edge as they had been at the end of the Carranza administration.[44]

Obregón and the Problem of Diplomatic Relations with the United States

During the Obregón regime the oil companies were to remain the chief obstacle in the effort to get diplomatic recognition from Washington.[45] The violent change of government in 1920 which led to Carranza's death and the end of the modus vivendi between the big American interests and the Mexican government had prompted the Americans to again urge for a solution once and for all. Pressure to withhold diplomatic recognition came not only from the oil firms but also from the organized bankers, who held most of the Mexican foreign debt bonds.[46] The various interests (oil, mining, agriculture) represented through the American Association of Mexico (AAM) declared openly that it was preferable to let the civil struggle go on than to allow the Obregón government to become more firmly established unless and until the necessary assurances were given.[47]

The oil companies' stand with respect to Obregón was the same as it had been in regard to De la Huerta: in their opinion, it was up to the State Department to get a formal commitment from the Mexican president that the 1917 constitutional provisions would not be applied retroactively.[48] At meetings held in Galveston, Texas, on March 16 and 17, 1921, the Association of Producers of Petroleum in Mexico formally resolved not to comply with the new oil laws, which they regarded as illegal, and went on record with the statement that in no case could this or any other legislation affect property acquired prior to 1917. In addition, the meeting agreed: (1) to continue to insist on the full legality of the firms' rights acquired prior to May 1, 1917; (2) to appeal to the State Department to defend their legitimate interests; (3) to make payment of export taxes only under protest and as an "advance"; and (4) to stand firm on the position that concessions granted in the "federal zones" were unlawful.[49] In 1922 the APPM was to reiterate its position: it wanted all or nothing.[50]

At no time did Washington turn a deaf ear to the oil firms. Their problem was among those considered to affect the "national welfare," and for some time it was handled personally by the secretary of state, who gave it priority over all the other matters pending with Mexico.[51] Since Obregón gave no sign of changing the stand that had been taken by De la Huerta, Washington announced that it could not recognize his administration, giving as its reasons the fact that the government was the result of a violent overthrow, that the welfare of U.S. citizens in Mexico had not been assured, and, finally, that no guarantees had been given against the retroactive application of Article 27.[52] The basic aim of the recently elected Republican administration was to secure a pledge that the American interests already acquired would be respected; only secondarily was it concerned with reparation of the damages caused to its citizens during the ten-year struggle.[53] Washington put on the pressure in various ways. The Obregón government was to be threatened continually—not so much with intervention or aid to its opposition but rather, more subtly, with cutoff of American arms, which were vital to the maintenance of power in a country that was only partially pacified, where a rebellion could break out at any moment.

On assuming the presidency, Obregón sent a new envoy to Washington, Manuel Vargas. However, Vargas was not to have any better luck with negotiations than his predecessors Iglesias Calderón and Pesqueira had had.[54] A number of American businessmen suggested schemes to Mexico whereby diplomatic recognition could be obtained from Washington without a signed commitment, but they all turned out to be the work of their authors' fantasy or opportunism: there was no easy way out.[55] On May 27, 1921, the U.S. government revealed its own plan, and for the first time it formally submitted a draft treaty of friendship and trade for Obregón's consideration. In essence this document was not very different from the memorandum that had been given to Pesqueira extraofficially the year before. Its first two articles virtually annulled the reforms contained in Article 27.[56] The United States was proposing, under the guise of respect for equal justice, that the citizens of either of the two countries living in the other one be accorded the same rights as nationals; that reciprocal guarantees be given for protection in the event of nationalization, which could only be effected in the case of a public utility and on the condition of prior, prompt, and fair indemnization; and that a limit be set on the retroactive application of Carranza's decree of January 6, 1915, the Constitution of 1917, and any other legislation. Specific mention was made of the recognition of oil and mining rights acquired by foreigners in Mexico under the laws of 1884, 1892, and 1909, as well as the return of or compensation for any American property taken from 1910 onward. Obregón rejected this proposal and answered saying that he trusted the United States would apply in the case of Mexico the traditional policy of recognition enounced originally by Thomas Jefferson— namely, that relations should be entered into with any government constituted by the will of the people. He added, moreover, that legally he could not sign a treaty such as the one proposed because it deprived the Supreme Court of its authority as the sole interpreter of the constitution. He then declared publicly that he was in favor of maintaining the modus vivendi—in the belief that sooner or later his policy would lead Washington to see that its efforts were useless.[57] Secretary of State Charles Evans Hughes, apparently unable to appreciate the reasons behind this stand, refuted Obregón's arguments literally.[58] He did not seem to understand that the Mexican president could accept the main points in the Washington proposal in practice but that he could not acquiesce to them formally. For to bow in front of the eyes of the whole country to a treaty that had already been likened to the Platt Amendment—one which would divest the nation of any last pretense of sovereignty by preventing it from interpreting and applying its own constitutional law—was impossible.[59] In an attempt to erase all doubt of his sincerity in nationalist circles, which had reacted strongly against the Hughes proposal, Obregón declared publicly that under no condition would he amend the Carranza oil laws or Article 27 in return for recognition by the U.S. government.[60]

The official correspondence exchanged between the Mexican and U.S. governments from May 17, 1921, to March 21, 1923, on the subject of oil centered around the proposed treaty of friendship and trade, since Washington considered that any other alternative failed to provide adequate assurance that American interests would be protected.[61] Foreign Affairs Minister Alberto J. Pani, in a memorandum of May 11, 1921, and in subsequent communications, insisted that it was not the intention of any of the three powers of the Mexican government to apply Article 27 retroactively. With regard to the treaty, he said, Mexico was prepared to sign it, and there would be no problem to negotiate it as soon as relations between the two countries were back on a normal basis, but not before and not in the unconstitutional manner suggested by the U.S. government. In all of Pani's communications to the State Department between 1921 and 1923 assurance was given that the oil law would be formulated in a way that would fully satisfy the United

States and he even went to far as to hint at a constitutional reform to put an end to the possibility that the laws implementing Article 27 could affect any vested rights.[62] The memoirs of Adolfo de la Huerta—who from his interim presidency went on to occupy the post of treasury minister under Obregón—and other records in the Ministry of Foreign Affairs archives show that the United States almost reached the point of accepting Mexico's position. According to these documents, when the treasury minister traveled to the United States in midsummer 1922 to discuss the foreign debt, he took the opportunity to bring up the oil question with the president and the secretary of state. These talks, he maintained, were highly fruitful: Washington agreed at last to recognize Obregón without prior signature of a treaty. Moreover, it consented to ceding the rights acquired prior to May 1917 in exchange for fifty-year government franchises. How did such an abrupt and basic change come about in the American position? What was left out of the official correspondence? De la Huerta provides no answer to these questions, nor does he explain why the agreement never became a reality— since the fact is that diplomatic relations between the two countries continued to be suspended. Although one might be suspicious of these statements in view of De la Huerta's subsequent falling-out with Obregón, there are documents that back them up.[63] One possible explanation, then, is that pressure exerted later by the oil companies may have forced the U.S. government to reverse its stand.

While the Mexican government was insisting through its official exchanges that American interests in Mexico would be protected, Obregón launched a vigorous propaganda drive designed to get recognition from Washington on his own terms. His declarations to the Mexican and foreign press were an important part of the campaign.[64] Although the U.S. officials appeared to respond, these efforts did nothing in the end to change the attitude of Washington or the oil firms.[65] The Americans by this time had decided to hold out for a clear-cut and definitive solution through a formal commitment. The State Department had received new complaints that the Mexican government was continuing to grant concessions—although in fact only a very few—in "federal zones" traversing the American firms' lands, as well as numerous reports of drilling permits denied.[66]

Obregón's Efforts to Satisfy the United States and Still Avoid Signing a Formal Agreement

Ever since Obregón's presidential campaign in 1919 he had let it be known that he intended to follow a policy somewhat different from that pursued by Carranza in the matter of oil—one more in line with the foreign companies' wishes. The conservative *Excélsior* observed with considerable pleasure on June 9, 1920, that the new chief of state was moderating his views in all areas and that "no longer do we see socialist tendencies in him."[67] Prior to Carranza's ouster, Obregón had been regarded as the leader of the radical left wing in the former administration. Evidently now, with the power in his hands, he was becoming more prudent. According to Foreign Affairs Minister Pani, Obregón formally rejected Washington's terms not because he expected to continue the campaign against the oil enclave but rather because he was "patiently waiting for progress in the execution of the presidential program to make it unnecessary for the U.S. government to insist on the treaty that it was so obsessed with for the protection of its nationals."[68] A first step in this direction was the near suspension of concessions to third parties in the "federal zones"—a practice that had greatly incensed the American firms.[69] A decree of January 15, 1921, stipulating that drilling permits were to be granted only to those parties that had complied with the Carranza decree of August 18, 1918, was revoked the following month in response to pressure exerted by Standard Oil.[70] There were still some problems in these areas, but they were now very few. By way of reinforcing these pacification measures, Obregón wrote directly to President Harding on July 21 and August 18, 1921, informing him that he intended to honor his commitment not to apply Article 27 retroactively and reiterating the assurances in this regard that had been given to U.S. Chargé d'Affaires Summerlin by Obregón's minister of foreign affairs.[71]

Prior to the so-called Bucareli Agreement of 1923, probably the most important step taken by the Obregón government toward acceding to U.S. requests was the series of five Supreme Court decisions upholding a set of injunctions filed by the firms' lawyers against the Carranza decrees.[72] The Supreme Court decision of August 30, 1921, must not have been much of a surprise to the Americans, since a memorandum of August 9 from Pani to Summerlin had already insinuated that if the executive and the legislative powers were in favor of the principle of nonretroactivity, "What else could the Supreme Court do but join the other two branches of the government in such equitable intentions?" Pani went on to hint that such an event might perhaps take place before too long. Given the executive's traditional control over the judiciary, these assurances were tantamount to almost an accomplished fact. And, indeed, the Supreme Court handed down a ruling in favor of the firms on August 30, 1921. Although it came precisely at the time the government was starting up talks with the oil group, because of the haste with which the case had been dealt with, several weeks were to go by before its definitive text was available. In essence, the judicial verdict recognized the nonretroactive interpretation of paragraph iv, taking as its basis Article 14 of the same constitution, which states that no law can be made retroactive—although it does not specifically refer to constitutional precepts themselves. The decision did not totally neutralize Carranza's policy, however, since it only referred to those lands on which a "positive act" had been carried out—that is to say, on which some drilling or other kind of activity had demonstrated the owner's intention to extract oil prior to May 1, 1917. While this covered the companies' lands on which exploitation was already underway, it did not say anything about the rest of them.[73] The court had given in only to the extent it was in its interest to do so: it did not throw out the whole article, nor did it condemn retroactive application as such. It simply left the door open for nonretroactivity in some cases, requiring that in such instances it be respected.[74] Moreover, depending on what was understood to be a "positive act," between 80 and 90 per cent of all the oil firms' land—that is, all that held as reserves—could still be affected by the Revolutionary legislation if the question were to be raised.[75] Despite the legal arguments summoned in support of this decision, there is no doubt that it was American pressure and nothing else that led Obregón to secure an interpretation of Article 27 which was clearly not in keeping with the nationalist spirit that had originated it.[76] In order for the August 30 decision to set a precedent, it was necessary to have four consecutive additional rulings in the same sense. These did not take long in coming, and by 1922 there were already five decisions on the books in the companies' favor.[77]

Since the Supreme Court rulings did not constitute total accession to the American requests or have the binding effect of a treaty, the position of the State Department and the oil group remained unchanged. In their opinion the rulings had been basically a political move, and they could be annulled just as easily as they had been made. As long as subsoil ownership rights were not fully recognized for all the lands acquired prior to May 1, 1917, they felt, the law would continue to amount to confiscation.[78] And to an extent they were right: for in the Supreme Court's subsequent decisions on oil matters it did not always find in favor of the companies, although the rulings to the contrary were few and far between and never succeeded in setting a precedent.[79]

In the absence of any positive reaction to the Mexican court decisions on the part of the U.S. government or the oil firms, coupled with their continued insistence that the gesture be followed up with a treaty of friendship and trade, Obregón let it be known in his address to the Mexican Congress on September 1, 1922, that he could not go much further: the proposed treaty, he said, was not only unnecessary, it was an insult to the national honor.

Negotiations between the two governments were paralleled by informal meetings between Mexican officials and spokesmen for the large American firms. These meetings were intended rather to iron out specific differences than to reach an agreement about the oil legislation as such. Still, Mexico tried to take advantage of them to get Washington and the interested parties to give up on the famous treaty. The first direct contact between the companies and the Obregón government was prompted by the former's refusal to accept a tax increase decreed on June 7, 1921, to help redeem the Mexican foreign debt bonds. Mexico had thought that by supporting the bankers who held these issues it could offset the oil interests' influence in Washington and thus put a stop to the State Department's protests. Things did not work out that way, however.[80] The companies' reaction to the tax rise was much stronger than had been anticipated. On July 1 they halted all shipments, saying that it was impossible for them to pay it. In so doing they cut off a very important source of income to the government, since production was at its peak. Moreover, the move put twenty thousand men out of work,[81] while the country's largest export industry entered into a state of paralysis which was to last for two months. The firms once again appealed to the State Department for help.[82] The response was immediate, and ships from the U.S. fleet soon appeared off the Mexican coast. They were claimed to have been sent as a precautionary measure in view of the discontent among the workers in Tampico following the mass layoffs. No one was fooled, however: the ships were there to keep Obregón from taking any direct action against the companies. The Mexican president, for his part, announced that he was prepared to uphold the new tax despite the protests, pointing out that it was only fair that the oil industry share its enormous profits with the nation.[83]

The standoff was not to last for very long. After a meeting with officials from the State Department, a delegation of five very important oil executives set out for Mexico in August 1921 to try to come to an agreement.[84] Negotiations opened immediately upon presentation of a memorandum to De la Huerta in his capacity as treasury minister on August 21, and on September 3, after four sessions—which took place in a cordial climate, according to the reports sent to Washington—an agreement was reached. In essence, the export tax was to be paid with the Mexican foreign debt bonds, which would be accepted at 100 per cent of their nominal value, while the oil firms would acquire them on the New York market at 40 or 50 per cent of this value. The arrangement was kept more or less secret, and the companies resumed their normal activities.[85]

Despite the fact that the government had been forced to reduce the tax by 50 or 60 per cent, the official reaction in Mexico was one of satisfaction. The companies, it was said, had struck a bargain without recourse to intercession from Washington.[86] In some circles it was thought that this rapprochement with the oil interests—and with the bankers, since Mexico had agreed to resume payment on the foreign debt—would be construed as unconditional recognition of Obregón. However, since settlement of the tax question did not in any way solve the problem of subsoil ownership, the firms made no move to ask Washington for a change in its position.[87] In reality, not even the tax problem had been solved, and before long the oil representatives had to sit down once again with the treasury minister, this time keeping the conversations truly secret. On April 23, 1922, spokesmen for the five American oil consortia arrived in Mexico City. As it turned out, they were exactly the same individuals who had been present at the talks the year before.[88] After paying a courtesy call on Obregón, they took up their negotiations with Treasury Minister De la Huerta. The meetings lasted from April 24 to May 3. As on the previous occasion, the tax problem was the central question, since the five oilmen had still not come to an agreement among themselves with regard to the fiscal situation, some of them considering that the levies, based as they were on the value of American oil, were excessive. However, unlike those of the year before, the meetings were not limited to discussion of the tax; they branched out to cover the situation of the industry in general. The oilmen were already foreseeing the crisis which was to affect their activities in Mexico and which was to come to an end only some twelve years later. Since no new oil deposits had been discovered for some time, consideration was given to the possibility of joining forces with the Mexican government and establishing a Petroleum

Development Company to carry out an intensive exploration campaign.[89] However, the continued disagreement over the interpretation of Article 27 —as witnessed by the furor over the Carranza decrees and the concessions granted in "federal zones"—kept the plan from being put into practice, and the argument over the subsoil rights went on. Had the joint enterprise actually materialized, the oil story might have taken a course quite different from the one that led to expropriation in 1938. The only concrete result, as in the previous meeting, was that De la Huerta agreed to reduce the tax. In the press release that was issued at the end, only the fiscal accord is mentioned, and no reference is made to the proposed enterprise or to the differences of opinion over Article 27.[90]

The talks between De la Huerta and the oilmen held in New York from July 19 to 27, 1922, were in effect an extension of the ones held in Mexico the month before.[91] On this occasion, since the tax problem was now out of the picture, discussion centered around plans for opening new areas to exploration, and the possibility of a joint Mexican-American undertaking was reviewed once again. No agreement was reached, however. The companies demanded greater guarantees, saying that otherwise they could not speed up their work in new areas. Moreover, they asked for a tax break on the drilling being carried out in recently discovered beds. If their request was not accepted, they said, they would not have the necessary incentive to keep up the intensive exploration that everyone wanted. But this time De la Huerta refused to grant a further tax reduction—among other reasons because the previous one had been severely criticized in Mexico. When he asked the companies for an advance against taxes in the amount of 25 million dollars, the firms, as it was to be expected, refused.

Thus the third round of talks came to a close and still no accord had been reached. It was at this point that the large American companies began to turn their attention to Venezuela, partly for political reasons, but above all for economic ones.[92] The *New York Times* blamed the failure to come to an understanding on the continued disagreement over the interpretation of Article 27. The proposed joint enterprise was impossible as long as De la Huerta was asking for an increased share of profits, his demand being based on the argument that the state was giving up its right to the subsoil, while the companies for their part refused to recognize that Mexico had any right whatsoever over lands acquired prior to May 1917. The standoff was not regarded as definitive, however. Obregón had agreed to review the companies' arguments once again.[93] In August the rumor went around that he had decided not to insist any longer on the application of Article 27 to lands acquired prior to 1917, irrespective of their status regarding whether or not a "positive act" had been undertaken.[94] In other words, that the struggle to throw off the Porfirian legacy had been abandoned. However, it was soon discovered that the rumor was unfounded and that in fact the Mexican position had not changed at all.

Although the contact between Obregón's representatives and those of the American oil firms (El Aguila did not participate in these meetings) did not lead to a final solution of the problem, it did help to improve relations between the two sides. For example, a dispute between Doheny and a Mexican group over co-ownership of the valuable Juan Felipe section near Huasteca's Cerro Azul camp was decided in favor of the American.[95] In another instance the government lent a hand in a more or less violent breakup of an oil strike in Veracruz. These secondary concessions on Obregón's part were reciprocated by Doheny, who decided to advance a five-million-dollar loan to Mexico against future taxes despite his earlier unwillingness and the fact that the State Department was against the idea because it would enable Mexico to solve its immediate fiscal problems without making any major changes in its policy.[96] Thus, by the end of 1922 tension between the United States and Mexico had to a certain extent abated.

Obregón, however, was far from pleased with the situation: it was clear that his government would not be recognized until the basic questions were ironed out with the oil firms. "We can see," said the Mexican chief of state in speaking of relations with the United States at a cabinet meeting in November, "that [our neighbor to the north] is trying to exercise more authority over us every day."[97]

Mobilization of the Interested Sectors in Mexico and the United States

As it has already been seen, the oil policy decisions taken in Mexico and Washington were influenced not only by the firms in question but also, though to a lesser degree, by other groups that for various reasons were concerned with the problem. The effect of Carranza's nationalist oil policy had carried over into the Obregón administration, and pressure to keep it alive was exerted by officials in the Ministry of Industry such as Manuel de la Peña, head of its Legal Department, and others. The *Boletín del petróleo* continued to serve as a propaganda organ for this group of officials, who were convinced that the exploitation of oil must not be allowed to fall back into foreign hands. They preferred that this wealth be kept more or less intact until Mexico was able to exploit it on its own. The Supreme Court decisions had been greeted with little enthusiasm within this group, especially since they represented the policy of the executive. However, these critics did not give too much importance to the ruling, believing, along with Washington, that the ultimate interpretation of Article 27 rested in the hands of the legislative branch, which surely at the proper time would rectify the court's error.[98] Although the action and opinions of this sector were controlled by the president in the final analysis, Obregón did not fail to take their views into account in formulating his oil policy.[99] Within the president's circle of close advisers, General Plutarco Elías Calles was more or less the spokesman for the radicals who were in favor of a nationalistic interpretation of Article 27.[100] The oil companies, for their part, promoted their interests in Mexico through a campaign in the press aimed at getting Article 27 repealed, or at least amended in their favor,[101] but they were unable to offset the radicals' strong hold on public opinion.

Although the pressure brought to bear by the companies was undoubtedly the deciding factor in the formulation of Washington's oil policy at the time, it was not the only one. There were other groups whose interests coincided with those of Doheny and Standard Oil. Most notable among these were the bankers involved in the Mexican foreign debt and certain big landholders. Within the United States, support came from the chambers of commerce in states that were interested in the Mexican market, religious groups, intellectuals, labor unions, and other groups which for various reasons and in differing degrees were interested in shaping the conditions that the White House was imposing on Obregón in exchange for diplomatic recognition—particularly those relating to the rights of the oil firms.

The influence of the bankers in Washington was no less important than that of the oil firms in matters of foreign policy. Although the two groups agreed that recognition of the Mexican government should be conditioned on its meeting their demands, their interests from that juncture on were far from identical. The bankers, for their part, were not concerned with the defense of property rights against the Revolutionary legislation; they simply wanted to see that payments on the foreign debt were resumed—a point that was not objected to in principle by the new Mexican leaders. Obregón understood the difference between the two sets of demands, and he did his best to pit the oil firms, which were fighting desperately for matters of principle, against the bankers, who were not in nearly such threatened circumstances. The accords reached with the bankers in 1922, known as the Lamont–De la Huerta Agreement, were very onerous for Mexico, since the debt bonds were quoted at their nominal price even though, as it has already been seen, their real value on the New York market was less than half. Obregón had decided to accept these conditions—despite the opposition of Foreign Affairs Minister Pani—in the hope that such a move might induce Washington to recognize his government without Mexico's having to sign the treaty that the oil firms and other American investors were insisting on. Moreover, it was thought that the clause providing for payment of the debt in part from levies on oil exports would encourage the bankers to give their support to the Mexican oil tax increase in Washington.[102] In the end, however, no real schism developed between the two groups. The most friction that occurred was over the oil companies' acquiring the depreciated Mexican foreign debt bonds for payment of their taxes (which would keep the Mexican government from redeeming the issues at their nominal value) and the bankers finally succeeded in arranging it so that the bonds would not be used to pay the taxes.[103] But there were examples of cooperation between the two groups. Even though Doheny had lent five million dollars to the Obregón administration in mid-1922, the oil companies unitedly refused to grant Mexico a twenty-five-million-dollar loan after the bankers asked them to do so in order to keep up the economic pressure and oblige the government to accept their point of view in regard to the foreign debt.[104] The bankers did not care too much about making Obregón sign the treaty that the oil firms were so intent on. A less aggressive policy than that of their oil colleagues[105] was all the advantage that Mexico was able to extract from them. A softer line was to be adopted by the bankers again during the Bucareli talks the following year. According to George K. Lewis,[106] the Mexican delegates were able to get the U.S. representatives to accept certain aspects of the oil reform that the companies did not like simply because the bankers wanted the United States to assume a more flexible position in order to come to an agreement quickly. By the same token, there was no insistence on revocation of paragraph iv before diplomatic ties could be resumed. Still, the bankers felt it was important for Mexico to modify its oil policy so that foreign capital would be attracted to that activity once again, for to do otherwise, they maintained, was economic suicide.[107]

The chambers of commerce in the southwestern United States were another force within the American political system that Mexico attempted to take advantage of in order to neutralize the pressure of the oil firms. In this case the Mexican efforts were more successful. Like the bankers, the businessmen did not have any property rights at stake, whereas on the other hand they regarded the absence of regular diplomatic ties with Mexico as an impediment to trade. From the moment Obregón took office he launched on a campaign to win the support of this sector: various representatives of American interests were invited to his inauguration in December 1920 so that they could see for themselves the peaceful political climate, the new government's good faith, and the economic possibilities that Mexico offered for the expansion of their enterprises.[108] Some business interests did, in fact, lobby in Washington for a change in the State Department's Mexican policy, claiming that the oil industry was leading this agency's officials by the nose. Eight different state legislatures petitioned the White House for unconditional recognition of the Obregón government, and some of the chambers of commerce appealed directly to Washington for resumption of relations.[109]

In addition, thanks to the efforts of Luis N. Morones, leader of the Mexican Regional Workers' Confederation (CROM), the American Federation of Labor formally declared itself to be on Mexico's side and joined the chorus asking for recognition.[110] Also there was the small segment of the press that sympathized with the Mexican Revolutionary governments—partly voicing the genuine convictions of liberals in the United States and partly reflecting Obregón's successful efforts to counteract the work of his adversaries.

In July 1921 a society called Friends of Mexico was organized in New York for the purpose of pressuring the United States into resuming diplomatic relations with Mexico. The principal defender of the Mexican viewpoint continued to be the *Nation*, an influential public opinion journal which stood somewhat to the left of most of the American press. Opinions favorable to Obregón also appeared in other newspapers, although less systematically. At the end of 1921 Obregón won the backing of no less than the influential Hearst chain itself. William Randolph Hearst, who for a long time had been one of the most impassioned advocates of intervention in Mexico, had gone there on a trip, spoken with the Mexican chief of state personally, and come back with his mind completely changed. From that time on he marshalled the support of his entire newspaper empire in Obregón's behalf and waged an unrelenting crusade against all those who were standing in the way of diplomatic recognition—in his opinion, the "international bankers" and "certain big oil interests." The campaign in favor of Obregón was not limited to the press. Books by authors such as E. J. Dillon and T. S. Woolsey denounced Washington's "imperialist policy" toward Mexico and called attention to the oil companies' strategic role in its formulation.[111]

To the extent that the United States imposed its policy in Europe, it was forced in turn to deal with reactions from countries such as France which had no oil interests to defend but saw their trade with Mexico impeded by the interruption of diplomatic relations.[112] For a while Obregón was confident that this pressure coming from so many different sides, together with his more moderate approach to nationalism, would sooner or later bring Washington to its knees, even in the face of continued opposition from the oil firms. Indeed, he said so in so many words in his state-of-the-union message of September 1, 1921.[113] More than a year was to go by before his optimism gave out and he decided to change his tactics in order to break the stalemate.

The propaganda campaign conducted by the APPM in the United States, which had vast resources behind it, invoked a wide variety of legal and political arguments to combat the current of opinion in favor of unconditional recognition.[114] The oil firms were not alone in their desire to exact a formal commitment from Mexico regarding American property rights in that country. Their position was fully shared by the American Association of Mexico, whose attitude was so intransigent that it had broken with the companies when it heard that the APPM might be prepared to moderate its stand. For the AAM, whose members for the most part were less powerful than the oilmen and therefore wanted even greater assurances, the only possible solution was total and absolute repudiation of all Revolutionary legislation. Their position with respect to paragraph iv was even more radical than that of the oil firms: they insisted on the repeal of all those measures calling for nationalization of the privately owned subsoil and were even opposed to the oil deposits discovered and acquired *after* 1917 falling under what they considered to be the "sterile" influence of the government's "absolute dominion."[115]

Likewise, the American Catholics were in the same camp with the APPM and the AAM, and they too registered their opposition to the renewal of diplomatic ties. It was at their insistence that a clause guaranteeing religious freedom for the American community in Mexico was included in the draft treaty presented by the American chargé d'affaires in 1921. There are indications that the Catholic clergy in the United States not only demanded such an assurance as a condition for recognition but also for a while actively supported an armed intervention. Monsignor Francis C. Kelley, on return from a trip to Mexico in 1922, reportedly told Assistant Secretary of State Leland Harrison that in his opinion 80 per cent of the Mexican population would welcome a U.S. intervention that would put an end to the Revolutionary experiment and return the country to peace and tranquility.[116]

Other Oil Company Protests, 1921–1923

Aside from the legal question over subsoil rights, the main source of friction between the oil firms and the Obregón administration was the tax decreed in June 1921. The companies suspended operations in an attempt to press for its repeal and protested to the State Department that the measure was illegal and confiscatory.[117] In addition, the APPM complained that there appeared to be intentional delays in the issuing of drilling permits and claimed that leases were being granted to favorites of the regime in "federal zones" cutting across lands owned by its members, thus permitting newcomers to exploit deposits that had been discovered only after extensive investments in exploration.[118] The suspension of this practice ordered by Obregón at the beginning of his term was no longer in effect, and Standard Oil told the State Department that certain English and French groups seemed to be taking advantage of their contacts in high Mexican government circles to get concessions of this kind.[119] By July 1921 these suspicions were confirmed.

Soon afterward it was reported that the Canadian firm El Sol was drilling on some of the American companies' land which had been guaranteed against "federal zone" concessions. According to APPM Secretary Guy Stevens, Generals Calles and Treviño were interested in this undertaking.[120] Washington had been given reason to suspect that El Sol was controlled by none other than Royal Dutch–Shell, or the Rothschild interests, and was connected with Atlantic Gulf and West Indies,[121] and it had good reason to believe that the European oil firms and Obregón's intimates were conspiring to move in on the American companies. When El Sol started to exploit deposits to which Standard Oil held claim, the Anglo-American struggle was on again.[122] As in the tax dispute, the APPM wasted no time in passing on to the State Department a full bill of particulars against the Mexican government.[123] Washington's reaction was apparently not very vigorous at first, since in February 1924 the APPM was still asking the State Department to register its official objection to the activities being carried out by El Sol and other companies on what it considered to be its land.[124] After a while, however, the appeals stopped and, for reasons not entirely clear but probably not unrelated to the opposition put up by the APPM, El Sol disappeared from the Mexican oil scene. The association also lodged complaints against the incipient oil activities being carried out by the Mexican government firm Ferrocarriles Nacionales. On July 27, 1923, precisely while the talks were going on between U.S. and Mexican representatives that were ultimately to lead to resumption of formal diplomatic ties, the APPM approached Obregón directly and asked him to call a halt to the operations of this and other companies, such as Petrolera Marítima, in "federal zones" traversing its members' lands. The president felt that the association had no right to make such a demand and refused to give it any consideration.[125] Guy Stevens may have had to excuse himself for the language he used, but he stood his ground.[126] The Mexican government for its part was equally firm in upholding the "federal zone" concessions, despite repeated protests from the State Department.[127] In the end the American firms agreed to accept the government's own limited undertakings in the "federal zones" but not the operations of private companies such as El Sol or Marítima, which were eventually forced out of business.

The Draft Law Implementing Paragraph iv

Like Carranza, Obregón was to be unsuccessful in dealing with the problem posed by paragraph iv. Finally, after a series of abortive attempts to put through a law implementing its provisions, he gave up. While he saw that he would be unable to effect legislation consistent with the spirit of the new constitution, still he was determined not to yield totally to American pressure. The only alternative, therefore, was to carry on with the modus vivendi established during the closing years of the Carranza administration, the oil firms holding out hope that more favorable circumstances in the future would bring a solution to this question which was so fundamental to the Revolutionary platform. He only came to this decision, however, after failing in a final series of attempts to draft a law that would be acceptable to all the parties involved.

In 1920, immediately after Carranza's overthrow, De la Huerta in his capacity as interim president had presented a draft law to the Petroleum Consultative Council which in essence provided for the "internationalization" of Mexican oil. The idea was to strike a happy medium between the situation that had existed prior to the Revolution and the Carranza reforms: as long as Mexico did not have control of the oil industry, neither would any other one nation. The council, made up of Carranza men, rejected the compromise and insisted that nationalization, not internationalization, was the only answer.[128] At this point De la Huerta desisted in his efforts, leaving the problem to his successor.

No sooner was Obregón inaugurated than he declared that his administration had "very firm ideas" about the law on oil and that the last draft presented by Carranza, still under consideration in the Chamber of Deputies in the early months of 1921, would have to be amended.[129] Accordingly, the legislators appointed two committees to draw up a new bill. Foreign Affairs Minister Pani informed Chargé d'Affaires Summerlin that the Congress had no intention of giving a retroactive interpretation to Article 27, but that as long as Washington refused to recognize Obregón's government the law implementing it would have to be held in abeyance, since a decision in favor of nonretroactivity would be viewed in Mexico as capitulation to American pressure.[130] Thus, he pointed out, it was Washington's own attitude that was perpetuating the legal uncertainty in regard to the industry's status. In mid-1921 the U.S. embassy and the press reported that the Congress had started its debate on the oil question behind closed doors—although no results were expected for some time. Obregón and the lawmakers examined the desirability of granting extraordinary powers to the chief executive under the new law. That is to say, they looked into the tactical advantages of having the responsibility for its enactment rest with the president rather than the Congress. It was decided, however, that the former would be more vulnerable to pressure from vested interests than the latter, and that therefore the Congress should be the one to present the bill, even though in fact it would have originated with the executive.[131] Meanwhile, the so-called social democratic bloc introduced another draft that was clearly in the oil companies' favor. The fact that the majority took no notice of it indicates that the executive regarded it with scant interest.[132] In August 1921 the newspapers published the complete texts of all the various bills that presumably were being considered. The reports emphasized that none of the proposals fundamentally affected the companies' acquired rights. At about this time, on the other hand, one deputy, speaking for his fellow representatives in the Congress, declared that despite their intentions to avoid a reopening of the controversy, the presence of U.S. warships off Tampico was obliging them to postpone their vote on the law in order not to appear to be bowing to pressure.[133] In the midst of these contradictory pronouncements, Obregón in his annual message on September 1 assured the Mexican people that the law on oil would in fact be promulgated, although he did not give any details as to its content.

The companies, apparently well informed by their contacts within the administration, notified the State Department that it was Obregón's intention to press for nothing less than the Carranza proposal of 1919, which clearly threatened some of their ownership rights.[134] During the months of September and October 1921 the newspapers maintained differently—namely, that the criteria of the president and the Congress were similar and that hence the new oil code could not possibly affect the rights acquired under laws existing prior to 1917.[135] These statements far from placated the companies. In November Guy Stevens appealed to the State Department more than once, asking it to stop the Mexican government from promulgating the version then under consideration in the two houses of Congress, since according to his information it definitely did deprive the oil firms of their rights. Henry P. Fletcher, the former U.S. ambassador in Mexico, sent a memorandum to President Harding supporting the companies' stand and urging that the resumption of diplomatic relations be postponed for a while longer. In response, Chargé d'Affaires Summerlin informed the Mexican authorities that Washington had serious reservations about the various retroactive provisions in the bill being studied by the Congress, especially the first four articles, and suggested that the text be modified.[136] But by November the press had stopped referring to the much-discussed draft. The companies told Washington that there were no indications that this or any other plan would be approved in the near future. Almost a year went by, and in September 1922 the State Department received the text of a new proposal, which reportedly had the approval of the minister of industry. At the beginning of October Summerlin was ordered to look into the situation again.[137] Talks between Foreign Minister Pani and the U.S. chargé d'affaires on October 6 confirmed that work on the oil code was going ahead. Pani indicated it was impossible for his government to amend Article 27 as the companies wanted because the Congress was opposed, but he stressed that it was Obregón's intention to implement it in such a way that it would not be retroactive or confiscatory.[138] Six days later the chargé forwarded to Washington a copy of what he understood to be the definitive text of the bill, which had been handed to him by Pani himself with assurance that any "constructive criticism" would be welcome. However, in an unofficial note of October 22 Pani informed Summerlin that the executive was about to present a new text to the Congress, the contents of which he would communicate to him in advance—implying apparently that the October 12 version had already been superseded.[139] Before long Washington was in possession of still two more possible texts.[140] In early November the five companies which were in contact with the Mexican government through the joint committee of executives formulated their objections to the various versions which had been considered up to that time.[141] Washington remained on the lookout but decided not to exert any pressure for the moment.

The persistent rumors about a possible bill containing strongly nationalist provisions were not entirely unfounded. In early November Obregón met with his cabinet to discuss the problem of the oil code generally and in particular still another new text, which had been prepared by the Ministries of Industry and Treasury.[142] The proposal gave the executive broad discretionary powers that would permit it to invalidate even contracts entered into prior to May 1917 and to set taxes at 15 per cent or more of the value of production.[143] However, Obregón, Calles, and De la Huerta all leaned toward respecting the interests of those companies that were currently exploiting the oil. They believed that the only possible solution was to oblige the firms to accept a change in their legal status through the system of granting concessions.[144] From the minutes of this debate—the only ones that could be obtained on a cabinet meeting in which the oil question was discussed—it can be seen that Obregón had a clear understanding of the problem at hand. It seemed to him that the proposal under study would only make for trouble, since the extraordinary powers it was intended to give him would simply not be recognized by the oil firms and there would be no way of forcing them to comply with the executive orders that would be issued.[145] He insisted that the final authority in the matter should rest with the Congress, and that this body, and not the president, should make the laws to implement Article 27—not only in regard to hydrocarbons but also with respect to the land reform. This way, he felt, it would be more difficult for the Americans to exert pressure. Naturally, the Congress would follow his guidance. "We will have to watch carefully," he said in closing the meeting, "to make sure that the Congress in carrying out its mission does not weaken the intent of Article 27 in any way. At the present time this is our only salvation."[146] Obregón made it clear that it was important not to back down on Article 27 despite the difficulties it was causing for relations with Washington.[147] As a result of this discussion the bill was modified: the executive was no longer to have extraordinary powers in oil matters, and for one year following promulgation of the new law those who had acquired rights prior to May 1917 could ask to have them ratified.[148] In effect, the property titles were to be changed to concessions, although for the moment the companies' position would in practice remain unchanged.

The events immediately following this November cabinet meeting indicate that a concerted effort was made to carry the plan forward as agreed. However, this proposal, like its numerous predecessors, was doomed to failure. On November 15 the press reported that the president had no immediate plans for solving the problem of the oil law, but that he was in favor of dealing with all aspects of Article 27—that is, both the oil and the land reforms—at the same time.[149] That same day a communiqué from Chargé d'Affaires Summerlin to Foreign Affairs Minister Pani made it known that the White House had taken note of the new draft and objected to several of its clauses. Obregón decided to take advantage of this protest—which in fact was in no way different from any of the others before it—and, to Washington's amazement and displeasure, made its contents public, telling the U.S. government it had no right to protest legislation which had not yet been promulgated and that therefore in no way affected American citizens. This move won the applause of broad sectors of the Mexican populace.[150] In Summerlin's opinion, the intent behind it was not so much to vigorously defend Mexican sovereignty as it was to distract public attention from economic problems on the domestic front and, as a favor to Calles, to put De la Huerta in a bad light for having sent the last text to Washington.[151] Secretary of State Hughes was indignant at what he considered an act of bad faith on the part of the Mexican government, which had abused the confidentiality of a diplomatic exchange in order to solve an internal problem. Despite all these complications, however, the protest served its purpose: the proposal was dropped.[152]

The effort to get some form of oil legislation on the books was to go on for still a good while longer. In December 1922 the Mexican Congress informed the press that it was discussing a new bill which stipulated that rights acquired prior to 1917 would have to be confirmed by the issuance of a government concession.[153] Predictably, the deliberations had no sooner begun than the APPM informed Washington that the text under study was unacceptable.[154] The two houses of the Mexican Congress debated the oil question heatedly through March 1923, while at the same time the firms continued to lodge their objections with Treasury Minister De la Huerta.[155] Finally on April 26 the Chamber of Deputies approved a bill which in its Article 5 confirmed the rights acquired prior to 1917 but insisted that the property titles be exchanged for concessions—which, to make matters worse would be good only for fifty years.[156] The bill was passed in the Senate. With this development the APPM became really alarmed, and its members wasted no time in calling on Secretary of State Hughes to express their concern.[157] At the other end of the spectrum, however, the nationalist sectors in Mexico were still unsatisfied and continued to insist that none of the companies' claims to rights acquired prior to 1917 should be recognized.[158] In July, while the so-called Bucareli talks were going on, the Senate began its study of the bill which had been approved by the Chamber of Deputies. The talks had a direct effect on the lawmakers, who agreed that "vested rights" would be fully recognized for a given period of time.[159] In view of this decision, the draft law was returned to the Chamber of Deputies, where later it was to be shelved for good. By that time Obregón had succeeded in calming down the Americans, but he did not want the terms agreed to at Bucareli to be committed to law. Meanwhile, the APPM's protests had not subsided entirely, even though the bill had been changed in its favor. For all these reasons, the government decided to postpone the final vote on the law to another session.[160]

The situation in 1923 was a typical reflection of the Mexican government's dilemma during that decade. Any attempt to strike a compromise between the status quo under the Porfirian regime and the reform demanded by the Carranza legislation was to meet with the dissatisfaction of both the oil firms and the Mexican nationalists. The government could not act openly against Washington's wishes, nor could it disregard the powerful nationalistic sentiment that had been aroused by the Revolution. Thus, one after another the different proposals had to be thrown out, and the possibility of reaching an agreement seemed to become increasingly remote.

The Threat of a Violent Solution

The beginning of Obregón's term in office coincided with what appeared to be the end of the "united oil front," heralded by El Aguila's announcement that it was dropping out of the APPM. The Mexican press jubilantly predicted that this important British firm would soon be submitting itself to the new laws, thus setting a precedent that would once and for all trigger a process of erosion against the companies' intransigent opposition.[161] The rejoicing was short-lived, however, for the British firm soon reversed its stand and admitted that the time had passed when it could act independently or against the wishes of American interests in Mexico. The front therefore continued to remain united, and Obregón could not find a single chink in the ranks that he could take advantage of to divert the companies' campaign to put an end to what was left of the Carranza oil reform.

According to notes of Wilson's cabinet meetings taken by Navy Secretary Josephus Daniels, in January 1921 Doheny urged once again that Mexico be invaded in order to put a stop to the new government's confiscatory policies.[162] During the first months of that year several important American newspapers hinted repeatedly that the Obregón administration would be unable to maintain internal order much longer, thus indirectly supporting those who were calling for the use of force.[163] At the same time there were many who claimed that the oil firms were originating these rumors precisely to create an excuse for armed intervention in Mexico.[164] The anti-interventionists in the United States suspected that a conspiracy had been mounted to provoke a showdown with Mexico. For example, a mass layoff of oil workers in Tamaulipas in 1921 was seen as an attempt to incite them to violence so as to justify sending U.S. troops into the oil region.[165] The New York American revealed the contents of a confidential letter supposedly written on July 6, 1921, which helped to fan the flame. Claimed to be an exchange between two oil company representatives, it reviewed the details of a conversation between Henry Lane Wilson, former ambassador to Mexico, and Secretary of State Hughes. In view of Mexico's unwillingness to sign a treaty, the latter reportedly declared that the American government was prepared to back any group that would start a revolution to reinstate the Constitution of 1857. Without giving any further details, the newspaper concluded by saying that the plan had in fact been attempted but had not met with any success.[166]

As a result of the labor unrest following the 1921 layoffs, two U.S. warships (USS *Cleveland* and USS *Sacramento*) appeared in Tampico harbor. The new navy secretary, Edwin Denby, informed the press that the vessels' commanders had been authorized to use force, but he added that this did not have "any international significance," since the ships had been sent only as a precautionary measure to "remind" the Mexican government of its duty to protect foreigners within its territory.[167] In the end the ships withdrew without any incident that might have led to a confrontation.[168] Three years later *El Universal Gráfico* claimed that Charles Hunt, a close associate of Senator Albert B. Fall's, had revealed a plot carefully laid out by the companies in 1921 to get U.S. forces to invade the oil region in Mexico. This story confirmed the accusation of the anti-imperialists that had appeared in certain sectors of the American press. Supposedly, the idea had been to set up a separate republic comprising the northern states of Mexico —the old plan espoused by former ambassador Henry Lane Wilson—and, to this end, to provoke an incident in Tampico that would bring on a U.S. troop landing. (A minor rebel leader, Daniel Martínez Herrera, had been enlisted to fight on the Americans' side, it was said, but Obregón's lieutenant Guadalupe Sánchez dissuaded him.) Meanwhile, according to this story, other clearly subversive activities were also carried out; indeed, the oil firms were claimed to have entered into negotiations with rebel leaders Pablo González, Manuel Peláez, Francisco Murguía, and Esteban Cantú (former governor of Lower California). In the end, however, it appeared that Eusebio Gorozane, still another rebel chief, who operated in the Huasteca region, was the only one who actually received a certain amount of help, and he never came to represent a serious threat to the central government. Finally, what with division within the American ranks over the strategy to be followed and lack of enthusiasm on the part of the British members in the group, the plan presumably fizzled out.[169]

By the end of 1921 the situation began to change. Thanks no doubt to Obregón's manifest concern and repeated statements on the subject of vested rights, the companies' attitude toward the new government softened. Talk of an invasion of Mexico stopped.[170] At the beginning of the following year the State Department formally disclaimed any connection with the insurrectionist activities of Félix Díaz. It also denied that it had ever entertained any idea of supporting an anti-Obregón movement in order to solve the oil problem.[171] Still, for the rest of that year and on into the next the Mexican government continued to receive news through its consular service in the United States of subversive plots being organized by the companies—although nothing ever materialized.[172] Hence it was that for two years the Obregón government was pelted with rumors of invasions and subversive activities supposedly backed by the oil firms.

The Bucareli Talks

The protracted, difficult, and much-discussed meetings held between spokesmen for the Mexican and American chiefs of state in Mexico City (called the "Bucareli talks" because they took place in a building on Bucareli Avenue) began on May 14, 1923, and ended three months later, bringing a temporary solution to the controversy. The definitive solution to the oil problem, however, was to come much later under another Mexican administration. The sessions led neither to the formal treaty being demanded by Fall and the American groups nor to the unconditional resumption of diplomatic ties that Obregón had wanted. The actual results included some more or less formal concessions on Mexico's part, an accord on payment of the foreign debt, and several agreements in regard to certain specific grievances. Only later, some time after the talks were over, were formal relations renewed between Washington and Mexico. According to Aarón Sáenz, Obregón's minister of foreign affairs, the meetings were a necessary succedaneum in the absence of a law on the books to implement Article 27.[173] In the opinion of certain American authors, if Mexico had not come to some kind of terms in 1923, the U.S. government might very well have thrown its support to some counter-revolutionary faction or actually gone so far as to invade the country in order to put an end to the impasse that was tormenting its citizens.[174] As the events of December 1923 were to show, Obregón had indeed had good reason to be concerned lest the transfer of power to President-elect Plutarco Elías Calles open the way for a rebellion. He knew that in the event of an uprising Washington's attitude would be decisive. In the 1924 elections U.S. backing was essential to the Obregón group in order to remain in power.

The White House's real reason for not insisting on Fall's demands to the letter and for contenting itself with an informal agreement instead of a treaty may perhaps be found in a report filed by the U.S. consul general on January 23, 1923. In this document it is suggested that certain American groups in Mexico felt that Washington's diplomatic offensive had failed. They pointed out that Obregón had succeeded in staying in power for two years without U.S. recognition and that in the meantime his propaganda had struck a sympathetic chord in a growing and increasingly vocal sector of the American public. To keep this situation from being perpetuated, they claimed, the Mexican government would have to be recognized even without the formal agreement. There were those in the State Department who concurred with this line of thinking, and it was felt that, given Obregón's moderate attitude, little harm would be done by recognizing his government at this point. They reasoned that in any case pressure could always be applied to keep him from interpreting Article 27 retroactively, which was the main point at issue.[175]

The possibility of substituting some other kind of commitment for a formal treaty as a condition for recognition had been contemplated since 1921.[176] In February 1922, when Obregón insisted that the treaty be signed *after* recognition, Washington had replied that the terms must be fully negotiated beforehand. Obregón stood firm.[177] In a note dated August 3 of that year mention was made for the first time in the official correspondence of the possibility that the United States might drop its demand for a signed treaty. It was made clear, however, that an alternative formula must be found to guarantee the protection of American interests. The road that was to lead to Bucareli was beginning to open up. As it turned out, it was through General James Ryan, representative of Texas Oil in Mexico and a personal friend of Obregón's, rather than the U.S. chargé d'affaires, that the details of this meeting which was to air the problems between the two countries were finalized. The proposal was formally agreed to on April 9, 1923, but not without serious reservations on the part of Obregón. If the talks failed, he said, it was very possible that the breach between Washington and Mexico would widen.[178] The record shows that he had tried to keep the subject of the oil legislation off the agenda, but at Ryan's insistence he finally relented.

On the American side were Charles Beecher Warren, former ambassador to Japan, and John Barton Payne, former secretary of the interior; Mexico was represented by Ramón Ross and the renowned jurist Fernando González Roa.[179] Secretary of State Hughes' instructions to the U.S. emissaries set the tone of the talks. The secretary of state had said that while it was not the United States' intention to tell Mexico how to write its laws, in no way could his government consent to the confiscation of property protected by legally acquired titles. And these were the terms in which a definitive agreement was finally to be reached. In addition, Hughes had said, it would be necessary to arrive at a specific definition of "vested rights" as used in the case of oil, being careful not to let it imply the loss of any property rights acquired prior to May 1, 1917.[180]

The talks took place in an atmosphere of tension that did not once let up during the whole three months.[181] It is impossible to follow their development step by step, since the brief official minutes record only the points of agreement and not the process by which they were arrived at.[182] However, these and other documents would indicate that the discussion centered largely on: protection of the rights acquired by foreigners prior to the Constitution of 1917, especially in the case of the oil industry; review of the Supreme Court's decisions in regard to oil and possible extension of the doctrine to analogous cases; interpretation of the term "positive act"; payment of taxes; the problem of "federal zones"; and the matter of drilling permits. The APPM was in constant contact with Warren and Payne, going over the different questions and proposing solutions. The U.S. representatives maintained that the laws prior to 1917 gave the surface landholder full title to the subsoil and that there was no alternative but to respect this property right. The Mexican delegates contested the point, using the arguments that had been developed in Carranza's time. Prior to 1917, they said, the surface landholder had simply a potential right, which became a full right only on finding and extracting the petroleum. Moreover, many of the oil lands were located in areas along coasts and national borders in which it was forbidden for foreigners to hold ownership—in open violation of laws that unquestionably existed prior to 1917. For Warren, the Supreme Court decisions in the case of Texas Oil amounted to an absolute and clear-cut repudiation of retroactive application, and he felt that the executive and legislative powers should follow this criterion to the letter. González Roa, on the other hand, considered that the rulings applied only to paragraph iv of Article 27 and in no sense to the principle of retroactivity as such, as the American representatives were claiming. In the face of this irreconcilable difference of opinion, the U.S. emissaries took a stand and explicitly reserved their fellow citizens' rights to the subsoil on lands acquired prior to 1917. González Roa, for Mexico's part, stated that, while it was intended to respect the Supreme Court decisions, no more than preferential consideration would be given to those companies that had undertaken a "positive act" prior to 1917 in granting fixed-term subsoil concessions. In the end, he accepted the U.S. reservation of rights, at the same time reserving Mexico's right over those lands acquired or leased by the oil firms prior to 1917 on which no "positive act" had been established.[183]

Clearly it was the application of Article 27 to the oil industry, and not the agrarian problem or the foreign debt, that was foremost in the minds of the representatives at Bucareli. Strictly speaking, the fact that both sides made reservations shows that even after five months of intensive negotiations no definitive agreement had been reached on the interpretation of paragraph iv. However, in reality the position of the oil properties acquired by foreigners prior to the date the new constitution went into effect was largely settled. For the United States had agreed to let the absolute property titles be turned into "confirmatory concessions," thus recognizing a change in the status of their ownership. Mexico, on the other hand, agreed to accept a definition of "positive act" that was so broad that practically all the areas which were important to the companies were covered by it. The agreements did not constitute a "secret treaty" that renounced the nationalist goals of the Revolution behind the people's back, as some of Obregón's detractors would have had it. Nor were they the result of an innocuous exchange of views in which the constitution was followed to the letter, as others maintained. The Mexican government had been forced to call what appeared at the time to be a definitive halt to the most important aspects of the oil reform. Although the resumption of formal diplomatic ties after the talks was received in Mexico City with the pealing of bells and was in fact an unquestioned success for the Obregón administration—later to be translated into full U.S. support when the Adolfo De la Huerta rebellion broke out in December 1923—Bucareli was no great triumph in terms of the long-range national interest as conceived under any of the various interpretations of the Revolution.[184]

The appointment of Charles Beecher Warren, who had been one of the delegates at Bucareli, as the American ambassador was regarded in Mexico as a sign that the United States intended to watch closely to see that the terms of the agreement were kept.[185] Moreover, Secretary of State Hughes gave broad Latin American significance to the outcome at Bucareli when on November 30, in a speech commemorating the hundredth anniversary of the Monroe Doctrine, he stressed that his government had no intention of challenging the laws of its Western Hemisphere neighbors, but by the same token the rights acquired by foreigners under existing laws in those countries should be respected as an "international obligation."

Shortly before diplomatic ties between Washington and Mexico were fully reestablished, the oil firms had said that they were prepared to push their operations in Mexico and make up for lost time if an agreement on their rights were reached.[186] However, when the terms of an accord were finally announced the companies did little to conceal their disappointment. They claimed that failure to reach a written agreement was tantamount to perpetuation of the uncertainty that had existed all along. Their opposition to the results at Bucareli was made known in all quarters, both public and private.[187]

It was precisely in this compact of August 1923 that De la Huerta was to find the theoretical justification for his break with Obregón and Calles. The De la Huerta rebellion was essentially a personal power contest within the group that had overthrown Carranza. To the extent that it went beyond these limited confines, it was a conservative movement supported by perhaps half the army. In reality it had little or nothing to do with Obregón's relations with Washington, even though its leader attempted to make it look like a struggle between nationalists and traitors.[188] According to De la Huerta, it was when he learned about the "extraofficial" rapprochement at Bucareli that he presented his resignation to Obregón. The fight between their respective partisans over the governorship of San Luis Potosí—which was to end in bloodshed—came later. De la Huerta consistently maintained that his falling-out with Obregón had nothing to do with his frustrated presidential aspirations; that from the very outset he had been opposed to the Bucareli pact and had done everything within his power to try to persuade Obregón to go back on the terms of the agreement.[189] In the light of these claims, it is surprising that the De la Huerta manifesto of December 7, 1923, against Obregón made no reference whatsoever to the agreement—presumably the fundamental cause of the rebellion—whereas it did specifically mention the rebels' desire to guarantee the property rights of both nationals and foreigners.[190] However, the fact that the 1923 uprising is better explained by reasons other than retribution for Obregón's "treason" does not mean that Bucareli played no part at all. Cándido Aguilar, who had been personally connected with Carranza and was never any friend of Obregón's, had accused the president of having sold out to the Americans even before the rebellion started, and he gave this as his main reason for taking sides with De la Huerta.[191] In any event, it was not until February 20, 1924, when the fighting had been going on for two months and Obregón was winning on all fronts, that De la Huerta issued a nationalist manifesto at Aguilar's insistence. In it he accused Obregón of having sold the nation's sovereignty down the river and declared that what had begun as a movement "to vindicate the will of the people . . . [had been] exalted, through great and selfless inspiration to a sacred task—that of safeguarding our sovereignty."[192] The opportunism was evident.

While propaganda-wise the Bucareli Agreement had worked somewhat against Obregón, it came to be a real negative factor for De la Huerta. For

Washington considered that, with De la Huerta in the presidency thanks to U.S. backing, it could try for an even more favorable accord. However, the turmoil that would ensue made such a plan too costly.[193] Although the record shows that from the very beginning De la Huerta took pains not to interfere with the American interests, Secretary of State Hughes apparently decided it was best to make the U.S. position clear in any event. Accordingly, on January 23, 1924, he publicly accused the Mexican rebels of having no other aim but to resolve the presidential succession by violence. Far from caring about the Revolution, he alleged, they wanted only to wrest tribute from certain American groups in Mexico. In view of the situation, he went on, the United States would have no alternative, were it asked for help, but to furnish the Mexican government with arms to help to put them down.[194] De la Huerta's envoy in Washington, Juan Manuel Alvarez del Castillo, strove in vain to change the State Department's view.[195] It was only after Washington gave its open support to Obregón that De la Huerta brought up the Bucareli Agreement and accused the president of having sold out to the Americans.

Despite their dissatisfaction with the 1923 accord, the American oil firms lent a certain amount of support to Obregón in his struggle against De la Huerta by making advance payments on their taxes.[196] Alvarez del Castillo, representing the movement that had sworn vengeance against the "extra-official" pact of 1923, tried to stand in the way of this little bit of cooperation by accusing Obregón and Calles in the United States of a "bolshevist" policy designed to confiscate from the companies that to which they were entitled.[197] Naturally no one paid any attention to this charge. Despite the risk he knew he was incurring, De la Huerta began to try to raise funds by collecting taxes from the firms whenever his troops gained control of one of the ports they were using.[198] When the companies resisted, some of the rebel chiefs threatened to raze their installations—although nothing ever came of it. Confident that Washington would be able to get De la Huerta and his men to restrain themselves, the oil firms continued to hold out. It would appear that their confidence was justified, for the rebels were to cause only one small interruption in their activities, in mid-February.[199] Meanwhile, there are indications that the British may have tried to take sides against their American colleagues by extending a discreet offer of help, through the authorities in Belize, to Obregón's opponents. If this is true, the lesson that President Wilson had taught to Victoriano Huerta must have been still quite fresh in everyone's minds, for the rebels apparently declined the offer. Thus, De la Huerta was without the clear support of either of the oil groups, and indeed in the case of the Americans he had certain real opposition to face.[200]

The 1924 Accord

There was little official correspondence between Mexico and the United States in regard to the oil question from September 3, 1923, to October 29,

1925, and what there was would indicate that no serious problems came up during that period. The companies understood that it would be difficult for Washington to go beyond what had been agreed to at Bucareli and decided to enter into direct talks with Obregón. And so it was that once again, in September and October 1924, their representatives met with Mexican officials to work out a "definitive solution" to the various points of contention between them. Since April the firms had been saying that in order to increase production, which was falling off alarmingly, it would be necessary for Mexico to agree to take certain steps that would open the way for the sizable new investments that were needed—namely: (1) promulgate a "practical" law on oil that would uncontestably protect them against retroactive application of Article 27; (2) suspend once and for all the granting of concessions to third parties in the "federal zones" traversing or bordering on their lands; (3) stop the collection of the rents and royalties stipulated in the Carranza decrees; (4) give assurances that Article 123 of the Constitution, on the rights of workers, would be applied only "within reason"; and (5) guarantee that taxes would remain unchanged for the next ten years.[201] At the time, Obregón had little reason to reopen the question of the oil firms' rights, but the companies were determined to give him the incentive. At the beginning of 1924 Pani, by that time minister of the treasury, approached the U.S. bankers asking them for a loan of twenty million dollars repayable over five years, to be secured against the proceeds from the oil taxes. When the firms heard about this request they contacted the bankers and got them to agree to hold off approval until there was a definitive agreement concerning their rights in Mexico.[202] In June of that year, at Ambassador Warren's insistence, a delegation of oil company executives was chosen to go to Mexico and discuss the problem with the authorities there.[203] Warren had suggested a joint commission of bankers and oilmen so that the question of the loan that Mexico was asking for would be formally linked to the promulgation of adequate oil legislation, but in the end the party was made up of oil representatives only.[204] This decision had been motivated by recent signs of dissatisfaction with the oil firms on the part of the Mexican government. Obregón had just accused them publicly of having once again threatened the stability of Mexican institutions. The decline in production, and hence in national revenue, had annoyed the administration, as had the firms' intercession to keep Mexico from getting the loan from the U.S. bankers.[205] The talks, held at the oil delegation's initiative, began on October 14. Present for Mexico were Treasury Minister Alberto J. Pani and Industry Minister Manuel Pérez Treviño. The agenda (which was not announced publicly) covered the question of taxes (both for fields already known to have oil and for unexplored ones), labor conditions, and Article 27. The companies were particularly opposed to exchanging their property titles for mere concessions and to accepting the "positive act" principle. They also expressed concern over the possibility of being affected by agrarian expropriations under the land reform. The results of these direct negotiations were not wholly satisfactory for the oil firms. Although on the one hand they did secure considerable tax cuts, on the other Obregón did not agree to any change that would affect interpretation of the constitution or promulgation of the law on oil. Still, the companies considered that some progress had been made, and they looked forward to making a firm agreement later on.[206] Since Obregón had only a short time left in office, the pact was submitted to the president-elect, Plutarco Elías Calles, who gave it his approval.[207]

Obregón ended his presidential term in 1924 and retired temporarily from public life. However, his influence as a leader within the group in power continued, even though Calles was in the driver's seat. The oil problem, which had been one of the decisive questions in his relations with the United States, was no longer quite so urgent or threatening, but it had not been solved. Like Carranza, he had been unable to put the oil reform into effect. Feeling as he did the force of U.S. pressure at a time when this country had no serious extracontinental preoccupations and the government was manifestly more responsive than its predecessor to the oil firms' interests, he was obliged to resort to the Supreme Court rulings and the Bucareli talks to avoid concluding a treaty that would have spelled the end of paragraph iv forever. Those who feel that he made serious concessions to the Americans should bear in mind that he had made it clear they were not definitive. The door was left open, and Calles was soon to attempt a new solution to the oil question, with results just as controversial, if not more so, than those of his predecessor.

Chapter 6

Calles and His Attempts
to Put an Oil Law into Effect

At the time he took office the new president, Plutarco Elías Calles, was considered to represent the left wing of the Agua Prieta group.[1] Although Obregón's influence continued to be felt, Calles had sufficient latitude to put his own stamp on his administration and, in certain cases, to reformulate solutions to the political and economic reconstruction problems that had emerged in the wake of the Revolution.[2] In the process the oil question was to come up again, although not right away. The first steps after the presidency changed hands and the De la Huerta uprising had been suppressed were to purge the army of elements unsympathetic to the administration and to promote the establishment of workers' and peasant organizations so as to broaden the new chief executive's base of power. (As it happened, the government's support of the worker and peasant sectors was to have the effect of tying these groups down unconditionally to official policies and stifling any independent mobilization.) The political reorganization was followed in turn by a large-scale program of public works and fiscal and monetary reform, vigorous expansion of the secular education movement that had been started under Obregón, and, finally, a concerted effort to reach a definitive solution to the problem posed by the Church, relegating it to a secondary place through strict implementation of the anticlerical clauses in the new constitution and confiscation of its lands.[3] This last undertaking was to lead to the Cristero Rebellion of 1926, a three-year struggle between the government and the Catholic groups whose theater of operations was mainly in the central lowlands of Mexico—the Bajío. When it ended in 1929 the Church had not been entirely defeated but the state's supremacy was unquestionably confirmed. At the end of his term Calles was to crown his accomplishments with the creation of an official party designed to bring together all the various Revolutionary groups and resolve the discord among them. Thus his administration laid the institutional bases which, once the world crisis was over, were to make for a politically stable climate in which the official party was hegemonic and the power of the presidency undisputed and, at the same time, for a healthy upsurge in economic development. The Calles reconstruction program was favored by a sudden rise in the demand for Mexican products on the world market (especially minerals, except oil), which permitted a certain budgetary freedom and helped to strengthen the magistracy of a state that was rapidly increasing its participation in national economic life.[4]

Actually it was only during the first phase of his administration that Calles' actions were more or less in keeping with his reputation as a progressive Revolutionary leader. Starting in 1926 or 1927 he began to veer sharply to the right. At the same time corruption began to be evident in high circles and personal fortunes to grow. In the opinion of some observers of the Mexican experience, the new group had come to leadership without the necessary intellectual, psychological, political, or administrative preparation, and at the same time without a coherent ideology or a strong enough value system to resist the temptation to abuse the almost unlimited power at their disposal.[5] Not unrelated to this shift to conservatism was the tremendous American pressure that was once again aimed at Mexico during the years 1925, 1926, and 1927. Calles' relations with the White House fell roughly into two periods, corresponding to the internal phases just mentioned: first, the time up to the arrival of Ambassador Dwight W. Morrow at the end of 1927, and second, the years characterized by a marked lessening of tension between the two countries, which coincided with the beginning of a conservative phase in Mexico that was to last until the Lázaro Cárdenas takeover in 1935 and Calles' expulsion from the country. The first years of Calles' administration (1924–1926) were to see a renewed attempt to put the country's development in national hands and relegate foreign capital to a secondary position—and hence a resurgence of the old conflict.[6] In a statement by Calles published in *Foreign Affairs* magazine in 1926, the new president declared that his administration was dedicated to eliminating the advantages that small but powerful groups had come to enjoy at the expense of the majority and that the program would be carried out regardless of the opposition it met. Once again it was in the oil industry—which was fast losing its earlier dynamic impetus—that the most bitter struggle was to break out. The mining industry, which coincidentally was going through a prosperous phase, was left in peace. However, both domestic and international circumstances were to work against this nationalist effort, which ended in perhaps more serious failure than any of the ones before it.

Washington's Position at the Beginning of the Calles Administration

Calles had to deal with the Republican administration of Calvin Coolidge, a passionate advocate of the status quo and a sworn enemy of any progressive movement.[7] At the international level "dollar diplomacy" was revived.[8] The U.S. president made it clear from the outset that he was prepared to assure maximum protection for the investments of his fellow citizens abroad—interests that in his opinion were an integral part of the "general domain of the nation." On the basis of this principle, he announced publicly: "We must be prepared for armed intervention . . . in any portion of the globe where disorder and violence threaten the peaceful rights of our people."[9] Thus the situation left no doubt: if Mexico were to raise the question of American oil property rights again, it would be in effect attacking what Coolidge regarded as part of his country's national domain, in defense of which he was prepared to go the limit. As in the previous administration, the oil interests were again represented in the cabinet itself, this time through oil magnate Andrew W. Mellon, who was secretary of the treasury.[10]

Coolidge made no attempt to hide his regret over the fall of Porfirio Díaz, who, he said, had worked thirty years to establish American capital in Mexico. According to him, the current disorder was destroying the valuable foundation that had been laid by Díaz and posing a threat to legitimate U.S. interests.[11]

Against the nationalist stand taken by Calles during the early years of his administration, Washington was to uphold the concept of property as defended in the U.S. courts. The U.S. position hardened if not in fact at least in theory. It was made clear that in the matter of the rights of foreigners the rules of the game could be none other than those prevailing in the United States. Washington was to be selective, however, in the legal precedents it chose to invoke, referring to only one of the several theses accepted by the U.S. courts—namely, the one that most favored the oil firms in their claim that the hydrocarbons in the subsoil were the absolute property of the surface landowner. It conveniently forgot that these same courts had also handed down other decisions which supported Mexico's contention that the surface landholder only became owner of the fuel at the time it was extracted.[12]

Coolidge's first ambassador to Mexico, James R. Sheffield, was a perfect exponent of the "new imperialism" being touted by Washington and the Republican leaders. A financially well-off New York lawyer, Sheffield always sided with the American colony in Mexico, especially in the case of the oil firms, against any change that might threaten their control over the modern and dynamic sectors of the Mexican economy, defending their property zealously.[13] From the very outset the ambassador made it clear that he shared Coolidge's sympathy for the old Porfirian regime and felt that Mexico still needed an authoritarian, paternalistic government, since the people were clearly unable to govern themselves.[14] A review of his correspondence with the State Department shows that he systematically presented the worst possible image of the Mexican administration, characterizing the president variously as a "murderer," an "assassin," a "robber," and a "violator of his own pledged word."[15] In regard to the oil problem, the ambassador not only supported the companies' position unconditionally, he went so far as to pull them back to their initial stand whenever they gave signs of relaxing their resistance and thinking of accepting the Mexican legislation, at which point he would reiterate his intention to use force to keep Calles from "violating international law through confiscation." This drastic recourse had become necessary, he claimed, not only in order to defend the interests of a few American firms in Mexico but also "in the interests of civilization and peaceful commerce."[16]

Resumption of the Conflict: The Draft Oil Law

Despite the decline in production, oil still represented the country's most important industry in 1924. Its legal status remained uncertain, although after the Bucareli talks it had not been directly threatened. At the beginning of Calles' term it looked as if the question of the oil companies' rights was going to be settled on the basis of the 1924 agreements, which, though they had been made with Obregón, were subsequently ratified by Calles.[17] In the oil circles there were hopes that this arrangement would lead to the formulation of a law that would be in line with the Americans' wishes. But things were not to work out that way.

By the time Calles took office in 1924 the firms were convinced that the downturn in oil production which had begun in 1923 was irreversible. The U.S. Federal Oil Conservation Board pointed out, however, that there were still some promising geological formations in Mexico that had not yet been explored and that it would be well for the Americans to keep these lands under their eye.[18] Meanwhile, Obregón's "oil peace" was very tenuous. Those who were set on changing the industry's legal status had not abandoned their efforts. Luis Cabrera, one of Carranza's closest associates, warned: "Our oil wealth is not as great as we might think; what is great is the unconscionableness with which we exploit it." He maintained that Mexico's share in this wealth was insufficient by any and all standards and should be increased.[19] From Spain, Camilo Barcia Trelles wrote in his treatise on oil imperialism and world peace that Mexico could and should stand up to the oil firms and win its freedom.[20] Noting this restlessness and looking for a way to hold Calles to the 1923 and 1924 agreements, the State Department began once again to insist on a treaty of friendship and trade just as it had done earlier with Obregón. However, the new president had other plans and refused to go along with the idea.[21]

In 1925, friction between the United States and Mexico was to be rekindled in all the three big areas: oil, agrarian, and religious. Coolidge understood that the oil legislation drafted by the Calles administration that year was to apply retroactively, and he regarded the expropriation of agricultural lands without suitable compensation (of the 2.5 million hectares taken at the time, only 200,000 belonged to Americans) as a serious threat to the U.S. national interest. Thus he decided to put on pressure to get the two measures annulled.[22] A fourth point of contention entered the picture when Mexico stopped payment on its foreign debt shortly thereafter. But still the oil question, because of its importance and background, remained in the forefront. To a certain extent the State Department exaggerated the significance of the agrarian and religious problems in order to justify its stepped-up pressure for a favorable solution to the problem of the subsoil legislation.

Although the platform and speeches in Calles' 1924 presidential campaign had made no direct reference to the oil question, the candidate had publicly expressed his intention to support the "fundamental principles" of Articles 27 and 28 of the constitution—though always appearing to be referring to their agrarian aspect. As a matter of fact, there were a number of signs that the controversy which seemed to have been settled in 1923 would not be long in flaring up again:[23] his strong emphasis on nationalism; his criticism of the role of foreign capital, which he claimed had come to Mexico to "take everything and leave nothing"; his reiterated determination to "safeguard what belongs to Mexico" through increased public control of natural resources. These signs became even clearer a few months after his term began. He appointed a joint congressional committee to draft a brand-new proposal for the law on oil, thus rejecting all the versions that had been left pending from the previous regime.[24]

By the end of July 1925 Washington began to receive disquieting reports both from its diplomatic agents and from the oil companies regarding the nature of the text that was being considered. The news was alarming: no protection was being provided for anyone who had not established the famous "positive act"—which was defined in much stricter terms than those at Bucareli—and the parties in question were given only a preferential period within which to file their claims. And, what was worse, their rights were limited to a period of thirty years.[25] The rising concern was somewhat tempered, however, when still another bill was presented by Deputy Justo A. Santa Anna which discarded the "positive act" principle in favor of absolute recognition of all rights to the subsoil acquired prior to the date the new constitution went into effect[26]—although the companies did not fail to object to one of its provisions, which called for a 10 per cent tax on the value of the oil drilled.[27] The State Department, having heard that more than one hundred deputies were behind this new proposal, relaxed.[28] But the congressional joint committee paid no heed whatsoever to the Santa Anna version and presented its own definitive bill in early September. This latest text emphasized that only the rights of those who had actually begun to drill prior to May 1917 (the interpretation of having established a "positive act") could be confirmed, and it set a time limit on these vested rights.[29] In mid-October the State Department informed the Mexican ambassador that the oil firms were highly dissatisfied with the government's plans.[30] By mid-November Ambassador Sheffield was openly concerned. It was still not known which of the two proposals the administration planned to back. Treasury Minister Pani told him that it was highly unlikely a decision would be reached before the end of the current session and that the question would thus be tabled at least for a while.[31] However, these vague assurances were not enough for the ambassador, and on November 17 he called on Foreign Affairs Minister Aarón Sáenz personally. Appealing to the spirit of the 1923 talks, he urged that negotiations be started immediately on the famous treaty of friendship and trade, which would commit Mexico to maintaining the status quo in the foreign sector of its economy. Sheffield warned the minister that he saw dark clouds gathering on the horizon.[32] Sáenz replied that *he* didn't see any such clouds and that the 1923 agreements, which were mere exchanges of views and had no legal force, could not be invoked as the ambassador was doing.[33] In the end the idea of the treaty was neither thrown out nor acted on.

Still another draft oil law, this time submitted to the Congress by Calles himself, was soon added to the companies' worries. Although it did not refer directly to the industry's legal status, it reiterated an earlier provision prohibiting foreign individuals or corporations from owning land within fifty kilometers of the coast and one hundred of any national border,[34] and a number of the oil lands were very near the Gulf coast.

Contrary to what Pani had led Sheffield to think, Calles had decided that the Congress should approve a law as soon as possible, and that it should be based on the joint congressional committee's version rather than Santa Anna's. This development was not greeted with pleasure by either Santa Anna or the Americans. The latter were concerned most of all about the fifty-year limit which it set on the confirmation of subsoil rights.[35] When the Chamber of Deputies approved the bill at the end of November, the U.S. embassy protested directly to Sáenz. The Mexican minister replied that the protest was out of order, since the legislation had not yet gone into effect, adding that he hoped the United States was not attempting to exercise pressure.[36] On the basis of Pani's assurances to one of the oilmen, Sheffield continued to report to Washington up to the last minute that the bill was not going to pass in the Senate and that, even in the remote chance it did, it would be vetoed by Calles. Meanwhile, for good measure, the ambassador continued to enter verbal protests.[37] All these efforts were in vain, however: on December 31, 1925, nine years after the promulgation of the constitution, the first oil law under the new constitution was passed, and its specific regulatory legislation was to appear the following April.[38]

The provisions corresponding to paragraphs i and iv were to arouse controversy in various respects. To begin with, not only did property holders have to apply for confirmation of their rights but, to make matters worse, there was a fifty-year limit on these rights as well—counting from the time the operations began. The Americans were opposed in principle to any country having the right to alter the status of legally acquired property rights. Moreover, they objected to the change in the meaning of "positive act" from what had been agreed on at Bucareli. Still another point of friction was the application of the Calvo clause—which prohibited foreigners from appealing to their governments for protection in the event of a conflict with Mexico—to the oil firms. The companies also protested the apparent contradiction in the fact that all their "due" rights could be confirmed but yet these same rights were not recognized on lands along the coasts and national borders. And, finally, to all the rest was added the fact that it was now also necessary to comply with the old Carranza decree of January 15, 1915, which required that claims be filed for the oil lands.[39] It was to be two years before Calles showed any response to the oil firms' main objections.

In the second half of 1925, when the companies had seen that the new government really intended to pass a law that would affect their rights, they asked Washington to informally point out to Industry Minister Luis N. Morones, who had been entrusted with seeing after the new legislation, that the proposed bills in the Congress were contrary to the terms agreed on at Bucareli.[40] In November, with confidential Ministry of Industry documents now in hand, the companies firmly assured Secretary of State Kellogg that Mexico was preparing retroactive and unconstitutional oil legislation. Standard Oil told Washington that the Mexican regime was so hostile that unless its attitude changed the company would be forced to leave the country once and for all. (It should be kept in mind that at the time there was a worldwide surplus of oil and that Standard's activities in Mexico were not particularly important within the overall picture.)[41] In December 1925, when the two proposals under debate in the Mexican Congress became public knowledge, the APPM urged Washington to protest the joint committee's version strongly and unremittingly.[42]

During 1925 the oilmen saw to it that their complaints and fears were communicated directly to Calles. In a formal letter they reminded him that his support of the draft legislation denying them of their rights was contrary to his endorsement of the 1924 agreements. After a month's delay, Calles answered saying simply that he had nothing to do with the measures under discussion in the legislature.[43] On December 22 the representative of Pan American Petroleum and Transport placed a memorandum in Pani's hands listing one by one all of his company's objections to the bill that the Congress was about to vote on.[44] Pani assured the firms' directors, who at the time were meeting in New York, that the regulatory legislation to come later would mitigate the stronger provisions in the present organic law. However, the oilmen, by now solidly opposed to the Mexican government's plans and anxious to see them fail, rejected these assurances on the grounds that Pani apparently had little to say in any final decisions on oil policy.[45]

The State Department, in exerting pressure from the moment it believed there was evidence of an oil law which did not fully reflect its repeated demands, was technically intervening in Mexican affairs, since it was protesting legislation that had not yet been passed and had therefore not yet affected the rights of any Americans. On repeated occasions throughout 1925 Secretary Kellogg sent word to the Mexican authorities (through diplomatic channels, but unofficially) that his government did not intend to stand by and let the confiscatory oil legislation go through. Almost a year before the law was approved, the State Department expressed concern over its possible damaging effect on American interests to Foreign Affairs Minister Aarón Sáenz.[46] In May 1925 Ambassador Sheffield went to see President Calles personally and reminded him of the precedent in the Supreme Court rulings of 1922. The Mexican chief executive indicated that these decisions had not in fact set a legal precedent; they were merely a reflection of the government's policy at the time and were not binding on his administration in any way.[47] In October Washington again protested the retroactive provisions of the draft law that was under consideration.[48] In November and December the pressure mounted. Sheffield went to Sáenz and insisted on knowing once and for all whether or not it was intended to respect the terms agreed to under Obregón. If a confiscatory law was passed, he warned, his country would reserve the right to demand restitution for any damaging effects it might have on property owned by American nationals. To this Sáenz replied that Mexico had no intention of doing anything to affect its friendly ties with the United States. However, he did not say specifically that steps would be taken to prevent the bill under study from becoming law.[49] In the light of all these protests on the one side and evasions on the other, it is not surprising that relations between the two governments turned less than cordial in the latter half of 1925. A new crisis broke at mid-year when Kellogg, in a June 12 press conference, hinted at the existence of a gathering movement against Calles in Mexico, adding a reminder that because of its reform program the country was "on trial before the world."[50] Calles' reaction was immediate and irate: Mexico, he declared, would not allow its domestic policy to be judged by anyone, and less still did it recognize that the U.S. secretary of state had any right to intervene in its internal affairs. The Mexican people rallied enthusiastically in support of their president.[51] The bill that Washington was fighting had not yet become law, and a diplomatic break-off was feared. However, President Coolidge apparently did not think the time had come to go that far.[52] During the months from July until December relations seemed to be getting back on an even keel, although the specter of the forthcoming oil law made for a certain degree of tension. On September 1, in his annual state-of-the-union message, Calles referred to the "frank and cordial understanding" between Mexico and the United States.[53] But this cordiality was only apparent, and he was fully aware of the fact: consular reports were constantly being received of an anti-Calles movement being mounted in the United States, possibly supported by the U.S. government, the American oil firms, and other less important interests.[54] As it turned out, this subversive activity never actually came to anything, but Calles had no way of knowing that this would be the case.

U.S. Reaction to the Organic Law Implementing Article 27

In favoring an oil law that departed somewhat from the terms agreed to under Obregón, Calles sought to place U.S.-Mexican relations on a new footing that would make it possible once and for all to begin to reverse the dependent relationship that had taken hold back in the Porfirian regime. The oil legislation was the key to his program. Calles' position was seen in certain American circles not as anti-imperialistic but rather as anti*capital*istic.[55] The fact is that he was determined—and he let the oil companies know it—to be "master of his own house" and to show the people that he was prepared to push for certain changes that were not acceptable to the foreign sector.[56]

In December 1925, before the new oil legislation was presented or put to the vote, several of the leaders in the Mexican Congress had pointed out to Calles the possible international consequences of his plan. In reply he declared that if necessary he would step down from the presidency, but he would never compromise. And so the lawmakers went ahead. Calles, a one-time member of Carranza's and Obregón's inner circles,[57] was perfectly aware of the risks his project entailed. Precisely with this in mind he took the trouble, just before events began to gain momentum, to resume payment of the foreign debt so as to soften the impact of his move against the oil firms in Washington's eyes. The agreement reached with the bankers in the United States implied a great sacrifice for the Mexican economy; extremely limited resources would have to be stretched at the expense of needed infrastructure in order to pay a debt incurred before the Revolution. Nevertheless, Calles felt that the support of the U.S. bankers was vital to the success of his oil reform.[58]

It should be noted that the oil group did not always stand solidly together, and for a time Calles thought to take advantage of its lack of unity to help his plans along. In the beginning Royal Dutch and Transcontinental Petroleum, among the large companies, seemed to lean toward acceptance of the new law, but the uncompromising stand taken by Doheny and Gulf was soon imposed on the rest of the important producers and a united front was achieved.[59] In this new phase of the oil conflict the big American companies were definitely in the lead, the British firms following suit only after some hesitation. As a matter of fact, it was not until the end of 1926 that the APPM received full assurances from El Aguila and La Corona that the British companies were not going to go along with the new legislation.[60] The united front was reinforced by extensive consultations among the oilmen.[61] Apparently some of the American firms did consider avoiding a new confrontation with Mexico; Ambassador Sheffield brought up with Washington several times the importance of making sure that they all refused to submit to the new law, lest the Mexican government succeed in making deals with individual companies and cause the American protests to lose their effect.[62] Doheny's stand finally prevailed, and Calles was not to benefit from any division in the enemy's ranks.

Once the law was passed, the first thing the companies did was to file an injunction against it. By the end of January there were sixty suits waiting to be heard in the Mexican courts. That same month an APPM committee representing the biggest of the firms called on Calles and Industry Minister Morones and told them that harmony could still be regained if Articles 14 and 15 of the new law—those which limited the duration of the concessions and restricted the definition of "positive act"[63]—were withdrawn. During January and February a small team coached by Guy Stevens, secretary of the APPM, undertook to draft a new text for the law (by now already passed, it will be remembered) which would be acceptable to both sides, but nothing ever came of this project.[64] The companies' main reason for refusing to accept the new law was that they regarded it as the first step in a process that would end up depriving them of all their rights—as a precedent that could threaten their properties throughout the world.[65] If Articles 14 and 15 of the new law were retained, no compromise would be possible. They communicated their elaborately reasoned viewpoints to the State Department both directly and through Sheffield, asking for support and protection.[66] Washington was prompt in lodging a formal protest.

The exchange of correspondence between Mexico and the United States from the last months of 1925 up to November 17, 1926, was voluminous (250 pages as published shortly thereafter),[67] but the points around which the controversy actually turned were few. Although the agrarian question was brought up again, the oil situation was the central theme. From the beginning Secretary of State Kellogg tried to make the Bucareli Agreement stand up as an international treaty so as to have strong ground on which to object to those aspects of the 1925 law which ran contrary to it.[68] The Mexican government, for its part, systematically denied that these agreements —merely a statement of the former administration's position, it claimed, by no means with the status of an international compact—had any bearing on the policy of Obregón's successors. It took a similar stand with respect to the 1922 high court rulings. The U.S. objections were to the concepts of

"retroactivity" and "confiscation." Mexico maintained that this line of reasoning did not apply, since the companies' rights acquired prior to 1917
were in no way affected, and it promised that if the fifty-year period allowed
for under the new law was not enough time to exhaust the deposits already
being worked there would be an extension. Moreover, as long as the firms
were in business in Mexico they could keep their properties located in the
prohibited zone along the coasts and the borders—that is to say, they would
be exempt from compliance with section i of Article 27's regulatory law.
Concessions of this type, however, did little to alleviate the pressure. The
State Department roundly rejected the idea of singling out those lands on
which a "positive act" had been demonstrated for special treatment. What
was wanted was the unlimited confirmation of the oil firms' rights to all
properties they had either purchased or leased prior to May 1917. In time
Calles was to relent somewhat, and in a communiqué dated March 27,
1926, he hinted at the possibility of letting the Supreme Court decide, as it
had done in Obregón's time, whether or not the laws in question had retroactive force. It was an escape valve in the event the situation should become unbearable. In a note of October 30, 1926, Foreign Affairs Minister
Sáenz stated that it was his government's firm intention to see that the
rights acquired by the American companies prior to 1917 were upheld without any loss or damage to them whatsoever under the new code—but without going back on the legislation just passed. Nothing concrete came of this
voluminous correspondence filled with highly technical legal arguments,
and for all practical purposes it came to an end in late 1926 when the State
Department, highly exasperated, decided that this approach had been explored to the limit and that others should now be tried.[69] Mexico maintained that as long as the United States did not present a specific case in
which the new legislation had in fact prejudiced the interests of its citizens,
its objections were out of place: there had been no confiscation, and hence
the protests were unwarranted under prevailing international law. Washington, for its part, considered that the new law in itself was reason to claim
a case of confiscation, and it insisted on reserving all the rights of its citizens acquired prior to 1917 which were affected thereby, in effect refusing
to recognize its validity.

When in late 1925 Secretary of State Kellogg learned that despite his
warnings Calles had let the Congress go ahead and pass the oil law, he gave
serious thought to severing the diplomatic ties that had just recently been
reestablished. The American press spoke of such a move as imminent and
even desirable. Thought was also given to lifting the embargo on the sale of
weapons to Mexico, which would mean that Calles' enemies could get hold
of arms. This was in January 1926. By March Washington had changed its
mind and was no longer in favor of such drastic action. It was ready to negotiate.[70] As a matter of fact, back in mid-January the Mexican consulate in
New York had already heard from reliable sources, contrary to the news appearing in the press, that Washington had ruled out the idea of a diplomatic
break-off.[71] The European countries stood unconditionally behind the
State Department.[72] Both the United Kingdom and the Netherlands followed the U.S. example and presented formal protests, although in much

more conciliatory tones. The British firms, which had not yet discovered the Poza Rica beds, had little interest in Mexico at this point and, like the Americans, were planning to concentrate their efforts in Venezuela.[73] Indeed for a while they had been quite disinclined to get into a new conflict with the Mexican government. This may well have been the basis for the friction that developed between the U.S. embassy and the British envoy, Mr. Ovey, over the oil question: the Foreign Office had confirmed its readiness to act jointly with the United States in the case of Mexico, and Ambassador Sheffield probably felt that Ovey's vague and unconvincing protests did not correspond to this commitment.[74] In order to avoid any misunderstandings like those that had occurred in the past, England and the United States agreed once again that none of their nationals would take advantage of the situation and denounce fellow oil landowners who were in violation of the new law in order to curry favor with the Mexican government.[75]

Action of Interest Groups Not Directly Involved in the Oil Conflict

With the controversy reopened some of the groups in the United States that had exercised their influence back in Carranza's time took up thier old positions once again. In Mexico even Calles' own cabinet was divided: on one side Treasury Minister Pani was doing his utmost to prevent a new clash with the oil interests, while on the other Industry Minister Morones (who was also titular leader of the CROM, the largest labor organization in Mexico at the time, and architect of the legislation that had been presented in Congress' name in December 1925) was determined to win out over them.[76] Foreign Affairs Minister Sáenz consulted Morones repeatedly on the wording of the official notes exchanged with the State Department during the 1926 controversy.[77] As a result, Morones had become the strong influence.[78] The Americans were aware of the situation: according to their reports, Morones and the minister of agriculture, counting to a certain extent on the support of the president, had taken a stand in the cabinet in the name of the radical faction which had been in favor of modifying the oil companies' status ever since 1917. In the eyes of the firms, Morones—the labor leader who appeared to be more interested in controlling than representing the workers —was purely and simply a "bolshevik." (Later, at the end of 1927, just when the issue was on the point of being resolved, Ambassador Morrow told Secretary Kellogg confidentially that Calles had confessed that the 1925 law had been necessary in order to appease the radical wing of the Revolutionary group at a time when things were very tense on the domestic front.)[79] Ambassador Sheffield figured that Pani and Sáenz were the moderating elements in the cabinet, preferring not to endanger Mexico's relations with its neighbor to the north.[80] The American envoy would appear to have been right: at the end of 1925 Sáenz came out in favor of drafting a new oil law that respected the rights acquired prior to May 1917 in keeping with the Bucareli commitment.[81] Morones was opposed: like Porfirio Díaz and Victoriano Huerta, he had come to believe that it would be possible to offset

U.S. pressure by mobilizing the support of Europe and the rest of Latin America. The exact position of former president Obregón is not known, although undoubtedly he was in favor of the organic law insofar as it related to paragraph i, if not iv, of Article 27.[82] In any case, his opinion must have been very important.

Pani apparently tried to keep the two provisions in the regulatory law from passing—or at least to get the wording changed. In November 1925 the U.S. embassy informed Washington that he had promised to use his influence in the two houses of Congress to hold up passage of the bill that the companies were against. Later the ambassador interpreted the return of the Senate-revised bill to the Chamber of Deputies to be the result of his tactics. The effort was not to be successful, however,[83] undoubtedly because Calles had not given Pani the necessary latitude. In the decisive days at the end of 1925 Pani was in direct and constant contact with the oil firms and the U.S. embassy—in the latter case through an American businessman, Wallace Payne Moats—keeping them up to date on the situation.[84] It may well have been the role he took in this affair, as much as Morones' victory, that was to lead to Pani's resignation and the appointment of Luis Montes de Oca in his place some two years later.

The national press—that is, the large newspapers—which since Carranza's time had defended the administration's position, for some reason apparently was freed of government pressure, and for a while it boldly attacked the 1925 laws both in the Congress and after they were passed.[85] Later, however, when the conflict became more heated, this same sector, either willingly or under duress, reversed itself again and once more took the government's side.[86] The labor sector was also contradictory: on the one hand it should be remembered that it was Morones, also leader of the CROM, who had forged and promoted the government's oil policy; on the other, the oil workers' unions, most of them with no interest in the CROM, took the companies' side on more than one occasion. This position may be attributed in part to their rivalry with Morones and in part to the fact that experience had shown them that the firms' difficulties with the government frequently resulted in layoffs and mass firings.[87]

In the United States, as always, the picture presented by the pressure groups was more complex. Calles, as we have already said, tried to court favor with the bankers. In October 1925 Pani signed a new agreement for payment of the foreign debt which superseded the terms worked out by Adolfo de la Huerta as treasury minister under Obregón. As before, it was specified that proceeds from the oil taxes would be used in part for this purpose. Payments were resumed at once, although not for very long. As it turned out, Calles' goodwill gesture to his foreign creditors was not to do much good. When in the beginning of 1927 the Mexican ambassador in Washington asked Thomas W. Lamont, secretary of the International Committee of Bankers on Mexico, to mediate between the Mexican government and the oil firms, the latter said he could do nothing and suggested instead that the Mexican courts hurry up and hand down a verdict on the legality of the 1925 legislation.[88] Also Pani apparently tried to get the bankers to urge the oil companies to carry on their normal activities, saying that otherwise

Mexico would not have the means to keep up its payments on the foreign debt.[89] This move was likewise in vain. According to George K. Lewis,[90] the bankers did not go along with Ambassador Sheffield's aggressive policy, and indeed before the end of the year Dwight Morrow, a more conciliatory man with connections in these financial circles, was sent to take his place.

The importance of the opposition to Coolidge and Kellogg's Mexican policy in the U.S. Senate should not be underestimated. This movement was led by Senator William E. Borah, chairman of the Foreign Relations Committee, and Senator Robert M. La Follette, author of the resolution recommending an investigation into Interior Secretary Albert B. Fall's oil lease deals. The opposition in Congress was prompted both by partisan motives and by a sincere difference of opinion between Borah and La Follette, on the one hand, and the administration, on the other, over what the U.S. policy for Latin America should be. In the view of Borah and other members of Congress, the time had come to stop supporting the activities of the Knights of Columbus and the oil and banana companies abroad; such a policy, which was forever creating a climate for intervention, was prejudicial to U.S. interests in the hemisphere.[91] Senator Borah took the occasion more than once to point out that Coolidge and his secretary of state had exaggerated the seriousness of the Mexican situation in order to help the oil interests along. Calles, in the senator's opinion, was acting in good faith, and his government was far from "bolshevik," as it had been characterized in official Washington circles. He proposed that the State Department limit itself in the future to filing protests against Mexico only when there were concrete violations of American rights. His line of reasoning coincided with that of Foreign Affairs Minister Sáenz.[92] One of the devices that he and his allies in Congress used to temper Coolidge's policy toward Mexico was to pass a series of resolutions on the subject: one demanded publication of diplomatic correspondence on the subjects of oil, land, etc.; another insisted on arbitration of the differences with Mexico (in accordance with Calles' suggestion); a third called for Senate authorization of any armed move; and a fourth requested the oil firms to report on the extent to which they had complied with Mexican laws.[93] In March 1927 Borah opened hearings on the Mexican problem. In the course of these sessions he interrogated various State Department officials and made it quite clear that he was dissatisfied with the way in which relations were being handled with the neighbor to the south.[94] Meanwhile, another colleague in the Senate looked into the accusation that the State Department had told the American press to spread the rumor that the Mexican government was trying to establish a bolshevik regime in Nicaragua.[95] It was this questioning attitude in the Congress that, as Samuel Flagg Bemis has put it, "spiked the guns of the interventionists."[96] In their search for information to head off the offensive against Mexico, Borah and La Follette contacted the Mexican authorities directly on more than one occasion. Borah warned Calles that the situation was serious, however, and stressed the importance of the Mexican courts' coming to a speedy decision in the companies' favor if an open conflict was to be avoided.[97]

The congressional Democrats' opposition to the administration's Mexico policy was echoed in liberal and anti-imperialist circles. Articles appeared in various publications attempting to clarify the situation and impartially assess the stand that Calles had taken, which was being systematically attacked by the large U.S. dailies.[98] These liberal groups, made up of workers and the opponents of "dollar diplomacy," objected just as much to Coolidge's unconditional support of big business in Mexico as they did to such a policy at the domestic level.[99] To a certain extent they understood and justified Mexico's need to modify some practices of the foreign interests, which had to be done in order to end an anachronistic economic system that was keeping the country from developing a more modern and independent social structure. They argued that the United States during certain periods of its development had also been forced to infringe on the rights of interest groups in order to protect the people at large. In the specific case of oil, they said, Washington was trying to keep Mexico from putting into effect a legal doctrine that had been upheld repeatedly in the U.S. courts— namely, that the hydrocarbons in the subsoil only become private property once they have been extracted.[100] Soon whole books began to appear justifying Calles' nationalist and reform policies and emphasizing the injustice and pointlessness of resisting the forces of change in Latin America.[101] This campaign had a certain impact on the American public, since the Teapot Dome scandal involving Fall, Doheny, and Sinclair was still fresh in everyone's mind and the oil group with interests in Mexico had come out of it looking rather badly. Even a small sector of the American press, led by the *New York World*, went to bat and urged that the controversy with Mexico not be allowed to reach the point where it could break out into an armed conflict.[102] The result of all this was that larger and larger groups of the American public joined the stand against intervention and called for arbitration of the differences. As Morison and Commager have said, neither the specter of communism nor the rumors of Mexican interference in Nicaragua, fanned by Secretary of State Kellogg in an effort to get the public to favor an aggressive defense of the oil interests in Mexico, made much of an impression.[103] Moreover, the Mexican position was supported not only by liberal groups, labor organizations, and the like but also by some frankly conservative sectors, such as the Ku Klux Klan, which joined Coolidge's critics because of their opposition to the Catholics, who had taken a stand against Calles.[104]

As his predecessors Carranza and Obregón had done, Calles sent spokesmen for the Mexican administration on propaganda tours throughout the United States. These envoys, one of whom, Moisés Sáenz, was the deputy minister of education, based their defense on the same arguments used by the American liberal groups. "The first business of the Revolution," said Sáenz, "was to oust the dictator, then to reconquer the land and to put wealth under the control of the government for the benefit of the many." It was inevitable, he went on, that in this process certain foreign interests would be adversely affected.[105] This Mexican campaign did not go unnoticed by its opponents, and in March 1927 a congressman from Massachusetts took the floor in the House to accuse the Mexican ambassador and the consul general in New York of having spent two million dollars to spread lies and insult the United States on its own territory.[106]

Naturally Calles, like Obregón, sought the support of the sector in the United States that was responsible for trade relations with Mexico. To this group he stressed that the objective of his reform program—which might unintentionally in the process be prejudicial to certain foreign investors— was to increase the purchasing power of twelve million Mexicans, who would become an important market for American products.[107] His appeal was to no avail, however, and the exporters, unconvinced by his arguments, stuck with the campaign against him. In December 1925 the president of the U.S. Chamber of Commerce told his Mexican counterpart that unless his government respected the vested rights of American business it would be impossible to collaborate in the country's development.[108] The Mexican Chamber of Commerce Federation was therefore in the position of trying to allay the fears of its American colleagues and at the same time defend its government's position.[109] Although the American export-import sector was certainly not sympathetic to the Mexican viewpoint, the stand it took was far from the embargo that the oil firms had wanted.[110] Finally, the American Catholics, incensed by Mexican persecution of the clergy, asked Coolidge to intervene on behalf of their coreligionists, thereby joining the ranks of those in favor of a hard-line policy.[111] At the end of 1926 the Knights of Columbus announced that they had decided to invest a million dollars in a crusade against the Mexican regime.[112] The Catholics sought to create the image of an atheist communistic state that was threatening moral and ma- terial values in the hemisphere.[113] In effect, though for different reasons, their position coincided perfectly with that of the oil companies. In an ef- fort to counteract this campaign, Calles persuaded the Supreme Council of the 33° of the Scottish Rite in Mexico to ask their American fellows to try every means at their disposal to avert an open breach between the two countries, the chances of which were increasing daily as a result of the ac- tion of the American Catholics and the oil firms. The U.S. Masons respond- ed to the call, and before long articles were appearing in their publications along the lines requested by their Mexican brothers.[114] In addition, certain Protestant groups, such as the Federal Council of Churches of Christ in America, mounted campaigns to get their members to let Washington know they were against the threatened conflict with Mexico.[115]

Reaction of Washington and the Oil Firms

As soon as the organic oil law went into effect, the companies began to file injunctions with the courts—against Industry Minister Morones' specific request that they not do so.[116] At the same time they approached Morones, as a last resort, to see if the upcoming regulatory legislation could be word- ed so as to offset the "negative effects" of its Articles 14 and 15. On Janu- ary 15 a nineteen-man committee representing five of the big firms, including the British ones, began a series of talks with the Mexican government.[117] The conversations lasted throughout the month of February and on into March. The company spokesmen, who did not have full powers, refused to discuss anything whatsoever that might change the status of their vested rights and rejected five different redrafts of the regulatory law proposed by the Ministry of Industry on the grounds that none of them confirmed their rights acquired prior to 1917.[118] In view of the lack of progress in the negotiations, a new committee, this time of executives from the United States with greater decision-making authority, was sent to work directly with Morones.[119] However, at this level the difficulties arose within the committee itself: Standard Oil was not prepared to accept anything other than a change in the law itself. In any event, the group succeeded in presenting some suggestions to be incorporated in the regulations pending future modification of the organic law.[120] Pani assured the committee that the law would be amended in accordance with their wishes, but very soon it became clear that once again, despite Pani's commitment, neither Calles nor Morones had any intention of following through. Whereupon the committee totally rejected the draft text of the regulations presented to it on April 8.[121] Finally, in a last-ditch effort, a group of the companies' lawyers (the executives having already left Mexico) met with Mexican officials during the month of May, but this attempt was no more successful than the previous ones, and all direct negotiations came to an end.[122] The numerous diplomatic exchanges with Washington from March until August show that Mexico stood firmly by its position. In September, however, the U.S. embassy reported signs that Calles was beginning to show a more conciliatory attitude.[123] In his state-of-the-union message on September 1 he announced that, while it was his intention that the two organic laws implementing Article 27 remain unchanged, if the test of time or experience should dictate any modifications, the executive would take the appropriate steps.[124] In October the oil firms, which continued to reject the new legislation, asked the Ministry of Industry for an interpretation of the points in the law that were most under discussion. Morones, with instructions from the president, reported that in regard to the problem of ownership along the coasts and borders the companies with interests acquired before the new constitution went into effect could keep their property despite their foreign nationality, as could those Mexican companies that had a majority of foreign stockholders. In regard to the confirmatory concessions, they would not lapse after fifty years but rather continue in effect as long as the corporations themselves were in existence.[125] Morones' response shows that the Mexican position was in fact becoming more flexible—that a compromise was being sought and that the 1925 law might be substantially changed in the firms' favor. The minister of industry warned, however, that even so, if by December 31—the deadline for the companies to comply with the new law—they had not filed for their confirmatory concessions, they would still lose their rights.[126]

As the date approached, and at the same time it became evident that Mexico was prepared to yield a little, the companies tried once again to hold talks with the Mexican government—although not without first having considered and rejected the idea of an open ultimatum to Calles.[127] This time only the local representatives met with Morones, and the latter limited himself to repeating the assurances he had given in October. It seemed that Calles was not prepared to give in any further.[128] The decision to stand firm may well have been predicated on the belief that the oil firms really intended to comply with the new legislation and had had the necessary papers drawn up but were simply stalling until the last possible moment—as reported by the Mexican embassy in Washington.[129] Among the oilmen, however, precisely the same line of thought was being followed in regard to Calles: they believed that at the last minute Mexico, instead of taking away their rights, would have the new law revised and extend the validity of the concessions to seventy-five years.[130] Accordingly, they agreed unanimously in a meeting held on December 27, 1926, not to apply for a single concession. And so it was that they set the stage for a renewed confrontation as serious as the most critical ones under the Carranza regime. Two days later, when the deadline came for them to comply with the new legislation—by which time the atmosphere had become highly charged—the firms asked Calles for an extension so that the law could be amended to reflect Morones' commitments. They could not take a chance on compromising their rights, they said, by accepting the concession formula. Calles denied the extension forthwith.[131]

Thus at the end of 1926 the Mexican government was once again faced with the old dilemma: on the one hand the companies' resistance left it no choice but to take a firm stand, but on the other it lacked the necessary power to risk taking any steps that might lead to an open and possibly violent confrontation with an infinitely stronger neighbor against which it was defenseless. By way of a temporary solution, it was decided on January 4 simply to remand to the attorney general all those oil firms that had failed to apply for confirmation of their rights.[132] Thus violence was averted, the government saved face by placing the problem in theory at least in the hands of the judiciary, and time was gained to continue hammering out the compromise that had been eluding the two sides since 1925. All the big American and British companies were on the list turned over for prosecution.[133] Meanwhile, with the matter still in the hands of the courts, the Ministry of Industry suddenly began to cancel the provisional drilling permits that it had granted in 1926. It should be noted that the State Department had been in agreement with Mexico on this provisional solution, since it was afraid that the government had actually decided to seize the lands of the rebellious companies. As it stood now, the courts could hand down a decision similar to the one given in the case of Texas Oil, and the use of force or other drastic measures would thereby be avoided.[134] The tension let up still more when several demands for injunction filed by the companies in reaction to cancellation of the provisional drilling permits were settled promptly and favorably by the courts.[135]

The subsequent revocation of other drilling permits, however, renewed tension with the firms and with Washington. Harry F. Sinclair of Sinclair Oil approached the Mexican authorities personally to try to work out a solution, but apparently these talks, like all the ones before them, were unsuccessful.[136] According to the U.S. embassy, which claimed to have Mexican government documents from mid-1926 in its possession, Calles had decided that the oil law would have to be amended in order to calm down the American firms, but that the first step would have to be to take the case to the courts for a ruling in support of the companies' arguments, as had been done under Obregón.[137] Either these documents were not authentic or else Calles changed his mind, for as it turned out the decisions finally reached by the Mexican courts precisely reversed the rulings that had been handed down in the firms' favor at the beginning of the year and obliged them to suspend their drilling operations.[138] In January 1927 the companies seriously contemplated total suspension of their activities in order to apply even greater pressure on the Mexican government.[139] Perhaps the downturn in production that came shortly thereafter—which meant lower taxes and would therefore make it less of a problem for Calles to stand up against such a move—led them to think twice. In any case, on April 27 they decided on a completely different line of action: namely, to carry on business as usual and even go forward with new operations despite the fact that in a number of cases they did not have drilling permits.[140]

Clearly the APPM must have felt it had support from Washington in order to have defied the Mexican government so openly. The firms' intention, apparently, was to aggravate the situation even more so as to provoke decisive action on the part of the United States. Ambassador Sheffield went along wholeheartedly with the decision, pointing out to his superiors that if the Mexicans were to halt operations at this juncture such a step would finally furnish irrefutable proof that the rights of American citizens were being violated and hence justify any action that might need to be taken .[141] The Mexican response more or less followed the lines that had been predicted: the government imposed heavy fines on the rebellious companies and capped the wells that had been drilled without authorization.[142]

At this point the firms seemed prepared to escalate the situation even further, for in a new challenge they broke the seals on the wells and resumed their activities. The Calles government could not let such open defiance go unrebuked: it called up its troops and capped the wells once again. The American ambassador was away on a trip at the time, and it fell to the chargé d'affaires, Arthur Schoenfeld, to inform Washington that at last there was a "concrete case" of violation of the companies' rights—the condition stipulated by Foreign Minister Sáenz in order to justify the charge of confiscation. The United States was to waste no time in taking advantage of the situation.[143]

By mid-1927 the crisis point was at hand, and in certain Mexican and American circles it was really feared that the Coolidge administration would opt for an armed solution.[144] According to a number of authors, it is quite probable that the U.S. president would have taken this course if he had been able to count on domestic support. According to Frank Tannenbaum, the firms decided to retreat on July 14, when they learned that they did not have Washington's full backing. It would seem that the confrontation did not materialize mainly because the U.S. administration thought that there was too much opposition to intervention.[145] (Later this facet of the situation will be examined more fully.) On June 18 Morones told the Mexican press that the government was prepared to use force if necessary to see that its decisions were complied with, and immediately afterward Gulf and Transcontinental Petroleum were informed that their rights had been revoked. However, nothing was done to carry through on this important announcement. On the contrary, a standoff ensued that was to end only several months later in an agreement between Calles and Ambassador Morrow whereby the Mexican government renounced all intention to continue with the oil reform.

Before going into greater detail in regard to the crisis of mid-1927 and its ultimate resolution, it is well to clarify a few other minor points first. As it has already been mentioned, the Calles administration's negotiations, cancellations, and threats throughout 1926 and on into 1927 were paralleled by an effort to pit the firms one against another in order to break up the "united oil front." This policy was not without its possibilities. During 1926 El Aguila, La Corona, and some of the other smaller firms were doubtful about the extent to which the State Department was prepared to side with the oil industry against Calles and were in favor of a more flexible position so that an agreement could still be reached with Mexico in the event it were necessary to yield a little on the matter of their rights. In January of that year Morones had let it be known to Gulf that those companies which showed a more cooperative attitude would receive favored treatment.[146] Later the same year Manuel Calero, the Mexican counsel for Huasteca, indicated in coversations with Sáenz that he thought it would be a good idea to apply for the confirmatory concessions, since for all practical purposes his firm's operations would continue unaffected. His opinion was overruled, however, by his superiors in the United States.[147] The following year, when tension between the two countries reached new heights, the companies finally came together in a solid front against the Mexican administration.[148] El Aguila, La Corona, and Texas Oil were taken by surprise when they received word that their applications for confirmation of certain rights acquired prior to 1917 had been approved—by surprise because at that point they had already withdrawn their applications in a show of unity with the rest of the firms.[149] They refused to recognize the confirmations. Still, in April 1927 the U.S. embassy continued to have reservations and expressed the fear once again that El Aguila and La Corona, along with Sinclair, might decide at the last minute to bolt the ranks and come to a separate agreement with Mexico. By the end of June, however, with the crisis at its peak, the doubts had disappeared. In the opinion of Chargé d'Affaires Schoenfeld, factors unrelated to the Mexican problem—in particular worldwide overproduction—had kept the companies from being pressed into a compromise with Mexico.[150]

The steady decline of output in Mexico, contrary to the picture elsewhere —due both to the depletion of existing reserves and to the failure of new explorations—also had a certain effect on Calles' oil policy. The Mexican administration thought it was the result of a deliberate move on the companies' part to pressure the government into making even further concessions beyond those of 1923 and 1924. Since the firms did not deny these rumors, the impression remained that the downturn was really nothing but economic pressure, especially when at the same time the companies withdrew all the money they had deposited in Mexican banks.[151]

Rumors that the oil firms were once again thinking of bankrolling the government's opposition did nothing to help the situation. Some authors have tied the companies to subversive activities in support of Generals Arnulfo R. Gómez and Francisco Serrano, members of the Obregón-Calles circle who rose up against Obregón when his reelection was announced. Gómez, in particular, has been characterized as a "close friend" of the oil interests.[152] In reality there is not enough evidence to prove any link between the companies and these uprisings. Still, during the first years of the Calles administration the Mexican consular service's reports repeatedly cited rumors of movements against the regime—headed variously by Félix Díaz, Adolfo de la Huerta, Pablo González, and others—which were supposedly being plotted in the United States with the help of the oil companies.[153]

The Crisis of 1927

Since 1925 the oil firms had bombarded the State Department with an uninterrupted flow of demands for protection. As of the beginning of 1927 their brief against the Mexican government was based on five other points in addition to the impending confiscatory legislation: (1) its refusal to grant drilling permits until the firms agreed to accept legislation that was detrimental to their interests; (2) its cancellation of the provisional permits already granted based on the same conditions; (3) the subsequent capping of the wells by force; (4) the threat to impose an embargo if the companies continued to refuse to pay the fine for drilling without proper permits; and (5) the recognition of third-party claims to their lands.[154] Ambassador Sheffield was fully behind the firms. During the last months of 1926 and the early part of 1927 he urged Secretary of State Kellogg to hold to a hard line, maintaining that if the United States consistently kept up its stand Calles would not dare to make a move against the companies, even though theoretically they had lost their right to the oil deposits.[155] In 1927, just before his return to Washington, his position became even stronger: he was convinced that the time had come to step up U.S. protection of the firms.[156] Both he and the State Department's chief of Mexican affairs had for a long time been in favor of lifting the embargo on arms shipments to Mexico, a measure which would automatically give free rein to Calles' opponents.[157] When Coolidge refused to take such a radical step, the companies accused him of having abandoned them.[158]

By the end of 1926 the tone of the diplomatic exchanges had become sharp. A U.S. note of November 10 led the *New York Times* to hint that relations with Mexico were on the verge of rupture.[159] Other papers came out with similar allusions to an imminent break.[160] However, the Mexican consul general in New York, after a talk with Senator Borah, reported to his government that it was not Washington's intention to sever diplomatic ties.[161] Calles told a group of Americans on January 9, 1927, that the only way to solve the dispute between his country and its neighbor—a conflict stemming essentially from the oil problem—was to submit it to The Hague or some other international tribunal, even though strictly speaking Mexico had no reason to subject the exercise of its sovereign rights to arbitration. On January 20 the Mexican government informed the State Department officially that it was willing to put the matter before an international court.[162] While Congress and other sectors of the American public were in favor of this solution,[163] Coolidge roundly rejected the idea that the "property rights" of American citizens could be submitted to arbitration. Washington argued that there was no point anyway because even if the court were to find in favor of the U.S. companies and landowners the Mexican government was totally without the means to indemnify them.[164] The APPM backed Coolidge fully. According to its secretary, Guy Stevens, this was not the time to arbitrate; rather, it was the moment to put on more pressure still, since Calles, faced with an internal financial crisis, was showing signs that he was prepared to relent.[165] The American press, which was on the side of Coolidge and the companies, likewise argued against arbitration: it was contrary to the principles of international law, since protection of a country's citizens abroad is a sovereign right.[166] Coolidge's real reasons were somewhat different. In the first place, he wanted to continue pressuring Calles until he gave up entirely on the oil reform. But what was more to the point, he was afraid that the American arguments would not stand up very well in an international court of law. The State Department knew that Mexico stood a very good chance of obtaining a favorable decision. It seriously doubted that the tribunal would agree that the status of the oil firms' rights could be changed only after prior compensation. Hence the chances of getting an amendment in the unwanted legislation would be considerably diminished.[167] With the U.S. refusal to submit to arbitration, the threat of armed intervention was increased.

A number of observers, both Mexican and American, agree that it was Calles' oil and agrarian reform policies that led the Coolidge administration to consider resort to the use of arms in 1927, either by supporting one of the numerous rebel groups within the country or through an invasion.[168] Since 1926 the Mexican president had been pointing with concern to the fact that certain American interests, particularly the oil companies, seemed to be pressuring Washington to use force to solve their problems with Mexico.[169] But it was in 1927, when the deadline passed for the firms to comply with the new legislation, that the danger became acute. In January of that year Secretary of State Kellogg presented a report to the U.S. Congress entitled "Bolshevik Aims and Policies in Mexico and Latin America." This document, which had been prepared months earlier, pictured the Calles regime as a hotbed of communist agitation and, in the words of William English Walling, "a menace to American civilization."[170] Unquestionably, it constituted one more step in the campaign toward ultimate intervention. On January 10 President Coolidge himself declared that there was irrefutable evidence of Mexican aid to the "rebels" in Nicaragua—evidence that was never produced, however, and which the American press was to search for in vain.[171] The APPM wasted no time in loudly echoing the White House's accusations, insisting that an end must be put to Mexican interference in Nicaragua.[172] These developments greatly alarmed the Mexican ambassador in Washington, and in mid-January he asked his government to postpone any and all action against the oil companies, since the slightest move could trigger an open conflict between the two countries, or at the very least dash the hopes for a solution by arbitration. From Mexico he was told that his suggestions would be followed.[173]

It was in March and April, apparently, that the possibility of an armed conflict became a real likelihood. Added to the oil problem, the clash between Mexican and U.S. policy in Nicaragua (Mexico being in favor of Vice President Juan B. Sacasa and the United States on the side of General Adolfo Díaz in the power struggle that followed the president's forced departure from the country) brought relations nearly to the boiling point. In March, Ambassador Sheffield informed Washington that Calles was prepared to carry his "radical" policy as far as the United States would let him. It was up to Washington to stop him.[174] In April, when Industry Minister Morones announced that drilling permits would be denied to companies refusing to apply for concessions, the U.S. embassy, as it has already been seen, pleaded for direct action to protect the oil firms.[175] The possibility of intervention was so real that Calles went to the point of ordering his military commander in the oil zone, General Lázaro Cárdenas, to be prepared to set fire to the oil fields in the event of a U.S. invasion.[176] In the end the situation cooled off for two reasons: first, Calles did not do anything to take away the rights of the firms that had failed to comply with the new law, and, second, sentiment against an armed conflict in Mexico was strong in the U.S. Congress and with the public in general. But perhaps an important factor in changing Coolidge's mind was the discovery by Mexican agents of confidential U.S. embassy documents revealing past attempts on the part of the State Department to plot Calles' overthrow. The Mexican president let word reach Washington that he intended to make this material public if the United States sent troops to Mexico. Meanwhile the White House called for an investigation of the matter, in response to which the State Department roundly denied the authenticity of the documents.[177] On May 3, however, Senator Lynn J. Frazier of North Dakota declared in San Francisco that the papers in Calles' possession were genuine and constituted undeniable proof of Secretary Kellogg's hostility toward Mexico.[178] The Mexican government never made any official reference to their existence or even to their contents, but knowledge of them was allowed to leak to the press, and afterward members of Calles' circle—Emilio Portes Gil, for one—were to mention them from time to time.[179]

Much later Ambassador Josephus Daniels, though not going into the problem very deeply, wrote to his son that a Mr. Robins—who had set up the talks between Sheffield's successor Dwight Morrow and Calles at the end of 1927, just before the new ambassador's arrival in Mexico—reported that two Americans had told him, on the basis of direct information from Coolidge and Kellogg, that there was a strong chance of war with Mexico.[180]

The State Department documents show only that in September Chargé d'Affaires Schoenfeld had the impression that the Mexican government was little inclined to modify its position and that the internal situation in the country was ripe for a successful anti-Calles movement.[181] The entire situation was to change after September, although as late as January 1928 Industry Minister Morones was still insisting that the companies' sole aim was to involve Mexico in a war with its neighbor to the north.[182]

The arrival of Ambassador Dwight Morrow, Sheffield's replacement, was to usher in a new American approach to the problem, based on negotiation rather than threats. The instructions he had received from Secretary of State Kellogg strictly ruled out the possibility of violence. A cordial telephone conversation between Calles and Coolidge on September 30, 1927, marked the beginning of a new period in U.S.-Mexican relations.

Efforts of Obregón and Pani to Reach a Direct Agreement with the Companies in 1927

Before going into the negotiations between Calles and the new ambassador, it is of interest to review the attempts of Alberto J. Pani and former president Obregón to solve the controversy through direct negotiations with the oil firms. Obregón, although officially out of politics since 1924, had been regularly briefed on the oil question by Calles.[183] According to U.S. embassy reports, he was even present in cabinet meetings when the matter was discussed.[184] Thinking to take advantage of his prestige and the basis on which relations had rested at the end of his administration, he decided at the beginning of 1927 to personally make a trip to San Francisco, along with Pani, who was also on good terms with the Americans, and talk with top oil company spokesmen there.[185] These negotiations were kept relatively secret— that is to say, they were not made in public in Mexico, although they were in fact reported in the American press. By way of preparing the atmosphere for the opening of these talks on February 1, it was announced that Mexico had decided not to stand in the way of operations undertaken by the companies with provisional permits prior to December 31, 1926.[186] Obregón and Pani arrived in San Francisco with full power to negotiate. However, the oil firms, apparently realizing at the last minute that new high-level negotiations would give Calles a breathing spell at a time when the pressure on him was the greatest, decided to prolong the crisis. Thus, despite the fact that the initiative to hold the meeting had been theirs, they gave the order to their representatives in California not to go ahead.[187] Later Ambassador Sheffield was to claim, unbelievably, that Obregón had failed to come to terms with the companies because he lacked the necessary authority to formalize the agreement they wanted! The fact that the following year, even though he was not too enthusiastic about the idea, he was to break with the constitutional precept that had been his battle cry against Porfirio Díaz, run for the presidency again, and get elected shows beyond a doubt that he was still the undisputed leader of the group in power. It may be that the negotiations were not carried forward in San Francisco for other reasons, but not because Obregón lacked the necessary authority.[188]

After the San Francisco debacle Obregón returned to Mexico, but Pani went on to New York (his ultimate destination being Paris) and met with the company directors themselves and the International Committee of Bankers on Mexico. By the end of the month he had seen both the oil magnates and J. P. Morgan himself—one of whose associates, Dwight Morrow, was shortly thereafter to become the new ambassador to Mexico. The meetings took on a secondary nature, however, with Obregón absent. Pani did not feel he had made any remarkable progress that required him to go back to Mexico and decided to go to Paris as planned. He contented himself with promising he would cable Calles and suggest that his oil policy be modified to take into account the following points: (1) that the courts be urged to reach an early decision on the matter of the companies' injunctions; (2) that Obregón be authorized to conclude the negotiations interrupted in 1924; (3) that provisional drilling permits be issued; and (4) that no confirmatory concessions be granted until the Supreme Court handed down its ruling. (It is assumed that this last point referred to the case of the independent firms that had been prepared to abide by the new law.)[189] Pani's message, assuming he actually sent it as he said he would, failed to produce any results, and Obregón did not meet with the oil company representatives again. However, the points are similar to those contained in the agreement reached with the U.S. ambassador at the end of the year, which was to be translated into acceptance of the firms' demands for injunction and, later, modification of the 1925 law. Of perhaps even greater interest, however, is the fact that Pani's negotiations with the bankers, and with J. P. Morgan in particular, may well have had something to do with the appointment of a member of their own circle, Dwight Morrow, as the new ambassador to Mexico.[190]

Morrow and the New U.S. Policy

From the beginning of 1927 Coolidge was aware that, in addition to the faction in the U.S. Senate that was opposed to his Mexican and Nicaraguan policies, an increasingly large and influential sector of the American public was likewise demanding relaxation of the tension with Mexico.[191] According to Edmund David Cronon,[192] it was around July when Coolidge began to think about changing his approach to Calles. However, as it has already been seen, relations did not actually improve until the end of September. The Mexican public had not yet sensed this shift in the American position when Ambassador Morrow presented his credentials in October, and the local papers made no effort to conceal their qualms over the new envoy's connections with the House of Morgan. One of them warned ominously, "First Morrow, then the Marines." Before only, however, it became apparent that the ambassador—who for a time had aspired to a cabinet post in Washington—was the bearer of a new policy. His instructions from Coolidge had been laconic but explicit: "Keep us out of war with Mexico!"[193]

It was up to Morrow to develop the proper approach within this framework. He wasted no time in making it clear that relations between the United States and its neighbor to the south were entering on a new phase: Ambassador Sheffield's aggressive attitude, typical of the old-style imperialism, was to be replaced by a much more subtle and cordial approach. But, if the means had changed, the end remained unaltered.

Ambassador Morrow, according to his biographer, Harold Nicolson, conceived and applied a theory, characterized as "moral guardianship," which he believed to be the most suitable basis for relations between a strong power and a weaker one. He put aside the Marines and the legal arguments and set about working toward a solution to the oil controversy, using persuasion as his only tool. The first thing he did was to establish direct contact with the key figures in the Mexican political system, whom he considered to include not only Calles and the political elite but even the leaders of the Communist Party, and undertake to create an image of "sympathy and confidence" both with them and with the public in general.[194] Before long he had established an open and informal relationship with Calles and members of his cabinet such as Foreign Affairs Minister Genaro Estrada, Industry Minister Morones, and Treasury Minister Montes de Oca.[195] These contacts secured, he set about convincing the Mexican leadership that there was nothing basic in their programs that could not be reconciled with American interests.[196] His success in this undertaking was complete. According to José Vasconcelos, Obregón's minister of education—who by the time of Morrow's arrival had broken with the group in power—the U.S. ambassador, for sure a "Jewish-capitalist" agent, ended up personally directing Mexico's domestic and foreign policies.[197] These exaggerations, like others of Vasconcelos, were not entirely without basis. The U.S. military attaché under Morrow, Colonel Alexander MacNab, later asserted publicly that the ambassador had "put Mexico on her feet and given her a strong government," that there was not a single ministry or bureau in Mexico that had not had the benefit of his advice, and that he had taken the minister of the treasury "under his wing and taught him finance."[198]

Morrow showed keen concern with all matters that were in any way related to the American interest. His aim was to find a solution to the difficulties between the two countries that would be acceptable to Mexico and at the same time not impinge on the rights of his fellow American citizens in the country. Calles, for his part, conveniently forgot his public attack against foreign intervention in domestic affairs delivered at Morelia four years earlier. From Morrow he was to accept more than just suggestions. Starting at the end of 1927, relations between the two countries entered into a state of cordiality virtually without precedent. But everything has its price. As Frank Brandenburg has put it, "After Morrow arrived on the scene foreign ownership was encouraged, local capitalists depreciated, labor unions suppressed, anticlericalism abandoned, and the agrarian reform stopped dead in its tracks."[199]

Such a sharp volte-face was far from the work of one man alone, or even of the tremendous and unrelenting pressure from Washington. Morrow's work was greatly facilitated by changes that were taking place within the power structure itself. The transformation of the Calles machine "from an instrument of reform to one of reaction" was a process that was already occurring quite independently of the action of the U.S. ambassador. With his apostolic glorification of orthodox capitalism, the former member of the House of Morgan merely provided Calles and his associates with the justification they needed.[200] The group in power, by now more interested in reaching a compromise with the elements still remaining from the Porfirian system than in doing away with it completely, a few years earlier would have been far less receptive to Morrow's advice.[201] Meanwhile, starting in 1927, "the fat cats began to proliferate. Former Revolutionaries—followers of Orozco, Villa, Carranza and the others, all rolled into a single package held together but flimsily thanks to their opportunistic shifts from one camp to another—were becoming big businessmen."[202] José Vasconcelos' challenge of Pascual Ortiz Rubio's candidacy in 1929 shows the discontent that had been generated by then with the men who had overthrown Carranza. The Sonora group now in power gave lip service to the official line, which spoke of an improved distribution of the national wealth, but in actual fact they were committed to just the opposite: concentrating it more and more in their own hands and those of their friends.[203] This oligarchy's newly acquired benefits brought its interests increasingly in line with those of the foreign companies. The identification was far from total, however. Foreign capital continued to occupy the privileged position that the new leading group wanted for itself. The clash of interests was becoming less and less marked, but it did not disappear altogether.

Amendment of the 1925 Oil Law

On his arrival, Ambassador Morrow was confronted with four problems: oil, the debts and claims, the agrarian reform, and the religious question. He wasted no time in tackling the first of these, in which effort he had the valuable collaboration of his counselor, J. Reuben Clark, Jr.[204] Morrow had already studied the matter, and, in view of his instructions from Coolidge, he thought it would be best to establish a new modus vivendi as soon as possible that would enable the companies to keep up their normal rate of production. This done, his next task would be to work toward a permanent solution to the problem through a Supreme Court decision that would be favorable to the industry's interests.[205] Before broaching the matter with Calles, the new ambassador, accompanied by Clark, met with the companies' lawyers to hear their point of view.[206] Morrow concluded that the controversy turned around six main points: the fifty-year limit on concessions, the status of ownership in the "prohibited" zones along the coast and national borders, interpretation of the term "positive act," the Calvo clause, the need for a ruling on whether or not compliance with Carranza's order of 1915 could be regarded as a "positive act," and the exact status of the titles held by foreigners to lands acquired prior to May 1917.[207] The firms agreed that these were the main points and stressed the importance of getting a

Mexican court decision in their favor, which would pave the way for subsequent modification of the law. It was at this juncture that Morrow took his next step.[208]

On November 2, 1927, at the initiative of the Mexican president, the first informal meeting was held between Calles and the ambassador. Six days later Morrow accompanied the president on a tour of the states in the north (Calles' objective in taking him along, says Harold Nicolson, was to show the Catholics in arms that they could no longer look for support from the United States). It was in the course of this trip, on November 8, that the oil question was brought up—also at Calles' initiative. After three and a half hours of discussion, the long-awaited accord was reached. Morrow did not approach the matter from a strictly legalistic point of view as his predecessor Sheffield, working under close orders from Secretary Kellogg, had done.[209] Instead, in answer to one of Calles' questions, he suggested that the court ruling in the companies' favor handed down some time ago by a judge in Tuxpan, a small city in the state of Veracruz—which had provoked Industry Minister Morones' annoyance and the judge's subsequent dismissal —be ratified by the Supreme Court, in keeping with the precedent set by the Texas Oil case of 1922. The president assured Morrow that if a solution to the conflict could be reached in this way he would see that such a decision was announced within two months.[210] As it turned out, it did not even take that long. Through Morones, Calles asked the Supreme Court to proceed as discussed with Morrow, and on November 17 the judges handed down the verdict requested.[211] According to the U.S. embassy, they had been prepared for such an eventuality since March, when the crisis between Mexico and Washington had reached one of its most serious points, and this explained the seeming speed with which they acted.[212] They pointed out in the text of their decision that confirmation of oil rights in accordance with the 1925 law would amount to a greatly prejudicial change in the status of the companies' rights and that for this reason the law should be amended.[213] They went on to say that: (1) the firms' entitlement with respect to the subsoil was not merely a prospective right (the thesis that Foreign Minister Sáenz had propounded in his correspondence with Secretary of State Kellogg) but indeed a vested one; (2) the setting of a fifty-year limit on the confirmatory concessions would amount to retroactive action against the companies; (3) the firms' refusal to apply for confirmation of their rights was not in the nature of an illegal act and there was therefore no cause for them to be penalized; and (4) still, even under the new conditions, the companies would have to request confirmation of their rights with the Ministry of Industry.[214] On November 14 Calles informed Morrow that he would immediately arrange for amendment of the 1925 law in accordance with the court's decision.[215]

Washington was highly pleased with the new turn of events: the injunctions filed for following cancellation of the drilling permits would be settled favorably and operations could be resumed; the 1925 legislation would be changed.[216] The oil firms, however, were not quite so well satisfied. On November 21 the Mexican papers published statements by APPM secretary Guy Stevens indicating the association's dissatisfaction with the Supreme

Court ruling. The *Wall Street Journal*—which was to speak for the companies during this period when their points of view did not coincide with those of the State Department—declared that basically it reasserted Calles' confiscatory policy, since the firms still had to have their rights confirmed by the Mexican government before they could be sure they would be respected.[217] Under Secretary of State Robert Olds informed Ambassador Morrow that these expressions of discontent did not reflect the views of the State Department or even the consensus of the oil firms. Things were going along so well, he said, that the cabinet was going to consider the possibility of having Charles Lindbergh, hero of the first nonstop Atlantic crossing, make a goodwill flight to Mexico.[218] The next day, however, he received a memorandum signed by all the companies in which they informed him in no uncertain terms that their opposition to the Mexican court ruling was unanimous.[219]

From the end of November until December 26, the date on which Calles sent the texts amending Articles 14 and 15 of the 1925 oil law to the Congress, Morrow was in constant contact with the oilmen. He objected strongly when it was suggested that a delegation of company executives travel to Mexico to discuss the problem with Calles directly and explain to him the reasons for their continuing dissatisfaction. He was able to hold them off by getting the president's draft bill, by that time already in the Congress, modified by the addition of the term *confirmatory* to qualify the concessions to be given to the firms.[220] On January 3, 1928, the amendments went into effect. The rights acquired by those who had demonstrated a "positive act" were confirmed in perpetuity and guaranteed against cancellation in the future for any reason whatsoever. Six days later representatives of Huasteca asked Morones personally—so as to be assured from the lips of one who had been their most outspoken enemy and put an end to all possible doubts that the firms still harbored—whether the act of applying for such confirmatory concessions would imply the loss of any right whatsoever acquired prior to May 1917. Morones said that it would not.[221] In Mexico there was apparently little or no reaction to this change in policy. The press at large, as might be expected, given its conservative leanings, applauded the amendment,[222] while the nationalist sectors within the government, despite their displeasure, remained silent.[223]

But still the companies found the amended law unsatisfactory. They set about putting their influence to work to see that the forthcoming regulations would clear up once and for all the secondary points that still bothered them. For example, they felt that use of the word *concession* in conjunction with the concept of "confirmation" entailed a serious risk. As it now stood, they claimed, another government in the future could try all over again to take their rights away from them.[224] Morones and Calles, for their part, however, were not prepared to give in any more, and the former roundly rejected a suggested text for the regulations which the companies drew up and presented to him on February 8, 1928. On January 19 Standard Oil informed Ambassador Morrow, who was away on a trip to Havana, Cuba, that the amended law continued to be unacceptable, since in failing to resolve a number of vital points it endangered the status of the company's possessions in other Latin American countries as well. The pressure was not limited to Morrow: four days later, after holding a meeting in New York, the oil company spokesmen went to Washington as a group and told the State Department that unless a satisfactory text were approved for the regulations they would go back to filing injunctions against the amended law, thus undoing all the negotiations and agreements so far.[225] In the face of this threat and in view of Morones' refusal to accept the draft text that the oil firms had presented, the U.S. embassy intervened once again and succeeded in holding up the proposed bill that the minister of industry was about to submit to the Congress. Morrow, Clark, and representatives of the Mexican ministry met for three weeks and hammered out a final text. In this new version there was no "Calvo clause" and the definition of "positive act" was in line with what had been agreed to by the Mexican representatives at Bucareli, but the concept of confirmatory concessions was retained.[226] Washington was satisfied, and Obregón, who was getting ready to return to the presidency, publicly expressed his approval of all the changes in the oil legislation.[227]

The amendment and the new regulations were almost a complete victory for the Americans. Twelve years after the constitution was promulgated at Querétaro and after a long struggle at the international level, progress from the standpoint of those in favor of the oil reform had not been very great. The only gains had been that the foreign interests had accepted the "positive act" theory—although the definition was so broad that practically all oil fields were covered—and that they had agreed to exchange absolute title to the subsoil for confirmatory concessions. In actual practice, these legal changes did not represent very much. In reality the oil industry continued to retain all the "enclave" characteristics that it had had prior to 1917 and that had earned it the opprobrium of the nationalist groups which had emerged with the Revolution. It appeared that the Revolution had been unable to impose its precepts on the foreign sector of the national economy.[228] From 1928 until 1937—rather slowly from 1933 onward—the Mexican government was to grant confirmatory titles to 6,940,568 hectares of land, while ordinary concessions for lands fully owned were given for more than a million and a half hectares. Owing to the deliberate slowness with which the confirmation process was carried out, a sizable number of the requests filed were still pending when the industry was expropriated in 1938.

The Oil Firms and the Morrow-Calles Agreement

The State Department was now quite satisfied with the new version of the organic law and its accompanying regulatory legislation, and Morrow soon came to be regarded in certain U.S. official circles as one of the most competent members of the diplomatic corps in his time.[229] On March 28, scarcely five months after he had presented his credentials in the midst of a grave diplomatic crisis between his country and Mexico, Washington announced that the steps Mexico had taken in regard to its oil legislation appeared to put an end to the controversy that had been going on for more than a decade. This declaration was in effect a goodwill gesture in return for the concessions that Mexico had made. It went on to say that any conflicts arising in the future over application of the oil law would be settled in the Mexican courts and not through diplomatic intervention.[230] This struck the oil firms as excessive; for the first time since Wilson had turned the White House back over to the Republicans, they found themselves in sharp disagreement with Washington. In direct communications, as well as through the *Wall Street Journal* and other newspapers, they pointed out to the State Department repeatedly that the Mexican problem was far from being solved. Quite the contrary, they claimed, the pressure had been lifted while the job was still only half done. A conciliatory policy had been decided on behind their backs at the expense of their legitimate interests, since the amended legislation was still basically confiscatory in that it obliged them to give up an absolute property right in exchange for concessions and to accept the "positive act" principle. The consequences, they said, could endanger their possessions in other countries—Colombia, for example, already having shown signs of wanting to follow in Mexico's footsteps.[231] In the absence of any response to these complaints, the companies were forced to bow to the Mexican legislation against their will. They begun to apply for their concessions.[232] Their formal acceptance, however, did not keep them from continuing to ask the State Department for still another modification in the laws which would be more in keeping with what they wanted. They presented several draft texts which no longer contained even the slightest hint of national ownership. Standard Oil of New Jersey went so far as to tell Washington that it would rather lose its property in Mexico once and for all than irremediably jeopardize the fundamental principle of property and in so doing open the doors to confiscation throughout the world.[233] More than a year went by, with the firms continuing to attack the official Washington position and insisting, without much effect, that their problems with Mexico remained unsolved.[234] In the face of the companies' continuing dissatisfaction with the oil code as amended, Morrow and Clark as well as the State Department in general were in the difficult situation of having to defend the Mexican laws against their own intransigent American investors. In Clark's view, the firms looked on the situation with an air of "oil suprasovereignty" which, if it were taken seriously would make any peaceful agreement with Mexico impossible. In the opinion of the U.S. embassy, the confirmatory concessions did not go so far as to deprive the companies of any of their rights, and the "positive act" concept was not an idea suddenly and arbitrarily thought up by Calles but rather a principle that had been in effect for 370 years (dating from mining ordinances issued by Philip II of Spain). The kind of assurance that the firms were asking for, Clark said, could only be obtained by invading the country or doing away with its inhabitants. (He suspected that the companies' intransigence was prompted not so much by fear of a new problem with Mexico as it was by their desire to set an example for the other countries of the hemisphere, where their interests by this time were much greater than they were in Mexico.) Morrow shared his counselor's point of view, and on May 8, 1928, he wrote to

Under Secretary Olds in Washington: "The last six months have been quite a disclosure to me of the extent to which the responsible oil companies seem to believe that it is the duty of the State Department to run their business in foreign lands. I would not have believed it possible!"[235] Olds, acting as liaison between Morrow and the oil executives in New York, told the companies that the department still stood behind its March statements—although in the event it became convinced that Mexico was violating their rights it would take this fact into account and proceed as it saw fit. Shortly thereafter he complained to Morrow that what the firms were demanding amounted to a guarantee against any contingency that might affect their interests abroad.[236] Their protests no longer struck the same sympathetic chord as in the past. For example, the *New York Times* countered the *Wall Street Journal*'s campaign by fully supporting the Morrow accord. This influential paper took the position that the oil controversy was over at last.[237]

When the question flared up again at the end of the 1930's, the State Department tried once more to make the Morrow-Calles accord stand as a formal agreement. Mexico never accepted it as such, and Clark supported this line of thinking by declaring that technically there was no "Morrow agreement" and that if what was no more than an informal understanding had been taken as a formal commitment by some, they had done so on their own and unofficially.[238]

Relations between the Oil Firms and the Mexican Government Following Amendment of the Law

After a settlement had presumably been reached, the Mexican administration was confident that in return for its numerous concessions there would at least be an immediate upturn in fuel production—a rise that would be translated into increased fiscal income. Since no such event took place—inasmuch as the earlier decline had not been part of a deliberate political move, as it was thought, but rather the result of actual depletion of the reserves themselves and fluctuations in the world market—the Mexican authorities decided that this was part of the firms' plan to put on even further pressure. Declarations that the oil would soon run out were disbelieved and regarded as simply one more of the companies' maneuvers.[239] Thus relations between the oil firms and the Mexican administration did not improve in tandem with those between the two countries at the intergovernmental level. The companies thought that the legislation in effect was still confiscatory, and Mexico both resented the continued low rate of output and felt that the firms' demands were excessive. This state of affairs did not make for serious friction, but it was reflected in a series of small difficulties between the government and the industry.

Next to the oil law, the companies' main cause for complaint from 1928 onward was the tax rates. They repeatedly called the government's attention to the fact that they were far higher than in Venezuela, making it financially impossible to explore new fields, they maintained.[240] The firms also alleged that the government's support of organized labor was contributing in large measure to the rising costs of production.[241] And finally, they complained that the National Petroleum Administration was still drilling in "federal zones" which they claimed were really their land.[242] Although the processing of confirmatory concessions went along smoothly (albeit slowly) —as even the companies admitted—from time to time cases came up in the course of reviewing the titles that called for Morrow's or Clark's informal intercession with the minister of industry in order to assure a settlement in the companies' favor.[243]

In summary, the Calles years, despite the Bucareli Agreement and the factor of Obregón's influence in the background, saw renewed efforts to put an oil reform into effect. Even though there was a decline in production during the period, the oil industry continued to be one of the most important activities in the country. The tremendous pressure brought to bear by the Coolidge administration, coupled eventually with the Obregón-Calles group's own shift to the right, in the long run led to modification of the oil code to reflect the objections that the State Department had been voicing ever since before the first version was passed in 1925. The "Sonora" group may have become more conservative, but the government in Washington never wavered from its initial stand. At the end of 1927, after having given serious thought to the possibility of an armed intervention, it reviewed its policy toward Mexico and decided—perhaps in response to the bankers' lobby and the sentiments of the American public—to have a try at conciliation and stop supporting the oil interests unconditionally. As a result, it obtained assurance from Mexico that the status prior to 1917 would basically be maintained, while in exchange it yielded on the introduction of certain reforms with regard to ownership of the subsoil which for all practical purposes were innocuous. This transaction, known as the "Morrow-Calles agreement," was more than slightly unilateral, thanks to the realities of the power structure, but still it did not go far enough to win the oil companies' total satisfaction. Its acceptance by the U.S. government made for a temporary solution to the controversy which by then had been going on for more than a decade. At the end of 1928 it looked as if the oil reform, like other aims of the Revolution, was to be thwarted.

Chapter 7

In the Shadow of Calles, the "Supreme Leader of the Revolution": A Pause

From his victory over Carranza in 1920, through the Calles administration and his campaign for reelection, and up until his assassination in 1928, Alvaro Obregón maintained undisputed control over all the Revolutionary factions—even though from 1924 on he had shared the reins with Calles. When he announced his decision to return to the presidency as Calles' successor, many people thought that the principle of nonreelection would be abandoned again and that the case of Porfirio Díaz and Manuel González would be repeated, the two leaders taking turns in power indefinitely.[1] However, Obregón's death at the hands of a religious militant while he was president-elect not only put an end to this possibility but also produced a serious crisis within the leadership. Despite the solid front maintained by Obregón and Calles during the latter's presidency, the other members of the governing clique had begun to align themselves with one or the other of the two leaders—a schism that was to sharpen when Obregón was killed. Understandably, his death on the eve of his inauguration caused profound frustration among his immediate followers, who, apart from their shock, lost overnight their hopes of occupying high government posts. It was natural that they should blame Calles for the death of their leader, whether or not they really believed he was responsible. Calles, deeply anxious to prevent a split within the leadership, disregarded Ambassador Morrow's advice and publicly declared that he would not remain at the head of the executive, even in the capacity of interim president. Dismissing his chief of police, he left the investigation of the assassination in the hands of Obregón's known followers. These steps were effective at the time, but in the long run they only delayed the outburst of violence that was bound to come sooner or later. Obregón's generals, while publicly supporting the candidacy of former minister of government Gilberto Valenzuela against Calles' choice (General Pascual Ortiz Rubio), were busy in private mounting a revolt under the leadership of General José Gonzalo Escobar, chief of military operations in Coahuila.

Meanwhile, Calles' refusal to stand for reelection and the appointment of Emilio Portes Gil as interim president did not mean that the former chief executive was prepared to leave the power in the hands of his successors. Through the National Revolutionary Party (PNR—Partido Nacional Revolucionario), which had been formed in 1929 to bring together all the factions of the governing group during the crisis after Obregón's death, Calles eventually succeeded in filling the political vacuum that had been created by the assassination of the president-elect. Through this new structure the

"Supreme Leader of the Revolution," as he was called at the time, was to indirectly control the governments of Portes Gil, Ortiz Rubio, and, following the latter's resignation, Abelardo L. Rodríguez. It was not until 1935, when President Lázaro Cárdenas had acquired sufficient strength of his own through a policy aimed at reviving the Revolutionary reform program laid down at Querétaro, that Calles ceased to be the "power behind the throne" and went into exile.

Starting in 1928, right after reaching the agreement with Morrow, Calles seemed to change his outlook in a number of ways: he broke openly with the labor movement, lost all interest in the agrarian reform, and frankly devoted himself to developing the country in the traditional way, with himself and his group as the main promoters. The CROM, which had been built up and reached its height of glory under Obregón and during the early Calles years, suddenly lost all the ground it had gained between 1920 and 1928. A similar fate befell the agrarian movement. Whereas during the first years of his government Calles had redistributed more land than any of his predecessors (3,088,000 hectares), at the end he tried to put a total stop to the agrarian reform. Portes Gil, who earlier as governor of Tamaulipas had been interested in the land reform program, took advantage of a visit of Calles to Europe to resume redistribution of vast tracts—a move that far from pleased Ambassador Morrow. However, immediately after Portes Gil turned over the reins to his successor, Ortiz Rubio, Calles made his famous declaration to the effect that the agrarian reform had been a failure.[2]

At a meeting of the new president and his cabinet with the "Supreme Leader" on March 20, 1930, the latter informed the group present that in his opinion the breaking up of the large estates was causing serious damage to the national economy. This amounted to an order, and the agrarian program virtually stopped, although the official party continued to wave its banner.[3] As it happened, Ortiz Rubio was unable to serve out his term, his differences with Calles (which were not ideological) obliging him to resign. To take his place the PNR picked General Abelardo Rodríguez, already by that time one of the most prosperous men in the country and a high-ranking member of the Calles circle.[4] During Rodríguez' term in office the redistribution of agricultural land struck up a fair pace again due to pressures from the rank and file, but it was nothing spectacular. All real progress toward nationalization of the Mexican economy was halted, and for all practical purposes foreign capital continued to enjoy the same dominant position it had had under Porfirio Díaz.[5] It is difficult to imagine that in such circumstances the Calles group allowed itself to be inspired by Soviet and Italian economic programs as well as Roosevelt's New Deal and to undertake the famous "Six-Year Plan," with its strong Revolutionary and nationalistic overtones, which was to serve as the government program for the subsequent administration. This apparent inconsistency is explained by the fact that the text got out of the group's hands when it went to an assembly of the PNR and the final wording was the work of the party. The changes made at the end contrary to Calles' wishes clearly showed that within the leadership itself there was a current of dissatisfaction with the "Supreme Leader's" shift to the right which was strong enough to risk going against him.

And it was precisely this trend within the group in power that was to open the way for Lázaro Cárdenas' challenge in 1935.

Relations with the United States

From 1928 on the U.S. government was determined to avoid a new political upheaval in Mexico, and with this end in mind it threw all its support to the Calles group. The Escobar rebellion of 1929, which, like the De la Huerta uprising in 1924, had the aid of an important faction within the army, was put down in part—but hardly exclusively—thanks to political and military backing from the White House. The newly elected president, Herbert Hoover, felt that it was in the U.S. national interest to side with Calles, since he considered that his regime had been the most friendly one toward the United States since the times of Porfirio Díaz.[6] José Vasconcelos, the third candidate for president in the 1929 election, refused to recognize Ortiz Rubio's victory, claiming that it had been fraudulently engineered by the United States, through Ambassador Morrow, in order to protect the 1928 agreement.[7]

The sending of arms in 1929 was not the only way in which Washington contributed to the Calles group's stability and the creation of a strong government in Mexico. Equally important was the decision to work out difficulties with Mexico by using less disruptive methods than those employed in the past. For example, Morrow announced to the oil companies that the U.S. government was no longer prepared to go any further than arbitration even in the event of an outright denial of justice. Apparently the period of threats and aid to the enemies of the regime had passed.[8] And indeed, as it turned out, neither the debt nor the claims problem, which were the two main issues at the time, nor the continuing differences of opinion over oil, ever went beyond the stage of bilateral negotiation.[9] At most Morrow felt that his last days in Mexico were somewhat clouded by the fact that Ortiz Rubio did not accept his suggestions for working out the foreign debt problem. The disagreement was far from serious, however.[10] Morrow left the embassy to take a seat in the U.S. Senate, and Hoover appointed J. Reuben Clark, Jr., who had worked at Morrow's side during the 1928 talks, as his successor.

Revision of U.S. Latin American Policy under Hoover

There is no question that relations between the two countries improved following the Morrow-Calles Agreement of 1928. However, though the understanding may have been the main cause for the change, it was not the only one. When Coolidge turned over the reins of government to Hoover at the beginning of 1929, the White House took a new look at its policy toward Latin America. Pan Americanism had reached an all-time low a year earlier at the Sixth International Conference of American States in Havana, where U.S. interventionist attitudes were sharply criticized by a number of Latin American countries.[11] As a result it was felt that the United States could no longer hold onto its dominant position in the region on the basis of threats— that consensus with the governing groups must be sought instead. And so it was that in 1929 a new U.S. attitude, aimed at clearing the air of distrust and frustration, began to take shape. A step in this direction was the signing by the Latin American countries and the United States, in Washington, of a series of instruments providing for settlement of their differences by con- ciliation and arbitration. The groundwork had been laid for what was to be the Good Neighbor policy.

The Depression of 1929 also contributed indirectly to the birth of this new policy. The crisis called for totally overhauling certain aspects of the American economic structure, and since Hoover proved incapable of com- ing up with the bold solutions needed, he was forced to yield his place to Franklin D. Roosevelt in the election of 1932. The Democrats, who had been out of the White House since Woodrow Wilson's time, returned with the promise to pull the country out of its marasmic state and give a new bill of health to U.S. and world capitalism. Roosevelt's plan, broadly speaking, was to put some of Keynes' ideas into practice in the field of economics, throw out certain policies carried over from traditional capitalism, and give public spending a decisive role in offsetting the decline in private-sector activity. At the beginning of the 1930's it was thought that unless a radical change was effected in the U.S. economic system it would collapse alto- gether. To begin with, it would have to be divested of its most outdated and anarchic aspects. Private enterprise, if it was to survive, would have to ac- cept a new discipline imposed by the state. The measures called for under Roosevelt's New Deal met with strong opposition in certain business cir- cles and in the long run could not be fully implemented. The Depression was not to end entirely until the demand generated by World War II drew upon capabilities in the system that had never been tapped before. The im- portant point as far as the present study is concerned is that the New Deal created a political climate in official U.S. circles that not only favored con- tinuation of Hoover's conciliatory approach toward Latin America but actu- ally went so far as to culminate in the Good Neighbor policy. Although Roosevelt had thought of this policy at the beginning in global terms, vari- ous factors led him ultimately to limit it to the Latin American sphere— that is, to that area of the world where the United States had hegemony. Only there could its rules be imposed and observed. The Good Neighbor approach was basically no different from the long-established U.S. policy of hemispheric domination—just more subtle and refined, with a certain aura of idealism. It showed the receiving countries more of the "carrot" than the "stick," as Edmund David Cronon has put it.[12] It was to have a decisive ef- fect on the course of events when the problem of control of the oil industry came up once again in Mexico—this time in the form of expropriation.

As part of the review of the oil controversy under the New Deal, it is well to examine, in addition to the change in Washington's approach toward Latin America, the person who was to represent Roosevelt and the new policy in Mexico—namely, Ambassador Josephus Daniels. The fact that the young Franklin Roosevelt as assistant secretary of the navy from 1913 to 1920 had worked directly under Daniels created a special relationship between the two men—a relationship that had no parallel in the case of any other U.S. diplomatic envoy who had been involved in the oil conflict. Daniels' friendship with the president allowed him a fair amount of latitude with regard to the State Department's directives and gave his views exceptional weight in the formulation of U.S. policy, just as Ambassadors Wilson and Morrow had had a great deal of influence, but in a different sense.[13]

Daniels had been known for his liberal ideas since his days as secretary of the navy under Woodrow Wilson, and it was no surprise to anyone when in the 1932 presidential campaign he placed his Raleigh, North Carolina, newspaper, the *News and Observer*, at the service of Roosevelt and the New Deal. When Roosevelt was elected, many people thought that Daniels would be given a post in the cabinet. But the new president had other plans. His former chief, now seventy-one years old, was to be ambassador to Mexico.[14] Daniels' appointment came as a blow to the American colony there. His scant sympathy for some of the practices of big business was already well known. The oil firms' displeasure was especially understandable, since during the Wilson administration he had actively opposed the idea of landing in Tampico and also the leasing of U.S. naval oil reserves to Doheny and the others, who had had to wait until some years later for Fall to work out the deal.[15] On his arrival in Mexico he made it clear that he wholeheartedly supported the Good Neighbor policy and that the old "dollar diplomacy" was dead.[16] In his opinion, American companies abroad had the right to hope for a fair profit, but in no circumstances could they aspire to political control of the countries in which they were operating. A study of Daniels' speeches and correspondence during his years as ambassador reveals that from the very beginning he felt that the best policy to be followed in Mexico was the one originally formulated by Woodrow Wilson: support of a revolution to end all revolutions. From the outset he made it a point to present himself as an "ambassador of goodwill," emphasizing the concept of juridical equality among nations and showing sincere interest in the "new and well-considered experiment" that was the Mexican Revolution.[17] He soon made it clear that "the financial bosses, monopolizers of the fruit of community labor," did not have his sympathies either in Mexico or anywhere else. At first he avoided any direct reference to the oil industry, but only a few months had gone by when, in a speech on Roosevelt's program for the conservation of natural resources in the United States, he declared that "the natural resources . . . are of right and are the property of all the people, not to be sequestered or transferred or monopolized for the enrichment of any single group."[18] The Mexican press received this statement of President Roosevelt's representative with the greatest enthusiasm. With declarations such as this, together with his support of government programs that sought to improve the standard of living of the poor masses and his ingenuously personal touches (as when he appeared in public in *charro* dress),[19] the old liberal soon became a popular figure among the Mexicans. He also established a friendly relationship with Calles, rather much to the discomfit of

the president then in office, Abelardo Rodríguez. None of this meant that
when the time came Daniels failed to fulfill his role as defender of American property rights, both in oil and in agricultural land, but his political position and his personal relationship with Roosevelt, added to the fact that he
was not a career diplomat, enabled him to carry out this defense less aggres-
sively than any of his predecessors.

Relations between Mexico and the Oil Interests
Following the Morrow-Calles Agreement

Before discussing the oil industry as a whole under the three administrations during which Calles was in the background, we need to make one or
two points in regard to the British interests. Moisei S. Alperovich and Boris
T. Rudenko claim—although they do not offer any concrete proof—that
General Escobar had the backing of British capital, which had not yet given
up in its efforts to get control of Mexican oil.[20] However, it is difficult to
imagine that, at a time when Mexico was losing its place as an important
producer, the world market was in a state of surplus, and the industry's uncertainty about its property rights in Mexico had been put to rest thanks to
U.S. policy, Shell and His British Majesty would suddenly see fit to challenge Washington once again.[21] Moreover, the evidently cordial relations
between El Aguila and the Ortiz Rubio administration are difficult to explain if this company was bankrolling the opposition.[22] (With Abelardo
Rodríguez the situation was somewhat different, since the dispute between
El Aguila and the Mexican firm Compañía Petrolera Comercial over possession of Amatlán lot 113 had been decided in favor of the Mexican group.)[23]

With the oil problem essentially solved by Morrow, Washington having
made it clear that no further changes were sought in the Mexican oil legislation, the U.S. embassy stopped receiving anything but what might be considered routine complaints. In 1931 the APPM had to admit that the controversy had really been solved.[24] The secondary problems stemmed mainly
from the slowness with which the confirmatory concessions were being
granted, especially at the beginning.[25]

The companies repeatedly asked the Mexican authorities to speed up the
processing of their applications, and Morrow and Clark backed them up in
their requests. On more than one occasion the two diplomats called on the
ministers of industry and foreign affairs in this regard. Morrow even
brought the problem up with Ortiz Rubio personally. But in this secondary
area the embassy was not to have the same success it had had with the fundamental issues, and some of its appeals were ignored.[26] The industry minister explained that the delay was due to all the red tape involved in reviewing the titles rather than to any deliberate policy. In some cases in the
course of the review the treasury minister denied the validity of the documentation presented and the U.S. embassy was prevailed on to intervene on
behalf of the affected parties.[27] With Daniels' arrival, however, diplomatic
intervention in matters of this kind fell off notably[28]—partly because the

new ambassador did not look favorably on such action and partly because the Abelardo Rodríguez administration had applied itself more assiduously to the task of granting the concessions with a view to "clearing up as soon as possible the status of oil ownership in the Republic."[29]

The labor situation was another of the lesser causes for the companies' dissatisfaction. Following creation of the Federal Board of Conciliation and Arbitration (JFCA—Junta Federal de Conciliación y Arbitraje) in 1927, they had lodged a number of complaints. But the real problem in this area came in 1931 with passage of the labor law implementing Article 123 of the new constitution—a law rather advanced for its time which had come about as the result of an alliance between organized workers and the government. Its promulgation during the conservative administration of Abelardo Rodríguez should be viewed in the light of the situation at the time. On the one hand, it was a gesture to the workers in view of the recent difficulties between the CROM and the government. On the other, only 15 per cent of the country's manpower was employed in industry, which for its part was almost totally controlled by foreign capital. Hence the 1931 legislation may be regarded as an effort to increase Mexican participation in the profits of this sector. The government was hardly opposed to the betterment of its labor allies at the expense of foreign capital![30] Indeed, the firms' difficulties with the labor unions, which were to be the official cause of the expropriation in 1938, originated not under the Cárdenas regime but rather during the last part of Abelardo Rodríguez' term. In 1934 and 1935 the Huasteca and El Aguila unions struck against their respective companies and won their demands. These labor conflicts were the preamble to the serious confrontation that was to come two years later over the signing of a collective contract.[31]

Still another problem that the Morrow-Calles Agreement had failed to settle was the companies' chronic dissatisfaction with the tax rates. In early 1929 they had protested a levy on income and royalties, claiming that it was unconstitutional,[32] and on May 20, 1931, they suggested to the government that one of the best ways it could help the industry to recover was by granting greater fiscal incentives.[33] Even within the administration itself there were those who, taking note of the fact that some of the firms were having to import gasoline in order to supply the Mexican domestic market,[34] felt that tax cuts were necessary in order to provide the companies with an incentive. Eventually there were some readjustments made in this area, but they were not very significant.

Finally, the problem of the "federal zones" continued, although it was no longer as acute as before and did not contribute to any real friction.[35]

None of the foregoing sources of contention was sufficiently serious, however, to disturb the basic harmony that prevailed after 1929. Indeed, in 1931 and 1932 the companies made several loans to the Mexican government, to be considered advances against their taxes. The government had been asking the firms for help of this kind ever since 1930 and the Depression but Morrow had been opposed, maintaining in the interest of the debtors that Mexico should not receive any new credit until it paid off its previous commitments, since otherwise ultimate settlement with the International Committee of Bankers on Mexico would necessarily be delayed. At the beginning of 1931 Morrow's advice was still being heeded and no loan had been granted, but later that year Mexico reopened the question and made a special plea to the five firms that were selling oil—El Aguila, Huasteca, Pierce, Sinclair, and Standard Oil of California—for a loan of 10 million dollars.[36] Internal differences within the group kept the five from coming to an agreement among themselves: while four were producing oil in Mexico, Standard was importing it, and while the exporting firms were asking for tax cuts on exports as a condition for the loan, Standard was interested in relief on imports. In the end the government agreed to commit itself to not increasing the import tax, in return for which it received a loan of 2.8 million dollars at 4.8 per cent. While the ostensible purpose of the credit was to underwrite highway construction, the U.S. embassy claimed that its real aim was to stabilize the exchange rate.[37] In November of the following year the government received another seven million dollars from El Aguila, Huasteca, and Pierce at the same rate of interest, this time for the officially announced purpose of creating a national mortgage bank and underpinning the peso. The companies' goodwill gesture was again reciprocated by certain fiscal concessions,[38] and the new spirit of cooperation was lauded in the national press.[39]

Mexican Attempts to Create an Official Oil Enterprise

Prior to the 1930's it had not crossed anyone's mind that the Mexican government might relinquish its status as a small oil producer attending only to the needs of the railroads and undertake to form a big consortium that would compete with the established companies and attempt to meet the entire domestic demand, which had been more or less forgotten by the foreign firms. However, the Depression and the subsequent crisis on the world oil market prompted serious consideration of this possibility.[40] Morrow, on examining the question, came to the conclusion that Mexico would not be able to mobilize enough capital to realize such an ambitious plan—and on this point he was correct.[41]

The official publications of the time show that the Ortiz Rubio and Abelardo Rodríguez administrations were beginning to be concerned over the need to be sure of an adequate fuel supply—at a suitably low price—for national agriculture and industry.[42] Through the *Boletín del petróleo* the officials responsible for oil in the Ministry of Industry launched the idea of creating an official enterprise similar to the one that had been established in Argentina in 1922. Short of nationalization, they claimed, there was no other way to keep the international consortia from continuing to monopolize Mexican oil. There was a clear trend throughout the world, they said, for governments to take over national energy resources, and Mexico should keep up with the times.[43] In view of the government's failure to gain control of the oil industry through legislation, the new strategy was proposed. At the same time, it happened that Luis Cabrera, the old Carranza supporter, had also decided that it was a good idea to reopen the subject of national-ization of the oil.[44]

During 1932 and 1933 the government declared publicly more than once that it intended to take steps that would prevent the total monopolization of Mexican oil by foreign interests, assure against any shortage of fuel for domestic use, and provide the state with a new machinery for controlling its natural wealth. In order to accomplish these ends it was necessary to create private Mexican oil companies and also to establish a semiofficial enterprise which would see that the government's needs were fully met and help to take care of the private sector's demand as well. Also within the strategy, certain property taxes would have to be raised, on the one hand, so as to reduce the area of idle land under private concessions, and export levies lowered, on the other, in order to encourage increased production. The ordinary concessions—that is, those already subject to the provisions of the Constitution of 1917—were suspended: the government was acquir-ing its own fields.[45] This time the Mexican press sided with the govern-ment. It began to show signs of concern over the damage that could be done to the national economy as a result of totally depending on foreign com-panies for the national fuel supply. The program should begin, *Excélsior* urged.[46] The U.S. embassy witnessed these renewed manifestations of eco-nomic nationalism with certain misgivings, but it did not intervene. It was still too early to evaluate the new strategy—which in any case did not di-rectly threaten the rights of the firms already in existence.[47] Moreover, dur-ing 1933 and in the beginning of 1934 the Abelardo Rodríguez administra-tion attempted to enlist the participation of the oil companies themselves. Each of the large ones was sounded out informally to find out if it was inter-ested in joining the government in the new undertaking. Unfortunately, all the offers were rejected: the foreign firms had no interest in helping the Mexican government get into the oil production business.[48]

The establishment of Petromex, S.A., by Abelardo Rodríguez represented one more effort on Mexico's part to exploit the by then not-so-flourishing oil reserves in the nation's behalf. According to the plan, this semiofficial enterprise was to be run exclusively with national capital. Its objective was to create and maintain a "genuinely national" oil industry and see to it that Mexico was no longer "one big private preserve for the big foreign com-panies." As long as the sources of production and the means of transporta-tion, refining, and distribution were "in the hands of firms controlled by absentee capital, which set the prices of these products at will," the prob-lem of domestic supply could never be fully solved. The new enterprise would provide the country with the fuel it needed "at reasonable prices."[49]

The companies received this new turn in government oil policy with cer-tain apprehension. Thomas R. Armstrong of the APPM went to talk with Ambassador Daniels about the matter. In the oilman's opinion, the new en-terprise threatened to deprive the firms of the large government market. Moreover, he was afraid that the new program would revive the controver-sy over control of the "federal zones," since Mexico could claim possession of certain watercourses that only appeared during the rainy season and whose beds, since they traversed company land, were being exploited by the firms. In this way, Armstrong claimed, the companies could lose up to 40 per cent of their best oil fields. The ambassador refused to put any pressure on the Mexican government to abandon its scheme and merely pointed out that, according to the State Department's 1928 declaration, if this new policy affected the firms' rights in any way they should appeal through the Mexican courts.[50] Armstrong's misgivings turned out to be unfounded. As Morrow had foreseen much earlier, Petromex did not have the capital to become a large national enterprise like the one in Argentina. The expected flow of private national monies did not come, and the government could not—or did not want to—shoulder the project alone.

In conclusion, it may be said that the Portes Gil, Ortiz Rubio, and Abelardo Rodríguez administrations adhered quite faithfully to the terms of the Morrow-Calles Agreement of 1928. The oil reform and the rest of the Revolutionary program as well were bogged down by the conservatism of the period. The effects of the 1929 crisis on a world oil industry already handicapped by overproduction kept the companies from stepping up their operations as the Mexicans had hoped they would following the 1928 agreement. This turn of events, added to the threat of an oil shortage which would cripple the national industry, led the Ortiz Rubio and Abelardo Rodríguez administrations to decide on a different approach to the problem. They stopped insisting on nationalization of the subsoil and began to stress the creation of a large semiofficial enterprise whose immediate objective would be to take the domestic market out of the hands of the foreign consortia. The shortage of national capital, however, was to prevent this new solution from achieving the results expected.

Chapter 8

The Cárdenas Regime and Solution
Once and for All of the Oil Problem

After almost fifteen years in power, the Sonora group was still far from having fulfilled the program that formally constituted its political standard:
the Constitution of 1917. In 1934 Calles and his team had had to recognize
the serious fragmentation of the political elite and, in making plans for the
succession, the importance therefore of having a candidate who while still
a member of their group was not identified with the lack of Revolutionary
spirit and with the corruption that had characterized the last few years of
government. If they did not take this precaution, the existing discontent
could become a threat to their stability. Already there was an agrarian leadership working both within and outside the National Revolutionary Party
to unite the workers and peasants in order to combat the influence of the
Calles group and its policy. And so it was that Lázaro Cárdenas—onetime
governor of Michoacán, chairman of the party, and minister of war—was
nominated as the official candidate. The left wing of the PNR considered
him a new element, a representative of the younger faction that differed
with the older generation of Revolutionary leaders. His relative independence with respect to Calles was well known. For example, when the latter
called for a halt to land redistribution in 1929, Cárdenas, who was then governor of Michoacán, refused to respond.[1] Still, he had made it a point to
avoid a direct confrontation with Calles and his group, and for this reason
they saw in him a man who, under their tutelage, could put an end to the
restlessness in Mexico. A change would be made, but it would be a controlled one.[2]

While some claim that Cárdenas had Calles' wholehearted "goodwill,
affection, and consideration,"[3] the general consensus of those who have
studied the subject is that his candidacy was to some extent imposed on
Calles, who would have preferred General Manuel Pérez Treviño.[4] But
whether or not the nomination met with Calles' total satisfaction, the
"Supreme Leader" certainly was far from seeing Cárdenas as a possible
rival. He figured that the candidate's radical tendencies would soon disappear under his own traditional stewardship.[5]

At first Calles thought to use institutional means to hold Cárdenas in
check. Accordingly, with the idea of putting a broad government program
into effect under which the new president would have little to say, the "Six-
Year Plan" was drawn up in 1933, while Abelardo Rodríguez was still in
office. Authored by two commissions—one technical, made up of representatives from the various ministries, and the other political, composed of
members of the Congress and the PNR—the plan as it came out of the

hands of these two working groups fully met with the terms of Calles' mandate. However, on submission to the PNR convention in Querétaro it underwent a number of significant changes introduced by the agrarian wing of the party, all of them quite the opposite of what Calles wanted. In the end it was to become the instrument whereby Calles, not Cárdenas, was placed in the subordinate position.[6] The Six-Year Plan did not fail to arouse misgivings among certain foreign observers who were afraid that a socialist society, albeit somewhat different from the Soviet brand, was being established in Mexico.[7] Talk along these lines gained so much momentum that the Mexican government was prompted to communicate its reassurances to Washington, saying it was merely seeking to enforce the Constitution of 1917.[8]

The new administration began its activities with the same lack of independence from Calles in the cabinet, the Congress, and the PNR that had characterized its three predecessors. The small "leftist" groups that might have been thought to be closer to Cárdenas than to Calles appeared to be neutralized.[9] Very soon, however, Cárdenas began to show signs that he was not going to put up with this situation indefinitely. In shaking free of the Calles yoke he was to have the help not only of certain loyal sectors in the army—which had been the fundamental base of power in all the previous governments—but also, and more importantly, of the workers and peasants, in whose name he was to govern in the future. By mid-1935 he was fully able to stand up to Calles. The case of Ortiz Rubio was not to be repeated: the president used his followers in the army, the government, and the mass organizations in such a way that in a short time they had permanently frustrated Calles' efforts to hold onto the reins of power.[10]

Cárdenas decided to assure his victory over the "Supreme Leader" by rapidly eliminating all the remaining Calles elements in the cabinet, the armed forces, the legislature, the state governments, and the PNR. Support for the labor movement was channeled through the Confederation of Mexican Workers (CTM—Confederación de Trabajadores Mexicanos), by then under the leadership of Vicente Lombardo Toledano, but without antagonizing the independent trade unions. The same was done with the peasants, who for the first time had a forum of their own, the National Peasant Confederation (CNC—Confederación Nacional Campesina). From the beginning both these organizations were under government control. The CTM became an instrument in the fight against capital, and the trade unions got back the power they had had in 1928. The government's role in labor-management relations took on a new focus: it was prepared to intervene in order to maintain the balance between the two basically unequal sectors. The state, as final arbiter of such disputes, was now more on the side of labor than of capital—a fact that was to play a major part in future relations between the government and the oil companies. The Cárdenas administration, working with the Mexican Peasant Confederation and later the National Peasant Confederation (CNC), was convinced that the ejido was the ideal form of rural land tenure. It undertook to do away with the latifundium—and succeeded.[11]

At first Cárdenas attempted to modernize the country, following an approach quite different from the one used by Calles. He sought to bring about a thoroughgoing change in structure based on agricultural land redistribution, stronger trade unions, and an end to colonialism in the economy. By 1937 his policy had a clear nationalistic stamp, and between 1935 and 1938 a series of reforms were implemented that were to substantially modify the national economic system—which up to then had still held on to characteristics inherited from the Porfirian regime.[12]

As of 1935, foreign domination of the Mexican economy continued to be an undisputed fact and the agrarian reform had not made much of a dent in the old land tenure pattern.[13] The Cárdenas regime from the outset was determined to set the stage for the "socialist democracy" called for in the Six-Year Plan, in the official party platform, and in government rhetoric. The strategy for achieving this goal was never clearly defined, but basically it was thought to modernize the country through development of the agricultural sector, together with a light industry subordinate to its needs made up of small plants which would be in the hands of workers' cooperatives. Such a system, it was believed, would avoid the social ills attendant to industrial capitalism. The cooperative movement, according to this line of thinking, would carry Mexico from feudalism directly to some sort of socialism without having to go through the stage of capitalism.[14] Although as it turned out the changes made during the Cárdenas regime did not lead to the kind of society that had been hoped for, at least they remained on the books and in a suitably tamed form were used by subsequent administrations to stimulate a line of economic development that was more in accord with the traditional structures of the capitalist economies. The causes for this turn of events were many, and their analysis is beyond the framework of the present study. In any case, Cárdenas' efforts to take the leadership of the national economy out of the hands of foreign capital were to be rewarded. True, the mining sector remained an enclave until the end of the regime, but the outlook for the foreign owners was not very bright from the oil expropriation onward. With Cárdenas the government was once again to take up the war against colonial capital that had been suspended since the Morrow-Calles Agreement in 1928. The youngest and most modern of the national industries—namely, those producing for the internal market—joined labor and the middle class in support of the government's policy to put basic sectors of the Mexican economy—the railroads, oil, mining, agrarian development, electric power—under state control.[15] And despite numerous setbacks along the way, the final balance sheet showed that they had come out ahead.

Cárdenas and the Oil Industry

When Cárdenas took office he already had first-hand knowledge of certain aspects of the oil problem as a result of his experience as field general under Calles in the region where the wells were located. Indeed, from then on his relations with the foreign firms had been far from cordial.[16] As he was to say

much later, he had resented the companies' attitude toward their employees and the local authorities, which gave him the impression that they regarded Mexico as "conquered territory."[17]

When Abelardo Rodríguez turned over the presidency, it was understood
that the Morrow-Calles Agreement continued to be in effect. However,
there had already been signs—for example, the Six-Year Plan and certain
references in Cárdenas' campaign speeches—that the modus vivendi between the oil companies and the Mexican government was not to last much
longer. Still, the certainty that Calles would continue to be the "Supreme
Leader" apparently allayed the misgivings of those who were interested in
maintaining the status quo.

The Six-Year Plan, for its part, was permeated throughout with undisguised nationalism. It stated that, while Mexico could not isolate itself
from the rest of the world, every effort would be made to see that national
interests were placed over foreign ones within the country's borders. To this
end, the program for nationalization of the subsoil resources was to go
ahead, the nationally owned oil industry was to be expanded, and other
steps were to be taken.[18] During the election campaign Cárdenas had come
out openly in favor of this aspect of the Six-Year Plan, saying on more than
one occasion that he intended to follow the lines laid down in this document. He emphasized the need to place the sources of wealth and the means
of production in the hands of the workers and to end exploitation of the subsoil by "foreign capitalist usurers."[19] When Calles dropped out of the political picture the Americans began to regard the government's plan with
certain apprehension.[20]

The Undoing of the Morrow-Calles Agreement: First Signs

Even before Calles was removed from the wings, the oil firms had shown
signs of concern over the cancellation of some of their concessions.[21] In
September 1934 Standard Oil of New Jersey told the State Department that
in its opinion the Mexican government was trying to limit the effect of the
Morrow-Calles Agreement, if not strip it entirely of its force.[22] Two months
later the APPM suggested to Ambassador Daniels—and later to the State
Department directly—that in view of the difficulties the Mexican government was creating for the industry, it would be desirable to arrange a meeting between Calles and former ambassador J. Reuben Clark, Jr. (by this time
Morrow had died), so that the latter could point out to the Mexican "strong
man" the extent to which the 1928 understanding was being disregarded.
The U.S. government refused to back the companies' plan, though it was
not opposed to it in principle.[23] Soon afterwards a series of moves—the
suspension of certain tax exemptions that a number of the firms had been
enjoying, publication in January 1935 of the government's economic action
program containing measures for increased utilization of the oil by the nation, and the outbreak of a strike among the Huasteca workers—prompted
the APPM to appeal even more strongly to the State Department and ask it

to intercede in their behalf. The companies were afraid that Cárdenas was attempting to back down on the 1928 accord, and they asked Washington to take a firm stand. They went so far as to suggest that the U.S. threaten to lift the arms embargo unless the problems were straightened out.[24] According to Standard Oil, the strike against Huasteca was a first step toward forcing it to suspend operations in Mexico.[25] These appeals to Washington were not all. The companies decided, in the meantime, to also go ahead on their own and try to reaffirm the understanding with Calles directly—thus speeding up Clark's arrival in Mexico.[26] The former U.S. ambassador succeeded in meeting with Calles, but the old leader's fall from power immediately thereafter prevented him from doing anything to help the Americans. It has even been suggested that one of the reasons behind Calles' effort to block the Cárdenas program was precisely his disagreement with the new president over the policy to be followed with respect to oil.[27] This point is not easy to prove, however. What is a fact, in any case, is that the firms' spokesmen appealed to Calles—as many others had done over the years—when they found it difficult to deal with the president.[28] Although neither the embassy nor the U.S. government had sponsored the "Clark mission," they had not failed to observe the Mexican government's hostility toward the oil companies.

Standard Oil's persistent complaints and prodding finally convinced Secretary of State Cordell Hull that the old controversy might be in the process of reopening. Hull was concerned over the increase in taxes and the slowness with which the confirmatory titles were being issued. Ambassador Daniels conveyed Washington's fears to the minister of foreign affairs and Cárdenas himself, but the Mexican government gave no sign of willingness to change its policy in reponse to U.S. demands.[29] In 1938 the APPM accused Mexico of stopping the issuance of confirmatory titles in order to force the companies to pay royalties on the concessions that had not yet been formalized.[30] Which turned out to be true.

With the new administration now free of the "Supreme Leader's" influence, its whole program took on a much more radical tone, and no time was lost before this shift in trend was felt in the oil sector. For a while it had seemed that relations between Cárdenas and the companies were taking a turn for the better, but the amity did not last for long[31]—as indeed the U.S. embassy had feared. The American diplomats blamed the new atmosphere of hostility on the fact that the Mexican government seemed to have decided that indiscriminate oil exports were no longer in the national interest—that the domestic market should have preference.[32] The embassy was right: in his state-of-the-union message to Congress in September 1935 Cárdenas hinted at the desirability of changing the Calles oil legislation, although at the time he referred only to the ordinary concessions.[33] The official organ of the PNR, *El Nacional*, was much clearer on the subject. In editorials appearing in October and November of that year it maintained that Mexico could no longer be the exclusive preserve of big business, which varied the pace of its exploitation according to the ups and downs of the international market. Mexico needed to be able to count on a regular output. Moreover, it insisted that the wages and taxes which the companies were paying in Mexico should be no less than the rates prevailing in the United States.[34] At the end of 1935 the firms began to have still more trouble with labor—in which the government sided with the workers—as well as tax problems and increasing difficulties in the confirmation of their concessions.[35]

In 1936 the Mexican government embarked on a series of steps that were once and for all to set the future course of its relations with the oil firms. The first of these was the proposal in the Congress of an expropriation law —which apparently was not aimed directly at the oil industry.[36] This draft law, one of whose purposes was to make for a greater distribution of the national wealth, gave the government the right to expropriate any property whatsoever for public use, compensation to be paid in accordance with its fiscal value within a maximum of ten years. The industrial organizations opposed it, alleging that it was unconstitutional, but their efforts were in vain.[37] On learning about the bill, Acting Secretary of State Walton Moore protested the "almost unlimited extension of the right of expropriation" that the law would give to the Mexican federal government and immediately asked Daniels to discuss the problem with Cárdenas personally. The word came too late, however. The law had been passed by the Congress before the embassy could carry out Moore's instructions. In any case, Cárdenas assured Daniels that the State Department's misgivings were unfounded and that the sole purpose of the new legislation was to empower the government to take control of those industries essential to the public welfare that had suspended their operations for one reason or another. He explained that it was not the government's intention to follow a policy of unrestrained expropriation and pointed out, by way of example, how absurd it would be to take over the mining or oil industries.[38] Apparently the United States dropped the matter at this point. In a speech in November Daniels declared that relations between his country and Mexico had never been better.[39] The U.S. embassy was confident that the regulatory legislation yet to be passed would be "liberal" and would put an end to the ambiguity in the organic law that gave rise to different interpretations.[40]

Another of the decisions taken in 1936 that was crucial to the oil question was the one concerning the industry's labor unions. Since 1913 there had been a growing current in favor of establishing a single vertical union that would bring together all the workers in the oil industry. Nothing concrete had been done for two decades, however, owing to certain resistance in both the companies and the government.[41] By 1934 the oil industry had ten thousand organized workers belonging to nineteen independent unions.[42] The following year, thanks to the Cárdenas administration's labor policy, these groups were all brought together in the Syndicate of Oil Workers of the Mexican Republic (STPRM—Sindicato de Trabajadores Petroleros de la República Mexicana). In 1936 the new organization was incorporated into the CTM and thereby placed under official aegis. On July 20 of that year the STPRM's general assembly, representing almost eighteen thousand workers, met at Mexico City and drew up its first collective bargaining contract. In principle the firms had no objection: quite the contrary, they looked on such a document as a good thing, since it would stabilize labor conditions even if it did mean higher wages.[43] Publicly, however, they declared that the demands were outrageous and rejected them flatly. According to their calculations, the increases in wages and benefits that the STPRM was asking for represented a total of 65 million pesos.[44] Undoubtedly the demands were intended to allow room for negotiation. In any case, the STPRM's action had had Cárdenas' blessing from the outset.[45] His thesis, expressed in his annual message to the Congress, was that each country should set its workers' wages on the basis of its economic capacity, not simply the law of supply and demand.[46]

In keeping with its past practices, the Petroleum Bureau in the Ministry of National Economy came out in no uncertain terms against the situation in the oil industry. The bureau's chief stated in an interview that for several decades Mexico had been watching its hydrocarbon resources disappear without leaving any lasting benefit for the nation. The oil region itself was ruined: its agriculture was no longer what it once was.[47] The government newspaper also voiced official dissatisfaction with the low levels of wages and taxes.[48] Hostility against the oil firms was clearly building up. Huasteca told the U.S. embassy that if this attitude persisted it would not take much for the firm to leave the country.[49] Now, however, the embassy no longer automatically blamed the Mexican government for the dark clouds that were gathering on the horizon. Daniels felt that part of the problem had grown out of the fact that the management in the oil companies, as well as in the rest of the American and British firms in Mexico, continued to hold onto an old-style imperialistic mentality that precluded any improvement in the situation of their workers.[50]

At the beginning of 1937 there were good signs for the companies economically but bad ones politically. It was precisely at this time that the differences with the Cárdenas government crystallized. The conflict was based on two different questions: one, the proposal to change the existing legislation, and the other, the labor problem, which was to be the crucial factor in the new confrontation. Still, from a review of the documents available it would seem that at least up until August 1937 the firms were worried more about the legal aspect of the question than about the labor situation. It is interesting to see what was the cause of their concern.

Early in the year the U.S. consulate in Mexico City received word that the Ministry of National Economy was drawing up a bill to strengthen the national oil enterprise.[51] In addition, it seemed that leftist General Francisco Múgica, by now minister of communications, was preparing a text that was even more ambitious. From a third party the oil companies had obtained a copy of this latter version, which would have inevitably reopened the old controversy. To begin with, it stipulated that all the oil reserves, whether or not they were covered by confirmatory concessions, belonged to the nation. Second, it provided that all the reserves would be exploited by a National Corporation of Mexican Oil.[52] To the displeasure of the Mexican government, the existence of these plans was exposed publicly through the American press. While the Mexican government did not deny that thought was being given to a reform in the oil legislation, Cárdenas personally insisted that nothing was being contemplated that would affect the legally acquired rights of the foreign companies.[53] As it may well be imagined, these rumors put an end to the Múgica proposal, and the only concrete outcome in the end was the creation in March of that year of the General Petroleum Administration.[54] The foreign firms hardly reacted with pleasure to the appearance of this agency, since its objective was clearly none other than to pressure them through competition (both domestically and abroad, it being suspected that Mexico was ready to set up a barter trade with other countries, particularly Italy and Germany) so as to ultimately gain control over production in Mexico.[55]

By the middle of the year tension had risen even more. The government made it known through the press that it was preparing a new tax law calling for payment of royalties to the federal government by any person or company engaged in exploitation of the subsoil, as called for under Article 27 of the constitution, and also requiring that regular work be kept up on the lands for which the new concessions had been granted.[56] The royalties would have to be paid by all, regardless of the kind of concessions they had, and they were set at 10 per cent of the gross value of output: in effect, the government was entering into "partnership" with the companies. And so the controversy resumed. The latest bill was different in its details from the one being considered at the beginning of the year, but the intent was the same: to do away with all privileges relating to concessions acquired prior to 1917.

As it might have been expected, the oil firms, with Washington's support, violently protested the new plan. The State Department asked the embassy to point out verbally to the Mexican government that the indiscriminate collection of royalties was against the Morrow-Calles Agreement, as was the requirement to keep up regular operations on the lands for which confirmatory concessions had been granted. The minister of foreign affairs, however, gave no sign of being prepared to yield in the face of the protest; he merely indicated that this decree which was of concern to Washington was not going to be approved in the immediate future anyway.[57] At this point the company spokesmen warned the minister of national economy that they would "not take the new decree lying down." Mexico still gave no indication of being ready to compromise.[58] The Cárdenas administration and the oil firms were headed straight for a new clash. Standard Oil described the situation to the State Department in just these terms.[59]

With the decree clearly going to be promulgated soon, despite assurances to the contrary, the companies got together and petitioned Secretary of State Hull to use his good offices with Mexico to stop the legislation. The State Department studied the problem and concluded that the firms' position was defensible, but it pointed out that if Mexico were to put the new assessments into effect saying they were taxes rather than royalties, this would not be contrary to the Morrow-Calles Agreement and there was little that could be done.[60] Washington urged the Mexican government not to reopen the oil controversy, inviting its attention to certain points that went against agreed principles.[61] If what the Cárdenas administration wanted was to increase its revenue, as Deputy Foreign Affairs Minister Ramón Beteta had indicated to the counselor at the U.S. embassy, then the oil problem could be solved by a moderate rise in oil taxes without their being regarded as royalties—Washington was not opposed to this.[62] The pressure brought results, at least temporarily: the controversial decree was stopped, although not abandoned. In September a Mexican Supreme Court decision ruled that the confirmatory concessions could not be kept valid unless the deposits were being worked.[63] The State Department was afraid that a real controversy would flare up unless at the same time the dispute between the companies and the newly formed STPRM, a problem that was becoming increasingly knotty, was solved.[64]

The Oil Workers' Strike

Before Cárdenas came to power relations between the oil workers and the government had left much to be desired. The state had not always had the workers' support in its efforts to put Article 27 into practice, since they saw it as a threat to their jobs, the companies generally having reacted by threatening to cut back production and lay off some of the labor force. On occasion their strikes had been hindered and even stopped by the government. The CROM and the oil workers had never established very harmonious relations, and Morones, unable to exercise control over the union, had actually exerted pressure against it whenever he had a chance.[65] By 1936, however, the situation was different. When in November of that year the government intervened in the dispute to keep the industry from being paralyzed, for the first time, it took the workers' side.[66]

The immediate purpose of the administration's intercession in 1936 had been to get the two parties to agree to come to the bargaining table. The effort was to no avail: the representatives met until May 1937 without coming to any terms. The companies had set the sum of 14 million pesos as the top amount they were prepared to concede, and they stood firm. The CTM was on the point of accepting the offer but at the last minute decided to turn it down, making it impossible to avoid a walkout.[67] With a strike thereby in existence, the federal government ruled that the firms were obliged to pay the workers' regular wages during the time they were away from their jobs. Once again the public mood was strong for total compliance with paragraph iv.[68] Fuel was added to the fire when in a speech at Monterrey Cárdenas let it be known to all industrialists that if the dispute between labor and management got much worse either the workers or the government would take over. The APPM informed the U.S. embassy that it was hoping for the best but feared for the worst. At a meeting between Cárdenas and the company spokesmen the president informed them that unless they came to an agreement with their workers the government would have to intervene directly —which would mean putting the industry in the hands of official supervisors for as long as necessary.[69] Ambassador Daniels didn't believe that Mexico would take such a radical step, but the situation could, he thought, get to be very difficult. In any case, the firms would have to grant a wage raise, whether or not they thought the levels were high enough already.[70]

Through all this the companies gave the impression of great confidence in their strength: they did not think that Mexico would dare to intervene or expropriate. What is more, they threatened to halt production if the union insisted on its original fantastic demands.[71] As far as their communications with the State Department were concerned, until then they had limited themselves to merely reporting on the progress of the negotiations; they had not asked it to intercede on their behalf in regard to the labor question.[72] It appeared that their assessment of the situation was correct. In May 1937 Cárdenas informed Francisco Castillo Nájera, the Mexican ambassador in Washington, that despite the circumstances it was not his intention to take over the industry.[73] In July Communications Minister Francisco Múgica and Treasury Minister Eduardo Suárez reiterated this position to an officer at the U.S. embassy.[74]

The Labor Conflict and Direct Government Intervention

The strike did not last long. Before the country's economy had a chance to become endangered, the CTM asked the Federal Board of Conciliation and Arbitration to declare the dispute a national emergency in view of its economic implications. The petition was accepted immediately; the strikers went back to their jobs; and the companies were required to submit their books to an audit by the authorities in order to determine whether or not they were in fact in a position to meet the workers' demands.[75] Since thirty days had been allowed for the report to be filed, a team of experts was set up and went to work immediately. Clearly the fact that this team—made up of Deputy Treasury Minister Efraín Buenrostro, Deputy Minister of National Economy Mariano Moctezuma, and Jesús Silva Herzog—had been established amounted to one step more toward government intervention; the firms were no longer dealing with the STPRM or the CTM but now rather with the Cárdenas administration directly.

In no one single respect did the interests of the Mexican government coincide with those of the oil firms. The two sides differed on wages, optimum utilization of the oil resources, destination of the earnings—everything. It is not surprising, therefore, that the labor-management dispute was used to try to force the companies to operate more in accordance with the nation's needs. The report of the experts reflects the situation very well. Their study went beyond a strictly financial investigation and reviewed the whole current oil situation as seen by the government. Their conclusions were no more or less than the administration's evaluation of the state of things in the industry—a view, naturally, that had little to say for the companies. The forty conclusions at the end of the 2,700-page report emphasized the discrepancy between the Mexican economy's needs and the oil firms' policy ever since they began their activities in the country and pointed to a large number of fiscal and political irregularities. As far as the labor problem itself was concerned, the experts considered that the companies were well able to bear the cost of a wage increase amounting to 26 million pesos a year—that is, 12 million more than they had been prepared to give.[76] Cárdenas appeared to be in agreement with the findings and recommendations of the report.[77] Shortly afterward Castillo Nájera informed Daniels that reports from London on the firms' last capital remittances confirmed the fact that they did indeed have the means to grant the wage increase which had been recommended.[78] Cárdenas told Castillo Nájera that there could not be any solution to the oil controversy that did not provide for increased government control over the industry and the setting of future wages and taxes in accordance with studies carried out by official federal agencies.[79]

While naturally the workers accepted the report on the industry's economic status without any fundamental objection, the companies pointed out that they were already paying nearly the highest wages in the country and took strong exception to the president's theory that the salary scale should be set in accordance with the industry's economic capacity.[80] They challenged every single one of the study's conclusions, both those referring to their own ability to pay the raises and those related to other political and economic aspects. Moreover, according to them, the real increase that the recommendations were calling for was 41 million pesos, not 26.[81] Using the local and foreign press, they mounted a campaign against the report, maintaining as their central argument that their earnings in 1936 were only 18 million pesos and not 77, as it had been alleged.[82]

While the experts' findings were being discussed, the companies had gone ahead and offered the union a 20-million-peso increase. Hence the amount in dispute was now only 6 million. But the firms were not prepared to give in any further, since they felt that to do so would open the way for more state control still. Cárdenas, for his part, was prepared to push for full compliance with the report's recommendations.[83] For the next four months the debate continued, but in the meantime the Federal Board of Conciliation and Arbitration, through its Special Group 7, had carried out a new on-the-spot investigation to assess the validity of the earlier team's conclusions. As a result of this second inquiry, the findings of the first one were upheld.[84]

While the legal machinery ground out its course, representatives of the big companies met with Cárdenas several times during the months of August and October in an effort to come to an understanding. In these talks the firms made their position clear: they were neither prepared nor able to go beyond the pay increase they had already granted. In a more or less veiled way they let Cárdenas know that they would suspend operations if the Mexican government were to insist on putting the recommendations into effect. The president showed little reaction. He simply listened to the companies' arguments and said that he would try to find a solution to the problem which he hoped would be an equitable one. He did, however, express his displeasure at the fact that the firms were trying to involve their own governments in the matter.[85] Indeed, the Americans had met with officials from the State Department to present their case. Two points stood out in their line of argument: on the one hand, they believed that the Mexican policy of threatening a national takeover was jeopardizing American oil investments throughout all of Latin America and therefore endangering the vital interests of the United States. Moreover, they said, strict compliance with the experts' recommendations meant an increase of not 26 but 41 million pesos.[86] The State Department remained calm. Ambassador Castillo Nájera assured Under Secretary Welles in October 1937 that Mexico hoped soon to come to an understanding with the companies.[87]

In response to an inquiry from the Netherlands in September of that year, Washington said that for the time being there was no thought of intervening formally and that the firms were being encouraged to work out their differences directly with Cárdenas.[88] The State Department's passivity was not total, however: in the course of an international press conference Daniels made it clear that the United States would not like to see any change take place in the oil status quo such as it had been established in the Morrow-Calles Agreement.[89]

Regardless of Castillo Nájera's assurances, the fact was that the talks between the president and the company spokesmen were stalled. Both sides held steadfast to their positions. In November an officer of Standard Oil brought the disagreement out in the open by declaring publicly that if the firms were forced to grant the 26-million-peso increase they would have to close down their operations. "We cannot and we will not pay," he said.[90] They were sure that in the end the government would have to give in as it had always done before, and this is what they told Ambassador Daniels. They believed that Cárdenas would not seize their properties simply because he did not have the specialized personnel to run the industry or the means of transportation to export the product. Also, although they did not say so, they knew they could see to it that the international markets were closed to Mexican oil.[91]

Cárdenas' Attempt to Break up the United Oil "Front": The Agreement with El Aguila

By the end of 1937 the hostility between the Mexican government and the oil companies was unconcealed. Added to the sharp disagreement over the report of the experts and the delay in granting the remaining confirmatory concessions was the fact that in November a 350,000-acre concession held by Standard Oil of California was taken back and the lands turned over to the National Petroleum Administration.[92] What was significant about this move was that although 200,000 of the 350,000 acres corresponded to a concession granted in 1930, the other 150,000 were from one dating back to 1909—in other words, a confirmatory concession. The Mexican government was attempting a new strategy (new to this phase, that is, since Carranza had also tried it some time ago)—namely, to divide the ranks of the oil group by offering especially attractive concessions to certain of its members. El Aguila was the obvious target for its overtures. For one thing, of all the firms in Mexico it had the greatest amount of capital invested. In addition, it had relatively less protection, since neither the British nor the Dutch government had much freedom of movement in this U.S. sphere of influence, especially at a time when Washington wanted to put an end to direct intervention in the Latin American countries.

Up to November 1937 El Aguila in its relations with the Cárdenas administration had not been particularly different from the rest of the companies. Since 1934 it had been engaged in a fruitless legal battle with a Mexican firm over control of some lands in Amatlán.[93] This conflict was to last up to the end of the Cárdenas administration. In addition, in March 1937 the Mexican courts had ruled that certain other tracts to which El Aguila laid claim were in fact federal property.[94] These reverses, however, did not prevent the Anglo-Dutch company and the government oil agency from entering into an agreement in 1936 regarding the exploitation of the important Poza Rica beds that was convenient to both sides.[95] The negotiations were prolonged and did not get much publicity, and on November 11, to the American firms' surprise and displeasure, a compact signed by Cárdenas and El Aguila for the joint exploitation of Poza Rica was made public. According to its terms, the company gained possession of thirteen thousand acres of oil lands whose reserves were estimated at 500 million barrels.[96] This meant, in the view of the *New York Times*, that El Aguila had acquired the second most important oil deposit in the world.[97] In exchange, the British recognized that the Mexican nation was entitled to the hydrocarbons in the subsoil and that the government had the power to decide on the confirmatory concessions. El Aguila agreed to give the state a share equivalent to between 15 and 35 per cent of the output.[98] It was expected that this government participation would contribute sizably to the public treasury, but, what was more important, it was figured that El Aguila, in order not to jeopardize its control of Poza Rica, would be obliged to depart from the positions taken by Standard Oil and the other American companies.[99]

At least this was the way the U.S. embassy and the rest of the oil companies saw it.[100] At the end of November, Daniels reported to Washington that it was possible that El Aguila had already agreed to go along with the Mexican courts' decision regarding the oil conflict.[101] This idea was reinforced when it was learned that Mexico was negotiating a similar agreement with an independent British group made up of the London firms of Stephens and Hardy, Corry Brothers, and Lambert-Vendell. Former treasury minister Alberto J. Pani was the liaison with the Mexican government. The U.S. embassy suspected that the group was not so independent after all and that it was linked with El Aguila. It proposed to build three refineries in Mexico, buy ten tankers, and drill between thirty and forty wells, from which it expected to produce 100,000 barrels a day; the Mexican government would receive a 50 per cent share plus a loan of 5 million dollars.[102]

The Mexican maneuvers did not stop here. Every effort was made to exploit any suspicions arising between the American and British firms. In July 1937 National Economy Minister Rafael Sánchez Tapia pointed out to the U.S. chargé d'affaires, Pierre Boal, that if the oil companies would only accept the Mexican government as a partner in the exploitation of the oil, official policy would be redirected so as to facilitate the solution of problems such as the labor issue instead of interfering in the industry's progress. The

State Department refused even to pass the message on to the companies.[103] In December Treasury Minister Eduardo Suárez hinted to the U.S. embassy that the Mexican government was disappointed in El Aguila and was prepared to enter into an accord with some of the American firms (based on certain government participation in their operations) in order to halt the British company's expansion. Suárez mentioned the Sinclair group or Huasteca as possible candidates, and on another occasion he spoke of Richmond Petroleum. The Mexican suggestions fell on deaf ears.[104] And in the end the courtship with El Aguila also proved to have been in vain, since after some hesitation it finally decided that the best way to protect its interests was to remain on the side of its American confreres.

The Decision of the Federal Board of Conciliation and Arbitration

On December 18, 1937, Special Group 7 of the Federal Board of Conciliation and Arbitration (JFCA) duly handed down its decision on the oil industry's labor-management dispute.[105] The award, as it has been said, closely followed the recommendations in the expert group's report: it approved an overall increase of 26,332,756 pesos in the cost of the contract and set a ceiling of 1,100 on the total number of nonunionized office staff allowed for all the companies.[106] The firms' reaction was immediate: they had been the victims of a clear miscarriage of justice. It was materially impossible, they claimed, to meet the terms of what they felt was the most outrageous collective contract ever awarded to workers in any industry anywhere in the world. In their opinion, the Mexican government had been baldly partial to the workers.[107] Later the companies were to point out that if they had complied with the board's decision they would have been accepting virtual expropriation, since the ceiling on nonunion office staff would have meant that in reality it was the union that controlled the industry.[108] It was clear that the eye of the storm had shifted from the question of wages and benefits to the fact that the oil firms had decided to continue their traditional policy of keeping the Mexican government out of their financial affairs and general policy. According to Raymond Vernon, they believed that if they yielded this once they would end up being pushed around throughout all the years to come.[109]

In Mexico the firms reacted by putting on the economic pressure and at the same time having their lawyers marshal all the possible legal arguments in their favor. In a protest, in the form of a request for injunction, filed on December 29, they challenged both the procedure and the award itself, continuing to maintain that the real increase was 41 million pesos, not 26—an amount that in their financial condition they could not agree to.[110] This time production did not stop, but when the economic situation began to threaten the stability of the exchange rate the companies seized on the opportunity to withdraw their bank deposits and create uneasiness in industrial and banking circles so as to trigger a drain on foreign exchange. The Bank of Mexico's reserves, which appeared to have been falling off dangerously since March, were depleted still further by this new blow.[111] Cárdenas noted in his journal that the situation was bad indeed, but still not as serious as the oil firms had wanted.[112] The government was forced to impose tariffs in order to keep down imports and compensate for the shortage of foreign exchange.[113] Climbing prices and an economic slowdown were soon to follow.[114]

The STPRM and the CTM reacted to the companies' defiant attitude by calling for the Supreme Court to rule in the matter—in their favor, of course.[115] But in the climate created by the 1938 labor dispute it was clear that the courts could no longer be used as they once had been by Obregón and Calles. The high tribunal's decision of March 1, 1938, hardly came as any surprise. Its eighteen points systematically refuted each and every one of the companies' arguments. While the court did hold that the firms were not obliged to pay more than the 26 million pesos, this still left them with nothing to work with, because their claim that the real amount was much greater had been simply ignored.[116] With this ruling to back it up, the Federal Board of Conciliation and Arbitration set March 7 as the deadline for the firms to comply with its award.

The Attitude of the U.S. Government

Up until 1936 the main bone of contention between the Cárdenas administration and the United States had been the agrarian reform, whereas in 1937 the oil controversy came to occupy first place. The agrarian question had been of concern because approximately 40 million acres of the land expropriated up to 1937, valued at about 5 million dollars, belonged to Americans.[117] But the investment at stake in the oil controversy was far greater. For a time the companies had been content to keep the State Department informed of their labor problems without asking for any assistance. However, on receiving the report of the expert committee, they appealed to Washington immediately. During August 1937 a series of exchanges took place between the oil firms and both Secretary Hull and Under Secretary Welles. The companies made it clear that if the Mexican recommendations were put into effect they would be so hard pressed financially that they would have no alternative but to halt their operations. In their view, Cárdenas unquestionably intended to confiscate the oil industry and was using the workers' demands as a smokescreen. Such a move would obviously infringe on U.S. national interest. Standard Oil's chairman of the board pointed out to Hull that if Mexico were to nationalize the oil industry its action could inspire other Latin American countries to follow suit, and the United States could end up being deprived of its only really available oil resources abroad. Welles, in turn, informed the companies that the State Department would be following developments carefully but that for the time being it would refrain from intervening unless a clear-cut denial of justice should occur.[118] The under secretary's refusal must have referred only to a formal protest, however, since he immediately told the U.S. ambassador in Mexico to inform the Mexican government that the United States was trusting the Morrow-Calles Agreement would be respected. Daniels met with Cárdenas, Foreign Affairs Minister Eduardo Hay, Deputy Minister Beteta, and Ambassador Castillo Nájera, who was in Mexico at the time, and told the Mexican officials that his country was confident that an agreement would be reached that was fair to both sides.[119] On December 30, Welles, in talks with Castillo Nájera and Eduardo Suárez, asked that the solution of the labor aspect of the controversy be left entirely in the hands of the courts and that the companies not be forced to pay the employees' wages for their work days lost during the walkout.[120] At the end of 1937, despite the fact that the firms by now were claiming that they had already suffered a denial of justice, Welles told the British ambassador in Washington that the United States was making it a point not to exercise any undue pressure on Mexico in the oil conflict and that it had no wish to unnecessarily disrupt the good relations prevailing between the two countries.[121] Nevertheless, certain pressure had already made itself felt: the State Department, which until that time had done no more than stand in readiness, began to make definite moves.

It should be remembered that economically Mexico was in a highly vulnerable position at the time. The 1934–1937 rally had run its course and the situation had begun to deteriorate again.[122] Silver exports to the United States had been worth 30 million dollars in 1937, but the Treasury Department could suspend them at any moment. In December of that year Eduardo Suárez went to Washington to renegotiate the silver agreement with Treasury Secretary Henry Morgenthau and at the same time ask for a loan to help offset the balance-of-payments deficit. Morgenthau turned down Suárez' proposal for a long-term silver purchase agreement and insisted on continuing with the monthly contract, his motive being to provide the State Department with the means to pressure Mexico in the matter of oil. He also took the occasion to point out to Suárez that Mexico's problems would only be solved once a suitable atmosphere for private capital had been assured. Meanwhile Cárdenas sent a message insisting that there was no reason to tie the oil controversy to the silver question.[123] Suárez did not leave Washington empty-handed, however: Morgenthau agreed to an immediate purchase of 35 million ounces of silver. Still, the threat that such transactions could readily be suspended was clear.[124]

Neither the oil firms nor the U.S. government gave any serious thought to the possibility of expropriation. The most radical move expected from Cárdenas, in the event an agreement failed to be reached, was intervention in the industry in the form of appointment of an overseer to make sure that the proper taxes were paid on output and that the wage increase called for by the Federal Board of Conciliation and Arbitration was actually put into effect. It was believed, however, that an understanding would be reached before any such step was taken.[125]

During this phase of the labor conflict, it should be noted, Ambassador Daniels' view of things was a little bit different from that of the companies. In September 1937 he spoke his mind not to the State Department but to

Roosevelt himself. He said that from the beginning the oil firms in Mexico had adopted a rather unscrupulous attitude, purchasing properties by means that were not always very clear and keeping high returns for themselves while paying low wages and, even before Carranza, only a small share in taxes. He felt that they could and should agree to pay a wage increase in the amount being asked: they were doing everything within their power to maintain the status quo, from which they were benefiting far above and beyond what was normal. In effect they were asking Washington for continuation of the old "dollar diplomacy" toward Mexico.[126] Daniels expressed this same point of view in his communications to Secretary of State Hull, although somewhat less vehemently.[127] In a way it can be said that the U.S. ambassador understood and accepted the Cárdenas government's position, in the sense that he thought it was inevitable that the oil industry should render greater profits to the Mexican economy. But at the same time, somewhat contradictorily, he believed up to the very end that the conflict could be settled without a serious crisis between Mexico and his country.[128]

A point of view so flexible and so contrary to that of the oil firms sat poorly with the State Department, where thinking was more in line with the traditional policy of protecting American interests abroad. By the end of 1937 Hull had decided that the conflict had gone beyond the labor-management level and taken on the status of a new confrontation between the companies and the Mexican government. And it was up to him to keep the interests of his fellow citizens from being affected. He had little sympathy for the Mexican position; as he saw it, the wages paid by the oil industry were already the highest in the country, and this was what the government should take into account, rather than the fact that the firms were capable, as it were, of paying even more. He was less optimistic than the ambassador, and he did not rule out the possibility of an expropriation or some other major interference in the industry's operations. In such case the United States would respond simply by demanding adequate, effective, and immediate compensation—which Mexico was unable to give. He did not feel that the time was yet at hand to use diplomatic intervention as the companies were asking; all internal legal recourses should be exhausted first.[129]

As it has been seen, this strict stand did not prevent Hull from taking advantage of the economic crisis at the end of 1937, provoked in part by the oil companies themselves, to try to force Cárdenas to give up on his attempts to change the industry's status quo. Neither Daniels nor Treasury Secretary Morgenthau had been in favor of using silver policy to put pressure on the Mexican government. They were afraid, among other things, that the resulting economic difficulties might oblige Cárdenas to turn to the fascist powers for support. Likewise, they were against putting the American mining firms (which controlled practically all the silver production in Mexico) at a disadvantage simply in order to help out the oil companies. This difference of opinion led to a compromise: Washington continued to buy Mexican silver, but through contracts that had to be renewed monthly—which could serve as a means of forcing Mexico, when the time came, to accept a reasonable arrangement with the oil firms.[130]

The Last Efforts to Reach an Understanding

In Cárdenas' 1938 New Year's message to the nation he announced that the Mexican government, although it had nothing against foreign capital, could not stand by and let it continue in the privileged position it had been enjoying so far.[131] Shortly afterward the APPM brought down a man from New York, Thomas Armstrong, to try to reach a compromise with Mexican officials. At the same time the heads of the big American firms called on the U.S. embassy and urged moderation with Cárdenas, since they were afraid that by now he wanted nothing less than to take over the whole industry.[132] Daniels refused to believe that Mexico was prepared to go that far.[133] As for the State Department, according to reports by the British ambassador in Washington, it had decided to remain on the sidelines and not make any formal representation: Mexico was acting "within the law."[134]

There was considerable tension in the air by the time the talks between Armstrong and Cárdenas got under way. The Mexican president's patience was being tried to the limit by the economic pressure that the firms were exerting through their bank withdrawals and periodic suspensions of sales. In a speech before the CTM he had denounced the companies' maneuvers and said that his government would abide by the courts' decision in the labor dispute regardless of what it might be.[135] The Armstrong-Cárdenas talks were fruitless. The oil magnate maintained that the industry's profits in 1937 had been only 19 million pesos and that the companies were not in any condition to increase wages by the amount indicated in the official study, which was based on figures that were totally unreal.[136] According to a memorandum from Daniels, at one point Armstrong had conceded to raise the sum to 22 million pesos, but Mexico held firm on its initial stand. In the face of this impasse, Cárdenas bowed out and referred Armstrong to his subordinates. Negotiations at this lower level were never undertaken[137] —even though Labor Minister Morones pointed out threateningly that if a solution was not reached Cárdenas would not hesitate to take over the industry.[138] At the end of February Deputy Foreign Minister Beteta suggested that it would be desirable for Armstrong to come back to Mexico and resume his talks with Cárdenas. If the companies would agree to pay 26 million pesos, Mexico was prepared to concede other points in the controversy.[139] Armstrong did not return, however. The firms told Daniels that they would definitely not reopen negotiations or pay the 26 million pesos.[140] In view of this stalemate, there was no alternative but to go ahead with a court ruling on the case the companies had filed. On March 1 the Supreme Court gave its verdict: an injunction could not be considered; the firms were given seven days to comply with the law. This left them virtually no way out: as private parties they could hardly challenge an unappealable court ruling. The very essence of the power of the state was involved.[141]

Contacts between the two sides were immediately renewed. On March 3 the companies' representatives met with Cárdenas and his ministers of treasury and labor.[142] Ambassador Daniels took an active part, serving as mediator between the oil industry and the Mexican government. He asked the firms to consider paying the 26-million-peso increase in order to avoid a rupture with Mexico. He thought that perhaps the British, who had more to lose, might be prepared to accept the terms of the board's decision and get the Americans to follow their example.[143] On this point he turned out to have indeed judged the situation quite well. On March 6 a second meeting was held, with Cárdenas, the oilmen, and other Mexican officials, but still no solution was reached. However, the representative of El Aguila saw Beteta the following day and agreed to an increase of 22 million pesos plus an additional investment of 4 million pesos in projects for the workers' benefit, such as housing, hospitals, and the like. The Englishman promised to obtain the concurrence of the Americans, and Beteta, that of his government.[144] Mexico turned the idea down, claiming that the 4 million pesos was really nothing but an extension of the firms' own investments.[145] At a third meeting, on March 8, the president insisted that in no case would more than 26 million pesos be paid. He added, however—and this was a new commitment on Mexico's part—that the board's decision would be put into effect in such a way as to ensure that no further difficulties were caused between the firms and their workers. Apparently this offer took care of another problem: that of the nonunion staff. But the companies did not budge.[146] The next day they told Daniels that they would rather lose their interests in Mexico than give in to the government's demands.[147] Meanwhile on March 8 the First District Court in Mexico City extended the effective date of the Supreme Court's ruling to March 12, stipulating that it would be decided at that time whether or not to suspend it indefinitely. In this way the pressure was lifted temporarily so that negotiations could continue.

Also on March 8, after the interview with the oil representatives was over, Cárdenas called in his cabinet ministers to discuss the problem with them. Opinions differed, but it was agreed to draw up an emergency scheme that could be put into effect in the event the companies should halt their activities. After the meeting, in view of the lack of unanimity among his ministers, Cárdenas took the ultimate decision alone: if necessary, the oil industry would be expropriated. He made the following entry in his diary that evening:

> Today Mexico has its great opportunity to shake off the political and economic yoke that the oil companies have placed upon us while exploiting one of our most important resources for their own benefit and holding back the program of social reform set forth in the Constitution.

The "opportunity" to which Cárdenas referred was created by both domestic and international factors. It is interesting to see how he regarded this special set of favorable circumstances:

> Various administrations since the Revolution have attempted to do something about the subsoil concessions being enjoyed by foreign firms, but up until now domestic problems and international pressure have mitigated against this effort. Today, however, the circumstances are different: there are no internal struggles going on, and a new world

war is about to begin. It is a good time to see if England and the United States, which talk so much about democracy and respect for the sovereignty of other countries, will in fact stand up to their spoken convictions when Mexico exercises its rights. The government over which I preside, knowing that it has the support of the people, will carry out the responsibility that is incumbent upon it in this hour.[148]

The next day a message signed by Deputy Foreign Affairs Minister Beteta informed the Mexican missions abroad that there were only two possible ways to solve the oil problem: either by appointing an inspector in each of the different companies to watch over the workers' interests, or else by voiding all contracts and proceeding with expropriation. A marked preference for the latter alternative could be felt in the message. "If this should be the solution," it went on to say, referring to a national takeover, "certain economic difficulties, and perhaps some international protests, are likely to follow, but the government is confident that its efforts will be rewarded with success and it considers that this is a key opportunity to fulfill one of the fundamental postulates of the Revolution—namely, that Mexico's natural resources should be utilized in the nation's behalf."[149]

On March 10, after visiting a sugar-cane refinery in the state of Morelos, Cárdenas discussed the oil problem once again with General Múgica, who had been advocating a hard line with respect to the companies right along. They both agreed that the approaching world conflict would keep the United States and England from attacking Mexico in the event of expropriation. Cárdenas then asked him to draft a statement to the Mexican people announcing nationalization of the oil industry.[150] Two days later the First District Court decided not to postpone the effective date of the court's ruling against the companies any longer.

In reaching the decision to take over the oil industry, Cárdenas and his advisers had assumed that international pressure against the move would not be great. As late as March 9 the U.S. and British envoys had limited themselves to expressing their concern in an amicable manner and voicing the hope that a solution would be found.[151] The fact is—as it was to be admitted later—that the American embassy did not really expect Cárdenas to carry through with his threat, especially in view of the country's precarious economic situation.[152] As of March 15 Roosevelt was still planning a state visit to Mexico.[153] On the eve of the expropriation there had been widespread rumors that the workers—not the government—intended to take over the mining, oil, and electric power industries, and the U.S. consulate wrote them off as unduly pessimistic.[154] Actually, the embassy had been caught off guard, since in the past it had always had advance knowledge of the Mexican government's important decisions in regard to the oil problem. Cárdenas' calculations, on the other hand, were basically realistic and proved to be valid, although they might be characterized as somewhat optimistic in view of the diplomatic and economic pressures that were exerted on Mexico during the years that followed. The political and above all the economic difficulties that were to stem from the decision were not inconsiderable.

Once the suspension of the Supreme Court decision was halted, events began to snowball. On March 15 the Federal Board of Conciliation and Arbitration informed the oil companies that they had to comply with the terms of the decision on that same day by five o'clock in the afternoon. The firms refused. The following day, at the request of the STPRM, they were declared to be "in rebellion." Meanwhile their negotiations with Cárdenas continued. On March 16, according to Daniels, they finally conceded to the 26-million-peso wage increase. However, it was still impossible to agree on the administrative clauses.[155] Technically the companies were on the wrong side of the law, but Cárdenas postponed his final decision one day more. On March 18 he met with the oilmen once again, but the same thing happened: differences over the administrative points kept an accord from being reached.[156] That night Cárdenas called one last cabinet meeting and informed his ministers that he had decided to proceed with the takeover. He said to Foreign Affairs Minister Hay that it was preferable to destroy the oil fields than to let the industry go on being the obstacle to national development it had been up until then.[157] At 9:45 P.M. the expropriation act was signed, and at 10:00 P.M. the president announced his decision to the nation in a radio broadcast from the Yellow Room of the presidential palace.

Nationalization of the Oil Industry

Mexico's act in taking over the properties of sixteen oil companies[158] was in reality more of a nationalization than an expropriation. That is to say, it was not individualized or directed at any particular firm; rather, it was a broad measure designed to bring about a basic change in the country's economic structure through takeover by the state, which is the outstanding characteristic of nationalization.[159] In his radio address to the nation Cárdenas said that this bold step had had to be taken in order to keep the decisions of the highest Mexican courts from being rendered meaningless by a simple declaration of insolvency (referring to the companies' claim that they were unable to pay the wage increase). The conflict, Cárdenas added, had threatened the national interest both politically and economically. If he had not gone ahead with nationalization, Mexican sovereignty would have continued indefinitely to be at the mercy of foreign capital.[160] The decision caused great commotion both in Mexico and abroad. Surprise was followed by jubilation, doubt, fear, or rage, depending on the case.[161]

The expropriation decree referred only to the companies' surface properties. The petroleum in the subsoil was considered to have belonged to the nation all along. As a result, the debate over the application of paragraph iv was to flare up again in full force. The companies felt that the commitments in the Bucareli and Morrow-Calles agreements had been broken, and this claim was to be the main issue in the last bitter round of the controversy—namely, the discussion over the amount of compensation that the companies should receive. From the outset the firms, backed in a sense by the State Department, demanded indemnization for the subsoil deposits, which they regarded as their absolute property. Unofficially they announced that on March 18 the Mexican government had contracted a debt with them ranging between 500 and 600 million dollars.[162]

The firms maintained that the takeover on March 18, 1938, was the culmination of a plan mounted by the Cárdenas administration years earlier—in 1936, to be exact—back when the United States and the Latin American countries had signed the nonintervention protocol at the Inter-American Conference for the Maintenance of Peace in Buenos Aires.[163] However, as the story is pieced together of how the decision was reached—and of the subsequent shortage of technical personnel and innumerable other problems—it becomes clear that the Mexican government had not seriously considered the possibility of expropriating the vast and complex oil establishment before the beginning of 1938. The State Department, for its part, thought that the decision was the result of pressure exerted by Lombardo Toledano and the CTM.[164] Daniels in turn believed that the main factor behind the move was Mexico's fear that the mining and oil industries were going to join forces to paralyze the economy.[165] All this speculation subsided, however, with the passing of time. Although it cannot be said that there was a Cárdenas "plan" conceived and set in motion long before the takeover, neither can the expropriation be considered a mere accident. It was the culmination of the Revolutionary governments' more or less determined resolve down through the years to change the colonial structure of an industry that was vital to the Mexican economy. "Now," wrote Cárdenas on March 19, "the nation will at last be able to use the oil industry to get a fair share of its returns and develop its economy on a broad scale." He went on to say, "If the people can muster the determination and the little bit of sacrifice needed to stand up to the attacks of the interests affected, Mexico will come out on top."[166] With an understandable sense of satisfaction and optimism, he made ready to defend a measure that Carranza, Obregón, and Calles had all considered impossible.

As it has already been seen, the Mexican move took Washington completely by surprise. Daniels, in responding to a U.S. Congressional resolution in 1939, said that he had had no advance warning whatsoever of the expropriation decree. Nor did the firms themselves ever tell him officially that they were expecting a takeover.[167] On the eve of March 18 Thomas Armstrong of the APPM had boasted to the Mexican ambassador in Washington: "Cárdenas wouldn't dare expropriate us," adding that the most serious thing that might happen was a temporary embargo.[168] He saw no way that Mexico could administer such a vast industrial complex.

The oil companies' and the U.S. government's conviction that Mexico would not go so far as to nationalize the oil industry would seem to have been based more on wishful thinking than on the facts at hand, since there had been a number of signs indicating that this was quite a real possibility. For example, when the firms filed for an injunction against the ruling of the Federal Board of Conciliation and Arbitration, one of the Supreme Court justices, Xavier Icaza, stated that in his opinion the matter had already gone beyond any strictly legal considerations: if Mexico gave in to the oil interests on this occasion its sovereignty would be compromised once and for all.[169] On February 22 Lombardo Toledano declared in the CTM general assembly that if the firms lost their case in court they would have no alternative but to turn everything over to the state and the workers. Still more important were Cárdenas' own words to a group of senators: "We have a great opportunity before us to put the country in a position of real political and economic independence vis-à-vis the constant intervention in our affairs that has prevailed with the oil firms."[170] In the first days of March Icaza and Lombardo Toledano again pointed out publicly that the companies' intransigence would only hasten the day when the industry was entirely in Mexican hands.[171] And while the expropriation of the large landholdings and plantations in La Laguna and Yucatán was nothing compared with the magnitude of a similar action in the oil industry, still it showed that the Cárdenas government was indeed prepared to invoke the 1936 law when there was no other solution. Through all this the Americans had failed to sense the changes in the international climate during the 1930's that now made it impossible to use the same open pressure tactics as in the past.

It is also conceivable that the U.S. embassy and the local oilmen had heard about the opposition to the move among some of Cárdenas' close advisers and were confident that their view would prevail. Their arguments had considerable weight: expropriation would place Mexico in competition with one of the most powerful international consortia in the world; as a result, the market for Mexican oil would disappear and the flight of capital would be worse than ever. Moreover, the possibility that the United States would react with armed violence, though not very likely, still could not be entirely ruled out.[172]

Thus the decision of 1938 was the culmination of a long effort which had never really been abandoned.[173] When Cárdenas finally decided to enforce Article 27, he went about it differently from the way his predecessors had —namely, through Article 123. His approach to the oil conflict was consistent with a policy that called for fulfillment to the letter of the principles set forth in the Constitution of 1917. The situation in the United States at the time was a decisive factor. The Good Neighbor policy and all the international instruments that were being signed in an effort to settle differences peacefully within the inter-American system—an outgrowth of U.S. reaction to the Depression—gave Mexico relative assurance for the first time that the "Colossus of the North" would not dare to use force to defend the oil companies' interests.

Expropriation implied a commitment for which the country was not yet entirely ready. If the undertaking failed, the whole Revolutionary economic system would be endangered. Cárdenas felt the risk was worth it as long as it meant putting an end to the contradiction existing between the behavior of certain sectors of international capital and what the Revolutionary governments regarded as basic principles of national sovereignty. It was not an easy course to follow: Mexico would have to face the hostility not only of Washington but also of a vastly powerful group of multinational enterprises that controlled more than 90 per cent of the world's oil production and hence the market abroad, the means of transportation, the sources of equipment, and the technology needed to keep the industry going. The struggle was to be relatively brief but intense, and its effects were to range far beyond the mere confines of the oil sector.

Chapter 9

From Nationalization to World War II

Mexico's decision to expropriate the foreign oil companies has been said to be the boldest one taken, from the international standpoint, since the beginning of the Revolution.[1] The support that Cárdenas won from it had few precedents in the country's modern history. While it is true that the jubilant demonstrations both immediately after March 18 and in subsequent years were partly organized by the government, still they exceeded all expectations and swelled into one great massive display of united acclaim, spanning the political spectrum and bringing together such divergent sectors as business groups and the hierarchy of the Church. A rapprochement between the Church and the Revolutionary governments had been brewing since before the end of the Calles administration, and the clergy took advantage of the expropriation climate to secure its reconciliation with the state. Collections were taken up in the streets to raise money to pay the companies' indemnization and, although the proceeds far from met the purpose, they were in any case impressive manifestations of the people's enthusiasm.[2] This almost unanimous approval of Cárdenas' course of action did not go unnoticed by the U.S. embassy. On more than one occasion Ambassador Daniels reported to Roosevelt, Secretary of State Hull, and others that public support of the national takeover was formidable: Cárdenas' position was more solid than ever and no power under the sun could make him turn back now. In Daniels' opinion, only a severe economic crisis that would further depress the people's standard of living, now already low, could threaten the government's stability.[3] Daniels' view was backed by the consul general in Mexico City.[4] The State Department took these evaluations to be correct and never doubted that Cárdenas had widespread support in his decision to nationalize the oil industry.[5]

The takeover was a fundamental step toward consolidation of the nationalist spirit that had given rise to the Revolution of 1910. It was, so to speak, "the historic moment in which the Nation's sense of self-worth was reborn."[6] Nationalization was interpreted by a broad sector of the people as a shaking off once and for all of the imperialist shackles that had held Mexico back for so long and prevented the nation from developing and relying on its own strength and ability.[7]

The fact is that support of the expropriation was widespread but not unanimous. In some sectors the decision was received with alarm or outright hostility. According to the U.S. consul in Monterrey, only those "who had nothing to lose" were fully in favor of it.[8] Businessmen in general, along with a number of public officials and knowledgeable observers, predicted catastrophe: reprisals on the part of the companies and the United States would force down the value of the peso to the point that there would be no more confidence in it on the world market, paralyze economic activity, and plunge the country into bankruptcy.[9] During the days immediately following the takeover word went around that the United States and Great Britain were thinking of sending troops to Mexico. Cárdenas and his ministers had all they could do to check the rumors. In official speeches a great effort was made to keep the people calm: expropriation, they were assured, would not mean chaos, nor would there be any foreign invasion.[10] Cárdenas was banking not only on the fact that intervention in Mexico would put an end to Roosevelt's new hemispheric policy—at a time when solidarity in the Americas was especially important to the United States—but also on the direct assurances which Under Secretary of State Sumner Welles had given to Ambassador Castillo Nájera on March 25.[11] Although no military action was expected, still the Mexican field commander in the oil region had standing orders to set fire to the wells in the event that foreign forces should try to land at Tampico or Veracruz.[12]

Internally, the greatest opposition to Cárdenas' oil policy came from General Saturnino Cedillo, a strongman from San Luis Potosí and former minister of agriculture who at first had backed Cárdenas in his conflict with Calles but began to drift away as the two men's views on reforms grew further and further apart. He had left his post in Cárdenas' cabinet in August 1937, ostensibly because of a difference of opinion over handling of a student riot at the National School of Agriculture.[13]

Neither the Cárdenas administration nor the Americans disregarded the possibility of a Cedillo revolt.[14] On May 15, a month and a half after the nationalization act, the legislature in San Luis Potosí, spurred by Cedillo and the governor of the state, issued a decree proclaiming that it no longer recognized Lázaro Cárdenas as president of the republic. Among the reasons it invoked to justify this action was the oil takeover, which it considered not only undesirable for the national economy but also, when looked at "in a practical and realistic light, . . . antieconomic, unpolitic, and unpatriotic." The Cedillo rebellion was doomed from the start, however, because it was never able to coordinate with the other foci of resistance against Cárdenas. The general from San Luis Potosí had started his military preparations long before the expropriation—back in 1937, in fact, right after he left the cabinet. In mid-September 1937 the Ministry of War had sounded an alert and gotten a plan ready to deal with his forces—peasants organized in paramilitary fashion—and those elements in the army that were expected to side with him.[15] And indeed it worked: by keeping Cedillo from getting the combat planes and matériel he needed while at the same time deploying large contingents of loyal troops throughout the state,[16] Cárdenas was able to stay the rebellion. Given the appearance of things at the end of October, Washington assumed that the threat had blown over—a state of affairs not entirely to the liking of some of the officials there, who assumed that this meant agrarian reform would be imposed in San Luis Potosí, where Americans owned sizable tracts of land that could be affected.[17] In any case, in Mexico City the Ministry of War continued to keep an eye on Cedillo. In

April 1938, in a speech in honor of Soldiers' Day, Cárdenas issued him a veiled threat when he warned that the army would not hesitate to put down any traitors who might be thinking of acting outside the law.[18]

Seeing that Cedillo was still going ahead with his preparations, Cárdenas decided to take even stronger action. He asked Cedillo to accept a command in Michoacán, but the general turned it down. The president then announced that he personally was going to San Luis Potosí. At that point Cedillo had to decide whether to go ahead in open rebellion or fade out of the political picture forever.[19] He chose the first alternative and took to the mountains with several thousand men—though quite a number of his irregulars failed to follow him. For a number of months his bands waged guerrilla attacks in the hills of San Luis Potosí, as well as Michoacán, Guanajuato, and other nearby states, but they never came to be the serious problem that some had expected.[20] Cárdenas kept the use of force against these groups to a minimum, trying instead for negotiation whenever possible. By the time of his death a few months later, Cedillo was practically alone.[21]

Although to all appearances the San Luis Potosí rebellion, prevented from becoming a military threat, had helped to make Cárdenas' position even stronger, the shadow cast by the Cedillo movement was more serious than it might have seemed at first sight. For some time thereafter it was rumored that Cedillo was only one of several generals in the army who planned to rise up against Cárdenas. Since the end of 1937 the U.S. embassy had been reporting that Cedillo was on good terms with other important conservative military leaders, among them former president Abelardo Rodríguez and General Juan Andreu Almazán in Nuevo León.[22] The State Department estimated that if his movement became strong enough locally he would be joined by Generals Abelardo Rodríguez and Joaquín Amaro (minister of war during the Calles administration, builder of the new Mexican army, and for a while sworn rival of Cedillo).[23] According to information received from the oil companies in April and May, there was a good chance that both these men, as well as General Román Yocupicio (governor of Sonora) would cast their lot with Cedillo,[24] and some talk even suggested that War Minister Manuel Avila Camacho would join them. But there are no hard data to back these rumors, least of all with respect to Avila Camacho's lack of loyalty.

The possibility of a schism within the army similar to the ones that had taken place during the De la Huerta and Escobar rebellions was for a time a real one, although it was never actually imminent. Probably Cárdenas' swift victory over Cedillo (it took only seventy-two hours) discouraged other more cautious military chiefs from following his example. In any case, the president repeated his tactics of before and garrisoned large numbers of loyal troops in Sonora as a warning to Yocupicio. Of less importance but more public notice were Cedillo's contacts with General Nicolás Rodríguez, leader of a fascist-leaning group called the "Gold Shirts." Rodríguez, who was in Texas (closely watched by the U.S. authorities), contented himself in the end simply with conducting propaganda campaigns against Cárdenas.[25]

The Cedillo threat and these other rumors after the oil takeover precipitated a reorganization—which had been being talked about since the year before—of the National Revolutionary Party (PNR). It was now more important than ever to have a solid political front with which to face subversion and promote the Cárdenas reforms.[26] In March 1938 the PNR became the Party of the Mexican Revolution (PRM—Partido de la Revolución Mexicana). Its declaration of principles advocated progressive nationalization of all the large industries in foreign hands as a means of achieving full national independence.[27] As it happened, the anti-Cárdenas forces at work both at home and abroad were to prevent this program from being carried out. Still, the reorganization of the party gave the president increased control over the political situation at what was a critical time. The interaction between its four very different sectors—the military, the peasants, the workers, and the middle-level public servants and office employees—was limited, and their dependence on the chief executive was great. In the event that one of the groups were to take an independent position, the president could quickly neutralize its effects by mobilizing the support of the others.[28]

The new party structure's effectiveness for maintaining discipline and unity among the various factions of the dominating group was soon put to the test—not only by Cedillo but also, not too long after, by a coalition of military groups which banded together to form the so-called Mexican Constitutional Front. Although not going so far as to openly declare themselves against Cárdenas, they mounted a campaign against the CTM and against Vicente Lombardo Toledano in particular. At the head of this movement, which warned that Mexico was taking a strongly leftist course and made veiled criticisms of the administration's oil policy, were generals like Fortunato Zuazua, Francisco Coss, and Ramón F. Iturbe.[29] During 1939 and 1940 the rumors abounded: threatened uprisings were imputed to every source from Calles and Joaquín Amaro at the one extreme to the Communist Party at the other.[30] The situation reached its most difficult point for Cárdenas and the new PRM when General Juan Andreu Almazán decided not to go along with the party's nomination of Avila Camacho and launched his own independent campaign. He succeeded in getting the backing of important military and economic elements in the north and won considerable sympathy among some of the urban sectors as well.[31] His movement reflected the most conservative trends within the governing group. (At the time he had a tremendous personal fortune which he had amassed through public works contracts, not to mention mining and fishing concessions, during his years as minister of communications and in the army.[32] His interest in putting an end to any "socialist" experiment was understandable.) He was a more subtle and hence a more dangerous enemy than Cedillo. Going about his campaign slowly and deliberately, he succeeded in appealing to broad sectors of the population. He created a split within the official party and later was to allege that there had been a fraud in the presidential election in which he was the opposition candidate. In regard to the oil problem, he knew better than to attack nationalization outright, but in his public declarations he pointed out that Mexico needed foreign capital in order to develop, making it clear that he was prepared to scrupulously respect its legitimate rights. The U.S. embassy understood perfectly well that this general-turned-entrepreneur was holding out assurances to the American interests in Mexico and seeking their support.[33] However, Washington refrained from establishing contact with his group.[34]

Faced with the possibility of a united big-business front with the U.S. government and part of his own army joined against him in the midst of a grave economic crisis, Cárdenas had no alternative but to support the candidacy of the other general, who was practically as conservative as Almazán but whom he felt he could try to commit up to a certain point to the administration's program: Manuel Avila Camacho. From the beginning this candidate was well regarded by the American groups with interests in Mexico. They identified him with a program of reconstruction, order, and hard work—that is to say, he was safe.[35]

The presidential campaign for the July 1940 elections began early, precipitated by the crisis of 1938. Within the PRM, factions had already formed by early 1939 to promote the candidacies of Manuel Avila Camacho, Juan Andreu Almazán, Rafael Sánchez Tapia, Román Yocupicio, Francisco Castillo Nájera, Gildardo Magaña, Francisco Múgica, and other less important figures. The contest soon boiled down to three: Avila Camacho, Almazán, and Múgica. The first two represented a marked shift to the right, while Múgica, the weakest politically, stood for continuity of the Cárdenas program. The internal discord within the party led to the resignation of its chairman, Luis Rodríguez, who openly favored Avila Camacho. He was replaced by General Heriberto Jara, a definite Cárdenas man. Still, however, the friction was considerable, and the Almazán group felt that it had enough strength to bolt the party. In January 1939 Avila Camacho, Múgica, and Sánchez Tapia resigned from their official posts in order to devote themselves fully to the election campaign. Cárdenas to all appearances remained neutral. By January Avila Camacho had rounded up the support of the majority in the two houses of Congress, some of the governors, and several peasant groups, whereas Múgica could count on a handful of legislators, a large number of peasant groups, and the Communist Party. Cárdenas' nod would tip the scales, and indeed in February Lombardo Toledano and the CTM, following Cárdenas' advice, gave their endorsement to Avila Camacho, thus eliminating Múgica and all the rest. And so it was that in March 1939, a year after nationalization of the oil industry, the U.S. embassy was able to report to its government that the leftward trend in Mexico had come to an end and that the coming years would see a shift back again toward the right.[36] This analysis was not altered by the fact that Almazán became a strong contender soon afterward, since regardless of the outcome of the election the winner would basically be conservative and pro-American.[37] However, Almazán gave the State Department cause for concern on another account: far to the right of the more reasonable Avila Camacho,[38] he had known Nazi sympathizers among his partisans, whereas Avila Camacho appeared inclined to support the United States unreservedly.[39]

The Mexican political picture became even more complicated at the end of 1939 with the threat of a broad anti–Avila Camacho front outside the PRM made up of Almazán, Amaro, and Sánchez Tapia.[40] In the United

States it was even thought that Cárdenas, under this pressure from the extreme right, might feel obliged to either stand for reelection himself or else put a puppet in the presidency,[41] and that the advantage of Avila Camacho's moderating influence would be lost.

In July 1939 the State Department began to hear rumors of a possible Almazán revolt supported by one or another of the anti-Cárdenas generals mentioned.[42] At the beginning of 1940 the U.S. consul in Monterrey, who was following Almazán's moves closely, suggested that the latter might be plotting a "Franco-type" coup. The U.S. naval attaché confirmed this observation.[43] Even the world press had commented on the situation. A rebellion was considered probable.[44] The minister of government attempted to minimize the rumors and assured Washington that the administration had everything under control. There was no chance of an uprising, although there was, he admitted, some local restlessness.[45] And, indeed, following Avila Camacho's victory at the polls there was talk of an Almazán rebellion in the north—originally to have started on September 16, but, presumably after a meeting with his coconspirators in Los Angeles, postponed until November in the hope of encountering a more favorable climate in the United States after the election that month. The U.S. intelligence services closely followed this group's moves,[46] but the scheme did not get very far. Roosevelt was reelected, and his decision to send Vice President Henry A. Wallace to Avila Camacho's inauguration seemed to be evidence that, for all its differences with Cárdenas, Washington was prepared to support his successor.[47] In November Daniels was able to report that Almazán's armed bands in the north had not made much of an impact and that their operations had been brought to a halt more as a result of negotiations than through the use of force.[48]

Within Mexico the success of the expropriation depended less on neutralizing the opposition than on being able to keep the enormous industrial complex going despite the critical shortage of trained personnel. The country's course of development up to that time had not allowed for the preparation of national technicians who could now step in and run the oil industry. However, the restrictions that had been imposed for some number of years on the entrance of foreign technicians had obliged the companies to train some national staff at least, and these cadres were the key to the successful outcome of nationalization.[49] In the beginning the government had to depend almost entirely on the STPRM to keep the industry supplied with workers. Many occupied the posts abandoned by the foreign technicians: some of them were not up to the task, but others were. It did not take long to see—contrary to the dire predictions of a great number of people, especially those in the foreign colony—that the technical difficulties, countless as they were, would not be the undoing of the recently nationalized industry.[50] The government's dependence on the oil workers' union did cause certain problems, however. The labor leaders came to think that it was they, not the state, who controlled the industry, and before long there were difficulties between the government management and the workers. The STPRM, even though a number of its leaders simultaneously held posts in the General Petroleum Administration, chose to forget the industrial—and to some extent national—crisis brought on by the foreign companies' boycott and demand immediate satisfaction in regard to the various benefits that had been awarded in the 1937 JFCA decision. Their demands were impossible to meet: the newly nationalized industry could not bear the economic burden. The government, after weathering a series of strike threats and acts of sabotage, finally succeeded in imposing its stand.[51]

Attitude Taken by the Affected Parties

In keeping with tradition, the companies' reaction to the national takeover was acted out on various levels, one of them juridical. In this final phase, however, the legal controversy was not as interesting as it had been before. It was concentrated on getting the executive to use the courts to change its position—the first idea that had come to mind after the initial shock of the expropriation. Recalling their earlier experiences, the oilmen thought during the first few months that they might try to pressure Cárdenas into ordering the courts to declare the expropriation decree illegal.[52] At first they kept their representatives stationed in Mexico, paid certain taxes, and continued to explore all possible legal recourse so that they could establish a denial of justice and give greater force to their protests with the State Department and the Mexican government.[53] Their first step, taken in April, was to file for an injunction against the 1936 expropriation law and the decree of March 18, 1938, claiming the unconstitutionality of both the acts themselves and the way in which the Treasury and National Economy ministries had gone about seizing the oil properties without prior compensation.[54] In June the courts upheld the legality of the decree and declared that immediate compensation was not required; Mexico had ten years in which to pay.[55] Within a month the companies' attorneys had appealed.[56] While all this was going on the Supreme Court handed down two decisions, one in May and the other in September, involving the injunctions filed earlier by Huasteca and Tuxpan Petroleum. In them, the retroactivity of the 1918 Carranza decrees was upheld, as was their legality in general. Thus they ran directly counter to the interpretations given by the Mexican courts in the 1920's in the case of Texas Oil, when the decrees were declared illegal precisely because of their retroactive nature. For the first time it was affirmed, and upheld, that paragraph iv did in fact affect the status of concessions granted prior to 1917.[57]

The legal dispute lasted on into 1939. In March of that year the courts handed down another decision against an injunction filed for by the companies. Finally in December 1939 the Supreme Court ruled that both the expropriation law and the decree of March 18, 1938, were legal, pointing out that the next step was to go ahead with an assessment based on the value of surface properties.[58] Thus it had backed the stand taken by Cárdenas in September and October 1938 in denying the firms administrative recourse to appeal the March 18 decree. In the high court's decision, as well as in the subsequent state-of-the-union message to the Congress, it was pointed out that the hydrocarbons in the subsoil had never belonged to the companies; they had merely enjoyed the right to exploit them.[59] The State Department was convinced that Cárdenas had personally dictated the terms of this ruling in order not to leave any legal loophole that might give his successor a chance to undo the steps that had been taken.[60] The next move, taken in 1940, was to declare the companies "in rebellion" for not having cooperated with the assessment.[61] Huasteca appealed this decision, but it lost its suit.[62] As was only natural, the firms accused the Mexican courts of being partial and maintained that their action corresponded to a clear case of justice denied.[63] The State Department, which was closely following the entire proceedings, indeed had had in its hands from the beginning the necessary documentation to claim that justice had been denied—as the companies had been wanting it to do for some time—but it never presented the case officially, having decided to seek a solution to the problem through other, more flexible means.[64]

The expropriation had scarcely been decreed when the word began to go around that an armed move against the Cárdenas government and in support of the affected oil interests was being mounted. Although these rumors, to an extent wishful thinking on the part of administration opponents, were somewhat exaggerated, they were not entirely without basis.[65] In the opinion of Ambassador Daniels, the big investors in Mexico had wanted, if Roosevelt was not prepared to send in troops, at least to see the establishment of a conservative, even fascist, government through a coup d'état. The oilmen told Daniels at the beginning of April that an armed revolt against Cárdenas—a movement that of course would have the sympathy of the foreign business community[66]—would break out in thirty days.[67] Their prediction was partially fulfilled by the Cedillo rebellion, but not with the magnitude or force that they had expected. Since the government in Washington had decided not to encourage any subversive activity, the plot had much less chance for success. The firms by themselves did not dare to go very far in showing their enthusiasm for a change of government in their favor.

Contrary to the claims of the Mexican government, various authors have maintained that the expropriated companies gave no more than moral support to the Cedillo movement. There is no conclusive proof one way or the other, but there would seem to have been more than a casual connection between the San Luis Potosí uprising and the national takeover. Some five or six months earlier the Mexican government had said it had knowledge of certain contacts between El Aguila and the general from San Luis Potosí.[68] Immediately after the expropriation a spokesman for Huasteca informed the U.S. embassy that the chance of the Cárdenas government's falling was not remote.[69] In April a representative of the companies suggested to the State Department that the pressure against Mexico be stepped up, this being the best way to create a suitable climate for a revolt. The idea met with little success in Washington.[70] Talk about possible anti-Cárdenas uprisings continued throughout May and June.[71] When the Cedillo movement finally did break out, the oil firms seemed to be well informed on the nature and capability of the forces involved, which they considered to be a serious threat to the government.[72] Just before this Cárdenas had alluded publicly to the subversive activities of the oil groups, which had also been the subject of a complaint by the Ministry of Foreign Affairs to the State Department.[73] Later the oilmen were to deny roundly that they had supported Cedillo. On the contrary, they insisted, they had urged him not to go through with his plan, since they would inevitably be blamed—as indeed they were—for any kind of trouble occurring at that time.[74] Publicly the Mexican government only charged the oil companies with having given Cedillo six Howard airplanes, which had been captured by the army.[75] It is possible that the Gold Shirts, apparently connected with Cedillo,[76] may have approached the firms for political and economic support, but, if in fact such contacts did take place, they never led to any notable results.[77] The U.S. government's decision not to consider Cárdenas' ouster as a suitable solution to its differences with Mexico sharply reduced the options of those who would oppose the reforms by force, but it did not prevent certain elements in the oil group from keeping in touch with the discontents. In 1939 some U.S. consular reports referred to contacts between the companies and Almazán's men, despite the fact that the latter had already openly declared his intention to stand behind the Cárdenas oil policy.[78] It would appear that before entering into contact with Almazán the oilmen had attempted—unsuccessfully—to come to an agreement with Avila Camacho.[79] In any case, at the end of that year the Mexican government told the U.S. embassy that it had good reason to believe that arms, possibly intended for Amaro, were being brought in on the Pacific coast and that the companies, as well as certain British agents, were not strangers to this activity.[80] In mid-1940 the U.S. Department of Justice learned that Almazán's brother and others in his group had approached the oil firms for economic aid.[81] The Mexican government took the opportunity to remind Washington about Almazán's fascist sympathies and the fact that he had German support.[82] Finally, in 1939 there were intermittent rumors about contacts between the oil firms and spokesmen for former president Calles and General Rafael Sánchez Tapia to discuss the possible financing of anti-Cárdenas activities.[83] In general, it would appear that the companies' efforts to foment an uprising against Cárdenas were sporadic and noncommittal at best in the absence of Washington's support;[84] they appeared to be focused more on taking advantage of, rather than actually stimulating, the internal rivalries within the Mexican leadership.

The oil firms definitely sought to capitalize on still another kind of internal difference to sabotage the recently nationalized industry—namely, the conflict between the government and the STPRM. They wasted no time in getting to the union's leaders and offering them funds in exchange for their opposition to the industry's reorganization. The strike threats and sabotage that occurred during these years were attributed at least in part to agitation by company agents.[85] Although the hoped-for rupture between the PEMEX administration and the oil workers never took place, the labor difficulties were amply exploited by the companies to show that not even the Mexican government itself could meet the terms of the JFCA decision that had led to expropriation.[86] In this point the firms were quite right. The economic crisis into which the industry had fallen as a result of nationalization made it impossible for PEMEX to pay the wages that the workers had failed to receive during the time they were on strike—or for that matter even to pay the famous increase. The workers embarked on a sabotage campaign (hardly discouraged by the companies) which only came to an end in 1941 when the Allied Powers joined Mexico in the task of safeguarding the oil fields.[87]

Unlike the U.S. government, the oil firms never came to accept Mexico's right to take away their properties, above all because Washington refused in principle to discuss the possibility of compensating them for the hydrocarbons that still remained in the subsoil, which they considered to be an integral part of what belonged to them.[88] They went so far as to charge Roosevelt and the State Department with selling them out.[89] They maintained that their properties had been taken not under a general and impersonal law but rather as a punishment for what the government regarded as their "rebellious" attitude. This, they claimed, added to the lack of prompt and adequate payment, made the Mexican action tantamount to confiscation, and the only admissible solution was return of their properties.[90] During the first weeks their propaganda hammered on the fact that Mexico was not in a position to keep the expropriated industry going and that therefore it would be wise both politically and economically to undo what had been done before it was too late, lest the entire country have to pay for the mistake.[91] This insistence on return of the properties as the only acceptable solution was based partly on their fear that the Mexican case would set an example for other Latin American countries where their oil interests were really important.[92] It is well to remember that the Mexican conflict had been preceded by the expropriation of Standard Oil in Bolivia. The two almost simultaneous takeovers, together with the groundswell of public reaction in support of Cárdenas ranging from labor organizations to intellectual circles throughout Latin America,[93] must have given them quite a turn.[94] The American press echoed their concern, pointing out that the Mexican nationalization could well be followed by a takeover of the nitrate industry in Chile or of oil in Argentina, Colombia, or Ecuador.[95]

Indeed, Cárdenas' action was unparalleled in the hemisphere and served as an inspiration to the other countries which over the years were to modify their laws on oil. For the companies the potential risk involved in letting Mexico get away with the expropriation was evident.[96] But while they were genuinely concerned over the precedent that the Mexican move might set for other countries in the hemisphere, it is also true that their emphasis on this point helped to give them one more argument with which to work on the State Department. At the end of 1938 Standard Oil of New Jersey informed Washington that Mexico was attempting to form a bloc with Venezuela and Colombia. Although it did not say outright that Mexico was maneuvering to provoke new expropriations, the inference was clear.[97] Unfortunately for the oil firms, the State Department consulted with its officers in Caracas and Bogotá and decided it was best not to propagate the image of 1927—namely, one of a government willing to undermine order in the hemisphere—which in the long run would be detrimental to U.S. interests.[98]

Reaction of the European Governments

To understand the position taken by the U.S. government in defense of American oil interests it may be well to review, as background, the policies followed by the other powers concerned—namely, Great Britain and the Netherlands.

British Prime Minister Neville Chamberlain gave El Aguila all his support, the government firmly refusing to recognize the legality of the national takeover. Extraofficially, discreetly, and on a friendly basis, its envoy in Mexico, Owen St. Clair O'Malley, had done what he could up to the end to reach a solution.[99] On the eve of the expropriation he had gone to see the minister of foreign affairs and expressed his deep concern over the impasse which the oil controversy had come to. After the takeover, however, the Foreign Office adopted quite a different attitude—virtually a "hard line." The first thing it did was to urge Washington not to let Mexico "get away with it." England was fully aware that only the United States could effectively put pressure on Mexico. In subsequent communications during the month of March a very special appeal was made to the U.S. government to fight for restoration of the status quo ante, and immediate joint diplomatic action against Mexico was proposed. Since the United States was not prepared to take an inflexible stand and claim that a denial of justice had occurred, as the British were asking, Secretary of State Hull turned down the suggestion.[100] However, in view of the strategic considerations (the British deposits in Mexico being the only ones that England could reach without having to cross the Mediterranean), he assured His Majesty's ambassador in Washington that the U.S. government would not allow Mexican oil to be taken by a hostile nation.[101] As in the past, British interests were subordinated to those of the United States—which because of the Good Neighbor policy demanded a more flexible and tolerant approach—while at the same time the former's strategic concerns were taken care of to the extent they could be. Once the positions of the two governments were clear, England launched on a sharp exchange with Mexico, which, though it gained very little of a practical nature, established a precedent of firmness that could later be used to its advantage in other parts of the world where its influence was more direct. By a month after the expropriation British officials and business circles were resigned to the fact that nothing could be done—except for a rebellion or an economic crisis—to get the El Aguila properties back.[102] In April and May 1938 England presented three notes drafted in very severe terms. While they did not deny Mexico's right to expropriate, emphasis was placed on the illegal way in which the takeover had been accomplished, and return of the oil industry to its legitimate owners was demanded as the only acceptable solution under international law. By the time these notes were received Mexico already knew that Washington was not behind the British position and that the two countries had been unable to agree on a joint policy.[103] Accordingly, the Ministry of Foreign Affairs had nothing to lose by replying to them in equally brusque terms, saying that His Majesty's government had no right to protest an action taken against a company that was legally Mexican. In its next communication England complained not very politely about the delay in the last payment on the Mexican reparations debt (for damages incurred by British subjects during the Revolution). This was the last straw: on May 12 Cárdenas consulted with Foreign Affairs Minister Hay and decided to break off ties with England. Shortly afterward the minister of foreign affairs delivered the sum in question to O'Malley, but not without reminding him that his own country still had similar debts pending with the United States from World War I. Mexico withdrew its diplomatic representatives in London, whereupon the Foreign Office did likewise with its personnel in Mexico. For several years relations between the two countries were suspended.[104] At the beginning of 1939 the Ministry of Foreign Affairs received word from its envoy in France that that country was prepared to mediate between Great Britain and Mexico. Mexico accepted the offer, though without much enthusiasm, and only on the condition that England recognize the legality of the nationalization. The French plan was dropped.[105]

The situation with the Netherlands was similar, although this latter country did not use quite such strong language in its notes. Like the United States and Great Britain, Holland had communicated its concern over the oil problem in the days before the takeover. After March 18, Dutch Chargé d'Affaires Mothöfer presented four notes, the last of which was transmitted in October. The most important one, that of July 12, roughly followed the British line: it questioned the legality of the 1936 expropriation law, of the JFCA ruling, and of the expropriation of March 18—and went on to point out that the problem had only two possible solutions, either the return of the properties or immediate compensation. Except for the answer to this July note, in which the points were refuted one by one,[106] Mexico's replies were extremely laconic—just a few lines acknowledging receipt and indicating disagreement with the Dutch position. During the last months of the year the Mexican envoy at The Hague was afraid that relations with the Netherlands would suffer the same fate as those with England, but in the end they did not, and the exchange of notes soon ceased.[107]

Although the Anglo-Dutch interests affected by Mexico in 1938 were much more sizable than the American ones, since at that time they controlled the important Poza Rica beds, their political action in Mexico had to be completely subordinated to what Washington wanted. The burden of the conflict was on U.S. shoulders, even though the interests being defended represented less in actual value than what the Europeans had at stake and were less vital to the American economy and defense. Hence it was that Mexico could afford to ignore the British and Dutch demands and put off a decision on the terms of indemnization until 1947, five years after a settlement had been made with the Americans.

Washington's Reaction

This then was the backdrop against which the situation unfolded with Washington. Cárdenas' decision to expropriate the oil industry produced an acutely irate reaction in the Department of State. Not only were agricultural properties being seized from American citizens, not only were labor protests against the mining and public service industries receiving the Mexican government's blessing, but now the oil controversy was reopening, and in a much more serious and spectacular way than in 1917 or 1925. On March 22, 1938, the companies transmitted a document to Secretary Hull in which they declared that they had been victims of a denial of justice on the part of the Mexican government and asked that the necessary steps be taken to redress the injury.[108] Six days later in a personal meeting with Hull they said they did not care to negotiate with Mexico and that a favorable solution to the problem depended entirely on whatever pressure Washington might be able to exert for prompt and adequate indemnization—or failing this, since the country was not in a position to meet such a demand, immediate return of their properties. Hull listened but did not commit himself.[109] While it is true that, as on previous occasions, the State Department was inclined to identify itself with the companies' position and would normally have pressured Mexico by various means until it succeeded in getting the properties returned, it had to take into account the different positions within the U.S. administration as well as the world situation, all of which meant in the end that it was important to stay on good terms with Latin America.

The nationalization brought out the fact that Ambassador Daniels was indeed a new kind of diplomat—an authentic representative of the New Deal and stout partisan of the Good Neighbor policy. He struggled unceasingly to promote a more up-to-date and enlightened form of capitalism than up to then had been practiced by the oil firms and largely defended by the State Department.[110] He believed that U.S. policy in Mexico had to stop being based on crude nineteenth-century "enclave"-type relations; it was time to change. He saw in the Mexican government's reform program—including the expropriation—a means of providing the masses with greater purchasing power and turning Mexico into a stable neighbor and a good customer of the United States.[111] Improvement of the distribution of wealth was the ideal way to combat the attraction of the fascist and communist doctrines that were threatening Western democratic institutions. While he did think that the expropriation had been a mistake, he felt that basically Cárdenas was right in trying to integrate the wealth from the Mexican subsoil—acquired by the companies by means open to question and exploited without regard for local needs—into the national economy. As he saw it, the 1938 crisis was the end result of the firms' systematic refusal to review the basic suppositions on which they had built up the industry back in the beginning of the century.[112]

Daniels tried to make both Roosevelt and the State Department see that it was virtually impossible for Cárdenas to reverse his decision.[113] He was convinced it would be wrong for the United States to adopt the "hard line" that the affected parties were calling for or to demand immediate compensation, which was impossible in view of the status of the Mexican treasury.[114] In the midst of a grave world crisis the "Good Neighbor" should be above such matters; the situation with Mexico would be the "trial by fire" for the new inter-American solidarity.[115] He felt, in the first place, that the State Department should moderate both the form and the content of its protests: the more Cárdenas was pushed back against the wall the more inflexible he would become.[116] In the second place, he thought the companies should be urged to come to an agreement with the Mexican government as soon as possible because the situation was undermining U.S. foreign policy throughout the world.[117]

Daniels' conciliatory position was reflected both in his statements to the press and in his reports to the State Department. The career diplomats in the embassy and in Washington were very much against his attitude, which they were afraid could be interpreted as acceptance of Mexico's action.[118] During the three and a half years following the takeover Daniels sought to act more as an intermediary or liaison between the two sides than as a representative of the interests affected. In his anxiousness to ward off a rupture he tried everything possible, even urging Roosevelt to come and pay a state visit, and took unprecedented decisions upon himself—such as agreeing, without Hull's knowledge, to consider that Mexico had not received the State Department's first note of protest.[119] Despite the problems that Cárdenas' reform program caused for relations between the two countries, Daniels continued to recognize its importance.[120] Because of this viewpoint, both the companies and the U.S. Congress were to accuse him of negligence in the oil conflict and even of complicity with the Mexicans.[121]

Just the opposite of Daniels' attitude was that adopted by a U.S. agency which, though it had little influence on the oil problem, does not fail to be of some interest—namely, the Federal Bureau of Investigation, headed since 1924 by J. Edgar Hoover. The companies' thesis that the takeover was the work of communists in the Mexican government[122] was fully backed by the FBI, which maintained that the Cárdenas government was not only seriously "tainted" by communism but also dangerously infiltrated by Nazi agents, both of which elements had great freedom of action. This arm of the Justice Department, which watched over the activities of these two groups in Mexico, believed that Cárdenas had systematically deceived Daniels concerning the true nature of Nazi and communist activities in Mexico and that his real sympathies were with these two groups.[123] The FBI's assessment of the Cárdenas regime was so extravagant that even the officials in the State Department, little given to sympathize with Cárdenas, agreed that Hoover had probably overstated the case and dismissed his accusation.[124]

Roosevelt's stand in regard to the expropriation seems to have been somewhere midway between that of Daniels and the State Department's. For after all the purpose of the New Deal, in the final analysis, was to help American private enterprise get reestablished in a world emerging from the Depression of 1929. This approach, a product of classical liberalism, called for putting an end to some of the more negative and abusive practices of big business. The Cárdenas program, however, was not exactly what had been in mind. Roosevelt received constant petitions from Daniels urging him not to break off relations. Mexico could not compensate the companies in the form they were insisting on, but neither could it turn back without putting national stability at stake. The Mexican regime firmly supported Roosevelt's international policy, Daniels said. It was indispensable to keep up Latin America's confidence in the United States and not fall back into the old imperialist practices.[125] The ambassador went on to tell his president that the State Department was reluctant to abandon the "big stick" in favor of the Good Neighbor policy.[126] His advice seems to have been heeded, but only up to a point, since there were forces pulling in the opposite direction that had to be taken into account as well.

Even before the oil crisis peaked, when the agricultural lands were expropriated in 1936, Roosevelt had not only shown himself averse to continuing his predecessors' rigid defense of the American landholders but had even seemed for a while to be prepared to let them be treated on the same basis as nationals.[127] Although in the end Mexico did compensate the American ranchers, the amount was probably less than the real value of the land expropriated.

When the nationalization took place Roosevelt immediately recognized Mexico's right to take the action, but he refused to agree to payment of the indemnization in the form prescribed by Mexican law—that is, over a period of ten years.[128] Also, contrary to the companies' wishes, he agreed that indemnization, although it should be immediate, need only take into account the capital invested less depreciation—that is to say, it did not have to include "prospective profits," which was another way of referring to the hydrocarbons in the subsoil.[129] (Still, as it turned out, when a solution was finally reached in 1942, Mexico did have to make partial compensation for the subsoil reserves.) Generally speaking, Roosevelt did not appear to be willing to sacrifice inter-American unity on the eve of a world conflict for the return of the companies' property. On the other hand, however, he was not opposed to a policy of systematic economic and diplomatic pressure by the State Department to get the firms back into Mexico.

The State Department, under Hull's stewardship, was determined to follow a "hard line" with Cárdenas, within the bounds set by Roosevelt. The idea of resorting to force was rejected from the outset. An anti-Cárdenas coup was also out of the question, since it could only too easily open the way for the fascists.[130] Still the State Department felt that something had to be done to impose the companies' rights.[131] Hull is reported to have told Treasury Secretary Morgenthau in private that he was determined to teach "those communists" in the Mexican government to respect international law[132] (Hoover not being the only one to see a communist hand in the matter). On receiving word of the national takeover, the department quickly drew up a three-point plan: a strong protest would be lodged not against the expropriation itself but over failure to make immediate compensation; the purchase of Mexican silver would be suspended; and the ambassador would be called to Washington for consultation.[133] Later another point was added: the department would support the firms' boycott by discouraging potential purchasers of Mexican oil, seeing that it was not used by U.S.

government agencies, and keeping Mexico from getting any loans in the United States.[134]

The four phases of the plan met with varying success. Daniels' scheduled trip to Washington in March 1938, a move that might have been regarded as a prelude to a diplomatic breakoff, did not take place. The ambassador, interfering with the State Department's plans, delayed his departure until it no longer would have any effect.[135] The economic protests and sanctions, on the other hand, were put into effect right away and had a serious impact. Immediately after the expropriation Daniels was ordered to protest it verbally in the strongest terms, while also exploring the possibility of having the measure annulled.[136] At the same time, on March 21 Under Secretary of State Sumner Welles met with Ambassador Castillo Nájera in Washington and warned that the political line being taken by Cárdenas was suicidal. He could not continue to seize the property of foreigners in Mexico without giving them suitable compensation. The step to expropriate had been taken at a time, Welles pointed out, when it was not needed: the firms had already agreed to pay the wage increase, the U.S. government had been prepared to continue its purchases of silver, and the annoying matter of the claims which for so long had plagued relations between the two countries was on the point of finally being solved. He hinted to Castillo Nájera that there was still time to reverse the decision and grant an injunction to the companies when they appealed to the courts. The Mexican ambassador, according to Welles' report, appeared to agree that the expropriation ought to be rescinded and that an overall change in the Cárdenas policy should be made, since otherwise the government could not remain in power much longer.[137] Despite Castillo Nájera's encouraging indications, Cárdenas showed no intention to retract, and four days later the ambassador had to inform Welles that the expropriation was final and ask him to try to persuade the firms to enter in contact with the Mexican government and negotiate the indemnization.[138] What Daniels had been saying right along was confirmed: namely, that this time it was highly unlikely Mexico would go back on its decision.[139] As the next step, Secretary of State Hull, following the policy outlined by Roosevelt, publicly declared that the United States government recognized Mexico's right to take the companies' properties—much to the firms', and to Great Britain's, displeasure[140]—but not without going on to condition this recognition on prompt, effective, and adequate indemnization, knowing full well that the country's economic plight made such a thing impossible. Thus, without challenging Mexico's sovereign rights, Washington placed itself in a very convenient position to effectively but not openly pressure Cárdenas into giving the companies' property back to them. It should be stressed that the firms had wanted even greater support from the State Department. They were asking not only for Mexico to give them immediate and adequate compensation but also for State to refuse to recognize the legality of the takeover and protest the sale of oil from the expropriated fields.[141] The American press demanded restitution.[142]

Unlike the exchange during the Calles administration, the official correspondence between the State Department and Mexico this time was not voluminous. Generally speaking, the atmosphere was less tense. The informal negotiations, however, took on much greater importance. The first U.S. note of protest was transmitted on March 26. Its delivery was preceded by talks by Daniels with Cárdenas and Deputy Foreign Minister Beteta, conducted at Hull's request. Daniels stated that the expropriation had come as an unpleasant surprise to the U.S. government and that the consequences of this action could be disastrous for Mexico and would undoubtedly affect its economic relations with the United States. He went on to say, however, that he was confident a prompt and satisfactory solution would be found. Beteta and Cárdenas replied that Mexico would not shrink from its obligations and was prepared to open talks with the firms immediately so as to reach an agreement on the amount of compensation and the form it was to take. They stressed that the measure had not been taken on the spur of the moment—that the long-range interests of the country were being taken into consideration and that in no circumstances would the decision be reversed. With respect to the international situation, since Mexico had no wish to undermine the United States' position in the impending world conflict, it was prepared to restrict the sale of its oil to the democratic countries and turn down any offers received from Germany or Japan.[143]

Thus the positions of the two sides were clear: The United States, specifically the State Department, requested a reversal of the decision on pain of serious economic pressure. Mexico refused and threatened to sell its oil to the United States' enemies if any such sanctions were applied. Before long the two respective courses of action were to unfold, and the conflict that ensued was to last until 1942, when a satisfactory formula was finally found. The U.S. note of March 26 did not limit itself to the oil question: it protested Mexico's entire policy in relation to the foreign sector. The United States, though recognizing that the Cárdenas government was unable to compensate the American interests in the form it considered most desirable, felt that at least international law should be respected. It concluded by asking how Mexico planned to indemnify the oil companies.[144] (This document coincided with a report filed by the Mexican ambassador in which he warned that Washington's attitude toward Mexico was deteriorating rapidly and seriously.)[145] The U.S. note, written in severe tones, was to meet with a strange fate: on its being presented to Cárdenas, the Mexican president asked that it be withdrawn, since it made no reference to the verbal assurances he had given the ambassador some days earlier that the firms would indeed be properly compensated. Hull had authorized Daniels to keep the delivery of the document secret, but Daniels went even further and agreed, without prior consultation with Washington, to consider that the note was not received. As he explained later to Hull, he made this decision bearing in mind that the tone of the communication would have obliged Mexico to respond in like manner, and this would have endangered all chances of reaching a satisfactory agreement.[146] The U.S. press learned of the note's existence and published a summary of its contents. Meanwhile, Daniels' action kept Mexico from having to answer it. A brief communiqué delivered to Daniels on March 31 (moments after the American ambassador presented Cárdenas with the document that was "not received") merely expressed appreciation of the U.S. government's understanding attitude with respect to the problem and reiterated Mexico's intention to compensate the expropriated firms—it being only a matter of waiting for the firms' representatives to come and begin negotiations.[147] As was to be expected, the companies were furious at Daniels, and they asked Hull to rectify his error by making the note public. Otherwise, they claimed, Cárdenas would be free to give the impression that his action had had the endorsement of the U.S. government.[148] The State Department did not go along with this request, but at the same time neither was it satisfied with the Mexican reply, and Castillo Nájera was so informed. Washington did not care so much about Mexico's assurances that it would indemnify the firms as it did about having the manner of payment clearly specified.[149] At the beginning of May Under Secretary of State Sumner Welles sent a memorandum to the Mexican ambassador urging his government to come forward with a concrete plan for compensation.[150] Some two months later Cárdenas took advantage of the ambiguous status of the famous "undelivered" note, precisely as the companies predicted he would, and publicly denied that the United States had officially protested the expropriation.[151] Hull, who considered that the document contained the bases of the U.S. position in the conflict, then insisted that it be formally accepted by Mexico. In order to do this, however, he had to agree that officially it had never been made public,[152] which profoundly incensed the firms because they had already referred to it on various occasions.[153] This belated solution did not keep the Cárdenas government from insisting up to the last minute, much to the State Department's annoyance, that the differences with Washington were minimal.[154]

The exchange of notes continued, but the central points did not vary. The ineffectiveness of the official correspondence was evident from the beginning, and the real efforts were concentrated on the informal negotiations. From time to time the United States tried to use the formal correspondence as a means of putting on pressure, but Mexico paid little attention and even went ahead, in the midst of the American protests, and expropriated some of the secondary oil properties that had not been included in the original decree of March 18.[155]

Throughout the exchange of notes over the period from March 26, 1938, to April 3, 1940, the U.S. tone was so strong that at times it nearly provoked a diplomatic breakoff.[156] The correspondence was not limited to the oil problem: it also referred to the other points of contention between the two countries—namely, the takeover of agricultural lands and the damages caused to Americans in the course of the Revolution. But everyone knew that the oil problem was at the bottom of all the discussions. Already on other occasions before the agrarian question had been used as a means of adding pressure in the oil matter.[157] (The sum claimed for the expropriated agricultural lands was sizable: 30 million dollars. Demands for prompt compensation were reiterated throughout the period from 1934 to 1940. An agreement was reached in 1941, but for an amount smaller than had been claimed.)[158] The bankers who held Mexican foreign debt bonds also tried to involve their problem in the settlement of the oil question, but they were not as successful.[159]

The State Department stressed two main points in its notes: first, Mexico had apparently failed to recognize the fact that the Good Neighbor policy was not unilateral; and, second, in seizing the oil and agricultural properties of American citizens when it did not have the means with which to make due compensation, it had undertaken to exercise a right without meeting the necessary conditions to assure that it was legally entitled to do so. International law required prompt, effective, and adequate payment, Washington said, in order for an expropriation to be accepted and not regarded as a confiscation (the traditional U.S. position). In order to comply fully with this, Mexico would once again have to subordinate its domestic needs to international capital; it would even have to write off the agrarian reform. Such a requirement in effect denies economically weak countries the right to expropriation.[160] The Mexican government countered by saying that compensation could not be demanded when the companies had systematically refused to discuss the value of the lands expropriated. But what was even more important, Mexico did not recognize the universal rule of law to which the U.S. notes referred—one that apparently obliged a country to make immediate compensation to all parties affected by a general and impersonal nationalization. (It took advantage of the occasion to call attention to certain expropriations by the U.S. government for which indemnization had never been made.) Finally, Mexico was to refuse to submit the conflict to arbitration, since it considered that there were still other courses open for arriving at a solution and it did not want to sign any agreement under which it would be obliged to act against its own national laws. The truth was that the Cárdenas government could not run the risk of a decision that would call for immediate payment for what had been expropriated, since it did not have sufficient funds with which to meet such terms.[161] Even in the last note—the one that Mexico sent to Washington on May 1, 1940—the positions of the two sides remained unchanged. The next document that was made known was a joint communiqué dated November 19, 1941—the General United States–Mexico Agreement. It announced the settlement of the agrarian claims and declared that a definitive solution to the oil conflict would be sought through a direct accord between the two governments based on an assessment of the nationalized properties by a joint commission of experts. This solution was in fact closer to the Mexican position than to that of the United States, since the payment was not to be made immediately but rather over a period of several years and formally no account was taken—although in reality it was—of the value of the hydrocarbons in the subsoil.[162] Thus, while up to the end in the official diplomatic notes neither side gave in on what were regarded as fundamental principles, in actual practice both of them did modify their respective initial stands.

The Effect of the World Situation

It has been seen already that in 1938 the oil companies had less influence over Washington's Mexican policy than they had ever had before.[163] This was not so much because Secretary of State Hull and his advisors were less disposed to defend the status quo than his predecessors Kellogg and Hughes had been, as it was that the crises in Europe and Asia were obliging the government to use restraint. The last thing they wanted was to jeopardize the stability of the Mexican administration or sell out their new inter-American policy. An open intervention would have been against the principles of solidarity and nonintervention recently subscribed to in inter-American conferences. A covert one was likewise inadvisable: as it has been said, the fall of Cárdenas could easily open the way for the fascists to come into power, and this would represent a greater danger to the United States than the success of the oil expropriation. Hence, if this time the companies did not find in Washington all the backing to which they were accustomed, it was in large measure because the international situation had relegated their interests to second place. Of course the firms did not fail to consistently point out the connection between their own interest and that of the U.S. government. When the expropriation took place Standard Oil not only predicted that it would set off a wave of takeovers elsewhere in Latin America but also called attention to the fact that the special quality of the Mexican oil made it indispensable for certain uses in the United States and that without it activities such as highway construction would be seriously affected.[164] By the end of 1938 the companies' appeals had become more dramatic, claiming that for strategic reasons it was essential to regain control of the Mexican oil fields, since they were in reality a geographic extension of those in the United States.[165] However, apparently Washington continued to view the national interest from a slightly different angle, and, like it or not, it had to give priority to hemispheric solidarity.

At the VIII International Conference of American States (Lima, December 1938) and the First Meeting of Consultation of Ministers of Foreign Affairs of the American Republics (Panama City, September–October 1939), where the main theme was unity against the Nazi threat, Secretary of State Hull relaxed his pressure on Mexico and the latter made it a point to show its support of the Good Neighbor policy. Roosevelt, Daniels, and Hull, in varying degrees, never ceased to bear in mind the threat of fascist influence in Latin America and the dangerous effect that U.S. pressure could have on the development of local fascist groups.[166] The Cedillo rebellion and later the Almazán movement had shown Washington that the anti-Cárdenas elements which were apparently prepared to respect and reestablish American capital were at the same time connected with local fascist groups, which in turn were infiltrated by agents from Europe.[167] Roosevelt had repeatedly warned the firms against aligning themselves with any antigovernment movement,[168] since despite Cárdenas' vigilance the Mexican fascist organizations and the agents from Germany, Italy, and Spain were very active.[169] For example, two of the most important anti-Cárdenas groups were under the influence of the Spanish Falange.[170]

The Mexican government, though decidedly anti-Nazi, did not fail to take advantage of the situation, fanning Washington's fear of a fascist-type movement from time to time so as to get some relief from the constant pressure. When the occasion presented itself, it would point out that too much pushing from the United States could easily force it to cultivate ties with the Axis despite its fundamental desire to cooperate in the fight against totalitarianism.[171] Cárdenas accompanied these warnings with gestures of approximation toward the Third Reich—such as, for example, sending back the Mexican ambassador to Berlin at the very moment when Roosevelt was recalling his envoy in protest over Hitler's anti-Semitic policy, or exchanging New Year's greetings with the Führer. The German government, ideological differences notwithstanding, showed its enthusiastic support of the oil nationalization through statements in the press, pronouncements in official circles, and the like.[172] The German embassy in Mexico City also played the game, and on several occasions it defended the Mexican position vis-à-vis the United States, emphasizing how the expropriation controversy had weakened American prestige.[173]

While trade between Mexico and the United States was more and more hampered by the economic sanctions imposed by the U.S. government and the oil companies, barter with the Axis powers—oil in exchange for merchandise—increased. In 1937 Mexico had been the United States' number-one client in Latin America, but by the end of the following year purchases had fallen off 35 per cent, while trade with Germany and Italy was on the rise.[174] Daniels warned Hull that, if the trend continued, American interests in Mexico, both political and economic, were going to be seriously affected. Again and again he urged acceptance of the Mexican offer to stop selling oil to the Axis countries and form a united front against them in exchange for an end to the boycott.[175] As it happened, the ultimate solution was to be more or less along these lines.

Negotiations with the Oil Firms

Starting only days after the expropriation, the Mexican embassy in Washington began to receive what were to be endless numbers of suggestions for reaching an agreement with the companies. Mostly the work of opportunists, none of them were acceptable to Mexico and they never led to anything.[176] From the very beginning Cárdenas had invited the companies to enter into direct talks,[177] Ambassador Castillo Nájera having been given full power to deal with their spokesmen in Washington.[178] At the end of March the State Department insisted that Mexico offer a concrete plan of compensation both for the oil companies and for the U.S. landholders affected by the agrarian reform. In reply, Mexico said it was prepared to make an initial payment in cash and the rest in oil. This proposal was in line with an earlier suggestion of Under Secretary Welles' that perhaps if the firms were offered a share in the foreign distribution of the oil they might be encouraged to negotiate.[179] The State Department had apparently misinterpreted the companies' position, since all they cared about was the return of their property. To judge from a statement by El Aguila in the British press, the oil firms had believed at first that the interruption of their activities was temporary and that their properties would soon be turned back over to them.[180] Some time was to pass before they were convinced to the contrary. By the end of March Cárdenas had made three unsuccessful attempts to establish contact with the company spokesmen to discuss the amount and form of payment.[181] In view of the firms' resistance, Mexico informed the U.S. government directly that it was prepared to send a delegation to Washington if such a step would help to speed up negotiations. In keeping with the U.S. request for a concrete plan for compensation contained both in its note of March 26 and in informal communications,[182] Deputy Foreign Minister Beteta presented a scheme formally to Ambassador Daniels on April 19. The document provided for payment to be made on the basis of fiscal value of the companies' installations plus what had been invested in exploratory drilling but without taking into account the value of the deposits still in the subsoil. Payment was to be made in oil, of course.[183] While this plan was being presented to the State Department, Treasury Minister Eduardo Suárez had finally succeeded in reaching the oil company spokesmen directly in New York and was offering them a slightly different plan. He proposed an arrangement whereby the firms would go back to operating the installations, but under a contract with the Mexican government.[184] As might be expected, the idea fell on deaf ears. It was never to be brought up again. Mexico's position throughout 1938 was that it was prepared to compensate the companies by letting them handle the exportation of the oil without interfering in this aspect of the industry.[185] The firms, however, were not prepared to accept anything short of full control as before. They decided to wait, confident that the various steps that had been taken against the Cárdenas administration would soon produce a change at least in attitude if not in the government itself. Roosevelt and Daniels did not share their optimism and advised them to enter into talks with the Mexican authorities as soon as possible. The U.S. president made it very clear that they should accept the expropriation as an irreversible fact and that there was no sense in waiting and hoping for Cárdenas' overthrow.[186] The State Department was not as firm as the chief executive, and it let more than two years go by before it began to insist seriously that the companies negotiate. Pressure to get them to the bargaining table came not only directly from Roosevelt and Daniels but also, indirectly, from the changing situation—that is, circumstances within the group itself. Sinclair was the first to give up hope and show signs of wanting to break from the united front and begin negotiations with Mexico. This created a problem for the rest of the companies: if Sinclair were successful in its efforts—and everything indicated that Cárdenas would see to it that it was—they could no longer allege that it was impossible to reach an agreement with the Mexican government without Washington behind them.[187]

It was through the State Department that in November 1938 contact was made between Ambassador Castillo Nájera and a spokesman for the oil group, Donald R. Richberg, in order to seriously begin negotiations. The firms' representative, a lawyer and former official in the National Recovery Administration, was an able negotiator and a flexible man who understood what was at the bottom of the conflict—namely, Mexico's need to modify its political and economic system.[188] Since June he had been trying to persuade the companies to discuss Mexico's proposals for reaching an agreement, but Standard Oil of New Jersey resisted, preferring to hold out for hoped-for changes in government.[189] In December Colonel Patrick J. Hurley, former secretary of war under Hoover, arrived in Mexico to negotiate compensation for Sinclair and some of the independent firms. This move set Standard, Shell, and the rest of the big companies in a scramble to see what they should do next lest Sinclair, which had a much more flexible point of view, enjoy all the advantages of the initiative it had taken.[190] Hurley was persuaded to postpone his mission, given the fact that Richberg was ready to go to work. Daniels informed Roosevelt in January 1939 that the main firms were still basically reluctant to enter into serious negotiations, continuing to hope that the U.S. president or Cárdenas, or both, would be replaced by men whose thinking was more in line with their own in the respective upcoming elections.[191] In any case, on February 6, 1939, Richberg delivered a memorandum to the Mexican ambassador in Washington that had the concurrence of the oil companies and the sanction of the State Department and was to serve as a basis for the talks that were later to take place with Cárdenas. Essentially it proposed the following: (1) exploitation of the oil on the basis of a long-term contract between the companies and the government; (2) tax rates and labor terms and conditions to be agreed on in advance for the entire duration of the contract; (3) compensation to the firms for the damages caused as a result of the expropriation; and (4) mutual determination of the bases on which, once the contract expired, the company properties would be turned over to the Mexican government.[192] As it is easy to see, this first plan of Richberg's did not fare very well. The firms wanted nothing short of return of their properties, in exchange for which they were prepared to agree to some slight changes in the way in which they had been doing business with Mexico since the beginning of the century. Richberg had instructions not to discuss a plan for compensation, since they would only consider full return to the status quo ante, or at least continuation of the impasse.[193] Still, the fact that they had at last decided to sit down at the bargaining table gave the U.S. government reason to hope that an early settlement might be reached.[194] Roosevelt, who did not want to be accused of having allowed Mexico to violate international law with impunity, informed Cárdenas through the U.S. embassy that in his opinion Richberg's plan was worth a try. The proposal was fair, the president said, and he regarded it "of the utmost importance in the interest of the two countries that an agreement be found at a very early moment."[195]

The negotiations took place in two stages. The first consisted of a series of eight talks held between Richberg and Cárdenas, conducted over the period from March 8 to 22. They mostly served to underscore the wide gap between the two positions. Cárdenas did not openly oppose the companies' return to Mexico, but he asked that before anything else an assessment be made of the expropriated industry. The resulting figure, he explained, would provide a basis for determining the government's and the firms' respective participation in the new enterprise to be jointly formed. As he envisaged it, both parties would invest in the undertaking, but the government would be the principal shareholder by virtue of the fact that it was contributing the oil deposits.[196] Richberg was opposed to an assessment.[197] He preferred the idea of a fifty-year contract under which the industry would be reorganized: the government would still have a major share, but it would not be on a partnership basis with the companies. Once the contract had expired, Mexico would be able to take over the oil properties once and for all without any payment entering into the picture. Richberg was attempting to soft-pedal the nationalization, while Cárdenas was trying to consolidate it. No common ground having been reached, the president finally told Richberg that he was constitutionally unable to accept the proposal, since it involved setting taxes and working conditions for a period of fifty years in advance, and that therefore it was impossible to go on discussing the matter.[198] The real problem, of course, was the question of control of the industry. Richberg returned to the United States.

Days later the second phase began. No sooner had Richberg reported his stalemate to the companies and the State Department than he received a telephone message from Cárdenas on April 12. The latter had decided to postpone the assessment. Apparently Mexico had given in. This new turn of events made it possible to resume negotiations. Richberg and Castillo Nájera met at San Antonio, Texas. The companies' envoy presented the Mexican ambassador with a new memorandum to serve as a basis for future negotiations. In March the two men traveled to Saltillo to meet with Cárdenas.[199] In informed circles it was rumored that an agreement was about to be reached: the firms were coming back to Mexico and were going to put in 20 million dollars to get the industry back on its feet.[200] At the end of June Castillo Nájera informed Under Secretary Welles that the talks were going well. Whereas Richberg's plan had called for each company to go back to administering its respective installations, Castillo Nájera succeeded in having it agreed that they would merge into four big firms (originally Mexico had wanted them all to join together in a single enterprise). However, the central question now was who was to be in charge of each of the newly merged companies and serve on the Board of Supervisors that was to oversee all of them. Richberg wanted the firms to name their own heads, while the supervisors would be Mexican, appointed by the government. Cárdenas did not agree. Without either accepting or rejecting the plan, he promised to study it, and the talks came to an end. Shortly afterward he told Richberg that he felt it was necessary that both the company managers and the supervisors be appointed by the government, but the American representative turned the idea down.[201] During the period from the meeting in Saltillo up until November 1939 Richberg and Castillo Nájera got together from time to time in the United States, but both sides continued to insist on control of the future enterprise.

From the beginning the plan really had had little chance for success. Richberg's clients never had complete confidence in him. They felt he was making too many concessions to Mexico and that the modifications proposed by Cárdenas were unacceptable.[202] The STPRM, for its part, did not like the proposal very much because the companies' return would mean loss of some of the control it had gained over the industry.[203] And to add still one more factor, the PRM committee responsible for drafting the second Six-Year Plan made it more difficult than ever to turn back by declaring on November 1, 1939, that the oil had been nationalized once and for all and that it must remain so entirely and unequivocably.

With the talks having broken down again, the companies declared that Cárdenas had kept them from reaching a solution and that they could now do nothing more. They said that at this point the defense of their rights rested entirely in the hands of the government in Washington.[204] Cárdenas, for his part, wrote to Roosevelt on July 29 and again on October 7 of that year outlining what had happened in the course of the talks and saying that it was the companies that had stood in the way of a solution by insisting on unacceptable conditions, such as the points on taxes and labor matters. At the same time, he reiterated his wish to indemnify the firms for the fair value of their property and gave his assurance that the government would not interfere with the companies' foreign trade. It was clear that he was trying to open the door for renewed negotiations.[205]

When it became clear that the talks between Richberg and Cárdenas were leading nowhere, the State Department finally decided to intervene. The first step it took was to send a note to Castillo Nájera at the end of May maintaining that the Richberg plan was reasonable and that it would behoove Mexico to give it early and favorable consideration.[206] This move prompted Deputy Foreign Minister Beteta to go to Washington and meet with officials in the State Department. He was very blunt: if the United States continued to insist, it could succeed in arranging the companies' return, but only if the Cárdenas administration were overthrown, and before his administration fell he personally would see that the "crude imperialist" maneuver was exposed—which of course would be the end of the Good Neighbor policy. The U.S. authorities hastened to assure him that they had no such thought in mind. Beteta then went on to inform them that the Richberg plan could not be accepted for two reasons. In the first place, it was impossible for political reasons to leave the management of the oil industry in the hands of the companies. Second, there was no way to make the assessment—which was necessary in any case, either to determine the government's participation in the new enterprise or to make compensation —since the companies refused to accept the fact they no longer had any right over the subsoil deposits.[207] The Mexican stand was firm, but still the State Department's wishes had to be respected, and contact with Richberg continued. But, as it has already been seen, nothing was accomplished. Taking the initiative once again, Welles met separately with Castillo Nájera and Richberg and urged both of them to try to be more flexible. To Mexico he reiterated Washington's desire to reach an early agreement and warned Castillo Nájera that in the absence of an accord Roosevelt might be forced by Congress to take strong steps in regard to the purchase of silver.[208] Richberg, for his part, was made to see the need to reach an agreement before people would think that the companies were marking time until the elections. It was unwise to mix the oil problem with the presidential campaign, Welles warned. In any case, there was no assurance that Almazán would win or that the next government would be disposed to accept the companies' point of view, while indeed the opposite could very well happen.[209] He went one step further: he himself came up with a compromise proposal, the "Welles Plan." With Roosevelt's concurrence, the under secretary of state presented a new scheme for consideration by the two sides on August 2. He proposed a new Board of Administration, one-third of whose members would be appointed by the Mexican government, one-third by the firms, and the remaining third by a neutral group of persons who would be neither Mexicans nor Americans. The proposal was rejected by both sides, which were equally wary of the "neutral" group.[210] Welles insisted, in spite of everything, that the parties continue to negotiate.[211] However, the companies did not follow through, and in August 1939 Standard Oil of New Jersey informed Washington officially that the talks had broken down and it was now up to Washington to put the pressure on Mexico.[212]

Taking the reins again, the State Department told Mexico that it regretted its proposals had been rejected and reiterated that the government was obligated to make prompt and adequate compensation, pointing out this time that if the controversy continued much longer it could affect the "close and friendly understanding" between the two countries. The Mexican embassy hastened to make it clear that its government had not closed the doors to further negotiations and that its earlier proposals concerning payment for the nationalized property were yet to be acted on.[213]

In mid-1940 a new Mexican plan combining elements from both the Richberg and the Welles proposals was presented to Washington for consideration—though not by the companies. It was put before the State Department by Luis Legorreta, president of the Banco Nacional de México, the largest private banking institution in the country. Since the beginning of 1939 Legorreta had offered his services as an intermediary between Mexico and the oil firms, but at first he had had no concrete proposal to offer.[214] The essence of his plan now consisted of a bond issue that would be subscribed to in equal parts by Legorreta's banking group, the oil companies, and an official U.S. agency. Operations would be supervised by a group of experts appointed by the firms, which would have veto power over the decisions taken by the directors, who would be Mexicans. The plan was discussed at length. The State Department was in favor of it, and it obviously had the support of the Mexican government as well. However, there is no indication that the companies ever considered it seriously, and in the end nothing came of it.[215]

Standard Oil and Shell had thought that by sending Richberg to Mexico they would avoid being accused of systematically resisting all attempts to reach a direct agreement. The failure of these talks and of the Welles Plan led the State Department finally to propose arbitration. (The British were against such a course, feeling that it was essential to insist on the return of the nationalized property.) The points to be arbitrated would be two: the amount to be paid, and the form in which payment would be made. In December 1939 a draft arbitration convention, based on the recently signed General Treaty on Inter-American Arbitration, was prepared in consultation with oil company representatives. One major point of disagreement arose:

Standard Oil was in favor of including the British, whereas the State Department was not.[216] Since England could not keep Washington from taking this step, it wanted to participate, together with the Netherlands, in any possible agreement on arbitration. Standard did what it could to support this request, but to no avail.[217] At this juncture, then, the idea of arbitration was rejected both by the firms and by England. Mexico had also been opposed: it was prepared to accept the good offices of the State Department in the solution of the conflict, but not in an arbitration proceeding, since it did not feel that the case was of an "internationally justiciable character."[218] Welles regarded the Mexican position as "inconceivable," since all other possible means for reaching a solution had definitely been exhausted (Cárdenas had said to Daniels in September 1939 that only when it was clear that all other alternatives had failed would Mexico consent to arbitration).[219] Daniels now asked Washington not to insist any further.[220] At this point, with Sinclair accepting a more flexible position than Standard Oil, Cárdenas had the advantage and could afford to take this stand. The chances that Sinclair—which had very few interests outside the United States and was therefore less concerned about setting a precedent that could be copied in other countries—might reach an agreement were considerable, and Standard was worried. If this were to happen, the onus of being "inflexible" would fall on the companies' shoulders rather than Mexico's.[221] As it will be remembered, Sinclair's man, Patrick J. Hurley, had traveled to Mexico at the end of 1938, but the presence of Richberg and other events had prompted his return to the United States. Shortly after Standard had announced the failure of the Richberg talks, Colonel Hurley once again entered into contact with Castillo Nájera and began a new series of negotiations.[222] Already since the end of 1938 it had been known that the Sinclair group (five companies in all) was prepared to go along with the Mexican government.[223] Thus when Hurley reopened the talks abandoned by Richberg it came as no surprise to anyone. These negotiations were difficult, since in exchange for breaking ranks with the other firms Sinclair had set its mind on getting a sizable compensation: more than 30 million dollars in cash and oil.[224]

The bargaining advanced slowly but surely. The two sides were finding an increasingly broader common ground of agreement and Sinclair was backing down on its ambitious claims.[225] So it can be seen that Cárdenas was in a comfortable position to reject Secretary of State Hull's proposal for arbitration. At this point, however, the conclusion of an early agreement with Sinclair became essential to Mexico, since any delay could be seized on by the other companies or the State Department to foil the negotiations or push through the arbitration bid.[226] In the end, on May 1, 1940, a document was signed. Mexico agreed to pay the Sinclair group 8.5 million dollars, which was to be paid in cash within a period of three years; part of it had to be paid in oil, the fuel to be delivered at a price of 25 to 35 U.S. cents a barrel, which was lower than the price on the world market.[227] Thus Mexico reached a more or less satisfactory agreement with a group of firms that in 1938 had accounted for 40 per cent of the American oil investment and 15 per cent of the total value of the industry.[228]

The agreement with Sinclair may have been costly from a strictly economic standpoint, but it had the advantage for Mexico that at least formally Sinclair had not been compensated for the subsoil deposits—although in fact the payment corresponded to far more than the real value of the firm's investment in surface land and installations. Moreover, it did not have to be made immediately, as the State Department and the other oil companies were insisting. And, finally, part of the payment was to be made in the form of oil. The Mexican government wasted no time in pointing out to the U.S. embassy that this agreement showed, first of all, the needlessness of arbitration and, second, its favorable disposition toward making similar compacts with the rest of the firms.[229] At the end of May that same year Mexico reached an agreement with another somewhat less important American group: Cities Service.[230] Standard was far from pleased, and a campaign was launched to keep the oil that Sinclair was to receive from entering the United States. The effort got nowhere, however, and the agreement stood.[231]

Richberg's negotiations with the Mexican authorities were in fact the last formal talks with the major companies—that is, those in the Standard Oil group—although there were various later attempts to resume them. The accord with Sinclair did not alter Standard's position. William S. Farish, president of Standard Oil of New Jersey, saw the Mexican ambassador in Washington at the end of 1940 and the beginning of 1941, but the meetings served no other purpose than to harden the two opposing stands. While Mexico insisted on an agreement similar to the one reached with Sinclair and Cities Service, Farish maintained that there were only two possible alternatives: Richberg's original plan or else arbitration.[232] With pressure from the State Department mounting, Farish decided to personally visit the newly inaugurated Mexican president, Manuel Avila Camacho, at the end of 1941. However, the Mexican embassy in Washington was not very enthusiastic about the idea: the situation had entered a new phase, since the agreement was now being sought by Mexico through direct negotiations with the State Department.[233] Farish ended by canceling his trip.

Economic Pressure against Mexico

The 1938 national takeover brought the Cárdenas regime under both political and economic pressure—the latter the work of the companies and the U.S. government. Standard Oil of New Jersey, Royal Dutch–Shell, and, for a while, Sinclair were the instigators of a boycott that was immediately imposed on the recently nationalized industry. Their transnational scope and their economic power made it possible for them to adopt measures that seriously threatened the success of the expropriation. This boycott, whose architects refused to recognize it publicly as such, affected not only the oil industry but the rest of the economy as well.[234]

It should be remembered that the exercise of pressure by Washington and

the oil firms took place in the midst of an economic crisis which made
Mexico's position all the more vulnerable. The officials in the State Department were well aware of this; they knew that the United States could permanently cripple the Mexican economic system.[235] Apparently Washington's intention—although not the companies'—was to keep up a certain
amount of pressure and yet not push to the breaking point. The years 1937
and 1938 had seen a recession in Mexico. Since 1935 the economy had been
caught in an inflationary spiral as a result of the expenditures for Cárdenas'
reforms. By 1937 the budget was badly in the red, and in 1938 the situation
was aggravated even further by the slackening off of private investment
owing to the uncertain political climate, the flight of foreign exchange
caused by the withdrawal of the oil companies' funds, the drop in revenue
from the decline in the oil and silver exports, and, finally, the need to increase food imports because of a bad crop year. At mid-1938 things appeared
to be quite critical, but toward the end of the year the situation improved.
Starting in 1939 the economy began to be slightly—but only slightly—less
vulnerable to outside pressure.

It is important to have a look at the nationalized industry's economic
problems. The greatest blow was the cutting off of the traditional markets
abroad. To cope with this problem, a national oil exporting company (Compañía Exportadora de Petróleo Nacional) was formed in 1938. While it is
true that in 1938 exports were down as compared with the levels of the
early 1920's, still at the time of expropriation between 50 and 60 per cent of
the oil being drilled was for consumption outside the country. In 1937 foreign sales of petroleum and petroleum products amounted to 18.2 per cent
of all national exports. Much of this market was lost after March 1938, and as
a result the production of oil, which was the third most important economic activity in the country,[236] had to be curtailed considerably: the number
of wells in service was reduced from 981 to 756.[237] Exports, which had been
24,960,335 barrels in 1937, fell to 14,562,250. The situation improved a little in 1939: between January and August of that year 1,750,000 barrels a
month were being sold to foreign buyers, and in August PEMEX stopped
taking orders because its output was entirely spoken for.[238] However, the
outbreak of war in Europe changed matters again, and with the loss of the
German market exports fell off by one-third. Shortly afterward the Italian
market went by the boards as well. Although these were severe setbacks,
new customers were found in time. Still, sales did not return to the pre–
August 1939 levels.[239] To get around the boycott, resort was had to barter
and undercutting. Eventually domestic consumption was to become the industry's mainstay.
   Cárdenas was unable to hold to his intention to keep the expropriated oil
away from the Axis countries. Months before the expropriation he had informed Washington that the United States had first claim to Mexican oil
if it were to go to war against Japan and Germany.[240] (It should be remembered that at the time German companies were making attractive offers in
an effort to gain a foothold in the Mexican oil industry.)[241] His offer was

repeated several times after March 1938 but continued to receive no reply. Finally when hostilities broke out in Europe he made a similar offer to France. Again there was no response.[242]

Meanwhile, Standard Oil and Shell had succeeded in erecting an almost insurmountable embargo against Mexican oil exports. Their campaign was waged on various fronts. To begin with they attempted to convince Washington that the sale of Mexican oil abroad should be stopped until its legitimate ownership was established.[243] Although the State Department did not follow this suggestion, still on various occasions tankers loaded with Mexican fuel were seized at the firms' request. Protests against these actions were filed by Mexico in courts in the United States, the Netherlands, France, Belgium, and Sweden, and in no case was there a decision in the companies' favor,[244] but the prospect of possibly getting involved in a legal battle was enough to scare away customers.[245] Although Standard Oil and Shell did not actually find the legal means to halt the sale of Mexican oil, their other efforts had considerable practical effect. In the United States relatively little Mexican oil was consumed during the years immediately after the expropriation (although from the beginning fair-sized quantities were imported for reshipment to Europe). While the companies could not get Germany or Italy to say no to Mexican oil, they did succeed in a British ban—over objections from the independent firms.[246] France never came out formally against Mexican oil, but it simply refused to grant entry permits.[247] Prime Minister Edouard Daladier believed that England should be supported in the matter.[248] Only after the war broke out in 1940 was any serious consideration given to purchasing fuel from Mexico. The Vichy government sent an emissary to negotiate a sizable contract, but this time Mexico was on the refusing end, citing lack of transport as its reason.[249] Meanwhile the Dutch government persuaded its importers not to accept any offers of Mexican oil,[250] although some shipments of it did slip past surveillance and were sold in the Netherlands.[251] When Denmark proposed a trade of oil in exchange for ships and electrical equipment, Standard and Shell gave their permission in view of the energy shortage in that country. Problems connected with the war, however, kept the agreement from being signed.[252]

Mexico tried hard to place its petroleum products in Latin America, and extensive negotiations were carried out to this end with Argentina, Brazil, Chile, Costa Rica, Cuba, El Salvador, Guatemala, Honduras, Nicaragua, Paraguay, and Uruguay through both the diplomatic missions and special PEMEX representatives. Invariably, however, these initiatives ran up against interference by the State Department and the American companies, which were systematically following the course of events with a view to blocking progress wherever possible. In some cases they succeeded in preventing agreements from being reached; in others they temporarily lowered the prices of their own products in order to undercut and thereby shut out the Mexican industry.[253] Despite all this, it was possible to partially break through the embargo, and sales were made—at least for a while—to Brazil, Chile, Cuba, Guatemala, Nicaragua, Uruguay, and, in smaller quantities, other Latin American countries such as Panama and Paraguay.

Standard Oil also went after the firms that bought Mexican oil in defiance of its campaign—especially Davis and Company of New York and the Eastern States Petroleum Corporation of Texas.[254] Davis was buying the petroleum and selling it in Europe after processing it in its Hamburg refinery, while Eastern States was bringing it into the United States first, refining it there, and then exporting it to Europe. Standard used various tactics: for example, it succeeded in getting the commissioner of customs in Washington to conduct an investigation of Eastern States to see if it was in violation of the Antidumping Act of May 1921 for having purchased its product at less than the market price, while at the same time it put pressure on the banks that were financing the transaction to get them to suspend credit. In the case of Davis, it tried to have the firm called in under the Trading with the Enemy Act of 1917, since it was shipping most of its oil to Germany and Italy,[255] but these efforts were unsuccessful. Davis continued its activity up until the war itself put a final halt to it, and Eastern States also carried on with its operations, although U.S. Treasury agents had to travel to Mexico to make sure that its purchase prices were not below cost.[256]

The boycott was not limited to stopping the sale of oil. It was also directed toward cutting off Mexico's sources of supply for the materials to keep the industry running. By the end of 1938, twenty-four U.S. firms had refused to sell PEMEX the equipment it needed, despite the fact that the Mexican industry was offering to pay in cash. In 1939 at least fifteen companies continued to say no to orders from Mexico.[257] However, a number of equipment producers wanting to sell on this market protested the boycott. They lodged their complaints with the State Department, but their objections had no effect and the ban went on for several years.[258] Mexico had to cope with this obstacle by getting the needed equipment from Germany, in exchange for oil, or by seeking out intermediaries who would have the purchases sent to Cuba, from where they were reshipped to Mexico.[259] The sale to Mexico of tetraethyl lead, an essential antidetonant used in the processing of gasoline, was cut off by the Ethyl Gasoline Corporation (a firm controlled by Standard Oil of New Jersey and General Motors). Efforts to get the antidetonant through intermediaries were to no avail; it was impossible to get past the surveillance that the manufacturers had set up.[260] This development put an end to exportation of the refined product and made it necessary to downgrade the quality of the fuel consumed domestically and import gasoline for aircraft and a few other specialized purposes.[261]

The shortage of transportation equipment—railroad tank cars and ocean-going tankers—was also a serious drawback. As far as the first were concerned, for a time the tank cars belonging to the expropriated companies still gave some service, while others were bought or rented. But the problem of the tankers was a little more difficult; many lines, even though they had available space, refused to lease it to Mexico. In some cases it was necessary to purchase the vessels outright.[262] On other occasions the big firms paid any price to rent them ahead of time and keep them from falling into Mexican hands.[263] It was not until 1940, with bottoms purchased from Norway and Italy, that PEMEX finally had the nucleus of its oil fleet.

The big companies' machinations also extended to areas that had nothing directly to do with oil. General Electric and Westinghouse, which had interests in Mexico, had to close down a sizable part of their operations there because of the uncertain climate created by the expropriation and the firms' countermeasures.[264] (Westinghouse cited exchange difficulties, not the takeover, as the reason for its decision to withdraw, but no one believed this explanation.)[265] The companies' action also affected the tourist industry and the influx of foreign exchange, their propaganda campaign having discouraged people from visiting the country. The total dollar income from tourism in 1938 was down one-third from the year before.[266] The hotel industry, in which American capital was also present, protested what it considered to be false reports of killings and terrorism in Mexico which were being spread by Standard Oil.[267]

The State Department from the beginning backed up its notes of protest with pressure. Three days after the expropriation Under Secretary Welles informed Ambassador Castillo Nájera that the United States would not be able to sign the recently negotiated trade treaty, which had been to Mexico's advantage.[268] The next step was to call for suspension of the Treasury Department's silver purchases, which had been going on regularly since 1934.[269] When this buying program first began five years earlier, the Bank of Mexico took over control of silver exports to make sure that the U.S. Treasury got the bulk of the national output.[270] The purchases were sizable: in 1936 they amounted to a value of 30.5 million dollars. As it happened, the announcement of this cutoff was the first official communication that Mexico was to receive from Washington after the expropriation. The Bank of Mexico, which for some time had been sorely pressed to keep the exchange rate firm, was obliged to withdraw the peso from the world market.[271] In vain Daniels argued with Roosevelt and the State Department that this move, which created a serious threat to the Mexican economy, would put an even greater strain on U.S.-Mexican relations without accomplishing anything toward the return of the expropriated property.[272] The president disregarded his ambassador's advice and went along with Hull's decision, which, in addition to suspending direct purchases from Mexico, called for forcing a considerable drop in the world price of silver.[273] By the end of March the international rate had fallen from 45 to 43 U.S. cents an ounce, thanks to the Treasury Department's maneuvers,[274] and within less than a year it was down to 40 cents, later hitting a low of 38.5.[275] The silver policy proposed by Hull was partly the result of pressures brought to bear by the oil and banking groups[276] and partly from the workings of the internal machinery in the State Department itself. His decisions were based on a study presented to him by the department's economic adviser, which was targeted at forcing a reduction in Mexican fiscal income, weakening its currency, and aggravating the already extremely serious economic crisis that the country was going through. The plan was to be implemented in such a way that it would not affect any of the other silver-producing countries.[277] It had only been partially thought through, however, for while on the one hand the U.S. Treasury stopped buying silver directly from the Bank of

Mexico and a dip in world prices was achieved, on the other three weeks later this same entity began to acquire the metal on the world market with no restrictions as to its origin.[278] In any case, in 1938 Mexican silver exports were 50 per cent lower than they had been the year before; in 1939 they fell even more; and in 1940, when the pressure reached its peak, they were only one-sixth the level of 1937.[279] For the companies and their allies this was still not enough: they wanted a total embargo on Mexican silver.[280] Their pressure was countered, however, by the silver lobby in the United States, which represented Americans with mining interests in Mexico.[281] Mexico made it known that total discontinuation of silver purchases would be catastrophic for its economy and pleaded for relief.[282] The fact that silver production in Mexico was largely controlled by American interests precluded the application of further pressure on this sector by the U.S. government. The State Department knew that the American miners would end up paying for the Mexican government's losses through increased taxes and wages. Also there was the danger that if the situation became financially unbearable for the mine owners, the organized workers might form cooperatives and take over their companies. The ultimate outcome could be a mining nationalization similar to the one that had just taken place in the oil sector.[283] This was not mere speculation. As a result of the suspension of the silver purchases, the Mexican government had decreed a new tax in July 1938 that affected mainly the American mining interests.

From the outset the State Department had let Mexico know that an agreement with the oil companies would be followed by a resumption of the silver purchases.[284] In 1938 and 1939 the pressure was great but not intolerable, but in December 1939 word came that the United States intended to step up its campaign and completely block the purchase of Mexican silver on the world market, and panic spread through official and private business circles in Mexico. This, on top of falling exports in general, was all that was needed to set off economic pandemonium. The rumor turned out to be unfounded, but the State Department deliberately refrained from denying it, seeing that the Bank of Mexico had just then withdrawn from the exchange market unable to meet the demand for dollars triggered by the speculation.[285] At the end of 1941, when the oil problem was nearing solution, a new silver agreement was reached whereby the U.S. Treasury promised to acquire up to a monthly total of 6 million ounces at a price to be set each day.[286]

The suspension of silver purchases was only one of the economic sanctions imposed by the U.S. government. Another, paralleling the tactics applied by the companies, was likewise designed to thwart Mexico's efforts to find markets for its oil in the United States, Latin America, and Europe. During 1938 and a large part of 1939 there was no legal barrier that prevented Mexico from looking for new clients in the United States. However, more or less open pressure on Washington's part put an end to these initiatives. To begin with, talks about the possible sale of Mexican oil to the U.S. Navy were discontinued when the expropriation took place. Next the State Department asked all government agencies to refrain from purchasing Mexican oil. This applied even to U.S. ships taking on stores at Tampico. Wash-

ington gave first preference in its oil imports to Venezuela and Dutch possessions.[287] When independent American companies showed that they were
prepared to defy Standard Oil and buy the lower-priced Mexican fuel, they
did not encounter any legal obstacles, but the State Department warned
them that to enter into any deals with Mexico would be "fishing in dangerous waters."[288] Some of the firms listened to Washington's warnings, but
others did not.[289] A large part of the oil acquired in this way was then exported to Europe to avoid protests from those who felt that its sale within
the United States would depress domestic prices. Also by this maneuver the
oil, once it was refined in the United States, could be regarded as an American product and thus get past the boycott imposed by Standard Oil and
Shell.[290] Since because of PEMEX's low prices entrance into the U.S. market still remained ajar, Standard asked the State Department to once and for
all put a stop to the importation of Mexican oil.[291] The request was not
granted, however. Meanwhile, the Treasury Department forced the largest
of the companies that were importing Mexican oil, Eastern States Petroleum, to post a bond until it could prove that the prices at which it was buying were not in violation of the antidumping laws. (To help this company
out, Mexico had to agree to an informal Treasury Department audit of
PEMEX's books.)[292] The State Department also asked the Port of New York
Authority to refuse permission to build tanks for storing Mexican oil which
was to be exported to Europe.[293] Eastern kept on bringing in the embargoed
product for some time, but it was always in financial difficulty owing to the
pressure from the big companies. A representative of Eastern's bank was
told by State Department officials that it was unwise to continue extending
credit to this company.[294] Eastern's problems, however, did not keep Mexico from selling to other independent American groups.[295]

In November 1939 the U.S. government stepped up its pressure by setting
import quotas on oil. Only 3.8 per cent of the petroleum entering the country was not subject to the quota restrictions, and this small proportion theoretically had to be divided up among all the potential suppliers, Mexico being but one of them (although in actual practice it took up almost the entire
share).[296] The rest of the Mexican oil was subject to a tariff of 100 per
cent—whereas the imports under the quota system (including the 3.8 per
cent) had the benefit of a 50 per cent discount on duty, pursuant to the
Venezuela Trade Agreement and a subsequent executive order of December
12. One of the results expected from these measures, of course, was a reduction in the entry of Mexican hydrocarbons. When Mexico asked to come
under a quota, it was told that these preferences had been reserved mainly
for countries such as Venezuela and Colombia that had made certain friendly concessions to the United States.[297] Mexico did not give up. An increased
allowance was obtained, but it was minimal: only a million barrels more. In
these negotiations Ambassador Castillo Nájera had the support of Sinclair.
This company alone, however, could not offset the tremendous influence of
Standard Oil, which was brought to bear particularly on the State Department's Office of the Legal Adviser—the source of the decision to veto Mexico's request for 22 million barrels. Castillo Nájera's protests were in
vain.[298] However, the disadvantages created by the import quotas were not

insurmountable. In 1940, perhaps owing to the outbreak of World War II, Standard Oil of Indiana, through a subsidiary, signed a 20-million-dollar contract for the purchase of Mexican oil.[299] In the same year one-seventh of the fuel that was reaching the United States from abroad was Mexican. Moreover, at the beginning of 1941 the press mentioned the possibility of the United States' picking up the oil that Mexico was refusing to sell to Japan.[300] In February 1942 the State Department declared officially that there was no objection to the U.S. Navy's buying Mexican fuel,[301] and accordingly in June steps in this direction were initiated. (After the war was over the navy continued its purchases.)[302] In any case, for a variety of economic and political reasons, PEMEX ceased to depend on exports as the decade progressed. Its activities began to center instead on supplying the domestic market, and the problem of introducing oil into the United States became of secondary importance.

The State Department's interference in Mexico's efforts to find foreign markets also went on outside U.S. borders, in the other countries of Latin America and in Europe. Not infrequently the emissaries in Washington of the countries interested in buying Mexican oil sought the department's opinion prior to making any purchase agreements. In most cases the U.S. officials limited themselves to pointing out that although they could not oppose such a purchase it should be kept in mind that the ownership of the oil was still in question and that the country would be buying it at its own risk.[303] Despite the warning, more than one of them took the chance. On seeing these developments, Standard urged the government to stop all sales of Mexican fuel to third countries.[304] The State Department, however, did not feel it would be wise to do so: if the United States were to impose such a blockade, it could become involved in unpleasant difficulties with a lot of countries.[305] Still, though officially Washington did not go along with the idea of the embargo, in reality it exercised considerable pressure on some of the Latin American countries that were buying Mexican oil.

Nicaragua was a case in point. In September 1938 the U.S. legation in that country reported that President Anastasio Somoza had turned down Mexico's offers, which were being made at very low prices, although a certain private party had bought a small quantity of the oil. In January of the following year it was learned that the Nicaraguan government itself had acquired 1,200 tons of Mexican asphalt, despite the fact that at that moment it was building a highway with U.S. aid. The purchase was made by an import firm whose partners included some of Somoza's closest associates. When the U.S. envoy in Managua raised the question of disloyal conduct with Somoza, the Nicaraguan president said he had had to do it to keep Mexico from supporting his political enemies—an excuse that failed to satisfy Washington. The Nicaraguan government did not make any more direct purchases from Mexico, but before long a private company was set up to distribute Mexican oil in that country, and it began to crowd out West Indies Oil. Washington protested again, and this time Somoza had to agree to take definitive steps to keep out the Mexican product.[306]

A similar course of events took place in Cuba when military groups close to President Fulgencio Batista established a company to import Mexican fuel in spite of Washington's opposition. It operated on the island for a while, but then it closed down.[307]

The U.S. interference did not stop even after the oil problem was solved with Mexico itself. At the beginning of 1942 a transportation crisis in the Caribbean, brought on by the war, had caused an acute energy shortage in that area and in Central America. Costa Rica, Cuba, the Dominican Republic, Honduras, and Nicaragua immediately appealed to Mexico.[308] Lack of tankers prevented PEMEX from meeting some of these requests, but in other cases pressure from Washington was behind the fact that the oil was not supplied. Both Cuba and Costa Rica were warned that if they were to buy the Mexican product an equivalent amount would be taken off the respective quotas of U.S. oil which they were receiving and that their collaboration with Mexico would prolong the oil controversy and be looked on unfavorably by Washington. As it turned out, Mexican oil did not reach Cuba, or, apparently, Nicaragua, and the trade with Costa Rica was short-lived.[309]

The case of Guatemala was slightly different. While here the U.S. government does not seem to have exerted any pressure to keep out Mexican oil, Shell did to some extent, attempting to convince Guatemalan officials that such purchases were bad business. The first load of gasoline arrived at the end of 1938. The Guatemalan government made half-hearted attempts to stop the entry of new shipments, but protests from the Mexican embassy put a stop to these efforts.[310] In 1939 a Guatemalan firm was set up to distribute PEMEX oil. Unfortunately, delays in filling the orders and poor relations between the enterprise and its representatives in Guatemala prevented Mexico from taking greater advantage of this market—the only one that could be reached by rail and where pressure on the part of Washington or the companies was not decisive.[311]

With Argentina the State Department pointed out that the United States had refrained from putting its wheat on the same market with Argentine grain in Brazil and, appealing to the principle of reciprocity, expressed the hope that Mexican oil would be kept from competing with the U.S. product in the River Plate country.[312] Taking the hint, Argentina informed the Mexican embassy that it could not allow foreign exchange to be used for importing Mexican oil unless Mexico were to agree to buy more products in return.[313] In Brazil, on the other hand, the U.S. embassy took the approach of courting the minister of foreign affairs, who they knew would oppose the cabinet members who wanted to make a deal with Mexico. However, the attraction of low prices outweighed the minister's arguments and a fairly large company was established for the distribution of Mexican oil.[314] The Brazilian market was maintained until the end of 1941, when the trade broke down not as a result of American pressure but rather because the Brazilian firm that was representing PEMEX ran into difficulties.[315] The Chilean government bought small quantities of Mexican fuel for its navy from 1939 until 1942 without any interference from Washington.[316] The shortage of tankers was an obstacle to selling oil in the Southern Tier.[317]

Outside Latin America Washington's interference in Mexico's efforts to export oil was more discreet, being limited to expressing concern over the possibility to the government in question—Switzerland being a case in point.[318] The principal intermediary between Mexico and a number of the European countries, independent American oilman William R. Davis, was followed throughout the continent by U.S. intelligence agents. Although there was no direct interference in his activities, he and his associates were warned not to go "fishing in troubled waters."[319] The United States was not alone in its efforts to spike the sale of Mexican oil abroad: the British government was also committed to this objective, and London in fact had better luck than Washington at dissuading potential buyers.[320]

Like the oil companies, Washington did not limit its campaign just to those transactions directly related to oil; it tried to interfere with any arrangement that might alleviate the general economic crisis that Mexico was going through. The State Department vetoed a proposed Export-Import Bank loan for the purchase of 750,000 dollars' worth of equipment for an iron and steel foundry in Monterrey. The same thing happened with credits being considered for a rayon factory in Guadalajara and with government requests for the purchase of electrical material, sugar refining equipment, and a pipeline.[321] With the private U.S. banking institutions there was no such thing as a direct veto, but whenever the opportunity presented itself the State Department pointed out to the parties concerned that it was not a good idea to make loans to Mexico.[322] When it suited the parties concerned, however, there were exceptions to this policy—as, for example, when certain private American banks wanted to finance a large Mexican purchase of armaments from the United States at the end of 1939.[323] Still, the interference, though not carried to the ultimate extreme or to the point of conflicting with the defense of the hemisphere, was significant.

If PEMEX still had some foreign customers, despite the opposition of Standard Oil, Shell, and the State Department, this circumstance was due largely to the world political crisis which had been developing since the early 1930's. This international situation enabled the Mexican oil industry to count on sizable foreign markets in Germany, Italy, and Japan. Although at first Cárdenas was reluctant to deal with these countries, the blockade that was being set up around him left him no alternative, and in July 1938 he let it be known that he was prepared to sell oil to any party that would buy it.[324] The Axis market was vital to Mexico from the time of nationalization up to the outbreak of World War II. Of total oil exports over this period, Germany accounted for 48 per cent; Italy, 17 per cent; the United States, 20 per cent (16 per cent was reexported, only 4 per cent being consumed internally); and Japan, a somewhat smaller share.[325] Standard Oil and Shell had thought that the Axis countries would not risk their good relations with the two consortia for the temporary advantage of buying Mexican oil below world market prices, but they miscalculated.[326] A few days after the expropriation the German shipping companies announced that they intended to disregard the boycott and carry Mexican oil.[327] Already in May 1938 the Mexican consul in Hamburg reported that there was a favorable climate in Germany for the purchase of Mexican oil.[328] The first sign was when the German government granted permission for an import firm, Hamburger Mineralöl Import, to buy several shiploads of Mexican oil.

It had been agreed ahead of time that the German courts would not find the company at fault in the event the British or the Americans attempted to enforce the embargo.[329] Trade increased when Germany and Italy decided to buy large quantities of Mexican oil below the world market price. Moreover, payment was to be made partially in kind. In exchange for its oil, Mexico was prepared to receive German drilling equipment, Italian rayon, or Japanese beans. (Barter was also attempted with nontotalitarian countries, oil being offered in trade for Swiss and Swedish machinery, Argentine wheat, and Uruguayan rice and wool, but these efforts did not fare as well.)[330]

Germany had already begun to buy Mexican oil in small amounts as far back as 1937. The large post-expropriation transactions were made through a U.S. company with interests in Germany, Davis & Co., over the objections of Shell and Standard Oil. By mid-1939 the German government decided to do without the go-between and deal directly with Mexico, but the outbreak of war put a stop to this idea.[331] In September 1938 a meeting, attended by various high German officials and representatives of Standard Oil of New Jersey and Shell, was held in the Ministry of Economic Affairs in Berlin to set a policy with regard to Mexican oil. It was decided to continue importing it not only in order to keep up the level of German exports to that country but also to meet the needs of the navy (which was doing what it could to accumulate reserves), with the advantage that part of the payment was to be made in kind. The break with Standard Oil and Shell was not total, however, since Germany agreed that it would not increase its purchases from Mexico beyond what was necessary to maintain its exports at the 1937 level.[332]

On October 28, 1938, a formal agreement was concluded with Italy to trade oil for goods from that country, and on December 8 a similar compact was made with Germany. It was thanks to these accords that in 1939 Mexico was able to enjoy export levels no lower than they had been in 1937. Relations between Mexico and Germany became strained when a delay occurred between delivery of the fuel and receipt of the materials being sent in payment, and the Mexican legation in Berlin began to press for liquidation of the debt as soon as possible lest a war in Europe make settlement impossible.[333] As it turned out, Mexico's worst fears were realized. With the outbreak of World War II economic ties between the two countries were cut off, although some Mexican oil probably did reach Germany afterward by way of Italy. The last shiploads of oil that left Tampico for Germany in the beginning of November were sunk by the British fleet.[334] For a while Germany continued to send the materials it owed to Mexico through Italian channels,[335] but delivery in full was not possible, and almost 500,000 marks' worth of goods reserved for Mexico stood waiting in German warehouses until war between the two countries was declared.[336]

Instrumental in the first sales of oil to Germany and the Scandinavian countries was William R. Davis, president of the independent firm Davis & Co., which had interests in Oklahoma and Texas, and of the company Parent Petroleum Interests, Ltd., in London. Davis also had an interest in a German firm. This astute and opportunistic American oilman appeared on

the Mexican scene in 1937 with an offer to trade PEMEX oil for 100 million pesos' worth of German railroad equipment. The transaction never actually took place, but in the course of the negotiations he acquired a firm
of secondary importance, Sabalo Transportation Company, through which
it was agreed he would work the Poza Rica beds in collaboration with
PEMEX. Poza Rica finally ended up in the hands of El Aguila, and Davis got
into a dispute with PEMEX which was still unsettled on March 18, 1938,
when Sabalo was expropriated along with the rest of the foreign companies.[337] Davis, a man of independent and adventurous spirit, did not react like the rest of the parties that were affected by the takeover. Quite the
contrary: when he realized that Mexico was desperate to export its oil at
any price, he met with Cárdenas in May and offered to take charge of the
entire recently nationalized industry. Conscious of the acute shortage of
tankers (sixty would normally have been needed to export the output in
question whereas only six were available), he sweetened the bid by saying
he had twenty-seven vessels that Mexico could use.[338] Cárdenas did not
accept the first part of the proposal, but he did agree to take advantage of
Davis' fleet and his refinery in Hamburg. The name of his company was
Eurotank, and its product was sold mainly in Germany, Italy, and the Scandinavian countries. In April Davis began to ship Mexican oil purchased at
quite attractive prices, and on June 5 he signed a 10-million-dollar agreement with PEMEX, payment to be made in the form most convenient for
Germany: 40 per cent in cash and the rest in goods.[339] By June Davis had
been named PEMEX distributor for Europe.[340] His relationship with Mexico was not without difficulties, however. Sometimes PEMEX's deliveries to
Davis were late. Also, given the nature of the arrangement, more than once
the Mexican authorities refused to let his tankers sail from Tampico until
payment for the oil had been guaranteed.[341] In July 1939 PEMEX had the
idea of taking Davis—and Germany—out of the picture and doing business
with France instead, but this latter country did not show any interest.[342]
With Mexico's reluctance to extend him any credit, Davis was forced to
seek help in American banking circles—a rather awkward situation in view
of the pressures being exerted by Standard Oil and the State Department.
Despite his precarious financial position, he continued to have big plans. At
the end of 1938 he was buying from Mexico at a rate of more than a million
dollars a month. He planned to double this volume in 1939 and increase it
even more in 1940, claiming that Mexico had the capacity to export as
much as 70 million dollars' worth of oil a year.[343] But these ambitious
dreams were never to be realized. While for a few months he was bringing in
a fortune as the number-one exporter of Mexican oil for Eastern States
Petroleum, the outbreak of war in Europe put an end to the German bonanza: his long-term contracts with Mexico were canceled. For a while he continued to buy small amounts of oil for a refinery in Sweden, and an attempt
at the end of 1939 to arrange for the shipment of Mexican oil to Italy (the
State Department had well-founded suspicions that its ultimate destination
was Germany)[344] was unsuccessful. Although his deals with Italy and Germany during those last months created considerable problems for him with
the U.S. and British governments, he apparently came out of the situation

unscathed, because in 1940 he was back in Mexico with a new proposal: construction of a pipeline, which would be under his control, across the isthmus of Tehuantepec. Nothing ever came of this, the last of his schemes involving Mexico.[345]

Germany and Italy were certainly Mexico's largest customers during the period 1938–1939. Although Japan figured much less importantly, its plans were bolder than those of the other two Axis powers and were of great concern to the government in Washington. Indeed, Japan's interest in Mexican oil dated back to earlier times: already some two years before the expropriation it had been rumored that there were Japanese in Mexico trying to buy up oil concessions, and apparently around 1936 they succeeded in acquiring a share in the Mexican firm La Laguna.[346] Even after nationalization Japan continued to be interested both in getting control over some of the deposits and in buying large quantities of the fuel.[347] Two weeks after the expropriation the first of this country's tankers left Tampico with a load of Mexican oil, and the press hinted at Japanese negotiations to acquire the Chontla Company in Minatitlán, Veracruz. The newspapers and the U.S. embassy reported that the Japanese had also offered to build a pipeline across Tehuantepec Isthmus so as to help Mexico cater to the countries in the Pacific. And according to still other rumors, a high-ranking official in the Petroleum Administration Council was in close contact with the Japanese and not ill disposed toward the expansion of their influence.[348] But for all this there was little concrete evidence. Oil sales to Japan in 1938 were very low, and the State Department's adviser on international economic affairs, after a study of the situation, concluded that it was unlikely Japan would enter into relations with Mexico simply in order to solve its energy problem.[349] Still, U.S. suspicions continued unallayed. Word went around in the United States that Mexico was thinking not only of granting oil concessions to the Japanese but also of letting them have the use of Magdalena Bay. Mexico denied the rumors,[350] but they persisted. The sale of oil to Japan, small as the quantities were, gave rise to protests on the part of Chinese nationalist organizations.[351] In 1939 Washington continued to suspect that Japan was interested in getting into the production end of the industry as well as in buying the oil. It was thought that Japanese interests —specifically the Nippon Loda Oil Company—were operating under the protection of a certain highly placed Mexican politician and the Compañía Petrolera Veracruzana. Ambassador Daniels succeeded in getting National Economy Minister Efraín Buenrostro to promise, as a show of Mexico's goodwill, to stop all Japanese interference in the latter firm.[352] In 1940, despite the fact that small quantities of oil continued to be sold to the Japanese (with rayon being received in exchange), Mexico informed Washington that it wanted to coordinate its oil policy with the United States. Shortly thereafter the company's concessions were canceled when its ties with Japan were confirmed. In addition, Mexico turned down a large Japanese bid for several million barrels of oil and eighteen thousand tons of scrap iron.[353]

The sale of Mexican oil to Germany, Italy, and Japan caused displeasure and concern in official and private business circles in the United States— mainly, of course, because these purchases neutralized some of the economic pressure with which it was intended to force Mexico to come to an agreement in the terms wanted by the expropriated companies. They also caused concern because they gave the Axis powers a toehold in Latin America. And they affected U.S. trade: Mexico's receipt of food and manufactured products from these countries in exchange for oil had meant a lowering of imports from the United States.[354] At the same time, Washington suspected that part of the German machinery received in Mexico was being reexported to other Latin American nations at prices competing with those of U.S. products.[355] Finally, American exporters were worried about the possible depressing effect on the U.S. foreign trade picture if Mexico's bartering were to give ideas to other countries, especially ones with controlled economies, which might choose to follow its example in order to open up new markets.[356]

Propaganda

The campaign launched by the oil companies after March 18, 1938, was worldwide, but it was felt especially in the United States. Standard Oil's task was helped in the United States by the fact that the Cárdenas administration's efforts at agrarian reform and in behalf of labor had already given it a "radical" taint long before the expropriation. Even with the situation in Europe and Asia taking the public's attention away from events in Mexico, the companies were still able to spread an anti-Mexican message that was no small cause for concern among those who did not share their point of view.[357]

At first the aim of the oil firms' propaganda had been to create an atmosphere of crisis that would induce the Roosevelt administration to use force against Mexico.[358] When it was clear that Washington was not going to resort to violence, the campaign then concentrated on maintaining constant pressure on the U.S. government to press for an agreement with Mexico on the companies' terms. To implement their strategy, the firms started by hiring a public relations man, Steve Hanagan, who had the distinction of having been the prime mover in turning the state of Florida into a tourist mecca. Under him an information office was set up in Rockefeller Center and charged with the mission of giving a "suitable orientation" to news related to the oil controversy. For several years the office put out a free-of-charge biweekly newsletter, called *Looking at Mexico*, which reprinted all the items appearing the American and foreign press that reported or commented on the oil problem from the companies' point of view. In addition, the firms' agents met with editors from the big U.S. dailies in an effort to enlist their support.[359] The press throughout the country was constantly publishing articles that the office had written. Also as part of the campaign, lectures were given in opinion-making forums. The basic plan of attack was as follows: (1) to show that the expropriation was against U.S. national interest in that it set a precedent and was part of an international plot (communist or fascist, depending on the context or the audience); (2) to spread the image of a Mexico governed by a band of thieves—a country where no foreign property was safe from confiscation and all would eventually be taken by the state (the mining industry being the next target); and (3) to demonstrate that Cárdenas and his associates were wrecking the Mexican economy. These ideas found their way into hundreds of editorials published throughout the nation, from local dailies and sensationalist sheets to such respected publications as *Foreign Affairs*, the *New York Times*, the *Washington Post*, and the *Wall Street Journal*.[360] The papers in the Hearst chain distinguished themselves by their virulent and constant attacks against Mexico. This press coverage was duplicated in England, and to a lesser extent in other European countries where the British had fairly strong influence.[361] Perhaps one of the biggest achievements of the entire campaign was a special issue of the *Atlantic Monthly*, paid for by the companies in 1938, which bore the following title: *The Atlantic Presents: Trouble below the Border*. Although it purported to be a study on Latin America, the bulk of its sixty-four pages was devoted to an analysis of the oil controversy from the companies' point of view.[362] This well-organized and wide-ranging effort did not take long to bear fruit: soon sizable sectors of the American public began to show their exasperation over the "perverse attitude" of the Mexican government, and the anti-Roosevelt politicians, Democrats as well as Republicans, started to call for a revision of the Good Neighbor policy.[363] In general the oil firms found a sympathetic ear among business groups, which since 1934 had been watching the new "Mexican radicalism" with great misgiving, and in the Catholic hierarchy, still resentful over the clergy's struggle with the Revolutionary governments. Both these sectors joined the chorus which was clamoring for Roosevelt to use an "iron hand" in dealing with Mexico.[364]

The activities of the Fall Committee during 1918–1920 had shown that the U.S. Congress could be an excellent forum for dissemination of the oil companies' position in their conflict with Mexico. This approach was tried again in 1939. In January of that year Senator Robert R. Reynolds of North Carolina proposed that the Senate investigate whether or not the Mexican government had violated international law and the basic rights of the individual in confiscating property belonging to U.S. citizens.[365] The proposal failed to win much support, however. A month later Representative Martin J. Kennedy, a Democrat from New York, took the floor to ask for Daniels' recall—an indirect way of criticizing Roosevelt's Mexican policy.[366] But this suggestion was also voted down. Kennedy then appealed directly to Secretary of State Hull and urged for a solution to the Mexican problem in view of the growing threat of German activity south of the border.[367] Three days later another proposal for an investigation, this time within the Senate's Foreign Relations Committee, was presented, now citing the question of transactions between certain U.S. citizens and Mexico for the purchase and sale of oil.[368] But thanks to a deciding vote cast by Senator Key Pittman in August 1939, the committee did not entertain the request. This seemed to be the end of the companies' efforts to involve the U.S. Congress directly in the oil problem.[369] On its own initiative, however, Congress was to make several suggestions—none of them very practical—for a solution of the problem. In January 1940 a representative from Arizona advanced the suggestion that Mexico settle its oil debt by ceding to the United States a piece of territory that would give his state an outlet to the sea.[370] This idea of acquiring Mexican territory was not new: it had been raised confidentially with the State Department by one of the senators in April 1938, to which Secretary Hull had replied that such a proposal would incense Mexico greatly and make matters far worse.[371]

The Mexican government, for its part, took the same approach it had used on previous occasions and sent out a series of missionaries—among them Moisés Sáenz and Alejandro Carrillo—to propagate the Mexican point of view by giving informal talks, interviews, and the like in the course of which they explained the factors that had led to the takeover.[372] In addition, pamphlets and other materials were printed in English and French for distribution in the United States and Europe.[373] The drive was not very successful, however, for Mexico did not have the preparation or the financial means to effectively combat the companies' propaganda on their home ground. The campaign conducted through the Mexican diplomatic missions in Latin America yielded more rewarding results.[374]

In the United States the Mexican position received support from liberal groups that sympathized with the Revolution's social reforms. In their opinion, Cárdenas was committed to his own New Deal. If he was having economic relations with the Axis countries, it was because he had no other choice, while his aid to the Spanish Republicans was the best real proof of his antifascist convictions. These groups understood the events that had led up to the nationalization and were in favor of the decision. Mexico, they felt, had a right to have the use of its own resources, recovering them, if need be, from the hands of those who had appropriated them with the aid of a dictatorial government.[375] The organized workers in the United States also showed their support of the expropriation, and John L. Lewis frankly expressed his sympathy with Cárdenas' policy during his visit to Mexico in 1938. If these sectors did not openly applaud the nationalization, they at least showed that they understood the Mexican social reform program and continued to support the Good Neighbor policy.[376] Pacifist organizations such as the National Council for the Prevention of War, the Keep America Out of the War Congress, and the American League for Peace and Democracy lobbied in Washington for a friendlier attitude toward Mexico and urged opposition to any open or clandestine violence against the Cárdenas government.[377]

The oil companies and the Mexican government also carried on the propaganda struggle within Mexico itself, but in this case the balance was in the government's favor, partly owing to its control over the mass organizations and the media. Meetings, demonstrations, and rallies in support of nationalization were supplemented by an information drive mounted by the Presidency's Department of Press and Propaganda (DAPP—Departamento Autónomo de Prensa y Propaganda).[378] The companies, for their part, along with the administration's critics, tried to show that the takeover was responsible for the rising cost of living, the decline in exports, and the general depression into which the country's economy had fallen. They insisted that Mexico was totally unable to run such a complex, modern undertaking as the oil industry and predicted the imminent ruin of PEMEX.[379] However, their efforts never really detracted from the expropriation's great popularity with the Mexican public.

Chapter 10

World War II and Final Settlement of the Oil Controversy

The outbreak of World War II brought pressure on Washington to reach full agreement with Mexico on the different matters that were pending, among the most important of which was the oil controversy. With the Germans walking across Europe and the Japanese threatening in the East, the U.S. government decided it was important to build up a united Western Hemisphere to combat any Axis infiltration. Moreover, it was necessary to have both political and military pacts with the countries that were strategic for the defense of the Panama Canal and other vulnerable sites. This meant Mexico—even if concessions had to be made on points that Washington had been insisting on since the outset. For a long time Ambassador Daniels had been urging a prompt settlement so as to be able to close up ranks against the fascist threat. In October 1939 he pointed out that the time was right for reaching an agreement, and by 1940 his speeches hammered relentlessly on the need to strengthen hemispheric unity in the face of the developing conflict in Europe.[1]

Daniels' view regarding the importance of a prompt settlement was shared by the embassy's counselor, Pierre Boal, a career foreign service officer who was not necessarily known for his flexibility with regard to Mexico. In a personal letter written in August 1939—that is, a month before the outbreak of hostilities in Europe—to Laurence Duggan, chief of the State Department's Division of the American Republics, Boal said that an agreement had to be reached with the Mexican government even if it were interpreted as U.S. support of Cárdenas, since it was urgent to get U.S. air forces down there to protect the air and sea lanes to Panama and Central America in the event of war. It was important to keep Nazi submarines from taking on fuel at Mexican ports and to prevent German technicians from entering the country to operate the air fields. He went on to say that the same precautions should be taken in relation to the Japanese. Duggan agreed.[2] In February 1940, with the conflict in Europe now out in the open, the U.S. military attaché in Mexico suggested that settlement of the oil controversy be speeded up by trying for an agreement at the intergovernmental level without waiting for the expropriated companies to participate in the negotiations.[3]

It was from this point on that the U.S. government's position began to depart from that of the companies.[4] The outbreak of the war coincided with the end of Cárdenas' term in office, and an administration supposedly more friendly toward the United States would be coming into power. This, plus Daniels' wish to bring the oil question to a close before returning to the

United States (his wife's ill health was obliging him to leave his post), led the ambassador to urge once again with Roosevelt for settlement of the conflict. Otherwise, he maintained, Latin America would lose faith in the Good Neighbor policy. Roosevelt agreed with him, and suggested to Daniels that he inform Secretary Hull accordingly.[5] In the State Department, Duggan was also in favor of solving the problem quickly and was prepared to accept a Mexican proposal as the basis—namely, appointment of an intergovernmental commission to decide on the amount and form of payment of the indemnization.[6] Roosevelt personally helped to set a conciliatory climate through a speech on Pan American Day in which he stressed the importance of settling conflicts in the hemisphere without recourse to coercion of any kind. In October Under Secretary of State Sumner Welles presented Mexico with a proposal for reaching a direct agreement between the two countries without arbitration or the presence of the affected companies.[7]

The declarations of inter-American solidarity made at the Second Meeting of Consultation of Ministers of Foreign Affairs in Havana in July 1940, together with the need for military coordination with Mexico, mitigated strongly against continuation of the U.S.-Mexican controversy. In the United States there was gathering awareness of the need to reach an agreement so as to demonstrate the viability of the Good Neighbor policy to the rest of Latin America.[8] Moreover, the Defense Department was anxious to obtain Mexico's cooperation in plans for the protection of Panama and the rest of the hemisphere, which called for having bases in Mexico for U.S. planes flying to the Canal. Also, thought had been given to building a highway that would link the United States with that part of Central America and of establishing military bases on Mexican territory as well.[9] In March 1939 Ambassador Francisco Castillo Nájera told the under secretary of state that Mexico was ready to align itself with the antifascist powers but that there was still one problem: the oil controversy.[10] Not until the following year were the Americans ready to talk. In May 1940 the possibility of military coordination between Mexico and the United States was discussed with Castillo Nájera, this time at the initiative of the United States. By June State Department representatives, together with a group of U.S. military officers, were meeting with the Mexican ambassador to explore the possibility of economic and military cooperation between the two countries. Although only a few weeks earlier Cárdenas had reiterated Mexico's intention to remain neutral with respect to the conflict in Europe, he had privately let Daniels know that his government was prepared to detain any persons found to be engaged in Nazi activities in Mexico. As a result, Castillo Nájera could say to the U.S. military officers at the meeting shortly thereafter that Mexico was prepared to cooperate unreservedly in the mutual defense against fascism, but that first it was necessary to reach a general political agreement—that is, to settle the oil controversy. By the end of 1940 plans for the creation of a Joint U.S.-Mexico Defense Commission were already being discussed.[11]

It is well to bear in mind that Mexico, to the extent it could, had shown itself to be disposed to cooperate with the United States in regard to the world crisis since long before the beginning of the war. From as far back as 1938 Cárdenas' letters to Roosevelt had consistently made it clear that he stood behind his American colleague.[12] Mexico had assured the State Department right along, and especially in preparation for the inter-American meetings, that it would cooperate with U.S. representatives in every way possible to assure hemispheric solidarity and the common defense. In Lima, at the VIII International Conference of American States in 1938, the Mexican delegation had made it a point to avoid any argument with the United States when the subject of the right of expropriation came up.[13]

In March 1941 Daniels informed Roosevelt that the Mexican government was fully prepared to cooperate with the United States in the anti-Nazi struggle but that there was still one problem: the conflict with the oil companies, of course. The ambassador stressed the importance of taking advantage of the fact that President Avila Camacho was favorably disposed— adding it was useless to defend a status that was "as dead as Julius Caesar."[14] The ambassador's hand was strengthened when the following month the Mexican Congress approved a treaty that would permit U.S. military planes en route to Panama to stop at Mexican bases.[15]

By 1941 Secretary of State Hull was no longer quite so disposed to go on supporting the oil firms unconditionally; he had begun to get impatient with their lack of cooperation.[16] The companies, for their part, held to their ground unyieldingly and maintained that no intergovernmental commission such as the one the State Department had accepted had the right to decide on the amount and form of payment for their properties.[17] On September 27 of that year Hull informed the oil firms that national interest demanded an immediate solution to the problem with Mexico and that concessions in principle would have to be made, since there was a real threat of fascist subversion south of the Rio Grande. In addition, Mexican cooperation was urgently needed in order to get the use of air and naval bases within its territory and to prevent any possible sale of strategic materials to the Axis countries. Standard Oil answered that it would prefer to lose its property in Mexico forever rather than give in on the principle that was the basis of its claim.[18] In October Hull informed the firms that the United States was considering entering into an agreement with Mexico for assessment of the nationalized industry,[19] and in fact on October 19, having decided that the strategic national interest could no longer continue to depend on the oil companies' say, Washington announced the first in a series of accords with Mexico leading to assessment by an intergovernmental commission. The second one, signed on November 17, although it did not settle the oil conflict, did lay the groundwork for its eventual solution. It provided for: cancellation of all pending general claims on payment by Mexico of a global indemnization in the amount of 40 million dollars; extension of a credit to Mexico in the same amount to stabilize the value of the peso; the signing of a new agreement for the purchase of 6 million ounces of Mexican silver each month by the U.S. government; and the granting of a 20-million-dollar loan for rehabilitation of the country's railroad network. With regard to oil, it was agreed that the matter would not be submitted to arbitration but that the value of the firms' properties, rights, and interests would be assessed "internationally."[20] At the end of 1941 it appeared for the first time in this long controversy that Mexico was going to win out against the oil companies—and definitively. Washington's decision to enter into this Good Neighbor Agreement, as it was called, was to be rewarded not long afterward when President Avila Camacho announced to a surprised and not very enthusiastic public that Mexico had declared war on the Axis powers.

In some American circles Washington's shift in policy had been foreseen. From the beginning of October the press had been referring to a soon-to-be-signed agreement with Mexico. Anticipating its terms, the *New York Times* went on record against any kind of loan to Mexico, which it claimed would amount to "financing" the expropriation of American property.[21] When the agreement was in fact concluded, this influential paper commented that Mexico had charged dearly for its collaboration in the defense of the hemisphere.[22]

The Question of Compensation

Not a month had elapsed following the national takeover when, on April 13, 1938, the Treasury Ministry circularized the sixteen companies affected with a letter urging them to initiate the necessary negotiations in order to decide on the amount and form of payment to be made in settlement. The firms did not respond, refusing to recognize the validity of the March 18 decree. In May the Mexican government announced its intention to compensate only for the value of the surface property, not taking into account the hydrocarbons in the subsoil. This decision, it said, was in accordance with recognized international precepts, and the fact that in some cases title had been acquired prior to 1917 did not alter the matter in any way.[23] While Mexico was taking this position officially, unofficially and secretly it was submitting a plan for Washington and the companies' consideration. The proposal envisioned paying the firms for equipment and drilling and exploitation costs but not for the value of the subsoil petroleum. In addition, it called for formation of a trusteeship, to be headed by Mexicans but with the foreign firms participating, to administer the property, handle the sale thereof, and indemnify the companies.[24] The State Department discussed this plan with the firms, and Standard refused to accept it. Secretary of State Hull pointed out that save through the use of force, which no one wanted, the only alternatives left to the companies were (1) to come to an agreement with Mexico on the basis of the terms it was proposing or (2) to hold things in suspense and wait until the situation was more favorable in the future. In 1938 the State Department did not yet see any reason for pressing for a settlement. The firms accepted Hull's analysis and decided that, in view of the ramifications that a solution to the problem with Mexico could have with respect to their other possessions abroad, it was better to wait.[25] Supposedly this meant that in time diplomatic and economic pressure by

Washington and the companies, respectively, would bring about a change in the Mexican government and/or policy.

In view of the failure to reach an agreement over the amount and manner of payment in the talks held between the Mexican government and the companies during May and June 1938,[26] Cárdenas ordered the solicitor general and the ministers of the treasury and national economy to proceed with an assessment on their own.[27] Before long it became clear that the obstacles to reaching a formula acceptable to all sides were insurmountable. To begin with, the American and British firms were pointing out that the real value of their combined property was between 400 and 500 million dollars, the American part representing something upward of 200 million.[28] This was the figure that the U.S. press was to pick up and use for a long time in referring to the problem with Mexico.[29] The State Department, which attempted to make its own calculations, came up with 76,297,105 dollars according to one method (the Adams formula) and 101,729,473 dollars according to another (the sixteen-times-earnings formula). In both cases the value of the subsoil hydrocarbons was taken into account.[30] As it can be seen, the discrepancy between these two figures and those of the companies was rather large. The State Department did not disclose the results of its calculations: publicly Secretary Hull continued to insist that the nationalized property was worth 400 million dollars.[31]

The official Mexican government inventory was initiated in the firms' absence, and over their objections, at the beginning of 1939. With the preliminary findings in hand, Cárdenas let it be known that Mexico considered itself obligated to pay the companies, after subtracting the debts that were pending with the Mexican government and the workers, a total of 40,208,813 dollars.[32] This figure, which in the firms' eyes was ridiculous and inadmissible, coincided fairly closely with the State Department's low estimate, which Mexico knew nothing about. Even though it represented only one-twelfth of what they were asking for, the Mexican treasury could not pay it immediately, and Cárdenas repeated his offer to settle the debt by making oil available—approximately 60 per cent of the total output—at prices below the world market.[33] The companies again turned it down, saying they could not agree to be paid in installments—and certainly not with their own oil. Although the assessment was completed at the beginning of 1939, Mexico did not formalize the matter right away, perhaps because conversations were being held with company representatives at the time. After the talks fell through in 1940 the figures were made known officially. By then a settlement had already been made with the Sinclair group, and the value of the rest of the nationalized property was estimated at 33.6 million dollars, of which only 6.5 million corresponded to the American part.[34] Since the firms' representatives had not been present during the assessment process, the courts ordered that the president of the republic appoint a commission to act in their name. Interestingly, it was at this point that for the first time a U.S. publication estimated the value of the American companies' nationalized property, exclusive of the Sinclair interests, at a figure lower than 100 million dollars—namely, 35 million.[35]

After the breakdown of the Richberg negotiations the firms never again dealt directly with the Mexican government. The State Department took the initiative from there on. In 1938 Under Secretary Welles had suggested the establishment of a commission to set the amount of the indemnization,[36] but the plan did not turn into anything concrete at the time, perhaps because of opposition by the companies. Little by little, between their inflexibility and the world situation, the State Department began to change its stand; World War II was making it increasingly urgent to come to a solution that was acceptable to all sides. The arrangements reached with Sinclair and Cities Service in 1940, together with the precedent set when compensation for the expropriated American ranchers was decided on by an intergovernmental agreement, made it possible to lay the groundwork for the final settlement in 1942.[37] Internal State Department records show that by March 1941 its officials were more than anxious for the oil firms to admit that the time had come to agree on a solution and stop dragging the matter out.[38] Indeed, their impatience was showing.[39]

Washington's attitude was translated into a new plan for compensation that was close to the Mexican position—payment to be made in oil with no participation by the companies either in administering the industry or in any other respect. It was simple: to the remaining uncompensated American firms Mexico would make an initial payment of 8 or 10 million dollars in cash and deliver 5 million barrels of oil a year at cost.[40] Mexico was not averse to the plan itself, but it refused to agree that the 8 or 10 million dollars would be taken as only 10 per cent of the total which the companies were to receive; it considered that their property was worth a maximum of 13 million dollars, although it was prepared to pay up to 16 million if by doing so an agreement could be reached.[41] In 1941 the State Department again attempted to assess the American properties that had not yet been compensated for. This time the study was more complex, and the results only added to the confusion. If the value of the subsoil deposits was not taken into account—a point on which Roosevelt had already conceded—the American investments still in dispute were worth 6 million dollars. However, counting the hydrocarbons still in the subsoil, the estimates were 20, 28, and 108 million dollars, depending on the formula used.[42] Finally in June the State Department arrived at a figure that took into account both the surface and the subsoil property: 13.5 million dollars.[43] To the State Department and the firms' chagrin, an American magazine saw fit to publish some of the data from this study.[44]

Although there was still no agreement on the amount to be paid, by mid-1941 a decisive step had been taken toward final settlement: both the United States and Mexico had accepted that: (1) the companies were not to return to the country; (2) payment would not be made immediately but rather over several years; and (3) the matter was to be handled between the two governments. The only points to work out were the exact amount and the form in which it was to be paid. It was at this juncture that Mexico began to yield. By July 1941 the Mexican embassy had already agreed that the initial amount would be 9 million, although the ability to make this payment hinged on the outcome of its request then being discussed with the U.S. Treasury and the Export-Import Bank, for a loan under the Good Neighbor Agreement. The final figure was yet to be worked out.[45]

The negotiations were intense and complicated. During the months of July, August, September, and October 1941 there was constant contact between the Mexican embassy and the State Department's Division of the American Republics, and in turn between these two and the spokesmen for Standard Oil of New Jersey. The main purpose of the talks was to decide on the wording of a document that the United States planned to present to Mexico asking for appointment of a commission to set the amount and terms of the indemnization.[46] Although formally speaking the document was only supposed to propose that the commission be set up, the idea was to agree on the assessment beforehand so as to avoid any difficulties once the matter was made public. The figures that Mexico came forward with as a basis for the discussion ranged between 8 and 381 million dollars, while the State Department's gamut was even broader still: 7 to 408 million.[47] By the end of September almost full agreement had been reached. The amount was to be set at 24 million. With the note now drafted to Mexico, Under Secretary Welles met with the representatives of Standard Oil of New Jersey and California and also those of Huasteca and told them that in the interest of hemispheric defense it was necessary to come to an immediate agreement. He went on to point out that Mexico had already shown it was prepared to cooperate with the United States in keeping Japan from acquiring strategic matériel and that as soon as the oil problem was solved it would be possible to ask Mexico for permission to establish U.S. naval bases on its territorial shores. Welles stressed that, although Mexico would not say in so many words, it was going to compensate the companies for the deposits in the subsoil and that in actual fact the figure to be paid reflected their value. The man from Standard Oil of New Jersey, speaking in the name of all the firms, rejected Welles' arguments—also invoking national interest. He pointed out that the United States was at war with Hitler precisely to defend the rights of property and human freedom, and that not to defend them with Mexico was to betray the valiant resistance being put up by the British people. In the opinion of Standard, it was better to leave things as they were than to bow to an agreement of the kind the State Department was proposing. If it went ahead in these terms the companies would have no alternative but to oppose the action of their own government.[48] These protests were disregarded and the plan went ahead. In November 1941 the proposed text was formally presented to Mexico—although not without one more try to get the firms to support it.[49] For some time Standard considered appealing to the courts to keep Washington from formalizing the agreement,[50] but apparently it gave up. The terms of the final agreement, on which accord had already nearly been reached in principle, were hammered out by a joint commission which began its work in January and concluded it on April 17, 1942, a few months after the attack on Pearl Harbor.[51] The commission's report set a value of 24 million dollars on the property of the American oil companies that had not yet been compensated, and it proposed that one-third of this amount be paid on June 1, 1942, and the rest over the next five years.[52] (When this report was presented Mexico had just concluded a 226,000-dollar settlement with a group of small oil firms.)[53]

In the final text it was not stated specifically whether or not the indemnization included the value of the deposits in the subsoil, although practically speaking it did. This was the concession that Mexico made in return for Washington's support against the express wishes of the American companies—that is, Standard Oil. After the report was presented Secretary of State Hull informed the firms that they were under no obligation to accept the terms of the agreement, which were the best that Washington had been able to get, but that they should know that from there on they would not have official support for any other moves they might want to make.[54] More than a year went by before Standard decided to accept the solution. This delay was possibly due to the fact that in July 1942 two small companies, Titania and Mercedes, won injunctions against the expropriation and there was a brief hope that Avila Camacho might go back on Cárdenas' decree. However any such ideas were quashed by the Mexican embassy, which announced that there was going to be no change in its country's oil policy.[55] In December 1942 Standard let Washington know that it was prepared to accept the agreement almost in its entirety, although it would not approve it officially.[56] Finally, on October 1, 1943, it accepted the State Department's solution. With this decision taken, the precise settlement was not very long in coming. The terms of the final agreement signed a month later were very close to those in the commission's original text. The Mexican government was to pay the companies 30 million dollars in annual installments until the total sum was reached in 1947.[57] Still, after the agreement was signed, the firms let Washington know indirectly that they were not at all pleased with what had happened: the government had originally encouraged them to invest beyond the U.S. national borders and in a time of crisis it had not been able to provide them with the necessary support.[58]

Earlier, after the commission's terms had been presented to Standard and the other remaining firms but before the agreement had been formally concluded, the U.S. government had decided to approach Mexico on another kind of deal in regard to its oil. The recently established Office of the Petroleum Coordinator for War apparently had an eye on Mexico's reserves in the event of an emergency. This idea was not entirely new: back in early 1941 the State Department had realized the United States might come to need Mexican oil and decided it was important to see that the industry was safeguarded.[59] Accordingly, it began to take steps to protect the Mexican fields against sabotage.[60] The Interior Department, for its part, went so far as to propose that the government negotiate to purchase the Mexican industry outright. Under Secretary of State Welles, astounded, refused to even consider the idea,[61] but he did ask Mexico for permission to send down a group of experts to inspect PEMEX on the spot. In July 1942 Avila Camacho gave his consent. The Interior Department continued to take an active interest in the Mexican industry—now no longer in buying it but rather in building it up as a hedge against a possible energy shortage. The U.S. mission in Mexico studied the newly nationalized industry's different problems and capabilities and filed a report of its findings with Washington.[62] Shortly afterward, at the express order of President Roosevelt, the State Department entered into protracted negotiations with Mexico for the construction of a refinery on the Gulf which would produce 100-octane gasoline to be used by American air-craft.[63] At the same time that Mexico's receptivity to this project was being sounded out, Avila Camacho was approached in very exploratory terms to see if he might consider agreeing to the return of the expropriated compan-ies. The State Department thought it was worth a try, now that the new Mexican president was well established in power.[64] (As it has been noted, rumors to this effect had appeared in the press and elsewhere following the award of injunctions to Titania and Mercedes in 1942.)[65] The documenta-tion available does not make it clear whether Avila Camacho actually went so far as to consider reversing the decision of his predecessor. The only thing certain is that the U.S. government did not get any result from the feelers it sent out: although the proposed refinery was finally established at the end of the war, the companies did not return to Mexico. Only later, un-der the administration of Miguel Alemán (1946–1952), was Mexico to show interest in once again establishing contact with foreign oil capital. Al-though PEMEX very much held the reins, between 1949 and 1951 five con-tracts were signed with as many American companies for the exploration, drilling, and rebuilding of wells in areas around the Gulf. Under these ar-rangements, PEMEX agreed to sell them all or part of the output of any wells they might discover. From the outset there were groups in Mexico that looked askance on the presence of these firms in Mexico, and in 1958, after Alemán had left office, a constitutional amendment was put through forbidding future contracts of this kind. At the end of 1969 and the begin-ning of 1970 those contracts still in effect were rescinded and indemniza-tion made.

Thus the last two decades of conflict ended with tacit recognition of the theses that Mexico had been insisting on ever since 1917. But the victory was not complete; the sum that the country was obliged to pay was con-siderably in excess of the real value of the American properties that had been nationalized in 1938 and did indeed, according to Washington's calcu-lations, taken into account the value of the deposits in the subsoil. Still, this did not totally invalidate the fact that officially what was basically covered was the value of the surface properties. From the Mexican standpoint the settlement implied acceptance by the United States of the principle that the hydrocarbons in the subsoil belonged to the nation independently of any concession that might have been granted before or after 1917. From the Ameri-can point of view it is equally valid to assume that the agreement tacitly recognized that the oil not yet extracted belonged to the companies, since they were compensated in an amount that corresponded to more than the value of their investments alone. In regard to form of payment, the Mexican position prevailed totally: it was not immediate. For this reason, the agree-ment reached between the Mexican government, the U.S. government, and the American oil companies had far-reaching implications. This accord, to-gether with one between Sweden and the Soviet Union signed in May 1941, gave recognition to a new way of making compensation for nationalized property which departed from the traditional standard of international law that calls for "prompt, effective, and adequate payment."[66] However, the agreement had repercussions more in international business circles than in the legal sphere because of its broad implications for foreign investors engaged in exporting natural resources from the developing countries. The Mexican move was one of several which served to point up the possibility and desirability of expropriation as part of a new concept of national interest. Influenced undoubtedly by the climate created by direct U.S. involvement in the war, Roosevelt recognized the growing acceptance of this principle in a speech on April 20, 1943, at Monterrey, when he said, "We know that the day of the exploitation of the resources and people of one country for the benefit of any group in another country is definitely over."[67]

The oil expropriation was the last serious confrontation between the United States and Mexico brought on by implementation of the Revolution's reform programs. The agreement that led to its solution meant that Washington had accepted, against the opposition of the British and American oil interests, Mexico's post-1917 nationalist policy. This ultimate triumph for the Mexican government was attributed not only to Cárdenas' skillful handling of the matter and to a degree of flexibility in the interpretation of certain pinciples but also to favorable circumstances beyond its control. One of these was the election of Franklin D. Roosevelt. Under the New Deal relations between the White House and the big oil companies were cooler than they had been in years past. There was a sharp difference between their respective interpretations of the "national interest." Some of the measures that Roosevelt had taken to get the United States out of the Depression turned him into a political enemy for a large sector of the business world, including the oil firms.[68] The United States' participation in World War II was another favorable factor, perhaps more important than the first, for it provided Mexico with a certain margin of independence. During the critical years following nationalization it permitted PEMEX exports to get around the embargo imposed by Standard and Shell and their governments. When normal conditions returned after the war the big companies once again exercised absolute control in the world market, accentuating Mexico's secondary position as an exporter of hydrocarbons, but by that time PEMEX was getting on its feet thanks to the domestic market. Since the country depended almost entirely on oil as a source of energy, the growing internal demand was able to take the place without too much difficulty of the markets lost abroad, so that starting in the 1940's the nationalized industry enjoyed a period of rapid and uninterrupted recovery. Indeed PEMEX contributed decidedly to the country's economic development in the period after World War II. Mexico became an exception to the pattern throughout the Western world of domination by the transnational consortia. The World War, besides providing foreign markets during a difficult time, helped in other ways as well. Germany and Japan's expansionist policies had obliged Roosevelt to counter by adopting a new style in the United States' relations with its Western Hemisphere neighbors. During the 1930's, worried that some extracontinental power might establish a foothold in its own backyard, the United States embarked on a crusade of inter-American solidarity. If it was to win the full support of the Latin American countries it had to be more flexible in its dealings with its neighbors and react less intransigently to independent decisions that might be somewhat against U.S. preferences. Moreover, in order to keep the fascist groups within the countries from becoming more powerful, it had to support their adversaries. The Cárdenas government was a case in point. In Washington's view of its own interest, hemispheric security came first, and the defense of a few but important private American groups working in Latin America had to take second place when these two principles clashed. Within the context of this new inter-American policy, the handling of the oil industry takeover in Mexico became the touchstone for the policy of the recently elected Democratic administration toward the republics to the south. Roosevelt, and Daniels even more so, felt that this time it was important to deny the oil companies any official support so that they would see the government really meant to turn over a new leaf in the history of the inter-American system.

The Effect of Expropriation on the Cárdenas Program in General

Nationalization of the oil industry was one of the key steps in the process designed to put an end to the type of economic colonialism inherited from the days of Porfirio Díaz. In this sense it was unquestionably a triumph. However, the timing of the move was unfortunate. The economic picture in Mexico at the beginning of 1938 was bleak. In addition to the heavy deficits from the public works and agrarian reform programs, crops had failed the year before and the declines in silver and oil exports had taken their toll of the national treasury. The crisis of confidence in the foreign and some of the national private sectors had led to a flight of capital and a sharp cutback in investments.[69] In some business circles it was believed that Mexico was headed for socialism and that the days of private capital were numbered.[70] For a while the foreign press spoke of "socialist Mexico." In this climate of fear the value of the peso fell 39 per cent (the exchange rate dropped from 3.6 to 5 pesos to the dollar) and both domestic prices and unemployment skyrocketed. The crisis was felt mostly in the urban centers; the rural areas, precisely because of their isolation from the more modern sectors of the economy, were at least apparently less affected.[71]

The economic situation had its political counterpart: agrarian reform, public works, and health and education projects all came to a slowdown. The government repeatedly reassured private industry that the oil expropriation had been prompted by extraordinary circumstances and that there was no thought of extending nationalization to the other private sectors; capitalism would not be abolished.[72] The workers' campaign against capital was kept low key in the name of national unity. Unofficially it was recognized that the economic crisis had changed the administration's political orientation.[73] The political program that was to have put Mexico "on the road to socialism" made a complete about-face. The movement to uplift and integrate the worker and peasant sectors through a broad revision of the economic and social structure was virtually halted. Instead, starting in 1938, Cárdenas increasingly focused his efforts on the re-creation of a favorable climate for private investment. The popular organizations, which had flourished less thanks to their own independent activity than to encouragement from the executive, lacked the strength and class awareness to resist the forces of the right that went to work following the expropriation. Indeed, the government turned them into tools for the implementation of its new policy. The swerve to the right was confirmed all the more when Cárdenas selected as his successor a candidate who had no commitment whatsoever to the sectors of the left. Apparently he intended by this move to keep the even more intransigent right wing, led by General Juan Andreu Almazán, from being provoked into seizing power by violent means. In the end, much to the surprise of those who had listened to the Cárdenas socialist rhetoric, the reforms introduced at the beginning of his regime were eventually used by his successors to build a capitalist society in which political stability was guaranteed by a dominant party and an authoritarian executive. The shift to the right during Cárdenas' last years in office was not due exclusively or above all to the oil expropriation. The explanation is much more complicated. However, there is no doubt that one factor which must be taken into account is the crisis provoked by the conflict with the powerful foreign industries that were exploiting Mexico's oil.

Chapter 11

Final Considerations

The withdrawal of Spanish authority following Mexican independence in 1821 left a vacuum that was not to be filled for half a century. Numerous different groups, more often than not with assistance from foreign powers, vied for the right to impose their model of development on the new nation. Only after the military and political defeat of the Church and of the conservative party that supported it were the liberals able to summon enough power to re-create a relatively stable national system. But the political disintegration that the former Viceroyalty of New Spain had experienced in the meantime left a number of far-reaching consequences. One of them was that the links between this peripheral region and the nerve centers of the world economy were almost entirely severed. After nearly three hundred years of dependence on Europe, Mexico found itself adrift, and the internal state of flux made it difficult if not impossible to establish new economic ties with other parts of the world.

After Benito Juárez' death General Porfirio Díaz came to power—though not without a struggle—and succeeded in remaining there for more than three decades. Only then was it possible to achieve the internal stability needed so that the political elite could take the time to reflect calmly on the nature of relations with the rest of the world. The opening of Mexico to foreign industries was a deliberate move, and the companies in question became the central pivot in a rapid process of modernization. American, British, and French participation was encouraged, while Spain was relegated to an increasingly minor role. By the end of the nineteenth century a new dependent relationship had already been established. The most dynamic sectors of the Mexican economy—namely, the mining industry and related activities—had become enclaves of the U.S. and to a lesser extent the European industrial system. The national elite centered its efforts on agriculture and was only marginally interested in industry. Lacking apparently both the resources and the initiative to operate effectively in this latter area, it left it in the hands of foreign capital. By the time the Díaz regime fell, the visible degree of foreign control over Mexican development was unparalleled anywhere in Latin America.

The first attempts at curtailing foreign domination in the country's economic life began prior to the Revolution of 1910, but they were notably intensified after that date. For the Revolution created a sudden and sharp awareness in both the leadership and the population at large of the extent to which national interests had become subordinated to those of the foreign companies. Despite the heterogeneous nature of the Revolutionary forces, the feeling with regard to the prosperity of the foreigners, especially the Americans, vis-à-vis the standstill in the local Mexican economy was nearly unanimous. Indeed, the Revolutionary movement was focused largely on turning around the situation in which the national interest, as defined by the new society, had been allowed to take second place to the needs of the enclave economy. The state was regarded as the appropriate instrument for changing this order of priorities—in other words for gaining control over the key sectors of the economy that up to then had been under foreign domination.

The size and importance of the American interests in Mexico, the geographic proximity of the two countries, and the emergence of the United States as a world power all came together to evoke a systematic opposition on the part of the American companies and the government in Washington to the Revolutionary development model. It was believed that as a result of putting the Revolutionary reforms into effect, particularly those called for by the Constitution of 1917, not only would the material interests of the American capitalists be impaired but also the political hegemony of the United States in its small but growing area of influence would be trimmed back. Moreover, in the long range the precepts of international law and trade themselves—the rules of the worldwide game as set by the dominant powers—would be undermined as well.

The Constitutionalist leaders and their successors, who represented the interests and attitudes of the middle class which had been slowly gathering strength during the Porfirian regime, succeeded in awakening the nationalism of the worker and peasant groups and mobilizing them in the struggle against the vested foreign interests. Within the picture of the Mexican economy as seen by the triumphant revolutionaries, a number of sectors had taken on the nature of enclaves. Of these, the most notorious—and the most productive—was the oil industry. Around this activity, whose rapid and astounding development had curiously coincided with the rise of the Mexican Revolution, raged the main battle between the new order and the foreign interests. The expropriations under the agrarian reform program, though they involved the same principles as those at stake in the oil reform, were of lesser economic and political significance. The same may be said of those issues which, although they were the subject of controversy, did not call into question the validity of prevailing principles in the international system, such as payment of the foreign debt and of compensation to those citizens of other countries who had suffered damages in the course of the civil conflict.

The Revolutionary leaders came to regard the oil reform as the touchstone for a new style of relations between Mexico and the rest of the world. The companies and their embassies, on the other hand, saw it as an unfair attempt to confiscate legitimately acquired wealth. To them the Mexican Revolution was merely a fight over the booty among unprincipled politicians—the trophy being the oil industry, created by their superior efforts and technology. Thus they looked on their effort to remain in Mexico not as crass imperialism but rather almost as a crusade against nefarious forces that were attempting to destroy the very principles of international life and perhaps of civilization itself. Both reason and a sense of justice demanded that they put an end to the "confiscatory" nationalist policies of the post-1910 Mexican regimes, born under the sign of violence and unlawfulness.

Moral arguments also carried weight within the Mexican Revolutionary group. The oil properties might, they admitted, have been acquired by dubiously legal means, but the benefits from the exploitation of this nonrenewable natural resource had up to then redounded very little to the country's good. However, this argument alone is hardly enough to justify the persistent efforts of the different Revolutionary governments to gain contol of the oil industry. A broader explanation would take into account both the legal and ideological vulnerability of the industry's position and also the fact it had been expanding rapidly while the rest of the economy was going through a period of relative stagnation. Although production began to fall off in 1922, the Mexicans were never sure of the origin of this phenomenon and always suspected tht it was due more to maneuvers on the part of the companies than to natural causes. The high profits that were correctly or incorrectly attributed to the oil activity were a great attraction to the different Mexican administrations, which were faced with constant budgetary deficits. Finally, the arrogance with which the firms responded to Mexican laws and decrees—an attitude that they also demonstrated in their own countries—is still one more factor that should be taken into consideration in explaining the acute and continuing resentment that was harbored both by the Mexican government and by the people at large.

Washington supported the oil companies to the hilt, although care was taken not to interfere any further than was felt wise within the international context at the different times in question. This backing, together with the power that the firms got from the sheer magnitude of their resources, made the nationalization process a protracted and hazardous one. That the oil industry finally did end up in the hands of the state was due mostly to the decisive attitude of certain Mexican leaders and to the fact that they knew how to take advantage of favorable international situations —namely, the two world wars. In both instances the international power structure had been altered in such a way that it was possible to neutralize to a considerable extent the pressures that the foreign countries were bringing to bear against Mexico.

The claims of certain American authors that the United States exercised restraint when it could well have resorted to armed intervention in defense of its nationals' interests ought to be somewhat tempered. Throughout the present study it has been shown that, except for the period under Franklin Roosevelt, the U.S. government never really rejected the possibility of using military force. Roosevelt's attitude stemmed from the revision that was taking place in U.S. policy toward Latin America and also from the overall international situation, with the great world powers divided into two opposing camps competing for the support of the peripheral countries. It should be remembered, however, that economic and diplomatic pressures did not cease to be used during the Good Neighbor period. The fact that the military and subversive alarms never actually led to anything beyond the occupation of Veracruz and the Pershing expedition is of secondary importance, since during most of the period in question Mexico had to act on the assumption that the threats could be fulfilled at any moment. As long as the oil firms had the total and unconditional support of the State Department and the Revolutionary forces were not fully mobilized, the new regime was helpless to change the status quo.

The evolution of the oil reform may be broken down into five different phases. The first, during which the foreign companies established control over the oil deposits (exploited up to 1938) could be said to run from 1901 to 1917. Up to 1911 it corresponded to the Porfirio Díaz regime, and afterward it was governed by a strategy that was basically no more than an extension of the same policy: namely, development of the country's natural resources by opening up their exploitation to foreign capital. The second period begins in 1917, when Carranza established the legal bases for nationalizing the hydrocarbon deposits through the new constitution, and ends after a long and frustrating controversy, with enactment of the first law on oil and the Morrow-Calles Agreement in 1928. At the close of this phase it looked as if the vested interests had put a halt once and for all to any attempts to change the situation inherited from the old regime. Mexico's sole and modest triumph was the recognition of its "positive-act" principle, which in reality meant very little. The third phase corresponds to the years following Calles' administration when he ran things from the sidelines as the "Supreme Leader." During this time, from 1928 to 1935, no serious problems with the oil companies came up, and it appeared as if the idea of a genuine reform in the subsoil ownership system had been abandoned, especially after the attempt to form a national oil enterprise—a scheme on which hopes had briefly been pinned as a new approach to the sought-for reform—fell through. Cárdenas' victory over Calles in 1935 marks the beginning of the fourth phase, when the broad program of Revolutionary reforms, including particularly the struggle for control of the oil industry, was revived. This period culminated in the decree of March 18, 1938. The fifth and last period covers the years 1938 to 1942, when, after serious difficulties, the takeover was solidly established and accepted by the parties involved as an irreversible fact—thanks largely to the pressures on Washington at the time stemming from World War II.

Generally speaking, the two periods when the greatest progress was made in the oil nationalization process, namely the years following Carranza's victory and those of the Cárdenas administration, had several characteristics in common. They both coincided with serious international crises between the great powers which culminated in world wars. They also coincided with the two most liberal administrations in the United States: those of Woodrow Wilson and Franklin D. Roosevelt. Contrariwise, Obregón and Calles' abortive efforts to carry forward the oil reform took place during times when relations among the great powers were on a fairly even keel and when the United States was under conservative Republican administrations. Paralleling these international trends, internally in Mexico the Revolutionary currents were strongest—and the mobilization of the marginal sectors most intense—during the Carranza and Cárdenas periods (despite the former's conservative line), while the 1920's and early 1930's, except for the very beginning of the Calles phase, were characterized more by accommodation of the vested interests and lack of Revolutionary impetus. These circumstances did not fail to play a part in the outcome of the oil controversy.

Historically, the Bolshevik Revolution and the Mexican struggle to end foreign control of its oil and of certain large agricultural holdings were the first assaults on the international investment system established by the capitalist industrialized countries of the West. Up until the first decade of the twentieth century the peripheral countries had never questioned the legitimacy of this system. Mexico's weak position with respect to the pressures exerted by the foreign interests and their governments obliged the post-Revolution administrations to focus on legal arguments in backing up their challenge. In doing so, they had to work within an international code made up by the industrialized nations themselves, which in the long run restricted their maneuverability. The system of international norms on which the United States based the defense of its interests permitted no change whatsoever in the oil companies' status as owners of the hydrocarbons unless Mexico provided immediate compensation, in cash, in an amount that was beyond its ability to pay. The Mexican position boiled down to the argument that the intended reforms were justified purely and simply because they were necessary for the good of the people. This new concept of national interest that grew out of the Revolution was never accepted by the United States. The struggle that ensued was one of the first episodes in a much broader controversy between the great powers, on the one side, and some of the peripheral and dependent countries, on the other, that has continued up to the present time. Within this conflict the latter have sought to reduce their dependence and forge a new system of international law that takes into account the needs of their developing societies—societies that must either remodel or get rid of the anachronistic structures inherited from the past.

The 1938 takeover was the culmination not only of the reform process set in motion at Querétaro twenty-one years earlier but also to a certain extent of the Mexican Revolution itself. The country gained control of its own economic system and relegated foreign capital to a secondary position—at least for the next two decades. In terms of U.S.-Mexican relations, it marked the end of an epoch. Never again, after the compensation agreement was signed, were the interests of the two governments to be polarized; never again were relations to take on the brutal and violent aspects they had seen in the past.

The success of the Mexican oil expropriation was looked on at the time as even more than the beginning of a new era in relations between the two neighboring countries. Some observers went so far as to believe that it heralded a whole new pattern of dealing between the weak nations and the strong, since one of the former had demonstrated that it could stand up to international big business without incurring an armed attack. However the realities of the postwar period were to show that its significance was in fact much more modest. It was only one of the first of the cases to point out that the old-style imperialism which had governed relations between the powerful and the less developed nations—between the industrialized capital-exporting economies and the dependent ones on the receiving end—was in the process of transformation. There were still to be many examples showing that the old system had not disappeared. One of them was Iran's frustrated attempt at petroleum nationalization in the early 1950's. Still, it is true that the attitude of the international oil consortia toward the underdeveloped countries in which they were operating did change somewhat after 1938, and there is reason to believe that the conflict with Mexico was not completely unrelated to their new attitude.

The nationalization of the oil industry in 1938 and the subsequent agreements definitely served to put Mexico in a less dependent position. Foreign capital ceased to control the key sectors in the economic system, which then shifted from raw materials to the production of consumer goods for the domestic market. In the two decades that followed, the new national bourgeoisie and the state together controlled the production system. Little by little, however, the picture of dependency was to return as the strategic sectors of the Mexican industrial complex were taken over again by transnational enterprises, which had the technological know-how and resources that the country needed in order to carry forward the industrialization it had opted for at the time of World War II. Thus the oil controversy was not the beginning of the end of Mexico's bondage but rather, apparently, a transition period to be followed by a new stage in its dependent development.

Appendix: Chronology 1910–1942

Year	Mexican President	Mexican Minister of Foreign Affairs or Equivalent
1910	Porfirio Díaz, 1877–1880, 1884–1911	Enrique C. Creel, 1910–1911
1911	Francisco Madero, 1911–1913	León de la Barra, 1911
		Manuel Calero, 1911–1912
1912		Pedro Lascuráin, 1912–1913
1913	Victoriano Huerta, 1913–1914	Francisco León de la Barra, 1913
1914		Provisional Period*
	Venustiano Carranza, 1914–1920	
1915		Jesús Urueta, 1915
1916		Jesús Acuña, 1915–1916
		Cándido Aguilar, 1916–1917
1917		Ernesto Garza Pérez, 1917–1918
1918		Cándido Aguilar, 1918
1919		Ernesto Garza Pérez, 1918–1919
		Salvador D. Fernández, 1919
1920	Adolfo de la Huerta, 1920	Hilario Medona, 1919–1920
1921	Alvaro Obregón, 1920–1924	Cutberto Hidalgo, 1920
		Alberto J. Pani, 1921–1923
1922		
1923		Aarón Sáenz, 1923–1927
1924	Plutarco Elías Calles, 1924–1928	
1925		
1926		
1927		Genaro Estrada, 1927–1932
1928	Emilio Portes Gil, 1928–1930	
1929		
1930	Pascual Ortiz Rubio, 1930–1932	
1931		
1932	Abelardo L. Rodríguez, 1932–1934	Manuel Téllez, 1932
1933		José M. Puig Casauranc, 1933–1934
1934	Lázaro Cárdenas, 1934–1940	Emilio Portes Gil, 1934–1935
1935		José Angel Cisneros, 1935
1936		Eduardo Hay, 1935–1940
1937		
1938		
1939		
1940	Manuel Avila Camacho, 1940–1946	Ezequiel Padilla, 1940–1945
1941		
1942		

*Also, for short periods, Francisco León de la Barra, Federico Gamboa, Querido Moheno, José López Portillo y Rojas, and Francisco S. Carvajal.

U.S. Ambassador	U.S. Secretary of State	U.S. President	Year
Henry Lane Wilson, 1910–1913	Philander C. Knox, 1909–1913	William Howard Taft, 1909–1913	1910
			1911
			1912
	William Jennings Bryan, 1913–1915	Woodrow Wilson, 1913–1921	1913
Diplomatic Relations Interrupted, February 1913–March 1917			1914
	Robert Lansing, 1915–1920		1915
			1916
Henry P. Fletcher, 1917–1919			1917
			1918
			1919
Diplomatic Relations Interrupted, January 1919–March 1924	Bainbridge Colby, 1920–1921		1920
	Charles Evans Hughes, 1921–1925	Warren G. Harding, 1921–1923	1921
			1922
		Calvin Coolidge, 1923–1929	1923
Charles Beecher Warren, 1924			1924
James R. Sheffield, 1924–1927	Frank B. Kellogg, 1925–1929		1925
			1926
Dwight W. Morrow, 1927–1930			1927
			1928
	Henry L. Stimson, 1929–1933	Herbert Hoover, 1929–1933	1929
			1930
J. Reuben Clark, Jr., 1930–1933			1931
			1932
Josephus Daniels, 1933–1941	Cordell Hull, 1933–1944	Franklin D. Roosevelt, 1933–1945	1933
			1934
			1935
			1936
			1937
			1938
			1939
			1940
			1941
George S. Messersmith, 1942–1946			1942

Notes

Introduction to the First Edition

1. *Economic imperialism* is understood here to mean the peaceful penetration of foreign capital in countries that are politically weak and economically less developed to the point that they are prevented from managing their own resources as they best see fit. The term *economic enclave* is used to characterize the situation in which an industrial complex from an investing country exploits some natural resource of a peripheral country for consumption by markets abroad, such markets usually being located in the investing country or in others of a similar level of development. Thus the enclave is an integral part of the other economic system or systems, virtually cut off from the country in which it is physically located.

2. The situation will be potentially more precarious still if the investment in question is for extracting a nonrenewable natural resource and if the fiscal income received by the country whose resources are being exploited is not considered by this country to be adequate compensation.

3. Daniel Cosío Villegas, *Extremos de América*, p. 12.

4. The papers consulted in the Josephus Daniels collection were found under the following headings: Diaries; Correspondence with Franklin D. Roosevelt, 1913–1945; Correspondence, 1933–1941; Correspondence with Mexican and U.S. Officials, 1933–1941; Correspondence on U.S.–Mexican Relations, 1933–1942; Speeches, Press Conferences, and Interviews; Speeches and Articles; Dossiers Relative to Problems with Mexico (Oil, Expropriation, etc.), 1933–1941; Memoranda on Problems Pending between the United States and Mexico, 1934. [N.B.: The collection was reorganized in 1974, and the foregoing headings no longer apply.]

Introduction to the Second Edition

1. Lorenzo Meyer, "Cambio político y dependencia: México en el siglo XX," in *La política exterior de México: Realidad y perspectivas*, pp. 1–38 (Mexico City: El Colegio de México, Centro de Estudios Internacionales, 1972).

1. Evolution of the Mexican Oil Industry

1. American politicians and businessmen were already looking forward to the day when their country, while still maintaining its status as a net importer, would be one of the financial centers in the world (Cleona Lewis, *America's Stake in International Investments*, pp. 1–2).

2. Daniel Durand, *La política petrolera internacional*, p. 29; James Neville Tattersall, "The Impact of Foreign Investment on Mexico," p. 60; C. Lewis, *America's Stake . . .* , p. 218.

3. For a more detailed study of this first period, see Carlos Díaz Dufoo, *México y los capitales extranjeros;* José Domingo Lavín, *Petróleo;* Miguel Manterola, *La industria del petróleo en México.*

4. Colegio de México, ed., *Estadísticas económicas del porfiriato: Comercio exterior de México, 1877–1911,* p. 249.

5. Doheny's testimony before the U.S. Senate can be consulted in United States, 66th Congress, 2nd session, Senate Committee on Foreign Relations, *Investigation of Mexican Affairs: Preliminary Report and Hearings . . . Pursuant to Senate Resolution No. 106 Directing the Committee . . . to Investigate the Matter of Outrages on Citizens of the United States in Mexico.*

6. Taken in its entirety, the U.S. investment was almost always larger than the British, but the British company El Aguila was the single most important one in Mexico.

7. In the opinion of his biographer, Pearson was, after Cortés, the individual who probably amassed the largest fortune in Mexico (Desmond Young, *Member for Mexico: A Biography of Weetman Pearson, First Viscount Cowdray,* pp. 4–5).

8. Carlos Díaz Dufoo, *La cuestión del petróleo,* p. 100; Clarence W. Barron, *The Mexican Problem,* p. 94.

9. A detailed description of the formation of the Doheny and Pearson enterprises appears in Doheny's testimony, United States, 66th Congress, 2nd session, Senate Committee on Foreign Relations, *Investigation of Mexican Affairs.* See also Young, *Member for Mexico.*

10. Pearson held onto a certain amount of stock (Young, *Member for Mexico,* pp. 188–190; Arthur C. Veatch, "Oil, Great Britain, and the United States," *Foreign Affairs* 9 (July 1931): 66). According to a report filed by the U.S. consul general in England on December 10, 1920, Shell paid 10 million pounds sterling for Pearson's holdings (NAW 812.6363⅛774).

11. Doheny was also in touch with certain bankers and British oil firms that were interested in his holdings (*New York Times,* March 11, 1925).

12. The literature on the rivalry among the oil companies is copious. Titles of interest include: Harvey O'Connor, *El imperio del* petróleo; Frank C. Hanighen, *The Secret War;* Pierre l'Espagnol de la Tramerge, *La Lutte mondiale pour le pétrole;* Francis Delaisi, *Oil: Its Influence on Politics;* Ludwell Denny, *We Fight for Oil.*

13. Willy John Feuerlein and Elizabeth Hannan, *Dólares en la América Latina,* p. 68.

14. In 1920 the British companies had more than 1.25 million hectares in oil lands, or about half of all the property claimed by the foreign industry (Manuel de la Peña, *La cuestión palpitante: Estudio jurídico, político y económico sobre el artículo 27 constitucional,* pp. 100–101). In 1933 El Aguila, the largest of the British firms, was producing 37 per cent of the oil being extracted in Mexico (report of the commercial attaché to Ambassador Daniels, April 24, 1934, JDP). According to Lavín, in 1926 El Aguila and Standard Oil of New Jersey agreed on their respective areas of influence in Mexico—a reflection of the fact that they had been able to come to agreement on the worldwide level. The British area was to the south of the Tampico parallel, whereas Standard's was the more promising one to the north. When the Poza Rica beds were discovered a few years later, the British were then in the more advantageous situation (Lavín, *Petróleo,* p. 84).

15. Durand, *La política petrolera internacional,* p. 31.

16. Report of the Association of Producers of Petroleum in Mexico (APPM), May 20, 1931, NAW 812.6363/2731.

17. The Shell group controlled Compañía Mexicana de Petróleo El Aguila, S.A., which in 1927 had ten subsidiaries plus the rights that Porfirio Díaz had granted to

Pearson. Before acquiring Pearson's rights, Shell was present in Mexico in the form of La Corona and its three subsidiaries. Standard Oil of New Jersey began its activities there through General Petroleum Corporation of California and Transcontinental Petroleum Company and its subsidiaries. With Doheny's acquisition of Pan American Petroleum and Transport and its seven subsidiaries—among them Huasteca—Standard's interests in Mexico increased considerably. Also Standard of Indiana, of California, and of New York were present at different times. The Gulf group had two subsidiaries plus contracts with other firms. Sinclair had three subsidiaries. Cities Service, which belonged to Henry L. Doherty, controlled twelve subsidiaries, but it did not have any pipelines or refineries of its own. Warner-Quinla controlled Atlantic Gulf and West Indies, which it acquired from Atlantic Gulf in 1927, plus two other subsidiaries. The detailed structure and importance of these groups and the other lesser companies in Mexico up to 1927 may be consulted in a report of the U.S. consul in Tampico to the Department of State, December 15, 1927, NAW 812.6363/2462. See table, page 239.

18. Díaz Dufoo estimated that in 1921 there were five hundred such companies (*La cuestión del petróleo*, p. 95). After that date the number declined.

19. Lavín, who at that time belonged to the group of "independent" oilmen, describes the hostility of the large firms toward the smaller ones in his *Petróleo*, pp. 120 ff.

20. In 1921, at the peak of the industry's boom, Mexican companies represented only 1 per cent of the total capital. The proportion increased to 3.02 per cent in 1926, but it dropped again two years later to 1.04 per cent and remained at this level until 1938 (*Boletín del petróleo* 10:306; 14:185; AREM L-E-533, vol. 1, Leg. 2, f. 195; Manterola, *La industria del petróleo en México*, p. 41; Max Winkler, *Investments of United States Capital in Latin America*, p. 225).

21. During the period 1920–1927 minerals accounted for 78 per cent of all Mexican exports, and of this total 60 per cent corresponded to oil. In the following decade silver and gold took first place over oil (Joaquín Santaella, *El petróleo en México: Factor económico*, pp. 48–50).

22. Mexico, Secretaría del Patrimonio Nacional, *El petróleo de México: Recopilación de documentos oficiales de orden económico de la industria petrolera con una introducción que resume sus motivos y consecuencias*, p. 45. In 1921, 78 per cent of Mexican oil exports were for the United States; in 1927 the proportion went down to 69 per cent, but by the end of the decade it was up again, this time to a high of 90 per cent. It is possible that the discovery of the Poza Rica beds by the British a few years later caused the share for Europe to go up in time (*Boletín del petróleo* 18; 21; 24; 25; Winkler, *Investments of United States Capital . . .* , p. 222; NAW 812.6363/2731).

23. John Ise, *The United States Oil Policy*, p. 455.

24. Emilio Alanís Patiño, "La energía en México," *Investigación económica* 14 (January–March 1954): 42.

25. In 1936, 16.9 per cent of the heavy oil went for internal consumption and 99 per cent of the light; together, this amounted to 43.5 per cent of all the refined output (Wendell C. Gordon, *The Expropriation of Foreign-owned Property in Mexico*, p. 80).

26. See Chapter 8.

27. In 1925, 3 per cent of the domestic demand was met with imports; by 1928 this proportion had increased to 10 per cent, and in 1932 it was up to 14 (*Boletín del petróleo* 22; 24; 35). Only on the eve of the expropriation did El Aguila lay a pipeline—from Papantla, Veracruz, to its refinery in the interior, in Azcapotzalco, D.F.—in an effort to take care of local needs.

28. The lack of any other cheap and abundant energy at the time Mexico's industrial development got underway helped to keep the nationalized oil enterprise from

Principal Petroleum Groups in Mexico in 1927

	Oil-bearing Lands Acquired before 1917 (Hectares)	Refining Capacity (Barrels per Day)	Pipeline Capacity (Barrels per Day)	Storage Capacity (Barrels)	Investment in Equipment (Dollars)
El Aguila	850,000	85,000	90,000	11,500,000	63,000,000
Standard Oil (N.J.)	850,000	—	—	—	20,000,000
Huasteca	31,000	162,000	205,000	8,500,000	115,000,000
Gulf	100,000	—	12,000	500,000	15,000,000
Sinclair	62,000	—	—	1,250,000	30,000,000[a]
City Services	500,000	None	None	—	—
La Corona	—	—	—	—	62,500,000[a]
Warner-Quinla	—	—	—	—	16,000,000[a]

[a] Pesos in gold.

—: Not found in the source consulted.

Source: Report of the U.S. consul in Tampico to the Department of State, December 15, 1927, NAW 812.6363/2462.

feeling any great impact from the loss of foreign markets. Mexico's dependence on hydrocarbons made it "the most oil-oriented country on earth" (Ernesto Lobato López, "El petróleo en la economía," in *México: 50 años de Revolución*, vol. 1, *La economía*, p. 314).

29. In 1910 sizable oil deposits were discovered in the Pánuco River basin. These, together with the Alamo and Cerro Azul fields discovered in 1913 and 1916, respectively, were to be the reason for the boom during the second phase.

30. At the end of this second period the twenty one largest companies had twenty eight terminals in the Mexican ports, pipelines with a capacity to carry 942,000 barrels a day, and fifteen refineries capable of turning out 400,000 barrels a day—all of this to handle the output of only 250 wells, most of which were located in five fields: Ebano (east of Tampico), Pánuco, Huasteca, Tuxpan, and Telmontepec-Tabasco (APPM report, May 20, 1931, NAW 812.6363/2731, pp. 5–6; Díaz Dufoo, *La cuestión del petróleo*, p. 107).

31. This fear arose during World War I and continued to inspire competition between the American and British firms throughout the world for some time to come (Durand, *La política petrolera internacional*, p. 9).

32. J. C. White, *Boletín de la Unión Panamericana* (July 1916) as cited in *Boletín del petróleo* 3 (January–June 1917). The same view was contained in a report presented by the Spanish embassy in Mexico through Miguel Bertan on July 3, 1918 (CDHM R51, Caja 351, Leg. 3, no. 31). Other more serious estimates also put the Mexican reserves in an outstanding position: in 1920 the U.S. Geological Survey's Foreign Minerals Section estimated them at more than 4.5 billion barrels, while the American reserves, the largest in the world, were set at 7 billion.

33. Spanish embassy in Mexico City to minister of state, August 14, 1918, CDHM R51, Caja 351, Leg. 3, no. 39.

34. L'Espagnol de la Tramerge, *La Lutte mondiale . . .* , pp. 121–124

35. NAW 812.6363/880. In a report of November 12, 1921, the U.S. consul in Tampico indicated that the companies had insufficient reserves to keep up such a high rate of production, since they had failed to carry on the necessary exploration owing to "political uncertainty" (?). In any case, the report went on, the days of the big profits with little effort were undoubtedly past; in the future, exploration would be more costly, and the firms were therefore dropping the competition among each other and joining forces (NAW 812.6363/1039).

36. U.S. embassy in Mexico City to Department of State, April 7, 1937, NAW 812.6363/2932.

37. The companies pointed out that the hostility of the Mexican government, added to the uncertainty about their rights stemming from the Constitution of 1917, had obliged them to turn their sights to Venezuela and other countries. They also complained about the excessive taxes, which amounted, they claimed, to 62 and 45 per cent of the light and heavy oil, respectively; about the labor legislation; about the regulations; etc. (APPM report to the Mexican government, May 20, 1931, NAW 812.6363/2731; Huasteca Petroleum Company and Standard Oil of California, *Expropiación: Un estudio de los hechos, causas, métodos y efectos de la dominación política de la industria en México*, p. 9; Gordon, *Expropriation . . .* , p. 54).

38. *El Universal*, November 2, 1938; Jesús Silva Herzog, *México y su petróleo*, p. 25. Government officials responsible for oil matters stated that the companies had decided to hold the Mexican deposits in reserve and not drill from them for the time being in view of the depressed world oil market (*Boletín del petróleo* 27 (January–June 1929): 169).

39. To a certain extent the Mexican output figures did not reflect the real situation (Antonio J. Bermúdez, "The Mexican National Petroleum Industry: A Case Study in Nationalization," *Hispanic-American Report* (1963): 202–203).

40. In 1926 the companies drilled a record of 800 wells, but even so they failed to find any rich deposits like the ones they had exhausted (*Boletín del petróleo* 33 [January–June 1927]: 122; NAW 812.6363/R226/E0472). The reports of the U.S. diplomatic service show that Washington was well informed of the situation. A memorandum from the Division of Mexican Affairs, Department of State, points out that the production decline in Mexico was due to technical and economic reasons rather than political ones (April 8, 1924, NAW 812.6363/1506). The same view was advanced by Ambassador Morrow in a letter to J. Reuben Clark, Jr., in the Department of State (October 30, 1928, NAW 812.6363/2597½), as well as in a report of the U.S. consul in Tampico (February 10, 1926, NAW 812.6363/1760).

41. Transcontinental Petroleum, for example, turned over its interests in Tampico to Huasteca in 1929, and Cortés-Aguada sold its holdings to El Aguila (report of U.S. consul in Tampico, July 25, 1929, NAW 812.6363/2655).

42. By 1930, 19 of the 28 terminals that were in operation in 1922 had been closed; the pipeline capacity was down to 387,000 barrels a day, only 28 per cent of which was being used; the refineries were operating at only 30 per cent of their capacity; and the number of workers in the industry had declined from an estimated peak of 50,000 to 13,745 (APPM report, May 20, 1931, NAW 812.6363/2731, pp. 5–6). The companies' situation at the beginning of the crisis in 1923 is described in a report filed the following year by the U.S. consul in Tampico (NAW 812.6363/2156).

43. The first of these views is set forth in Ise, *The United States Oil Policy*, p. 452, and James Fred Rippy, *The United States and Mexico*, p. 384. The latter is found in Albert D. Brokaw, "Oil," *Foreign Affairs* 6 (October 1927): 93.

44. According to the companies' calculations, the f.o.b. cost of a barrel of Mexican oil was 1.05 (U.S. dollars) in 1931, whereas in Venezuela it was only .56. The taxes should be lowered especially, they said, when exploitation of new beds is involved, since otherwise they cannot risk the tremendous investment needed (APPM report, May 20, 1931, NAW 812.6363/2731, pp. 6–39).

45. APPM report, May 20, 1931, NAW 812.6363/2731, pp. 6–39.

46. It is possible that the British Admiralty encouraged Shell to develop this rich new field, since the problems of Japanese expansion in Asia, the Spanish civil war, the invasion of Ethiopia, etc., might have led the British strategists to see the advantage of having fuel reserves in areas less potentially dangerous than the Middle East.

47. Association of Producers of Petroleum in Mexico, (APPM), *Current Conditions in Mexico*, pp. 37–40. In a report submitted to Ambassador Daniels by his commercial attaché it was again stated that Mexico was one of the richest countries in oil in the world (Josephus Daniels, *Shirt-Sleeve Diplomat*, p. 216). In 1943 Graham H. Stuart expressed a similar view (*Latin America and the United States*, pp. 191–192).

48. U.S. embassy to Department of State, April 7, 1937, NAW 812.6363/2932.

49. Mexican secretary of industry, commerce, and labor to Mexican ambassador in Washington, (1926?), AREM III/628 (010)/I L-E-533, Leg. ff. 117–119.

50. Luis Nicolau d'Olwer, "Las inversiones extranjeras," in *Historia moderna de México: El porfiriato; La vida económica*, ed. Daniel Cosío Villegas, pp. 1137–1147.

51. In 1914, for example, the Doheny group represented 70.5 per cent of the total U.S. oil investment in Mexico (C. Lewis, *America's Stake . . .* , p. 220).

52. Ibid., pp. 588–589.

53. Cleona Lewis, referring to the American oil companies that had been in Mexico and were picking up operations in Venezuela, pointed out that they had already made fabulous profits (ibid, pp. 427–428).

54. Oscar Morineau estimates that the earnings were on the order of 5 billion dollars (*The Good Neighbor*, p. 6), but, according to the calculations of Stocking, based on information from Silva Herzog, they were only slightly over 1 billion for the period

1901–1938 (George Ward Stocking and Jesús Silva Herzog, *Mexican Expropriation: The Mexican Oil Problem*, p. 512). Paul Boracrès, for his part, sets the figure at 7.1 billion pesos, which at the prevailing rate of exchange would have been 2 billion dollars (*Le Pétrole mexicain . . . un bien volé!*, pp. 95–96). Neville estimates the average annually repatriated by the companies at 75 million dollars and the overall sum at 2.75 billion (*The Impact of Foreign Investment . . .* , p. 152).Frank Brandenburg speaks of returns ten times the value of the capital invested (*The Making of Modern Mexico*, p. 273).

55. Daniels to Secretary of State Hull, September 9, 1937, JDP.

56. Mexico, Cámara de Senadores, Sección Estadística y Anales de Jurisprudencia, *El petróleo: La más grande riqueza nacional*, p. 300. These estimates seem to be exaggerated. However, the *Economist* pointed out that in 1919–1920 the world oil industry had had one of its highest profits indexes, with an average of 33.9 per cent. See also Díaz Dufoo, *La cuestión del petróleo*, p. 340; Manuel López Gallo, *Economía y política en la historia de México*, pp. 438–439.

57. Unsigned and undated document on the financial situation of El Aguila, AREM III/628 (010)/1 L-E-541, Leg. 28, f. 6; *Boletín del petróleo* 3 (January–June 1917): 471; J. Vázquez Schiaffino in *Petroleum* 7 (August 1919): 104; L'Espagnol de la Tramerge, *La Lutte mondiale . . .* , p. 107; Boracrès, *Le Pétrole mexicain . . .* , p. 9; De la Peña, *La cuestión palpitante*, p. 107.

58. Manuel González Ramírez, *El petróleo mexicano: La expropiación petrolera ante el derecho internacional*, p. 21.

59. Estimates by Boracrès, cited by López Gallo (*Economía y política . . .* , p. 447). For the period 1934–1936, Lobato López sets the profits in relation to capital invested at 32, 39, and 31 per cent a year, respectively ("El petróleo en la economía," p. 323).

60. Raymond F. Mikesell, ed., *U.S. Private and Government Investment Abroad*, pp. 5–6, 32–34.

61. Jesús Silva Herzog Flores, "Consideraciones sobre la industria petrolera y el desarrollo económico de México" (Master's thesis, National University of Mexico, 1957), p. 42.

62. For a more complete study on this point, see Manterola, *La industria del petróleo en México*, pp. 312 ff.; Gordon, *Expropriation . . .* , pp. 59–62; Santaella, *El petróleo en México*, pp. 39–42.

63. Mexico, Secretaría del Patrimonio Nacional, *El petróleo de México*, p. 78.

64. In 1919, for example, Doheny's Mexican Petroleum paid 2 million dollars to Mexico and 5 million to the United States in taxes on Mexican oil introduced into the United States.

65. *Boletín del petróleo* 1; 10; 11; 18; 24; 33; 35; Gustavo Ortega, *Los recursos petrolíferos mexicanos y su actual explotación*, pp. 10–11; Mexico, Secretaría del Patrimonio Nacional, *El petróleo de México*, pp. 113–117.

66. In 1917 an editorial in the *Boletín del petróleo* declared: "If it is not possible to refine the oil in Mexico and use its products in Mexican industries, better then that the inheritance in our subsoil from the prehistoric ages be saved for other generations in the future." Twenty years later, in an expert report on the status on the industry, it was urged that in the end "all or at least most of these valuable [petroleum] products be consumed in the country" (Mexico, Secretaría del Patrimonio Nacional, *El Petróleo de México*, p. 94).

67. Silva Herzog Flores, "Consideraciones sobre la industria petrolera . . . ," p. 40. Up until 1931 only 15 per cent of the oil extracted had been for domestic consumption (*El Universal*, February 25, 1931); in 1936, however, 43 per cent of all the petroleum products refined went to the domestic market (Gordon, *Expropriation . . .* , p. 80).

68. Jesús Silva Herzog, *Historia de la expropiación petrolera*, p. 76; Guy Stevens, *Current Controversies with Mexico: Addresses and Writings*, p. 136; Santaella, *El*

petróleo en México, pp. 54–56; Manterola, *La industria del petróleo en México,* pp. 70–74.

69. Report of Miguel Bertan to the Spanish embassy, July 3, 1918, CDHM R51, Caja 351, Leg. 3, no. 931.

70. Miguel Acosta Saignés, *Petróleo en México y Venezuela,* p. 16.

71. Daniels, *Shirt-Sleeve Diplomat,* pp. 213–214.

72. APPM, *Current Conditions in Mexico,* pp. 37–40. The firms did not accept this estimate, however. Later, when they were expropriated, they still claimed ownership of 18.5 million hectares more, which had been acquired prior to May 1917 (Lobato López, "El petróleo en la economía," p. 323; Manterola, *La industria del petróleo en México,* pp. 30–36).

73. U.S. consul in Yucatán to Department of State, December 6, 1928, NAW 812.6363/2617; U.S. consul in Mexicali to Department of State, July 24, 1923, NAW 812.6363/R18/Aug.; U.S. consul in Nogales to Department of State, June 3, 1920, NAW 812.6363/M34. These efforts led to formation of the Compañía Petrolera de la Baja California and the Yucatan Petroleum Corporation.

74. Unsigned memorandum of August 1938, AREM III/628 "938"/2 L-E-555, part 1, f. 149.

75. In 1937 the net value of oil exports was 40 million dollars, of which 17.6 million was paid abroad (Patiño, "La energía en México," p. 56).

2. Establishment of the First Oil Companies: 1900–1914

1. Howard F. Cline, *The United States and Mexico,* pp. 52–53.

2. José Luis Ceceña, "La penetración extranjera y los grupos de poder en México, 1870–1910," *Problemas del desarrollo: Revista latinoamericana de economía* 1, no. 1 (October–December 1969): 62.

3. Ibid.

4. Moisés González Navarro, *Estadísticas sociales del porfiriato, 1887–1910,* pp. 40–41, 217–219; Jesús Silva Herzog, *El agrarismo mexicano y la reforma agraria: Exposición y crítica,* p. 502.

5. Raymond Vernon, ed., *How Latin America Views the United States Investor,* p. 97.

6. Fernando Rosenzweig, "El desarrollo económico de México, 1877–1911," *Trimestre económico* 32 (July–September 1965): 405–406. During the Porfirian regime the gross national product increased by an annual 2.7 per cent and the population growth rate was 1.4.

7. See also Ceceña, "La penetración extranjera . . ."

8. Ibid., p. 59.

9. Raymond W. Goldsmith, *The Financial Development of Mexico,* p. 73; Charles C. Cumberland, *Mexico: The Struggle for Modernity,* pp. 232–233.

10. Ceceña, "La penetración extranjera . . ."

11. Ibid., pp. 51–53.

12. Raymond Vernon, *The Dilemma of Mexico's Development,* p. 53.

13. *Nation* 123, no. 3207 (December 22, 1926): 656.

14. Pan American Petroleum and Transport Company, *Mexican Petroleum.*

15. *Nation* 123, no. 3207 (December 22, 1926): 656.

16. United States, 66th Congress, 2nd Session, Senate Committee on Foreign Relations, *Investigation of Mexican Affairs: Preliminary Report and Hearings . . . Pursuant to Senate Resolution No. 106 Directing the Committee . . . to Investigate the Matter of Outrages on Citizens of the United States in Mexico,* pp. 230–231.

17. Fritz Hoffman, "Edward Doheny and the Beginning of Petroleum Development in Mexico," *Mid-America* 13 (1942): 98.

18. Luis Nicolau d'Olwer, "Las inversiones extranjeras," in *Historia moderna de México: El porfiriato; La vida económica*, ed. Daniel Cosío Villegas, p. 1127.

19. Mexico, Secretaría del Patrimonio Nacional, *El petróleo de México: Recopilación de documentos oficiales de orden económico de la industria petrolera, con una introducción que resume sus motivos y consecuencias*, pp. 86–87.

20. For further details on this subject, including Doheny's statements before the Fall Committee, see, among others, Moisei S. Alperovich and Boris T. Rudenko, *La Revolución Mexicana de 1910–1917 y la política de los Estados Unidos;* José Domingo Lavín, *Petróleo;* Miguel Manterola, *La industria del petróleo en México;* d'Olwer, "Las inversiones extranjeras."

21. In 1906 Pearson signed a contract with the Mexican government agreeing to turn over to the state, in the form of royalties, 10 per cent of the value of the output corresponding to nationally owned lands in exchange for complete exemption from any taxes thereon. At the last minute, thanks to a deal made with a deputy in the Mexican congress, he succeeded in having a clause added extending the tax exemption to oil extracted on private land. Pearson never worked the federal lands (Jesús Silva Herzog, *México y su petróleo*, p. 28).

22. More detailed information on Pearson's early days in oil is available in Desmond Young, *Member for Mexico: A Biography of Weetman Pearson, First Viscount Cowdray*, pp. 119–139; Mexico, Secretaría del Patrimonio Nacional, *El petróleo de México*, pp. 84–86.

23. Daniel Cosío Villegas, ed., *Historia moderna de México: El Porfiriato; La vida política exterior*, pt. 2, pp. xxii–xxiii; James Neville Tattersall, "The Impact of Foreign Investment on Mexico" (Master's thesis, University of Washington, 1956), pp. 128–129.

24. The Spanish mining code, which envisaged mainly metals, made all minerals the patrimony of the monarch. The Aranjuez ordinances of 1793, the first mining legislation to refer exclusively to New Spain, upheld this principle. The oil companies were to claim later that when subsequently Charles IV turned over the rights to coal to the surface landholder in 1803 he did so for the hydrocarbons as well. They went on to maintain, therefore, that when the rights of the Spanish crown were passed to Mexico in the Treaty of Peace and Friendship of 1836 oil was not among them, since it had already been ceded previously. They did not take into account that Charles IV's provisions referred only to Metropolitan Spain. Nor did they emphasize the fact that later President Benito Juárez clearly decreed that coal was on a par with all the other minerals and its exploitation had to be authorized by the state —a provision that was still in effect when Porfirio Díaz came to power.

25. In 1884 it was considered that legally speaking oil was on a par with water and should therefore have the same status. The U.S. State Department from that date on, up to 1917, was to regard the rights acquired by the companies as irrevocable and perpetual, whereas the Revolutionary groups claimed that the 1884 law was invalid owing to certain defects in its enactment (Merrill Rippy, "El petróleo y la Revolución Mexicana," *Problemas agrícolas e industriales de México* 6 [July–September 1954]: 20, 23; Salvador Mendoza, *La controversia del petróleo*, p. 172).

26. Ambassador Daniels was among those who considered this law a product of the oil firms' maneuvers (Josephus Daniels, *Shirt-Sleeve Diplomat*, p. 212).

27. Edmund David Cronon, *Josephus Daniels in Mexico*, p. 36.

28. The validity of the 1909 law is attacked in Fernando González Roa, *Las cuestiones fundamentales de actualidad en México*, p. 88. There is a large bibliography on mining and oil legislation from the colonial period up to the expropriation in

1938, including: J. Reuben Clark, "The Oil Settlement with Mexico," *Foreign Affairs* 6 (July 1928); Lavín, *Petróleo;* González Roa, *Las cuestiones fundamentales* . . . ; Manuel González Ramírez, *El petróleo mexicano: La expropiación petrolera ante el derecho internacional;* Manuel de la Peña, *El dominio directo del soberano en las minas de México y génesis de la legislación petrolera mexicana;* M. Rippy, "El petróleo y la Revolución Mexicana"; Mexico, *La cuestión petrolera mexicana: El punto de vista del Ejecutivo Federal;* Mexico, Cámara de Senadores, Sección de Estadística y Anales de Jurisprudencia, *El petróleo: La más grande riqueza nacional.*

29. United States, 66th Congress, 2nd session, Senate Committee on Foreign Relations, *Investigation of Mexican Affairs,* p. 217; M. Rippy, "El petróleo y la Revolución Mexicana," p. 25.

30. For a review of the rationale behind the bill, see Lorenzo Elízaga, Luis Ibarra, and Manuel Fernández Guerra, *Proyecto de ley del petróleo y exposición de motivos de la misma que presentan al Ministerio de Fomento los señores licenciados* . . .

31. The arguments set forth in 1905 were basically the same that were to be used up until 1938 by both the companies' opponents and their defenders. Studies against the need to pay indemnization were presented by Miguel Mejía, Francisco Béistigui, Isidro Rojas, and Alfredo Mateos Cardeña. These jurists maintained that the oil belonged to the nation and therefore that the legislator could take back a concession granted to the surface landholder whenever he judged it necessary. A more detailed study of the respective positions taken in this debate may be found in Mendoza, *La controversia del petróleo.*

32. Andrés Molina Enríquez, Wistano Luis Orozco, Antonio Caso, and other intellectuals of the time were concerned about the extent of American penetration. According to a U.S. diplomat, they were afraid that Mexico would meet with the same fate as Panama and Hawaii (William F. Sands and Joseph M. Lalley, *Our Jungle Diplomacy,* p. 143).

33. On the eve of the Revolution the climate in the oil region was already hostile to Doheny and Pearson (Cosío Villegas, ed., *El Porfiriato; La vida política exterior,* pt. 2, p. 398).

34. Anita Brenner, *The Wind That Swept Mexico: The History of the Mexican Revolution 1910–1942,* p. 16; Cosío Villegas, ed., *El Porfiriato; La vida política exterior,* pt. 2, pp. 251 ff.; Jorge Vera Estañol, *La Revolución Mexicana: Orígenes y resultados,* p. 111; James Fred Rippy, José Vasconcelos, and Guy Stevens, *American Policies Abroad: Mexico,* pp. 11–12; Toribio Esquivel Obregón, *México y los Estados Unidos ante el derecho internacional,* p. 94.

35. Brenner, *The Wind That Swept Mexico,* pp. 16–17; Cosío Villegas, *El Porfiriato; La vida política exterior,* pt. 2, pp. 251 ff.

36. Mexico, Secretaría del Patrimonio Nacional, *El petróleo de México,* pp. 12–13.

37. Cosío Villegas, ed., *El Porfiriato; La vida política exterior,* pt. 2, p. 405; Young, *Member for Mexico,* pp. 127–133.

38. A detailed description of the rivalry between the two oil magnates may be found in Young, *Member for Mexico,* pp. 127–133.

39. Ludwell Denny refers to Doheny's hostility toward Pearson (*We Fight for Oil*), but the latter's biographer denies that there was any problem between the two and points out that they cooperated to the extent of even sharing pipelines (Young, *Member for Mexico,* pp. 138–139). Veatch also contradicts Denny's view (Arthur C. Veatch, "Oil, Great Britain, and the United States," *Foreign Affairs* 9 [July 1931]: 666).

40. In 1887 the State Department asked the Mexican Ministry of Foreign Affairs to cancel the oil refining concession granted to Compañía Martínez in view of the fact that it impinged on the interests of the American firms J. Findlay and Company and

Waters-Pierce. Mexico refused to retract the concession, but the Martínez enterprise never did well (D'Olwer, "Las inversiones extranjeras," p. 1126).

41. Henry W. Taft (brother of the U.S. president) and Attorney General George W. Wickersham were on El Aguila's board of directors (D'Olwer, "Las inversiones extranjeras," p. 1129–1184).

42. Cosío Villegas, ed., *El porfiriato; La vida política exterior*, pt. 2, pp. 404–409. According to A. Vagts, Pierce gave Madero 685,000 dollars and Standard Oil also made some contributions (as cited in Alperovich and Rudenko, *La Revolución Mexicana . . .*, p. 91). Merrill Rippy indicates that upon his victory Madero paid back the 685,000 dollars to Pierce ("El petróleo y la Revolución Mexicana," p. 80). These loans were mentioned before the Fall Committee in 1920 (United States, 66th Congress, 2nd session, Senate Committee on Foreign Relations, *Investigation of Mexican Affairs*, II, 2554–2557).

43. Young, *Member for Mexico*, p. 159. The view of those who saw the struggle for control over the oil as the cause of the Mexican Revolution may be studied in, among others, Pierre l'Espagnol de la Tramerge, *La Lutte mondiale pour le pétrole;* Denny, *We Fight for Oil*.

44. Shortly before the fall of the Díaz regime Treasury Minister Limantour gave a press conference in New York in which he said that apparently the Americans had allied themselves directly or indirectly with the Madero movement in the hope of avenging some resentment they had against the Mexican government, and he predicted that in the long range their support of the Revolution would backfire (Vera Estañol, *La Revolución Mexicana*, p. 164).

45. Charles C. Cumberland, *The Mexican Revolution: Genesis under Madero*, p. 243.

46. Cline, *The United States and Mexico*, p. 133.

47. James Fred Rippy, *The United States and Mexico*, p. 349.

48. Cline, *The United States and Mexico*, p. 128.

49. Examples of Spanish press reaction to Díaz' fall may be seen in *El Liberal*, June 16, 1911, *Mañana*, June 17, 1911; *La Correspondencia*, June 17, 1911.

50. J. F. Rippy, *The United States and Mexico*, pp. 334–336; José Vasconcelos, *Ulises criollo*, in *Obras Completas*, I, 690.

51. Cumberland, *The Mexican Revolution*, p. 200.

52. President Taft never wanted to intervene directly in Mexico except as a last recourse. He pointed out in August 1912 that this would imply an expenditure of hundreds of millions of dollars and the loss of thousands of lives—an expenditure which would be far greater than the interests that it was intended to protect (Henry Fowles Pringle, *The Life and Times of William Howard Taft*, p. 709).

53. Frank Tannenbaum, *Mexico: The Struggle for Peace and Bread*, p. 254; Vasconcelos, *Ulises criollo*, pp. 690–691; Henry Lane Wilson, *Diplomatic Episodes in Mexico, Belgium, and Chile*, p. 240.

54. The Madero family controlled one of the few Mexican mining firms of any importance, Compañía Metalúrgica de Torreón. Even so, with a capital of 5 million pesos, it was hardly a serious competitor of the Guggenheim interests.

55. J. F. Rippy, Vasconcelos, and Stevens, *American Policies Abroad*, p. 21; Alperovich and Rudenko, *La Revolución Mexicana . . .*, pp. 64–65; Frank C. Hanighen, *The Secret War*, p. 60.

56. In a note transmitted on April 15, 1912, the State Department protested the aggression of the Orozco group and blamed the Madero government for not controlling its opposition.

57. Cumberland, *The Mexican Revolution*, p. 229.

58. Ibid., pp. 238–243.

59. In 1911 Luis Cabrera cited among the six main causes leading to the Revolution

what he called "foreignism"—that is, "the predominance and competitive advantage enjoyed by foreigners over nationals in all branches of activity" (*Veinte años después*, p. 50). With Madero the expression of the national bourgeoisie's resentment against the privileged position of foreign capital was tepid at best. In his book *La sucesión presidencial* only vague criticisms are made of the Porfirian policy with respect to foreign interests. Nor in the San Luis Plan is there any direct reference to the problem, which only comes up indirectly in the promise to review the titles to agricultural land—but not without due respect for the commitments entered into by the Díaz administration with foreign governments and corporations (point 3).

60. Ambassador Wilson to Department of State, August 22, 1912 (Alperovich and Rudenko, *La Revolución Mexicana . . .* , p. 140).

61. This charge was contained in the Empacadora ("Packinghouse") Pact of March 1912.

62. The Empacadora Pact referred to supposed aid given to the Madero movement by Waters-Pierce.

63. *Mexican Herald*, November 18, 1911.

64. U.S. consul in Tampico to Department of State, November 21, 1911, NAW 812.6363/0.

65. The decree and its corresponding regulations are found in Mexico, Secretaría de Industria, Comercio y Trabajo, *Legislación petrolera, 1783–1921*.

66. Federico Bach and Manuel de la Peña, *México y su petróleo: Síntesis histórica*, p. 13.

67. A detailed presentation of the companies' objections is contained in a booklet published by Mexican Petroleum and Huasteca, *Los impuestos sobre la industria petrolera*.

68. Letter from Hagsett to Tanis, Division of Mexican Affairs, Department of State, August 14, 1937, NAW 812.512/3919.

69. In 1914 an American writer, Edward J. Bell, observed that by that time not a single foreign economic group supported the Mexican government: "Madero was on trial for his official life, and every substantial businessman with a Mexican connection was [his] prosecuting attorney" (*The Political Shame of Mexico* [New York, 1914], p. 219, cited in Wilfred H. Callcott, *Liberalism in Mexico, 1857–1929*, p. 205).

70. Clark, "The Oil Settlement with Mexico," p. 600.

71. The companies' protests obliged the governor of Veracruz to modify his decree of June 29, 1912, which had imposed certain taxes on them.

72. U.S. consul in Tampico to Department of State, May 10, 1912, and Secretary of State Knox to Ambassador Wilson, June 3, 1912, NAW 812.6363/3.

73. U.S. consul in Tampico to Department of State, May 25, 1912, NAW 812.6363/4. For an example of the kinds of attacks that appeared against Waters-Pierce, see the Tampico paper *El Eco del Golfo*, May 11, 1912.

74. U.S. consul in Tampico to Department of State, July 18 and 27, 1912, NAW 812.6363/6.

75. Ambassador Wilson to Department of State, August 9, 1912, NAW 812.6363/8.

76. The note said, in effect, that American businesses in general were not well looked upon by certain parties, which were persecuting them and stealing from them at every chance. In the particular case of the oil firms, it mentioned what it called the almost unbearable taxes and demanded immediate assurances that the anomalous situation would be remedied (Samuel Flagg Bemis, *La diplomacia de Estados Unidos en la América Latina*, p. 181; NAW 812.11/834A).

77. J. F. Rippy, Vasconcelos, and Stevens, *American Policies Abroad*, p. 30; M. Rippy, "El petróleo y la Revolución Mexicana," p. 83.

78. Pringle, *William Howard Taft*, p. 711.

79. Manuel Márquez Sterling, *Los últimos días del presidente Madero*, p. 281.

80. The *Mexican Hearld* was an American-owned paper published in Mexico City.

81. In their characterization of Wilson, Samuel Eliot Morison and Henry Steele Commager write that he was "born an aristocrat, bred a conservative, trained a Hamiltonian" (*The Growth of the American Republic* II, 425).

82. Although in principle Wilson repudiated "dollar diplomacy," in actual practice the change in policy was difficult to see: the Marines remained in Nicaragua; the United States intervened in Haiti and continued to occupy the country until 1930; a similar fate befell the Dominican Republic; and the famous Bryan-Chamorro Treaty was signed with the Nicaraguan government.

83. Bemis, *La diplomacia de Estados Unidos . . .* , pp. 183–184; Samuel Eliot Morison and Henry Steele Commager, *Historia de los Estados Unidos de Norteamérica*, III, 21; J. L. Busey, "Don Victoriano y la prensa yanqui," *Historia mexicana* 4 (April–June 1955): 590.

84. According to Josephus Daniels, in 1913 President Wilson and most of his cabinet had become aware of the underlying causes of the Mexican conflict: it would not end until the large landholdings were divided up, the labor laws were improved, and foreigners were kept from monopolizing the natural resources of the country (*The Wilson Era*, pp. 184–185). In a conversation with Samuel G. Blythe in April, 1917, Wilson declared that the old Mexican system was dead and that he intended to do what he could to see that the new one was founded on respect for freedom and human rights (Frederick Sherwood Dunn, *The Diplomatic Protection of Americans in Mexico*, pp. 316, 319). During his 1916 campaign he came out and said, in effect, that although some of the leaders of the Revolution may have often been wrong, violent, or selfish, the Revolution itself was inevitable and right. In regard to American interests in Mexico, he added that the country's leaders, like Porfirio Díaz, had used them as a stimulus for development and had discovered that they were the servants not of Mexico but of foreign concessionaires. Wilson said that, if he had to make the choice, the rights of the oppressed Mexicans came before the property claims of his fellow citizens (Josephus Daniels, *The Life of Woodrow Wilson, 1856–1924*, p. 187; Mexico, *La verdad sobre la expropiación de los bienes de las empresas petroleras*, p. 15).

85. Typical examples of this view may be found in Sands and Lalley, *Our Jungle Diplomacy*, and Graham H. Stuart, *Latin America and the United States*. Howard F. Cline, for his part, flatly denies that Wilson had any such policy for Mexico (*The United States and Mexico*, p. 166).

86. Cline, *The United States and Mexico*, p. 141.

87. President Wilson never stuck to the traditional diplomatic channels, believing that they had proved to be inadequate for implementing his intentions (Edith O'Shaughnessy, *Une Femme de diplomate au Mexique*).

88. John Lind wrote to Secretary of State Bryan on September 19, 1913, that recognition of Huerta would not lead to the pacification of Mexico. He said that there could be no lasting peace until certain basic and judicious economic and social reforms were effected. It was necessary, therefore, to support Huerta's opponents. The Revolutionary leaders, he went on, might not have any special value as men, but the movement as a whole had a lot more merit than the Huerta government (John P. Harrison, "Un análisis norteamericano de la Revolución Mexicana en 1913," *Historia mexicana* 5 [April–June 1956]: 613–614).

89. It was Ambassador Wilson who was responsible for the idea of taking advantage of Huerta's difficult situation to get favorable settlement of such matters as the Chamizal border dispute and claims for damages caused to Americans in the course of the Revolution (Wilson, *Diplomatic Episodes*, pp. 297–298; J. F. Rippy, *The United States and Mexico*, pp. 354–355).

90. President Wilson was convinced that the "embassy pact" between Ambassador Henry Lane Wilson and General Félix Díaz (nephew of the former dictator who had his forces in the Veracruz region) contained such a provision.

91. In a speech delivered on October 27, 1913, in Mobile, Alabama, President Wilson declared that in no circumstances whatsoever would the material interests of the United States be allowed to prevail over human freedom or deny a nation the chances to which it is entitled.

92. The strong anti-American sentiment in Mexico prevented Carranza from collaborating openly with President Wilson in Huerta's overthrow. With respect to Europe, and mainly England, there was still the hope of being able to compete with the United States for control of the Western Hemisphere. The Latin American countries, for their part, followed the lines laid out by Washington, but with little enthusiasm.

93. O'Shaughnessy, *Une Femme de diplomate au Mexique*, pp. 5, 55, 192–193.

94. According to Josephus Daniels, then secretary of the navy, President Wilson never considered the possibility of war with Mexico, even though some members of his cabinet—War Secretary Lindley Garrison, Secretary of State Robert Lansing, Interior Secretary Franklin K. Lane, and Treasury Secretary William Gibbs McAdoo—had advocated armed intervention (Daniels to Franklin D. Roosevelt, May 4, 1940, JDP).

95. Vera Estañol, *La Revolución Mexicana*, pp. 356–359.

96. According to Jorge Vera Estañol, who had been Huerta's minister for a time, it was not too far-fetched to say that if the U.S. government had recognized Huerta as provisional president, in the knowledge that definitive elections would soon be held, the Revolution would have died aborning ("El carrancismo y la Constitución de 1917," in Gastón García Cantú, *El pensamiento de la reacción mexicana: Historia documental, 1810–1962*, p. 87).

97. Edmund David Cronon, ed., *The Cabinet Diaries of Josephus Daniels, 1913–1921*, pp. 43–44.

98. In a cabinet meeting held on May 23, 1913, during the course of which it was definitely agreed not to recognize the Huerta government, President Wilson stressed that he was not defending any interests in particular—that he was president of the United States and not of a group of Americans with interests in Mexico (Daniels, *The Wilson Era*, p. 182).

99. Ibid., p. 181; Daniels to his son, April 16 and September 7, 1938, JDP.

100. According to Alperovich and Rudenko, Wilson's hostility toward Huerta stemmed from the fact that the American president had uncovered a British plan to take over the American oil firms in Mexico—although why it was Wilson and not Taft who had discovered the plan, or what Huerta's motives were for having agreed to it were not explained (*La Revolución Mexicana . . .* , pp. 178–179). The U.S. consul in Mexico during the Huerta regime was to testify some years afterward that the Mexican leader never failed to protect American interests and that it was only after Wilson launched a campaign against him that he began to show certain antagonism toward the firms (United States, 66th Congress, 2nd session, Senate Committee on Foreign Relations, *Investigation of Mexican Affairs*, pp. 1764–1765). Merrill Rippy ("El petróleo y la Revolución Mexicana," p. 85), Stuart Alexander MacCorkle (*American Policy of Recognition towards Mexico*), and other authors consider that Huerta was on good terms with the American oil companies at the time he came to power.

101. The Chiapas delegation proposed that the state corporation absorb or expropriate the private companies and suggested that for this purpose a loan in the amount of 50 million pounds sterling be applied for. Luis Zubiría y Campa and Félix Palavicini asked that a special commission be set up to review the law in this respect and pro-

pose appropriate amendments (Manuel Flores, *Apuntes sobre el petróleo mexicano*, pp. 30–33).

102. Department of State to Chargé d'Affaires Nelson O'Shaughnessy, November 20, 1913, NAW 812.6363/15.

103. On October 14, 1913, the U.S. consul in Veracruz reported that the tax was being increased from .20 to a full dollar a ton. On November 12 the oil firms called for the support of the U.S., British, and Netherlands governments in their protest against the tax, which in the end went from .20 to .65 (Canadian government to Department of State, October 14, 1914; oil companies to Department of State, November 12, 1913, NAW 812.6363/12).

104. U.S. consul in Veracruz to Department of State, November 12, 1913, and Department of State to chargé d'affaires in Mexico, November 21, 1913, NAW 812.6363/14.

105. See note 128 below.

106. Jean-Baptiste Duroselle, *Política exterior de los Estados Unidos: De Wilson a Roosevelt, 1913–1945*, p. 78. President Wilson was extremely displeased to learn that England had so ostensively disregarded his Mexico policy, and he did not hesitate to place public blame on the British oil firms in a speech delivered at Mobile, Alabama, on October 27, 1913 (Cronon, *The Cabinet Diaries* . . . , p. 83). Meanwhile, the U.S. chargé d'affaires referred to the British ambassador in Mexico as the traditional enemy of American interests in the hemisphere (O'Shaughnessy to Department of State, October 14, 1913, WWP).

107. On January 10, 1914, John Lind, writing from Mexico, told President Wilson: ". . . if the Huerta government, or rather what the Huerta government stands for in principle, should prevail, Mexico would continue to be a European annex industrially, financially, politically, and in sentiment" (George M. Stephenson, *John Lind of Minnesota*, p. 253). In the event that all indirect methods failed, Lind proposed armed intervention in order to get rid of Huerta (Bemis, *La diplomacia de Estados Unidos* . . . , pp. 185–186).

108. Bach and De la Peña, *México y su petróleo*, p. 17.

109. Stephenson, *John Lind of Minnesota*, p. 240; Alperovich and Rudenko, *La Revolución Mexicana* . . . , p. 180; Young, *Member for Mexico*, pp. 153–158. Henry Lane Wilson accused an American oil firm connected with Madero of being among the first of the American interests to influence the U.S. president's envoys against Huerta (*Diplomatic Episodes*, p. 237). Pierre l'Espagnol de la Tramerge—who exaggerated the role of the oil firms in Mexican politics in order to emphasize their imperialist attitude—claimed that Standard tried to make an agreement with Huerta whereby it would call off all activity against him in exchange for a monopoly on oil exploitation in Mexico; Huerta supposedly turned it down, for unknown reasons, and Standard thereupon resolved to see him out of power (*La Lutte mondiale* . . . , p. 113).

110. Young, *Member for Mexico*, pp. 4, 153–168.

111. O'Shaughnessy, *Une Femme de diplomate au Mexique*, p. 9; J. F. Rippy, Vasconcelos, and Stevens, *American Policies Abroad*, p. 44.

112. On June 17 Churchill pointed out on the floor of the House of Commons that the Mexican oil reserves were vast and that the Admiralty could not afford to disregard them (Alperovich and Rudenko, *La Revolución Mexicana* . . . , p. 179).

113. President Wilson persuaded Congress to abolish discriminatory tariffs being levied on Panama and on non-American bottoms through a law which it passed in 1912.

114. Secretary of State Bryan to U.S. consul in Tampico, May 20, 1914, NAW 812.6363/70A; British and Netherlands embassies to Department of State, June 2, 1914, NAW 812.6363/87–88; Swedish embassy to Department of State, July 7, 1914, NAW 812.6363/124A.

115. Young, *Member for Mexico*, p. 161.

116. Nathaniel and Silvia Weyl, "La reconquista de México: Los días de Lázaro Cárdenas," *Problemas agrícolas e industriales de México* 7 (October–December 1955): 282.

117. In the Woodrow Wilson Papers in the U.S. Library of Congress there is a large volume of letters received both against and in favor of recognition of the Huerta government, as well as invasion of Mexico.

118. Young, *Member for Mexico*, p. 176. This relative tranquillity did not keep 245 American residents in Tampico from petitioning Wilson on July 14, 1913, for protection so that there wouldn't be another "Alamo," claiming that they were at the mercy of "hordes of bandits" (WWP).

119. Daniels, *The Wilson Era*, p. 192; Department of State to Secretary of War, February 14, 1914, NAW 812.6363/26.

120. Mexican Petroleum Producers, Resolution Adopted at a Meeting of Mexican Petroleum Producers and Allied Industries," May 7, 1914, New York, N.Y.

121. Oil companies to Department of State, April 28, 1914; British embassy to Department of State, April 30 and May 1, 1914, NAW 812.6363/46–47; Secretary of State Bryan to U.S. consul in Tampico, April 9 and 28, 1914, NAW 812.6363/73 9/2; Senator Morris Sheppard to President Wilson and Congressman J. H. Eagle to Secretary of State Bryan, April 30, 1914, NAW 812.6363/38–40.

122. British embassy to Department of State, May 6 and 8, 1914, NAW 812.6363/49, 52; Miller to Department of State, May 1 and 15, 1914, NAW 812.6363/32.

123. Department of State to U.S. consul in Tampico, NAW 812.6363/55.

124. On May 21, 1914, Consul Canada (*sic*) informed the State Department that, in spite of the forced evacuation of the foreign technicians, the Mexican personnel could have the wells running almost without any problem (NAW 812.6363/72).

125. The other two options offered by the ambassador were to force Huerta to give in on all the American demands or to invade the country (J. F. Rippy, *The United States and Mexico*, pp. 354–355).

126. According to Ambassador Wilson, Huerta demanded "excessive and irregular" payments from the oil industry (*Diplomatic Episodes*, pp. 306–307). During the course of the struggle the Constitutionalists charged much lower taxes than the Huerta administration did (U.S. consul in Tampico to Department of State, June 3, 1914, NAW 812.6363/90).

127. United States, 66th Congress, 2nd session, Senate Committee on Foreign Relations, *Investigation of Mexican Affairs*, p. 777.

128. Ibid., pp. 277–284; Weyl and Weyl, "La reconquista de México," p. 282. On January 8, 1914, a group of American oil firms—which pointed out that they had no connection with Standard Oil—wrote to the State Department that it was not a good idea to pay the tax being imposed by the Huerta government, which was clearly high and arbitrary, because it would give Huerta vast monetary resources (WWP).

129. In a letter dated August 9, 1913, Fall told the State Department that he firmly believed it was best to pursue a policy of zealous protection of American interests, and even of armed intervention, in order to restore peace and order in Mexico, which would be in the best interests of both countries (WWP).

130. Senator Fall had had his first contact with Mexican affairs during the Porfirio Díaz regime as a personal friend of the dictator—a situation that had not failed to be of help for his business activities in that country (United States, 66th Congress, 2nd session, Senate Committee on Foreign Relations, *Investigation of Mexican Affairs*, p. 1131). With regard to the Teapot Dome scandal, see Robert Engler, *La política petrolera: Un estudio del poder privado y las directivas democráticas*, pp. 94–95).

131. The letter from Payne to President Wilson cited moral, not economic, reasons

in support of temporary military intervention in Mexico (December 30, 1913, WWP).

132. Alperovich and Rudenko, *La Revolución Mexicana . . .* , p. 194.

133. Daniels wrote to his son that Paul Young had mentioned this rumor to him but that he considered it totally unfounded (August 18, 1933, JDP).

3. The Formulation of a New Oil Policy

1. Frank Brandenburg, *The Making of Modern Mexico*, p. 54.

2. For a detailed study of this problem, see, among others, Robert E. Quirk, *The Mexican Revolution, 1914–1915: The Convention of Aguascalientes*; John Womack, *Zapata and the Mexican Revolution*, pp. 191–330; Jean Meyer, "Les Ouvriers dans la Révolution mexicaine: Les Bataillones rouges," *Annales* 25 (January–February 1970): 30–55.

3. Howard F. Cline, *The United States and Mexico*, p. 151.

4. Edith O'Shaughnessy, *Une Femme de diplomate au Mexique*, p. 18.

5. Immediately after Victoriano Huerta's coup, the U.S. consul in Saltillo, Coahuila, met with Governor Carranza, on the ambassador's instructions, to discuss recognition of the new regime. Carranza, in addition to refusing, let the U.S. official know how he felt about his embassy's role in the recent victory (José Mancisidor, *Historia de la Revolución Mexicana*, pp. 236–237).

6. There were many such incidents of disagreement. Among the most important ones were those that stemmed from the taking of Veracruz and the attempts by the State Department and the ABC powers to arrange an armistice between Huerta and the Constitutionalists.

7. P. E. Haley, *Revolution and Intervention: The Diplomacy of Taft and Wilson with Mexico, 1910–1917*; Kenneth J. Grieb, *The United States and Huerta*; Josephus Daniels, *The Life of Woodrow Wilson, 1856–1924*, p. 180.

8. There were other abortive attempts to solve the problem—in one case by conciliation of the two factions and in another by putting the main leaders aside and supporting a secondary figure who would agree to reach a conciliation.

9. Up until the United States recognized Carranza, Villa consistently sought to maintain good relations with Washington (report of George C. Carothers, special State Department agent assigned to follow him). In 1914 he promised another U.S. agent, P. Fuller, that in the event he became president he would protect the vested rights of American citizens. There are other similar examples of this attitude (Manuel González Ramírez, *La revolución social de México*, I, 497; Cline, *The United States and Mexico*, p. 171; Clarence C. Clendenen, *The United States and Pancho Villa: A Study in Unconventional Diplomacy*, pp. 160–186). With regard to Zapata, see O'Shaughnessy, *Une Femme de diplomate au Mexique*, p. 181.

10. Quirk, *The Mexican Revolution*, pp. 279–285; Jean-Baptist Duroselle, *Política exterior de los Estados Unidos: De Wilson a Roosevelt, 1913–1945*, p. 79.

11. Carranza had to agree to protect American interests in Mexico and also to pay a settlement for damages caused to foreign property in the course of the Revolution (Cline, *The United States and Mexico*, p. 179).

12. Ibid., p. 171.

13. For example, on November 11, 1918, Secretary of State Lansing warned the U.S. consul in Tampico of possible German sabotage on an oil train (NAW 812.6363/317).

14. Spanish embassy to minister of state, May 22, 1917, CDHM R50, container 332, sole leg., no. 2

15. On October 12, 1917, President Wilson's ambassador in London reported a German plot to bring Mexico into the war against the United States, starting with des-

truction of the oil wells and other sabotage (Ray Stannard Baker, *Woodrow Wilson: Life and Letters*, VI, 304).

16. This point is contained in Article 22 of the Additions to the Plan of Guadalupe.

17. In the opinion of the Spanish embassy, Carranza's supporters were staunch Germanophiles, whereas the upper classes were more in sympathy with the Allies (April 12, 1917, CDHM R50, case 331, sole leg., no. 35; Emilio Portes Gil, *Autobiografía de la Revolución Mexicana*, p. 217).

18. Spanish embassy to minister of state, April 12, 1917, CDHM R50, container 33, sole leg., no. 35.

19. The *New York Times* (March 15 and April 12, 1917) accused Carranza of being opposed to oil exports for the British fleet, saying that the Mexican economy and the country's political life as well were dominated by Germans—who were responsible for the oil clauses in the Constitution of 1917. For these reasons, it editorialized, force should be used if necessary in order to maintain control over Mexican oil.

20. Baker, *Woodrow Wilson*, VI, 25–26.

21. González Ramírez, *La revolución social de México* I, 671–688. General Félix Díaz, as "commander-in-chief of the National Reorganization Army," claimed that a plot had been hatched between Carranza and the Germans (Manuel González Ramírez, *Fuentes para la historia de la Revolución Mexicana*, vol. 1, *Planes y otros documentos*, pp. 233–242.

22. Oil companies to Department of State, September 9, 1918, NAW 812.6363/312; United States, 66th Congress, 2nd session, Senate Committee on Foreign Relations, *Investigation of Mexican Affairs: Preliminary Report and Hearings . . . Pursuant to Senate Resolution No. 106 Directing the Committee . . . to Investigate the Matter of Outrages on Citizens of the United States in Mexico*, p. 944; *New York Times*, November 16, 1917.

23. On July 31, 1917, the *New York Times* claimed that the strikes among the oil workers were the work of German agents. There was also a rumor that an army of German reserves was standing in readiness to repel any Allied landing in the Mexican oil region (Desmond Young, *Member for Mexico: A Biography of Weetman Pearson, First Viscount Cowdroy*, p. 180).

24. On July 23, 1919, a representative of Huasteca wrote to the State Department saying that there was a plan afoot to take away the property of the American firms and turn it over to certain German and Mexican interests.

25. Statements by W. E. Black, vice president of Tampico Petroleum Pipe Line and Refining Company, appearing in the *Dallas Morning News*, December 14, 1941.

26. Cline, *The United States and Mexico*, p. 154.

27. A telegram from the Canadian consul in Tampico to the State Department pointed out that with the taking of the port by the Constitutionalists the danger of the British getting control of Mexican oil was passed (May 18, 1914, NAW 812.6363/69).

28. In November 1913 Cándido Aguilar, governor of Veracruz, ordered suspension of the sale of fuel for Huerta's railroads and demanded payment of certain taxes. Shortly afterwards he withdrew his request for the taxes, but he stood firm on his ban despite the protests of Henry Clay Pierce, who was afraid of reprisals by the Huerta forces.

29. Anita Brenner, *The Wind That Swept Mexico: The History of the Mexican Revolution, 1910–1942*, p. 43; Secretary of State Bryan to George C. Carothers, May 16, 1914, NAW 812.6363/68.

30. Secretary of State Bryan to Consul Silliman, April 3, 1915, NAW 812.6363/179.

31. Both Félix F. Palavicini (*Historia de la Constitución de 1917*, p. 605) and Pastor Rouaix (in *El Heraldo de México*, July 30, 1920) point out that it was in 1914 with

Carranza that the policy was embarked on that was to lead eventually to "renational-ization" of the subsoil.

32. Brenner, *The Wind That Swept Mexico*, p. 37; United States, 66th Congress, 2nd session, Senate Committee on Foreign Relations, *Investigation of Mexican Affairs*, p. 797.

33. Committee members Joaquín Santaella and Mauricio Langarica believed that the juridical tradition of subsoil ownership by the nation, broken during the Porfirian regime, should be upheld because (clearly they did not want to attack the companies directly) the new system only benefited landholders and speculators. They went on to point out that property rights were not absolute, and that expropriation and taxation were instruments that the state could legally use to restrain them for the general good if necessary (*Boletín del petróleo* 3 [January–June 1917]: 220; Isidro Fabela, "La política internacional del presidente Cárdenas," *Problemas agrícolas e industriales de México* 7 [October–December 1955]: 46).

34. The tax was demanded in gold because the parties wanted to make their payments in Constitutionalist money.

35. According to the U.S. consul in Tampico, the tax was so burdensome that all the companies except El Aguila were on the point of "disappearing" (NAW 812.6363/124). Eventually payment was made under protest and none of the companies disappeared. Although the new taxes came to 300 per cent of what the levies had been under Madero, it should be remembered that these latter had been insignificant. The tax had been decreed in order to raise funds to pay for the struggle against Villa.

36. Stanley R. Ross et al., *Historia documental de México*, II, 545.

37. J. Reuben Clark, "The Oil Settlement with Mexico," *Foreign Affairs* 6 (July 1928): 600.

38. Secretary of State Bryan to Hanna, June 29, 1914, NAW 812.6363/532; Secretary of State Bryan to Canada, December 24, 1914, NAW 812.512/525.

39. The U.S. consul in Veracruz reported to the State Department on various occasions that both he and the companies had tried to persuade Cándido Aguilar not to make his decree retroactive (Bevan to Department of State, November 5, 1914, NAW 812.6363/144).

40. Department of State to Admiral Fletcher, November 19 and 23, 1914, NAW 812.6363/103.

41. Clark, "The Oil Settlement with Mexico," p. 600.

42. Isidro Fabela, *Documentos históricos de la Revolución Mexicana*, IV, 122–124.

43. Venustiano Carranza, *Informe del C . . . , Primer Jefe del Ejército Constitucionalista, encargado del Poder Ejecutivo de la República, leído ante el Congresso de la Unión, en la sesión de 15 de abril de 1917*.

44. The State Department attempted to gain assurances from Mexico that the measure would not affect operations already under way (Department of State to Canada, January 13, 1915, NAW 812.6363/146; Canada to Department of State, January 16 and 17, NAW 812.6363/162; Bevan to Department of State, January 22, 1915, NAW 812.6363/154; Secretary of State Bryan to Bevan, January 25, 1917, NAW 812.6363/154.

45. U.S. consul in Tampico to Department of State, January 14, 1915, NAW 812.6363/161; Canada to President Carranza, January 13, 1915, NAW 812.6363/178.

46. NAW 812.6363/173.

47. Huasteca to Department of State, March 11, 1915, NAW 812.6363/175.

48. The U.S. consul in Tampico reported to the State Department that the confusion was such that often there wasn't even an authority from which to request the necessary permission (February 13, 1915, NAW 812.6363/171).

49. This information included a declaration of capital invested, output, size of

properties, number of wells, pipelines, refineries, etc. (AREM L-E-547, vol. 4, Leg. 2, f. 2).

50. A Veracruz state decree dated May 16 and a federal one issued by the Ministry of Treasury on September 2 both insisted on the requirement that the companies register their holdings.

51. Consul Silliman to Department of State, February 3, 1916, NAW 812.6363/220; U.S. consul in Tampico to Department of State, NAW 812.6363/211.

52. Compañía Petrolera Marítima to Department of State, May 17, 1916, NAW 812.6363/231; Secretary of State Lansing to Consul Silliman, January 21 and March 13, 1916, and January 19, 1917, NAW 812.6363/205, 221, 532; Secretary of State Lansing to Rogers, August 16, 1916, NAW 812.5034/6.

53. Department of State to Consul Silliman, January 19, 1916, NAW 812.6363/202A; Consul Silliman to Department of State, January 21 and 26, 1916, NAW 812.6363/203, 208.

54. *El Luchador*, February 25, 1916; *World*, February 10, 1916.

55. On May 30 the U.S. consul in Tampico reported that Pastor Rouaix had been conducting certain investigations in the region with a view to drafting a decree that would nationalize the oil as of January 1917 (NAW 812.6363/235; Netherlands ambassador to Department of State, November 25, 1916, NAW 812.6363/254).

56. In the Aguascalientes Convention it was agreed that the state should be given a proportional share in the gross profits from the mining industry in general. The Revolutionary Convention, for its part, meeting in Jojutla in April 1916, called for reform of the mining and oil legislation in order to put an end to monopolies and, similarly, give the state a share in the profits. Some of the conservative sectors, led by Jorge Vera Estañol and Toribio Esquivel Obregón, were in favor of a policy that would guard against the hydrocarbon deposits running dry, which would justify nationalization if necessary (Víctor Alba, *Las ideas sociales contemporáneas en México*, p. 171; González Ramírez, *Fuentes para la historia . . .* , I, 125; Mexico, Cámara de Senadores, Sección de Estadística y Anales de Jurisprudencia, *El petróleo: La más grande riqueza nacional*, p. 126.

57. From the floor of the Congress Luis Cabrera, the prominent Carranza supporter, called the companies "our enemies" and blamed them for the rebellion in the oil region (Carlos Díaz Dufoo, *La cuestión del petróleo*, pp. 177–179).

58. Oil companies to Department of State, March 8, 1918, NAW 812.6363/372.

59. Estimates vary as to how much the oil firms paid to Manuel Peláez. In 1917 Josephus Daniels set the sum at 35,000 dollars a year (Edmund David Cronon, ed., *The Cabinet Diaries of Josephus Daniels, 1913–1921*, p. 214). The League of Free Nations Association, on the other hand, claimed that the amount actually reached 200,000 dollars a month (Association to Department of State, August 15, 1919, NAW 812.6363/508). A report sent from the warship USS *Nashville* to the State Department on January 26, 1917, noted that Peláez was receiving 10,000 dollars a month from Huasteca and a matching amount from El Aguila (NAW 812.6363/259).

60. USS *Annapolis* to Department of State, November 12, 1917, NAW 812.6363/319.

61. The British consul in Tampico reported on February 1, 1918, that the companies did not want the Mexican government to fall to Manuel Peláez (NAW 812.6363/359, 0829). On August 20, 1917, the State Department received a request from the firms that war matériel not be supplied to Carranza without first checking with them, since Peláez was threatening reprisals (NAW 812.6363/303).

62. See the companies' repeated statements before the Fall Committee in this regard in United States, 66th Congress, 2nd session, Senate Committee on Foreign Relations, *Investigation of Mexican Affairs*; also Dawson in Tampico to Department

of State, August 11, 1916, NAW 812.6363/245.

63. Cándido Aguilar to Ambassador Fletcher, March 12, 1917, NAW 812.6363/269.

64. On January 25, 1917, the U.S. consul in Tampico reported to Washington that the Carranza forces were threatening to destroy the oil properties if the firms continued paying tribute to Manuel Peláez (NAW 812.6363/256).

65. Secretary of State Lansing to Parker, January 27, 1917, NAW 812.6363/257; Department of State to Ambassador Fletcher, February 15, 1918, NAW 812.6363/341.

66. According to a September 1919 communication from the State Department to the League of Free Nations Association, the U.S. government had left it up to the companies to decide whether or not to pay tribute to Manuel Peláez (NAW 812.6363/522), but the firms for their part insisted that the payments had the State Department's backing (Huasteca Petroleum Company and Standard Oil of California, *Expropiación: Un estudio de los hechos, causas, métodos y efectos de la dominación política de la industria en México*, p. 33; United States, 66th Congress, 2nd session, Senate Committee on Foreign Relations, *Investigation of Mexican Affairs*, pp. 280–285).

67. On August 11, 1916, the U.S. consul in Tampico reported to the State Department that apparently Manuel Peláez wanted to make a proposal to the United States: arms in exchange for protection of the oil fields. This news had reached the consul in Tampico through an agent working for El Aguila and from his colleague in Tuxpan. According to them, Peláez was sincere, since he himself had property in the area; in any case, Peláez' defeat would definitely heighten the threat to the oil fields (NAW 812.6363/245).

68. On Feburary 29, 1918, Consul Dawson reported certain damages to the companies' properties caused by Peláez (Dawson to Department of State, NAW 812.6363/344).

69. A Mr. Green, working for Huasteca, reported to the company on March 1, 1918, that he had spoken with Manuel Peláez personally and that it was the Mexican rebel's intention to put several of the oil fields out of operation in order to bring on U.S. intervention. Green attempted to dissuade him, pointing out that this strategy would only play into Carranza's hands (NAW 812.6363/373).

70. Already by March 14, 1918, the *New York Times* had ceased to speak of Carranza as an ally of Germany and appeared to be optimistic about an early defeat of the rebel leader, who was demanding larger and larger payments from the companies.

71. Jesús Romero Flores, *Anales históricos de la Revolución Mexicana*, III, 87.

72. Report from El Paso to Department of State, August 22, 1914, NAW 812.6363/129; Department of Justice to Department of State, June 24, 1914, NAW 812.6363/115.

73. *San Antonio Express*, June 8, 1914.

74. This theory originated with *Everybody's Magazine* (May 1916—cited by Moisei S. Alperovich and Boris T. Rudenko, *La Revolución Mexicana de 1910–1917 y la política de los Estados Unidos*, pp. 247–248). Similar suspicions were voiced by Frank C. Hanighen (*The Secret War*, p. 72).

75. The *New York American*, February 12, 1922, referred to the existence of a series of unpublished congressional documents that showed evidence of the oil companies' efforts since 1919 to enter into an understanding with Villa.

76. On May 31 the U.S. consul in Tampico asked that a warship be sent down to force Cándido Aguilar (governor of Veracruz) into providing protection for the employees of Penn-Mex Oil. In June the request was withdrawn, since the U.S. naval authorities had succeeded in negotiating the necessary assurances from Aguilar (NAW 812.6363/82, 89).

77. Frederick Sherwood Dunn, *The Diplomatic Protection of Americans in Mexico*, pp. 324–325.

78. During these years the Woodrow Wilson correspondence shows that opposition to intervention in Mexico was considerable (WWP).

79. Merrill Rippy, "El petróleo y la Revolución Mexicana," *Problemas agrícolas e industriales de México* 6 (July–September 1954): 85.

80. Alperovich and Rudenko, *La Revolución Mexicana . . .* , p. 240; WWP.

81. Quirk, *The Mexican Revolution*, p. 196.

82. This message was transmitted to the State Department by the British embassy in Washington (June 12, 1915, NAW 812.6363/196).

83. Baker, *Woodrow Wilson*, V, 71–72, 79.

84. James Morton Callahan, *American Foreign Policy in Mexican Relations*, pp. 566–567; Duroselle, *Política exterior de los Estados Unidos*, p. 80.

85. Baker, *Woodrow Wilson*, V, 71.

86. J. D. Short, of New Mexico, to Congressman J. H. Stephens, March 30, 1916, WWP.

87. Baker, *Woodrow Wilson*, V, 74–75.

88. In June the State Department wrote that the only forces which could be landed in Mexico were the Marines, which were currently tied up in the Dominican Republic and Haiti, and that in any case it did not see the need for an armed intervention (Polk in Department of State to businessman J. H. Byrd, June 10, 1916, NAW 812.6363/240).

89. NAW 812.6363/226. The U.S. consul in Tampico reported to the State Department on June 23, 1916, that Mexico had made contingency plans for a U.S. invasion (NAW 812.6363/237).

4. Carranza and the Oil Reform

1. This group was headed by General Francisco J. Múgica.

2. One of the authors of the Carranza text, Manuel Rojas, insisted publicly that it had not been the chief executive's intention to nationalize the oil in any way (*El Universal*, July 12, 1931).

3. "It is understood," Pastor Rouaix wrote, "that in proposing the clause on oil, I, as minister of state at the time, had the acquiescence and prior authorization of the chief of state, this trust having been placed by the Constitutional Congress with Venustiano Carranza, who was the author of the aforementioned policy of redressment of rights abused" (*Génesis de los artículos 27 y 123 de la Constitución Política de 1917*, p. 161).

4. Moisés Sáenz and Herbert I. Priestley, *Some Mexican Problems*, p. 120.

5. Isidro Fabela, "La Política internacional del presidente Cárdenas," *Problemas agrícolas e industriales de México* 7 (October–December 1955): 48.

6. Rouaix, *Los Artículos 27 y 123*, p. 167.

7. Mexico, Poder Legislativo, *Diario de los debates del Congreso Constituyente, 1916–1917*, II, 782.

8. On December 22 an amendment to Article 27 was proposed which declared that all subsoil natural resources belonged to the nation and that therefore the surface landholders were merely renters (Luis Melgarejo and J. Fernández Rojas, *El Congreso Constituyente de 1916–1917*, p. 491). When paragraph iv of Article 27 was presented to the assembly for approval, the only modification proposed—which was not accepted because it was considered to be of secondary importance—was one by delegate Federico Ibarra specifying the percentage of the total profits that the oil and mining

companies had up to then been paying to the surface landholders and should henceforth share with the Mexican nation (Rouaix, *Los artículos 27 y 123*, p. 190).

9. The proponents of this view refused to recognize that the basic characteristic of any revolution is precisely its intent to modify the legal property regime to the extent that the attainment of its goals may require, since "no state is obliged to allow its inhabitants, be they nationals or foreigners, perpetual enjoyment of the rights that its legislation may give them at any one moment" (Jorge Castañeda, "México y el exterior," in *México: 50 años de Revolución*, III, 276).

10. This interpretation of nonretroactivity which it was attempted to give to paragraph iv but not to the rest of Article 27—in which case the agrarian reform would have been impossible—was found not only in court rulings and opinions of the day but also, later, in works by authors connected in one way or another with the Obregón and Calles administrations who felt it necessary to insist on this thesis, apparently so as to give a highly orthodox patriotic image—denying, of course, that outside circumstances kept it from being applied. Among those who maintained that the Constitutional Assembly had accepted a twentieth-century principle of international law that prevented changing the system of oil ownership—although indeed in Querétaro Enrique Colunga had cited, in the name of the sponsors of Article 27, the assembly's power to take measures affecting acquired rights (Rouaix, *Los artículos 27 y 123*, pp. 209–211)—were Aarón Sáenz, Emilio Portes Gil, and historian Manuel González Ramírez (Aarón Sáenz, *La política internacional de la Revolución: Estudios y documentos*; Emilio Portes Gil, *Autobiografía de la Revolución Mexicana*, p. 346; Manuel González Ramírez, *El petróleo mexicano: La expropiación petrolera ante el derecho internacional*, pp. 201–206). On the other hand, Antonio Gómez Robledo and Luis Zubiría y Campa, among many others, demonstrated that even within the framework of traditional international law the Constitutional Assembly had the power to affect the legal status of any oil property whatsoever (Antonio Gómez Robledo, *The Bucareli Agreements and International Law*, p. 48; Luis Zubiría y Campa, *El artículo 27 y el petróleo*, pp. 3–4).

11. For Pastor Rouaix, as long as return of the value of the oil extracted prior to 1917 was not demanded, it was not possible to speak of retroactivity (Mexico, Cámara de Senadores, Sección de Estadística y Anales de Jurisprudencia, *El petróleo: La más grande riqueza nacional*, pp. 52–58). Francisco Múgica, Andrés Molina Enríquez, and Manuel Rojas also took the same position (Armando María y Campos, *Múgica: Crónica biográfica*, p. 134; *El Universal*, July 22, 1931; editorial in *El Reformador*, June 2, 1938). This view was also expressed by the renowned jurist Fernando González Roa, who, although he did not participate directly in the drafting of Article 27, had worked closely with Carranza on the matter (*Las cuestiones fundamentales de actualidad en México*, p. 115).

12. United States, 80th Congress, 2nd session, House of Representatives Committee on Interstate and Foreign Commerce, *Fuel Investigation: Mexican Petroleum*, pp. 117–118.

13. This total was distributed as follows: Compañía Franco-Española, 145,666 hectares; the Mestres group, 76,222; the Pearson group, 564,095; the Doheny group, 227,447; the La Corona group, 408,385; the Penn-Mex group, 67,110; Compañía Exportadora Petrolífera, 63,907; and the 273 remaining companies, 598,257 (NAW 812.6363/293). According to reports by the Association of Producers of Petroleum in Mexico (APPM), to the U.S. Shipping Board, the lands controlled in 1917 by the principal American companies came to about 1.5 million hectares (3.7 million acres), and practically all of them were proven oil lands (December 31, 1919, NAW 812.6363/ 618). For a list of the 47 American firms plus those with American capital registered in Mexico which had rights acquired prior to the date the new constitution went in-

to effect, see United States, 69th Congress, 2nd session, Senate Committee on Foreign Relations, *Oil Concessions in Mexico: Message from the President of the United States Transmitting Report of the Secretary of State in Response to Senate Resolution No. 330, Submitting Certain Information Respecting Oil Lands or Oil Concessions in Mexico*, pp. 3–4.

14. In the United Nations a new principle of international law is taking shape which gives the insufficiently developed countries the possibility of recovering their national resources being exploited by foreign capital (United Nations, International Law Commission, *Yearbook, 1960*, II, 17 ff.).

15. Félix Palavicini was the target of suspicions in this regard (María y Campos, *Múgica*, p. 134).

16. New England Fuel Oil to Department of State, NAW 812.6363/236.

17. An international committee bringing together the bondholders of the Mexican foreign debt was established in London in 1917. Two years later there appeared a National Association for the Protection of American Rights in Mexico, in which the oil firms had a controlling role. Also in 1919 the bankers with interests in Mexico got together and formed a group in Paris.

18. According to a report by the U.S. chargé d'affaires, the firms belonging to the APPM accounted for about 90 per cent of the total Mexican oil output (July 9, 1937, NAW 812.6363/2948).

19. This declaration was made after a meeting held in Galveston, Texas, on May 17, 1921 (Asociación Americana de México, *Condiciones de los americanos en México*).

20. H. Walker to Department of State, July 19, 1918, NAW 812.512/2120.

21. It was not only a question of the companies exerting pressure on the U.S. government—the channel worked both ways. For example, the director of the Oil Division in the U.S. Fuel Administration had urged from the beginning that the companies not give in to the Mexican demands, even if indemnization was offered, since it was vital for them to maintain control over the oil (NAW 812.6363/715).

22. AREM L-E-547, vol. 15, Leg. 3, f. 27.

23. Alberto J. Pani, *Mi contribución al nuevo régimen, 1910–1933*, pp. 231–236; Isidro Fabela, *Historia diplomática de la Revolución Mexicana*, I, 314–319.

24. Edmund David Cronon, *Josephus Daniels in Mexico*, p. 43; Wendell C. Gordon, *The Expropriation of Foreign-owned Property in Mexico*, p. 43; NAW 812.6363/2382.

25. The change in the legal status of the subsoil affected the oil companies most of all, but there were also protests from other kinds of enterprises, such as the United States Graphite Company, which claimed absolute ownership of the graphite deposits.

26. NAW 812.6363/2366; Howard F. Cline, *The United States and Mexico*, p. 186. These "assurances" that Carranza gave had to do with lands "then under exploitation." This led the Americans to think that they had been promised that all their rights acquired prior to May 1, 1917, would be respected, whereas Carranza had in mind a much more restricted application, as it will be seen later.

27. The literature on this point is rather abundant: see the *Boletín del petróleo*, especially the editorials by Salvador Mendoza in 7 (January–June 1919) and Joaquín Santaella in 8 (July–December 1919), as well as the study by Aquiles Elorduy in the same volume, pp. 11–14, and the editorial in 10 (July–December 1920); Manuel de la Peña, *El petróleo y la legislación frente a las compañías petroleras*; J. Vázquez Schiaffino, Joaquín Santaella, and Aquiles Elorduy, *Informes sobre la cuestión petrolera*.

28. This thesis appeared not only in articles and books but also in official documents. The draft regulations governing Article 27's oil clause which were presented to the Congress by Carranza on November 22, 1918, pointed out that "the basic laws

[in question] are necessarily retroactive because their intent is to reform." If the restitution of a right is considered retroactive, it is only legitimate that this should be so (Mexico, Secretaría de Industria, Comercio y Trabajo, *Proyecto de ley orgánica del artículo 27 constitucional en el ramo del petróleo aprobado por la H. Cámara de Senadores y enviada a la H. Cámara de Diputados para su discusión*). The Ministry of Industry took a similar stand in the preamble of its 1917 bill (Mexico, Secretaría de Industria, Comercio y Trabajo, *Proyecto de ley del petróleo de los Estados Unidos Mexicanos*). This view is also expressed in a document transmitted by Industry to Foreign Affairs on September 22, 1926, which says that the lawmaker is in no way prevented from passing retroactive legislation (AREM L-E, vol. 21, Leg. 1, ff. 151–152).

29. Examples constantly cited were the abolition of slavery and the prohibiton law, both of which affected vested rights (González Roa, *Las cuestiones fundamentales . . .* , pp. 120–121; Gómez Robledo, *The Bucareli Agreements . . .* , p. 31).

30. Those who maintained this point of view held that hydrocarbons were in the same category as wild animals in that they were constantly shifting and could only be said to be someone's property once they were "captured." It was pointed out, moreover, that even in the United States decisions had been handed down applying the *ferae naturae* principle to oil—that is, that it belonged to the state until it was extracted (Walter D. Hawk, "Aspectos de la cuestión petrolera que quedan comprendidos en la diplomacia mexicano-americana," manuscript translation of article in *Illinois Law Review* 22 [June 1927]).

31. It its brief presented to the courts the executive maintained that "no legislation may validly deprive the nation of ownership of the subsoil in order to attribute it to private parties" (Mexico, *La cuestión petrolera mexicana: El punto de vista del Ejecutivo Federal*). See also the preamble to the bill of November 22, 1918; articles appearing in *El Heraldo de México*, September 1, 2, 5, and 6, 1919; González Roa, *Las cuestiones fundamentales . . .*

32. Mexico, Secretaría de Industria, Comercio y Trabajo, *Proyecto de ley orgánica del artículo 27 . . .*

33. President's state-of-the-union message, September 1, 1919.

34. Ambassador Fletcher to Department of State, June 25, 1918, NAW 812.51/437.

35. José Domingo Lavín, *Petróleo*, p. 90.

36. In 1918 the tax payment increased to 12 million pesos, and the treasury minister estimated that this sum could well keep on going up to ten times as much, given the industry's prosperous outlook (*Revista Tricolor*, August 1918).

37. The preamble to the organic oil law bill drafted by the Ministry of Industry in 1917 said: "In Mexico the oil industry has special importance because, unlike the situation in other countries, the industrial application of petroleum can take place without the benefit of extensive deposits of coal; thus, the use of oil not only constitutes a saving but represents an indispensable basis for future industrial development" (Mexico, Secretaría de Industria, Comercio y Trabajo, *Proyecto de ley del petróleo de los Estados Unidos Mexicanos*, p. 18). "To let stand the monopolies established by the dictatorship," said the Technical Commission on the Nationalization of Oil in 1916," would be tantamount to stifling the economic independence of Mexican industry" (*Boletín del petróleo* 3 [January–June 1917]: 220). Statements in this tone appeared throughout the *Boletín del petróleo* during the period in question.

38. On this point see, among others, Carlos Díaz Dufoo, *México y los capitales extranjeros*, p. 7; Frederick Sherwood Dunn, *The Diplomatic Protection of Americans in Mexico*, p. 327.

39. Pani, who in reality was never in favor of a radical stand with respect to the companies, pointed out in a cabinet meeting on November 4, 1922, that Carranza's

extreme position—unconstitutional according to him—had been aimed only at a "fair middle ground" in negotiations with the firms; the radical climate of the time had obliged him to take this extreme position (AREM C-3-2-43, Exp. III/625 (011)2-1, Leg. 1, ff. 21, 26–27).

40. This tax, decreed on April 13, 1917, imposed levies on the output itself, on the derivatives, and on the fuel waste, according to the value of the product. To get around the Porfirian tax exemption laws, which applied to everything but stamp taxes, Carranza made it payable precisely in stamps.

41. Ambassador Fletcher reported to the State Department that the measure had been the subject of much discussion among Industry Minister Pani, Deputy Treasury Minister Berlanga, and acting Foreign Affairs Minister Cándido Aguilar, and that the last-mentioned was in favor of a less radical approach (NAW 812.1562/1977).

42. These powers were granted to him on May 8, 1917, with a view to facilitating salary payments to government employees, but they hardly could have been considered the most ideal basis for implementing measures of this kind.

43. The decree, which was the "first effective attempt at constitutional restoration of the nation's direct domain," was issued by the Ministry of the Treasury but in reality it had been prepared by the Ministry of Industry, which had failed to reach an agreement with the companies prior to its publication. It called for the payment of royalties equivalent to 5 dollars a hectare and 5 per cent of the value of output (Alberto J. Pani, *Las conferencias de Bucareli*, p. 101).

44. The period was extended under the decree of May 18. On June 8 the regulations corresponding to Article 14 of the February decree, which fully upheld it in spirit, were published. Since the companies stood by their position, on July 31 a deadline for filing the claims was proposed once again. On August 8 it was announced that within a week any Mexican citizen could file claim with respect to any oil lands for which their present owners or renters had not done so. Still the companies refused to change their stand.

45. Ambassador Fletcher reported to the State Department that the Mexican government, unable to enforce the point, had prepared this decree on the eve of the deadline (NAW 812.6363).

46. See Mexico, *La cuestión petrolera mexicana*; [Oil companies], *Alegatos que presentan ante la Suprema Corte de Justicia de la Nación las siguientes compañías y personas . . . en los juicios de amparo promovidos contra leyes y actos del Ejecutivo de la Unión y de sus dependencias, la Secretaría de Gobernación, La Secretaría de Hacienda y Crédito Público y la Secretaría de Industria, Comercio y Trabajo*.

47. In 1919 the companies filed a total of eighty suits for injunction.

48. On January 13, 1919, forty-six of the principal companies sent a telegram to Carranza asking, in view of the need to dig new wells in order to keep up production levels, that the Mexican government grant provisional permits without the firms having to renounce what they considered to be their rights (NAW 812.6363/628A). A year later, on January 20, 1920, Carranza answered them in the affirmative (NAW 812.6363). The text of the decrees and executive orders mentioned may be found in Mexico, Secretaría de Industria, Comercio y Trabajo, *Legislación petrolera, 1783–1921*.

49. Pani, *Las conferencias de Bucareli*, p. 103.

50. The Mexican government went so far as to propose granting the drilling permits if the companies agreed beforehand to abide by the regulatory law that the Congress was to approve. Needless to say, the firms refused.

51. Circular of May 16, 1919.

52. Merrill Rippy, "El petróleo y la Revolución Mexicana," *Problemas agrícolas e industriales de México* 6 (July–September 1954): 29.

53. U.S. consul in Tampico to Department of State, June 19, 1919, NAW 812.6363/476; Department of State to U.S. embassy in Mexico, June 18, 1919, NAW 812.6363/476.

54. U.S. consulate in Tampico to Department of State, August 23, 1919, NAW 711.12/196.

55. One cause for friction between the government and the oil firms, although it was only of secondary importance, was the granting of concessions under the March 12 decree and the circular of April 21, 1919, allowing third parties to work "federal zones"—rivers, streambeds, estuaries, lakes, and swamps that cut across the companies' lands. The purpose was to open up a new source of income for the government, which claimed that to date the firms which had exploited the oil had given virtually no return whatsoever to the nation. The firms, for their part, maintained that this maneuver was nothing but robbery (Manuel Calero and Delbert J. Haff, *Concesiones petroleras en las zonas federales*, p. 13).

56. In the interim a fair degree of anarchy reigned, since all the oil transactions were governed by a casuistic series of presidential agreements that gave rise to contradictions and confusion.

57. It was the Industry Ministry's first important effort in this area (Pani, *Mi contribución . . .* , p. 245).

58. It was said that they were not within the "Revolutionary criteria" (Arturo Pani, *Alberto J. Pani: Ensayo biográfico*, pp. 120–121).

59. In the cabinet meeting of November 4, 1922, Pani, defending his characteristic point of view, said that the law was promulgated with full knowledge that it was "absolutely radical, unconstitutional, and retroactive" and it "produced the consequent scandal and protests" (AREM C-3-2-43, Exp. III/625 (011)/2-1, Leg. l, f. 26).

60. Mexico, Secretaría de Industria, Comercio y Trabajo, *Proyecto do ley del petróleo de los Estados Unidos Mexicanos*.

61. See Carlos Díaz Dufoo, *La cuestión del petróleo*, pp. 209–211.

62. U.S. embassy to Department of State, May 30, 1917, NAW 812.6363/281; oil companies to Polk, June 6, 1917, NAW 812.6363/285.

63. Simpson, Brown and Williams to Department of State, July 11, 1917, NAW 812.6363/291.

64. Cándido Aguilar, *Iniciativa de ley orgánica del artículo 27 constitucional en lo relativo a petróleo que presenta el C. General . . . , Gobernador Constitucional del Estado de Veracruz a la H. Legislatura del mismo Estado, para ser enviada por ésta al Congreso de la Unión*.

65. *Boletín del petróleo* 5 (January–June 1918): 128–135, 136–139. Other comments on the proposal are found in Mexico, Secretaría de Industria, Comercio y Trabajo, *Documentos relacionados con la legislación petrolera mexicana*, pp. 331–396.

66. Spanish embassy to the minister of state, February 14, 1917, CDHM R50, container 331, sole leg., no. 16.

67. *El Universal*, June 4, 1917.

68. NAW 812.6363/415.

69. Owners of lands on which the type of investment indicated had not been made only had preferential rights for making their claim during one year (Mexico, Secretaría de Industria, Comercio y Trabajo, *Proyecto de ley orgánica del artículo 27 . . .*). The companies pointed out that the bill did not guarantee all their rights, it improperly charged them royalties, and it did not cover the 90 per cent of their holdings on which no investment had been made prior to 1917 (Association of Producers of Petroleum in Mexico, *Documents Relating to the Attempt of the Government of Mexico to Confiscate Foreign-owned Oil Properties*).

70. NAW 812.6363/415.

71. According to Carlos Díaz Dufoo, this decision was the result of external pressure (*La cuestión del petróleo*, pp. 310–312). Whether or not this is true, there is no doubt that the U.S. embassy was in contact with members of the Senate committee, according to reports filed by Chargé d'Affaires Summerlin in September 1919 (NAW 812.6363/537).

72. The deputy minister of industry, whose stand was extremely radical, like that of many of the senators, was present at the discussion. The sponsors of the new bill were accused in the press and on the Senate floor of being in league with the oil firms (*El Heraldo de México*, September and October; *Boletín del petróleo* 7 [July–December 1919]: 233; Díaz Dufoo, *La cuestión del petróleo*, pp. 315–322; M. Rippy, "El petróleo y la Revolución Mexicana," p. 39).

73. U.S. embassy to Department of State, October 8, 1919, NAW 812.6363/646.

74. Mexico, Secretaría de Industria, Comercio y Trabajo, *Proyecto de ley orgánica del artículo 27 . . .*

75. Manuel de la Peña, *El dominio directo del soberano en las minas de México y génesis de la legislación petrolera mexicana*, II, 209–210.

76. On the centralist and authoritarian nature of the Carranza regime, see Manuel Moreno Sánchez, *Crisis política de México*, pp. 33–35.

77. For details on the firms' position with respect to the Carranza measures, see [Oil companies], *Alegatos . . .*; APPM, *Documents . . .* ; memorandum prepared by oil attorney Frederick R. Kellogg, NAW 812.6363/688.

78. United States, 66th Congress, 2nd session, Senate Committee on Foreign Relations, *Investigation of Mexican Affairs: Preliminary Report and Hearings . . . Pursuant to Senate Resolution No. 106 Directing the Committee . . . to Investigate the Matter of Outrages on Citizens of the United States in Mexico*, p. 540.

79. Doheny pointed out that the tax was really 33 per cent and not 10, as the Mexican government maintained. Apparently he based this calculation on the total value of the tax vis-à-vis the total value of the oil at the well, which was when it was at its lowest point—.10 or .15 (U.S. cents) a barrel as compared with .80 by the time it reached Tampico (Gordon, *The Expropriation . . .* , p. 74).

80. Frederick R. Kellogg, "The Mexican Oil Problem," *Nation*, October 5, 1918.

81. Carranza was accused of all manner of things in the American press—of being a bolshevik, of cooperating with the Central Powers, etc.

82. The findings of the investigation are reported in United States, 66th Congress, 2nd session, Senate Committee on Foreign Relations, *Investigation of Mexican Affairs*.

83. Carlos Díaz Dufoo relentlessly fought all measures contrary to the companies' interests, calling attention to the goodwill of an industry that had never done anything to hurt the country and indeed had done much to benefit it (*La cuestión del petróleo*).

84. See, for example, the views expressed in *Excélsior*, August 21, 1919, with respect to Articles 27 and 123.

85. *Boletín del petróleo* 5 (January–June 1918): 452–457; NAW 812.6363/300.

86. It is well to bear in mind that this "united front" did not include all the companies. In 1921 the independent producers, backed by Senator Joseph F. Guffey and E. W. Marland, launched a campaign of protest against the big firms' maneuvers with respect to the Mexican law (M. Rippy, "El petróleo y la Revolución Mexicana," p. 36). Carranza attempted to widen the rift by supporting the establishment of a company that would go along with the government's measures—a plan that eventually saw some fruition with Atlantic Gulf and West Indies. AGWI, a merger of these two firms, took issue with the State Department over the Carranza provisions, for which it was roundly attacked by the rest of the companies. It was never a very important

firm (Mexico, Secretaría del Patrimonio Nacional, *El petróleo de México: Recopilación de documentos oficiales de orden económico de la industria petrolera, con una introducción que resume sus motivos y consecuencias*, p. 16; oil companies to U.S. Shipping Board, December 30, 1919, NAW 812.6363/618).

87. Department of State to U.S. embassy in Mexico and Ambassador Fletcher to Department of State, November 6 and 7, 1918, respectively, NAW 812.512/2190A, 2191.

88. The following documents may be consulted: Mexico, Secretaría de Industria, Comercio y Trabajo, *Documentos relacionados con la legislación petrolera mexicana*, pp. 427–439; Alberto J. Pani, *Apuntes autobiográficos*, p. 264; United States, 66th Congress, 2nd session, Senate Committee on Foreign Relations, *Investigation of Mexican Affairs*, p. 387; *Boletín del petróleo* 7 (July–December 1918): 6; AREM L-E, vol. 1, Leg. 1, ff. 20, 25, 39–40; NAW 812.512/2004.

89. See, for example, oil companies to U.S. Fuel Administration, August 4, 1919, NAW 812.6363/532; oil companies to Senator D. U. Fletcher, May 29, 1919, NAW 812.6363/464; oil companies to secretary of the president, November 22, 1919, WWP; letter signed by President Wilson, December 1919, NAW 812.6363/600.

90. Oil companies to Polk, May 5, 1917, NAW 812.6363/236, 0510; Panuco-Boston Oil Fields to Secretary of State Lansing, July 29, 1918, NAW 812.6363/407; APPM to Department of State, September 22 and November 15, 1919, NAW 812.6363/543, 581; oil companies to Senator F. M. Simmons, December 8, 1919, NAW 812.6363/598.

91. James Fred Rippy, José Vasconcelos, and Guy Stevens, *American Policies Abroad: Mexico*, pp. 192–193. The companies maintained that Article 27, as well as Mexico's oil policy in general, was the work of the German minister (AREM L-E-533, vol. 1, Leg. 1, ff. 39–40). The representative of Panuco-Boston Oil Fields testified before the Fall committee that with the United States at war the oilmen, as patriotic Americans, could not take any step that would imply agreeing that the hydrocarbons belonged to the Mexican nation, since such a step would endanger the Allies' fuel supply (United States, 66th Congress, 2nd session, Senate Committee on Foreign Relations, *Investigation of Mexican Affairs*, pp. 590–591).

92. NAW 812.6363/591; APPM, *Documents . . .* , p. 80; Manuel González Ramírez, *La revolución social de México*, I, 680.

93. Doheny went to Versailles in 1919 as representative of the National Association for the Protection of American Rights in Mexico and the Association of Producers of Petroleum in Mexico. There was more than a billion dollars' worth of U.S. investments in that country to be protected (*New York Times*, January 18, 1919; *El Universal*, April 29, 1921).

94. In 1917 the bulk of the Mexican oil output went to meet the war needs of the United States and the countries in Europe. In February 1918 the State Department's Division of Mexican Affairs warned that the oil problems in Mexico could have grave repercussions in Europe (report of Mexican Petroleum Company of Delaware, 1917, NAW 812.6363/401).

95. Samuel Eliot Morison and Henry Steele Commager, *Historia de los Estados Unidos de Norteamérica*, III, 99.

96. NAW 812.6363/605, 592. Reacting to one of the Mexican oil-law bills, the *New York Times* came out with the following front-page headline: "Mexican Oil Seizures Menace Our Merchant Marine" (December 11, 1919). The companies did their best to perpetuate this attitude (Edward L. Doheny, *The Mexican Question: Its Relations to Our Industries, Our Merchant Marine, and Our Foreign Trade*; Clarence W. Barron, *The Mexican Problem*, p. 88). The State Department instructed its consuls to report on the oil prospects in their districts as well as to give all possible aid to any Americans wishing to engage in exploitation.

97. Ambassador Fletcher reported on August 2, 1917, that Carranza had promised he would not nationalize either of these two industries (NAW 812.63/481). The Spanish embassy, for its part, reported to Madrid on March 12, 1917, that the United States intended to pressure Carranza into signing a treaty that would to a great extent undo the provisions of the new constitution (CDHM R5, container 333, Leg. 2, no. 6).

98. J. F. Rippy, Vasconcelos, and Stevens, *American Policies Abroad*, p. 65.

99. Spanish embassy to minister of state, August 13, 1917, CDHM R50, container 332, sole leg., no. 22.

100. In a note dated July 16 Ambassador Fletcher let Mexico know that the taxes would be paid, albeit under protest, since the companies' contracts provided for their payment (AREM 42-15-2, Exp. A/628 (010)/1–2, f. 4; NAW 812.6363/250, 251, 281½). Another, somewhat less important problem came up when Mexico refused to recognize the sizable property acquired by Americans between February 1, 1917, the date when the new constitution was promulgated, and May 5, when it went into effect; following a series of U.S. protests, Mexico eventually reversed its decision (NAW 812.6363/292).

101. The plan was British, according to a Spanish embassy report to Madrid (July 28, 1917, CDHM R50, container 332, sole leg., no. 18).

102. Ambassador Fletcher to Department of State, April 3, 1918, NAW 812.512/ 1935.

103. NAW 812.6363/532.

104. Spanish embassy to minister of state, June 19, 1918, CDHM R51, container 351, Leg. 3, no. 26.

105. Secretary of State Lansing to Ambassador Fletcher, March 19, 1918, NAW 812.6363/376, 812.512/1894.

106. Carranza emphasized that the measures were purely fiscal in nature and that he would not admit any diplomatic interference; at most the companies could appeal through the courts, but they could not turn to their governments (Ambassador Fletcher to Secretary of State Lansing, NAW 812.512/2058A). This stand was reiterated in a Mexican note of August 17, 1918 (NAW 812.512/2089).

107. Department of State to U.S. embassy in Mexico, April 4, 1918, and June 15, 1919, NAW 812.6363/532, 463.

108. Ambassador Fletcher to Secretary of State Lansing, March 1, 1918, NAW 812.512/1894.

109. Polk to Ambassador Fletcher, December 21, 1918, NAW 812.032/41.

110. Department of State to U.S. embassy in Mexico, June 18, October 1, November 18, and December 29, 1919, NAW 812.6363/470, 538A, 581, 312, 115 4/11; Ministry of Foreign Affairs to Mexican embassy in Washington, July 21, 1919, NAW 812.6363/448.

111. Ambassador Fletcher pointed out that if Mexico did not accept this suggestion it would not be possible to get the State Department to agree to a more liberal stand with respect to the export of arms and other manufactures that the country needed (NAW 812.6363/444).

112. Department of State to U.S. embassy in Mexico, March 18, April 14 and 16, and October 1, 1919, NAW 812.6363/2366.

113. Leander Jan de Bekker, *The Plot against Mexico*, pp. 213 ff.

114. United States, 66th Congress, 2nd session, Senate Committee on Foreign Relations, *Investigation of Mexican Affairs*, pp. 267, 404–409, 1000.

115. Josephus Daniels, *Shirt-Sleeve Diplomat*, p. 41.

116. United States, 66th Congress, 2nd session, Senate Committee on Foreign Relations, *Investigation of Mexican Affairs*, p. 605.

117. Leander Jan de Bekker is representative of the sector in the United States that was opposed to the companies' interventionist stand. He wrote several articles and a

book in defense of this viewpoint, but he was unable to present any conclusive evidence to the Fall Committee.

118. Hunt reported that he had presented the proposal to Pancho Villa, but that the latter had not been interested. Carranza knew about the scheme (*El Universal Gráfico*, March 11 and 14, 1924).

119. Ambassador Daniels to Department of State, March 4, 1938, NAW 812.504/ 1717.

120. Spanish embassy to minister of state, May 3, 11, and 12, 1917, CDHM R50, container 331, sole leg., nos. 40, 41, 42.

121. Cline, *The United States and Mexico*, p. 187.

122. On April 14, 1917, the *New York Times* denied the rumor that the War Department had recommended the occupation of Tampico. Six days earlier, however, the State Department's Division of Mexican Affairs had suggested that the Navy undertake surveillance of the Tampico-Tuxpan route and send 6,000 troops to Galveston or Corpus Christi, Texas, to stand ready in the event it was necessary to take over the oil region in Mexico (NAW 812.6363/308). Josephus Daniels, who was then secretary of the navy, says in his diary that the companies tried to force him into taking action, but President Wilson stood behind him in his refusal (Edmund David Cronon, ed., *The Cabinet Diaries of Josephus Daniels, 1913–1921*, p. 328).

123. Farwell, preface to Leander Jan de Bekker, *The Plot against Mexico*, p. 16.

124. The interrogation of witnesses in favor of Carranza, such as Leander Jan de Bekker and Samuel Guy Inman, was aggressive and completely one-sided.

125. Among the witnesses on behalf of the companies were Doheny, a representative of Penn-Mex Oil, the director of the National Association for the Protection of American Rights in Mexico, and representatives of Continental Mexican, International Petroleum, Texas Oil, Tal Vez Oil, and Panuco-Boston Oil Fields. They accused the Mexican government of trying to confiscate their rights and characterized it as corrupt, thieving, bolshevik, pro-German, etc.

126. United States, 66th Congress, 2nd session, Senate Committee on Foreign Relations, *Investigation of Mexican Affairs*, pp. 9–10; H. Walker to J. P. Tumulty, secretary to President Wilson, November 22, 1919, WWP; I. Jewell William to Department of State, NAW 812.6363/634.

127. Hobby to Department of State, August 25, 1919, NAW 711.12/210.

128. Memorandum of a conversation between Secretary of State Lansing and oil company representatives, January 9, 1920, NAW 812.6363/641.

129. Department of the Navy to Department of State, August 7 and 16, 1919, NAW 711.12/194½, 195½.

130. It was pointed out in the course of their meeting that the oil firms were seeking intervention in order to have greater security over their properties, which would thereby increase greatly in value (Cronon, ed., *The Cabinet Diaries . . .* , p. 461).

131. William Jenkins, U.S. consul in Puebla, was kidnapped by a rebel group which then demanded a ransom. The State Department and the American press, especially the Hearst papers, demanded that the Mexican government secure his release and criticized it severely for being unable to protect the lives of foreigners (*New York Times*, December 17, 1919). Manuel González Ramírez voices the suspicion, which appears to have some basis, that the incident was "fabricated" (*La revolución social de México*, I, 663–666).

132. Department of State to President Wilson, December 19, 1919, NAW 812.6363/ 620; Cronon, ed., *The Cabinet Diaries . . .* , pp. 465, 467.

133. Cronon, ed., *The Cabinet Diaries . . .* , p. 501; J. F. Rippy, Vasconcelos, and Stevens, *American Policies Abroad*, pp. 59–61; James Morton Callahan, *American Foreign Policy in Mexican Relations*, pp. 578–579.

134. Ambassador Daniels to President Roosevelt and Secretary of State Hull,

March 22, 1938 (JDP). Secretary of State Lansing and Senator Fall were not the only ones who were calling for a "hard-line" policy with Mexico: Attorney General A. M. Palmer, the U.S. minister in Cuba, and Ambassador Fletcher were also of the same view, as was the governor of Texas, who demanded intervention "for Mexico's own good" (WWP). In the Senate there were also Albert B. Cummins of Iowa, James E. Watson of Indiana, and N. J. Gould of New York.

135. According to Frank Tannenbaum, this was the deciding factor in the U.S. decision against the use of armed intervention to solve the controversy with Carranza; moreover, the United States was already opposed to any new military commitment in principle (*Mexico: The Struggle for Peace and Bread*, p. 275). The incursion into Soviet territory had been a lesson; it was not impossible that the same thing could happen in Mexico. All this showed that the American public and the world at large was for the most part against any new conflict.

136. Emile Joseph Dillon, *México en su momento crítico*, pp. 142–143.

137. Walker to U.S. Shipping Board, April 23, 1920, NAW 812.6363/0642; Cronon, ed., *The Cabinet Diaries . . .* , pp. 525, 528.

138. Other members were Andrés Molina Enríquez, who had abandoned his 1909 position that the vested interests of foreigners could not be impinged on; Joaquín Santaella; J. Vázquez Schiaffino; Aquiles Elorduy; Fernando González Roa; Manuel de la Peña; and Calles himself.

139. Pani's attempt to get the February decree amended in order to avoid a clash with the companies was unsuccessful (Callahan, *American Foreign Policy in Mexican Relations*, p. 575; Díaz Dufoo, *La cuestión del petróleo*, p. 260).

140. Aguilar asked Carranza to withdraw his bill from the Congress and have another one drawn up to reflect the requirements of the moment; otherwise, he warned, a conflict with the United States was imminent (AREM L-E-533, vol. 1, Leg. 1, ff. 40–46).

141. See Díaz Dufoo, *La cuestión del petróleo*; idem, *México y los capitales extranjeros*.

142. The companies were in contact with Senator Castelazo and possibly with Senators Barroso and Frías; Deputy Reynoso undertook their defense in his *El Demócrata* (NAW 812.6363/446, 547).

143. Another example of some of the Protestant churches' activity in support of Carranza's nationalist policy was the establishment of the League of Free Nations Association—one of the Fall Committee's targets—which took the view that intervention in Mexico would undo all their work in that country (United States, 66th Congress, 2nd session, Senate Committee on Foreign Relations, *Investigation of Mexican Affairs*, pp. 41–42). The labor movement in the United States was on the whole on Mexico's side (M. Rippy, "El petróleo y la Revolución Mexicana," p. 90).

144. Different arguments were given: while the *Nation* and the *Baltimore Evening Sun*, among others, condemned the intrigues of big business, in principle, the *New Republic* was against intervention for reasons of economy, since more would be spent on American holdings in Mexico than they were actually worth and the cost would fall on the taxpayers.

145. The *Revista Mexicana* and other publications were financed by the Mexican embassy (United States, 66th Congress, 2nd session, Senate Committee on Foreign Relations, *Investigation of Mexican Affairs*, p. 424).

5. From Obregón's Victory to the Bucareli Agreement and the 1924 Accord

1. The "Sonora dynasty" had control over the Mexican Regional Workers' Confederation (CROM—Confederación Regional Obrera Mexicana), which was estab-

lished in 1919 and had become the strongest workers' organization in the country. The peasants, more numerous but less well organized, were represented by such leaders as Aurelio Manrique and Antonio Díaz Soto y Gama.

2. This Revolutionary phraseology, quite divorced from reality, more than once led Washington to take Obregón for a truly socialist, and even bolshevik, leader (Henry Bamford Parkes, *A History of Mexico*, pp. 371–372; William S. McCrea, "A Comparative Study of the Mexican Oil Expropriation (1938) and the Iranian Oil Nationalization (1951)" (Doctoral dissertation, Georgetown University, 1955), p. 13.

3. Tulio Halperin Donghi, *Historia contemporánea de América Latina*, pp. 321–323; Anatol Shulgovski, *México en la encrucijada de su historia*, pp. 37–68.

4. John W. F. Dulles, *Yesterday in Mexico: A Chronicle of the Revolution, 1919–1936*, pp. 109–117; Edwin Lieuwen, *Mexican Militarism: The Rise and Fall of the Revolutionary Army, 1910–1940*.

5. Among the main declines were those in silver, copper, lead, and henequen.

6. Before formally taking office as president, Obregón told the *Chicago Commercial Herald and Examiner* that his country was anxious to have any foreign capital that sought to bring with it just retribution (September 22, 1920). Once in the presidency, he appealed specifically to American capital for cooperation in the new endeavor (Alvaro Obregón, *Campaña política del C. . . . , candidato a la presidencia de la República, 1920–1924*, V, 235; idem, *Discursos del general . . .* , pp. 311, 331).

7. Howard F. Cline, *The United States and Mexico*, p. 194; Manuel Moreno Sánchez, "Comentarios al estudio de Paul Nathan, 'Un estudio norteamericano sobre Cárdenas,'" *Problemas agrícolas e industriales de México* 7 (July–September 1955): 239. Obregón had to deal with uprisings led by Francisco Murguía and Lucio Blanco in 1922 as well as that of Adolfo de la Huerta at the end of his incumbency. All of them, especially the last, could have been taken advantage of by the U.S. government—if it had been so inclined—to get him out of office.

8. Other problems were the national debt, the railroad debt, and the damage claims.

9. George K. Lewis, "An Analysis of the Institutional Status and Role of the Petroleum Industry in Mexico's Evolving System of Political Economy" (Doctoral dissertation, University of Texas [Austin], 1959), p. 9.

10. The Republican platform declared: "We should not recognize any Mexican government unless it be a responsible government willing and able to give sufficient assurances that the lives and property of American citizens are respected and protected, that wrongs will be promptly corrected." The Democratic Party, on the other hand, was only prepared to recognize the Mexican government when it had "signified its willingness to meet international obligations and written upon its statutes just laws under which foreign investors shall have rights as well as duties." In both cases the demands amounted to exemption of American interests from the reforms in the new constitution (*Boletín de la Asociación Americana de México* [1921]: 11–12).

11. Samuel Eliot Morison and Henry Steele Commager, *Historia de los Estados Unidos de Norteamérica*, III, 83.

12. Cline, *The United States and Mexico*, pp. 194–195; T. H. Reynolds, "México y los Estados Unidos, 1821–1951," *Historia mexicana* 2 (January–March 1953): 417.

13. Samuel Eliot Morison and Henry Steele Commager, *Historia de los Estados Unidos de Norteamérica*, III, 85. Henry Bamford Parkes characterized Harding as an "especial friend of the oil industry" (*A History of Mexico*, p. 377). Albert B. Fall, in his capacity as secretary of the interior, gave the oil firms and other members of the big business community a direct voice in the meetings of the cabinet. The person immediately responsible for Mexican affairs, Secretary of State Charles Evans Hughes, was also on the best of terms with the oil industry, and on leaving office he was to serve on the boards of the American Petroleum Institute, Standard Oil, and other

large oil corporations (Ludwell Denny, *We Fight for Oil*, p. 42).

14. Other commitments aimed at maintenance and confirmation of the world status quo and prevention of a new holocaust were the treaty signed at the Washington Conference on the Limitation of Armament in 1922, which undertook to limit the naval power of the signatory nations, and the Naval Treaty of London, drawn up for the same purpose a few years later.

15. Samuel Flagg Bemis, *La diplomacia de Estados Unidos en la América Latina*, p. 233.

16. In 1920 the Federal Trade Commission, Senators Albert B. Fall and James D. Phelan, and, of course, the oil companies came out in support of a plan to give the United States a position similar to that of Great Britain with respect to world oil reserves (John Ise, *The United States Oil Policy*, pp. 481–482; Harvey O'Connor, *El imperio del petróleo*, p. 354).

17. Mark Lawrence Requa, *The Petroleum Problem*, pp. 20–21.

18. NAW 812.6363/643A. A similar study was done again in 1921 (NAW 812.6363/847A).

19. U.S. consul in Salina Cruz to Department of State, February 14, 1920, NAW 812.6363/652. In 1921 the U.S. Shipping Board was still interested in the project, but the plans were abandoned the following year (U.S. Shipping Board to Department of State, August 15, 1921, NAW 812.6363/449).

20. On March 17, 1921, the American press reported the rumor that the Mexican government had been recognized by France. The following day the Associated Press went on to editorialize that recognition of Mexico by France would come as a surprise to the State Department, since for years there had been an understanding between the principal European powers and the United States that the formers' relations with Mexico would be largely governed by whatever position the United States took. It was pointed out that one of the immediate effects of the recognition would be serious repercussions among the world's large banking houses on the lending of money to Mexico. And so it seemed that Fall's policy had been adopted in Europe.

21. A report of the U.S. Shipping Board mentioned the possibility of Doheny's interests passing into British hands and stressed the importance of avoiding such an event (December 24, 1920, NAW 812.6363/994).

22. This stand taken by President Wilson, which according to MacCorkle was to turn him into a champion of American economic imperialism, has been explained by Rippy with the suggestion that by the end of his term in office Wilson was no longer in control of the State Department (Stuart Alexander MacCorkle, *American Policy of Recognition towards Mexico*, p. 96; James Fred Rippy, *The United States and Mexico*, p. 362).

23. Memorandum of a conversation between Fernando Iglesias Calderón and the under secretary of state, July 6, 1920, WWP 470–472; memorandum from the Division of Mexican Affairs, Department of State, October 26, 1920, NAW 812.6363/734½.

24. In addition to relief from the retroactive application of Article 27, the State Department asked for establishment of a joint commission that would review all claims for damages caused by the Revolution, as well as acceptance and payment of the foreign debt (Dulles, *Yesterday in Mexico*, p. 91).

25. Ibid. According to Miguel Alessio Robles, Obregón, Calles, and De la Huerta held a series of meetings in their homes to discuss the U.S. demands, at the conclusion of which it was decided to inform Wilson's lawyer and envoy, Mr. King, that it was not possible to enter into any treaty with the United States prior to diplomatic recognition (*Historia política de la Revolución*, pp. 341–342).

26. *El Universal*, April 28, 1921.

27. De la Huerta personally denied before the Chamber of Deputies, in a session on October 26, 1921, that the movement had any connection with the oil firms (*Excélsior*, October 27, 1921).

28. *New York Times*, July 13, 1920.

29. Gulf to Department of State, July 13, 1920, NAW 812.6363/694.

30. Department of State to Chargé d'Affaires Summerlin, August 11, 1920, NAW 812.6363/2366.

31. Following a meeting between Treviño and A. C. Ebie of Magnolia Petroleum, the latter declared that the end of the controversy was near (Obregón, *Campaña política. . .*, V, 316–317).

32. Frederick Sherwood Dunn, *The Diplomatic Protection of Americans in Mexico*, p. 345.

33. Jesús Silva Herzog, *Petróleo mexicano*, p. 82.

34. In a meeting between De la Huerta and Chargé d'Affaires George T. Summerlin on September 14, 1920, the Mexican said that from the beginning he had been against the Carranza oil law regulations, but that now he had changed his mind: it was necessary that concessions be granted by the government (NAW 812.6363/722½). When Transcontinental Petroleum protested to the Ministry of Industry that drilling permits had been granted to third parties on land belonging to it prior to 1917 but for which no claim had been filed, it was informed that the Carranza decrees remained in force until such time as they might be legally repealed. The ministry also took the opportunity to say once again that the hydrocarbons were public domain and that it was necessary to get a concession from the executive in order to extract them (Manuel de la Peña, *La cuestión palpitante: Estudio jurídico, político y económico sobre el artículo 27 Constitucional*, pp. 43–46.

35. C. O. Swain to Department of State, December 21, 1920, NAW 812.6363/778; Department of State to Chargé d'Affaires Summerlin, August 13, 1920, NAW 811.127/359.

36. According to a memorandum of the State Department's Division of Mexican Affairs, De la Huerta's attitude stemmed from the companies' refusal to pay certain taxes in exchange for derogation of the Carranza decrees (August 9, 1920, NAW 812.6363/888).

37. Department of State to Chargé d'Affaires Summerlin, August 18, 1921, NAW 812.6363/707; Summerlin to Ministry of Foreign Affairs, August 31, 1921, NAW 812.6363/1550½.

38. The State Department, in a communication of December 10, 1920, to its envoy in Mexico, reported that certain British and Dutch firms had gotten almost all the concessions that the De la Huerta administration had granted for exploration of the "federal zones." They had been able to do so with the help of Industry Minister Jacinto Treviño, General Benjamín Hill, and others. Chargé d'Affaires Summerlin reported on December 17 that a Canadian company by the name of El Sol had obtained some of these concessions on agreeing to pay the government 40 per cent of its profits (NAW 812.6363/755A). The American firms complained to Washington that El Aguila and La Corona had benefited from concessions granted by De la Huerta and that it was for this reason that El Aguila had had to withdraw from the APPM. It was very important, they said, to watch the moves of the British (oil companies to Department of State, December 8, 1920, NAW 812.6363/761).

39. Oil companies to Department of State, December 10, 1920, NAW 812.6363/756. For a more detailed study of the problem, see Manuel Calero and Delbert J. Haff, *Concesiones petroleras en las zonas federales; Excélsior*, June 30, 1920.

40. Industry Minister Treviño was persistent in his efforts to see that royalties were collected from the firms in accordance with the Carranza decree (Carlos Díaz Dufoo,

La cuestión del petróleo, pp. 368–369). In statements appearing in *El Heraldo de México* on June 10, 1920, Joaquín Santaella and J. Vázquez Schiaffino claimed that the companies had maneuvered to get him out of the way through their participation in Carranza politics. On July 17, De la Huerta set up a consultative board to deal with oil problems; its members were all Carranza's old advisers—namely, Santaella, Vázquez Schiaffino, Manuel de la Peña, and Salvador Urbina (*Diario oficial*, July 26, 1920).

41. See, for example, the statements by Industry Minister Treviño and Joseph F. Guffey published in *El Heraldo de México*, August 11 and 12, 1920.

42. Department of State to U.S. embassy in London, December 20, 1920, NAW 812.6363/775.

43. Report of the U.S. Shipping Board, December 24, 1920, NAW 812.6363/994.

44. On November 19, 1920, Roberto Pesqueira gave a speech in which he declared that his country was prepared to arbitrate its differences with the United States, but it was not ready to let one small group [the oil firms] dictate the conditions on which diplomatic relations between the two countries would be resumed. The following day the oil companies wrote to the State Department saying that the Pesqueira speech reaffirmed Mexico's illegal policy of nationalization (NAW 812.6363/739½). The reply by Mexico to a speech delivered by oil industry attorney Frederick R. Kellogg before the American Petroleum Institute on November 19, 1920, which was published later that same month in *El Universal*, contains a good statement of the provisional government's position with respect to the oil controversy.

45. James Fred Rippy, José Vasconcelos, and Guy Stevens, *American Policies Abroad: Mexico*, p. 134.

46. According to William Randolph Hearst, American banker Thomas W. Lamont recommended to his government that before reestablishing diplomatic relations with Mexico it should insist on payment of the foreign debt bonds at 120, despite the fact that they were being quoted on the New York market at 40 (NAW 812.00, p. 81/131).

47. The AAM considered that the Constitution of 1917 had been adopted illegally and that the United States should not recognize it to be in force, since to do so would set a precedent leading to incalculable harm (*Boletín de la Asociación Americana de México*, no. 15 [1921]: 3).

48. C. O. Swain to Department of State, November 9, 1920, NAW 812.6363/755.

49. Guy Stevens, secretary of the APPM, declared on March 17 that the new Mexican government should not be recognized until it gave an absolute guarantee that it would protect the oil firms against confiscation. The APPM gave its total support to the recommendations of the Fall Committee (NAW 812.6363/815; *New York Times*, March 17, 1921; *El Universal*, March 3, 1921).

50. NAW 812.6363/1074.

51. According to the *New York Times* (January 1, 1921), the State Department was considering the oil question separately from Mexican problems in general, having placed it on a par with those that had arisen in connection with the Anglo-French agreement in Mesopotamia, the Dutch operations in Java, or Canadian activities in Latin America. It was regarded as a matter directly affecting the national interest, not just investments abroad.

52. MacCorkle, *American Policy of Recognition . . .* , p. 98.

53. On June 7, 1921, Secretary of State Hughes said: "The fundamental question which confronts the Government of the United States in considering its relations with Mexico is the safeguarding of property rights against confiscation." Later President Harding was to add that it was the wish of the United States to be able to acclaim a stable government in Mexico and help show its good neighbor the road that

would lead it to its greatest progress. He emphasized that it should not be difficult to reach a clear and friendly agreement—and that "there must be such an agreement, for otherwise there would be no recognition" (Dunn, *Diplomatic Protection . . .* , p. 346; Asociación Americana de México, *Condiciones de los americanos en México,* pp. 10–11).

54. On February 13, 1921, Secretary of State Bainbridge Colby told Wilson that the Mexican president's envoy did nothing but reiterate the position of his predecessors and oppose the idea of prior signature of a treaty (WWP 471).

55. J. P. Withers, who represented himself as an extraofficial spokesman for the State Department in Mexico, said that in February and March 1921 Secretary of State Colby and other officials had tried to obtain certain concessions from Mexico in exchange for recognition. On May 2 an American by the name of Phillippi offered to Foreign Affairs Minister Pani to set up a meeting between the two presidents that could lead to a solution of the problem. Senator Henry Cabot Lodge, outspoken opponent of the Mexican Revolutionary governments, was to be the go-between (NAW 812.00 81/82; AREM L-E-1574, vol. 2, Leg. iv, ff. 59–65).

56. NAW 812.6363/833.

57. Memorandum of Division of Mexican Affairs, April 27, 1922, NAW 812.512/274; Aarón Sáenz, *La política internacional de la Revolución: Estudios y documentos,* pp. 43–44. Upon his return from Texas, Obregón told the press that the United States would recognize Mexico unconditionally as soon as it saw in practice the goodwill of its policy toward foreign interests (*El Universal,* October 23, 1920).

58. Secretary of State Hughes failed to understand why Obregón turned down the draft bill that contained the very same points that he had set forth in his political platform (J. F. Rippy, *The United States and Mexico,* p. 366).

59. Vito Alessio Robles, *Los tratados de Bucareli,* pp. 15–16; Manuel González Ramírez, *Los llamados tratados de Bucareli: México y los Estados Unidos en las Convenciones Internacionales de 1923,* p. 18.

60. *Excélsior,* November 13, 1920.

61. Mexico from the beginning had proposed that a convention on claims for damages caused to U.S. citizens in the course of the Revolution be signed first, following which diplomatic relations would be resumed and a general agreement then negotiated governing claims from the previous century.

62. This hint was contained in a memorandum from Foreign Affairs Minister Pani to Chargé d'Affaires Summerlin dated July 4, 1921. The complete correspondence may be consulted in Mexico, Secretaría de Relaciones Exteriores, *La cuestión internacional mexicano-americana durante el gobierno del general don Alvaro Obregón.*

63. Adolfo de la Huerta, *Memorias de don Adolfo de la Huerta según su propio dictado,* pp. 212–215. De la Huerta's memoirs are in reality nothing more than a justification of his decision in 1923 to break with Obregón. The details of his negotiations in Washington as described by him may also be obtained from the shorthand transcript of the cabinet meeting of November 4, 1922—which was before his rift with Obregón. According to this document, in reply to Secretary of State Hughes' claim that the infringement on the oil firms' rights amounted to confiscation, De la Huerta insisted "that the assessment was incorrect and that, while it was true that the companies would have to fit into the new order of things, there was no intention on the part of the government to impede their activities—quite the contrary, it wants to encourage them. We only want—for the sake of academic discussion, if you will— for these men to dress in the clothes that we're offering them. They won't lose any of their rights by doing so, but we want them to recognize that we have the right to ask it. Hughes told me he thought this was fair" (AREM C-3-2-43, Exp. III/625(011)/2-

1, Leg. 1, ff. 15–17). According to this document and De la Huerta's memoirs, Hughes agreed to a change in the "modality" of oil ownership, assuring him that on his return from Brazil relations between Mexico and the United States would be resumed without any further complications.

64. Typical were the declarations in *World* to the effect that Mexico would fully protect any private right acquired prior to May 1, 1917. "The famous Article 27," said Obregón, "one of whose sections states that the subsoil hydrocarbons belong to the nation, will not be applied retroactively" (*El Universal*, June 29, 1921).

65. In June 1921 Doheny said categorically: "It's time that Mexico respected the wishes of [Secretary of State] Hughes and that these official statements repeated so often were put down in the form of an international treaty" (*El Universal*, June 21, 1921).

66. An example of the persistence of controversy in the "federal zones" is the case of the concessions granted to the firm El Sol. Since American interests were affected, Chargé d'Affaires Summerlin was asked to file a protest (Department of State to Summerlin, October 22, 1921, NAW 812.6363/1011; Pani to Summerlin, November 18, 1921, NAW 812.6363/1052). In February 1922 the State Department again complained to Mexico, because by now drilling permits had been denied to two companies whose rights had been acquired prior to May 1, 1917, but which had failed to begin operations by that date; Washington considered that the oil firms' rights should not be subject to any conditions whatsoever (Department of State to Summerlin, February 28, 1922, NAW 812.6363/1078; Pani to Summerlin, April 18, 1922, NAW 812.6363/1104; Department of State to Summerlin, June 6, 1922, NAW 812.6363/1104).

67. In a speech delivered at Nogales, Sonora, on July 1, 1919, Obregón promised with respect to the economic problem "full recognition of all legitimately acquired rights in our country, in absolute adherence to our laws, by all foreigners." He also stated that he was in favor of encouraging the entry of foreign capital for the development of natural resources (*Campaña política* . . . , I, 53, 76).

68. Alberto J. Pani, *Introducción a la cuestión internacional mexicano-norteamericana, durante el gobierno del general don Alvaro Obregón*, p. iv.

69. By a presidential agreement of December 13, 1921, these concessions were suspended until such time as the organic oil law went into effect. This event led the APPM to write to the State Department to express its appreciation (January 28, 1921, NAW 812.6363/790).

70. On May 20 and 23, 1921, letters were addressed to the State Department by C. O. Swain of Standard Oil and the APPM, respectively, protesting the requirements established for the issuance of drilling permits (NAW 812.6363/832, 833). On February 22, 1921, the press made it clear that it was only necessary to present documents proving that the parties requesting the permits were the owners or leaseholders of the lands in question.

71. On July 21, 1921, Obregón wrote to President Harding telling him that his statements in *World*, in which he promised that the interpretation of Article 27 would be in the sense that Washington was asking for, constituted "the strongest moral commitment that I can undertake in my capacity as chief executive of Mexico, not only before my country but before the world as well." He went on to assure him that the legislative and judiciary branches would follow suit. However, Obregón did not consider that he had bowed to conditional recognition. On August 18 he wrote again to his American colleague, this time saying that "before long the nonretroactive and nonconfiscatory nature of Article 27 will be clarified." He was referring to the regulatory legislation, which in the end was not passed (AREM C-3-2-43, Exp. III/625 (011)/2-1, Leg. 3, ff. 90–91; Leg. I, ff. 91–92).

72. More than 200 injunctions had been filed against the Carranza decrees.

73. The ruling was in connection with a protest filed by Texas Oil against the fact that a Mexican citizen was awarded an oil concession on lands belonging to it prior to 1917 because Texas Oil had failed to comply with the 1918 decrees. At first the case was decided against the American firm, but Texas Oil appealed to the Supreme Court and for several years the case remained in abeyance in the hope that in the meantime the political side of the matter would be settled. When it was in fact resolved, the court ruled that Article 27 was not retroactive "either in letter or in spirit" in those cases in which a "positive act" had been undertaken.

74. Stanley R. Ross et al., *Historia documental de México*, II, 547.

75. Dunn, *Diplomatic Protection . . .* , p. 349.

76. The defenders of the Obregón government, in their eagerness to polish the luster of their leader's nationalist image, claimed that he had not forced the Supreme Court to reach the decision that it did and that the ruling was 100 per cent in keeping with the spirit of the Constitution of 1917. Examples were González Ramírez, *Los llamados tratados de Bucareli*, p. 126; A. Sáenz, *La política internacional de la Revolución*, pp. 52–53. To attempt to ignore the traditional manipulation of the judiciary power by the executive in Mexico is, in the best of cases, to deny reality. With regard to the original spirit of Article 27, see Chapter 4 of this book.

77. The other four were two in relation to petitions filed by International Petroleum and two in the case of Tamiahua Petroleum.

78. On hearing the Supreme Court's first decision, the firms wrote to Washington urging that recognition continue to be withheld as long as their rights failed to be definitively protected (APPM to Department of State, September 6, 1921, NAW 812.6363/951). Chargé d'Affaires Summerlin shared this view: he felt that U.S. pressure should be kept up until a treaty was signed (Summerlin to former ambassador Fletcher, September 1, 1921, NAW 812.6363/951½). When the five 1922 decisions were handed down, the Doheny interests complained to the State Department that they were far from satisfactory. Hanna in the Division of Mexican Affairs agreed: as long as the subsoil rights were not fully recognized, the Mexican legislation did not cease to be confiscatory (press release of August 10, 1922; memorandum of the Division of Mexican Affairs, May 19, 1922, NAW 812.6363/1129; oil firms to Department of State, NAW 812.6363/1158, 1159).

79. On August 4, for example, the court ruled against an injunction that Doheny had filed for and another one requested by Gulf (*El Universal*, August 5, 1922).

80. In the accords that De la Huerta signed with Thomas W. Lamont, representative of the Mexican foreign bondholders, it was agreed that the bonds would be retired with the funds from a new tax on the exportation of oil. This tax was decreed on June 7, 1921, and it ranged from 1.50 to 2.50 (pesos) per cubic meter, depending on the market value of the product.

81. Mexico, Secretaría del Patrimonio Nacional, *El petróleo de México: Recopilación de documentos oficiales de orden económico de la industria petrolera, con una introducción que resume sus motivos y consecuencias*, p. 19; Chargé d'Affaires Summerlin to Department of State, August 26, 1921, NAW 812.6363/949.

82. APPM to Department of State, June 15, 1921, NAW 812.6363/1073.

83. In July Obregón declared that the taxes were legitimate "because for all the enormous dividends the oil industry has gotten from Mexican wells, it is fair that Mexico should have at least part of the benefit of its own natural wealth to help it meet the just demands of the foreign bondholders." Before going away, the oil should render at least some return to the country (*En pro del reconocimiento de México por el gobierno de los Estados Unidos*, p. 11; *El Universal*, August 18, 1921).

84. The delegation was made up of Doheny, representing Mexican Petroleum;

Harry F. Sinclair, for Sinclair Oil; J. W. Van Dyke, for Atlantic Refining; Amos L. Beaty, for Texas Oil; and W. C. Teagle, for Standard Oil of New Jersey.

85. The memorandums and other documents related to these meetings are filed under NAW 812.6363/1231.

86. *El Universal*, September 4, 1921.

87. The American Association of Mexico, in a definitive break with the oil firms, attacked the companies' agreement with Obregón, saying that it was a first step toward getting Washington to back down on prior signature of a treaty and thus leaving the agricultural interests and others without any protection (*Boletín de la Asociación Americana de México*, nos. 6–7 [1921]).

88. The delegation was made up of representatives from Standard Oil of New Jersey, Mexican Petroleum, Sinclair, Atlantic Refining, and Texas Oil.

89. The plan originally presented by the companies excluded the Mexican government; the joint activities of the five firms were to be carried on outside the area then under exploration.

90. The documents related to these talks are filed under NAW 812.6363/1550½.

91. The main purpose of De la Huerta's trip to the United States was to come to an agreement about the national debt, but at the end of his negotiations with banker Thomas W. Lamont he went on to meet with the five oil company spokesmen who had been in Mexico the month before.

92. De la Huerta wrote to Obregón on November 4, 1922, that in the New York talks the oil representatives looked at the problem only from the business point of view and did not take into account any of the legal aspects, since their original position totally "disregarded Article 27 of the Constitution and the Mexican government's obligation to ask the Congress for a constitutional amendment" (AREM III/625 (011)/2-1, Leg. 1, ff. 13–14). Obviously, as long as Obregón's government remained unrecognized, the legal problem, despite De la Huerta's claims, remained separate from the economic one. The documents on this subject are filed under NAW 812.6363/1550½.

93. *New York Times*, June 30 and July 8, 1922.

94. In August Texas Oil transmitted to Secretary of State Hughes the text of a telegram received from its representative in Mexico, General James Ryan, announcing Obregón's decision (August 22, 1922, NAW 812.6363/1176).

95. Doheny needed this land in order to protect his Cerro Azul oil field. In 1922 a special decree was issued which in practice applied only to this case, since Huasteca was the only firm that could meet the conditions indicated. The partiality of the measure was so obvious that the Chamber of Deputies, in a rare action, appealed to the deputy minister of industry in the matter (José Domingo Lavín, *Petróleo*, pp. 71–73).

96. Ramón Puente, *Hombres de la Revolución: Calles*, p. 128; Merrill Rippy, "El petróleo y la Revolución Mexicana," *Problemas agrícolas e industriales de México* 6 (July–September 1954): 93. In a State Department memorandum of July 11, 1922, reporting a conversation between Secretary Hughes and representatives from the oil companies, it was made clear that while Washington could not advise any loan to the Mexican government, at the same time it would not oppose one if the firms should decide to extend it (NAW 812.6363/1228). The same thing was said in a memorandum from the Division of Mexican Affairs to the Secretary of State (July 14, 1922, NAW 812.51/901).

97. AREM C-3-2-43, III/625 (011)/2-1, Leg. 1, shorthand transcript of the cabinet meeting of November 4, 1922, ff. 43–44.

98. In his published writings Manuel de la Peña maintained that the surface landholder had no right over the oil until after it was out of the ground and that therefore

the subsoil deposits had never belonged to the companies or to anyone else. For a fuller study of this thesis, see his *La cuestión palpitante* and *El petróleo y la legislación frente a las compañías petroleras; Boletín del petróleo* 10 (July–December 1920): 1–5; *Excélsior*, September 13, 1920. For a review of this group's position with respect to the Supreme Court's ruling on Article 27, see articles by Salvador Mendoza in *El Universal*, September 28, 1921; May 15, 1922. Additional examples of interest are the articles by Luis Zubiría y Campa, Felipe Llanas, Eduardo Castillo, Cepeda Medrano, and others in Mexico, Camara de Senadores, Sección de Estadística y Anales de Jurisprudencia, *El petróleo: La más grande riqueza nacional*. This nationalistic sector's view with respect to U.S. policy toward Mexico can also be seen in articles by Isidro Fabela appearing from March 1921 onward in *El Universal*, *Excélsior*, and *El Globo*.

99. Foreign Affairs Minister Pani wrote to Obregón on November 27, 1922, giving his opinion with respect to interpretation of paragraph iv and proposing that the oil companies' vested rights be recognized but that they not be exempted from full payment of taxes and compliance with the regulations regarding exploitation—in order to satisfy the "patriotic elements" that with good reason were attacking this interpretation (AREM C-3-2-43, Exp. 111/2225 (011)/2-1, Leg. 3, ff. 104–112).

100. Calles, minister of government at the time, accused the oil companies of trying to suborn some of the legislators in an effort to get Articles 27 and 123 revoked (*El Universal*, January 26, 1921). In his view the subsoil should always be regarded as belonging to the nation, and the government should exploit the hydrocarbons in the "federal zones." He was to make other similar statements later.

101. When the government was not pressing for it to do otherwise, *Excélsior* spoke out against the oil reform. In an editorial of June 21, 1921, it pointed out that Article 27, in failing to give the oil firms the guarantees they needed, was doing Mexico no good. On August 26 it called for abrogation of Article 27, which had become a *bête noire*, etc. Nor was *El Universal* a stranger to this campaign, as witnessed by its editorial of August 11.

102. Alberto J. Pani, *Introducción a la cuestión internacional . . .* , pp. v–vi.

103. Thomas W. Lamont, International Committee of Bankers on Mexico, to W. C. Teagle, Standard Oil of New Jersey, September 19, 1921, and Lamont to Department of State, September 23, 1921, NAW 812.51/794.

104. Division of Mexican Affairs to Secretary of State, July 14, 1922, NAW 812.51/901.

105. According to Anita Brenner, the 1921 plans to land in Tampico fizzled out because of the bankers' opposition. According to her, the landing never took place because an American miner-banker (whose name she did not divulge) persuaded the oil firms that it was better to continue negotiating with the Mexican government than to resort to direct action (*The Wind That Swept Mexico: The History of the Mexican Revolution, 1910–1942*, p. 67).

106. G. K. Lewis, "Analysis of the Institutional Status . . . ", pp. 46–47.

107. Thomas W. Lamont, International Committee of Bankers on Mexico, to Secretary of State, November 13, 1922, NAW 812.51/923.

108. Present at the ceremony were representatives from the states of Alabama, Arkansas, Arizona, Colorado, Indiana, Iowa, Kansas, Mississippi, and Oklahoma and also the governors of New Mexico and Texas (Obregón, *Campaña política*, I, 587–588).

109. In February 1922 Representative Thomas Connally from Texas asked Congress to recognize Obregón and accused the administration of having sold out to the oil firms. On July 19 Senator E. F. Ladd expressed the same point of view. Under pressure from business interests, the state legislatures in Arizona, California, Illinois,

Kentucky, Maryland, Michigan, Oklahoma, and Texas followed suit. (In the case of Arizona, for example, the decision was the result of a petition signed by a group of businessmen, ranchers, and miners.) The chambers of commerce that made themselves heard directly in Washington were those from the cities of Los Angeles, San Francisco, and St. Louis (*New York American*, February 24, 1922; *En pro del reconocimiento de México . . .* , p. 6; MacCorkle, *American Policy of Recognition . . .*).

110. In Los Angeles 40,000 workers demonstrated in favor of recognition of Obregón on January 26, 1922.

111. J. Kenneth Turner and E. J. Dillon wrote in the *Nation* that the State Department's policy gave Mexico only the alternatives of becoming an American protectorate or of being the object of aggression. The *Mexican Post*, August 1, 1921, claimed that the only things standing in the way of improved trade relations with the U.S. were Standard Oil and Mexican Petroleum. Hearst, in an editorial of November 1, assured that Obregón was prepared to respect American interests and that it would be difficult to find a more capable man in the Mexican presidency.

112. Rodolfo Nervo, Mexican chargé d'affaires in France, reported to Foreign Affairs Minister Pani that he had met with the director of political affairs in the Ministry of Foreign Affairs, who had told him that France considered the Mexican position perfectly normal and regular and that it would be in order for Ambassador J. J. Jusserand in Washington to speak with the State Department urging that the United States yield to the considerations of law and national honor that motivated the Mexican opposition to Washington's demands. He added that France would ask for England's cooperation in the matter (June 18, 1922, AREM L-E-1874, vol. 2, Leg. 4, ff. 77–77v).

113. Referring to the demands of certain American groups, Obregón said: "This makes us hope that it will not be long before the American nation's spirit of justice and its good sense win out and Mexico is finally treated the way it should be" (Alvaro Obregón, *Informes rendidos por el C. Presidente Constitucional al Congreso de 1921–1924 y contestación de los Presidentes del Congreso en el mismo período*, p. 33).

114. Ise, *The United States Oil Policy*, p. 482.

115. The AAM was formed in January 1921, almost immediately after Obregón formally took office as president. From the beginning it took the line promoted by Senator Fall and even went beyond that. Its platform is the best example of the position of the hard-core group in the American colony in Mexico. As a condition for recognition of any Mexican government, it called for return of all the confiscated properties, compensation for the damages incurred in the course of the Revolution, and elimination of all constitutional provisions restricting "the development of American enterprise in Mexico." This incendiary group proposed nothing less than to turn Mexico into a colony, preferring a counterrevolution, or even intervention, to continuing with the "current state of affairs" (Asociación Americana de México, *Condiciones de los americanos en México; Boletín de la Asociación de México*, no. 5 (August 1921); no. 6 (September 1921).

116. Elizabeth Ann Rice, *The Diplomatic Relations between the United States and Mexico as Affected by the Struggle for Religious Liberty in Mexico, 1925–1929*, pp. 17–18.

117. *New York Times*, June 21, 1921. Frederick R. Kellogg, attorney for the oil firms, prepared a memorandum for Secretary of State Hughes outlining all the possible legal and economic arguments against the decrees of May 24 and June 7, 1921 (NAW 812.6363/1449).

118. Chargé d'Affaires Summerlin to Department of State, February 23, 1921, NAW 812.6363/802.

119. Standard Oil to Department of State, February 3, 1921, NAW 812.6363/633.

120. Guy Stevens to Department of State, July 23, 1921, NAW 812.6363/720.

121. Report of a special agent to Department of State, August 12, 1921, NAW 812.6363/940½.

122. Standard Oil reported to the State Department on August 17, 1921, that El Sol was drilling in a stream that crossed its land which was almost always dry and which the government regarded as a "federal zone" (NAW 812.6363/923).

123. Association of Producers of Petroleum in Mexico (APPM), *Petroleum Concessions on "Federal Zones" of Mexican Rivers, Their Unconstitutional, Illegal, and Confiscatory Character: Memorandum Submitted to the Secretary of State of the United States of America*.

124. APPM to Department of State, February 29, 1924, NAW 812.6363/1489.

125. The APPM telegram of July 27 protested the drilling activity of the national railroad enterprise, Ferrocarriles Nacionales, and another Mexican government–connected firm, Petrolera Marítima. In his answer the following day Obregón called attention in the first place to the disrespectful tone of the wire and then went on to point out that the nation was the undisputed owner of the "zones" in question and that therefore no one had a right to protest their use by the federal government (NAW 812.6363/427).

126. Guy Stevens to President Obregón, August 1, 1923, NAW 812.6363/428.

127. Department of State to Chargé d'Affaires Summerlin, August 6, 1921, 812.6363/1427.

128. *El Heraldo de México*, October 13, 1920; *Excélsior*, November 4, 1920.

129. Statements by Vázquez Schiaffino published in *Excélsior*, February 14, 1921.

130. Arturo Pani, *Alberto J. Pani: Ensayo biográfico*, pp. 147–148.

131. Chargé d'Affaires Summerlin to Department of State, June 28 and July 28, 1921, NAW 812.6363/698, 881; *El Universal*, June 24, 1921.

132. Article 8 of the Social Democrats' bill presented on July 22, 1921, said: "Petroleum exploration and exploitation shall be carried on freely on those private lands with respect to which contracts for such activity were entered into prior to May 1, 1917, and also on those lands on which the surface owner has undertaken, prior to this date, operations directed toward obtention of the substances in the subsoil" (Salvador Mendoza, *La controversia del petróleo*, p. 410).

133. A draft text appeared in *El Heraldo de México*, August 10, 1921, and another one was published in *El Universal*, September 1, 1921. The statement, which was made by Deputy Aurelio Manrique, appeared in *Excélsior*, August 4, 1921.

134. Guy Stevens to Department of State, September 20, 1921, NAW 812.6363/1024. A memorandum from the Office of the Solicitor, Department of State, confirmed the points made by Stevens: the bill that the Mexican government was considering did not recognize "all" the lands acquired by the oil firms prior to May 1917 (September 21, 1921, NAW 812.6363/688).

135. *El Universal*, September 23, 1921; *Excélsior*, October 27, 1921.

136. Guy Stevens to Department of State, October 3 and 11 and November 4, 7, and 15, 1921, NAW 812.6363/1020, 1025, 1029; Ambassador Fletcher to President Harding, November 14, 1921, NAW 812.6363/1028E; Department of State to Chargé d'Affaires Summerlin, November 19, 1921, NAW 812.6363/1022.

137. Department of State to Chargé d'Affaires Summerlin, October 9, 1922, NAW 812.6363/1015–1016.

138. Chargé d'Affaires Summerlin to Department of State, October 6, 1922, NAW 812.6363/1016.

139. NAW 812.6363/1225, 1255.

140. Chargé d'Affaires Summerlin to Department of State, October 17 and 20, 1922, NAW 812.6363/1248, 1251.

141. Oil Companies to General James Ryan, NAW 812.6363/1257; Walker of Huasteca to Hanna, November 4, 1922, NAW 812.6363/2366.

142. This bill, according to De la Huerta, had been prepared by "three of the most knowledgeable and at the same time most radical men in the field of oil . . . and in no way reflected pressure from north of the Rio Grande" (AREM L-E-537, vol. 4, Leg. 3, shorthand transcript of the cabinet meeting of November 4, 1922, f. 18).

143. Article 5 gave the president the power, pursuant to the provisions of Article 27 of the constitution, to annul contracts entered into prior to May 1, 1917. Article 6 made it possible to confirm rights acquired prior to this date by means of a contract-concession, but the property holders would not retain the original title. According to Article 16, the executive could issue any supplementary provisions that might be necessary (ibid., ff. 11–15).

144. Ibid., ff. 9–10, 16–19.

145. Obregón observed: "Could the federal excutive say 'the rights acquired by such-and-such a company are null and void'? This is the point that we should discuss, . . . because this power of the executive would not be recognized by the companies any more than they have recognized the power that the constitution itself gives to the executive to issue regulations for the oil law" (ibid., f. 24).

146. In Obregón's opinion the regulations were already long overdue: "If we had issued the most radical possible regulations within a year or two after promulgation of the constitution, by now mankind would be familiar with them . . ." (ibid., f. 50).

147. "Unfortunately," said Obregón, "the article is already part of our body of fundamental law, and we cannot turn back now" (ibid., f. 50).

148. Ibid., ff. 44–50.

149. This was a report of statements made by Obregón to a committee of deputies (*Excélsior*, November 14, 1922).

150. Obregón reported the incident to the Congress, which at that moment was considering the oil problem. It immediately announced its support of the president, as well as its decision to pass a law on oil that was national in focus. Meanwhile, on November 16, 1922, Foreign Affairs Minister Pani told U.S. Chargé d'Affaires Summerlin that no foreign government had the right to censure the bill of a law that had not yet been promulgated. The State Department insisted that it was not intervening and that if Mexico wanted diplomatic recognition it would have to try to understand the U.S. point of view.

151. Chargé d'Affaires Summerlin to Department of State, November 18, 1922, NAW 812.6363/7286. The secretary of state informed President Harding that Treasury Minister De la Huerta had sent to Washington, via Thomas W. Lamont, the draft text of the bill which the Mexican executive hoped to present to the Congress on October 12 (memorandum of November 20, 1922, NAW 812.6363/1279).

152. *New York Times*, November 20, 1922.

153. The text of the bill, drafted by the Joint Committee on Oil, is reproduced in *Diario de los debates de la Cámara de Diputados* 1, no. 72 (December 11, 1922): 8–12.

154. APPM to Department of State, January 31 and February 5, 1923, NAW 812.6363/1336, 1337.

155. APPM to General James Ryan, March 14, 1923, NAW 812.6363/1362.

156. According to this version, the "vested rights" would have to be turned into contract-concessions within the next three years. Moreover, the executive could use the last paragraph of the section on oil in Article 27 to annul any titles acquired prior to 1917 (Mexico, Cámara de Senadores, Sección de Estadística y Anales de Jurisprudencia, *El petróleo*, pp. 319–320; *Boletín del petróleo* 15 (January–June 1923): 538 ff.).

157. On May 4, 1923, the APPM expressed its complaints to Hanna, and on May 14

directly to Secretary of State Hughes, to whom it presented a study prepared by Manuel Calero, Mexican adviser for Huasteca, against the bill (NAW 812.6363/1395, 1403, 1410).

158. See the article by Eduardo L. Castillo in *Boletín del petróleo* 15 (January–June 1923): 456.

159. According to the Senate modifications, these "acquired rights" could no longer be exchanged for concessions, but they could be confirmed; they were unlimited as to time; no mention was made of the possibility of annulling titles granted prior to 1917; and the oil industry was not declared as being in the public interest (*El Heraldo de México*, November 15, 1923).

160. Since the bill continued to fail to recognize the rights of those who had not demonstrated a "positive act," the Division of Mexican Affairs found it unsatisfactory (NAW 812.6363/1464). The APPM informed the State Department that it was opposed to the Senate-approved bill and that it was in violation of what had been agreed upon at Bucareli (November 30 and December 6, 1923, NAW 813.6363/ 1447½, 1469).

161. *El Heraldo de México*, January 3, 1921.

162. Edmund David Cronon, ed., *The Cabinet Diaries of Josephus Daniels, 1913–1921*, p. 590.

163. A typical example was Albert W. Fox's article in the *Washington Post*, March 28, 1921, in which he maintained that the situation in Mexico was deteriorating to such an extent that there would surely be a change in government within three or six months.

164. See article by John K. Turner in *El Universal*, April 30, 1921.

165. *New York Evening Post*, May 19, 1921.

166. Obregón reported that two of the companies' agents, Lee and Leroy, had had contacts with Pablo González and others of his opponents (*New York American*, January 25 and 28, 1922).

167. *El Heraldo de México*, July 6, 1921; *El Universal*, July 8 and 10, 1921.

168. The American Federation of Labor protested the display of force to intimidate the Mexican workers.

169. *El Universal Gráfico*, March 12 and 19, 1924.

170. In the face of persistent rumors that President Harding and Secretary of State Hughes were instigating a movement against Cárdenas, Washington was forced to deny the accusations. A *Universal* dispatch made it clear that their names and Senator Fall's had been used unfairly by conspiratory elements (*El Universal*, January 27, 1922).

171. April 23, 1922, NAW 812.6363/1260.

172. On January 22, 1923, the Mexican consul in Los Angeles reported to his colleague in Calexico that preparations were underway for a freebooting expedition in Lower California supported by a "known oil magnate." Three days later this report was confirmed: the leader of the expedition turned out to be Charles Downey, but the oilman remained unidentified (AREM L-E-863, R, Leg. 10, ff. 1–10). Consular Inspector Rafael Múzquiz wrote from Los Angeles to the Ministry of Foreign Affairs in May of that year that José Barrio Lope, who was being held in San Antonio, had been found with documents proving that the oil interests (unspecified) were planning to organize an uprising in Mexico headed by Generals Guillermo Rubio Navarrete and Guadalupe Sánchez (AREM L-E-709, R, vol. 100, Leg. 1, f. 1).

173. Sáenz, *La política internacional de la Revolución*, p. 135.

174. Daniel James, *Mexico and the Americans*, p. 223; Parkes, *A History of Mexico*, p. 378.

175. Rice, *Diplomatic Relations . . .* , pp. 25–27.

176. In August of that year former ambassador Fletcher declared in a speech in the United States that if Mexico had a better idea than a treaty for solving the problem, it was free to propose it, but in any case it was necessary that the United States have assurances that Article 27 would not be applied retroactively (*El Universal*, August 18, 1921). De la Huerta also announced that year that the United States was proposing a commission made up of two members from each of the countries to discuss policy in regard to foreign interests in Mexico. The reason behind this plan was never explained, nor was it put into effect (*Memorias* . . . , p. 218).

177. In January Juan Ochoa Ramos, speaking in the name of Obregón, proposed to Washington that the treaty be signed after diplomatic relations were resumed, but the United States continued to insist that the document had to be negotiated prior to recognition (memorandum of Division of Mexican Affairs, April 27, 1922, NAW 812.512/274).

178. General James Ryan to Secretary of State Hughes, April 13, 1923, NAW 812.6363/2289.

179. Ross, Obregón's personal friend, had been named by the president; González Roa was Pani's appointment. As it turned out, González Roa carried most of Mexico's side in the talks, using long and erudite juridical arguments (Alberto J. Pani, *Introducción a la cuestión internacional* . . . , p. 150). ·

180. These instructions said that it was necessary for "all" rights acquired prior to May 1917 to be recognized, not only those of parties that had been engaged in operations before this date. They also called for an end to the requirement for drilling permit applications and to the confiscatory taxes. And finally, the terms of the future organic law on oil had to be agreed upon (instructions from Secretary of State Hughes to John Barton Payne, May 5, 1923, NAW 812.6363/2289½).

181. On May 31, 1923, Obregón wired to Calles: "There are days when everything points to a favorable outcome, but there are more still when it looks as if all will end up like Rosario Amozoc. Anything would be better than to accept conditions that do injury to our national honor or our sovereignty" (Sáenz, *La política internacional de la Revolución*, pp. 65, 248).

182. According to Guy Stevens, Senator Henry Cabot Lodge examined lengthy notes of conversations that were never made public (J. F. Rippy, Vasconcelos, and Stevens, *American Policies Abroad*, p. 201). However, Secretary of State Frank B. Kellogg wrote to Senator Charles Curtis on January 18, 1926, that the only agreements reached at Bucareli are those contained in the publication *Proceedings of the United States-Mexican Conference Convened in Mexico City, May 14, 1923*—that is to say, the official minutes (AREM L-E-1576, vol. 4, Leg. 2, f. 12).

183. Mexico, Secretaría de Relaciones Exteriores, *La cuestión internacional* . . . ; Alberto J. Pani, *Las conferencias de Bucareli*, pp. 132–137; MacCorkle, *American Policy of Recognition* . . . , p. 96; Industry Minister Morones to Foreign Affairs Minister Sáenz, 1926, AREM L-E-522, vol. 21, Leg. 1, ff. 141–155; APPM to Charles Beecher Warren and John Barton Payne, May 24, June 26 and 27, July 6, and August 1, 1923, NAW 812.6363/1441, 1427, 0792; memorandum of Division of Mexican Affairs, NAW 812.6363/1438½; Warren to Department of State, July 21, 1924, NAW 812.6363/1515.

184. Technically, according to the credentials of Warren and Payne, the negotiating parties met to "exchange impressions" with a view to reaching an agreement between the two countries (NAW 812.6363/2289½). In practice, however, this exchange of impressions amounted actually to an "extraofficial pact," kept more or less in secret. When Obregón announced on September 1, 1923, that the resumption of relations with the United States was not the fruit of any compromise or agreement entered into against Mexican law, he was really telling a half-truth.

185. For personal reasons Warren had to leave his ambassadorial post in Mexico after only a short time (Graham H. Stuart, *Latin America and the United States*, p. 172).

186. *New York Times*, August 21, 1923.

187. On August 24, 1923, after having heard the reports of emissaries Warren and Payne, Guy Stevens wrote to Secretary of State Hughes expressing his displeasure at the fact that there was no provision for definitively abrogating the Carranza decrees and also that Mexico had been left free to set taxes in any amount on property acquired prior to 1917 (NAW 812.6363/1438; *New York Times*, August 24, 1924). Hughes calmed down the oil firms by pointing out that the United States had refused to recognize the Mexican "positive act" doctrine (Department of State to Gulf Oil, November 19, 1923, NAW 812.6363/1458). In 1924 Stevens told Ignacio Morán, De la Huerta's representative, that unless and until Article 27 was repealed the oil firms would not be able to support the Mexican government; he blamed Warren for the limited success at Bucareli (Obregón-Calles, AGN, R, Paq. 5-1, Leg. 8, Exp. 101, R2–Z2).

188. Although the revolt that broke out in December 1923 was more or less reactionary, it had the support of such Revolutionaries as Salvador Alvarado and Antonio Villarreal. This clash between De la Huerta and Calles had been expected since long before the Bucareli talks; the U.S. embassy foresaw it already in November 1922 (Chargé d'Affaires Summerlin to Department of State, November 20, 1922, NAW 812.6363/1279.

189. De la Huerta wired Obregón from Hermosillo on April 26, 1923, pointing out the mistake it had been to hold the talks and insisting that Secretary of State Hughes had already agreed to recognize Mexico on the condition that the foreign debt be paid, the vested rights confirmed, and the expropriated lands assessed. Obregón, offended, replied that he would not accept any such conditional recognition. Later, back in Mexico City, De la Huerta continued to hold to his view (A. Sáenz, *La política internacional de la Revolución*, pp. 189–191; De la Huerta, *Memorias . . .* , pp. 219–220, 230–233; M. Alessio Robles, *Historia política de la Revolución*, pp. 347–348).

190. De la Huerta later admitted that it had been unwise to launch this attack against Washington (*Excélsior*, January 30, 1958).

191. On January 3, 1924, Cándido Aguilar wrote to De la Huerta that what had begun as simply an ordinary rivalry between two factions had become a nationwide struggle over Obregón's policy. This statement had a history behind it: in June 1923, Aguilar had warned Fernando González Roa that the Revolution and the country must not be betrayed in order to get recognition from Washington. Later Aguilar, defeated and imprisoned in Texas, was to draft a manifesto in which he justified taking up the fight alongside De la Huerta by saying that he had wanted to see a return to nationalism after Obregón sold out Mexico's sovereignty at Bucareli (Adolfo Manero Suárez and José Paniagua Arredondo, *Los tratados de Bucareli: Traición y sangre sobre México*, pp. 326–327, 337–338, 350–351; Emilio Portes Gil, *Autobiografía de la Revolución Mexicana*, p. 374).

192. Mario Mena, *Alvaro Obregón: Historia militar y política, 1912–1929*, pp. 91–92.

193. Despite all that has been written suggesting that there was a secret treaty signed at Bucareli, this was not the case. A good review of what was agreed to is contained in a memorandum exchanged in 1926 between the Ministries of Foreign Affairs and of Industry. This documents states that "the commitments to which Secretary of State Kellogg refers can only be the result of some agreement reached at the 1923 talks. However, a careful study of the statements made in the 1921–1923 correspondence, a detailed look at the words of the Mexican representatives during the course of the talks, and, above all, a studious review of the final declarations of these

representatives and the terms approved by the executives and the senates of the two nations fail to reveal that there was any pact such as Secretary Kellogg is saying there was" (AREM L-E-552, vol. 20, Leg. 1, ff. 133–134).

194. When the rebellion broke out, Obregón sent Ramón Ross—his old friend and representative at Bucareli—to Washington to ask for military aid. Ross got everything he asked for except warships: sixteen De Havilland and Lincoln planes, machine guns, rifles, ammunition, and permission to march Mexican troops through Texas. De la Huerta was only able to get 300,000 loads of ammunition (Dulles, *Yesterday in Mexico*, pp. 228–229; James, *Mexico and the Americans*, p. 221; James Morton Callahan, *American Foreign Policy in Mexican Relations*, p. 595). According to De la Huerta, Washington agreed to recognize his state of belligerence on the condition that he in turn accept the terms of Bucareli, but he refused (*Memorias* . . . , pp. 263–265).

195. In January and February the anti-Obregón forces, faced with U.S. threats of intervention in the event that fighting should break out in Tampico and Veracruz, abandoned these ports without a struggle (De la Huerta, *Memorias* . . . , pp. 259–260; Denny, *We Fight for Oil*, p. 58).

196. Huasteca helped out the Obregón administration with a loan for 10 million pesos and other American groups came in with an additional 8 million (Alberto J. Pani, *Tres monografías*, p. 63; Dulles, *Yesterday in Mexico*, p. 230).

197. Obregón to Calles, AGN R Paq. 4, Leg. 2, exp. 101; Alvarez del Castillo to American Oil Export Co., March 26, 1924, AGN R2-A-22.

198. The Veracruz *El Dictamen*, December 31, 1923, published a decree requiring the oil firms to pay their taxes to the rebel forces and declaring invalid those paid to the Obregón government. The latter, for its part, likewise refused to recognize taxes paid to De la Huerta, although it had no way of keeping the companies from making such payments.

199. *New York Times*, January 21, 1924; U.S. consul in Tampico to Department of State, February 10 and 15, 1924, NAW 812.6363/1481–1485.

200. On February 27, 1924, the Ministry of Government informed the Mexican consul in Belize that reports had been received of possible aid being given to the rebels by El Aguila (AREM L-E-860, Leg. 1). De la Huerta in his memoirs confirms that the governor of Belize did in fact offer him assistance, but he goes on to say that he turned it down because he did not want to get into a situation with England similar to what Obregón was experiencing with the United States (*Memorias* . . . , p. 261).

201. Department of State to U.S. embassy in Mexico, April 15, 1924, NAW 812.6363/1497.

202. Oil companies to Thomas W. Lamont, International Committee of Bankers on Mexico, April 4, 1924, NAW 812.51/1031.

203. The committee was made up of Avery D. Andrews, C. O. Swain, and Dean Emery (Guy Stevens to Department of State, June 23, 1924, NAW 812.6363).

204. Ambassador Warren to Department of State, April 25, 1924, NAW 812.51/1039.

205. On June 8 Obregón declared in a speech in Nogales, Sonora, that certain interests were becoming a millstone and were holding back the development of any kind of noble idea in the country—this millstone being the oil companies; he also cited Wall Street as being a threat to his government (*New York Times*, June 9, 1924).

206. The final agreement was reached only after the negotiating team was already back in the United States. The plan contained many generalities that the companies hoped to make more specific once Pani was appointed ambassador in Washington. For example, it was agreed to lower taxes in new areas to be explored, but by how much was not stated. Nor was the situation definitively worked out with respect to the "federal zones" or the "positive act" test, etc. The minutes are on file under

NAW 812.6363/1534, 1541. See also oil companies to J. R. Clark, September 19, 1927, NAW 812.6363/2404.

207. Memorandum of a meeting of oil company representatives with officials from Department of State, May 19, 1928, NAW 812.6363/2570½.

6. Calles and His Attempts to Put an Oil Law into Effect

1. During these years Calles was often characterized by his opponents as a "bolshevik," whereas his partisans called him a "man of the left" (Henry Bamford Parkes, *A History of Mexico*, p. 379; José Manuel Puig Casauranc, *El sentido social del proceso histórico de México*, pp. 178–179).

2. Víctor Alba, *Las ideas sociales contemporáneas en México*, p. 221.

3. It was at that time that the National Roads and Irrigation Commissions were established and also the Bank of Mexico and the funds for agricultural and ejido credit.

4. Oil production, unlike most other areas of the economy, maintained a steady upward climb.

5. Marcos Kaplan, *Formación del estado nacional en América Latina*, p. 305.

6. William English Walling, *The Mexican Question: Mexico and American-Mexican Relations under Calles and Obregón*, pp. 147–150.

7. Samuel Eliot Morison and Henry Steele Commager, *Historia de los Estados Unidos de Norteamérica*, III, 88.

8. Coolidge's foreign policy was characterized by his contemporaries as the "new imperialism" (Walling, *The Mexican Question*, p. 17).

9. Ibid., p. 184; Josephus Daniels, *Shirt-Sleeve Diplomat*, p. 228.

10. Prior to assuming his cabinet post, Mellon declared that he had turned his holdings over to a member of his family—implying that therefore he would have no special interest to defend as a member of the cabinet! (Walling, *The Mexican Question*, p. 171)

11. Harold Nicolson, *Dwight Morrow*, p. 306.

12. John P. Bullington, "The Land and Petroleum Laws of Mexico," *American Journal of International Law* 22 (January 1928): 58.

13. Frank Tannenbaum, *Mexico: The Struggle for Peace and Bread*, p. 269; Anita Brenner, *The Wind That Swept Mexico: The History of the Mexican Revolution, 1910–1942*, p. 67.

14. Edmund David Cronon, *Josephus Daniels in Mexico*, p. 49.

15. Ibid., pp. 48–49.

16. Ibid.

17. On December 23, 1924, Industry Minister Morones and Treasury Minister Pani confirmed Calles' acceptance to the Oil Executives Committee (NAW 812.6262/R222/EO424).

18. Burt M. McConnell, *Mexico at the Bar of Public Opinion*, p. 4.

19. Cited by Manuel Villaseñor in Mexico, Secretaría de Educación Pública, *Sobre el petróleo de México: Conferencias* (1938).

20. Cited by Antonio Gómez Robledo, *The Bucareli Agreements and International Law*, trans. Salomón de la Selva, p. 46.

21. The official correspondence exchanged between Washington and Mexico City during the Calles administration appears in Mexico, Secretaría de Relaciones Exteriores, *Correspondencia oficial cambiada entre el Gobierno de México y los Estados Unidos con motivo de las dos leyes reglamentarias de la fracción primera del artículo 27 de la Constitución Mexicana*; also memorandums from Secretary of State Kellogg to Aarón Sáenz, November 17 and 27, 1925, AREM, L-E-533, vol. 1, Leg. 3.

22. Lesley Byrd Simpson, *Many Mexicos*, p. 280.

23. The speeches and programs in question may be consulted in Plutarco Elías Calles, *Mexico before the World*, pp. 3, 51–52, 55–56, 93.

24. The committee's members were Deputy Jesús Yépez Solórzano, Senator Ignacio Rodarte, Joaquín Santaella from the Ministry of the Treasury, and Manuel de la Peña from the Ministry of Industry.

25. U.S. consul in Nuevo Laredo to Department of State, July 23, 1925, NAW 812.6363/1566; Guy Stevens to Department of State, August 24, 1925, NAW 812.6363/1567; U.S. embassy in Mexico City to Department of State, August 28, 1925, NAW 812.6363/1569.

26. Mexico, Cámara de Diputados del Congreso de la Unión, Comisión Especial Reglamentaria del Artículo 27, *Proyecto de ley orgánica del artículo 27 de la Constitución Política de la República en la parte relativa a los combustibles minerales presentados por el C. diputado Justo A. Santa Anna* (1925).

27. Oil companies to Department of State, October 23, 1925, NAW 812.6363/1576.

28. Memorandum signed by the Solicitor, Department of State, November 7, 1925, NAW 812.6363/1580.

29. Mexico, Congreso de la Unión, *Proyecto de ley reglamentaria del artículo 27 constitucional en el ramo del petróleo formulado por la comisión mixta* (1925).

30. Ambassador Téllez to Ministry of Foreign Affairs, October 13, AREM III/628(010)/1, L-E-536, Leg. 17, ff. 19–20.

31. Ambassador Sheffield to Department of State, November 16, 1925, NAW 812.6363/1579, 1581.

32. Memorandum from Ambassador Sheffield to Foreign Affairs Minister Sáenz, November 17, 1925, AREM III/628(010)/1, L-E-534, Leg. 7, ff. 14–16.

33. Memorandum from Ambassador Sheffield to Foreign Affairs Minister Sáenz, November 17, 1925, and the latter's reply, AREM III/628(010)/1, L-E-536, Leg. 17, ff. 109–115.

34. The text of the bill appears in AREM III/628(010)/1 L-E-551, Leg. 51, with amendments in Leg. 52. The Mexican embassy in Washington reported that American business and official circles were still in a state of alarm over the two bills (October 14, 1925, AREM L-E-536, vol. 4, Leg. 7, f. 19; November 30, 1925, AREM Exp. A/628(010)/2, Leg. 3, A-O, f. 34).

35. *El Universal*, November 27, 1925.

36. Memorandum from Ambassador Sheffield to Foreign Affairs Minister Sáenz, November 28, 1925, and the latter's reply, December 5, 1925, AREM III/628(010)/1, L-E-539, Leg. 26, ff. 1–14, 102, 105.

37. Memorandum of conversation between Ambassador Sheffield and Foreign Affairs Minister Sáenz, December 18, 1925, AREM III/628(010)/1, L-E-536, Leg. 17, f. 189.

38. The texts of the approved laws appear in Mexico, Secretaría de Industria, Comercio y Trabajo, *La industria, el comercio y el trabajo en México durante la gestión administrativa del señor general Plutarco Elías Calles* V, 207 ff., 291 ff.

39. AREM L-E-547, vol. xv, Leg. 3, ff. 27–30; memorandum of conversation with Guy Stevens, Division of American Republics, Department of State, December 9, 1925, NAW 812.6363/1627.

40. Memorandum of Division of Mexican Affairs, Department of State, August 21, 1925, NAW 812.6363/1574.

41. Oil companies to Department of State, November 21, 1925, NAW 812.6363/1613; memorandum of Division of Mexican Affairs, December 1, 1925, NAW 812.6363/1600.

42. APPM to Department of State, December 9, 1925, NAW 812.6363/1601; Department of State to APPM, December 15, 1925, NAW 812.6363/1601.

43. Oil companies to President Calles, September 24, 1925, NAW 812.6363/1600; Calles to the oil companies, October 29, 1925, NAW 812.6363/1600.

44. NAW 812.6363/1648.

45. Memorandum of Division of Mexican Affairs, Department of State, December 29, 1925, NAW 812.6363/1643.

46. Memorandum from U.S. embassy to Minister of Foreign Affairs, January 17, 1925, AREM 42-15-3, Exp. A/628(010)/2, Leg. 4, f. 24.

47. Ambassador Sheffield to Department of State, May 16, 1925, NAW 812.6363/1564.

48. Ambassador Téllez to Foreign Affairs Minister Sáenz, October 30, 1925, AREM, L-E-536, vol. ix, Leg. 7, f. 19.

49. Memorandum of conversation between Ambassador Sheffield and Foreign Affairs Minister Sáenz, December 16, 1925, AREM 42-15-3, Exp. A/628(018)/2, Leg. 3, AO, f. 34; L-E-536, vol. iv, Leg. 7; NAW 812.6363/1614.

50. Kellogg's statement—totally uncalled for as far as Mexico was concerned—was given to the press on June 12, 1925, following a meeting with Ambassador Sheffield. Kellogg went on to say that his country could continue on friendly terms with Mexico only if the latter protected the lives and interests of American citizens. His threat became clearer when he added that he was aware a new revolution was brewing in Mexico—and in fact the De la Huerta forces were indeed attempting to organize a new campaign against Calles (Cronon, *Josephus Daniels in Mexico*, pp. 47–48; Isidro Fabela, "La política internacional del presidente Cárdenas," *Problemas agrícolas e industriales de México* 7 (October–December 1955): 66).

51. Support came not only from Obregón but also from the Congress, the army, the labor unions, and the peasant organizations. The Mexican press, either by choice or under pressure, was unanimous in its censure of Kellogg. In the United States the *World*, the *New Republic*, the *Washington Post*, and many others came out against the secretary of state's move.

52. Fabela, "La política internacional del presidente Cárdenas," p. 67.

53. Plutarco Elías Calles, *Informes rendidos por el C. General . . . , Presidente Constitucional de los Estados Unidos Mexicanos ante el H. Congreso de la Unión las días 1º de septiembre de 1925 y 1º de septiembre de 1926 y contestación de los C.C. presidentes del citado Congreso*, p. 30.

54. Arturo M. Elías and M. G. Prieto at the Mexican consulate in New York informed Calles that Guy Stevens had said that if conditions did not improve in Mexico, Secretary of State Kellogg would recognize one of the rebel groups as a belligerent, meaning that the oil companies would then be able to finance it generously (July 29 and 31, August 4, 12, 16, and 19, and September 11, 1925, AGN, R. Obregón Calles, Paq. 5, Exp. 101, R2-1-1). Washington was informed that General Enrique Estrada had contacted certain banking groups and discussed his plans for an uprising against Calles (G. E. Hoover to Department of State, November 2, 1925, NAW 812.00/1830). Carranza's old ally, Cándido Aguilar, in Cuba at the time, reported that U.S. agents there had asked for his collaboration in an anti-Calles movement (Adolfo Manero Suárez and José Paniagua Arredondo, *Los tratados de Bucareli: Traición y sangre sobre México*, p. 419).

55. See, for example: Wallace Thompson, "Wanted: A Mexican Policy," *Atlantic Monthly* (March 1927): 386.

56. Ambassador Sheffield to Department of State, December 24, 1925, NAW 812.032/251.

57. Statements of Vicente Lombardo Toledano cited by Nathaniel and Silvia Weyl, "La reconquista de México: Los días de Lázaro Cárdenas," *Problemas Agrícolas e industriales de México* 7 (October–December 1955): 284.

58. George K. Lewis, "An Analysis of the Institutional Status and Role of the Petroleum Industry in Mexico's Evolving System of Political Economy" (Doctoral dissertation, University of Texas [Austin], 1959), pp. 50–51, 70.

59. There were more firms that complied with the new legislation than rejected it, but the latter represented more than 70 per cent of the output and 90 per cent of the oil lands acquired prior to May 1, 1917 (Wendell C. Gordon, *The Expropriation of Foreign-owned Property in Mexico*, p. 78; John W. F. Dulles, *Yesterday in Mexico: A Chronicle of the Revolution, 1919–1936*, p. 319; Merrill Rippy, "El petróleo y la Revolución Mexicana," *Problemas agrícolas e industriales de México* 6 [July–September 1954]: 420).

60. Ambassador Sheffield to Secretary of State Kellogg, July 18, 1926, NAW 812.6363; El Aguila to APPM, November 18, 1926, NAW EO186.

61. *World*, December 7, 1926.

62. Ambassador Sheffield to Department of State, April 15, 1926, NAW 812.6363/1832.

63. *El Demócrata*, January 17, 1926; *El Universal*, January 27, 1926.

64. Guy Stevens to the Oil Executives Committee in Mexico, January 29 and February 8, 1926, NAW 812.6363/1741–1744; Ambassador Sheffield to Department of State, February 18, 1926, NAW 812.6363/1770; *El Universal*, March 27, 1926.

65. Guy Stevens, *Current Controversies with Mexico: Addresses and Writings*, p. 187.

66. Memorandum of conversation between the Under Secretary of State and C. O. Swain, December 30, 1925, NAW 812.6363/1640; Swain to Under Secretary of State, January 6, 1926, NAW 812.6363/2499; Ambassador Sheffield to Department of State, April 17 and May 3, 1926, NAW 812.6363/1842.

67. Mexico, Secretaría de Relaciones Exteriores, *Correspondencia oficial* . . .

68. Like the oil firms, the State Department took exception to Articles 14 and 15 of the law of December 31, 1925, and also to its transitory articles 2, 3, 4, and 6 (Re law of 1925: Department of State memorandum, undated, NAW 812.6363/2289; Re regulatory provisions of April 1926: Department of State memorandum, April 19, 1926, NAW 812.6363/1983).

69. *Washington Post*, November 17, 1926.

70. Secretary of State Kellogg to Ambassador Sheffield, January 2, 1926, NAW 812.6363/1622½; Under Secretary of State to British embassy, March 5, 1926, NAW 812.6363/1787; *Wall Street Journal*, January 15, 1926; *New York Times*, February 1, 1926.

71. Mexican consul in New York to Ministry of Foreign Affairs, AREM III/628(010)/L-E-549, Leg. 45, ff. 97–99.

72. The Spanish embassy told Sheffield on March 4, 1926, that it was up to the United States to protect European interests in Mexico, since the country was in the U.S. sphere of influence (NAW 812.6363/1791).

73. Federico Bach and Manuel de la Peña, *México y su petróleo: Síntesis histórica*, p. 20. The British and Dutch notes were dated January 12 and June 7, 1926, respectively (NAW 812.6363). The British note of December 24, 1926, and the Mexican replies may be consulted in AREM III/628(010)/1 L-E-538, Legs. 21 and 24, ff. 63–66 and 14–18.

74. U.S. embassy in London to Department of State, November 12, 1926, NAW 711.12/788; Ambassador Sheffield to Department of State, December 24, 1926, NAW 812.6363/2085.

75. British embassy to Department of State, November 30, 1927, NAW 812.6363/2442.

76. According to a letter from Elmer R. Jones, representative in Mexico of the In-

ternational Committee of Bankers on Mexico, to the committee's president, Thomas W. Lamont, during the period 1925–1927 it was Morones who was responsible for handling the oil problem (May 7, 1927, NAW 812.51/1345).

77. The archives of the Ministry of Foreign Affairs have a number of documents on file regarding this problem between Morones and Sáenz—for example, Morones' official communication to the Ministry of Foreign Affairs in which he discusses at length the content of the replies to one of the notes from Secretary of State Kellogg (September 22, 1926, AREM III/628(010)/1 L-E-553, Leg. 55, ff. 121–157).

78. G. K. Lewis, "Analysis of the Institutional Status . . . ," pp. 72–73.

79. Ambassador Morrow to Secretary of State Kellogg, November 8, 1927, NAW 812.6363/2421½.

80. Ambassador Sheffield to Department of State, January 11, 1926, and January 4, 1927, NAW 812.6363/2129, 2112; Sheffield to Department of State, January 26, 1926, NAW 812.6363/1728.

81. Memorandum from the legal adviser to Minister of Foreign Affairs on the organic oil law bill, August 20, 1925, AREM III/628 (010)/1 L-E-552, Leg. 53, ff. 1–9.

82. Obregón's approval of the bill for the organic law relating to Article 27, paragraph i, is contained in a memorandum to Calles (undated but probably sent at the beginning of November 1925, AREM III/628(010)/1 L-E-551, Leg. 52, f. 82).

83. Ambassador Sheffield to Department of State, November 23 and December 1, 1925, NAW 812.6363/1582, 1599.

84. Ambassador Sheffield to Department of State, December 11, 1925, NAW 812.6363/1617.

85. See editorials in *El Universal*, December 17 and 18, 1925; January 5, 1926.

86. See, for example, editorial in *El Universal*, November 15, 1926.

87. Chargé d'Affaires Schoenfeld to Department of State, August 24, 1927, NAW 812.6363/2353.

88. Memorandum of International Committee of Bankers on Mexico, May 25, 1927, NAW 812.6363/2282½.

89. Ambassador Sheffield to Department of State, January 28, 1927, NAW 812.51/1318.

90. G. K. Lewis, "Analysis of the Institutional Status . . . ," p. 71.

91. James Fred Rippy, *Latin America in World Politics: An Outline Survey*, p. 269.

92. Walling, *The Mexican Question*, p. 170; *United States Daily*, March 21, 1927; *Nation*, April 13, 1927.

93. The resolution proposing arbitration of the differences with Mexico was approved unanimously on January 25, 1927. The resolution calling for public disclosure of the diplomatic correspondence between the United States and Mexico over the period from November 17, 1925, to March 6, 1926, was approved on March 27, 1926. On February 3, 1927, the Senate asked for a report on the American oil firms' compliance with the Mexican legislation.

94. *United States Daily*, March 22 and 23, 1927.

95. In late 1926 word went around in the United States that the State Department had asked the press to emphasize the fact that Mexico was a center of bolshevik activity (*Editor and Publisher*, December 4, 1926).

96. Samuel Flagg Bemis, *La diplomacia de Estados Unidos en la América Latina*, p. 226.

97. Ambassador Sheffield to Department of State, May 4, 1927, NAW 812.6363/2258; AREM 42-15-3, Exp. A 628/(010)/2, Leg. 3, f. 27; *New York Times*, March 1, 1927.

98. Throughout 1926 and 1927 the *Wall Street Journal* systematically attacked Calles, calling him a crook and a murderer. In addition to linking him to a bolshevik movement in Mexico and Central America, the press accused him of negotiating

secretly with Japan for the cession of Lower California, which would be a direct
threat to U.S. security (*Cincinnati Inquirer*, March 30, 1926; *Richmond Times Dispatch*, April 2, 1926; etc.).

99. Walling, *The Mexican Question*, p. 190.

100. The following works are excellent examples of this position: Walter Lippman,
"Vested Rights and Nationalism in Latin America," *Foreign Affairs* 5 (April 1927);
Walter D. Hawk, "Aspectos de la cuestión petrolera que quedan comprendidos en la
diplomacia mexicano-americana," manuscript translation of article in *Illinois Law
Review* 22 (June 1927); John P. Bullington, "Problems of International Law in the
Mexican Constitution of 1917," *American Journal of International Law* 21 (October
1927): 694–705; idem, "The Land and Petroleum Laws of Mexico"; Moisés Sáenz
and Herbert I. Priestley, *Some Mexican Problems*; Isaac F. Morcosson, articles in *The
Saturday Evening Post*, February 26 and March 5, 12, and 19, 1927. See also the open
letter signed by 101 professors from 43 colleges calling for a peaceful solution to the
Mexican problem (*New York Times*, January 24, 1927); Carleton Beals, "Whose
Property Is Kellogg Protecting?" *New Republic* 50, no. 638 (February 23, 1927).

101. Examples are Walling, *The Mexican Question*; Charles Wilson Hackett, *The
Mexican Revolution and the United States, 1910–1926*; J. F. Rippy, *Latin America
in World Politics*.

102. This attitude was seen particularly in the southern and western press.

103. Morison and Commager, *Historia de los Estados Unidos . . .* , II, 80; Daniel
Cosío Villegas, *Extremos de América*, p. 71. A survey conducted by the National
Civic Federation at a period of great tension in U.S.-Mexican relations showed that
the majority of the American public was against armed intervention. Congressman
Huddleston claimed on the floor of the House that 99 per cent of the American
people were opposed to a war with Mexico (Walling, *The Mexican Question*, p. 173;
New York Times, January 9 and February 2, 1927). The groups in favor of arbitrating
the differences with Mexico were widely heterogeneous, giving an idea of the broad
range of opposition to Kellogg's policy; they included, for example, the Union of
Hebrew Congregations, the National Council of Jewish Women, the Federal Council
of Churches of Christ in America; labor organizations such as the American Federation of Labor and the National League of Farmers; and peace groups such as the
Union of Pacifist Women and the Anti-Imperialist League.

104. The position of the KKK (and that of many of the Protestant churches)
stemmed from Coolidge's support of the U.S. Catholics in their campaign against
Calles (Ludwell Denny, *We Fight for Oil*, p. 68).

105. Sáenz and Priestley, *Some Mexican Problems*, p. 6; also Guy Stevens, Santiago Iglesias, and Heberto M. Sein, *The Issue in Mexico Discussed by . . . : A Stenographic Report of the 87th Session . . . of the Foreign Policy Association*.

106. In the House of Representatives Congressman James A. Galliman accused the
Mexican embassy of having spent two million dollars on propaganda against the U.S.
president and secretary of state (March 9, 1927, Ambassador Téllez to Minister of
Foreign Affairs, AREM III/628(010)/1 L-E-554, Leg. 56, f. 215. Ambassador Sheffield in
Mexico reported to his superiors that Ambassador Téllez had a special fund for use in
influencing the American press (January 23, 1926, NAW 812.20218/18).

107. Calles, *Mexico before the World*, pp. 51–52.

108. December 19, 1925, AREM L-E-536, vol. iv, Leg. 7, ff. 207–210. The Los
Angeles Chamber of Commerce recommended to its members in clear-cut terms that
they suspend their transactions with Mexico (AREM 42-15-3, Exp. A/628(010)/2, Leg.
3, A-O, f. 34).

109. Confederation of Chambers of Commerce of Mexico to the U.S. Chamber of
Commerce, December 18, 1925, AREM III/628(010)/1 L-E-536, Leg. 17, f. 207.

110. Guy Stevens appealed to the U.S. Chamber of Commerce, asking it, in the

name of commercial ethics, to apply the same treatment to Mexico that was being given to Soviet Russia (August 3, 1927, NAW 812.6363/2334).

111. William S. McCrea, "A Comparative Study of the Mexican Oil Expropriation (1938) and the Iranian Oil Nationalization (1951)," (Doctoral dissertation, Georgetown University, 1955), p. 14.

112. See the statements by James A. Flaherty in the Detroit *Free Press,* November 7, 1926.

113. An example of this kind of propaganda is the voluminous and not very serious work by Francis McCullagh, *Red Mexico,* in essence a laundry list of every crime that by any stretch of the imagination could be attributed to the "tyrant" Calles. Another similar case is the book by Francis C. Kelley, *The Mexican Question.*

114. The Supreme Council's letter is dated January 13, 1927. On January 15 the Mexican consulate in Los Angeles received a letter from the editor of the magazine *Pan Pacific Progress* asking for material for the campaign requested by the Mexican confreres (AREM III/628(010)/1 L-E-533, Leg. 2, ff. 114–116, 119). Another Masonic magazine, the *New Age,* also published material in support of the Mexican point of view.

115. See AREM III/628(010)/1 L-E-554, Leg. 56, ff. 50–59.

116. Ambassador Sheffield to Department of State, January 16, 1926, NAW 812.6363/1704.

117. The firms represented were El Aguila, Standard Oil of New Jersey, Huasteca, La Corona, and Marland Oil Company.

118. See NAW 812.6363/1770, 1772–1773, 1781, 1796.

119. This time the firms represented were Gulf Oil and Pan American Petroleum and Transport.

120. In reality the committee wanted no more nor less than full preservation of their rights acquired prior to May 1917 (NAW 812.6363/1812–1817).

121. Ambassador Sheffield to Department of State, April 7, 1926, NAW 812.6363/1835.

122. Hackett, *The Mexican Revolution and the United States,* pp. 97–98.

123. Chargé d'Affaires Schoenfeld to Department of State, September 14, 1926, NAW 812.6363/1946.

124. Calles, *Informes redidos . . . ,* p. 16.

125. Industry Minister Morones to the oil firms, October 14, 1926, AREM III/628(010)/1 L-E-533, Leg. 2, ff. 144–148.

126. *Excélsior,* October 19, 1926.

127. NAW 812.6363/2041.

128. Oil firms to Industry Minister Morones, December 13, 1926, and his reply of December 16, NAW 812.6363/2077½.

129. Ambassador Téllez to Ministry of Foreign Affairs, December 15, 1926, AREM III/628(010)/1 L-E-538, Leg. 21, f. 39.

130. *New York Times,* December 29, 1926.

131. AREM III/628(010)/1 L-E-538, Leg. 1, f. 48; Leg. 2, f. 78.

132. *Boletín del petróleo* 23 (January–June 1927): 80.

133. The only companies that applied for confirmatory concessions at the time were Penn-Mex Oil, Texas Petroleum and Asphalt, East Coast Oil, and New England Fuel Oil. The first two were not producing anything as of that date and the other two had nothing but land. Later on, in September, Penn-Mex lent the Mexican government several million dollars (Chargé d'Affaires Schoenfeld to Department of State, September 30, 1927, NAW 812.6363/2372).

134. Memorandum from attorney general to Department of State, January 8, 1927, NAW 812.6363/2372.

135. Ambassador Sheffield to Department of State, January 21, 1927, NAW 812.6363/2145; U.S. consul in Tampico to Department of State, February 17, 1927, NAW 812.6363/2189.

136. According to documents that Ambassador Sheffield assured were authentic, Sinclair had made an agreement with Calles whereby Mexico would permit this firm to drill within the "prohibited" coastal zones in return for a 15 per cent royalty, a twenty-million-dollar loan, and support of the Mexican position; however, these documents were most likely apocryphal, since Sinclair did not break from the "united front" (NAW 812.6363/2269).

137. Ambassador Sheffield to Department of State, May 16, 1927, NAW 812.6363/ 2267, 2270.

138. On May 19, 1927, Ambassador Sheffield reported that the decision in favor of Gulf had been reversed (NAW 812.6363/2265). The ruling handed down by the judge at Villa Cuauhtémoc, Veracruz, in favor of Gulf was followed by pressure from the Ministry of Industry for his resignation, and it was his successor who rescinded the earlier decision (memorandum from Mexican Gulf, May 31, 1927, NAW 812.6363/ 2282; *Excélsior*, June 1 and 3, 1927).

139. Ambassador Sheffield to Department of State, January 24, 1927, NAW 812.6363/2140.

140. On April 14, 1927, the U.S. consul in Tampico reported that Mexico depended very little on revenue from the oil industry taxes (NAW 812.6363/2241). According to Chargé d'Affaires Arthur Schoenfeld, the decision to go ahead and drill without permits was taken by the APPM in New York (June 25, 1927, NAW 812.6363/2296).

141. Ambassador Sheffield reported on April 11, 1927, that the companies' attitude stemmed from the need to meet all their orders pending [at a time of excess production?] (NAW 812.6363/2238).

142. *El Universal*, July 21, 1927.

143. Chargé d'Affaires Schoenfeld to Department of State, June 15, 18, and 24 and July 7, 1927, NAW 812.6363/2238.

144. Daniel James, *Mexico and the Americans*, p. 239.

145. Tannenbaum, *Mexico: The Struggle for Peace and Bread*, p. 274.

146. Ambassador Sheffield to Department of State, April 15 and October 11, 1926, NAW 812.6363/1832.

147. Ambassador Sheffield to Department of State, December 21, 1926, NAW 812.6363/2094.

148. This collaboration gave rise to a series of meetings in New York among representatives of the sixteen principal companies (NAW 812.6363/2118).

149. U.S. consul in Salina Cruz to Department of State, February 21, 1927, NAW 812.6363/2204; Ambassador Sheffield to Department of State, April 7, 1927, NAW 812.6363/2278; *Diario oficial*, June 27, 1927.

150. Ambassador Sheffield to Department of State, April 12, 1927, NAW 812.6363/ 2233; Chargé d'Affaires Schoenfeld to Department of State, June 25, 1927, NAW 812.6363/2295.

151. See, for example, the statements issued by the Ministry of Industry claiming that the fall in production was deliberately triggered by the companies (*Excélsior*, June 11, 1926; see also Universidad Obrera de México, *El conflicto del petróleo en México, 1937–1938*, pp. 43–50; Merrill Rippy, "El petróleo y la Revolución Mexicana," *Problemas agrícolas e industriales de México* 6 (July–September 1954): 40; Mexico, Secretaría de Educación Pública, *Sobre el petróleo de México*, p. 17).

152. Nathaniel and Silvia Weyl mention a telegram from the U.S. embassy that referred to a compromise between General Gómez and certain American interests ("La reconquista de México," p. 171). Other authors that have mentioned a connec-

tion between the two are Denny, *We Fight for Oil*, p. 73; Frank C. Hanighen, *The Secret War*, p. 127; Walling, *The Mexican Question*, p. 15; Bach and De la Peña, *Mexico y su petróleo*, p. 19.

153. Berta Ulloa, *Revolución Mexicana, 1910–1920*, pp. 431 ff.

154. Memorandum from J. Reuben Clark in the Department of State, September 21, 1927, NAW 812.6363/2382; Pan American Oil Company to Under Secretary Olds, May 11 and October 26, 1927, NAW 812.6363/2389, 2409; memorandum of a conversation between Secretary of State Kellogg and oil company spokesmen, August 9, 1927, NAW 812.6363/2384; Standard Oil of New Jersey to Under Secretary Olds, June 28 and July 19, 1927, NAW 812.6363/2346.

155. Ambassador Sheffield to Department of State, December 2, 5, 22, 29, and 30, 1926, NAW 812.6363/2029, 2036, 2078½, 2089. Secretary of State Kellogg had to remind his ambassador that Washington could not force the companies to act in any given way (December 4 and 9, NAW 812.6363/2029). See also Sheffield to Department of State, February 9, 1927, NAW 812.6363/2166.

156. January 19, 1927, NAW 812.6363/1687.

157. Ambassador Sheffield to Department of State, July 19, 1926, NAW 812.113/10129; memorandum of the Division of Mexican Affairs, Department of State, July 31, 1926, NAW 812.6363/1909; Secretary of State Kellogg to President Coolidge, August 26, 1926, NAW 812.6363/1914–1915.

158. Oil companies to Department of State, May 28, 1926, NAW 812.6363/1875½.

159. *New York Times*, November 11, 1926.

160. *World*, November 27, 1926; *Washington Post*, November 29, 1926.

161. Mexican consul general in New York to Ministry of Foreign Affairs, November 26, 1926, AREM III/628(010)/1 L-E-538, Leg. 21, ff. 20–23.

162. AREM L-E-542, vol. 10, Leg. 1, f. 38.

163. See, for example, the pamphlet published by the National Student Federation of America, *The Present Dispute between Mexico and the United States: Is Arbitration the Way Out?*

164. According to this position, any economically weak country would have to abstain from resort to an international court of justice in similar circumstances (Bullington, "The Land and Petroleum Laws of Mexico," p. 69).

165. Stevens, *Current Controversies with Mexico*, pp. 202–203, 206–209. On August 10, 1927, Pan American Petroleum and Transport reminded the State Department of the importance of not going for arbitration (NAW 812.6363/2392).

166. David Lawrence warned in the *Saturday Evening Post* that if the United States allowed Mexico to bring vital international principles into question the result would be chaotic for relations between the two states (May 5, 1927). Similar arguments appeared in the *Washington Post*, in which Mexico's action against the oil companies was likened to the capture of a country's warship by a foreign power, calling for immediate retaliation rather than arbitration (January 5, 1927).

167. A State Department memorandum prepared by (future ambassador) J. Reuben Clark, Jr., warns not to take the oil conflict to the U.S.-Mexico General Claims Commission because Mexico would be able to cite many instruments of international law in its defense; moreover, the U.S. courts themselves had not always recognized compensation as intrinsic to the law of the eminent domain (January 25, 1927, NAW 812.6363/2156½).

168. According to a report filed by the president of Mexican Petroleum (by now a subsidiary of Standard Oil of New Jersey) following the national takeover in 1938, the U.S. government threatened Mexico that it would have to resort to force if it did not respect international law and insisted on enforcement of the laws of 1925 (Willy John Feuerlein and Elizabeth Hannan, *Dólares en la América Latina*, pp. 120–121).

The *Journal of Commerce* said the same thing (July 31, 1940). It should be kept in mind that the idea of using arms against governments impinging on U.S. interests abroad had come up in other instances too: for example, around this same time the American Chamber of Commerce in Shanghai had demanded a show of strength in order to recover its confiscated property there and get payment for damages incurred (Walling, *The Mexican Question*, p. 180).

169. James Morton Callahan, *American Foreign Policy in Mexican Relations*, p. 602.

170. Walling, *The Mexican Question*, p. 178.

171. Alexander de Conde, *Herbert Hoover's Latin American Policy*, p. 8.

172. Stevens, *Current Controversies with Mexico*, pp. 130–141.

173. Ambassador Téllez to Ministry of Foreign Affairs, January 18, 1927, AREM III/628(010)/1 L-E-538, Leg. 21, ff. 86–88.

174. Ambassador Sheffield to Department of State, March 21, 1927, NAW 812.6363/2228.

175. Tannenbaum, *Mexico: The Struggle for Peace and Bread*, pp. 273–274.

176. Callahan, *American Foreign Policy . . .* , pp. 607–608; Fabela, "La política internacional del Presidente Cárdenas," p. 70; Emilio Portes Gil, "Cómo se conjuró en 1927 una invasión armada," *El Universal*, May 28, 1950; idem, *Autobiografía de la Revolución Mexicana*, pp. 388–397; J. F. Rippy, *Latin America in World Politics*, p. 268.

177. *New York World*, March 29, 1927.

178. Mexican consul general in San Francisco to Ministry of Foreign Affairs, May 9, 1927, AREM III/628(010)/1 L-E-543, Leg. 34, f. 284.

179. In a memorandum summarizing the points that Kellogg and J. Reuben Clark, Jr., discussed with the APPM, the State Department's position was that it did not wish to go beyond diplomatic representations in urging Calles to amend the oil legislation (August 9, 1927, NAW 812.6363/2334–2385).

180. Daniels to his son, August 16, 1933, JDP.

181. Chargé d'Affaires Schoenfeld to Department of State, September 5, 8, and 12, 1927, NAW 812.6363/2363, 2365; 812.001/27. In his memoirs, De la Huerta says that the Americans offered him support during this period for an armed uprising against Calles (*Memorias de Don Adolfo de la Huerta, según su propio dictado*, pp. 279–283).

182. Ambassador Morrow to Treasury Secretary Andrew W. Mellon, April 11, 1928, NAW 812.6363.

183. See, for example, Ministry of Foreign Affairs to Alvaro Obregón in Cajeme, Sonora, October 15, 1926, AREM III/628(010)/1 L-E-553, Leg. 55, f. 545.

184. Ambassador Sheffield reported Obregón's presence in a cabinet meeting at which the oil question was discussed in a communiqué to Washington dated March 20, 1927, NAW 812.6363/2222½.

185. Obregón was also accompanied by Gonzalo Ramírez Carrillo and José Colomo.

186. *El Universal*, February 1, 1927.

187. *New York Times*, February 10, 1927.

188. Ambassador Sheffield to Department of State, April 6, 1927, NAW 812.6363/2235.

189. G. K. Lewis, "Analysis of the . . . Petroleum Industry . . . ," pp. 74–76; Pan American Petroleum and Transport to Department of State, February 24, 1927, NAW 812.6363/2209½.

190. G. K. Lewis, "Analysis of the . . . Petroleum Industry . . . ," p. 77.

191. Morison and Commager, *Historia de los Estados Unidos*, III, 80.

192. Cronon, *Josephus Daniels in Mexico*, p. 49.

193. Nicolson, *Dwight Morrow*, pp. 287–293; Daniels, *Shirt-Sleeve Diplomat*, p. 272.

194. Nicolson, *Dwight Morrow*, pp. 296–299.

195. Ibid., p. 336.

196. Stanley R. Ross, "Dwight Morrow and the Mexican Revolution," *Hispanic-American Historical Review* 38 (1958): 509–510.

197. José Vasconcelos, *Breve historia de México*, vol. 4 of *Obras completas*, pp. 1684–1695.

198. MacNab made these statements in a speech delivered on April 23, 1930, in support of Morrow's campaign for a seat in the U.S. Senate (Nicolson, *Dwight Morrow*, p. 382).

199. Frank Brandenburg, *The Making of Modern Mexico*, p. 75.

200. Parkes, *History of Mexico*, p. 391.

201. Nicolson, *Dwight Morrow*, p. 304; Ross, "Dwight Morrow . . ."

202. Mauricio Magdaleno, *Las palabras perdidas*, p. 103. Possibly Calles personally had shown certain moderation in the accumulation of wealth, but this was not true of his associates: Luis N. Morones, the powerful CROM leaders, Aarón Sáenz, Abelardo L. Rodríguez, Alberto J. Pani, Luis León, José Manuel Puig Casauranc, and others all acquired large holdings.

203. Cosío Villegas, *Extremos de América*, pp. 32–33.

204. According to a letter from Ambassador Morrow to Treasury Secretary Mellon, it had been the idea of the late former secretary of state, Philander C. Knox, that Clark be assigned to the embassy in Mexico. Knox considered him one of the best experts in international law in the United States (April 21, 1928, NAW 812.6363/2557½).

205. Confidential memorandum for the Department of State to Ambassador Morrow, October 10, 1927, NAW 812.6363/2378½. Morrow probably utilized a memorandum on the oil question prepared by Clark, September 21, 1927, NAW 812.6363/2382.

206. Ambassador Morrow to Treasury Secretary Andrew W. Mellon, April 21, 1928, NAW 812.6363/2557½.

207. Memorandum from Ambassador Morrow to the Secretary of State, September 12, 1930, NAW 812.6363/2698.

208. Palmer E. Pierce to Ira J. Williams, October 3, 1927, NAW 812.6363/2410½.

209. Morrow made a thorough study of the matter and came to the conclusion that Mexico had a valid argument in that more than once the American courts had handed down rulings that were no less "retroactive and confiscatory" than the Mexican legislation of 1925 was accused of being.

210. Ambassador Morrow to Secretary of State Kellogg, November 8, 1927, NAW 812.6363/2421½; Nicolson, *Dwight Morrow*, pp. 328–330; Ross, "Dwight Morrow . . . ," pp. 510–511.

211. According to Vicente Lombardo Toledano, Morones asked the chief justice to hand down the decision because "the government was in danger" (Weyl and Weyl, "La reconquista de México," p. 284).

212. In a memorandum prepared for Ambassador Daniels it is stated that the November 17 ruling was handed down according to instructions from Calles which had been in the chief justice's hands since March (April 16, 1934, JDP).

213. The injunctions the companies had filed for by the end of 1927 covered a wide range of protests, including those against the Carranza decrees of 1918, the Calles appropriation in early 1927, the cancellation of drilling permits, and third-party claims on "unconfirmed" property (memorandum signed by J. Reuben Clark, Sep-

tember 21, 1927, NAW 812.6363/2382; APPM report to Department of State, NAW 812.6363/2449).

214. The text of the decision appears in *Boletín del petróleo* 25 (January–June 1928): 256 ff.

215. Ambassador Morrow to Secretary of State Kellogg, November 20, 1927, NAW 812.6363/2429.

216. Department of State to Ambassador Morrow, November 16 and 28, 1927, NAW 812.6363/2421. The seven big American and British companies had requested 247 drilling permits, of which 208 had been denied and the rest were pending (Ambassador Morrow to Department of State, November 18, 1927, NAW 812.6363/2435).

217. See articles appearing on December 11, 12, and 13, 1927.

218. Under Secretary Olds to Ambassador Morrow, November 29, 1927, NAW 812.6363/2438A.

219. They were insisting on the elimination of Articles 14 and 15 and the amendment of others; above all, they refused to accept the "positive act" principle (NAW 812.6363/2443).

220. The draft amendments are transcribed in the *Boletín del petróleo* 25 (January–June 1928): 256 ff. On December 26 Morrow told the oil companies that, if they wished, he could get Calles to withdraw the bill and ask the Congress to give him "extraordinary powers" with respect to oil. The firms decided it was better to try for the best possible legislation once and for all. Ambassador Morrow to Treasury Secretary Mellon, April 11, 1928, NAW 812.6363/2557½; Ambassador Morrow to Department of State, December 8, 1927, NAW 812.6363/2445.

221. J. Reuben Clark, "The Oil Settlement with Mexico," *Foreign Affairs* 6 (July 1928): 611; *Diario oficial*, January 11, 1928; correspondence between Branch of Huasteca and Industry Minister Morones, NAW 812.6363/2475.

222. An editorial appearing in *Excélsior* on December 25, 1927, pointed out with satisfaction that that paper had some time earlier called attention to the defects in the oil law that the Supreme Court had just brought to light; it went on to hail the decision and urge for amendment of the law.

223. Morrow reported to Under Secretary Olds that Fernando González Roa was in profound disagreement with the Supreme Court decision, which he considered even more generous than the ruling handed down in 1922 in the case of Texas Oil (November 30, 1927, NAW 812.6363/2426½).

224. Oil companies to Under Secretary Olds, February 2, 1928, NAW 812.6363/2500½. It is unlikely that the injunction awarded to Huasteca and the other companies by the Third District judge in Mexico City on the day before the oil law was amended and Articles 2, 4, 14, and 15 were declared unconstitutional really reflected the companies' wishes. The Ministry of Industry was to appeal this ruling ("Documents Relating to the Petroleum Law of Mexico of December 26, 1925, with Amendments of January 3, 1928" [mimeographed], pp. 32–40).

225. Standard Oil to Ambassador Morrow, January 19, 1928, NAW 812.6363/2501½; Walker to Under Secretary Olds, January 23, 1928, NAW 812.6363/2498–2499; memorandum of talks with the companies on January 20, 1928, NAW 812.6363/2498.

226. The text of the amended regulations appears in the *Diario oficial*, March 28, 1928. See also Ambassador Morrow to Department of State, March 6, 1928, and September 12, 1930, NAW 812.6363/2524 and 2698, respectively.

227. *Excélsior*, March 29, 1928.

228. Years later Ambassador Daniels was to say that Morrow had succeeded in getting Calles to nullify the constitution with respect to its provisions on oil and pass laws that were virtually a copy of those in force in the United States (Daniels, *Shirt-*

Sleeve Diplomat, p. 274). According to Antonio Gómez Robledo, Calles had turned the Bucareli Agreement into law (*The Bucareli Agreements and International Law*, p. 93).

229. Nicolson, *Dwight Morrow*, pp. 332–349. On March 31 Secretary of State Kellogg congratulated Ambassador Morrow on his accomplishment (NAW 812.6363/2537a).

230. The chief of the Division of Mexican Affairs in the State Department informed Under Secretary Olds on March 28 that he did not agree with this way of "washing our hands" with respect to future problems with the companies (NAW 812.6363/2531).

231. *Wall Street Journal*, March 28 and 30, April 4 and 28, 1927; *Herald Tribune*, March 28, 1928; L. Mellon to Ambassador Morrow, April 11, 1928, NAW 812.6363/2557½; L. Mellon to M. Mellon, April 11, 1928, NAW 812.6363/2545½; Stevens, *Current Controversies with Mexico*, pp. 325–355.

232. *New York Times*, April 16 and 19, 1928.

233. Oil companies to Department of State, April 27, 1928, NAW 812.6363/2558; memorandum of conversation between J. Reuben Clark and Arthur B. Lane of the State Department and oil company spokesmen, May 19, 1928, NAW 812.6363/2570½; L. Mellon to Morrow, June 25, 1928, NAW 812.6363/2578.

234. Callahan, *American Foreign Policy*, p. 617; *Wall Street Journal*, January 11, 1929.

235. J. Reuben Clark to Ambassador Morrow, February 3, 1928, NAW 812.6363/2508½; Ambassador Morrow to Under Secretary Olds, May 8, 1928, NAW 812.6363/2563½.

236. Oil companies to Under Secretary Olds, April 27, 1928, NAW 812.6363/2558; Under Secretary Olds to Ambassador Morrow, May 1, 1928, NAW 812.6363/2558.

237. *New York Times*, January 7 and 28, 1928; March 29, 1928.

238. Memorandum of conversation between former ambassador J. Reuben Clark and William W. Schott, second secretary at the U.S. embassy in Mexico City, September 6, 1936, NAW 812.6363/2952.

239. Mexico, Secretaría de Industria, Comercio y Trabajo, *La industria, el comercio y el trabajo en México . . .* , I, 429–430; Denny, *We Fight for Oil*, pp. 88–89.

240. According to an APPM report, Mexican taxes were 38 cents a barrel whereas the Venezuelan levies were only 8 cents, August 30, 1928, NAW 812.6363/2662.

241. The same APPM report stated that the labor legislation had caused labor costs to increase (August 30, 1928, NAW 812.6363/2662).

242. U.S. consul in Tampico to Department of State, September 8, 1928, NAW 812.6363/2590; Walter to Ambassador Morrow, October 11, 1928, NAW 812.6363/2597½.

243. J. Reuben Clark, Jr., to Ambassador Morrow, October 30, 1928, NAW 812.6363/2597½; Morrow to Ramón P. de Negri, May 9, 1929, NAW 812.6363/2671; also, various communications from Clark to the minister of industry regarding the concessions applied for by F. A. Lilliendahl, May 16–September 13, 1929, NAW 812.6363/2748.

7. In the Shadow of Calles, the "Supreme Leader of the Revolution": A Pause

1. Mario Mena, *Alvaro Obregón: Historia militar y política, 1912–1929*, p. 102.

2. *El Universal*, December 26, 1929.

3. According to Stanley R. Ross, neither Morrow nor the United States had anything to do with this move of Calles' ("Dwight Morrow and the Mexican Revolution," *Hispanic American Historical Review* 38 [1958]: 524).

4. During his incumbency Abelardo Rodríguez became one of the richest men in Mexico, amassing a fortune through his banking activities and control of gambling houses and casinos.

5. Statement made by G. A. Palma in a speech given on March 14, 1938 (Mexico, Secretaría de Educación Pública, *Sobre el petróleo de México: Conferencias*, pp. 31–32).

6. President Hoover, on learning about the uprising led by Escobar, took immediate steps to stop the shipment of all arms except those going to the Mexican government. Secretary of State Kellogg refused to receive Escobar's envoys, at the same time dispatching more than eleven million dollars' worth of weapons to Calles. It was rumored that the United States also sent down pilots, who took part in the Torreón and Jiménez skirmishes—although Portes Gil maintained there was no basis for this rumor (Alexander de Conde, *Herbert Hoover's Latin American Policy*, p. 94; John W. F. Dulles, *Yesterday in Mexico: A Chronicle of the Revolution, 1919–1936*, p. 443; Mauricio Magdaleno, *Las Palabras perdidas*, p. 82; Emilio Portes Gil, *Autobiografía de la Revolución Mexicana*, p. 482).

7. Even though the Vasconcelos movement obviously would never have had a chance against Calles in an armed confrontation, its leader was to claim, shortly after he went to the United States in self-exile, that President Hoover had said the United States would stand by in the event of a civil conflict only in the event an uprising against Calles was underway prior to the scheduled visit of President-elect Ortiz Rubio to Washington (José Vasconcelos, *El proconsulado*, vol. 2 of *Obras Completas*, pp. 291, 315).

8. Memorandum of a conversation between Ambassador Morrow and Branch of Huasteca Oil Company, November 19, 1929, NAW 812.6363/2670½.

9. In 1933 the State Department was more interested in the problems stemming from the agrarian reform and in the debts and damage claims than it was in the oil question (Daniels to his son, April 17, 1933, JDP; Edmund David Cronon, *Josephus Daniels in Mexico*, p. 130). The clashes between the U.S. and Mexican delegations at the VII International Conference of American States in Montevideo in 1933 arose over Mexico's request for a moratorium on all Latin American foreign debts (Cordell Hull, *The Memoirs of Cordell Hull*, II, 335–336).

10. At Ambassador Morrow's behest, the U.S. naval attaché in Mexico City drew up a plan for reorganizing the Mexican national debt, but it was rejected by Ortiz Rubio. Morrow went so far as to oppose the government's expenditures on health until it had met its international commitments (Harold Nicolson, *Dwight Morrow*, pp. 381–382; Josephus Daniels, *Shirt-Sleeve Diplomat*, p. 176).

11. At this conference the attack against constant U.S. intervention in the hemisphere in general was led off by Argentina, El Salvador, and Mexico.

12. Cronon, *Josephus Daniels in Mexico*, p. viii. The formulation and practice of the Good Neighbor policy is outlined in Bryce Wood, *The Making of Good Neighbor Policy*.

13. When Roosevelt took office Daniels was in doubt as to how to address his old friend, but the president soon wrote him: "My dear Chief: That title still stands! And I am still Franklin to you." This was to be the tone of relations between the president and his ambassador in Mexico.

14. Daniels' role in the taking of Veracruz in 1914 had not been forgotten, and it was with reluctance that Abelardo Rodríguez received the credentials of the new ambassador (Cronon, *Josephus Daniels in Mexico*, pp. 14–15).

15. Cronon, *Josephus Daniels in Mexico*; Daniels to his son, January 21, 1939, JDP. During the course of the Fall Committee's investigation in 1920 the companies accused Daniels of having failed to give them the necessary guarantees (United States, 66th Congress, 2nd session, Senate Committee on Foreign Relations, *Investigation of*

Mexican Affairs: Preliminary Report and Hearings . . . Pursuant to Senate Resolution No. 106 Directing the Committee to Investigate the Matter of Outrages on Citizens of the United States in Mexico, p. 1002.

16. Daniels wrote to President Roosevelt: "We have had too much Dollar Diplomacy on this hemisphere" (September 9, 1933, JDP).

17. Speech on presentation of his credentials, JDP.

18. Speeches of June 22 and July 4, 1933, and July 4, 1935, JDP. Reactions to the speech of July 4, 1933, may be seen in the July 6 editions of *Excélsior, El Universal, El Nacional,* and *La Prensa*.

19. At one time the typical attire of the rural upper class in Jalisco and Michoacán, by 1932 the *charro* had become the national dress.

20. Moisei S. Alperovich and Boris T. Rudenko, *La Revolución Mexicana de 1910–1917 y la política de los Estados Unidos*, p. 312.

21. If it were true, even Adolfo de la Huerta preferred to yield to Obregón rather than accept British aid.

22. Richmond Petroleum suspected that the Mexican authorities were dragging their feet on the concessions in response to pressure from El Aguila (J. Reuben Clark to Chargé d'Affaires H. V. Johnson, May 19, 1930, NAW 812.6363/2688). It is also claimed that Ortiz Rubio deported Luis Cabrera to Guatemala because of his legal battle with the British firm (José Domingo Lavín, *Petróleo*, pp. 159–161).

23. While bringing to light what it maintained were a number of irregularities with respect to the English firm, Petrolera Comercial did point out that El Aguila had not turned to the British or Dutch governments asking for pressure to be put on the Rodríguez administration (Compañía Petrolera Comercial, *La sombra internacional de El Aguila,* pp. 6–7).

24. APPM to Department of State, May 20, 1931, NAW 812.6363/2731.

25. J. Reuben Clark to Department of State, November 16, 1929, NAW 812.6363/2671; Ambassador Morrow to Department of State, September 12, 1930, NAW 812.6363/2698.

26. APPM to Ministry of Industry and Commerce, April 17, 1929, NAW 812.6363/2643; J. Reuben Clark to Department of State, November 16, 1929, NAW 812.6363/2671; Ambassador Morrow to Department of State, July 15, 1930, NAW 812.6363/2693.

27. An example is the controversy that arose in the course of reviewing the titles for the Chapacao, Cerro Azul, and Juan Felipe fields, which dragged on for several years. The U.S. embassy intervened in the companies' behalf on several occasions (J. Reuben Clark to Department of State, November 16, 1929, NAW 812.6363/2671; Ambassador Morrow to Ministry of Industry, April 17, 1930, NAW 812.6363/2699; J. Reuben Clark to Department of State, December 30, 1930, NAW 812.6363/2706; J. Reuben Clark to Department of State, February 2, 1931, NAW 812.6363/2710).

28. Daniels, *Shirt-Sleeve Diplomat*, pp. 219–220.

29. Mexico, Secretaría de Economía Nacional, *Programa de los fundadores de Petróleos de México, S.A.,* pp. 8–9.

30. APPM report, May 20, 1931, NAW 812.6363/2731, p. 53; United States 80th Congress, 2nd session, House of Representatives Committee on Interstate and Foreign Commerce, *Fuel Investigation: Mexican Petroleum,* p. 120; George Ward Stocking and Jesús Silva Herzog, *Mexican Expropriation: The Mexican Oil Problem,* p. 601.

31. The strike against El Aguila began on May 9, 1934, shortly after which President Rodríguez was named arbiter. Conclusion of the conflict in July gave the union a reduction in the work week, paid vacations, the right to indicate who should be employed by the company, and other benefits. Not long afterward a similar movement against Huasteca yielded like results (Dulles, *Yesterday in Mexico,* p. 601).

32. On January 29, 1929, the U.S. consul in Veracruz reported that the oil firms were thinking of filing for an injunction against the new tax (NAW 812.6363/2731).

33. They also suggested a labor reform, a new policy regarding national reserves, amendments to the technical regulations, abolition of the "federal zones," etc.

34. *El Nacional*, February 17, 1931; *El Universal*, January 10, 1931. Importation of petroleum for refining and reexportation declined in 1932.

35. The U.S. consul reported to the Department of State on March 8, 1932, that Mexican Petroleum had filed for an injunction against a decision that excluded from their property all lands within "federal zones" (NAW 812.6363/2745).

36. U.S. embassy to Department of State, March 20, 1931, NAW 812.6363/2716; U.S. embassy to Department of State, December 8, 1932, NAW 812.6363/2755.

37. J. Reuben Clark to Department of State, June 24, 1931, NAW 812.6363/2727; J. Reuben Clark to Department of State, December 8, 1932, NAW 812.6363/2755; commercial attaché to Department of State, March 27, 1931, NAW 812.512/3566.

38. J. Reuben Clark to Department of State, December 8, 1932, NAW 812.6363/2755.

39. *El Universal*, November 12, 1932.

40. *Excélsior*, March 11, 1929.

41. Ambassador Morrow to Department of State, March 22, 1929, NAW 812.6363/2634.

42. Mexico, Secretaría de Economía Nacional, *Programa de los fundadores de Petróleos de México, S.A.*, p. 9.

43. *Boletín del petróleo* 30 (July–December 1930): 245–247, 250–251.

44. With regard to the oil situation, Luis Cabrera said in 1931: "This is perhaps the most difficult problem that Mexico has to solve, but at present I am addressing myself in particular to the importance of nationalizing the sources of production of our natural resources" (*Veinte años después*, p. 86).

45. *El Universal*, February 13, 1932; *Excélsior*, April 10 and 15, 1932; *Boletín del petróleo* 35 (January–June 1933): 221.

46. *Excélsior*, March 22 and April 11, 1932.

47. J. Reuben Clark to Department of State, March 9, 1932, NAW 812.6363/2746.

48. U.S. embassy to Department of State, February 2, 1934, NAW 812.51/1980.

49. Mexico, Secretaría de Economía Nacional, *Programa de los fundadores de Petróleos de México, S.A.*, pp. 3–9.

50. Daniels, *Shirt-Sleeve Diplomat*, pp. 217–219; Mexico, Secretaría del Patrimonio Nacional, *El petróleo de México: Recopilación de documentos oficiales de orden económico de la industria petrolera, con una introducción que resume sus motivos y consecuencias*, p. 557.

8. The Cárdenas Regime and Solution Once and for All of the Oil Problem

1. Mosés González Navarro, *La Confederación Nacional Campesina*, p. 100.

2. Anita Brenner, *The Wind That Swept Mexico: The History of the Mexican Revolution, 1910–1942*, pp. 83–84; Vicente Fuentes Díaz, *Los partidos políticos en México*, II, 60–62; Manuel Moreno Sánchez, *Crisis política de México*, p. 240; Moisés González Navarro, "La ideología de la Revolución Mexicana," *Historia Mexicana* 10 (April–June 1961); "Editorial," *Problemas agrícolas e industriales de México* 7 (July–September 1955): 10.

3. Victoriano Anguiano, "Cárdenas y el cardenismo," *Problemas agrícolas e industriales de México* 7 (July–September 1955): 200–201.

4. González Navarro, *La Confederación Nacional Campesina*, p. 99.

5. Silvano Barba González, "Hechos y no palabras," *Problemas agrícolas e indus-*

triales de México 7 (July–September 1955): 223; Edmund David Cronon, *Josephus Daniels in Mexico*, pp. 112–131; Paul Nathan, "México en la época de Cárdenas," *Problemas agrícolas e industriales de México* 7 (July–September 1955): 56; Henry Bamford Parkes, *A History of Mexico*, p. 399; Nathaniel and Silvia Weyl, "La reconquista de México: Los días de Lázaro Cárdenas," *Problemas agrícolas e industriales de México* 7 (October–December 1955): 188–190.

6. González Navarro, *La Confederación Nacional Campesina*, p. 105; Stanley R. Ross et al., *Historia documental de México*, II, 497.

7. George Howland Cox, "Mexico's Industrialization Program," *World Affairs* 97 (June 1934): 106–109.

8. Daniels to Department of State, April 17, 1954, JDP.

9. Within the cabinet Narciso Bassols and Francisco Múgica, regarded as "radicals," were in a minority vis-à-vis the "conservative" group of prominent Calles men such as Aarón Sáenz, Rodolfo Elías Calles, and Tomás Garrido Canábal.

10. The clash between Calles and Cárdenas reached its peak on June 11, 1935, when the press quoted comments by the former with regard to the strikes against the oil firms. Apparently he had said that the country was going through a "marathon of radicalism" and criticized the labor policy of Vicente Lombardo Toledano. The president responded quickly: by pitting strong generals like Juan Andreu Almazán and Saturnino Cedillo against those supporting Calles he kept the army from making any move in support of Calles. Soon thereafter the labor unions also rallied. By June 19 Cárdenas had the situation entirely under his control.

11. This agrarian policy was the first point on which Cárdenas and the United States were to clash, the latter being firmly opposed to expropriation of the large rural landholdings that were in the hands of U.S. citizens (Cronon, *Josephus Daniels in Mexico*, pp. 136 ff.).

12. Victor Alba, *Las ideas sociales contemporáneas en México*, p. 145. Ambassador Daniels believed that in Mexico, as in the United States, the time had come for the "forgotten man," and that the country could never progress as long as part of its population was enjoying a high standard of living while the rest remained in misery (speech delivered before a group of American students, July 10, 1935, JDP).

13. In 1935, 75 per cent of the investment in industry was from foreign sources; foreign capital controlled, among other things, 98 per cent of all mining operations, 99 per cent of the oil industry, 79 per cent of the rail and trolley system, and 100 per cent of the electric power (Association of Producers of Petroleum in Mexico [APPM], *Current Conditions in Mexico*; NAW 812.6363/2763; Alfredo Navarrete, "La inversión extranjera directa en México," *Mercado de valores* [October 1966]).

14. González Navarro, *La Confederación Nacional Campesina*, p. 113; Weyl and Weyl, "La reconquista de México," p. 191; Hubert Herring and Herbert Weinstock, eds., *Renascent Mexico*, pp. 81–82, 109; Daniel James, *Mexico and the Americans*, p. 252; Cox, "Mexico's Industrialization Program," pp. 106–109; Sanford A. Mosk, *Industrial Revolution in Mexico*, pp. 53–59.

15. Ever since his campaign for the presidency began, Cárdenas had come out in marked nationalist tones against foreign capital. Already in 1935 an American observer had commented on the extremely hostile climate that was building up against foreign investment. Cárdenas wanted Mexico's development to be basically the work of Mexicans. "Our country," he said in a speech before a group of miners, "will never prosper as long as it serves merely as a siren to attract foreign capital" (Herring and Weinstock, eds., *Renascent Mexico*, pp. 120–125; Weyl and Weyl, "La reconquista de México," pp. 200–201). This nationalist policy was possibly encouraged by the fact that ever since 1929, as a result of the Depression, the entering flow of foreign capital had been considerably curtailed and there was little risk of frightening

away potential investors in those areas where capital was needed. Ambassador Daniels, in a report to the State Department, attributed the decline of foreign investment in Mexico since 1929 and its accelerated pace starting in 1935 largely to the government's policy of expropriation and support of workers' demands—overlooking the worldwide nature of the trend (February 9, 1939, JDP).

16. On more than one occasion Cárdenas as a general in command of the area had taken a stand against oil company practices and turned down their attempts to buy him off (William C. Townsend, *Lázaro Cárdenas: Demócrata mexicano*, pp. 43–45).

17. Entries of March 10 and 13, 1938, in Cárdenas' personal diary as quoted by *El Universal*, October 22, 1970.

18. Article 97 of the Six-Year Plan called in effect for nationalization of the subsoil. The government was to closely regulate the activities of those parties engaged in the exploitation of natural resources and prevent monopolization of the oil deposits. At the same time, national reserves were to be increased. Article 98 emphasized the desirability of increased government participation in the profits derived from natural resources. Article 103 proposed a balance among the various economic interests involved in the oil industry; it was necessary to develop national enterprises, whether they be private or public. The next article stressed the need to keep up a regular output based on the volume of reserves. Finally, Article 106 proposed a ban on the exportation of those petroleum derivatives that were less refined (Gilberto Bosques, *The National Revolutionary Party of Mexico and the Six-Year Plan*, pp. 164–166).

19. Merrill Rippy, "El petróleo y la Revolución Mexicana," *Problemas agrícolas e industriales de México* 6 (July–September 1954): 98.

20. In 1935 Hubert Herring predicted that the oil industry was going to be subjected to an impressive series of restrictions imposed by the Mexican government that would virtually amount to its nationalization (Herring and Weinstock, eds., *Renascent Mexico*, pp. 120–121).

21. Nathan, "México en la época de Cárdenas," p. 123.

22. Cronon, *Josephus Daniels in Mexico*, p. 155.

23. Josephus Daniels, *Shirt-Sleeve Diplomat*, p. 221; Cronon, *Josephus Daniels in Mexico*, pp. 156–158.

24. Huasteca Petroleum Company to Department of State, April 25 and 26, 1935, NAW 812.6363/2846, 2840.

25. U.S. embassy in Mexico to Department of State, May 20, 1935, NAW 812.6363/2849.

26. The economic action program unveiled by Cárdenas on January 1, 1935, indicated that oil was to be put to use in behalf of the nation—through Mexican enterprises as much as possible. At the very least the state was to control the use to which it was put and the prices at which it was sold (Manuel de la Peña, *Necesidad de reformar la ley del petróleo orgánica del artículo 27 constitucional*, pp. 13–15; John W. F. Dulles, *Yesterday in Mexico: A Chronicle of the Revolution, 1919–1936*, p. 632).

27. According to Virginia Prewett, the Calles group had sizable interests in the foreign oil companies that were being threatened by the government (cited by M. Rippy, "El petróleo y la Revolución Mexicana," p. 99).

28. U.S. embassy in Mexico City to Department of State, June 11, 1935, NAW 812.6363/2851.

29. U.S. embassy in Mexico City to Department of State, May 14, 1935, NAW 812.6363/2844; Cronon, *Josephus Daniels in Mexico*, pp. 158–159.

30. Ambassador Daniels to Department of State, January 18, 1938, NAW 812.6363/3068.

31. During June, July, and August the company spokesmen had a series of meetings

with Cárdenas and his staff that served to temporarily dispel the threat of an armed conflict (U.S. embassy in Mexico City to Department of State, June 13 and August 23, 1935, NAW 812.6363/2853, 2859).

32. Chargé d'Affaires Ad Interim Henry Norweb to Department of State, June 11, 1935, NAW 812.6363/2851.

33. "The enforcement of the 1925 oil law with respect to the granting of ordinary concessions," Cárdenas said, "has not respected the spirit of Article 27 of the Constitution. Quite the contrary, vast tracts of land have been brought under their coverage that are not even being worked."

34. *El Nacional*, October 4 and November 7, 1935.

35. On the subject of confirmatory concessions: Chargé d'Affaires Ad Interim Henry Norweb to Department of State, October 28 and November 5, 1935, NAW 812.6363/2868, 2872; Ambassador Daniels to Department of State, February 4, 1936, NAW 812.6363/2880. In regard to the taxes: Consul C. E. Macy in Mexico City to Department of State, November 14, 1935, NAW 812.6363/2874. Documents relative to the Huasteca labor dispute are filed under NAW 812.6363/2865.

36. Armando María y Campos, *Múgica: Crónica biográfica*, pp. 296–297. Years later the oil firms and their defenders were to say that promulgation of the organic law was the first step in a grand scheme that led to expropriation of the industry (Eduardo J. Correa, *El balance del cardenismo*, p. 153).

37. *Compilation of Documents with Regard to the Draft of Expropriation Law*.

38. Cronon, *Josephus Daniels in Mexico*, pp. 123–125.

39. Speech delivered on November 9, 1936, JDP.

40. In a U.S. embassy study of the expropriation law it was pointed out that the text could be interpreted in such a way that virtually any expropriation was possible (December 14, 1936, JDP).

41. Starting in 1913, the year the Mexican Oil Workers Union appeared, the labor leaders were subjected to a series of pressures ranging from attempted subornation to threats of assassination (Antonio Rodríguez, *El rescate del petróleo; Epopeya de un pueblo*, pp. 59 ff.).

42. U.S. consul in Mexico City, May 2, 1936, NAW 812.51/2152.

43. U.S. consul in Mexico City to Department of State, May 21, 1936, NAW 812.504/1595.

44. The salary increase itself came to 28 million pesos; the rest corresponded to benefits. The union was asking for dining halls, medical services, round-trip travel for the worker and his family to a vacation spot of his choice, double pay for those working at altitudes above seven meters or in swamp areas, and provision of automobiles for union officers (Harlow S. Pearson, *Mexican Oil: Symbol of Recent Trends in International Relations*).

45. In 1938 Lombardo Toledano stated that the STPRM decision had been carefully studied from the outset and taken with Cárdenas' concurrence (Universidad Obrera de México, *El conflicto del petróleo en México, 1937–1938*, p. 45).

46. Standard Oil of New Jersey, *Present Status of the Mexican Oil Expropriation*, p. 35.

47. *Mexican Weekly News*, August 22, 1936.

48. See, for example, *El Nacional*, March 7, 1936.

49. Cronon, *Josephus Daniels in Mexico*, p. 161.

50. Daniels to his son, May 15, 1937, JDP. To Secretary of State Hull he had reported the year before that the American colony in Mexico was opposed to the Good Neighbor policy, resented paying even starvation wages, and felt that diplomatic protection to save their large enterprises was their due (Cronon, *Josephus Daniels in Mexico*, pp. 58–59). On this point the ambassador was right. According to a survey conducted in 1936 among the members of the American Club of Mexico, more than

90 per cent of the persons polled were against Roosevelt (*Mexican News Letter*, n.d.).

51. U.S. consul in Mexico City to Department of State, February 26, 1937, NAW 812.6363/2916.

52. U.S. embassy in Mexico City to Department of State, February 23, 1937, NAW 812.6363/2912.

53. U.S. embassy in Mexico City to Department of State, February 25, 1937, NAW 812.6363/2913; *El Universal*, February 24, 1937.

54. *Diario oficial*, March 2, 1937.

55. U.S. Embassy in Mexico City to Department of State, February 26 and March 2 and 3, 1937, NAW 812.6363/2914, 2918, 2919.

56. *El Nacional*, July 2, 1937.

57. Department of State to U.S. embassy in Mexico City, July 8 and 14, 1937, NAW 812.6363/2945; Pierre Boal to Department of State, July 10, 1937, NAW 812.6363/2947.

58. U.S. embassy in Mexico City to Department of State, July 9, 1937, NAW 812.6363/2948.

59. F. C. Pannell of Standard Oil of New Jersey to Laurence Duggan, Department of State, July 12, 1937, NAW 812.6363/2962.

60. Oil companies to Department of State, July 14, 1937, and memorandum from the legal adviser, Department of State, July 16, 1937, NAW 812.6363/2954.

61. Department of State to Pierre Boal, July 17, 1937, NAW 812.6363/2947.

62. Pierre Boal to Department of State, July 15, 1937, and Secretary of State Hull to Boal, August 2, 1937, NAW 812.6363/2956, 2968B.

63. *Excélsior*, September 1, 1937.

64. Pierre Boal to Department of State, July 12, 1937, NAW 812.6363/2965.

65. Juan Jacobo, "La huelga contra El Aguila en 1924," *El Día*, April 8, 1970.

66. Cárdenas on many occasions had pointed out that in the struggle between capital and labor the latter was at a disadvantage and that for this reason the state should show a certain partiality toward the workers, always deciding in their favor in the event of a real doubt (George Ward Stocking and Jesús Silva Herzog, *Mexican Expropriation: The Mexican Oil Problem*, p. 503).

67. Universidad Obrera de México, *El conflicto del petróleo . . .* , p. 61.

68. For example, Gilberto Bosques editorialized in a PNR publication that an oil industry in foreign hands was of little benefit to the national economy; the profits that it returned annually to its home country constituted a significant drain on resources. Bosques practically advised its expropriation (*The National Revolutionary Party . . .* , p. 283). Antonio Gómez Robledo, for his part, indicated that it was not desirable to delay total nationalization of the hydrocarbons any longer than necessary (*The Bucareli Agreements and International Law*, trans. Salomón de la Selva, pp. 38, 41–42).

69. Pierre Boal to Department of State, June 3, 1937, NAW 812.6363/2936.

70. Daniels to Department of State, March 6, 1937, JDP; Standard Oil of New Jersey to Department of State, June 22, 1937, NAW 812.6363/2950.

71. Townsend, *Lázaro Cárdenas*, p. 247; Daniels, *Shirt-Sleeve Diplomat*, pp. 223–224.

72. Standard Oil of New Jersey to Department of State, June 29, 1937, NAW 812.6363/2950.

73. Francisco Castillo Nájera, *El petróleo en la industria moderna: Las compañías petroleras y los gobiernos de México*, p. 40.

74. Pierre Boal to Department of State, July 9, 1937, NAW 812.6363/2949.

75. The companies protested, maintaining that only the employers had the right to initiate such an investigation.

76. In essence, the conclusions drawn from the investigation conducted by Silva

Herzog and his collaborators were as follows: (a) the companies under review were part of large foreign consortia whose interests were not shared by Mexico and indeed on occasions were in outright opposition; (b) in carrying forward their purposes the oil firms had interfered in Mexican internal politics on numerous occasions; (c) while the fall in production was due to the deposits under exploitation running dry, it was possibly also due to a deliberate policy on the part of the companies; exploration and drilling should be encouraged because of the number of wells running dry; (d) domestic consumption of Mexican oil was becoming a matter of increasing importance; (e) at the time of the investigation El Aguila was the biggest company, its output representing 59.2 per cent of the total; (f) the audit of the firms' books revealed a series of irregularities, such as the recording of sales prices below those on the world market, sales to subsidiaries at prices higher than normal, inflation of the payroll, etc.; (g) as far as the companies' financial state was concerned, the expert committee found that during the period 1934–1936 profits had represented 34.3 per cent of corporate capital and 16.8 per cent of unamortized capital investments, it being noted that in the United States profits were running at a rate of about 2 per cent (Mexico, Secretaría del Patrimonio Nacional, *El petróleo de México: Recopilación de documentos oficiales de orden económico de la industria petrolera, con una introducción que resume sus motivos y consecuencias*).

77. Chester Lloyd Jones, "Production of Wealth in Mexico," in *Mexico Today*, ed. Arthur P. Whitaker, p. 67.

78. Daniels to Secretary of State Hull, September 7, 1957, JDP.

79. Castillo Nájera, *El petróleo . . .* , p. 40.

80. According to this theory, the employees in high-productivity industries became a privileged caste; it was better to take out excess earnings in the form of taxes.

81. After a lengthy study of the report, the companies presented their objections. They insisted that it was economically impossible to grant the wage increase that was being demanded. Their profits during the period 1934–1936 had not reached anything like the 55-million-peso figure cited; rather, they were of the order of 22 million. Their earnings had been 4.25 per cent and not 16 per cent. The report's conclusions, they said, were impassioned. And they denied everything, even the fact that the firms in question were subsidiaries of other international consortia ([oil companies], *Objeciones de la industria petrolera al informe y dictamen de la comisión pericial*; Donald R. Richberg, *Alegato sobre la cuestión petrolera de México*; Wendell C. Gordon, *The Expropriation of Foreign-owned Property in Mexico*, pp. 83–85).

82. *Excélsior*, August 6, 1937; *El Universal*, August 7, 1937; *Times*, August 9, 1937.

83. Cronon, *Josephus Daniels in Mexico*, pp. 164–165.

84. This special group was made up of one representative each from the companies, the workers, and the Mexican government.

85. Pierre Boal to Department of State, August 30 and September 2, 1937, NAW 812.6363/2991, 3001; Ambassador Daniels to Department of State, October 20, 1937, NAW 812.6363/3024.

86. Walter Tagle of Standard Oil of New Jersey to Secretary of State Hull, NAW 812.6363/3002; Thomas R. Armstrong of the same firm to Green Hackworth, Legal Adviser, Department of State, September 1 and October 26, 1937, NAW 812.6363/3026.

87. Memorandum of a conversation between Under Secretary Welles and Ambassador Castillo Nájera, October 1, 1937, NAW 812.6363/3020.

88. Memorandum of a conversation between Laurence Duggan, Department of State, and the Netherlands chargé d'affaires, September 10, 1937, NAW 812.6363/3012.

89. Ambassador Daniels to Department of State, September 6, 1937, NAW 812.6363/2994.

90. Betty Kirk, *Covering the Mexican Front: The Battle of Europe versus America*, p. 162.

91. Daniels to his son, November 6, 1937, JDP.

92. *Diario oficial*, November 4, 1937.

93. See the spread paid for by Compañía Petrolera Comercial in *Excélsior*, March 12, 1936.

94. Ambassador Daniels to Department of State, March 3, 1937, NAW 812.6363/ 2924.

95. Ambassador Daniels to Department of State, May 2, 1936, NAW 812.6363/ 2896.

96. Stocking and Silva Herzog, *Mexican Expropriation*, p. 499.

97. *New York Times*, November 14, 1937.

98. The contract set an output figure of less than 12,600 barrels a day. Royal Dutch, in statements released to the press, declared that it would not pay royalties on confirmatory concessions and claimed that the Mexican government would thereby be "participating" in production (*New York Times*, November 17, 1937).

99. Gordon, *Expropriation . . .* , pp. 103–104; Jones, "Production of Wealth in Mexico," p. 67; M. Rippy, "El petróleo y la Revolución Mexicana," p. 112; Kirk, *Covering the Mexican Front*, pp. 162–163.

100. Ambassador Daniels to Department of State, November 17, 1937, NAW 812.6363/3042; commercial attaché to Daniels, November 17, 1937, NAW 812.6363/ 3045.

101. Ambassador Daniels to Department of State, November 19, 1937, NAW 812.6363/3046.

102. Ambassador Daniels to Department of State, November 13 and 18, 1937, NAW 812.6363/3042, 3043; commercial attaché to Daniels, November 17, 1937, NAW 812.6363/3045.

103. Luis G. Zorrilla, *Historia de las relaciones entre México y los Estados Unidos de América*, II, 469–470.

104. Ambassador Daniels to Department of State, December 18, 1937, NAW 812.6363/3049; 812.51/2237; Frank L. Kluckhohn, *The Mexican Challenge*, pp. 110–111.

105. According to the law, the board was to study the expert committee report, wait seventy two hours for any objections to be filed by the parties in conflict (in this case the period was longer), and then hand down its decision. In the case of any objections, both sides were to be heard, after which the decision would be given. The board had authority to call for an increase or a cutback in personnel, set working hours, change the wage scale, and generally introduce changes in the working conditions. If the employer did not accept its decision, the labor contract would be terminated and the employees given three months' wages as indemnization.

106. For a detailed study of the ruling, see Universidad Obrera de México, *El Conflicto del petróleo . . .*

107. The companies' position is set forth in their publication *The Mexican Oil Strike of 1937*, vol. 1.

108. Richberg, *Alegato . . .* , p. 40.

109. Raymond Vernon, "An Interpretation of the Mexican View," in *How Latin America Views the United States Investor*, p. 104.

110. In their petition for an injunction the oil company lawyers insisted that Special Group 7 had no authority to decide in the conflict—that this authority rested only with the JFCA. As for the award itself, they claimed that it violated no less than fifty articles of the Federal Labor Law, as well as six provisions of the constitution. The conflict, they maintained, had been unfairly presented as a financial one; there was no justification for asking for a wage increase corresponding to the firms' eco-

nomic capacity. The JFCA award, they went on, even stipulated fringe benefits that the workers had not originally asked for, and it rejected out of hand the proof offered by the companies with respect to their economic situation. The firms' spokesmen insisted that the real increase corresponded to 41 million pesos and not 26, and they rejected as unfair the limit on nonunion office staff (Universidad Obrera de México, *El conflicto del petróleo . . .* , pp. 35–39).

111. According to Jesús Silva Herzog, as of the end of 1937 the country had reserves only slightly in excess of the legal minimum, and with these it was hoped to stand up to the flight of capital, which at that time and up to early 1938 was about 500 million dollars (*Petróleo mexicano*, pp. 18–19; Weyl and Weyl, "La reconquista de México," p. 328; M. Rippy, "El petróleo y la Revolución Mexicana," p. 76). Lombardo Toledano accused the oil interests of having sought the cooperation of the Mexican National Bankers Association in their efforts to spark an economic crisis (Universidad Obrera de México, *El conflicto del petróleo . . .* , p. 46). Huasteca tried to get the number-one mining enterprise, American Smelting and Refining Company, to force a conflict with its workers in order to aggravate the crisis, but the bonanza that the firm was enjoying as a result of the silver sales kept it from cooperating (Cronon, *Josephus Daniels in Mexico*, p. 181). The companies claimed that the withdrawal of their funds had nothing to do with any effort to pressure the government; rather, they were afraid that it would freeze their deposits (Kluckhohn, *The Mexican Challenge*, p. 108).

112. Cárdenas' personal diary as quoted in *El Universal*, October 22, 1970.

113. These measures were decreed on December 31, 1937.

114. Gordon, *Expropriation . . .* , p. 48.

115. In a speech delivered before the CTM General Assembly on February 22, 1938, Lombardo Toledano went so far as to say, "I am sure that on Friday of this week the Supreme Court will hand down its decision confirming the JFCA's award."

116. The ruling may be consulted in Universidad Obrera de México, *El conflicto del petróleo . . .* , pp. 67–68.

117. Ambassador Daniels to Department of State, December 10, 1937, NAW 812.51/2237; memorandum signed by the adviser on International Economic Affairs, Department of State, December 10, 1937, NAW 812.51/2243.

118. Cronon, *Josephus Daniels in Mexico*, pp. 168–169; William S. McCrea, "A Comparative Study of the Mexican Oil Expropriation (1938) and the Iranian Oil Nationalization (1951)" (Doctoral dissertation, Georgetown University, 1955), p. 58; Standard Oil of New Jersey, *Respuesta de las compañías petroleras al documento del Gobierno Mexicano intitulado "La verdad sobre la expropiación de los bienes de las empresas petroleras."*

119. Daniels to Secretary of State Hull, September 7 and 9 and November 26, 1937, JDP; Daniels to his son, September 11, 1937, JDP.

120. Cárdenas' personal diary as quoted in *El Universal*, October 22, 1970.

121. Memorandum of a conversation between Under Secretary Welles and the British ambassador, December 29, 1937, JDP.

122. See annual reports of the National Bank of Mexico for this period and *Excélsior*, December 30, 1937.

123. Cárdenas' personal diary as quoted in *El Universal*, October 22, 1970.

124. Memorandums signed by the adviser on international economic affairs, Department of State, December 13 and 31, 1937, NAW 812.51/2242½, 2255.

125. Daniels to his son, December 23, 1937, JDP; idem, *Shirt-Sleeve Diplomat*, p. 226; Kirk, *Covering the Mexican Front*, p. 157.

126. Daniels to President Roosevelt, September 14, 1937, JDP.

127. Daniels pointed out to Secretary of State Hull that there was no reason for the

companies to be crying "confiscation" every time the workers asked for a raise, maintaining that it was only fair that Mexico get a larger share of the oil's value through wages and taxes (Daniels to Hull, September 9 and 24, 1937, JDP).

128. On September 18 the ambassador wrote to his son that the Mexicans were convinced the foreign oil companies were taking the cream and leaving them with just the skim milk (see also letter of December 23, 1937, JDP).

129. Secretary of State Hull to Daniels, November 17, 1937, JDP; McCrea, "Comparative Study . . . ," p. 67.

130. Cronon, *Josephus Daniels in Mexico*, pp. 175–177; Townsend, *Lázaro Cárdenas*, p. 163.

131. *Excélsior*, January 2, 1938.

132. Ambassador Daniels to Department of State, January 7, 1938, NAW 812.6363/ 3286.

133. Ambassador Daniels to Department of State, January 21, 1938, NAW 812.6363/3069.

134. Memorandum of meeting between Sumner Welles and the British ambassador, February 25, 1938, NAW 812.6363/3148.

135. *El Nacional*, February 25, 1935.

136. Daniels to his son, January 8, 1938, JDP. Armstrong rejected the Treasury Ministry's calculations, which indicated that the oil industry's profit margin was considerably higher and would, in fact, allow comfortably for the wage increase set by the JFCA (Cronon, *Josephus Daniels in Mexico*, pp. 178–179).

137. Ambassador Daniels to Department of State, March 19, 1938, NAW 812.6363/ 3107.

138. Ambassador Daniels to Department of State, January 31, 1938, NAW 812.6363/3072.

139. Ambassador Daniels to Department of State, February 24, 1938, NAW 812.6363/3075.

140. Ibid.

141. Zorrilla, *Historia de las relaciones . . .* , p. 473.

142. Memorandum from Ambassador Daniels to the consulates in Mexico, April 15, 1938, NAW 812.00/30559.

143. El Aguila had decided to bow to the terms of the JFCA award, but pressure from Standard Oil and other American companies forced it to change its mind (Bryce Wood, *The Making of Good Neighbor Policy*, p. 205; Cronon, *Jospehus Daniels in Mexico*, pp. 182–184).

144. Ambassador Daniels to Department of State, March 31, 1938, NAW 812.6363/ 3362.

145. Memorandum from Deputy Foreign Affairs Minister Beteta to Mexican foreign missions abroad, March 9, 1938, AREM III/628 "938"/2 L-E-555, part 1, f. 3.

146. Ministry of Foreign Affairs to Ambassador Castillo Nájera, March 8, 1938, AREM III/628 "938"/2 L-E-558, Estados Unidos, f. 6.

147. Daniels to his son, March 19, 1938, JDP.

148. Cárdenas' personal diary as quoted in *El Universal*, October 22, 1970.

149. Memorandum from Deputy Foreign Affairs Minister Beteta to Mexican foreign missions abroad, March 9, 1938, AREM III/628 "938"/2 L-E-555, part 1, f. 4.

150. Cárdenas' personal diary as quoted in *El Universal*, October 22, 1970.

151. Memorandum from Deputy Foreign Affairs Minister Beteta to Mexican foreign missions abroad, March 1, 1938, AREM III/628 "938"/2 L-E-555, part 1, f. 4.

152. Political report of the U.S. consul in Mexico City to Department of State, April 9, 1938, NAW 812.00/30557.

153. President Roosevelt to Daniels, March 15, 1938, JDP.

154. U.S. consulate in Mexico City to Department of State, March 9, 1938, NAW 812.00/30539.

155. Memorandum from Ambassador Daniels to the consulates in Mexico, April 15, 1938, NAW 812.00/30559.

156. Ambassador Daniels to Department of State, March 18, 1938, NAW 812.6363/3103.

157. *Ultimas noticias*, March 18, 1939.

158. *Diario oficial*, March 19, 1938. The legal bases for this measure were found in paragraph 2 of section vi of Article 27 and in Articles 1, 4, 8, 10, and 20 of the expropriation law of November 23, 1936.

159. United Nations, International Law Commission, *Yearbook, 1959*, II, 13.

160. The president pointed out in his message that the oil firms had turned down an agreement in which it was guaranteed that the increase would not be more than the 26 million pesos and instead were conducting a quiet campaign against the country's economic interest. They had interfered constantly in Mexican politics and as far as any social contribution was concerned the balance sheet was clearly negative. The government could not allow the conflict to deprive Mexico of its oil; if the state lost control of the nation's economic life, loss of political control could easily follow.

161. See description of press coverage in Rodríguez, *El rescate del petróleo*.

162. George K. Lewis, "An Analysis of the Institutional Status and Role of the Petroleum Industry in Mexico's Evolving System of Political Economy" (Doctoral dissertation, University of Texas, 1959), p. 137.

163. [Oil companies], *The Mexican Oil Strike of 1937*, IV, 54–55; Standard Oil of New Jersey, *Confiscation or Expropriation? Mexico's Seizure of the Foreign-owned Oil Industry*, pp. 20–28; Samuel Flagg Bemis, *La diplomacia de Estados Unidos en la América Latina*, p. 352; Roscoe B. Gaither, *Expropriation in Mexico*, pp. 8–9; Kluckhohn, *The Mexican Challenge*, pp. 96–97; Correa, *El balance del cardenismo*, pp. 153–154. One of the most curious versions of the reasons behind the expropriation, and one that has been relatively well circulated, is that set forth by Carreño and Manero Suárez, among others. According to these authors, the expropriation decree was the result of a scheme mapped by Roosevelt and Cárdenas to get rid of the British interests. Secretary of State Hull's protestations, according to them, were only a smoke screen to cover up the fact that there was such an agreement (Alberto María Carreño, *La diplomacia extraordinaria entre México y los Estados Unidos, 1789–1947*, XI, 263; Adolfo Manero Suárez and José Paniagua Arredondo, *Los tratados de Bucareli: Traición y sangre sobre México*, p. 509).

164. Memorandum from Laurence Duggan, Division of the American Republics, to Under Secretary Welles, April 5, 1938, NAW 812.6363/3374.

165. Ambassador Daniels to Department of State, March 19, 1938, NAW 812.6363/3104.

166. Cárdenas' personal diary as quoted in *El Universal*, October 22, 1970.

167. Daniels to Department of State, February 9, 1939, JDP.

168. Castillo Nájera, *El petróleo . . .* , p. 41.

169. Justice Icaza excused himself from sitting on the companies' suit for injunction, but his public statements reveal the attitude that prevailed in official circles in general and in the Supreme Court in particular.

170. Universidad Obrera de México, *El conflicto del petróleo . . .* , pp. 91–92.

171. Icaza declared on March 1 that, regardless of the stand taken by the companies at this point, Mexico had won. If they accepted the terms of the award, the success was obvious; if they didn't, there was at last justification for taking over the oil industry. Lombardo Toledano, for his part, stated in a speech delivered at the Hall of Fine Arts that the real significance of the conflict was that Mexico could finally bring

the oil into the service of the nation (Universidad Obrera de México, *El conflicto del petróleo* . . . , p. 63; Mexico, Secretaría de Educación Pública, *Sobre el petróleo de México: Conferencias*, p. 104).

172. Deputy Foreign Affairs Minister Ramón Beteta was not among those who were opposed to the expropriation. In Washington Ambassador Castillo Nájera was afraid that the measure would lead to armed reprisal on the part of the United States (Weyl and Weyl, "La reconquista de México," p. 280: Kluckhohn, *The Mexican Challenge*, p. 249; Jesús Silva Herzog, *México y su petróleo*, p. 44).

173. Gordon, *Expropriation* . . . , p. 102.

9. From Nationalization to World War II

1. Henry Bamford Parkes, *A History of Mexico*, p. 407.

2. One of the government's first steps toward collecting the funds to compensate the expropriated firms—which served also to rally public support in its favor—was to float a 100-million-peso issue of bonds for redeeming the debt (*Diario oficial*, April 25, 1938). Also, a Committee on Mexican Unity for Economic Liberation (CUMPLE—Comité de Unidad Mexicana Pro Liberación Económica), was formed to promote the sale of these bonds and other activities in support of Cárdenas. In June, however, the operation was canceled, the president maintaining that he could not ask the Mexican people to make any further sacrifices than necessary (*Excélsior*, June 8 and 28, 1938). Private industry, thinking that it would have to pick up the bonds, reacted by telling the government it was not prepared to cooperate (Pierre Boal to Department of State following talk with a representative of the Association of Foreign Enterprises in Mexico, April 25, 1938, NAW 812.6363/3785).

3. Daniels to President Roosevelt, March 22, 1938, JDP; Daniels to his son, April 9, 1938 and March 18, 1939, JDP; Josephus Daniels, *Shirt-Sleeve Diplomat*, p. 230.

4. U.S. consul general to Department of State, April 9, 1938, NAW 812.00/30557.

5. Memorandum of Division of the American Republics, Department of State, May 25, 1938, NAW 812.6363/3556.

6. Javier Rondero, "Características del nacionalismo," in *México: 50 años de Revolución*, III, 310.

7. Oscar Morineau, *The Good Neighbor*.

8. U.S. consul in Monterrey to Department of State, April 18, 1938, NAW 812.6363/3556.

9. According to this version, the decline in the value of the peso would make precious metals the only form of exchange, but since they would be monopolized by speculators, the government would have to issue even more paper money, which the people would refuse to use, leading to hunger and unemployment in the cities (Nathaniel and Silvia Weyl, "La reconquista de México: Los días de Lázaro Cárdenas," *Problemas agrícolas e industriales de México* 7 (October–December 1955): 294. Of interest in this regard are the reports of the U.S. consul in Monterrey to the State Department dated March 21 and April 18, 1938, and of the consul in San Luis Potosí of March 26, 1938. In both cases the business world's opposition to the national takeover is reviewed (NAW 812.6363/3134, 3556, 3244).

10. According to the U.S. ambassador, the fears were found mostly in the upper and middle bureaucratic sectors (Daniels to his son, March 26, 1938, JDP; William C. Townsend, *Lázaro Cárdenas: Demócrata mexicano*, p. 226; idem, *The Truth about Mexico's Oil*, pp. 28–31).

11. Ambassador Castillo Nájera to Ministry of Foreign Affairs, March 25, 1938, AREM III/628 "938"/2 C-E-558, Estados Unidos, f. 2.

12. Note from Department of State to Department of Justice, June 13, 1940, NAW 812.6363/6972.

13. Cedillo wanted to use force, whereas Cárdenas did not.

14. The U.S. consul in San Luis Potosí reported to the Department of State on March 26 that Cedillo was probably going to rise up in arms (NAW 812.6363/3224).

15. War Minister Manuel Avila Camacho reported to Ambassador Daniels that an armed uprising was expected around September 16 (Daniels to Department of State, September 13, 1937, NAW 812.00/30500).

16. Memorandum of a conversation between Ambassador Castillo Nájera and Under Secretary of State Sumner Welles, October 1, 1937, NAW 812.6363/3020.

17. Memorandum signed by R. C. Tanis, Division of the American Republics, October 5, 1937, NAW 812.00/30508.

18. Excélsior, April 28, 1938.

19. According to a U.S. embassy report, Cedillo was definitely planning to rise up against Cárdenas, but at a later date; in May his preparations were still underway (Pierre Boal to Department of State, June 14, 1938, NAW 812.00/30583).

20. On May 23, 1938, the New York Times predicted that Cárdenas was going to take quite a while to settle the Cedillo problem.

21. Cedillo was killed in a skirmish with the federal army at the beginning of 1939.

22. Chargé d'Affaires William P. Blacker to Department of State, August 17, 1937, NAW 812.00/30485.

23. Memorandum from Division of the American Republics, May 27, 1938, NAW 812.6363/4104.

24. In a communiqué from the U.S. embassy to the Department of State Generals Abelardo Rodríguez, Manuel Avila Camacho, Román Yocupicio, and Saturnino Cedillo were mentioned as possible conspirators, though the embassy considered that these rumors were not well founded (April 20, 1938, NAW 812.6363/3574; Pierre Boal, counselor of embassy, to Department of State, May 3 and 14, 1938, NAW 812.6363/3858; 812.00/30557; U.S. consul in Tampico to Department of State, May 3, 1938, NAW 812.6363/3816).

25. U.S. consul in Tampico to Department of State, May 13, 1938, NAW 812.6363/3905; memorandum of the Department of State, May 13, 1938, NAW 812.6363/3958. Prior to his uprising Cedillo had entered into contact with various fascist-type organizations such as the National Union of Veterans of the Revolution, the Middle Class Confederation, the Employers Center of Mexico, and Mexican Revolutionary Action. For a review of this situation see Manuel Fernández Boyoli and Enrique Marrón de Angelis, Lo que no se sabe de la rebelión cedillista; Betty Kirk, Covering the Mexican Front: The Battle of Europe versus America.

26. Editorial in Problemas agrícolas e industriales de México 7 (July–September 1955): 7, 15.

27. El Nacional, March 31, 1938.

28. The aim of the recently formed PRM, according to point 4 in its declaration of principles, was no less than to prepare the country for a workers' democracy, which in turn would lead eventually to a socialist regime.

29. See the manifesto Frente Constitucional Democrático Mexicano of September 15, 1938; U.S. consul in Ciudad Juárez, August 12, 1938, NAW 812.00/30608; U.S. consul in Nuevo Laredo, November 28, 1938, NAW 812.00/30650.

30. While in 1940 the FBI was preparing for a communist uprising, the earlier reports on file mentioned only rumors about Calles and Amaro (Department of Justice, January 31, 1939, NAW 812.00/310011½, 31073; Pierre Boal to Department of State, May 17, 1939, NAW 812.6363/5414).

31. Ambassador Daniels to Department of State, March 6, 1939, NAW 812.00/30704.

32. Military Attaché McCoy, August 1, 1939, NAW 812.00/30819.

33. Herbert Bursley of the Division of the American Republics, in a memorandum to Laurence Duggan of that same office, called these declarations "a double-barreled play for the sympathy of this government with Almazán's campaign" (August 2, 1939, NAW 812.00/30801).

34. Personal letter from Pierre Boal to Laurence Duggan, July 11, 1939, NAW 812.00/30774½.

35. Memorandum of a conversation between Herbert Bursley of the Department of State and William B. Richardson of the National City Bank in Mexico, May 18, 1940, NAW 812.00/31055.

36. Ambassador Daniels to Department of State, March 6, 1939, NAW 812.00/30704.

37. U.S. consul in Chihuahua to Department of State, June 24, 1940, NAW 812.00/31114.

38. Herbert Bursley to Laurence Duggan, Division of the American Republics, September 12, 1939, NAW 812.6354/14.

39. U.S. consul general to Department of State, July 10, 1939 and report of Naval Attaché Dillon, April 16, 1940, NAW 812.00/31010½.

40. For an example of Amaro's propaganda, see *Excélsior*, November 23, 1939.

41. See previous document and also Ambassador Daniels to Department of State, December 22, 1939, NAW 812.00/30874.

42. Pierre Boal to Department of State, June 13, 1939, NAW 812.248/286; U.S. consul in Ciudad Juárez to Department of State, July 6, 1939, NAW 812.00/30762.

43. U.S. consul in Monterrey to Department of State, April 20, 1940, NAW 812.00/31013; naval attaché to Department of Navy, May 17, 1940, NAW 812.00/31109.

44. See, for example, article in the London *Times*, March 14, 1940.

45. Report by Pierre Boal to Department of State of conversation with Ricardo Rubio in the Ministry of Government, NAW 812.00/31042.

46. See various reports filed by the U.S. consuls in Ciudad Juárez and Chihuahua during the month of September 1940 and memorandums of the Department of State of October 17 and 29, 1940, NAW 812.00/31398, 31422, 31423, 31507, 31544.

47. See General Juan Andreu Almazán's statements on his return from the United States, reported in *El Universal*, November 27, 1940.

48. Ambassador Daniels to Department of State, November 1, 1940, NAW 812.00/31547; U.S. consul in Chihuahua to Department of State, September 24, 1940, NAW 812.00/31442.

49. In June 1938 the State Department believed that Mexico was capable of solving the technical problems of its nationalized industry because its immigration policies had permitted the formation of an adequate nucleus of technicians (memorandum of the Division of the American Republics, June 23, 1938, NAW 812.6363/4286).

50. Right after the expropriation American businessmen predicted that the nationalized industry would be bankrupt within a short time (Laurence Duggan, Division of the American Republics, to Under Secretary of State Welles, March 30, 1938, NAW). Within the State Department it was also thought that the Mexican undertaking would fail, but not so much because of its inability to run the industry as because of contravening economic pressure (memorandum signed by the Adviser on International Economic Affairs, April 12, 1938, NAW 812.6363/3513). In the opinion of some observers the companies' equipment in 1938 was old and out of date, and it was precisely the fact that the machinery was relatively unsophisticated and less complicated to operate that contributed in some measure to the national enterprise's success (Paul Nathan, "México en la época de Cárdenas," *Problemas agrícolas e industriales de México* 7 (July–September 1955): 130.

51. Cárdenas met with the oil leaders in March 1940 and tried to make them under-

stand that it was impossible for PEMEX (Petróleos Mexicanos) to meet the terms of the 1937 award, and that it was necessary to go ahead with the reorganization of an industry whose work force had increased from 15,895 to 22,206, thanks to union maneuvers, despite the fact that its operations had fallen off considerably. The president asked the STPRM to release 2,592 unnecessary workers and return 22 million pesos lost through incompetence and corruption attributable to the union. The oil leaders refused to meet these demands and PEMEX had to go before the JFCA—an economic conflict! At the end of the year, as was to be expected, the JFCA approved the cutbacks on the work force and in the salaries. The threatened strike did not materialize, and the government won the day, although the problem continued to fester until as late as 1942 (Merrill Rippy, "El petróleo y la Revolución Mexicana," *Problemas agrícolas e industriales de México* 6 (July–September 1954): 141–152; Kirk, *Covering the Mexican Front*, pp. 65–69.

52. In a letter dated May 9, 1938, Thomas R. Armstrong of Standard Oil of New Jersey suggested to Under Secretary of State Welles that Cárdenas could use the courts to return the companies' property; other alternatives were arbitration or even direct and open return without recourse to any juridical subterfuge (NAW 812.6363/4003).

53. Memorandum signed by Herbert Bursley, Division of the American Republics, December 2, 1938, NAW 812.6363/5156.

54. See [Oil companies], *Demanda de amparo y recurso administrativo de revocación contra el Decreto de Expropiación de la industria petrolera*; Standard Oil of New Jersey, *The Mexican Expropriation in International Law*, pp. 38–50.

55. NAW 812.6363/4154.

56. NAW 812.6363/4379.

57. NAW 812.6363/4942.

58. *Excélsior*, December 5, 1939; NAW 812.6363/635.

59. NAW 812.6363/4998; Luis G. Zorrilla, *Historia de las relaciones entre México y los Estados Unidos de América*, p. 474.

60. Memorandum from Herbert Bursley to Laurence Duggan, Division of the American Republics, and to Under Secretary Welles, December 8, 1939, NAW 812.6363/6386.

61. Ambassador Daniels to Department of State, January 5, 1940, NAW 812.6363/6417.

62. Ambassador Daniels to Department of State, January 20, 1940, NAW 812.6363/6454.

63. Huasteca Petroleum Company and Standard Oil of California, *Expropiación: Un estudio de los hechos, causas, métodos y efectos de la dominación política de la industria en México*, pp. 19–32.

64. Memorandum signed by A. A. O'Neill, Legal Adviser, Department of State, April 11, 1938, NAW 812.6363/3359.

65. Actually these rumors had begun to circulate even before March 18. Early in 1938 Huasteca's Lawrence Anderson told the U.S. embassy it was impossible to keep operations going under the Cárdenas administration (Edmund David Cronon, *Josephus Daniels in Mexico*, p. 180). News of the expropriation brought predictions by *Paris Soir*, the *Houston Post*, and the London *Times* of an immediate uprising in Mexico. In some circles it was thought that General Juan Andreu Almazán, who had close ties with the oil firms, would try to mobilize part of the army on his side (Mexico, Secretaría del Patrimonio Nacional, *El petróleo de México: Recopilación de documentos oficiales de orden económico de la industria petrolera, con una introducción que resume sus motivos y consecuencias*, p. 24).

66. On August 30 Daniels reported to Secretary of State Hull that many of the Americans living in Mexico were in favor of using armed force to solve the oil con-

troversy (JDP). Shortly thereafter the ambassador wrote to his son that he had had a talk with Elmer R. Jones of Wells, Fargo and Company, whose views were representative of a certain sector of American investors, and that Jones was in favor of annexation of Mexico by the United States (September 7, 1938, JDP). A month later Daniels reported to his son a conversation with G. Maton of the British-American Tobacco Company—whom he qualified as one of the most intelligent members of the American colony—in which Maton advised a diplomatic breakoff. This businessman felt that Mexico would be better off with the kind of government that Guatemala had—namely, one headed by a benevolent despot. Daniels remarked that these investors would be just as happy if Latin America were governed entirely by fascists (October 22, 1938, JDP).

67. Ambassador Daniels, aware of the tremendous support that Cárdenas had, rejected these reports from an official of Standard Oil (Daniels to his son, April 9, 1938, JDP).

68. Prior to the expropriation, Noyola was negotiating with some of the oil firms for a 150,000-peso loan for Cedillo, which was apparently never made (Fernández Boyoli and Marrón de Angelis, *Lo que no se sabe . . .* , p. 171; Jesús Silva Herzog, *Petróleo mexicano*, pp. 156–157).

69. Ambassador Daniels to Department of State, March 28, 1938, NAW 812.6363/3228.

70. Memorandum of conversation between Assistant Secretary of State A. A. Berle, Jr., and oil company representative George McDonald, April 21, 1938, NAW 812.6363/3745.

71. U.S. consul in Tampico to Department of State, May 3, 1938, NAW 812.6363/3816; Pierre Boal to Department of State, June 14, 1938, NAW 812.6363/4227.

72. T. R. Armstrong, Standard Oil of New Jersey, to Laurence Duggan, Division of the American Republics, June 3, 1938, NAW 812.6363/4143.

73. The speeches were given on April 21 in Mexico City and May 12 in San Luis Potosí. In private Eduardo Hay and Ramón Beteta told U.S. Counselor of Embassy Pierre Boal that Cárdenas' information was reliable (memorandum of Division of the American Republics, May 20, 1938, NAW 812.6363/4025).

74. Pierre Boal to Department of State, May 17, 1938, NAW 812.6363/4017. A statement of denial by the companies appeared in *Novedades*, May 20, 1938.

75. *El Nacional*, June 17, 1938.

76. According to a memorandum to the Division of the American Republics, Cedillo told the head of American Bond and Share in San Luis Potosí that he was counting on support from the Gold Shirts and Mexican elements in Texas (May 19, 1938, NAW 812.6363/4021).

77. According to Nathaniel and Silvia Weyl, General Nicolás Rodríguez, leader of the Gold Shirts, promised the oil firms that he would revoke both the expropriation decree and Article 27 if he got to be president. This rebel leader was to receive between 2 and 10 million dollars from the companies, laundered through Cuba and Canada. In the end, for reasons that are not very clear, the plan never actually went forward ("La reconquista de México," p. 289; U.S. consul in Nuevo Laredo to Department of State, May 13, 1938, NAW 812.6363/3905).

78. U.S. consul in Chihuahua to Department of State, June 27 and 30, 1939, NAW 812.00/359, 361. Almazán came out in support of the expropriation in *El Universal*, August 18, 1939.

79. The oil firms' intention to bankroll Avila Camacho is reported in U.S. consul in Ciudad Juárez to Laurence Duggan, Division of the American Republics, June 26, 1939, and also in a State Department memorandum of June 30, 1939, NAW 812.6363/5873½; 812.00 Chihuahua/361.

80. Memorandum from Pierre Boal to Laurence Duggan, Division of the American

Republics, reporting a conversation with Villaseñor, December 1, 1939, NAW 812.00/30879½.

81. Report of Department of Justice, June 10, 1940, NAW 812.00/31102; report of special agent Don Owen to Department of State, July 13, 1940, NAW 812.00/31246.

82. Memorandum of a conversation between Under Secretary Welles and Ambassador Castillo Nájera, May 24, 1940, NAW 812.00/31005.

83. Department of Justice to Department of State, January 31, 1939, NAW 812.6363/5414; Herbert Bursley to Laurence Duggan, Division of the American Republics, December 15, 1939, NAW 812.00/30880.

84. Carroll Kilpatrick, in a letter to Ambassador Daniels dated September 5, 1938, insinuated that one of the oil firms was prepared to deliver 1 million dollars to anyone who would mount a rebellion against Cárdenas if the State Department would support the plan (JDP).

85. According to a confidential government report of July 29, 1940, cited by Silva Herzog, Standard Oil and El Aguila entered into contact with certain of the labor leaders and offered them economic support in exchange for their opposition to the government's plan for reorganization. According to the report, one of the leaders agreed with the companies to organize a strike in the event the government went forward with its scheme. In another similar document dated July 30 reference was made to an agreement with Standard Oil of New Jersey and California and El Aguila for the establishment of an aid fund for the STPRM in the eventuality of a strike: the British were to put up 50 per cent and the Americans the other half. The report also mentioned plans for sparking unrest in the oil camps. Several of the accidents that took place at that time gave the appearance of sabotage. In August 1940 Silva Herzog himself resigned from the board of Distribuidora after documents from several secret deals made by its employees were published in the United States (Silva Herzog, *Petróleo mexicano,* pp. 274–284).

86. Standard Oil of New Jersey, *Respuesta de las compañías petroleras al documento del Gobierno Mexicano intitulado "La verdad sobre la expropiación de los bienes de las empresas petroleras,"* p. 4. Standard sent propaganda to be distributed among the workers in Tampico (Pierre Boal to Department of State, June 21, 1938, NAW 812.6363/4280).

87. Kirk, *Covering the Mexican Front,* pp. 174–176. An example of the kind of problems that arose between PEMEX and the oil workers was the stoppage on the part of certain key employees in Tampico at the end of May 1939, which caused losses running in the thousands of pesos. It was claimed to be the work of the expropriated firms in *El Mundo* and *Excélsior,* June 1, 1939.

88. The fact that Washington was prepared to accept Mexico's right to expropriate as long as sufficient and immediate payment was made led the companies to claim that they had been abandoned (Daniels, *Shirt-Sleeve Diplomat,* p. 231).

89. Memorandum of a conversation between Secretary of State Hull and various oil company representatives, April 4, 1938, NAW 812.6363/3449.

90. Daniels to Department of State, April 16, 1938, JDP; Pierre Boal to Department of State, May 2, 1938, NAW 812.6363/3781; T. R. Armstrong, Standard Oil of New Jersey, to Secretary of State Hull, June 16, 1938, NAW 812.6363/4205. Through various channels the companies insisted up until 1942 that the only possibility for an agreement with Mexico depended on the return of their property.

91. According to the companies, Mexico had taken only their physical property but not such "intangible factors" as their technical know-how, managerial ability, etc., and therefore sooner or later the nationalized industry would go bankrupt. The firms' position was set forth in a series of pamphlets published by Standard Oil of New Jersey during 1938–1940: *Confiscation or Expropriation? Mexico's Seizure of the*

Foreign-owned Oil Industry; Denials of Justice; Diplomatic Protection; Empty Promises; Investments and Trade; The Fine Art of Squeezing; The Mexican Expropriation in International Law; The Reply to Mexico; The Solution for the Mexican Confiscation; They Took What They Wanted; Whose Oil Is It? The Question of Subsoil Rights in Mexico. See also Huasteca Petroleum Company, *Expropriation; New York Times,* March 22, 1938.

92. Standard Oil's pamphlet *Confiscation or Expropriation?* claimed that the very structure of world trade was in danger owing to the Mexican government's action, for if private property can be taken at will without prompt and adequate payment, it said, the whole basis of relations among sovereign states is undermined (pp. 93–94).

93. Some of the numerous messages of this kind which were received may be consulted in the respective country files in AREM III/628 "938"/2 L-E-555–558.

94. The Bolivian expropriation was less important in terms of both its magnitude and the fact that it was not the product of a predetermined policy. The 1938 Bolivian controversy was brought on by failure to pay taxes and illegal exportation of fuel; the most unfair part was that no compensation was paid to the affected firm. In the case of Mexico the U.S. government was able to give relatively effective support to Standard Oil, whereas with Bolivia it extended no help whatsoever and even kept third-party countries from giving any aid (Bryce Wood, *The Making of Good Neighbor Policy,* pp. 186–197).

95. *New York Times,* March 27, 1938.

96. The U.S. ambassador in Peru and the chargé d'affaires in Chile informed the State Department that if pressure were not put on Mexico their countries could easily follow its example (March 28 and April 5, 1938, respectively, NAW 812.6363/3380, 3425). The Bolivian Supreme Court's ratification of the expropriation decree on March 11, 1939, was an indirect result of the Mexican situation. However, the pressure placed on this country in 1944 led it to retract and return the expropriated holdings to Standard. Nor was the Mexican oil policy unrelated to the takeover of six British and American refineries in Uruguay—or for that matter to the relatively nationalist laws passed in Colombia, Cuba, Ecuador, and, to some extent, Venezuela in 1943 (Kirk, *Covering the Mexican Front,* pp. 200–201; Daniel Durand, *La política petrolera internacional,* p. 50). In Geneva in 1939, during the course of a labor congress, the Uruguayan delegate declared that if foreign capitalists in Latin America did not change their ways the other governments of the region would be obliged to follow Mexico's example (*New York Times,* June 21, 1939).

97. T. R. Armstrong, Standard Oil of New Jersey, to Laurence Duggan, Division of the American Republics, September 1, 1938, NAW 812.6363/4708.

98. Department of State to U.S. legation in Caracas and reply thereto, September 7 and 14, NAW 812.6363/4708, 4775.

99. Deputy Minister of Foreign Affairs Ramón Beteta to Mexican missions abroad, March 9, 1938, AREM III/628 "938"/2 L-E-555, part 1, f. 4.

100. U.S. embassy in London to Department of State, March 24, 1938, NAW 812.6363/3301; British embassy in Washington to Under Secretary Welles, March 25, 1938, and appended document dated March 28, NAW 812.6363/3311.

101. Memorandum of conversation between Secretary of State Hull and Sir Ronald Lindsay, British ambassador in Washington, March 30, 1938, NAW 812.6363/3321.

102. According to a report by the Mexican minister in London to the Ministry of Foreign Affairs, the British were hoping for an uprising against Cárdenas that would bring about a change of government; the chances of an economic collapse in Mexico were seen as less probable (March 3, 1938, AREM III/"938"/2 L-E-575, Inglaterra, part 2, f. 84).

103. Ambassador Castillo Nájera to Ministry of Foreign Affairs, March 31, 1938, AREM III/628 "938"/2 L-E-558, Estados Unidos, f. 100.

104. Cárdenas' personal diary as quoted in *El Universal*, October 22, 1970.

105. Mexico, Departamento Autónomo de Prensa y Propaganda, *Notas diplomáticas cruzadas entre los gobiernos de México y la Gran Bretaña con motivo de la expropiación de la industria petrolera;* M. Rippy, "El petróleo y la Revolución Mexicana," pp. 125–127; Manuel González Ramírez, *El petróleo mexicano: La expropiación petrolera ante el derecho internacional,* pp. 29–34; Silva Herzog, *Petróleo mexicano,* pp. 57–58. The original notes exchanged between Mexico and Great Britain are found in AREM III/628 "938"/2 L-E-600, Inglaterra. See also communication from Mexican minister in France to deputy minister of foreign affairs, January 13, 1939, and reply thereto of February 22, as well as note from the Mexican minister to the French minister of foreign affairs, January 12, 1939, AREM III/628 "938"/2 L-E-601, Francia, ff. 46, 53–58.

106. The Dutch notes of March 15, April 4, June 27, July 12, and October 27, 1938, together with the Mexican replies thereto, are on file under AREM III/628 "938"/2 L-E-560, Holanda, ff. 1–48.

107. Padilla Nervo at The Hague to Ministry of Foreign Affairs, November 10, 1938, AREM III/628 "938"/2 L-E-560, Holanda, f. 83.

108. Oil companies to Department of State, March 22, 1938, NAW 812.6363/3159. Strictly speaking, the companies were not justified in filing their petition, since they had not exhausted all their legal recourses.

109. Memorandum signed by Laurence Duggan, Division of the American Republics, March 28, 1938, NAW 812.6363/3337.

110. In a letter to Ambassador Claude Bowers in Spain, Daniels complained that in reality the philosophy of the New Deal and the Good Neighbor policy was scorned by the career diplomats, and that even among Roosevelt's appointees some of them practiced it only verbally (September 6, 1938, JDP).

111. Cronon, *Josephus Daniels in Mexico,* pp. 275–286.

112. Daniels wrote to Claude Bowers on September 27, 1938, that justice and honesty among the nations of America, which were the basis of the Good Neighbor policy, were not easy to come by when the bulk of the resources in the countries belonged to foreigners (JDP). In his earlier letter of September 6 Daniels had told his colleague that in Mexico the Spaniards had been succeeded by the Dohenys, the Cowdrays, and other exploiters who apparently thought that the Mexicans had been born to make foreigners rich and that God had put important natural resources in Mexican subsoil to enhance the fortunes already in their coffers (JDP). In his July 4 speech of that year the ambassador asserted that one of the reasons why democracy was in danger in the world was that, in addition to unemployment, the people were not receiving a fair share of the product of their natural resources or of their labor. Shortly afterward Daniels was to suggest to Secretary of State Hull that the companies should be agreeing to a salary raise for the workers instead of fighting the decisions of the Mexican courts (Daniels to Hull, July 26, 1938, JDP).

113. Daniels to Under Secretary of State Welles, March 25, 1938, JDP; Cronon, *Josephus Daniels in Mexico,* p. 187.

114. In a letter to Bowers, Daniels deplored the fact that the State Department was vigorously demanding payment from Mexico while Great Britain and France said nothing—adding that he did not understand this kind of diplomacy (September 6, 1938, JDP).

115. From 1938 up to the end of his assignment in Mexico, Daniels urged Roosevelt to follow Wilson's example and not be swayed by those who were demanding an aggressive policy toward Mexico. Such an attitude was not justified and seriously

threatened the Good Neighbor policy, which was the only hope for preserving democracy in Latin America (Daniels to Roosevelt, March 22, 1938, and May 4, 1940, as well as speech delivered by Daniels in Dallas, Texas, on December 2, 1939, JDP).

116. Pierre Boal to Department of State, March 30, 1938, NAW 812.6363/3319½.

117. Ambassador Daniels to Department of State, April 1, 1938, NAW 812.6363/3262. The ambassador proposed that he speak personally with John D. Rockefeller and attempt to persuade him to accept the expropriation as a fait accompli and begin negotiations with the Mexican government; the State Department was opposed (Daniels, *Shirt Sleeve Diplomat*, pp. 230–241).

118. An excellent document for seeing the difference in attitude between Ambassador Daniels and the personnel in the State Department is a memorandum reporting a telephone conversation between Pierre Boal, counselor in the embassy, and Laurence Duggan, chief of the Division of the American Republics (March 21, 1938, NAW 812.6363/3146).

119. Ambassador Daniels urged President Roosevelt on various occasions, without much success, to go ahead with the plan made before the expropriation for him to visit Mexico (Daniels to Roosevelt, May 12, July 24, and November 6, 1939, JDP). At the request of Foreign Affairs Minister Hay, Daniels agreed, without consulting with Secretary of State Hull, to consider that the note he delivered to Foreign Affairs on March 26, 1938, was not received. In this note the State Department had used a particularly offensive tone which Daniels felt could have led to a diplomatic breakoff (Daniels to his son, July 23, 1938, JDP; Daniels, *Shirt-Sleeve Diplomat*, pp. 235–236; Cronon, *Josephus Daniels in Mexico*, pp. 196–198). Bryce Wood regards this act as almost unique in the annals of modern U.S. diplomacy and suggests that Daniels got away with it only because of his friendship with Roosevelt (*The Making of Good Neighbor Policy*, pp. 210–213, 218).

120. In the fall of 1938 Daniels wrote to his son that he believed President Cárdenas had one of the most difficult jobs in the world and that he hoped this time he would accomplish his aims and give the Indians the chance they had never had (October 29, 1938, JDP). Later, when his assignment in Mexico was coming to an end in 1941, the old Democrat wrote a short farewell note to Cárdenas—who had already turned the reins over to his successor, Manuel Avila Camacho—in which he said, "Your place is safe in history along with [Benito] Juárez" (November 6, 1941, JDP).

121. On April 14, 1938, Thomas R. Armstrong of Standard Oil of New Jersey wrote to Laurence Duggan, Division of the American Republics, that Ambassador Daniels' public statements on the expropriation were giving the idea that Washington supported Mexico's action (NAW 812.6363/3562). Daniels, for his part, wrote to his son that a high-ranking oil company official was saying that the expropriation was the result of a scheme elaborated by Cárdenas, Francisco Castillo Nájera, Ramón Beteta, Francisco Múgica, Leon Trotsky, Vicente Lombardo Toledano, and Daniels himself (July 2, 1938, JDP). For a review of the debate on the subject in the U.S. Congress, see the *Congressional Record* 84, no. 37 (February 23, 1939): 2569.

122. Ambassador Daniels to Department of State, March 28, 1938, NAW 812.6363/3228.

123. Report of FBI to Department of Justice, June 12, 1940, NAW 812.00/31174. As an example of the FBI's activities in Mexico, see report of August 9, 1941, NAW 812.00/31759.

124. Memorandum signed by Herbert Bursley, Division of the American Republics, June 19, 1940, NAW 812.00/31174.

125. Daniels wrote to President Roosevelt shortly after the expropriation that the two main obstacles in U.S.-Mexican relations were the oil firms' intransigence and the Mexican government's empty coffers. In August he announced that for the first

time in a long while relations between the two countries were cordial; Mexico felt that Roosevelt understood its problems and its aims. He added that it would be a calamity if this spirit were lost, which had already been upset and threatened. The president, he said, should not give in to the companies' pressure but have patience instead; in reality, all that Cárdenas had in mind was to have his own New Deal. Later he conveyed the Mexican president's desire to enter into discussions with the United States so as to see if Latin America could keep from getting involved in the world conflict (Daniels to Roosevelt, March 30 and August 31, 1938, and November 4, 1939, JDP).

126. Daniels to President Roosevelt, September 15, 1938, JDP.

127. Secretary of State Hull did not agree with President Roosevelt because he considered that the Mexican properties were subject to the international code of justice (Cronon, *Josephus Daniels in Mexico*, pp. 146–147).

128. A year afterward, on October 7, 1939, Cárdenas sent a personal message to Roosevelt expressing his gratification at the understanding shown toward Mexico's right to expropriate the oil industry (Francisco Cuevas Cancino, *Roosevelt y la Buena Vecindad*, p. 286).

129. President Roosevelt to Daniels, February 15, 1939, JDP; *New York Times*, April 2, 1938.

130. On this point the State Department agreed with Ambassador Daniels, who warned Secretary Hull that to start an uprising in Mexico would be the worst crime perpetrated in the Western Hemisphere since the days of Victoriano Huerta (Daniels, *Shirt-Sleeve Diplomat*, p. 230). Assistant Secretary of State Adolf A. Berle, Jr., indicated in private that to help start a rebellion in Mexico would be "an extremely dangerous mistake" (Wood, *The Making of Good Neighbor Policy*, p. 221). Attempts to smuggle arms for Cedillo across the border were frustrated by the U.S. authorities (Nathan, "México en la época de Cárdenas," p. 153). According to Senator Dennis Chavez from New Mexico, the companies did not fail to show their dissatisfaction over the U.S. refusal to defend their interests (Daniels to President Roosevelt, April 4, 1938, JDP).

131. Daniels, *Shirt-Sleeve Diplomat*, p. 227.

132. Treasury Secretary Morgenthau wrote in his diary that Secretary of State Hull considered the Mexican government to be full of communists and that, even though Ambassador Daniels and President Roosevelt had given it to think it could get away with what it was doing, he, Hull, was determined to see that it did not (Wood, *The Making of Good Neighbor Policy*, p. 217).

133. Cronon, *Josephus Daniels in Mexico*, pp. 193–194.

134. The State Department made no effort to block the purchase of Mexican oil by private parties in the United States, but it did warn them that they were "fishing in dangerous waters" (Cronon, *Josephus Daniels in Mexico*, p. 203; Wood, *The Making of Good Neighbor Policy*, pp. 230–232).

135. Secretary of State Hull to Ambassador Daniels, March 26, 1938, and Daniels to Hull, March 27, 1938, NAW 812.6363/3159A, 3160; Cronon, *Josephus Daniels in Mexico*, p. 197.

136. Cronon, *Josephus Daniels in Mexico*, p. 187. Under Secretary of State Sumner Welles met with the Mexican ambassador and pointed out to him that if the decree were not revoked Mexico would be embarking on a suicidal policy since it was in no condition to run the industry that it had taken over. Whereupon Cárdenas informed Ambassador Castillo Nájera personally that there was no chance of Mexico turning back (Francisco Castillo Nájera, *El petróleo en la industria moderna: Las compañías petroleras y los gobiernos de México*, pp. 41–42; Wood, *The Making of Good Neighbor Policy*, p. 207; Cronon, *Josephus Daniels in Mexico*, pp. 187–188).

137. Memorandum of a conversation between Under Secretary of State Sumner Welles and Ambassador Castillo Nájera, March 21, 1938, NAW 812.6363/3153.

138. Ambassador Castillo Nájera to Ministry of Foreign Affairs, March 25, 1938, AREM III/628 "938"/2 L-E-558, Estados Unidos, ff. 50–51.

139. Ambassador Daniels to Department of State, March 20, 1938, NAW 812.6363/ 3097.

140. Mexico, Departamento Autónomo de Prensa y Propaganda, *Notas diplomáticas . . .* ; M. Rippy, "El petróleo y la Revolución Mexicana," pp. 125–127; González Ramírez, *El petróleo mexicano*, pp. 29–34; Silva Herzog, *Petróleo mexicano*, pp. 57–58. In September 1939 Holland and Great Britain, under pressure because of the European conflict, attempted to bring the State Department around to their side and get their property returned once and for all (pp. 235–236), but Secretary Hull refused to join in a "united front."

141. Oil companies to Department of State, April 8, 1938, NAW 812.6363/3386.

142. *Washington Post*, March 24, 1938.

143. Ambassador Daniels to Department of State, March 21 and 22, 1938, NAW 812.6363/3109, 3122, 3141.

144. NAW 812.6363/3190A.

145. On March 25 Ambassador Castillo Nájera had reported that the Department of State's reaction was not as strong as had been predicted, but in a telephone call to the Ministry of Foreign Affairs on March 28, following a conversation with Under Secretary Welles, he indicated that the situation was worsening considerably (AREM III/628 "938", L-E-558, Estados Unidos, ff. 20, 54).

146. Secretary of State Hull to Ambassador Daniels and Daniels to Hull, March 27, 1938; Daniels to Department of State, March 29; memorandum of a conversation between Pierre Boal and Daniels in Mexico and Hull in Washington, March 29—NAW 812.6363/3190B, 3163–64, 3203, 3270.

147. Ambassador Daniels to Department of State, March 31, 1938, NAW 812.6363/ 3245.

148. Memorandum of a meeting held between Under Secretary of State Welles and representatives of the oil companies, April 21, 1938, NAW 812.6363/3701.

149. Memorandum of a conversation between Under Secretary Welles and Ambassador Castillo Nájera, March 31, 1938, NAW 812.6363/3341.

150. Under Secretary of State Welles to Ambassador Castillo Nájera, May 9, 1938, AREM III/628 "938"/2 L-E-558, Estados Unidos, ff. 108–110.

151. *El Universal*, July 20, 1938.

152. Ambassador Daniels to Department of State and Secretary of State Hull to Daniels, July 21, 1938, NAW 812.6363/4424, 4441A.

153. Memorandum signed by Laurence Duggan, Division of the American Republics, November 4, 1938, NAW 812.6363/5098. The State Department was upset by the companies' lack of discretion.

154. This problem is reviewed in a personal letter of mid-August from Counselor of Embassy Pierre Boal to Laurence Duggan, chief of the Division of the American Republics. Boal felt that Cárdenas had to a considerable extent kept the Mexican public from understanding the real U.S. position (NAW 812.6363/30774½).

155. Ambassador Daniels to Department of State, April 7, 1938, NAW 812.6363/ 3417; memorandum of the Division of the American Republics, June 3, 1938, NAW 812.6363/4292; Laurence Duggan, Division of the American Republics, to Under Secretary of State Welles, October 10, 1938, NAW 812.6363/4835.

156. In a letter of March 27, 1938, Ambassador Daniels urged Secretary of State Hull not to provoke a diplomatic rupture with Mexico (NAW 812.6363/3167). The notes of March 26 and August 22, 1938, worried Daniels very much (*Shirt-Sleeve*

Diplomat, pp. 235–236; letter to his son, August 27, 1938, JDP). The August 22 note was viewed as an ultimatum by Merrill Rippy ("El petróleo y la Revolución Mexicana," p. 63). In September, Pierre Boal, then in the Division of the American Republics in Washington, warned Daniels that there was a good chance relations with Mexico would reach the "danger point" unless the ambassador changed his attitude (Boal to Daniels, September 21, 1938, JDP). The note of April 3 was characterized as "interventionist" by the Mexican press.

157. In the summer of 1938 Washington demanded payment of 10 million dollars in compensation for expropriated agricultural lands, turning down the Mexican proposal for settlement in installments (Howard F. Cline, *The United States and Mexico*, p. 245; Cronon, *Josephus Daniels in Mexico*, pp. 212–216). Cárdenas had not expected this reaction from the State Department; he thought the U.S. government realized it was impossible to hold back agrarian reform and the expropriation of foreign property and still keep domestic peace in Mexico (Professor Frank Tannenbaum to Daniels, July 6, 1938, JDP).

158. Ambassador Daniels to Department of State, April 5, 1938, NAW 812.6363/ 3358; memorandum of a conversation between Under Secretary Welles and Ambassador Castillo Nájera, December 11, 1939, and another of a meeting of Welles, Castillo Nájera, and Eduardo Suárez, January 11, 1940, NAW 812.6363/6354½, 6451.

159. On April 11, 1938, the Independent International Committee for Defaulted Mexican External Obligations asked Secretary of State Hull that they be included in any settlement of the oil debt, but on April 22 he turned them down and suggested that their claims be handled through the powerful International Committee of Bankers on Mexico (NAW 812.51/2278).

160. The U.S. note of April 3 was addressed to Ambassador Castillo Nájera and signed by Secretary of State Hull. On March 16 Castillo Nájera delivered a memorandum to Hull informing him that Mexico would not agree to arbitration; formal denial followed in a note of May 1, 1940 (AREM III/628 "938"/ 1 L-E-607, Arbitraje, ff. 6–14 and part 2, ff. 2–6. William C. Townsend characterized Hull's attitude as that of a Shylock demanding a pound of Mexico's flesh (*The Truth about Mexico's Oil*, p. 56).

161. Mexico, *La verdad sobre la expropiación de los bienes de las empresas petroleras*, p. 262; Daniels to his son, July 30, 1938, JDP. Ambassador Castillo Nájera told Secretary of State Hull on February 19, 1940, that his government would agree to arbitration only after all other possibilities for reaching a settlement were exhausted. In the Mexican note of May 1, 1940, Washington was reminded that when Mexico had consented to arbitrate the differences in the Chamizal border dispute the United States had failed to abide by the court's decision. In the capital the CTM organized demonstrations against arbitration.

162. Following Roosevelt's victory at the polls, Cárdenas sent a message congratulating him and letting him know that the American peoples, bowed down by the pressure of international capitalism aspiring to dominate national economies, were looking to the U.S. government for justice (November 27, 1940, JDP). For a study of the U.S. notes of March 26, June 29, July 21, August 22, and November 9, 1938, and April 3, 1940, together with the Mexican replies of August 3 and September 10, 1938, and May 1, 1940, see NAW 812.6363/6659A and 6836; United States, Department of State, *Foreign Relations of the United States: Diplomatic Papers, 1940*, vol. 5; Under Secretary of State Welles to Ambassador Castillo Nájera, June 29, 1938, JDP; Standard Oil of New Jersey, *Present Status of the Mexican Oil Expropriation*, pp. 50–51; M. Rippy, "El petróleo y la Revolución Mexicana," pp. 62–67; Cronon, *Josephus Daniels in Mexico*, pp. 22, 226–228; Isidro Fabela, "La política internacional del Presidente Cárdenas," *Problemas agrícolas y industriales de México* 7 (October–December 1955): 98–99; Jesús Silva Herzog, *Historia de la expropiación petrolera*, pp. 141–147; Daniels, *Shirt-Sleeve Diplomat*, pp. 232–235.

163. N. B. Tanner, "Diplomacy of the Expropriation of the American Oil Industry in Mexico" (Master's thesis, Texas College of Arts and Industries, 1940), p. 66.

164. Memorandum of a conversation between R. C. Tanis, Division of the American Republics, and the local representative of Standard Oil of New Jersey, March 19, 1938, NAW 812.6363/5149.

165. Memorandum of a meeting of Briggs and Herbert Bursley of the Division of the American Republics and a representative of Standard Oil of New Jersey, November 14, 1938, NAW 812.6363/5149.

166. For an understanding of Secretary of State Cordell Hull's views on fascist influence in the Western Hemisphere, see *The Memoirs of Cordell Hull*, pp. 493–503, 601 ff., 813 ff.

167. Alejandro Carrillo, *The Mexican People and the Oil Companies*, p. 28.

168. Cronon, *Josephus Daniels in Mexico*, p. 212.

169. The American press never ceased to be conscious of the fascist threat in Mexico (Kirk, *Covering the Mexican Front*, pp. 223, 275, 281, 285; *Dallas News*, June 13, 1940). Also, this threat was frequently exaggerated in the U.S. media as part of the campaign to discredit Cárdenas. Ambassador Daniels was obliged to deny these rumors on numerous occasions (Daniels to Secretary of State Hull, August 20, 1938, JDP). See also *San Francisco Chronicle*, May 15, 1940; *Washington Times-Herald*, June 15, 1940.

170. Kirk, *Covering the Mexican Front*, p. 275. Other similarly oriented groups were the Social Democratic Party (Partido Social Demócrata), the Confederation of Independent Parties (Confederación de Partidos Independientes), the Middle Class Confederation (Confederación de la Clase Media), the Spanish Anticommunist and Anti-Semitic Association (Asociación Española Anticomunista y Antijudía), the Countrymen's Phalanx (Falange Poblana), the Nationalist Civic Action (Acción Cívica Nacionalista), and the Nationalist Youth of Mexico (Juventudes Nacionalistas de México) (José Mancisidor, *Historia de la Revolución Mexicana*, pp. 322–323).

171. Cárdenas told Ambassador Daniels in February 1939 that Mexico could not meet Secretary of State Hull's request and compensate the firms immediately, but he could get a loan from the Axis powers for the purpose. This, of course, would mean a break in the hemisphere's united stand against fascism (Daniels to President Roosevelt, February 25, 1939, JDP). Deputy Foreign Affairs Minister Beteta later informed the U.S. ambassador that the embargo imposed by the companies had obliged Mexico to trade its oil for machinery from the Axis powers and in effect virtually thrown it into Germany's arms (Daniels to his son, October 29, 1938, JDP).

172. See the confidential report on the German market for Mexican oil prepared by the Mexican consulate in Hamburg, May 1938, AREM III/"938"/2 L-E-588, Alemania, ff. 28–29.

173. Cronon, *Josephus Daniels in Mexico*, p. 250; Frank L. Kluckhohn, *The Mexican Challenge*, p. 1.

174. Report of the U.S. consul general in Mexico City, January 30, 1939, NAW 812.6342/36.

175. Daniels to Secretary of State Hull, June 30 and September 27, 1938, and Daniels to President Roosevelt, September 29, 1938, JDP.

176. Castillo Nájera, *El petróleo . . .* , pp. 43–48.

177. See, for example, *New York Times*, October 22, 1938.

178. Pierre Boal to Department of State, April 23, 1938, NAW 812.6363/3697.

179. Ambassador Castillo Nájera to Ministry of Foreign Affairs, March 25, 1938, AREM III/628 "938"/2 L-E-558, Estados Unidos, f. 78.

180. *Sunday Express*, March 20, 1938.

181. Memorandum of conversation between Under Secretary of State Welles and Ambassador Castillo Nájera, March 30, 1938, NAW 812.6363/3338.

182. Telegrams from Secretary of State Hull to Ambassador Daniels, April 2 and 4, 1938, NAW 812.6363/3245, 3269; memorandum of conversation between Under Secretary Welles and Ambassador Castillo Nájera, April 4, 1938, NAW 812.6363/3367.

183. Memorandum of the Division of the American Republics, April 9, 1938, NAW 812.6363/3388½. The plan presented to Ambassador Daniels by Deputy Minister of Foreign Affairs Beteta on April 19 is on file under NAW 812.6363/3573.

184. Memorandum of a conversation between Assistant Secretary of State A. A. Berle, Jr., and Eduardo Suárez, April 20, 1938, NAW 812.6363/3700.

185. Ambassador Daniels to Department of State, December 1, 1938, NAW 812.6363/5214.

186. In April 1938 Ambassador Daniels wrote to Secretary of State Hull pointing out that the oil firms' refusal to negotiate with Cárdenas was against U.S. interests and even their own. The expropriation was an accomplished fact that could not be reversed unless the companies intended to start a revolution. According to Daniels, Roosevelt had met with oil company spokesmen in June and it had been agreed that: (a) Mexico's right to expropriate was recognized; (b) they were to negotiate with the Mexican government in regard to the amount and form of payment of the compensation; and (c) no uprising in Mexico would be countenanced (Daniels to Hull, April 2 and 9 and June 24, 1938, JDP).

187. Cronon, *Josephus Daniels in Mexico*, p. 238.

188. Donald R. Richberg explained that the nationalization of the oil industry was an essential part of the effort to establish a new political and economic system, the unrealized goal of the Mexican Revolution (*Alegato sobre la cuestión petrolera de México*, p. 23).

189. Memorandum of a conversation between Assistant Secretary of State A. A. Berle, Jr., and Donald R. Richberg, June 7, 1938, NAW 812.6363/4154.

190. Colonel Hurley was received immediately by the Mexican authorities and the talks were cordial, according to Daniels' report (Daniels to Department of State, December 17, 1938, JDP).

191. Daniels wrote to President Roosevelt that the companies were prepared to "lay that baby [the Mexico problem] on the doorstep of the State Department and make the Government take the initiative and full responsibility while they assume the role of innocent martyrs. If the baby dies, they wish our Government to be regarded as the murderer" (January 31, 1939, JDP).

192. Castillo Nájera, *El petróleo...*, pp. 53–55; Richberg, *Alegato...*, p. 47; Standard Oil of New Jersey, *Present Status of the Mexican Oil Expropriation*, p. 67.

193. Ambassador Daniels to Department of State, NAW 812.6363/5558.

194. Daniels, *Shirt-Sleeve Diplomat*, p. 263.

195. February 15, 1939, JDP.

196. The essential elements in Cárdenas' plan were (a) assessment of the expropriated property as the basis for setting the amount of compensation; (b) a long-term cooperative agreement between Mexico and the firms; and (c) commitment on both sides to make new investments, bearing in mind that control of the industry would remain in the Mexican government's hands.

197. Richberg was opposed because (a) it would not be possible to agree on the amount; and (b) even if an amount were settled on, Mexico did not have the resources with which to pay it (Ambassador Daniels to Secretary of State Hull, March 17, 1939, NAW 812.6363/5616).

198. Mexico, *La verdad sobre la expropiación...*, pp. 107–118; Fabela, "La política internacional del Presidente Cárdenas," p. 92.

199. It would seem that in the April 12 telephone conversation Cárdenas told Richberg that the assessment would be made immediately following the talks or not at

all, if a better solution could be found. The president also agreed, at Richberg's request, to give up the plan for a collective settlement with the companies, making individual arrangements instead (Tanner, "Diplomacy of the Expropriation . . . ," pp. 56–57; Richberg, *Alegato . . .* , pp. 47–49; Mexico, *La verdad sobre la expropiación . . .* , p. 121; M. Rippy, "El petróleo y la Revolución Mexicana," p. 157).

200. U.S. consul general in Mexico City to Department of State, May 6, 1939, NAW 812.00/30739.

201. Letter from Ambassador Castillo Nájera written in Lower California to Donald R. Richberg, July 5, 1939, and reply thereto, July 17, 1939, NAW 812.6363/6001; Mexico, *La verdad sobre la expropiación . . .* , pp. 119–128; U.S. vice consul in Saltillo to Daniels, May 3, 1939, JDP.

202. Memorandum signed by Laurence Duggan, Division of the American Republics, May 16, 1939, NAW 812.6363/5772½.

203. See *El Universal Gráfico* and *Ultimas noticias*, March 19, 1938; Ambassador Daniels to Department of State, May 20, 1939, NAW 812.6363/5795.

204. Standard Oil of New Jersey, *Confiscation or Expropriation?*; Richberg, *Alegato . . .*

205. NAW 812.6363/5636⅜ and 6233½.

206. Memorandum of conversation between Under Secretary of State Welles and Ambassador Castillo Nájera, May 29, 1939, NAW 812.6363/5808.

207. Memorandum of conversation between Laurence Duggan, Division of the American Republics, and Deputy Minister of Foreign Affairs Beteta, June 19, 1939, NAW 812.6363/5862.

208. Memorandum of conversation between Under Secretary of State Welles and Ambassador Castillo Nájera, August 2, 1939, NAW 812.6363/6078.

209. Memorandum of conversation between Under Secretary of State Welles and Donald R. Richberg, August 2, 1939, NAW 812.6363/6078.

210. "Welles' plan has the authorization of Roosevelt" (memorandum of conversation between Under Secretary of State Welles and Ambassador Castillo Nájera, NAW 812.6363/6078).

211. Wood, *The Making of Good Neighbor Policy*, p. 221.

212. W. S. Farish, Standard Oil of New Jersey, to Secretary of State Hull, August 10, 1929, NAW 812.6363/6001.

213. Under Secretary of State Welles to Ambassador Daniels, August 16, 1939, NAW 812.6363/6015.

214. Memorandum of conversation between Bursley, Division of the American Republics, and Luis Legorreta, February 15, 1939, NAW 812.6363/5536.

215. The first contacts between Luis Legorreta and the State Department are reported in NAW 812.6363/6886 1/11 and 8/11. The plan itself is summarized in the memorandum of a conversation between Under Secretary of State Welles and Ambassador Castillo Nájera, July 4, 1948, NAW 812.6363/6952.

216. Under Secretary of State Welles to the Department's Legal Adviser, December 27, 1939, and British embassy in Washington to Department of State, December 12, 1939, NAW 812.6363/6389½. For a view of the exchanges between the department and the oil firms, see W. S. Farish, Standard Oil of New Jersey, to Department of State, March 9 and 14, 1940, NAW 812.6363/6527, 6583.

217. Department of State to British embassy in Washington, January 11, 1940, NAW 812.6363/6509; memorandum of a conversation between Under Secretary Welles and the British ambassador, February 5, 1940, NAW 812.6363/6436; memorandum of a conversation between Welles and the Netherlands minister, February 9, 1940, NAW 812.6363/6490.

218. Ambassador Daniels to Department of State, January 31, 1940, NAW

812.6C 53/6470; memorandum of a conversation between Laurence Duggan, Division of the American Republics, and Ambassador Castillo Nájera, February 19, 1940, NAW 812.6363/6529; Castillo Nájera to Department of State, March 16, 1940, NAW 812.6363/6600.

219. Memorandum of a conversation between Under Secretary of State Welles and Ambassador Castillo Nájera, February 5, 1940, NAW 812.6363/6486; telegram from Laurence Duggan, Division of the American Republics, to Welles, September 29, 1939, NAW 812.6363/6177A.

220. Ambassador Daniels to Department of State, May 17, 1940, NAW 812.6363/ 6865.

221. It should be pointed out that Sinclair had already once before broken a "united front" when it refused to join the big consortia's blockade of Soviet Russia following nationalization of their property and entered into talks directly with the revolutionary government.

222. In December 1939 the negotiating team was joined by the American labor leader John L. Lewis, the Mexican minister of the treasury, and Jesús Silva Herzog (Castillo Nájera, *El petróleo* . . . , p. 65; Patrick J. Hurley, *La lucha por el petróleo mexicano: Declaración del coronel* . . . , *abogado de la Consolidated Oil Corporation ante la Comisión de Ferrocarriles del Estado de Texas*, pp. 10–11).

223. Memorandum from Herbert Bursley, Division of the American Republics, to Under Secretary of State Welles, December 23, 1938, NAW 812.6363/5280; report of the representative of Huasteca Petroleum to Pierre Boal, and Boal to Department of State, June 27, 1938, NAW 812.6363/4297.

224. In 1940 Harry F. Sinclair himself and some officers of Consolidated Oil were present at the meetings. On this occasion Sinclair agreed to reduce his firm's demands from 32 to 14 million dollars. In April 1940 Castillo Nájera reported that the American oilman had agreed on a compensation of 9 million dollars plus a sale-purchase contract for 20 million barrels of oil at prices below the market (Castillo Nájera, *El petróleo* . . . , pp. 66–67; Silva Herzog, *Petróleo mexicano*, pp. 173–175).

225. The State Department realized that the arrangement with Sinclair had turned the situation around in Mexico's favor (memorandum signed by Herbert Bursley, Division of the American Republics, May 2, 1940, NAW 812.6363/6845).

226. "If we come to an agreement with this company," said Jesús Silva Herzog, "we will have shown the State Department that we wanted to and could pay, and it could not help but have a salutary effect on domestic political conditions" (*Historia de la expropiación petrolera*, p. 165).

227. The settlement covered the following firms: Mexican Sinclair Petroleum Company, Pierce Oil Company, Compañía Terminal de Lobos, and Stanford y Compañía. In 1948 Sinclair agreed to modify the terms of the 1940 agreement because the price of oil on the world market had risen considerably. Instead of continuing to pay 90 cents a barrel, it agreed to go up—voluntarily—to as high as 1.90 and 2.25 (Antonio J. Bermúdez, "The Mexican National Petroleum Industry: A Case Study in Nationalization," *Hispanic American Report* [1963]).

228. The settlement nearly fell through because of a disagreement over principles: Mexico refused to allow the final document to state that Sinclair's property had not been expropriated but rather that its shares had been purchased by the Mexican government.

229. Daniels to his son, May 7, 1940, JDP. There is also a long memorandum from Ambassador Castillo Nájera to the Ministry of Foreign Affairs in which he reports in detail on the progress of negotiations with Sinclair (AREM III/628 "938"/2 L-E-609, Sinclair, ff. 18–38).

230. Pierre Boal to Department of State, May 24, 1940, NAW 812.6363/6912.

231. Standard tried to get the U.S. Senate to call for an embargo on all imports of

Mexican oil. Patrick J. Hurley had to defend the agreement he had signed with Mexico in proceedings before the Texas Railroad Commission, which refused to allow the entrance of Mexican oil (Cronon, *Josephus Daniels in Mexico*, p. 253; Hurley, *La lucha . . .*).

232. W. S. Farish to Under Secretary of State Welles, December 24, 1940, NAW 812.6363/7208.

233. Memorandum signed by Herbert Bursley, Division of the American Republics, October 24, 1941, NAW 812.6363/7369; memorandum signed by Under Secretary of State Welles, November 5, 1941, NAW 812.6363/7353; memorandum of a conversation between Welles and Ambassador Castillo Nájera, November 12, 1941, NAW 812.6363/7372 11/21.

234. Standard never admitted that the expropriated firms were engaged in a boycott against Mexico (Standard Oil of New Jersey, *Respuesta de las compañías . . .* , pp. 7–8).

235. On March 17 the commercial attaché reported to the State Department that the Mexican financial structure was so weak that it could not stand up to any severe diplomatic-economic pressure on the part of the United States (NAW 812.516/603). As an example of the care with which Washington was following the economic situation in Mexico, see Laurence Duggan, Division of the American Republics, to Under Secretary of State Welles, April 29, 1938, NAW 812.50/208; commercial attaché in Mexico to Department of State, October 1, 1938, NAW 812.6363/4889.

236. The other two most important activities were agriculture and mining.

237. The technical difficulties also had an impact on the decline in production, but its main cause was the loss of markets.

238. Distribuidora de Petróleos Mexicanos to Ministry of Foreign Affairs, August 4, 1939, AREM III/628 "938"/2 L-E-591, Estados Unidos, f. 290.

239. Pierre Boal to Department of State, January 11 and October 10, 1939, NAW 812.6363/5342, 6202; Ambassador Daniels to Department of State, August 8, 1939, NAW 812.6363 Davis and Company/194. On February 14, 1940, Daniels informed the State Department that Mexico had exported 1,501,000 barrels in January (NAW 812.6363/6519).

240. Memorandum of a conversation between Under Secretary of State Welles and Ambassador Castillo Nájera, October 1, 1937, NAW 812.6363/3020.

241. Counselor of U.S. embassy in Mexico City to Department of State, January 8, 1938, NAW 812.6363/3067.

242. Ambassador Daniels to Department of State, September 6, 1939, NAW 812.6363/6129.

243. Oil companies to Secretary of State, April 1, 1938, NAW 812.6363/3263.

244. Mexico, Secretaría de Relaciones Exteriores, *Tribunales extranjeros reconocen el indiscutible derecho con que México expropió los intereses petroleros*.

245. As an example of this tactic on the part of the companies, see the ad published by El Aguila in a Swiss newspaper announcing that it would take legal steps against anyone who purchased Mexican oil (*Nya Dagligt Allehanda*, October 24, 1938).

246. Shortly after the expropriation a British oil magnate, Francis M. Rickett, met with President Cárdenas and tried to make a deal with Mexico for several million barrels, but the scheme failed when the British press denounced it; he was unable to land in England with his first load of oil, and his account with the Bank of England was frozen (AREM III/628 "938"/2 L-E-575, Inglaterra, part 2, Mexican minister in London to deputy minister of foreign affairs, May 3, 1938, ff. 82–83).

247. France refused to buy Mexican oil so as not to antagonize the British oil interests, which had aided the country in the past on several critical occasions (memorandum of a conversation between the U.S. counselor of embassy in Paris and the French

representative of Standard Oil of New Jersey, September 21, 1938, and U.S. embassy in Paris to Department of State, October 26, 1938, NAW 812.6363/5936.

248. Mexican chargé d'affaires in France to Ministry of Foreign Affairs, May 21, 1938, AREM III/628 "938"/2 L-E-592, France, f. 49. A review of this file shows what Mexico went through to try to sell its oil in France despite the fact that there was no legal barrier against it.

249. Mexican legation in Vichy to Ministry of Foreign Affairs, July 11, 1940, and reply thereto, July 30, AREM III/628 "938"/2 L-E-592, Francia, ff. 268–292.

250. Padilla Nervo to Ministry of Foreign Affairs, May 16, 1938, AREM III/628 "938"/2 L-E-560, Holanda, ff. 15–16.

251. Mexican legation at The Hague to Ministry of Foreign Affairs, September 4, 1938, AREM III/628 "938"/2 L-E-593, Holanda, ff. 22–24.

252. Mexican legation in Copenhagen to Ministry of Foreign Affairs, October 30, 1938, September 8, 1939, and January 17, 1940, AREM III/628 "938"/2 L-E-590, Dinamarca, ff. 7, 22, 48.

253. The documentation illustrating this point is copious and shows very well the kind of intelligence that the oil firms had at their disposal in thwarting the efforts of the Mexican diplomats and PEMEX agents in Latin America (T. R. Armstrong of Standard Oil of New Jersey to Laurence Duggan, Division of the American Republics, September 30, 1938; U.S. embassy in Buenos Aires to Department of State, August 12 and 29, 1938; U.S. legation in Montevideo to Department of State, August 12, 22, 23, 27, and 29; U.S. embassy in San Salvador to Department of State, August 1938— NAW 812.6363/4610, 4684, 4619, 4690, 4629, 4691, 4656, 4617, 4618.) Standard went so far as to accuse Mexico of interfering in Chilean politics—that is, supporting a presidential candidate—in order to sell oil (U.S. embassy in Santiago, September 10, 1938, NAW 812.6363/4769.

254. These two firms controlled two-thirds of Mexico's oil exports after the expropriation (memorandum signed by Herbert Bursley, Division of the American Republics, November 23, 1938, NAW 812.6363/5123).

255. Standard Oil of New Jersey to Commissioner of Customs, September 16, 1938, NAW 812.6363/4832; Eastern States Petroleum to Export-Import Bank, September 27, 1938, NAW 812.6363/4902; memorandum signed by Laurence Duggan, Division of the American Republics, NAW 812 Davis and Company/136.

256. Mexican chargé d'affaires in Washington to deputy minister of foreign affairs, January 9, 1939, AREM III/628 "938"/2 L-E-591, Estados Unidos, ff. 415–416.

257. Report from Deputy Minister of Foreign Affairs Beteta to Ambassador Daniels, October 28, 1938, NAW 812.6363/5070; Eduardo Suárez to Ministry of Foreign Affairs, February 8, 1940, AREM III/628 "938"/1, L-E-606, *compra de maquinaria,* f. 21.

258. Hicks and Company complained to the State Department that there was a tacit agreement between the oil equipment manufacturers and the expropriated firms against the shipment of such machinery to Mexico and asked that the boycott be stopped. The State Department declined to interfere in the matter (Hicks and Company to Department of State, June 6 and 11, 1940, and the Department's reply, June 29, 1940, NAW 812.6363/6952½, 6962½, 6992).

259. For an example of this kind of operation see AREM III/628 "938"/2 L-E-557, Cuba, f. 34.

260. Mexican consul general in New York to Ministry of Foreign Affairs, AREM III/628 "938"/2 L-E-591, Estados Unidos, ff. 215–216.

261. PEMEX was forced to produce the tetraethyl that it needed at a higher cost and at much sacrifice. Only after this was accomplished did the American companies, seeing their monopoly threatened, agree to sell it again to Mexico.

262. Memorandum of the Division of the American Republics, May 5, 1938, NAW 812.6363/3866; memorandum of a conversation between Laurence Duggan of the Division and a representative of Socony-Vacuum, April 1, 1938, NAW 812.6363/3324.

263. Mexican consul general in Hamburg to Ministry of Foreign Affairs, May 1938, AREM III/628 "938"/2 L-E-588, Alemania, f. 154.

264. In the case of the two firms mentioned, their representatives traveled to Mexico to review the situation with authorities there. While General Electric was satisfied with the assurances given by President Cárdenas, Westinghouse, on the other hand, suspended its activities in Mexico for some time (Daniels to his son, March 6, 1939, JDP).

265. Ambassador Daniels to Department of State, February 22, 1939, NAW 812.6463/101.

266. Hubert Herring, *México: La formación de una nación*, p. 74.

267. Albert Nathan, president of the National Chamber of Hotels in Mexico, to Department of State, August 11, 1938, NAW 812.6363/4585.

268. Ambassador Castillo Nájera to Ministry of Foreign Affairs, March 21, 1938, AREM III/628 "938"/2 L-E-558, Estados Unidos, f. 19.

269. At the time, 95 per cent of the Mexican mining industry was in the hands of American companies, who controlled 70 per cent of the silver output (United States, 80th Congress, 2nd session, House of Representatives Committee on Interstate and Foreign Commerce, *Fuel Investigation: Mexican Petroleum*, pp. 3–4; Kirk, *Covering the Mexican Front*, p. 61).

270. U.S. consul general in Mexico City to Department of State, May 2, 1936, NAW 812.51/2152.

271. It was rumored that within an hour after the news was out the Bank of Mexico had sold 1 million dollars. Whether or not this is true, it very soon did have to drop out of the foreign exchange market in the face of the threat that the public might draw off all its reserves.

272. Daniels pointed out to President Roosevelt that, even though the Good Neighbor policy had almost succeeded in overcoming the traditional antagonism between the two countries, the suspension of silver purchases had gone a long way toward undoing the good results achieved. The ambassador urged that the United States renew its purchases of Mexican silver (March 29, 1938, JDP; memorandum of a telephone conversation between Pierre Boal in Mexico and Laurence Duggan, Division of the American Republics, March 29, 1938, NAW 812.6363/3415).

273. Treasury Secretary Morgenthau had been against Hull's plan, which was presented to Roosevelt on March 25, 1938. Since the president, who was not in Washington at the time, did not make any comment, Morgenthau assumed that he had approved it and went ahead with it on March 27 (Cronon, *Josephus Daniels in Mexico*, pp. 191–192; Daniels, *Shirt-Sleeve Diplomat*, pp. 199–200).

274. *New York Herald Tribune*, March 29 and 30, 1938.

275. *Financial Times*, June 29, 1939.

276. Mexican consul general in New York to Ministry of Foreign Affairs, March 25, 1938, AREM III/628 "938"/2 L-E-568, Estados Unidos, f. 20.

277. Cronon, *Josephus Daniels in Mexico*, pp. 190–191.

278. Treasury Secretary Morgenthau explained this situation by saying that it was necessary for Canada, China, and Mexico to keep up their demand for U.S. products (Wood, *The Making of Good Neighbor Policy*, p. 225; Burt M. McConnell, *Mexico at the Bar of Public Opinion*, 211).

279. Cuevas Cancino, *Roosevelt y la Buena Vecindad*, p. 155.

280. See, for example, the *New York Times*, February 10, April 11, and May 9, 1940; Wendell C. Gordon, *The Expropriation of Foreign-owned Property in Mexico*,

p. 97; William O. Scroggs, "Mexican Anxieties," *Foreign Affairs* 18 (January 1940): 175.

281. Robert Engler, *La política petrolera: Un estudio del poder privado y las directivas democráticas*, p. 205; Zorrilla, *Historia de las relaciones . . .* , p. 476.

282. Ambassador Daniels to Department of State, May 7, 1940, NAW 812.6363/6864.

283. U.S. consul general in Mexico City to Department of State, January 30, 1939, NAW 812.6342/36.

284. Memorandum of a telephone conversation between Pierre Boal and Laurence Duggan, Division of the American Republics, March 29, 1938, NAW 812.6363/3415.

285. Ambassador Daniels to Department of State, December 12, 1939, Herbert Bursley to Laurence Duggan, Division of the American Republics, December 16, 1939, and Department of State to Ambassador Daniels, December 16, 1939, NAW 812.51/2415.

286. *Times*, November 22, 1941.

287. Townsend, *The Truth about Mexico's Oil*, pp. 37–40; Department of State to Secretary of the Navy, April 25, 1939, NAW 812.6363/5736.

288. The prospect of acquiring lower-cost Mexican oil led Eastern Petroleum of Houston to sign a contract with PEMEX for the purchase of fifteen thousand barrels a day, while Cities Service formed a "straw" company to buy more than a million and a half barrels from Pánuco in 1939 and the First National Corporation of New York also acquired Mexican oil, as did Petroleum Heat and Power, the following year (Mexico, Secretaría del Patrimonio Nacional, *El petróleo de México*, p. 24; Jesús Silva Herzog, *México y su petróleo*, p. 53; idem, *Petróleo mexicano*, p. 28; M. Rippy, "El petróleo y la Revolución Mexicana," p. 140; Hurley, *La lucha . . .* , p. 25).

289. There were many American companies that approached Mexico with view to buying its oil. Their correspondence with PEMEX and the diplomatic emissaries make up a voluminous file in AREM III/628 "938"/2 L-E-591, Estados Unidos.

290. See, for example, the conversation between the State Department's Adviser on International Economic Affairs and a representative of International Paper, which was considering an exchange of paper for Mexican oil (NAW 812.6363/5454). There was also the opposition of the Texas firms which continued selling Mexican oil to the end of 1938 (*New York Times*, August 22, 1938). A legal defense of those who were buying the embargoed fuel was prepared by Eastern States Petroleum in order to protect its own position, the main points of which are cited in the memorandum of a conversation between Eastern States' representatives and State Department officials on September 19, 1938 (NAW 812.6363/4815, 4810). See also memorandum of the Division of the American Republics, November 4, 1938, NAW 812.6363/5078.

291. Memorandum of a conversation between Laurence Duggan and Herbert Bursley, Division of the American Republics, and Bohanon of Standard Oil of New Jersey, October 5, 1938, NAW 812.6363/4899.

292. Herbert Bursley, Division of the American Republics, to Under Secretary of State Sumner Welles, December 5, 8, 22, and 28, 1938, and January 7, 1939, NAW 812.6363/5282, 5283, 5285, 5286, 5323.

293. Mayor of New York City to Under Secretary of State Sumner Welles, December 12, 1938, and reply, December 14, 1938, NAW 812.6363/5240.

294. Memorandum of a conversation between Herbert Bursley, Division of the American Republics, and a banker connected with Eastern States Petroleum, April 28, 1939, NAW 812.6363/5727.

295. Examples are the contracts signed in July 1939 with Mexusa-Holland Corporation, subsidiary of Cities Service, and in April 1940 with Petroleum Heat and Power (Mexican consul general in New York to Ministry of Foreign Affairs, July 20, 1939,

and April 18, 1940, AREM III/628 "938"/2 L-E-591, Estados Unidos, ff. 249, 255–256.

296. Within the 3.8 per cent quota Mexico could introduce into the United States only an amount of oil corresponding to 5 per cent of the total refined in the country during the previous year.

297. Ambassador Castillo Nájera to Ministry of Foreign Affairs, December 11, 1939, AREM III/628 "938"/2 L-E-591, Estados Unidos, f. 410.

298. Ambassador Castillo Nájera to Ministry of Foreign Affairs, December 13 and 30, 1940, AREM III/628 "938"/2 L-E-591, Estados Unidos, ff. 44o, 467, 471–472.

299. The subsidiary was Petroleum Heat and Power Company.

300. *New York Herald Tribune*, January 10, 1941.

301. Department of State to Department of the Navy, February 11, 1942, NAW 812.6363/7486.

302. Ambassador Castillo Nájera to Ministry of Foreign Affairs, June 13, 1942, and June 12, 1945, and PEMEX to Ministry of Foreign Affairs, June 30, 1944, and June 23, 1947, AREM III/628 "938"/2 L-E-591, Estados Unidos, ff. 516, 538–540, 525, 561–562.

303. Memorandum of conversations held by Laurence Duggan, Division of the American Republics, and Nicaraguan and French envoys, August 4, 5, and 8, 1938, NAW 812.6363/4665.

304. These requests were prompted by Mexico's negotiations with Uruguay and Greece (memorandum of a conversation held by chiefs of the Division of the American Republics and of the Division of Near Eastern Affairs with representatives of Standard Oil of New Jersey, August 26 and October 28, 1938, NAW 812.6363/4757, 5703).

305. Assistant Secretary of State A. A. Berle, Jr., to Thomas R. Armstrong of Standard Oil of New Jersey, September 12, 1938, NAW 812.6363/4779.

306. U.S. legation in Managua to Department of State, September 13, 1938, and July 14 and August 7, 1939, NAW 812.6363/4764, 5937, 6008; memorandums signed by Beauloc and Herbert Bursley, Division of the American Republics, February 2 and June 6, 1939, NAW 812.6363/5393, 5937; Mexican consul in Managua to Ministry of Foreign Affairs, February 10, 1939, AREM III/628 "938"/2 L-E-594, Nicaragua, ff. 32–35.

307. U.S. embassy in Havana to Department of State, May 18, 1939, NAW 812.6363/5823; Ambassador Daniels to Department of State, February 1, 1940, NAW 812.6363/6477.

308. Mexican legation in Paris, representative of Standard Française, and Mexican chargé d'affaires in Tegucigalpa to Ministry of Foreign Affairs, July 22, 1942; Mexican embassy to Ministry of Foreign Affairs, July 27, 1942; Mexican chargé d'affaires in Managua to Ministry of Foreign Affairs, October 27, 1942—AREM III/628 "938"/2 L-E-590, Dominicana, f. 5; L-E-593, Honduras, ff. 24–26; L-E-589, Cuba, f. 95; L-E-594, Nicaragua, ff. 49–50.

309. Mexican legation in Costa Rica to Ministry of Foreign Affairs, July 7, 1943, AREM III/628 "938"/2 L-E-589, Costa Rica, f. 144; Mexican embassy in Havana to Ministry of Foreign Affairs, February 12, 1942, AREM/628 "938"/2 L-E-589, Cuba, f. 110. See also the Cuban daily *Acción*, February 11, 1943.

310. For a detailed account of shipments of Mexican oil to Guatemala, see Mexican embassy in Guatemala City to Ministry of Foreign Affairs and to President Avila Camacho, September 3, 1940 and March 5, 1942, respectively, AREM III/628 "938"/2 L-E-592, Guatemala, ff. 106, 178–183.

311. In regard to the Guatemalan case it is of interest to review the entire file on the oil situation there. In particular, for the negotiations with respect to the first shipment of gasoline, see Mexican embassy in Guatemala City to Ministry of Foreign Affairs, October 22, 1938, AREM III/628 "938"/2 L-E-592, Guatemala, ff. 28–29. For

pressure exercised by Shell see Mexican embassy in Guatemala City to Ministry of Foreign Affairs, October 19 and 28, 1938, AREM III/628 "938"/2 L-E-592, Guatemala, ff. 43–46, 64–65.

312. Memorandum of a conversation between Under Secretary of State Welles and the Argentine ambassador, July 26, 1939, NAW 812.6363/6006.

313. Salvador E. Altamirano, representative of Petróleos Mexicanos in Montevideo, to PEMEX, July 12, 1938, and report from Mexican embassy in Buenos Aires, June 7, 1940, AREM III/628 "938"/2 L-E-588, Argentina, ff. 19–20, 59. The latter document traces the opposition to the purchase of Mexican oil to an agreement between the head of the Argentine national oil enterprise (Yacimientos Petroleros Fiscales) and Shell.

314. Memorandum signed by Laurence Duggan, Division of the American Republics, October 5, 1938, NAW 812.6363/4780; U.S. embassy in Rio de Janeiro to Department of State, December 13, 1938, and May 6, 1940, NAW 812.6363/5260, 6860.

315. Following difficulties with Mexico in 1942, the PEMEX representative in Brazil, Correa e Castro, suspended operations. PEMEX demanded a settlement of thirty thousand dollars.

316. Mexican embassy in Santiago to Ministry of Foreign Affairs, October 14, 1939, April 8 and October 23, 1940, August 4, 1941, and March 18, 1942, AREM III/628 "938"/2 L-E-584, Chile, ff. 74, 132, 150, 184, 272.

317. In 1941 Mexico was forced to turn down orders from Argentina and Uruguay because it didn't have tankers (Petróleos Mexicanos to Ministry of Foreign Affairs, July 1, 1941, AREM III/628 "938"/2 L-E-588, Argentina, f. 84).

318. Secretary of State Hull to U.S. legation in Berne, June 24, 1939, NAW 812.6363/5861A.

319. All the documents on Davis' operations are on file under NAW 812.6363 Davis and Company. The warning is contained in a memorandum from Herbert Bursley, Division of the American Republics, October 27, 1938, NAW 812.6363 Davis and Company/142.

320. British oilmen D. A. Thomas and Harrison of Harrison, Ltd., called off their negotiations with PEMEX under pressure from their government (Pierre Boal to Department of State May 6, 1938, NAW 812.6363/3878). British pressure kept Norway from buying Mexican oil in 1939 (Mexican chargé d'affaires in Oslo to Ministry of Foreign Affairs, December 20, 1939, AREM III/628 "938"/2 L-E-594, Noruega, ff. 26–28.

321. Laurence Duggan, Division of the American Republics, to the State Department's Adviser on International Economic Affairs, July 7, 1938, and memorandum signed by the Adviser on International Economic Affairs, July 11, 1939, also Herbert Bursley, Division of the American Republics to Under Secretary of State Welles, October 31, 1939, and Under Secretary Welles to Ambassador Daniels, November 13, 1939, NAW 182.6511/9; 812.655 Rayon Yarn/2; 812.51/2406.

322. Memorandum of a conversation between Laurence Duggan, Division of the American Republics, and a representative of National City Bank, June 23, 1939, and memorandum signed by Duggan, June 24, NAW 812.51/2378, 2379.

323. Memorandum of Department of State, August 29, 1939, NAW 812.248/296.

324. The occasion was a luncheon given by President Cárdenas for the foreign press on July 27, 1938. The reference to Germany, Italy, and Japan was implicit.

325. Ambassador Daniels to Department of State, September 12, 1939, NAW 812.6363/6155.

326. Shortly after the expropriation the Italian envoy in Mexico stated that it was unlikely his country would go against the wishes of the big consortia, which had helped Italy out in its Ethiopian campaign, by purchasing Mexican oil (Kirk, *Covering the Mexican Front*, p. 166).

327. Mexican consul general in Hamburg and chargé d'affaires in Berlin to Ministry of Foreign Affairs, March 28 and May 9, 1938, respectively, AREM III/628 "938"/2 L-E-588, Alemania, ff. 2, 21.

328. Confidential report on the German market for Mexican oil sent by the Mexican consul general in Hamburg to the Ministry of Foreign Affairs, May 1938, AREM III/628 "938"/2 L E-588, Alemania, ff. 28–29.

329. Ibid., f. 29.

330. Memorandum of Division of the American Republics, September 24, 1938, NAW 812.6363/4903.

331. Mexican legation in Berlin to Ministry of Foreign Affairs, June 27, 1939, AREM III/628 "938"/2 L-E-Alemania, f. 209.

332. U.S. embassy in London to Department of State, September 15, 1938, NAW 812.6363/4903.

333. Mexican legation in Berlin to Ministry of Foreign Affairs, April 26 and August 1, 1939, AREM III/628 "938"/2 L-E-588, Alemania, ff. 194, 213.

334. *Evening Standard*, November 2, 1939.

335. Ambassador Daniels to Department of State, October 25, 1929, NAW 812.6363/6251; Pierre Boal to Department of State, May 24, 1940, NAW 812.6363/6921.

336. Mexican consulate general in Hamburg to Ministry of Foreign Affairs, May 27, 1942, AREM III/628 "938"/2 L-E-588, ff. 251–252.

337. Davis' early activities in Mexico may be reviewed in NAW 812.6363 Davis and Company/1–30.

338. Pierre Boal to Department of State, May 2, 1938, NAW 812.6363/3781.

339. *New York Times*, April 7, 1938; *Excélsior*, July 7, 1938.

340. *Times*, June 29, 1938.

341. The institution financing it was the First National City Bank of Boston.

342. Ministry of Foreign Affairs to Mexican legation in Paris, July 24, 1939, AREM III/628 "938"/2 L-E-592, Francia, f. 165.

343. Davis presented these plans to the U.S. secretary of state in a meeting held with him on August 17, 1938 (NAW 812.6363/4592½).

344. Memorandum signed by Laurence Duggan, Division of the American Republics, October 6, 1939, and report of the U.S. embassy in Rome, November 3, 1939, NAW 812.6363 Davis and Company/209, 12, 241.

345. Ambassador Daniels to Department of State, August 30, 1940, NAW 812.6363/7079.

346. U.S. embassy to Department of State, March 5 and April 16 and 24, 1936, NAW 812.6363/2885; 812.823/174; 812.6363/2894.

347. Ambassador Daniels to Department of State, January 4, 1938, NAW 812.6363/3061.

348. Ambassador Daniels to Department of State, March 21 and 26 and October 28, 1938, NAW 812.6363/3111, 3175, 5027; *Ultimas noticias*, March 25, 1938; *New York Times*, April 8, 1938.

349. Memorandum to Department of State, April 19, 1938, NAW 812.6363/3823.

350. Ambassador Castillo Nájera to Ministry of Foreign Affairs, March 29, 1938, and Deputy Minister Beteta to Castillo Nájera, April 5, 1938, AREM III/628 "938"/2 L-E-583, Japón, ff. 1–2.

351. Mexican legation in Shanghai to Ministry of Foreign Affairs, September 6, 1938, AREM III/628 "938"/2 L-E-594, Japón, ff. 56–57.

352. Ambassador Daniels to Department of State, March 27, 1939, NAW 812.6363/5631.

353. Ambassador Daniels to Department of State, April 10 and October 24, 1940, NAW 812.6363/6689, 7146; memorandums signed by Herbert Bursley, Division of

the American Republics, August 14 and 15, 1940, and January 27, 1941, NAW 812.6363/7065, 7067, 7280; memorandum signed by Donovan, Division of the American Republics, NAW 812.6363/7090; Japanese legation in Mexico to Ministry of Foreign Affairs, October 30, 1940, AREM III/628 "938"/2 L-E-594, Japón, f. 51; *St. Louis Dispatch*, October 22, 1940.

354. *New York Times*, August 15, 1938.

355. U.S. vice consul in Tampico to Department of State, December 14, 1938, NAW 812.6363 Davis and Company/159.

356. National Foreign Trade Council, Inc., to Department of State, August 11, 1938, NAW 812.6363/4592.

357. Daniels wrote to his son that an American professor, Frank Tannenbaum, had arrived in Mexico and warned Cárdenas that the oil companies' campaign had created strong feelings against his government; he urged for an early settlement of the controversy (February 6, 1939, JDP).

358. Daniels, *Shirt Sleeve Diplomat*, p. 225.

359. William Miller, a journalist from Cleveland, informed Ambassador Daniels that Standard Oil's David Henshaw was meeting with the heads of the most important papers in the country as part of the campaign. Miller cited the articles of Henry J. Allen, former governor of Kansas, in the *New York Herald-Tribune* as an example of the kind of material being put out by the oil firms (November 28, 1938, JDP).

360. A very clear idea of the extent of this campaign can be gotten from Burt M. McConnell's *Mexico at the Bar . . .* , which was based on editorials appearing in the U.S. and foreign press. The *New York Times*, for its part, provides an example of the more "objective" propaganda, which, without failing to mention the positive human aspect of Cárdenas' policy, insisted on the impossibility of Mexico's running the expropriated industry, the unnecessary harm it was causing to the national economy, the corruption prevailing in the Mexican administration, and the threat of an alliance between "socialist Mexico" and "totalitarian Germany" to American interests and prestige, among other arguments (for example, March 22, June 25, September 9, and December 10, 1938, and January 20, 1939). Other examples are the book published by the *New York Times* correspondent in Mexico, Frank L. Kluckhohn, *The Mexican Challenge*, and the article by Graham Hutton, "The New-Old Crisis in Mexico," *Foreign Affairs* 16 (July 1938).

361. See the report of the Mexican legation in France on the effects of the anti-Mexican propaganda being put out by the British press (Mexican legation in Paris to Ministry of Foreign Affairs, March 15, 1939, AREM III/628 "938"/2 L-E-573, France, ff. 442–443).

362. *Atlantic Presents* 1, no. 1 (July 1938). Ambassador Daniels was informed by a State Department official that, according to reports received, this publication was paid for by the oil companies, and the *Atlantic Monthly* agreed to do it because of its precarious financial situation (Daniels to Claude Bowers, September 6, 1938, JDP).

363. Even a National Citizens Committee on Mexico was organized to raise 20 million dollars from the firms in order to lobby with Congress in favor of armed intervention in Mexico (Daniels, *Shirt-Sleeve Diplomat*, p. 232).

364. A detailed study of the attitude of these groups is contained in James Dunbar Bell, *Attitudes of Selected Groups in the United States toward Mexico, 1930–1940*, pp. 177–188.

365. United States, 76th Congress, 1st session, Senate, *Resolution Authorizing an Investigation of Conditions in Mexico as Affecting Property Rights of American Citizens* (January 27, 1939).

366. *New York Herald Tribune*, February 2, 1939.

367. M. J. Kennedy to Secretary of State Hull, July 28, 1939, NAW 812.6363/5961.

368. United States, 76th Congress, 1st session, Senate, *Resolution Authorizing an*

Investigation of Negotiations by American Citizens or Officials with the Mexican Government Concerning Certain Oil Sales.

369. The vote on the resolutions was taken on August 2, 1939. See United States, 76th Congress, 1st session, Senate, Resolutions 174 and 177.

370. Memorandum signed by Herbert Bursley, Division of the American Republics, January 10, 1940, NAW 812.6363/6445.

371. NAW 812.6363/3696.

372. Townsend, *Lázaro Cárdenas*, p. 291; Alejandro Carrillo, "Pasado, presente y futuro de nuestro pueblo," *Problemas agrícolas e industriales de México* 6 (July–September 1954): 89.

373. One of the first pamphlets, *Oil: Mexico's Position*, was printed by the Mexican consulate in New York. Similar publications were Morineau's *The Good Neighbor* and Carrillo's *The Mexican People* . . . In France Mauricio Fresco, a consular officer there, came out with *Synthèse du conflit de pétrole au Mexique.*

374. Townsend, *The Truth about Mexico's Oil*, pp. 65–66. See also a State Department circular to its missions in Latin America (April 1, 1938, JDP). An excellent view of Mexican propaganda abroad may be gleaned from a study of the classified material filed under AREM III/628 "938"/2 L-E-605.

375. Samuel Guy Inman, who ever since Carranza's time had been noted for his defense of Mexico's nationalist measures in the field of oil, went so far as to suggest that the U.S. government itself should compensate the companies in the amount of 200 million dollars (*Democracy versus the Totalitarian State in Latin America*). Waldo Frank also defended Cárdenas skillfully; see his "Cárdenas of Mexico," *Foreign Affairs* 18 (October 1939). Townsend's book *The Truth about Mexico's Oil* belongs to this genre as well.

376. Bell, *Attitudes of Selected Groups* . . . , pp. 178, 188–190. In April 1938 A. E. Edwards, in the name of 413 labor organizations representing 1,600,000 AFL and CIO workers, came out in support of Mexico in its struggle against the oil "pirates" (*Excélsior*, April 4, 1938). The support of labor throughout the rest of Spanish America was expressed through the Confederation of Workers of Latin America (CTAL—Confederación de Trabajadores de América Latina) and through many individual messages as well. There were also demonstrations of solidarity from labor groups outside the hemisphere, such as the one expressed in Oslo on May 21, 1938, and transmitted by the General Council of the International Federation of Trade Unions.

377. The views of these three organizations may be seen in NAW 812.6363/3323, 4311; 812.00/30639.

378. One of the Mexican government's biggest propaganda efforts was the publication *La verdad sobre la expropiación de los bienes de las empresas petroleras*, which contains a complete rundown of all the legal, historical, and political arguments that the Cárdenas administration was able to marshal in defense of its position and in response to the attacks of the oil companies.

379. The expropriation gave rise to the monthly review *El Economista*, which was nothing but a propaganda organ of the oil companies. Also, the Institute of Economic and Social Studies produced a long series of articles against the expropriation and Cárdenas' policies in general. See, in particular, those appearing in *Hoy* (September and October 1938), which also published writings by Luis Cabrera and M. H. Güereña. The rightist *Omega* epitomized the height of the campaign against the expropriation.

10. World War II and Final Settlement of the Oil Controversy

1. Speeches of April 12 (given at the Ministry of Foreign Affairs), March 5 (to the

Rotary Club), July 4, September 15, October 22, November 8 and 26 (the last delivered in the presence of Cárdenas), JDP.

2. Pierre Boal to Laurence Duggan, Division of the American Republics, Department of State, August 22, 1939, and the latter's reply, September 13, 1939, NAW 815.50/235½, 236A.

3. Memorandum signed by Donovan, Division of the American Republics, March 27, 1940, NAW 812.6363/6635.

4. Josef L. Kunz, *The Mexican Expropriations*, p. 3.

5. Josephus Daniels, *Shirt-Sleeve Diplomat*, p. 267.

6. Both Herbert Feis and M. W. Thornburg, economic and petroleum counselors respectively, were opposed to the United States setting such a precedent (Bryce Wood, *The Making of Good Neighbor Policy*, pp. 245, 247–249).

7. Memorandum signed by Sumner Welles, June 22, 1941, NAW 812.6363/7346 1/9.

8. William O. Scroggs, "Mexican Anxieties," *Foreign Affairs* 18 (January 1940): 266–267.

9. Edmund David Cronon, *Josephus Daniels in Mexico*, p. 258; Daniels to his son, October 28, 1939, JDP.

10. Ambassador Castillo Nájera to Under Secretary Welles, March 21, 1939, NAW 812.6363/5636, 5638.

11. Documents on this subject are reproduced in United States, Department of State, *Foreign Relations of the United States: Diplomatic Papers, 1940*, vol. 5, *The American Republics*, pp. 133–145; see also Wood, *The Making of Good Neighbor Policy*, p. 251.

12. On September 28 Ambassador Daniels received a letter from Cárdenas for transmittal to Roosevelt in which the Mexican president expressed his support of the U.S. chief of state's appeal to Czechoslovakia and Germany for a cease-fire and suggested a boycott against Germany and other aggressors (JDP). On several occasions Daniels received assurances that the Mexican government was prepared to cooperate in the fight against fascist aggression (Daniels to Roosevelt, June 28, 1940, JDP; Daniels to his son, July 6, 1940, JDP).

13. Daniels to his son, November 6 and 26, 1938, and September 6, 1939, JDP; Daniels to President Roosevelt, September 12, 1939, and July 28, 1940, JDP; Cordell Hull, *The Memoirs of Cordell Hull*, I, 260.

14. Daniels to President Roosevelt, March 11, 1941, JDP.

15. In July 1941 President Avila Camacho had declared that Mexico would go to war if the United States were attacked.

16. Cronon, *Josephus Daniels in Mexico*, p. 260.

17. This view was also set forth in a booklet published by Standard Oil of New Jersey, *The Mexican Expropriation in International Law*.

18. Wood, *The Making of Good Neighbor Policy*, pp. 254–256; Cronon, *Josephus Daniels in Mexico*, pp. 264–265.

19. *New York Times*, November 20, 1941.

20. Stanley R. Ross et al., *Historia documental de México*, pp. 530–531.

21. *New York Times*, October 3, 1941.

22. Ibid., November 20, 1941.

23. This ruling can be consulted in Standard Oil of New Jersey, *Present Status of the Mexican Oil Expropriation*. On December 2, 1939, the Supreme Court upheld the thesis. Justice Ignacio García Téllez, in a communication to Cárdenas dated August 15, 1938, set forth the following line of reasoning for the Mexican government's position: since the subsoil is within the nation's direct domain, expropriation cannot include what already legitimately belongs to it. On December 12 García Téllez submitted a proposal to Cárdenas for a constitutional amendment that would clearly

stipulate that oil exploration was the exclusive right of the nation in order to prevent future administrations from tampering with this policy (Merril Rippy, "El petróleo y la Revolución Mexicana," *Problemas agrícolas e industriales de México* 6 (July–September 1954): 179–180).

24. The text of this plan is reproduced in AREM III/628 "938"/2 L-E-558, Estados Unidos, ff. 111–131.

25. Memorandum of a meeting of Secretary of State Hull with spokesmen from Standard Oil of New Jersey, May 25, 1938, NAW 812.6363/4123.

26. NAW 812.6363/4079.

27. Communication of July 21, 1938, AREM III/628 "938"/2 L-E-555, part 1, f. 130.

28. Memorandum signed by R. C. Tanis, Division of the American Republics, March 22, 1938, NAW 812.6363/3266; Ambassador Daniels to Department of State, April 18, 1938, NAW 812.6363/3552; Thomas R. Armstrong of Standard Oil of New Jersey to Secretary of State Hull, August 6, 1938, NAW 812.6363/4548.

29. *New York Times*, March 27 and 30, 1938.

30. Memorandum of Division of the American Republics, April 12, 1938, NAW 812.6363/3489A.

31. *San Antonio Light*, August 19, 1938.

32. Paul Nathan, "México en la época de Cárdenas," *Problemas Agrícolas e industriales de Mexico* 7 (July–September 1955): 135. According to Jesús Silva Herzog (*Petróleo mexicano*, pp. 152–156), the oil debt was calculated on the basis of the assets of the sixteen companies involved, which as of the end of 1936 came to 323.8 million pesos, or, after subtracting the capital in circulation (which was not affected), 221.8 million pesos. Any sums owed by the firms to the Mexican government or to the workers at the time of expropriation were then deducted from this amount. The debt assumed by Mexico on March 18 was therefore approximately 150 million pesos (a little more than 33 million dollars). According to the figures of the Mexican courts, the value of the property expropriated in 1938 came to 160 million pesos. Other sums increased the total to 203,278,185 pesos (45 million dollars). This amount did not include the payment made in 1940 to four of the sixteen firms affected. The companies' protest against this assessment is contained in a communication to the Department of State (February 16, 1939, NAW 812.6363/5507, 5514).

33. Memorandum of Division of the American Republics, May 20, 1938, NAW 812.6363/4025.

34. Memorandum signed by Herbert Bursley, Division of the American Republics, June 10, 1941, NAW 812.6363/7354 2/11.

35. *Affairs*, January 19, 1940.

36. The commission proposed by Welles would be made up of a representative from each of the two governments and a third one selected by the three White House-accredited diplomats with the greatest seniority (M. Rippy, "El petróleo y la Revolución Mexicana," p. 156).

37. In 1938 Mexico and the United States had agreed on settling the agricultural expropriation problem on the basis of an intergovernmental assessment.

38. Memorandum from Herbert Bursley and Bonsal, Division of the American Republics, to Under Secretary Welles, March 21 and 24, 1941, NAW 812.6363/7229½.

39. *Washington Post*, February 2, 1941.

40. Memorandum from Laurence Duggan to Dowson, Division of the American Republics, NAW 812.6363/7308½.

41. Memorandum of a meeting held between Laurence Duggan, Herbert Bursley, and Ambassador Castillo Nájera, July 2, 1941, NAW 812.6363/7317 6/11.

42. Memorandum signed by Herbert Bursley, Division of the American Republics, April 24, 1941, NAW 812.6363/7267½.

43. According to these calculations, the value of the U.S.-owned properties—not including those of the Sinclair group, which had already been paid off—came to 13.5 million dollars, while the British ones were estimated to be worth 115.3 million (memorandum signed by Bursley, Division of the American Republics, June 6, 1941, NAW 812.6363/7308.

44. *Newsweek*, August 25, 1941.

45. Mexican embassy to Department of State, July 22, 1941, NAW 812.6363/7346 1/9.

46. There is copious documentation on this point, filed under NAW 812.6363/ 7230½ through 7365 20/21.

47. Memorandum signed by Herbert Bursley, Division of the American Republics, July 1, 1941, NAW 812.6363/7354 2/11.

48. Memorandum signed by Herbert Bursley, Division of the American Republics, September 27, 1941, NAW 812.6363/7365 4/2.

49. Department of State to Ambassador Daniels, November 5, 1941, NAW 812.6363/7402.

50. *Times*, November 22, 1941.

51. The representatives were Manuel J. Zevada for Mexico and Morris L. Cooke for the United States. The agreement is on file under NAW 812.6363/7656.

52. The commissioners came up with the following figures: 18,391,641 dollars for Standard Oil of New Jersey, 3,589,158 dollars for Standard Oil of California, 630,151 dollars for Consolidated Oil Company, 897,671 dollars for the Sabalo Transportation group, and 487,370 for the International Petroleum Company—including in each case the respective affiliates operating in Mexico (M. Rippy, "El petróleo y la Revolución Mexicana," p. 166).

53. These firms were Compañía de Gas y Combustible "Imperio," Compañía Mexicana de Oleuductos "Imperio," Gulf Coast Company, Southern Fuel and Refining Company, Atlantic Gulf and West Indies Corporation, Mexican Atlas Petroleum Company, and Moctezuma Terminal Company.

54. Betty Kirk, *Covering the Mexican Front: The Battle of Europe versus America*, p. 352.

55. The Ministry of Foreign Affairs informed Ambassador Castillo Nájera that the injunctions had been granted because the decree of March 1938 did not make any mention of Titania or Mercedes (July 31, 1942, AREM III/628 "938"/2 L-E-556, part 4, f. 60).

56. Messersmith to Department of State, December 4, 1942, NAW 812.6363/7814.

57. This agreement also included indemnization for several firms not mentioned in the commissioners' report of 1942—namely, J. A. Brown; Green and Company; Doheny, Bridge and Company; Naviera Transportadora de Petróleo; Titania; and Mercedes.

58. These views are set forth in *Guaranty Survey* 23, no. 11 (February 24, 1944), a publication of the powerful Guaranty Trust Company of New York, which had close ties with the oil companies.

59. Memorandum from Herbert Bursley to Bonsal, Division of the American Republics, February 25, 1941, NAW 812.6363/7215½.

60. An example of Washington's cooperation with Mexico can be seen in a report on possible sabotage transmitted by the Department of State to Ambassador Castillo Nájera and forwarded by the latter in turn to the Ministry of Foreign Affairs, March 4, 1942, AREM III/628 "938"/2 L-E-591, Estados Unidos, f. 504.

61. Department of Interior to Department of State, February 20, 1942, and memorandum signed by Under Secretary of State Welles, February 24, 1942, NAW 812.6363/7616.

62. Memorandum from the Petroleum Adviser, Department of State, June 25, 1942, NAW 812.6363/7706; Messersmith to Department of State, July 28, 1942, NAW 812.6363/7700; final report of the commission headed by E. de Golyer, NAW 812.6363/7801.

63. Documentation on the plan to build a refinery for aircraft gasoline is copious, some of the most important references being found in NAW 812.6363/7802, 7854, 7867, 7932, 7968, 7969, 7989.

64. Memorandums signed by Herbert Bursley, Division of the American Republics, September 11 and October 20, 1941, NAW 812.6363/7325 5/11, 7362; report by Bursley, now as counselor in the U.S. embassy in Mexico City, to Department of State, January 6, 1943, NAW 812.6363/7826.

65. *New York Times*, January 31, 1942.

66. United Nations, International Law Commission, *Yearbook, 1960*, VII, 22–23. The convention also changed somewhat the traditional requirements with respect to "suitable and effective" payment.

67. James Fred Rippy, *British Investments in Latin America, 1822–1949*, p. 213. The problem with respect to the British interests took a little longer to be settled. In this case there was no intergovernmental agreement to cite because, despite the fact that diplomatic relations between England and Mexico had been resumed, the latter continued to insist that El Aguila was a Mexican firm. In 1940, 1941, and 1946 the British companies entered into talks with Mexican officials with a view to settling the problem, but the conditions were rejected as being far too onerous. In 1947, when Miguel Alemán took office, the Mexican government changed its position and agreed to compensate El Aguila in the amount of 130 million dollars, which was paid in full by 1962. (Antonio Bermúdez sets the figure at almost 200 million dollars.) This agreement has been widely criticized, since if the British investments in 1938 represented 50 per cent of the oil interests, they should have corresponded to the same amount of indemnization the Americans received, but not more. Bermúdez defends the agreement on the basis that in 1938 the British controlled more like 70 per cent of the oil industry (Antonio J. Bermúdez, "The Mexican National Petroleum Industry: A Case Study in Nationalization," *Hispanic American Report* [1963]: 27; *El Universal*, June 13, 1940; U.S. embassy in London to Department of State, October 23, 1941, NAW 812.6363/7395; Jesús Silva Herzog, *Mexico y su petróleo*, p. 59; idem, *Historia de la expropiación petrolera*, p. 170; Isidro Fabela, "La política internacional del presidente Cárdenas," *Problemas agrícolas e industriales de México* 7 [October–December 1955]: 108–109).

68. In a confidential letter to U.S. Attorney General Robert H. Jackson, Josephus Daniels repeated what he had said to Roosevelt: "We must destroy Monopoly or Monopoly will destroy Democracy." Within this line of thinking he recommended a thoroughgoing attack against the U.S. oil companies in general in order to break up their monopolies (September 20, 1940, JDP).

69. Sanford A. Mosk, *Industrial Revolution in Mexico*, pp. 83–85; Chester Lloyd Jones, "Production of Wealth in Mexico," *Mexico Today*, ed. Arthur P. Whitaker, p. 67.

70. As an example of this view, see *Diario de los negocios*, June 21, 1938.

71. William O. Scroggs, "Mexico's Oil in World Politics," *Foreign Affairs* 17 (October 1938): 172–173; Nathan, "México en la época de Cárdenas," p. 133.

72. *El Universal*, March 22, 1938.

73. Nathaniel and Silvia Weyl, "La reconquista de México: Los días de Lázaro Cárdenas," *Problemas agrícolas e industriales de México* 7 (October–December 1955): 298.

Sources Cited

Archives

AGN. General Archives of the Nation, Mexico City.
AREM. Archives of the Mexican Ministry of Foreign Affairs, Mexico City. (The symbols L-E indicate that the material is filed under its topographic heading; otherwise the numbers refer to the decimal classification system.)
CDHM. Mexican-Spanish Diplomatic Correspondence, El Colegio de México, Mexico City.
JDP. Josephus Daniels Papers, Manuscript Division, U.S. Library of Congress, Washington, D.C. [N.B.: Collection was reorganized in 1974.]
NAW. Records of the Department of State, U.S. National Archives, Washington, D.C.
WWP. Woodrow Wilson Papers, Manuscript Division, U.S. Library of Congress, Washington, D.C. [N.B.: Collection was reorganized in 1974.]

Books, Pamphlets, Articles, and Theses

Acosta Saignés, Miguel. *Petróleo en México y Venezuela*. Mexico City: Ediciones Morelos, 1941.
Aguilar, Cándido. *Iniciativa de ley orgánica del artículo 27 constitucional en lo relativo a petróleo que presenta el C. General . . . , Gobernador Constitucional del Estado de Veracruz a la H. Legislatura del mismo Estado, para ser enviada por ésta al Congresso de la Unión*. Mexico City: Imprenta Escalante, 1917.
Alba, Víctor. *Las ideas sociales contemporáneas en México*. Mexico City: Fondo de Cultura Económica, 1960.
Alessio Robles, Miguel. *Historia política de la Revolución*. 3rd ed. Mexico City: Ediciones Botas, 1946.
Alessio Robles, Vito. *Los tratados de Bucareli*. Mexico City: A. del Bosque, 1937.
Alperovich, Moisei S., and Boris T. Rudenko. *La Revolución Mexicana de 1910–1917 y la política de los Estados Unidos*. Mexico City, Editorial Popular, 1960.
Anguiano, Victoriano. "Cárdenas y el cardenismo." *Problemas agrícolas e industriales de México* 7 (July–September 1955).
APPM. *See* Association of Producers of Petroleum in Mexico.
Asociación Americana de México. *Condiciones de los americanos en México*. Special number of the *Boletín de la Asociación Americana de México*. New York: American Association of Mexico, 1921.
Association of Producers of Petroleum in Mexico (APPM). *Current Conditions in Mexico*. Mexico City, June 24, 1933.
———. *Documents Relating to the Attempt of the Government of Mexico to Confiscate Foreign-owned Oil Properties*. 1919.

———. *Petroleum Concessions on "Federal Zones" of Mexican Rivers, Their Unconstitutional, Illegal, and Confiscatory Character: Memorandum Submitted to the Secretary of State of the United States of America*. New York, 1921.

Bach, Federico, and Manuel de la Peña. *México y su petróleo: Síntesis histórica.* Mexico City: Editorial México Nuevo, 1938.

Baker, Ray Stannard. *Woodrow Wilson: Life and Letters*. Vols. 5, 6, 7. New York: Scribner's, 1946.

Barba González, Silvano. "Hechos y no palabras." *Problemas agrícolas e industriales de México* 7 (July–September 1955).

Barron, Clarence W. *The Mexican Problem*. Cambridge, Mass.: Houghton Mifflin, 1917.

Beals, Carleton. "Whose Property Is Kellogg Protecting?" *New Republic* 50, no. 638 (February 23, 1927).

Bell, James Dunbar. *Attitudes of Selected Groups in the United States toward Mexico, 1930–1940*. Chicago: University of Chicago Press, 1945.

Bemis, Samuel Flagg. *La diplomacia de Estados Unidos en la América Latina*. Mexico City: Fondo de Cultura Económica, 1944. (Translation of *The Latin American Policy of the United States*. New York: Harcourt, Brace, 1943.)

Bermúdez, Antonio J. "The Mexican National Petroleum Industry: A Case Study in Nationalization." *Hispanic-American Report* (1963).

Boracrés, Paul. *Le pétrole mexicain . . . Un "bien volé"?* Paris: Editions Internationales, 1939.

Bosques, Gilberto. *The National Revolutionary Party of Mexico and the Six-Year Plan*. Mexico City: Partido Nacional Revolucionario, 1937.

Brandenburg, Frank. *The Making of Modern Mexico*. Englewood Cliffs, N.J.: Prentice-Hall, 1964.

Brenner, Anita. *The Wind That Swept Mexico: The History of the Mexican Revolution, 1910–1942*. New York: Harper and Brothers, 1943.

Brokaw, Albert D. "Oil." *Foreign Affairs* 6 (October 1927).

Bullington, John P. "The Land and Petroleum Laws of Mexico." *American Journal of International Law* 22 (January 1928).

———. "Problems of International Law in the Mexican Constitution of 1917." *American Journal of International Law* 21 (October 1927).

Bussey, J. L. "Don Victoriano y la prensa yanqui." *Historia mexicana* 4 (April–June 1955).

Cabrera, Luis. *Veinte años después*. 3rd ed. Mexico City: Ediciones Botas, 1938.

Calero, Manuel, and Delbert J. Haff. *Concesiones petroleras en las zonas federales*. Mexico City: Imprenta Nacional, 1921.

Call, Tomme C. *The Mexican Venture: From Political to Industrial Revolution in Mexico*. New York: Oxford University Press, 1953.

Callahan, James Morton. *American Foreign Policy in Mexican Relations*. New York: Macmillan, 1932.

Callcott, Wilfred H. *Liberalism in Mexico, 1857–1929*. Stanford, Calif.: Stanford University Press, 1931.

Calles, Plutarco Elías. *Informes rendidos por el C. General . . . , Presidente Constitucional de los Estados Unidos Mexicanos ante el H. Congreso de la Unión los días 1° de septiembre de 1925 y 1° septiembre de 1926 y contestación de los C.C. presidentes del citado Congreso*. Mexico City: Talleres Gráficos de la Nación [1926].

———. *Mexico before the World*. New York: Academy Press, 1927.

———. "The Policies of Mexico Today." *Foreign Affairs* 5 (October 1926).

Campa, Valentín. "El cardenismo en la Revolución Mexicana." *Problemas agrícolas e industriales de México* 7 (July–September 1955).

Cárdenas, Lazaro. Excerpts from personal diary reprinted in *El Universal*, October 22, 1970.

———. *Mensaje a la Nación, dirigido el 4 de junio desde la ciudad de San Luis Potosí*. Mexico City: Talleres Gráficos de la Nación, 1938.

Carranza, Venustiano. *Informe del C. . . , Primer Jefe del Ejército Constitucionalista, encargado del Poder Ejecutivo de la República, leído ante el Congreso de la Unión en la sesión de 15 de abril de 1917*. Mexico City: La Editora Nacional, 1917.

Carreño, Alberto María. *La diplomacia extraordinaria entre México y los Estados Unidos, 1789–1947*. Vol. 11. Colección Figuras y Episodios de la Historia de México. Mexico City: Editorial Jus, 1961.

Carrillo, Alejandro. *The Mexican People and the Oil Companies*. Mexico City: DAPP, 1938.

———. "Pasado, presente y futuro de nuestro pueblo." *Problemas agrícolas e industriales de México* 6 (July–September 1954).

Castañeda, Jorge. "México y el exterior." In *México: 50 años de Revolución*, vol 3, *La política*. Mexico City: Fondo de la Cultura Económica, 1961.

Castillo Nájera, Francisco. *El petróleo en la industria moderna: Las compañías petroleras y los gobiernos de México*. Mexico City: Cámara Nacional de la Industria de Transformación, 1949.

Cerceña, José Luis. "La penetración extranjera y los grupos de poder en México, 1870–1910." *Problemas del desarrollo: Revista latinoamericana de economía* 1, no. 1 (October–December 1969).

Clark, J. Reuben. "The Oil Settlement with Mexico." *Foreign Affairs* 6 (July 1928).

Clendenen, Clarence C. *The United States and Pancho Villa: A Study in Unconventional Diplomacy*. Ithaca, N.Y.: Cornell University Press, 1953.

Cline, Howard F. *The United States and Mexico*. Cambridge, Mass.: Harvard University Press, 1953.

Close, Upton. "La expropiación petrolera y los Estados Unidos." *Excélsior*, November 7, 1938.

Colegio de México, ed. *Estadísticas económicas del porfiriato: Comercio exterior de México, 1877–1911*. Mexico City, 1960.

Compañía Petrolera Comercial. *La sombra internacional de El Aguila*. Mexico City, 1935.

Compilation of Documents with Regard to the Draft of Expropriation Law. Mexico City, 1936.

Correa, Eduardo J. *El balance del cardenismo*. Mexico City, 1941.

Cosío Villegas, Daniel. *Extremos de América*. Mexico City: Tezontle, 1949. (Translated by Américo Paredes as *American Extremes*. Austin: University of Texas Press, 1964.)

———, ed. *Historia moderna de México: El porfiriato*. Mexico City: Editorial Hermes, 1963–1965.

Cox, George Howland. "Mexico's Industrialization Program." *World Affairs* 97 (June 1934).

Cronon, Edmund David. *Josephus Daniels in Mexico*. Madison: University of Wisconsin Press, 1960.

———, ed. *The Cabinet Diaries of Josephus Daniels, 1913–1921*. Lincoln: University of Nebraska Press, 1963.

Cuevas Cancino, Francisco. *Roosevelt y la Buena Vecindad*. Mexico City: Fondo de Cultura Económica, 1954.

Cumberland, Charles C. *The Mexican Revolution: Genesis under Madero*. Austin:

University of Texas Press, 1952.

———. *Mexico: The Struggle for Modernity*. New York: Oxford University Press, 1968.

Daniels, Josephus. *The Life of Woodrow Wilson, 1856–1924*. Philadelphia and Chicago: John C. Winston, 1924.

———. *Shirt-Sleeve Diplomat*. Chapel Hill: University of North Carolina Press, 1947.

———. *The Wilson Era*. Chapel Hill: University of North Carolina Press, 1944.

De Bekker, Leander Jan. *The Plot against Mexico*. New York: Alfred A. Knopf, 1919.

De Conde, Alexander. *Herbert Hoover's Latin American Policy*. Stanford, Calif.: Stanford University Press, 1951.

De la Huerta, Adolfo. *Memorias de don Adolfo de la Huerta según su propio dictado*. Mexico City: Ediciones Guzmán, 1957.

Delaisi, Francis. *Oil: Its Influence on Politics*. London: Labour Publishing, 1922.

De la Peña, Manuel. *La cuestion palpitante: Estudio jurídico, político y económico sobre el artículo 27 constitucional*. Mexico City: Cámara de Diputados, 1921.

———. *El dominio directo del soberano en las minas de México y génesis de la legislación petrolera mexicana*. 2 vols. Mexico City: Secretaría de Industria, Comercio y Trabajo, 1928–1932.

———. *Necesidad de reformar la ley del petróleo orgánica del artículo 27 constitucional*. Pamphlet. Mexico City, 1936.

———. *El petróleo y la legislación frente a las compañías petroleras*. Mexico City: Secretaría de Gobernación, 1920.

Denny, Ludwell. *We Fight for Oil*. New York: Alfred A. Knopf, 1928.

Díaz Dufoo, Carlos. *La cuestión del petróleo*. Mexico City: Eusebio Gómez de la Puente, 1921.

———. *México y los capitales extranjeros*. Mexico City: Librería Viuda de C. Bouret, 1918.

Dillon, Emile Joseph. *México en su momento crítico*. Mexico City: Herrero Hermanos Sucesores, 1922. (Translation of *Mexico on the Verge*. New York: George H. Doran, 1921; Arno Press, 1970.)

"Documents Relating to the Petroleum Law of Mexico of December 26, 1925, with Amendments of January 3, 1928." Mimeographed. Mexico City, 1928.

Doheny, Edward L. *The Mexican Question: Its Relations to Our Industries, Our Merchant Marine, and Our Foreign Trade*. Los Angeles, 1919.

D'Olwer, Luis Nicolau. "Las inversiones extranjeras." In *Historia moderna de México: El porfiriato; La vida económica*, edited by Daniel Cosío Villegas. Mexico City: Editorial Hermes, 1965.

Dulles, John W. F. *Yesterday in Mexico: A Chronicle of the Revolution, 1919–1936*. Austin: University of Texas Press, 1961.

Dunn, Frederick Sherwood. *The Diplomatic Protection of Americans in Mexico*. New York: Columbia University Press, 1933.

Durand, Daniel. *La política petrolera internacional*. Buenos Aires: Editorial Universitaria, 1965.

Duroselle, Jean-Baptiste. *Política exterior de los Estados Unidos: De Wilson a Roosevelt, 1913–1945*. Mexico City: Fondo de Cultura Económica, 1965.

Elízaga, Lorenzo, Luis Ibarra, and Manuel Fernández Guerra. *Proyecto de ley del petróleo y exposición de motivos de la misma que presentan al Ministerio de Fomento los señores licenciados . . .* Mexico City: Talleres El Tiempo, 1905.

Engler, Robert. *La política petrolera: Un estudio del poder privado y las directivas democráticas*. Mexico City: Fondo de Cultura Económica, 1966. (Translation of *The Politics of Oil: A Study of Private Power and Democratic Directions*. New York: Macmillan, 1961.)

En pro del reconocimiento de México por el gobierno de los Estados Unidos. Pamphlet. Mexico City, 1922.

Esquivel Obregón, Toribio. *México y los Estados Unidos ante el derecho internacional.* Mexico City: Herrero Hermanos Sucesores, 1926.

Fabela, Isidro. *Documentos históricos de la Revolución Mexicana.* Vol. 4. Mexico City: Fondo de Cultura Económica, 1963.

———. *Historia diplomática de la Revolución Mexicana.* 2 vols. Mexico City: 1958–1959.

———. "La política internacional del presidente Cárdenas." *Problemas agrícolas e industriales de México* 7 (October–December 1955).

Fernández Boyoli, Manuel, and E. Marrón de Angelis. *Lo que no se sabe de la rebelión cedillista.* Mexico City, 1938.

Feuerlein, Willy John, and Elizabeth Hannan. *Dólares en la América Latina.* Mexico City: Fondo de Cultura Económica, 1944. (Translation of *Dollars in Latin America: An Old Problem in a New Setting.* New York: Council on Foreign Relations, 1941.)

Flores, Manuel. *Apuntes sobre el petróleo mexicano.* 1913.

Frank, Waldo. "Cárdenas of Mexico." *Foreign Affairs* 18 (October 1939).

Fresco, Mauricio. *Synthèse du conflit de pétrole au Mexique.* Pamphlet. Paris, 1938.

Fuentes Díaz, Vicente. *Los partidos políticos en México.* Vol. 2, *De Carranza a Ruíz Cortines.* Mexico City: published by the author, 1956.

Gaither, Roscoe B. *Expropriation in Mexico.* New York: William Morrow, 1940.

García Cantú, Gastón. *El pensamiento de la reacción mexicana: Historia documental, 1810–1962.* Mexico City: Empresas Editoriales, 1965.

García Granados, Jorge. *Los veneros del diablo.* Mexico City: Ediciones Liberación, 1941.

Glade, William P., and Charles W. Anderson. *The Political Economy of Mexico.* Vol. 2. Madison: University of Wisconsin Press, 1963.

Goldsmith, Raymond W. *The Financial Development of Mexico.* Paris: Development Center, Organization for Economic Cooperation and Development, 1966.

Gómez Robledo, Antonio. *The Bucareli Agreements and International Law.* Translated by Salomón de la Selva. Mexico City: National University of Mexico Press, 1940.

González Aguayo, Leopoldo. *La nacionalización en América Latina.* Mexico City, 1965.

González Aparicio, Enrique. *Nuestro petróleo.* Mexico City: Editorial Masas, 1938.

González Navarro, Moisés. *La Confederación Nacional Campesina.* Mexico City: Costa-Amic, 1968.

———. *Estadísticas sociales del porfiriato, 1887–1910.* Mexico City: Dirección General de Estadística, Secretaría de Economía, 1956.

———. "La ideología de la Revolución Mexicana." *Historia mexicana* 10 (April–June 1961).

González Ramírez, Manuel. *Fuentes para la historia de la Revolución Mexicana.* Vol. 1, *Planes políticos y otros documentos.* Mexico City: Fondo de Cultura Económica, 1954.

———. *Los llamados tratados de Bucareli: México y los Estados Unidos en las convenciones internacionales de 1923.* Mexico City, 1939.

———. *El petróleo mexicano: La expropiación petrolera ante el derecho internacional.* Mexico City: Editorial América, 1941.

———. "La política exterior del presidente Obregón." *Problemas agrícolas e industriales de México* 7 (October–December 1955).

———. *La revolución social de México.* Vol. 1. Mexico City: Fondo de Cultura Económica, 1960.

González Roa, Fernando. *Las cuestiones fundamentales de actualidad en México.* Mexico City: Secretaría de Relaciones Exteriores, 1927.

Gordon, Wendell C. *The Expropriation of Foreign-owned Property in Mexico.* Washington: American Council on Public Affairs, 1941.

Grieb, Kenneth J. *The United States and Huerta.* Lincoln: University of Nebraska Press, 1969.

Hackett, Charles Wilson. *The Mexican Revolution and the United States, 1910–1926.* Boston: World Peace Foundation, 1926.

Haley, P. E. *Revolution and Intervention: The Diplomacy of Taft and Wilson with Mexico, 1910–1917.* Cambridge: Massachusetts Institute of Technology, 1971.

Halperin Donghi, Tulio. *Historia contemporánea de América Latina.* Madrid: Alianza Editorial, 1969.

Hanighen, Frank C. *The Secret War.* New York: John Day, 1934.

Harrison, John P. "Un análisis norteamericano de la Revolución Mexicana en 1913." *Historia mexicana* 5 (April–June 1956).

Hawk, Walter D. "Aspectos de la cuestión petrolera que quedan comprendidos en la diplomacia mexicano-americana." Manuscript translation of article in *Illinois Law Review* 22 (June 1927).

Herring, Hubert. *México: La formación de una nación.* Mexico City: Ediciones Minerva, 1943. (Translation of *Mexico: The Making of a Nation.* New York: Foreign Policy Association, 1942.)

————, and Herbert Weinstock, eds. *Renascent Mexico.* New York: Covici Friede Publishers, 1935.

Hoffman, Fritz. "Edward Doheny and the Beginning of Petroleum Development in Mexico." *Mid-America* 13 (1942).

Huasteca Petroleum Company and Standard Oil of California. *Expropiación: Un estudio de los hechos, causas, métodos y efectos de la dominación política de la industria en México.* Pamphlet. [1938]. (Translation of *Expropriation: A Factual Study of the Causes, Methods, and Effects of Political Domination of Industry in Mexico.* New York: Marben Press, 1938.)

Hull, Cordell. *The Memoirs of Cordell Hull.* 2 vols. New York: Macmillan, 1948.

Hurley, Patrick J. *La lucha por el petróleo mexicano: Declaración del coronel . . . , abogado de la Consolidated Oil Corporation, ante la Comisión de Ferrocarriles del Estado de Texas.* Mexico City: Editorial Cultura, 1940. (Translation of *The Struggle for Mexican Oil: Statement by Attorney for the Consolidated Oil Corporation, . . . , Made before the Railways Commission of the State of Texas.* Mexico City: Editorial Cultura, 1940.)

Hutton, Graham. "The New-Old Crisis in Mexico." *Foreign Affairs* 16 (July 1938).

Inman, Samuel Guy. *Democracy versus the Totalitarian State in Latin America.* Philadelphia: American Academy of Political and Social Sciences, 1938.

Ise, John. *The United States Oil Policy.* New Haven: Yale University Press, 1926.

Jacobo, Juan. "La huelga contra El Aguila en 1924." *El Día,* April 8, 1970.

James, Daniel. *Mexico and the Americans.* New York: Praeger, 1963.

Jones, Chester Lloyd. "Production of Wealth in Mexico." In *Mexico Today,* edited by Arthur P. Whitaker. Philadelphia: American Academy of Political and Social Sciences, 1940.

Kaplan, Marcos. *Formación del estado nacional en América Latina.* Santiago, Chile: Editorial Universitaria, 1969.

Kelley, Francis C. *The Mexican Question.* New York: Paulist Press, 1926.

Kellogg, Frederick R. "The Mexican Oil Problem." *Nation,* October 5, 1918.

Kirk, Betty. *Covering the Mexican Front: The Battle of Europe versus America.* Norman: University of Oklahoma Press, 1942.

Kluckhohn, Frank L. *The Mexican Challenge*. New York: Doubleday Doran, 1939.

Kunz, Josef L. *The Mexican Expropriations*. Contemporary Law Pamphlets. New York: New York University School of Law, 1940.

Lavín, José Domingo. "Notas al libro de Merrill Rippy." *Problemas agrícolas e industriales de México* 6 (July–September 1954).

———. *Petróleo*. Mexico City: EDIAPSA, 1950.

L'Espagnol de la Tramerge, Pierre. *La Lutte mondiale pour le pétrole*. Paris: Editions La Vie Universitaire, 1921.

Lewis, Cleona. *America's Stake in International Investments*. In collaboration with Karl T. Schlotterbeck. Washington: Brookings Institution, 1938.

Lewis, George K. "An Analysis of the Institutional Status and Role of the Petroleum Industry in Mexico's Evolving System of Political Economy." Doctoral dissertation, University of Texas (Austin), 1959.

Lieuwin, Edwin. *Mexican Militarism: The Rise and Fall of the Revolutionary Army, 1910–1940*. Albuquerque: University of New Mexico Press, 1968.

Lippman, Walter. "Vested Rights and Nationalism in Latin America." *Foreign Affairs* 5 (April 1927).

Lobato López, Ernesto. "El petróleo en la economía." In *México: 50 años de Revolución*, vol. 1, *La economía*. Mexico City: Fondo de Cultura Económica, 1960.

López Gallo, Manuel. *Economía y política en la historia de México*. Mexico City: Ediciones Solidaridad, 1965.

McConnell, Burt M. *Mexico at the Bar of Public Opinion*. New York: Mail and Express Publishing Company, 1939.

MacCorkle, Stuart Alexander. *American Policy of Recognition towards Mexico*. Baltimore: Johns Hopkins Press, 1933.

McCrea, William S. "A Comparative Study of the Mexican Oil Expropriation (1938) and the Iranian Oil Nationalization (1951)." Doctoral dissertation, Georgetown University, 1955.

McCullagh, Francis. *Red Mexico*. N.p.: Louis Carrier, 1928.

McHenry, Patrick J. *A Short History of Mexico*. New York: Doubleday, 1962.

Madero, Francisco I. *La sucesión presidencial de 1910*. Mexico City: Los Insurgentes, 1960.

Magdaleno, Mauricio. *Las palabras perdidas*. Mexico City: Fondo de Cultura Económica, 1956.

Mancisidor, José. *Historia de la Revolución Mexicana*. 4th ed. Mexico City: Libro Mex, 1964.

Manero Suárez, Adolfo, and José Paniagua Arredondo. *Los tratados de Bucareli: Traición y sangre sobre México*. 2 vols. Mexico City, 1958.

Manterola, Miguel. *La industria del petróleo en México*. Mexico City: Secretaría de Hacienda y Crédito Público, 1938.

María y Campos, Armando. *Múgica: Crónica biográfica*. Mexico City: CEPSA, 1939.

Márquez Sterling, Manuel. *Los últimos días del presidente Madero*. Havana: Imprenta Nacional de Cuba, 1960.

Melgarejo, Luis, and J. Fernández Rojas. *El Congreso Constituyente de 1916–1917*. Mexico City, 1917.

Mena, Mario. *Alvaro Obregón: Historia militar y política, 1912–1929*. Mexico City: Editorial Jus, 1960.

Mendoza, Salvador. *La controversia del petróleo*. Mexico City: Imprenta Politécnica, 1921.

Mexican Petroleum Company and Huasteca Petroleum Company. *Los impuestos sobre la industria petrolera*. Mexico City, 1912.

Mexico. *La cuestión petrolera mexicana: El punto de vista del Ejecutivo Federal*.

Mexico City: Talleres Gráficos de la Nación, 1919.

———. *La verdad sobre la expropiación de los bienes de las empresas petroleras.* Mexico City: Talleres Gráficos de la Nación, 1940.

———, Cámara de Diputados del Congreso de la Unión, Comisión Especial Reglamentaria del Artículo 27. *Proyecto de ley orgánica del artículo 27 de la Constitución Política de la República en la parte relativa a los combustibles minerales presentado por el C. diputado Justo A. Santa Anna.* Mexico City, 1925.

———, Cámara de Senadores. *Dictamen de las Comisiones Unidas del Petróleo y Primera de Puntos Constitucionales acerca del proyecto de ley orgánica del artículo 27 en la parte relativa al petróleo.* Mexico City, 1923.

———, Cámara de Senadores, Sección de Estadística y Anales de Jurisprudencia. *El petróleo: La más grande riqueza nacional.* Mexico City, 1923.

———, Congreso de la Unión. *Proyecto de ley reglamentaria del artículo 27 constitucional en el ramo del petróleo formulado por la Comisión Mixta.* Mexico City: Cámara de Diputados, 1925.

———, Departamento Autónomo de Prensa y Propaganda. *Notas diplomáticas cruzadas entre los gobiernos de México y la Gran Bretaña con motivo de la expropiación de la industria petrolera.* Mexico City, 1938.

———, Poder Legislativo. *Diario de los debates del Congreso Constituyente, 1916–1917.* Mexico City: Talleres Gráficos de la Nación, 1960.

———, Secretaría de Economía Nacional. *Programa de los fundadores de Petróleos de México, S.A.* Mexico City: Talleres Gráficos de la Nación.

———, Secretaría de Educación Pública. *Sobre el petróleo de México: Conferencias.* Mexico City: Departamento Autónomo de Prensa y Propaganda, 1938.

———, Secretaría de Gobernación. *Seis años de gobierno al servicio de México, 1934–1940.* Mexico City, 1940.

———, Secretaría de Hacienda y Crédito Público, Dirección General de Ingresos. "Egresos e ingresos del Gobierno Federal, 1900–1958." Mimeographed. Mexico City, 1959.

———, Secretaría de Industria, Comercio y Trabajo. *Documentos relacionados con la legislación petrolera mexicana.* Mexico City, 1919.

———, ———. *La industria, el comercio y el trabajo en México durante la gestión administrativa del señor general Plutarco Elías Calles.* Vols. 1, 5. Mexico City: Tipografía Galas, 1928.

———, ———. *Iniciativa de ley orgánica del artículo 27 constitucional en el ramo del petróleo: Exposición de motivos y fundamentos.* Mexico City, 1938.

———, ———. *Legislación petrolera, 1783–1921.* Mexico City: Secretaría de Educación Pública, 1922.

———, ———. *Ley del petróleo y su reglamento: Edición oficial.* Mexico City: Talleres Gráficos de la Nación, 1926.

———, ———. *Proyecto de ley del petróleo de los Estados Unidos Mexicanos.* Mexico City: Secretaría de Hacienda, 1918.

———, ———. *Proyecto de ley orgánica del artículo 27 constitucional en el ramo del petróleo aprobado por la H. Cámara de Senadores y enviada a la H. Cámara de Diputados para su discusión.* Mexico City: Talleres Gráficos de la Nación, 1920.

———, ———, Departamento de Petróleo. *Junta celebrada el día 13 de octubre de 1917, en el salón de juntas de la Secretaría de Industria y Comercio, a que fueron convocados los industriales petroleros por medio del circular num. 3, de fecha primero del mismo mes.* Mexico City: Talleres Gráficos de la Secretaría de Comunicaciones, 1917.

———, Secretaría del Patrimonio Nacional. *El petróleo de México: Recopilación de documentos oficiales de orden económico de la industria petrolera, con una introducción que resume sus motivos y consecuencias*. Rev. ed. Mexico City, 1963.

———, Secretaría de Relaciones Exteriores. *Correspondencia oficial cambiada entre el Gobierno de México y los Estados Unidos con motivo de las dos leyes reglamentarias de la fracción primera del artículo 27 de la Constitución Mexicana*. Mexico City, 1926.

———, ———. *La cuestión internacional mexicano-americana durante el gobierno del general don Alvaro Obregón*. 3rd ed. Mexico City: Editorial Cultura, 1949.

———, ———. *Tribunales extranjeros reconocen el indiscutible derecho con que México expropió los intereses petroleros*. Mexico City: Talleres Gráficos de la Nación, 1940.

Meyer, Jean. "Les Ouvriers dans la Révolution mexicaine: Les Bataillones rouges." *Annales* 25 (January–February 1970).

Meyer, Lorenzo. "Cambio político y dependencia: México en el siglo XX." In *La política exterior de México: Realidad y perspectivas*, pp. 1–38. Mexico City: El Colegio de México, Centro de Estudios Internacionales, 1972.

Mikesell, Raymond F., ed. *U.S. Private and Government Investment Abroad*. Eugene: University of Oregon Press, 1962.

Molina Enríquez, Andrés. *Los grandes problemas nacionales*. Mexico City: A. Carranza, 1909.

Moreno Sánchez, Manuel. "Comentarios al estudio de Paul Nathan, 'Un estudio norteamericano sobre Cárdenas.'" *Problemas agrícolas e industriales de México* 7 (July–September 1955).

———. *Crisis política de México*. Mexico City: Editorial Extemporáneos, 1970.

Morineau, Oscar. *The Good Neighbor*. Mexico City, 1938.

Morison, Samuel Eliot, and Henry Steele Commager. *Historia de los Estados Unidos de Norteamérica*. Vols. 2, 3. Mexico City: Fondo de Cultura Económica, 1951. (Translation of *The Growth of the American Republic*. 4th ed. New York: Oxford University Press, 1950.)

Mosk, Sanford A. *Industrial Revolution in Mexico*. Berkeley and Los Angeles: University of California Press, 1950.

Nathan, Paul. "México en la época de Cárdenas." *Problemas agrícolas e industriales de México* 7 (July–September 1955).

National Student Federation of America. *The Present Dispute between Mexico and the United States: Is Arbitration the Way Out?* Pamphlet. N.p., 1927.

Navarrete, Alfredo. "La inversión extranjera directa en México." *Mercado de valores* (October 1966).

Nicolson, Harold. *Dwight Morrow*. New York: Harcourt, Brace, 1935.

Obregón, Alvaro. *Campaña política del C. . . . , candidato a la presidencia de la República, 1920–1924*. 5 vols. Mexico City, 1923.

———. *Discursos del general . . . .* 2 vols. Mexico City: Biblioteca de la Dirección General de Educación Militar, 1932.

———. *Informes rendidos por el C. Presidente Constitucional al Congreso de 1921– 1924 y contestación de los presidentes del Congreso en el mismo período*. Mexico City: Talleres del Diario Oficial, 1924.

O'Connor, Harvey. *El imperio del petróleo*. Mexico City: Editorial América Nueva, 1956. (Translation of *The Empire of Oil*. New York: Monthly Review Press, 1955.)

[Oil companies]. *Alegatos que presentan ante la Suprema Corte de Justicia de la Nación las siguientes compañías y personas . . . en los juicios de amparo promovidos contra leyes y actos del Ejecutivo de la Unión y de sus dependencias, la*

Secretaría de Gobernación, la Secretaría de Hacienda y Crédito Público y la Secretaría de Industria, Comercio y Trabajo. Mexico City: J. Escalante, 1919.

———. *Demanda de amparo y recurso administrativo de revocación contra el Decreto de Expropiación de la industria petrolera.* N.p. [1938?].

———. *The Mexican Oil Strike of 1937.* Vol. 1; vol. 3, *The Decision of the Labour Board;* vol. 4, *The Expropriatory Decree.* N.p., 1938.

———. *Objeciones de la industria petrolera al informe y dictamen de la comisión pericial.* Mexico City, 1937.

Ortega, Gustavo. *Los recursos petrolíferos mexicanos y su actual explotación.* Mexico City: Talleres Gráficos de la Nación, 1925.

O'Shaughnessy, Edith. *Une Femme de diplomate au Mexique.* Paris: Plan-Nourrit, 1918. (Translation of *A Diplomat's Wife in Mexico.* New York and London: Harper and Brothers, 1916; Arno Press, 1970.)

Palavicini, Félix F. *Historia de la Constitución de 1917.* 2 vols. Mexico City, 1938.

Pan American Petroleum and Transport Company. *Mexican Petroleum.* New York, 1922.

Pani, Alberto J. *Apuntes autobiográficos.* 2 vols. Mexico City: Librería de Manuel Porrúa, 1950.

———. *Las conferencias de Bucareli.* Mexico City: Editorial Jus, 1953.

———. *Introducción a la cuestión internacional mexicano-americana, durante el gobierno del general don Alvaro Obregón.* 3rd ed. Mexico City: Editorial Cultura, 1936.

———. *Mi contribución al nuevo régimen, 1910–1933.* Mexico City: Editorial Cultura, 1936.

———. *Tres monografías.* Mexico City, 1941.

Pani, Arturo. *Alberto J. Pani: Ensayo biográfico.* Mexico City, 1961.

Parkes, Henry Bamford. *A History of Mexico.* Cambridge, Mass.: Riverside Press, 1938.

Patiño, Emilio Alanís. "La energía en México." *Investigación económica* 14 (January–March 1954).

Pearson, Harlow S. *Mexican Oil: Symbol of Recent Trends in International Relations.* New York: Harper and Brothers, 1942.

Pérez López, Enrique. "El producto nacional." In *México: 50 años de Revolución,* vol. 1, *La economía,* pp. 487–588. Mexico City: Fondo de Cultura Económica, 1960.

"El petróleo y la economía mexicana: Informe del Comité Wolverton a la Cámara de Diputados de los Estados Unidos." Translated by Manuel Sánchez Sarto. *Problemas agrícolas e industriales de México* 6 (October–December 1954).

Portes Gil, Emilio. *Autobiografía de la Revolución Mexicana.* Mexico City: Instituto Mexicano de Cultura, 1964.

———. "Como se conjuró en 1927 una invasión armada." *El Universal,* May 26, 1950; May 28, 1950; *El Nacional,* October 30, 1950; November 1, 1950; *Mañana,* August 22, 1953; August 29, 1953.

Powell, Richard J. *The Mexican Petroleum Industry.* Berkeley: University of California Press, 1956.

Pringle, Henry Fowles. *The Life and Times of William Howard Taft.* 2 vols. New York: Holt and Rinehart, 1939.

Puente, Ramón. *Hombres de la Revolución: Calles.* Los Angeles, 1933.

Puig Casauranc, José Manuel. *El sentido social del proceso histórico de México.* Mexico City: Ediciones Botas, 1936.

Quirk, Robert E. *The Mexican Revolution, 1914–1915: The Convention of Aguascalientes.* New York: Citadel Press, 1963.

Requa, Mark Lawrence. *The Petroleum Problem*. Philadelphia: Curtis Publishing, 1920.

Reynolds, T. H. "México y los Estados Unidos, 1821–1951." *Historia mexicana* 2 (January–March 1953).

Rice, Elizabeth Ann. *The Diplomatic Relations between the United States and Mexico as Affected by the Struggle for Religious Liberty in Mexico, 1925–1929*. Washington, D.C.: Catholic University Press, 1959.

Richberg, Donald R. *Alegato sobre la cuestión petrolera de México*. Mexico City: Comisión de Estudios de la Presidencia, 1940.

Rippy, James Fred. *British Investments in Latin America, 1822–1949*. Minneapolis: University of Minnesota Press, 1959.

———. *Latin America in World Politics: An Outline Survey*. New York: Alfred A. Knopf, 1928.

———. *The United States and Mexico*. New York: F. S. Crofts, 1931.

———, José Vasconcelos, and Guy Stevens. *American Policies Abroad: Mexico*. Chicago: University of Chicago Press, 1928.

Rippy, Merrill. "El petróleo y la Revolución Mexicana." *Problemas agrícolas e industriales de México* 6 (July–September 1954). (Translation of *Oil and the Mexican Revolution*. Leiden: Bill, 1972.)

Rodríguez, Antonio. *El rescate del petróleo: Epopeya de un pueblo*. Mexico City: Ediciones Revista Siempre, 1958.

Romero Flores, Jesús. *Anales históricos de la Revolución Mexicana*. 3 vols. Mexico City: Libro-Mex, 1960.

Rondero, Javier. "Características del nacionalismo." In *México: 50 años de Revolución*, vol. 3, *La política*. Mexico City: Fondo de Cultura Económica, 1961.

Rosenzweig, Fernando. "El desarrollo económico de México, 1877–1911." *Trimestre económico* 32 (July–September 1965).

Ross, Stanley R. "Dwight Morrow and the Mexican Revolution." *Hispanic-American Historical Review* 38 (1958).

———, et al. *Historia documental de México*. Vol. 2. Mexico City: Universidad Nacional Autónoma de México, 1964.

Rouaix, Pastor. *Génesis de los artículos 27 y 123 de la Constitución Política de 1917*. Mexico City: Biblioteca del Instituto Nacional de Estudios Históricos de la Revolución, 1959.

Rudenko, Boris T., et al. *La Revolución Mexicana: Cuatro estudios soviéticos*. Translated from Russian by Arnoldo Martínez Verdugo and Alejo Méndez García. Mexico City: Ediciones Los Insurgentes, 1960.

Sáenz, Aarón. *La política internacional de la Revolución: Estudios y documentos*. Mexico City: Fondo de Cultura Económica, 1961.

Sáenz, Moisés, and Herbert I. Priestley. *Some Mexican Problems*. Chicago: University of Chicago Press, 1926.

Sands, William F., and Joseph M. Lalley. *Our Jungle Diplomacy*. Chapel Hill: University of North Carolina Press, 1944.

Santaella, Joaquín. *El petróleo en México: Factor económico*. Mexico City: Lebrija y Aguilar, 1937.

Schneider, Franz. "The Financial Future of Mexico." *Foreign Affairs* 7 (October 1928).

Scroggs, William O. "Mexican Anxieties." *Foreign Affairs* 18 (January 1940).

———. "Mexico's Oil in World Politics." *Foreign Affairs* 17 (October 1938).

Shulgovski, Anatol. *México en la encrucijada de su historia*. Mexico City: Fondo de Cultura Popular, 1968.

Silva Herzog, Jesús. *El agrarismo mexicano y la reforma agraria: Exposición y crí-*

tica. Mexico City: Fondo de Cultura Económica, 1959.

———. *Historia de la expropiación petrolera*. Mexico City: Cuadernos Americanos, 1963.

———. *Meditaciones sobre México: Notas y ensayos*. Mexico City: Cuadernos Americanos, 1948.

———. *México y su petróleo*. Buenos Aires: Universidad de Buenos Aires, 1959.

———. *Petróleo mexicano*. Mexico City: Fondo de Cultura Económica, 1941.

Silva Herzog Flores, Jesús. "Consideraciones sobre la industria petrolera y el desarrollo económico de México." Master's thesis, National University of Mexico, 1957.

Simpson, Lesley Byrd. *Many Mexicos*. Berkeley: University of California Press, 1961.

Standard Oil of New Jersey. *Confiscation or Expropriation? Mexico's Seizure of the Foreign-owned Oil Industry*. Pamphlet. New York, 1940.

———. *Denials of Justice*. Pamphlet. New York, 1938–1940.

———. *Diplomatic Protection*. Pamphlet. New York, 1939.

———. *Empty Promises*. Pamphlet. New York, 1940.

———. *The Fine Art of Squeezing*. Pamphlet. New York, 1938–1940.

———. *Investments and Trade*. Pamphlet. New York, 1938–1940.

———. *The Mexican Expropriation in International Law*. Pamphlet. New York, 1938.

———. *Present Status of the Mexican Oil Expropriation*. Pamphlet. New York, 1940.

———. *The Reply to Mexico*. Pamphlet. New York, 1938–1940.

———. *Respuesta de las compañías petroleras al documento del Gobierno Mexicano intitulado "La verdad sobre la expropiación de los bienes de las empresas petroleras."* New York, 1941.

———. *The Solution for the Mexican Confiscation*. Pamphlet. New York, 1938–1940.

———. *They Took What They Wanted*. Pamphlet. New York, 1938–1940.

———. *Whose Oil Is It? The Question of Subsoil Rights in Mexico*. New York, 1939.

Stephenson, George M. *John Lind of Minnesota*. Minneapolis: University of Minnesota Press, 1935.

Stevens, Guy. *Current Controversies with Mexico: Addresses and Writings*. N.p. [1929].

———, Santiago Iglesias, and Heberto M. Sein. *The Issue in Mexico, Discussed by . . . : A Stenographic Report of the 87th Session . . . of the Foreign Policy Association*. Foreign Policy Association Pamphlet 38. New York, 1926.

Stocking, George Ward, and Jesús Silva Herzog. *Mexican Expropriation: The Mexican Oil Problem*. New York: Carnegie Endowment for International Peace, Division of Intercourse and Education, 1938.

Stuart, Graham H. *Latin America and the United States*. New York and London: Appleton-Century, 1943.

Tannenbaum, Frank. *Mexico: The Struggle for Peace and Bread*. New York: Alfred A. Knopf, 1956.

Tanner, N. B. "Diplomacy of the Expropriation of the American Oil Industry in Mexico." Master's thesis, Texas College of Arts and Industries (Kingsville), 1940.

Tattersall, James Neville. "The Impact of Foreign Investment on Mexico." Master's thesis, University of Washington, 1956.

Thompson, Wallace. "Wanted: A Mexican Policy." *Atlantic Monthly* (March 1927): 386.

Townsend, William C. *Lázaro Cárdenas: Demócrata mexicano*. Mexico City: Editorial Grijalvo, 1959. (Translation of *Lázaro Cárdenas: Mexican Democrat*. Ann Arbor: G. Wahr, 1952.)

————. *The Truth about Mexico's Oil*. Los Angeles: Summer Institute of Linguistics, 1940.

Turlington, Edgar. "Foreign Investments." In *Mexico Today*, edited by Arthur P. Whitaker. Philadelphia: American Academy of Political and Social Sciences, 1940.

————. *Mexico and Her Foreign Creditors*. New York: Columbia University Press, 1930.

Ulloa, Berta. *Revolución Mexicana, 1910–1920*. Mexico City: Secretaría de Relaciones Exteriores, 1963.

United Nations, International Law Commission. *Yearbook, 1960*. A/CN.4/Ser.A/ 1960. New York, 1960.

United States, 66th Congress, 2nd session, Senate Committee on Foreign Relations. *Investigation of Mexican Affairs: Preliminary Report and Hearings . . . Pursuant to Senate Resolution No. 106 Directing the Committee . . . to Investigate the Matter of Outrages on Citizens of the United States in Mexico*. Senate Document 285. Washington, D.C., 1920.

————, 69th Congress, 2nd session, Senate Committee on Foreign Relations. *Oil Concessions in Mexico: Message from the President of the United States Transmitting Report of the Secretary of State in Response to Senate Resolution No. 330, Submitting Certain Information Respecting Oil Lands or Oil Concessions in Mexico*. Senate Document 210. Washington, D.C., 1927.

————, 76th Congress, 1st session, Senate. *Resolution Authorizing an Investigation of Conditions in Mexico as Affecting Property Rights of American Citizens*. Senate Resolution 72. Washington, D.C., 1939.

————, 76th Congress, 1st session, Senate. *Resolution Authorizing an Investigation of Negotiations by American Citizens or Officials with the Mexican Government Concerning Certain Oil Sales*. Senate Resolution 177. Washington, D.C., 1939.

————, 80th Congress, 2nd session, House of Representatives Committee on Interstate and Foreign Commerce. *Fuel Investigation: Mexican Petroleum*. House Report 2470. Washington, D.C., 1949.

————, Department of State. *Foreign Relations of the United States: Diplomatic Papers, 1940*. Vol. 5, *The American Republics*. Washington, D.C., 1961.

————, Tariff Commission. *Foreign Trade of Latin America*. Washington, D.C., 1942.

Universidad Obrera de México. *El conflicto del petróleo en México, 1937–1938*. Mexico City, 1938.

Vasconcelos, José. *Obras completas*. Vol. 1, *Ulises criollo*; vol. 2, *El proconsulado*; vol. 4, *Breve historia de México*. Mexico City: Libreros Mexicanos Unidos, 1961.

Vázquez Schiaffino, J., Joaquín Santaella, and Aquiles Elorduy. *Informes sobre la cuestión petrolera*. Mexico City: Cámara de Diputados, 1919.

Veatch, Arthur C. "Oil, Great Britain, and the United States," *Foreign Affairs* 9 (July 1931).

Vera Estañol, Jorge. *La Revolución Mexicana: Orígenes y resultados*. Mexico City: Editorial Porrúa, 1957.

Vernon, Raymond. *The Dilemma of Mexico's Development*. Cambridge, Mass.: Harvard University Press, 1963.

————, ed. *How Latin America Views the United States Investor*. New York: Praeger, 1966.

Walling, William English. *The Mexican Question: Mexico and American-Mexican Relations under Calles and Obregón*. New York: Robin Press, 1927.

Weyl, Nathaniel and Silvia. "La reconquista de México: Los días de Lázaro Cárdenas." *Problemas agrícolas e industriales de México* 7 (October–December 1955).

Whitaker, Arthur P., ed. *Mexico Today*. Philadelphia: American Academy of Political and Social Sciences, 1940.

Wilson, Henry Lane. *Diplomatic Episodes in Mexico, Belgium, and Chile*. New York: Doubleday, Page, 1927.

Winkler, Max. *Investments of United States Capital in Latin America*. Boston: World Peace Foundation, 1929.

Womack, John. *Zapata and the Mexican Revolution*. New York: Alfred A. Knopf, 1969.

Wood, Bryce. *The Making of Good Neighbor Policy*. New York: Columbia University Press, 1961.

Woolsey, T. S. "Some Thoughts on the Mexican Oil Question." *American Journal of International Law* 16 (January 1922).

Young, Desmond. *Member for Mexico: A Biography of Weetman Pearson, First Viscount Cowdray*. London: Cassell, 1966.

Zorrilla, Luis G. *Historia de las relaciones entre México y los Estados Unidos de América*. Vol 2. Mexico City: Editorial Porrúa, 1966.

Zubiría y Campa, Luis. *El Artículo 27 y el petróleo*. 1922.

Periodicals

Acción (Havana).
Affairs (Washington, D.C.).
Atlantic Monthly (Cambridge, Mass.).
Baltimore Evening Sun.
Boletín de la Asociación Americana de México (Mexico City).
Boletín de la Unión Panamericana (Washington, D.C.).
Boletín del petróleo (Mexico City).
Chicago Commercial Herald and Examiner.
Congressional Record (Washington, D.C.).
Dallas Morning News.
Demócrata, El (Mexico City).
Día, El (Mexico City).
Diario de los debates de la Cámara de Diputados (Mexico City).
Diario de los negocios (Mexico City).
Diario oficial (Mexico City).
Dictamen, El (Veracruz).
Economist (London).
Economista, El (Mexico City).
Evening Standard (London).
Excélsior (Mexico City).
Financial Times (London)
Foreign Relations of the United States (Washington, D.C.).
Globo, El (Mexico City).
Guaranty News (New York).
Heraldo de México, El (Mexico City).
Houston Post.
Hoy (Mexico City).
Journal of Commerce (New York).
Luchador, El (Tampico).
Mañana (Mexico City).
Mexican Herald (Mexico City).

Mexican Post (Mexico City).
Mexican Weekly News (Mexico City).
Mundo, El (Tampico).
Nacional, El (Mexico City).
Nation (Washington, D.C.).
New Republic (New York).
Newsweek (New York).
New York American.
New York Evening Post.
New York Herald Tribune.
New York Times.
Nya Dagligt Allehanda (Stockholm).
Omega (Mexico City).
Paris Soir.
Prensa, La (Mexico City).
Prensa, La (San Antonio).
Reformador, El (Mexico City).
Revista mexicana (Mexico City).
Revista tricolor (Mexico City).
St. Louis Dispatch.
San Antonio Express.
San Antonio Light.
San Francisco Chronicle.
Saturday Evening Post (Philadelphia).
Sunday Express (London).
Time (New York).
Times (London).
Times-Herald (Washington, D.C.).
Ultimas noticias (Mexico City).
United States Daily (Washington, D.C.).
Universal, El (Mexico City).
Universal Gráfico, El (Mexico City).
Wall Street Journal (New York).
Washington Post.
World (New York).

Index